EMINENT ECONOMISTS II

The sequel to *Eminent Economists*, this book presents the ideas of some of the most outstanding economists of the past half-century. The contributors, representing divergent points of the ideological compass, present their life philosophies and reflect on their conceptions of human nature, society, justice, and the source of creative impulse. These self-portraits reveal details of the economists' personal and professional lives that capture the significance of the total person. The essays represent streams of thought that lead to the vast ocean of economics, where gems of the discipline lie, and the volume will appeal to a wide array of readers, including professional economists, students, and laypersons who seek a window into the heart of this complex field.

Michael Szenberg is Distinguished Professor of Economics and Chair, Business and Economics department, Touro College and University System. He is Distinguished Professor Emeritus, Lubin School of Business, Pace University. Professor Szenberg is the recipient of many awards, including the 2013 John R. Commons Award, 2013 Homer and Charles Pace Award, 1983 Kenan Award for excellence in teaching, and the 1971 Irving Fisher Monograph Award. He also served as the editor-in-chief, Emeritus, of *The American Economist* (1973–2011). Professor Szenberg is the author or coauthor with Lall B. Ramrattan of more than seventeen books and many journal articles and encyclopedia entries.

Lall B. Ramrattan holds a PhD from The New School for Social Research. He is an instructor at the University of California, Berkeley. He has published articles in several major journals and has served as an associate editor of *The American Economist*.

Eminent Economists II

Their Life and Work Philosophies

Edited by

MICHAEL SZENBERG

Touro College and University System

LALL B. RAMRATTAN

University of California, Berkeley Extension

CAMBRIDGE
UNIVERSITY PRESS

32 Avenue of the Americas, New York, NY 10013-2473, USA

Cambridge University Press is part of the University of Cambridge.

It furthers the University's mission by disseminating knowledge in the pursuit of education, learning, and research at the highest international levels of excellence.

www.cambridge.org
Information on this title: www.cambridge.org/9781107656369

© Cambridge University Press 2014

First published 2014

Printed in the United States of America

A catalog record for this publication is available from the British Library.

Library of Congress Cataloging in Publication Data
Eminent economists II: their life and work philosophies / [edited by] Michael Szenberg, Lall Ramrattan; foreword by Robert Solow.
pages   cm
Includes bibliographical references and index.
ISBN 978-1-107-04053-3 (hardback) – ISBN 978-1-107-65636-9 (paperback)
1. Economists – Biography.   2. Economics – Philosophy.   I. Szenberg, Michael.   II. Ramrattan, Lall, 1951–
HB76.E452   2014
330.092′2–dc23   2013027354

ISBN 978-1-107-04053-3 Hardback
ISBN 978-1-107-65636-9 Paperback

B'H

Once again, to my mother, Sara, who gave birth to me – twice;
my father, Henoch, for his wisdom;
my sister, Esther, for bringing me to these shores;
my two children, Naomi and Avi, and
their spouses, Marc and Tova;
and my wife, Miriam

And most of all to my grandchildren,
Elki and now Chaim, Batya, Chanoch, Devorah, Ephraim, Ayala, and Jacob

And to the Righteous Anonymous Austrian-German Officer who took my
immediate family to a hiding place just days before the last transport to
Auschwitz, where most of my family perished

In Memoriam
To my late elder sister, Balwanty Deolall,
and brother, Deonarine Ramrattan,
who have always directed me on the traditional path

No bird soars too high, if he soars with his own wings.

William Blake

Contents

Contributors

Alan S. Blinder Gordon S. Rentschler Memorial Professor of Economics and Public Affairs at Princeton University

Clair Brown Professor of Economics and Director of the Center for Work, Technology, and Society at the Institute for Research on Labor and Employment, University of California, Berkeley

John Y. Campbell Morton L. and Carole S. Olshan Professor of Economics at Harvard University

Vincent P. Crawford Drummond Professor of Political Economy and Fellow of All Souls College at the University of Oxford and Distinguished Professor Emeritus and Research Professor at the University of California, San Diego

Paul Davidson Holly Professor of Excellence, Emeritus, at the University of Tennessee in Knoxville

Angus Deaton Dwight D. Eisenhower Professor of Economics and International Affairs at the Woodrow Wilson School of Public and International Affairs and the Economics Department at Princeton University

Harold Demsetz Professor Emeritus of Economics at the University of California, Los Angeles

Peter Diamond Institute Professor at the Massachusetts Institute of Technology

Avinash Dixit John J. F. Sherrerd '52 University Professor Emeritus of Economics at Princeton University

Barry Eichengreen George C. Pardee and Helen N. Pardee Professor of Economics and Political Science at the University of California, Berkeley

Jeffrey Frankel James W. Harpel Professor of Capital Formation and Growth at Harvard Kennedy School

Richard B. Freeman Herbert Ascherman Professor of Economics at Harvard University, Co-Director of the Labor and Worklife Program at Harvard Law School, and Senior Research Fellow on Labour Markets at the Centre for Economic Performance, London School of Economics

Benjamin M. Friedman William Joseph Maier Professor of Political Economy at Harvard University

John Hull Professor of Finance and Maple Financial Group Chair in Derivatives and Risk Management at the University of Toronto

Michael D. Intriligator Professor Emeritus of Economics, Political Science, and Public Policy at the University of California, Los Angeles

Peter B. Kenen Walker Professor of Economics and International Finance, Emeritus, at Princeton University

Anne O. Krueger Professor of International Economics at the School for Advanced International Studies, Johns Hopkins University, and Senior Fellow of the Center for International Development and the Herald L. and Caroline Ritch Emeritus Professor of Sciences and Humanities in the Economics Department at Stanford University

Helen F. Ladd Edgar Thompson Professor of Public Policy Studies and Professor of Economics at Duke University's Sanford School of Public Policy

Harry M. Markowitz Professor of Finance at the Rady School of Management, University of California, San Diego

Frederic S. Mishkin Alfred Lerner Professor of Banking and Financial Institutions at the Graduate School of Business, Columbia University

Elinor Ostrom Distinguished Professor at Indiana University, Arthur F. Bentley Professor of Political Science and Co-Director of the Workshop in Political Theory and Policy Analysis at Indiana University in Bloomington, and Research Professor and Founding Director of the Center for the Study of Institutional Diversity at Arizona State University in Tempe

Anwar Shaikh Professor of Economics at the Graduate Faculty of the New School

Jeremy J. Siegel Russell E. Palmer Professor of Finance at the Wharton School at the University of Pennsylvania

Vernon L. Smith Professor of Economics and Law at George Mason University, Research Scholar at the Interdisciplinary Center for Economic Science, and a Fellow of the Mercatus Center, all in Arlington, VA

Robert M. Stern Professor Emeritus of Economics and Public Policy at the University of Michigan

Myra H. Strober Professor in the School of Education at Stanford University

Hal R. Varian Emeritus Professor in the School of Information, the Haas School of Business, and the Department of Economics at the University of California, Berkeley

Michelle J. White Professor of Economics at the University of California, San Diego, and Research Associate at the National Bureau of Economic Research

Marina v. N. Whitman Professor of Public Policy, Gerald R. Ford School of Public Policy & Professor of Business Administration, Stephen M. Ross School of Business Administration at the University of Michigan

Foreword

Only the oldest readers and perhaps a few antiquarians will remember Helen Hokanson. She was a cartoonist for *The New Yorker* long ago whose specialty was suburban matrons in flowered dresses saying things that we, but not they, found funny. The particular cartoon I have in mind shows a typical Helen Hokanson lady in conversation with several Navy sailors, all in blue uniforms and round white caps. She is saying, "How do you tell one another apart?" What brought all this to mind was reading the autobiographical essays in this book. There is no such problem for economists: they come in enormous variety, apparently no two alike. Some are breezy, some formal, some in between; some are technical, some are meditative; some are men and some, at last, are women. They are very easy to tell apart.

They do, however, have rather similar ideas. Economists and civilians come at problems in distinct, recognizable, even stereotypical ways. That is not incompatible with great diversity within the profession. We call it a "discipline" for a reason, after all. It is supposed to put some limits on "anything goes." From the outside, some of those limits seem pretty narrow.

What struck me particularly is that most or all of these ("eminent") economists seem to be skeptical about the same limitations in conventional economics: especially rigid assumptions about greed, rationality, and the ubiquity of equilibrium. They seem to treat them not as assertions to be uncritically believed, but rather as convenient, simplifying starting points. Presumably they should be abandoned when they begin to cost more than the benefits they confer. Not always, though: you and I, who are always paragons of intellectual detachment, know that even economists are subject to waves of belief. As Robert Frost observed (in "The Black Cottage"): "Most of the change we think we see in life / Is due to truths being in and out of favor." This is, of course, a complicated matter. It is interesting to follow, in these essays, the various ways in which their eminent authors deal with the

interplay between the conventions of the "discipline" and their own observations, intuitions, and analytical needs.

Maybe the picture that emerges from these autobiographies is a bit too
optimistic. The institutions of academic life, especially the appointment
process, do create pressure for uniformity. Frost was right but, to coin a
phrase, there can be long and variable lags.

Here are some not quite random observations that bubble up from the
reading of these stories.

One is about the changing role of women in the profession. The older
women were clearly victims of overt and covert discrimination, conscious
and unconscious, usually casual. My wife, who is slightly older, remembers
the same or even worse: there were leading law schools that did not accept
women as students, let alone as faculty. There is much less of that now, and
what remains is at least shamefaced, in considerable part because of the
achievements of the cohort represented in this book. Here is a lead back to
what I was saying earlier. There are alternative interpretations of this piece
of progress.

One school of thought might say: there you see the market having its
usual benign effect. Another school of thought replies: the market didn't
jump, it was pushed. Also half-truths come in and out of favor.

Another observation: I was struck by the important role that policy applications (and other applications) play in the work even of those whose mark
has been made primarily in theory. It rings true.

In my own experience, involvement with policy issues has been a fertile
source of research questions, even fairly abstract questions, to be thought
about later. One has to hope that this is one of the mechanisms that warns
many active economists not to take those simplifying assumptions too
seriously.

I suspect that outside critics of economics are generically unaware of all
this; they are forever beating a dead horse, at least partially dead. I suppose it is natural that graduate students start off by reacting to the literature
instead of to the world. The literature is what they know about. Eventually
that changes.

Lastly, this sample of successful careers suggests that there is no single
path to success. Some of the protagonists just started off well and went from
one good idea to the next, with only a rare dead end. Others didn't stumble onto pay dirt until considerably later, and sometimes in unexpected
places.

Some are hedgehogs, some are foxes. My impression is that talent (or good luck) in choosing promising problems to work on is just about as important as talent (or good luck) in finding solutions. Of course that insight, if it is an insight, does not offer a lot of practical help in the How to Make Good department.

There are many interesting stories here, many people worth getting to know, even apart from their published work. I can think of some missing tales that I would like to hear. So can you. Maybe they will come along in due course. Let's hope so.

Robert Solow
February 2013

Preface and Acknowledgments

Some time ago we came across Paul Sartre's play *Huis-clos* (*No Exit*), which contains the famous line "L'enfer c'est les autres": "Hell is other people."[1] This is only half true. Rereading the essays that appear in this volume and interacting with the contributors, we suggest a complementary line, "Heaven is other people." Juxtaposing both lines forms one of life's great equations.

Our contributors traverse continents and cultures and disciplines, and ultimately end up making major inroads in economics by cultivating their own garden. They heed Voltaire's wise words expressed in *Candide*, "Il faut cultiver notre jardin." Our interest in learning, analyzing the various paths the contributors have taken is to discover the wellspring of creative impulses in order to cultivate our own garden. Besides being scholarly, the vivid mosaic essays presented here are inspiring, engaging, meditative, affecting, and even entertaining. They point the path to scholarly success. The scholars presented here are "round" in the way E. M. Forster describes in *Aspects of the Novel*. Such characters are dynamic and "capable of surprising in a convincing way." Robert Frost noted that "[p]oetry begins in delight and ends in wisdom." The same can be said about reading the essays written for this volume: they make us well aware how wisdom is gained in the scholarly world. Given the turbulent times of the world we live in, we are reminded of Anatole Frances's line: "He is a truly great historian; he has enriched his subject with a new uncertainty."

This volume owes a great debt to Scott Parris, former senior editor of Cambridge University Press, for his belief in the project and constant encouragement. Thank you, Scott. *Eminent Economists II: Their Life and Work Philosophies* is a sequel to the 1992 volume, still in print, which was translated into many languages. This is the third book coming to fruition under Scott's stewardship. Also, we would like to acknowledge the cooperativeness of the contributors to this volume with thanks and gratitude.

We are grateful to Bob Solow, who adorns this work with an encore foreword after he did the same for our *Franco Modigliani: A Mind That Never Rests*, which was also translated into several languages.

Szenberg is profoundly grateful to Ben Friedman and Victor Fuchs for being his champions.

Our intellectual debt continues with the members of the Executive Board of Omicron Delta Epsilon, the Honor Society in Economics, for being an important source of inspiration, encouragement, and support – Professors Mary Ellen Benedict, Tina Das, Alan Grant, Paul W. Grimes, Katherine A. Nantz, Farhang Niroomand, Robert Rycroft, Joseph M. Santos, and Ali Zadeh – and the Coordinator of the ODE Central Office, Phyllis Carter. We are grateful for their collegiality and deep friendship.

Pace's library is a superbly run unit where efficiency and kindness dwell together. We are grateful to the librarians of Pace University – Adele Artola, Yakov Bibichkov, Steve Bobich, Wanda Castaner, Amernal Denton, Michelle Fanelli, Gladys Gonzalo, Alicia Joseph, Sanda Petre, Chloe Pinera, Rey Racelis, and Ann Wilberton – for being extraordinarily supportive.

Thanks are extended to colleagues at Pace University: Lew Altfest, Arthur Centonze, Natalia Gershun, Elena Goldman, Aron Gottesman, Iuliana Ismailescu, Tamara Kelly, and Joe Salerno. They are a constant source of affection. Szenberg would like to especially recognize Carmen Urma, the Coordinator of the Finance and Economics Department, for her zest in work, great assistance, and friendship. We also want to recognize Michelle Cheung, Natalie Hedden, Elki Herzog, Batya Kunin, and Devora Szenberg. They did their work with diligence, character, good humor, exactitude, and patience. They all have lightened many a task. Their assistance was incalculable and we are grateful to them.

Szenberg's heart still warms with gratitude toward Ester Robbins (Budek), Leo Faleev, Lisa Ferraro, Laura Garcia, and Marina Slavina, my past talented and devoted graduate research assistants who have helped directly and indirectly in more ways than I can list to make this book the offspring of our partnership. Their input lives on in these pages.

Lastly, Szenberg's deep gratitude is expressed to Stephen J. Friedman, President of Pace University, for his rare combination of effective leadership, efficiency, humility, kindness, and cheerfulness.

Notes

1 It is important to note that in 1964 Sartre refused the Nobel Prize in literature. Boris Pasternak was the only other winner in literature who declined the Nobel, in 1958. However, he was forced to do so by the Soviet authorities.

Introduction

Michael Szenberg and Lall B. Ramrattan

The former collection of *Eminent Economists* edited by Michael Szenberg (1992), profiling twenty-two preeminent economists of the preceding decade, has been successful in whetting the appetite of readers but not satiating it. Rather, the idea of such a compilation has created such a niche for itself among economists, readers, and students that it stands to become a genre in itself. Just as William Shakespeare questions the law of diminishing returns in his play *Twelfth Night; or, What You Will* when Duke Orsino asks for an excess of music that may sicken his appetite for love, readers here seem to want more philosophies and stories of the lives and times of eminent economists. Just as more music will not kill Orsino's love for the beautiful Lady Olivia, these compilations will keep inspiring new generations of economists bridging times.

Finance and economics combine to form the bedrock of modern-day society, and these economists occupy an important podium attempting to satisfy limitless human wants within the limits of Mother Nature in a sustainable and incremental way. They formulate ideas drawing knowledge from other fields such as mathematics, computer technology, and human behavior, collecting and collating hundreds of bytes of data to understand the forces of the market and make human life just a bit better.

These eminent economists are prominent faces in electronic media today, trying to explain the economic problem-solution paradigm to the public, in the classroom preparing the next generation of leaders, and advising policy makers in the government. Behind the curtains they toil, burning the midnight oil to build economic models and explain situational logic and empirical facts. A compendium like this one is a beautiful attempt to bring several ideologies together on a single platform so that the reader is able to compare, contrast, critique, and perhaps identify with, and advance, a particular school of thought.

Readers can seek to identify levers that propelled these economists and how some of them used even life-threatening experiences to evolve groundbreaking theories. Anne Krueger writes how she was influenced by news and events of the Second World War as well as by graduate students in regard to "disguised unemployment," which channeled her thought processes in the direction of the international economy. For another group of economists, it may have been just a book that intrigued them enough to explore further. Harold Demsetz was influenced by Edward Chamberlin's *Theory of Monopolistic Competition* (1933), and Michael Intriligator tells us how his teacher had him read Roy Harrod's *Life of Keynes* and how it changed his life.

In his seminal masterpiece, *The Open Society and Its Enemies*, Karl Popper wrote: "The analysis of the situation, the situational logic, plays a very important part in social life as well as the social sciences. It is, in fact, the method of economic analysis" (Popper 2003: 107).

Quite a few of the contributors to this volume have appealed to situational logic.

Vernon Smith, anchoring his learning in faith, writes that "if the universe had always existed it seemed that there was room aplenty for Einstein's impersonal God, the deism of natural rules, order, and beauty, to say nothing of agnosticism and atheism." His view of determinism is coupled with situations as well. For instance, his experiment revealed that the Great Recession can be explained by the situational logic of the Great Depression: "These data are just a rerun of comparable movements in new housing expenditures before and during the Depression, when the investment boom in housing was shorter-lived than in the recent run … starting in 1922 it rose to fraternal twin peaks in 1925 and 1926, when expenditures stood almost 60 percent above their 1929 level. By 1933 new housing expenditures had catered to more than 85 percent below their 1929 level."

In a similar fashion Avinash Dixit writes: "Economics is all around you, and it is not the least bit dismal. Learn to recognize it, appreciate it, and enjoy it." Having grown up in a Berkeley environment and always surrounded by professors, Barry Eichengreen surmises: "Put an undergraduate in an unstructured environment and he or she will go in one of two directions. One is off the deep end, which for my classmates meant making candles in Ben Lomand. The other is in search of more structure. This is my best explanation for how I ended up in economics." Drawing more upon situational logic Clair Brown writes, "The Vietnam War helped women enter the economics field because when the draft lottery began in 1970 and graduate studies no longer provided draft deferment, the universities were scrambling to replace male graduate students who were drafted and others who decided not to apply." In the same vein, Elinor Ostrom relates how conditions during the Great Depression taught her "a lot about the household economics of a poor family – long before [she] studied these problems in developing countries," while Anwar Shaikh describes how meeting with Joan Robinson set the stage for his important contribution known as the "Humbug production function."

Though only a shade away from faith, luck plays a role in states of eminence as well, and at least two of the eminent financial economists in this compilation seem to clearly assert themselves in this category. John Campbell opens his piece with the claim that he accidentally entered the field of economics, while John Hull emphasizes the chance events that brought him into economics, such as: "The job at London Business School, which led to my move back to academia, happened by chance; my move from the UK to Canada happened by chance; my derivatives research with Alan started by chance; and so on." He cautions us, however, that "we should not underestimate the importance of education, industriousness, perseverance, pragmatism, search for opportunities, and taking full advantage when they present themselves.... Luck tends to happen more often when we are doing what we enjoy."

In a similar vein, Alan Blinder, states, "This essay has emphasized how accidents here and there shaped my career, opening some pathways while foreclosing others." He started studying mathematics before he switched to economics and presented a Keynesian point of view that is grounded in his dissertation on distribution and confronted Keynesian fiscal and monetary policy with economic reality. In particular, when he was a member of President Ford's Council of Economic Advisers (CEA), he got the "Aha" sensation from Alan Greenspan, chairman at the time, that the 1973–1975 recession was sourced to a decline in inventory investment for which Keynesian polices brought closure. But this did not square with the disinflation recessions of the 1980s. For those observations, he turned to the "rational expectations models of business cycles."

For the current and future generations of economists, these authors are good exemplars who, through their life stories, show us how to bridge unknown rivers. They have cleared pathways so that others may have fewer detours and will be able to efficiently navigate avoiding errors and superstitions in the discipline to reach new areas of knowledge and novelties. Some are scientific while others are instrumental and artistic, but at the very least we will gather a constellation of facts, theories, and methods that will serve as a springboard for the future.

CATEGORIZING

Through their works Adam Smith and David Ricardo urge us to specialize in absolute and comparative advantage, respectively. Some eminent economists easily fall into known specialties whose work has a focus and commonality. In this group it is easy to locate Peter Kenen, Anne Krueger, Harry Markowitz, Peter Diamond, Paul Davidson, Vernon Smith, and a few others. Just at the mere mention of their names, economists rattle off their achievements.

Some have taken up aspects of economics from their direct experience of economic events, while others follow Isaac Newton's (1642–1727) absolute space-time reference. The time of the Great Depression is a soundly fixed point for Mary Strober, who writes: "Unemployment was a recurrent topic at dinners in my family, not only possible unemployment for my dad but also the Great Depression and the suffering faced by my parents' siblings and friends during those years. The topic intrigued me." From the present time value approach, Richard Freeman wrote that "at age seventeen I calculated the expected present value of lifetime earnings from economics and other plausible careers ... and determined that economics was the best fit."

Some have used prior subject measures to classify their works, like the categorical imperative of Immanuel Kant (1724–1804), who had self-selected his field. Elinor Ostrom writes, "Basically, I believe that solving problems related to the long-term sustainability of common-pool resources and the efficient provision of public goods is difficult but not impossible." Helen Ladd adds, "By the early 1990s, my publications and other professional activities had established my reputation within the field of state and local public finance." Marina Whitman states, "[M]y father [Von Neumann] impressed on me, virtually from my earliest conscious moment, the moral imperative of making full use of whatever intellectual capacities we were endowed with, whether man or woman, paid or unpaid." John Hull emphasizes the influence of mathematics in his career, from high school: "Math skills have been really important to me in my research, and readers may be surprised to learn that I consider the most important part of my math education to have been in high school and not in university." Frederic Mishkin attributes his career choice in part to family influence: at the age of twelve, his father exposed him "to technical analysis of the stock market where you looked for patterns in stock prices like the ones called 'head and shoulders,' which supposedly would tell you where stock prices would head in the future."

Some require us to find relations among their work in order to categorize, for example, the use of some measure, such as Gottfried Wilhelm Leibniz's (1646–1716) metric, which defines a field or discipline to categorize a work. Harold Demsetz's writing, which was confined to three categories of subject matter – "(1) markets and firms; (2) property rights and externalities; and (3) financial markets and transaction costs" – seems to be heavily utilized in industrial organization. In the same way, we find that Benjamin Friedman's work spans macro policy and religious thinking, which he packaged into the classical field of Smithian thought. Michael Intriligator lists several fields upfront in his contribution, but his work in mathematical economics is popular. Jeffrey Frankel writes: "First I ventured into other parts of macroeconomics, including, for example, the coordination of monetary and fiscal policy when different policy makers believe in different models. Then I ventured into other parts of international economics, such as the circumstances under which the 'trade-creating' advantages of regional free-trade areas outweigh the 'trade-diverting' disadvantages."

The hardest group to classify involves those who move with the events of economics. They appear to follow something like Jules Henri Poincaré's (1854–1912) group theory view, where the observer of economic events moves with the events he or she is observing. Hal Varian's interest spans statistics, mathematical economics, macroeconomics, microeconomics, industrial organization, and public finances, and he is now working in the field of information theory at Google. He might not mind being listed as a microeconomist, as he has written two best-selling college texts – *Microeconomics* and *Intermediate Microeconomics*.

Vincent Crawford calls his contribution a "safety net" approach. He examines the advice he has given to others – students, colleagues, and authors – in order to distill his "professional philosophy." Anwar Shaikh relates how he moved away from perfect and imperfect competition to discover his view of the vision of the classical economists. He has added a new set of terms to the economists' lexicon – moving limits, systemic order and disorder, turbulent regulation, macrodynamics, and pattern recurrence.

In this classification, we cannot say that all the eminent economists can be classified into a genus following the maxim that all eminent economists are working on practical and useful results. Some are interested in theory and experiment, while others prefer explaining the forces at work in the economy. Some seek out historic causes of the state of the economy, while others deal with how events are historicized in the economy. This brings up the issue of possible paths to economics.

PATHS TO ECONOMICS

Just as there are many streams that lead to the ocean, we see how the contributors came to choose economics as their playground. Alan Blinder asserts that his career was path dependent. He means a somewhat linear career path from undergraduate straight through graduate studies.

Some started in the hard sciences before entering economics. Michelle White entered Harvard as a chemistry major, but soon signed up for economics. Vincent Crawford was interested in research at the tender age of eight, which took him to mathematics and science. Paul Davidson graduated from college in chemistry and biology. He completed graduate courses in biochemistry at the University of Pennsylvania before he decided to do an MBA at the City University of New York. He thus came to economics with a strong science background. Anwar Shaikh taught math, physics, and social studies in high school. After arriving in the United States in 1943, Marina Whitman found herself in the lucky and unusual circumstance of being influenced by her parents, John and Mariette von Neumann. She, however, did not want to pursue the path of growth and game theory that her father overshadowed, but a more judicious mix of economics and journalism. Vincent Crawford, too, was influenced by his parents, who presented him with game theory materials from Newman's *World of Mathematics*. The strategic experience he gained as a Boy Scout and later from competitive sailing influenced his strategic communication aspects in game theory. Having read Isaac Asimov's *Foundation Trilogy* around the age of twelve, Hal Varian writes: "The idea that one could construct mathematical models of human behavior made a big impression on me; perhaps this is why I eventually became an economist." Richard Freeman explains: "What set me up to choose economics was Isaac Asimov's *Foundation* series of science fiction books," in which he learned how to construct science from history. Moreover, "Equations based on verified knowledge could predict the flow of history," and "the aggregation of individual actions rather than the decisions of kings and queens determined the flow of history and ... it was possible at least in the far-off future to write down equations that would predict how those actions determined the flow of history. Wow!"

The eminent mind can arise out of curiosity. Harry Markowitz pondered throughout his high school days the question "What do we know and how do we know it?" He heard the call of "uncertainty" in economics when he entered the University of Chicago. Peter Diamond, for instance, exposed the methodology of how to read the literature – read to find error in the proof or to transform the idea. Equally important is his approach to teaching as an enhancement of and not as a hindrance to research.

Some had economics thrust upon them. Economists usually pair themselves with peers or schools of thought. Helen Ladd tells how she was influenced by Carolyn Shaw Bell to turn to many subdisciplines of economics – taxation, public finance, urban policies, and education. Angus Deaton relates how he was influenced by the work of Modigliani and Brumberg. John Campbell gives credit to "effort and skill and dedicated mentors."

A few others seem to have simply stumbled upon the subject. Robert Stern tells how he left linguistics for economics while managing his father's butcher business. Angus Deaton moved from music to mathematics to rugby and finally to economics. Peter Kenen considered economics in the final two years of college at Columbia. He writes: "In my last two undergraduate years at Columbia, I divided my time between courses in politics and economics, and it was not until my senior year that I decided to go on to graduate work in economics." While John Hull explicitly credits his luck, he stumbled from studying math to business and, finally, finance.

Necessity is the mother not only of science but of eminence as well. Peter Diamond identifies strategic thinking as a necessary prerequisite. "This essay reports my memory of how I have proceeded strategically over the past fifty years, both before and after recognizing a need to think directly about these choices." He operationalizes this method through "[t]eaching, working on policy questions, leaving subjects when diminishing returns appear to have set in, and returning to them with a fresh mind later." John Hull advocates learning mathematics early at the high school level as sufficient for eminence at a later age.

One need not live, eat, and dream about economics to be eminent. When we look back, Francis Quesnay was a medical doctor, Adam Smith lectured on jurisprudence, David Ricardo was a stockbroker and parliamentarian, T. R. Malthus was a reverend, J. M. Keynes was a probability specialist, and

Milton Friedman came to economics from physics. The stories in this compilation of eminent economists reflect similar circumstances. It appears that one can generalize that to be an eminent economist one simply has to get out of one's field of specialization, but that is only an illusion.

EXPANDING SPHERES OF KNOWLEDGE

The contributors to this book share a variety of paradigms. Most modern economists are of the two major schools, namely monetarist and Keynesian. Keynes himself used Aristotelian/Marxian CMC and MCM circuits to characterize the monetary and real sides of the economy which have ontological implications for a worldview of economics (Meikle 2001: 41). The post-Keynesian economist Paul Davidson noticed that Keynes supported a nonergodic method in his writings, exorcising probability and stochastic processes from economics. On the other hand, stochastic analysis is the cornerstone for financial economists such as Harry Markowitz. Jeremy Siegel is self-described as a light libertarian, who we would expect to separate the enterprises of mathematics from economics.

The works of these contributors are what legends are built on. We normally find them improving existing solutions, solving anomalies, and offering novel facts that either are new or were not confirmed before. While they propose ideas and concepts to refute some of the anomalies they solve, their theoretical or empirical progress stands out. Some of the contributors provide novel, dramatic, and stunning facts (Meikle 2001: 41). Paul Davidson provided some when he identified Keynesian thought as nonergodic. He quoted John Hicks as saying, "You have now rationalized my suspicions and have shown me that I have missed my chance of labeling my own point of view as non-ergodic. One needs a name like that to ram a point home." Anwar Shaikh, who is sometimes at odds with post-Keynesian and Marxian ideas, has worked within the domain of nonergodic models providing a somewhat dialectic view of the economy. Robert Stern pioneered computation general equilibrium models, setting the stage for doing economic modeling with numbers. Harry Markowitz exemplifies several of these points when he writes: "[S]ince I believe in maximizing expected utility (using probability beliefs where objective probabilities are not known), then how dare I recommend the use of the mean and variance of return in choosing portfolios of securities?" The mean-variance approach to portfolio analysis was a revolution at that time, and subsequent work made it consistent with utility analysis.

In general, the knowledge to be gained in this collection straddles both the existential and ontological dimensions. On the existential side, the eminent economists care not only about themselves but also about their fellow beings and society solving economic problems that portend dead-weight losses, poverty, and inequality. Anwar Shaikh is very explicit on the existential point of view. He finds "a big difference between gravitation around an ever-moving balance point and equilibrium-as-a-state-of-rest ... one cannot assume that agents make their decisions as if they are in equilib-rium." On the causal side of existence stands Harold Demsetz, who remarks that "we are powerless to affect time and place of birth," implying that one has to work with what one has been endowed with in order to become emi-nent. Barry Eichengreen worked with materials he heard at the dinner table of his parents and other economists. As much as she tried to eschew the strong influence of her father, John von Neumann, Marina Whitman did not escape the academic influence in her background: besides her engage-ment in the public life she became an economist. Another aspect of exis-tence is concerned with how to relate to others, their essential needs. Elinor Ostrom and Mary Strober exemplified that regard working with influences of the Great Depression.

The ontological or the essential side of eminence is concerned with things prior to positive economics. For instance, the eminent economists are ontological when they are concerned with what is to be produced because, ideally, production should endure through time. This does not preclude production for consumption but appeals to a regular way of doing so, like the concept of a Kuhnian normal science that can be changed with scien-tific revolution. In short, the eminent economists, by "dealing with things in a way that brings them into tune with our and their context discloses them" (Spinosa et al. 1997: 180). For example, labor market analysts now see social factors such as "gender bias" as important elements to include in their theory (Maki 2001: 370). On the ontological side, we find Helen Ladd and Myra Strober questioning the "inner working" of the economic world, transforming questions "about the economic world view ... into ques-tions about economic theory" (Maki 2001: 6, 371). Some strong exemplars include Paul Davidson exorcising the ergodic models from the essence of post-Keynesian economics and Hal Varian specifying a new model of sales. For Anwar Shaikh, equilibrium is not a reality; it is only the dominant reg-ulative principles and system dynamics that are real, manifesting through nonergodic processes such as counteractive tendencies and cycles.

The eminent economists are abreast with the philosophy of critical real-ism in economics. Critical realists are interested in how well mainstream economics explains social reality. As developed by Roy Bhaskar, the old dia-lectic process of identity, negativity, and totality extended into other realms, which include ontology, existence and causality, science and social science (Bhaskar 1993: xiii). Practical application of this concept such as by Tony Lawson has focused on "finding and using methods" and emphasizing the major differences between studying social and natural sciences (Fullbrook 2009: 1).

The ontological wing of critical realism involves social processes that possess emergent powers and are also structured, internally related, and process oriented (Fullbrook 2009: 5). Fullbrook illustrated how this categorization of the social process fits in with gender concepts, an area of research highlighted by the works of Helen Ladd and Myra Strober. The process is open due to its historical development. Gender issues emerge in the process of becoming a woman in society. One needs a social structure to study women from an existential viewpoint. It is from defining oneself that the other is studied and known (Fullbrook 2009: 6). In another context, Paul Davidson recognizes that the time for openness in Keynesian analysis has arrived. He writes: "In 1980, I decided that Keynes's *General Theory* analysis had been (wrongly) discussed primarily in a closed-economy context. With the growth of a global economic prospective, I decided Keynes's analysis had to be presented in a clear and unambiguous open-economy context." Avanish Dixit also subscribes to the open view, writing that "[e]conomists have broadened their perspective to include other-regarding preferences and several forms of behavior that were once dismissed as irrational and to include the political process squarely in their analysis of economic policy making." In the same vein, we find Harry Markowitz opening up expected utility analysis to approximation with mean-variance analysis.

The ontological critical realism viewpoint places a bind on the sphere of mathematics in mainstream economics. Harold Demsetz writes: "Cold logic, imagination, and exposition by way of words, simple geometry, and basic statistics are the tools on which I have mainly relied throughout most of my career. I do not feel fully in command of a problem or a resolution of it until I can state both clearly in words and/or geometry." Along with other eminent mathematical works such as Markowitz's maximizing individual, Robert Stern's CGE approach to modeling, Richard Friedman's analogy with the sciences, and Vincent Crawford's strategic games, the bound ontological viewpoint highlights a closed system rather than an open one. According to Tony Lawson, mathematical analysis can deal with only a closed system, "meaning those in which event regularities or correlations occur" (Lawson 2009: 126). An open system would put more emphasis on heterodoxy, such as the post-Keynesian viewpoint Paul Davidson advocates. As Lawson puts it: "The sense in which various traditions like post Keynesians are heterodox is precisely that they reject the mainstream or orthodox doctrine that methods of mathematical modeling should be used more or less always, and by all of us, whatever the context" (Lawson 2009: 125). Some, such as J. Siegel, would prefer a separation of math and economics. Basically, Lawson emphasizes the major differences between studying the social sciences and the natural sciences (Fullbrook 2009: 1). Overall, this view is not anti-mathematics but anti-misuse of mathematics in economics.

Another ontology view that characterizes the eminent economists is the view advanced by Philip Pettit, that economists have both a self-regarding and a common mind (Pettit 2001: 90). Pettit brings to light the idea that self-regarding is not an actual, but a virtual cause of economic behavior. Behavior has a standby cause that makes self-regarding behavior resilient. It is likened to rolling a ball down an inclining plane. Because of Newton's law, the ball should follow a straight line path. If the ball deviates from that path, then one can place on the side of the incline some posts to steer the ball in the right direction, making the straight line motion resilient (Pettit 2001: 91). Paul Davidson's proposal for an International Monetary Clearing Unit institution exemplifies that resiliency. The clearing unit will act as a post for openness in Keynesian policies for the purpose of "changing the rules of the economic game so that the onus of adjusting to persistent deficits in a nation's current account was shifted primarily to the creditor and not the debtor nation." Davidson proceeds to identify the "money contract," which highlights money illusion as the primary cause of the meandering of the capitalist economy. Avinash Dixit has another take on this view that demonstrates the common mind at work. He writes: "In economics, traditional Keynesianism with price stickiness and other forms of inertia, on the one hand, and the rational expectations theorists' emphasis on forward-looking behavior, on the other, have similarly merged into a fruitful synthesis in the hands of a new generation of researchers like Michael Woodford."

We have attempted to delineate the boundaries of the contributions of the eminent economists. None of them wanted to be philosophical in asserting that they seek the truth in their work. But we see that tendency in their endeavors; however, we must add that their truths vary. Some seek mathematical truth, such as mathematical equilibrium, while others look at dialectical processes. There is one instance of experimental truth. As Adam Smith did not care to say what precisely is the invisible hand or the spectator that rules the market, some eminent economists have followed him, while others dare to assert that it might be culture, historical and evolutionary forces, or the deity itself. Avinash Dixit mentions consideration of behavior that once appeared irrational. John Campbell says that he values "underlying forces rather than superficial variation." Anwar Shaikh looks for dominant regulative principles and system dynamics. Harry Markowitz probes the uncertain. Frederic Mishkin reviews several philosophical principles that guided his research, which reminds us of the Cartesian maxim on the investigation of truths: "You never know where your research ideas are going to come from." And "You never know which of your papers will have an impact and how long it will take for them to do so."

We absorb how one's immediate environment, such as family influence or economic circumstances, can be a driver to eminence. We are also told how immense love for a subject, such as science, creates a desire to apply those methods and economics, allowing one the opportunity to attain the desired objective.

The study of eminent economists is as fundamental as the squaring of economic reality with economic methodology. The eminent economists represent all moments in a continuum of changing economic methodology over positivism, paradigm, research program, critical realism, and ontology. They are concerned with what economic laws should be and how they explain and predict the changing economic reality.

From the ontological point of view, some would agree with Uskali Maki that "[c]ausal processes, causal interactions, and causal laws provide the mechanisms by which the world works" (Maki 2001: 372), while from the point of view of Tony Lawson such causal processes with mathematical characterization can court only a closed social system.

Few will deny that the eminent economists provide methods and synthesis that make practical men and women secure in their activities in the daily business of living. When we no longer criticize their work, we are apt to make it a part of our day-to-day curriculum of study and are disposed to accept and retain the knowledge they contribute readily.

REFERENCES

Bhaskar, Roy (1993). *Dialectic: The Pulse of Freedom*. London: Verso.

Fullbrook, Edward (2009). *Ontology and Economics: Tony Lawson and His Critics*. London: Routledge.

Lawson, Tony (2009). "Contemporary Economics and the Crisis," *Real-World Economics Review* 50: 122–131.

Maki, Uskali (ed.) (2001). *The Economic World View*. Cambridge: Cambridge University Press.

Meikle, Scott (2001). "Quality and Quantity in Economics: The Metaphysical Construction of the Economic Realm," in Uskali Maki (ed.), *The Economic World View*, 32–54. Cambridge: Cambridge University Press.

Pettit, Philip (2001). "The Virtual Reality of *Homo Economicus*," in Uskali Maki (ed.), *The Economic World View*, 75–97. Cambridge: Cambridge University Press.

Popper, Karl (2003 [1945]). *The Open Society and Its Enemies*, vol. 2. London: Routledge.

Spinosa, Charles, Fernando Flores, and Hubert L. Dreyfus (1997). *Disclosing New Worlds: Entrepreneurship, Democratic Actions, and the Cultivation of Solidarity*. Cambridge, MA: MIT Press.

1

Being There: An Intellectual Journey

Alan S. Blinder

My *life and work philosophies*, you say? Do I have such things? And if I do, who would care to read about them? Tough questions. But until you know for whom you are writing, it's hard to know what to write. The best answer I could come up with is that, maybe, some students of economics, both undergraduate and graduate, could benefit from my experiences and postjudices.[1] So, mindful of the dangers of self-indulgence, I have penned this essay with students in mind. It's a career road map, of sorts, but one that benefits from the 20–20 vision of hindsight.

We economists believe deeply in equilibrium models – not to mention *rational* equilibrium models *without hysteresis*. But life is not like that. More commonly, it is governed by accidents that leave lasting imprints – paths taken and not taken. That certainly includes my own professional career even though, on paper, it looks like I marched lockstep through a boringly preprogrammed life cycle: an economics major in college, straight on to graduate school in economics, and then straight onto the Princeton economics faculty, where I remain to this day. No apparent deviations or afterthoughts.

In truth, accidents mattered greatly.

GETTING EDUCATED

Most of us economists are dropouts from mathematics – the differences being in how long you lasted in math. I owe a deep debt of gratitude to a then-young boy of about sixteen, whose name I no longer remember, for pushing me out of mathematics early. It's a decision I've never regretted.

When I enrolled at Princeton University, I didn't know what mathematics was really like, but I thought I was pretty good at it. Since Princeton offered beginning calculus at three different levels, I signed up for the highest, most abstract version. For three semesters, I struggled to remain in that rarefied math track, all the while earning the equivalent of A+ (Princeton didn't use the A–F scale then) by getting about 45 percent on exams. Princeton mathematicians like to keep students humble.

Then, in the fall semester of my sophomore year, a sixteen-year-old freshman, whom I'll call Tommy, showed up in my fancy math class. Tommy and I were the two star students. But there was a difference. While he was two years younger, I was getting A+ by scoring about 45 percent while he was getting A+ by scoring about 98 percent. Sometime during that term, I said to myself, "Blinder, there is one guy in this class who's going to be a mathematician, and it's not you." The next term, I dropped down to the more practical, science- and engineering-level math. Without Tommy's obvious superiority, who knows how much longer I would have stubbornly persevered in an activity in which I have no comparative advantage? Lesson: believe in David Ricardo.

The other life-changing accident in my college days derived from the need to earn some money. An organization called the University Press Club then (as now) provided stringers for major newspapers and wire services. The pay was excellent, and the work looked very attractive – especially compared with, say, waiting on tables (the next-best alternative?). So I tried out and won a spot. The Press Club brought me what was, for a college kid at the time, quite a bit of money. More important, it trained me to write clearly, quickly, and well. Precious few economists are known for their writing skills. It was newspaper work, not anything I ever wrote for an economics course, that taught me how to write.

I graduated from Princeton in 1967 as an economics major with good but not great math skills, an unusual talent for writing, and, thank heaven, a wife to support me. Graduate school in economics seemed the logical next step, and the professoriate seemed an attractive occupation to prepare for. So off I went on a Fulbright Scholarship to the London School of Economics, deferring my admission to MIT's PhD program for a year. After a second one-year hiatus due to Vietnam era draft problems (don't ask), I finally enrolled at MIT in September 1969.

The choice of MIT was *not* an accident; here, rational equilibrium theory really applies. With Paul Samuelson, Bob Solow, Franco Modigliani, and others there, why would anyone choose anyplace else? My years as a PhD student, 1969–1971, probably came just after MIT's ultimate heyday (the cohorts leaving in 1965–1969). But as compensation, it was no longer *de rigueur* to do a growth model for your dissertation.[2] In fact, I was much more interested in the size distribution of income – which turned out to be my dissertation topic even though MIT offered no teaching in the subject.

As I look back on that brief but intense period, a few things stand out. One sounds like a laugh line: my major field of study was "advanced economic theory." Since MIT didn't even have a field called "mathematical economics" then, that choice placed me at the techno-mathematical frontier. The idea that I was then a *theorist* sounds, and is, ludicrous by modern standards. And at the risk of sounding like an old man passed-by by modern technology, I remain skeptical that raising the technical bar has been entirely salutary. Even back in my graduate school days, economic theory was stark, sharply constrained both by mathematics and by a dominant neoclassical paradigm, and sometimes even ethereal. Compared with today, however, what we "theorists" did back then looks pretty down to earth.

By the time I showed up at MIT, I was two years behind my age cohort and getting tired of being a student – a young man in a hurry. So I rushed through the program at breakneck speed, finishing everything and getting my PhD in two years.[3] My dissertation came out as a book.[4] But I also more or less completed the empirical paper that would become my most-cited journal article ever,[5] a minor theoretical paper that would soon be published in the *Quarterly Journal of Economics*,[6] and I made a good start on a major theoretical paper that, with indispensable help from coauthor Yoram Weiss, would appear a few years later in the *Journal of Political Economy*.[7]

The third notable feature of my time at MIT was another fortuitous accident. Early in the spring of 1971, well after the main job market was virtually over, I could see that I would not need another full year to finish my dissertation. Thinking about putting food on the table, I asked Bob Solow, who was my main thesis adviser, to keep his eyes open for any teaching jobs that might become available in one of the local colleges – which often sought Harvard or MIT graduate students to fill one-year teaching needs.

Solow's response a few weeks later took me aback: "Harvard's got a vacancy." *Harvard*? That was not exactly what I meant by a "local college." I took the interview at Harvard, of course, and by dint of that found myself on the job market a few months after it had all but closed for the year. As it turned out, Harvard could offer me only a futures contract: the promise of a job the following year. Given the vagaries of university budgets, and my need to eat, that wasn't a gamble I cared to take.

Luckily, a few weeks later, Princeton found itself with a late vacancy when one of its assistant professors resigned. Richard Quandt, who was then Princeton's chairman, heard I was available and phoned me at MIT. "Can you teach graduate macro?" he inquired. Remember, I had been a *theorist* writing a dissertation on *income distribution*. So I gave the only reasonable answer: "Of course, I can." I was soon hired. No fuss, no muss, no bother, but plenty of accidental hysteresis.

Like virtually every other major department in America, the Princeton Economics Department offered no teaching in the "field" of income distribution. In truth, there was no such field; the economics profession was not much interested in it. For example, no major journal was a natural home for research on inequality. But macroeconomics was different. A huge field, it was relatively "hot" at the time (when isn't it?), with plenty of publication outlets, research colleagues, and teaching needs all over the country. Thus, it was the pull of demand, rather than any innate desire to supply on my part, that turned me into a macroeconomist. (Demand rules the roost in Keynesian models, doesn't it?) That choice was cemented by yet one more accident.

WORKING HARD AND PLAYING BY THE RULES

In the summer of 1971, just before my wife, Madeline, and I decamped for Princeton, Bob and Barbara Solow invited us out to their home in Concord for a barbeque. It was a mini-celebration, of sorts, of the imminent completion of my dissertation. But the famous Professor Solow had something else in mind, too. Over a glass of wine on the deck after dinner, he offered me a proposition that I couldn't refuse.

It seems that, some months earlier, the Brookings Institution had contracted with Paul Samuelson and him to produce a survey essay on fiscal policy for a volume that eventually became *The Economics of Public Finance*, a book that received some notice at the time but has since been lost to history.[8] As I listened, I learned that Solow had made a good start on his part of the paper, but Samuelson had lost interest in the project. Bob wanted a new coauthor. Would I take over for Samuelson and finish this essay with him?

I don't think I dropped my wine glass, but I was flabbergasted. There I was, twenty-five years old, without a publication to my name, being offered a guaranteed joint publication with the world-renowned Robert Solow – and replacing Paul Samuelson, no less! I didn't stop to ask whether the paper would be "Blinder and Solow" or "Solow and Blinder"; I just said yes.[9] That paper produced, as a spin-off, the then-famous Blinder-Solow paper "Does Fiscal Policy Matter?"[10] which was reprinted in several places and widely discussed in the ensuing years. It gave my career an important early boost and pushed it strongly toward macroeconomics.

A part of my professional philosophy was forming, I suppose. It was the Yogi Berra Principle: when you come to a fork in the road, take it. I've taken many such forks since then.

After graduation, my career went "by the book" for a while. I worked hard and played by the rules. The rules for a young academic at the time, as now, were to devote yourself single-mindedly to publishing in all the best places. So I did, publishing papers in the *Brookings Papers on Economic Activity* in 1972; in the *Quarterly Journal of Economics*, the *Journal of Public Economics*, and the *Journal of Human Resources*, which was then the top journal for labor economics, all in 1973; in the *Journal of Political Economy* in 1975; and another in the *JPE* plus two in the *American Economic Review* in 1976. These papers constituted exactly what a budding young scholar is supposed to produce: a steady stream of papers that display high productivity and some originality but that fall squarely within the predominant paradigm. Had there been Google searches at the time, crossing "Blinder" with "unconventional" probably would have turned up nothing. Following the formulaic path to academic success, I was granted tenure at Princeton in 1976. I was thirty years old.

THE BIRTH OF A TEXTBOOK

Just before that, another fortuitous accident happened. It was eerily similar to the deal Bob Solow had offered me in 1971.

Sometime in 1975, a publisher then known as Harcourt Brace Jovanovich[11] contacted me about a textbook project. In seems that, years earlier, they had contracted with four famous economists – my colleague Will Baumol, who had been my undergraduate thesis adviser, Walter Heller, Harry Johnson, and James Tobin – to collaborate on a principles-of-economics textbook. Each would write a quarter of a book, and somehow (don't ask me how) it would all get stitched together. A crazy idea. After seven years of futile waiting, the publisher had received about a quarter of a book from Baumol and nothing from anyone else. They were looking for a macroeconomist to help Baumol finish the book. So now I was being asked to replace Heller, Johnson, and Tobin in order to compete with Samuelson! Life does have its twists and turns.

As a young scholar still short of tenure, I had not been thinking about textbook writing at all. But after mulling it over and inspecting my nearly empty bank account, I took the deal. After all, writing textbooks is something professors do, isn't it?

Writing *Economics: Principles and Policy* (first edition: Harcourt, 1979) brought me an advance that, while puny by today's standards, was well above my paltry Princeton salary. More important, it drew me for the first time into teaching principles of economics – where, I quickly became convinced, the social value of an economics professor is *vastly* higher than anywhere else. In principles, you ignore all the arcana and teach the absolutely most important lessons of economics: supply and demand, opportunity cost, comparative advantage, the invisible hand, the time value of money, ... The list goes on and on. These lessons are intellectual eye-openers for many students, and life changers for some. Compare doing that with, for example, teaching PhD students the minutiae of advanced macroeconomic theory – which I did for more than twenty years.

I still teach Economics 101 at Princeton, and *Economics: Principles and Policy* is still going strong in its twelfth edition – an outcome I never dreamed of when I signed the original contract in 1975. My business partnership with Will Baumol has thus been going on for about thirty-seven years, with nary a harsh word exchanged between us. Was there ever a more agreeable and productive man? (I'll answer that: no.)

Once I was seriously engaged in the textbook business, it did not take me long to appreciate the wisdom of Samuelson's famous words: "I don't care who writes a nation's laws, or crafts its advanced treatises, if I can write its economics textbooks."[12] He was in this, as in most things, exactly right. By now, well over 2 million students have learned economics from "Baumol and Blinder." Hardly a week goes by that I don't meet either a person who took Economics 101 from me or someone who studied economics from our book. Some of them tell me it changed their lives. It's gratifying.

MACROECONOMIC STAR WARS

The great pitcher Lefty Gomez once allegedly said that he'd "rather be lucky than good." My early professional career certainly had elements of both. But it was utterly conventional. Beneath the surface, however, two almost-contradictory forces were stirring. On the one hand, the real world was pulling me in. On the other hand, academic macroeconomics was drifting ever further away from reality. Talk about cognitive dissonance!

In the mid-1970s, I was far too young to have anything approaching a professional philosophy; that's for older folks. I had not, however, lost sight of what attracted me to economics in the first place: the idea that mathematical techniques could *and should* be put to work on social problems. The *should* was important. Economics, I thought, was not just an intellectually demanding parlor game, like chess. It was supposed to be relevant to real-world problems. When I entered the macroeconomic fraternity, I thought I was signing on to a progressive program of Kuhnian normal science that would improve our ability to control the business cycle. So I was blindsided by what followed. The decades after my PhD years turned out to be incredibly tumultuous. Unbeknownst to me when I opted for macroeconomics, I had enlisted in intellectual trench warfare. In a perfect foresight model, I would have chosen something else.

In the spring and summer of 1975, the United States was just emerging from its worst recession since the 1930s. Never imagining what would come later, some of us were calling it the "Great Recession."[13] To me, getting out of that recession was the most important policy issue of the day, and figuring out how to avoid future recessions was the most important intellectual issue of the day. What was already considered "old-fashioned" Keynesianism seemed to offer the most promising answers – by a mile – even though important details and better microfoundations remained to be worked out.

In the academy, however, the winds of change were blowing strongly in the opposite direction. Robert Lucas had already argued that *anticipated* increases in the money supply – precisely what the Fed was doing to fight the recession – had no effects on real variables, and Thomas Sargent and Neil Wallace had recently developed that idea further into the famous "policy ineffectiveness" proposition.[14] The Lucas critique, which would usher in an era of macroeconometric nihilism, was just a year away from publication.[15]

I had a very negative intellectual reaction to these developments, perhaps too negative. My rejection of what came to be called "new classical macroeconomics" was bolstered, first, by watching monetary and fiscal policy help bring the 1973–1975 recession to a close and, then, by watching the *pre-announced* Thatcher and Volcker disinflations cause deep recessions. How could this have happened if anticipated monetary policy doesn't matter and recessions are really mass vacations? As Groucho Marx once asked, though in a rather different context, "Who you gonna believe, me or your own eyes?"

Groucho notwithstanding, I went with my own eyes, which drew me to old-fashioned Keynesian economics because it provided *much* better explanations of what was happening than did newfangled new classical economics. So I found myself fighting a rearguard action for an intellectual doctrine that was apparently out of fashion. As I wrote a few years later, "By about 1980, it was hard to find an American academic macroeconomist under the age of 40 who professed to be a Keynesian."[16] But, at the age of thirty-five, I was one of them.

It got worse. As the fiftieth anniversary of Keynes's *General Theory* in 1986 approached, more and more conference organizers, editors, and the like started asking me (and a few others) to pen defenses of Keynes against the Lucasian attacks. In a few cases, I let my feistiness get the better of me and agreed.[17] One such presentation, I recall, led to some testy exchanges with Bob Lucas before a packed house at the December 1986 meetings of the American Economic Association.[18]

All this macroeconomic warfare taught me several lessons. Actually, one of them was an old lesson dating back to all those forgettable growth theory dissertations piled up in the MIT library: academic research runs in fads and exhibits strong herding behavior. OK. But the corollary was worse: in academia, I saw, while it is marginally better to be right than wrong, the real sin is to be seen as behind the times, to appear technologically obsolete or old-fashioned.

Meanwhile, back in the real world, I agreed to become one of the founding fathers of the Congressional Budget Office (CBO) in the summer of 1975, working under the newly appointed founding mother, the remarkable Alice Rivlin. It was not a good career move, I knew – I didn't have tenure yet! But I gave only one long summer to the CBO. The CBO's analysis of the recession and what to do about it, written partly by me, was strictly Keynesian,[19] and it came out just as modern academics were beginning to sneer at that approach.[20]

But it was a very different lesson from that summer that affected my research career. It came from Alan Greenspan, who was then chairman of President Ford's Council of Economic Advisers (CEA). While we at the

CBO were drafting our first report on the economy, Greenspan asserted that the mega-recession that was just ending was mostly an inventory cycle. An *inventory cycle*? we scoffed. That was for minor recessions. Surely the big recession of 1973–1975 was a lot more than that! Then I checked the data. Greenspan was right. Not only was the violent contraction of 1973–1975 mostly accounted for (in an arithmetic sense) by declining inventory investment, so were most other US recessions.

For me, that realization was an "Aha moment" that turned my research career on a dime. I immediately started working like mad on a subject that virtually no one else was researching – inventories[21] – eventually churning out eleven scholarly papers on the subject when I could have been where the crowd was, working on rational expectations models of business cycles.[22] That was truly a bad career move. Swimming against the tide is guaranteed to hold down your citation count.

INTO THE PUBLIC ARENA

There was another respect in which I allowed the real world to impinge upon my academic career around that time. Academic economists generally speak to one another rather than to anyone else; and we often speak in our own impenetrable dialect, guaranteeing that no one else will understand, anyway. There are pros and cons to this insularity. On the plus side, it enables academics to sit quietly in corners, making scientific progress. On the minus side, it allows academics to become almost monastically disengaged from public discourse. That, in my estimation, is healthy neither for society nor for economists. Besides, it grated against my emerging "philosophy."

When the Reagan revolution began, I found myself grousing about the nonsense that was being spouted daily, including frequent attacks on mainstream economics. (Remember supply-side economics?) One day, my wife urged me to stop complaining privately and go public with an op-ed. I took her good advice, dusted off my newspaper training, and published my first op-ed column in the *Boston Globe* in 1981.[23] It would not be my last. After about four years as a *Globe* regular, I was invited to join a four-economist rotation in *Business Week*, which greatly enhanced my journalistic visibility. Now I was *really* going outside the fraternity, becoming a bit of a public person.

Perhaps that early journalistic experience emboldened me to stray even further from the fold and write a trade book – a book that ordinary people might read! In *Hard Heads, Soft Hearts*,[24] I sketched and extolled what I saw as the unwritten but common philosophy of liberal economists, which combined healthy respect for market efficiency (the hard head) with genuine concern over income inequality (the soft heart), my old flame from graduate school. As I wrote in the introductory chapter of that book:

> The many policy changes that I advocate in this book are not easily classified as "conservative" or "liberal," as Democratic or Republican. They derive nonetheless from a coherent underlying philosophy, a vision of what economic society could and should be. This world view, and the consistent set of policies that comes with it, cuts neatly across party lines and is available on equal terms to any politician who will embrace it and sell it to the electorate.[25]

At last I had a philosophy.

But that's about all I had. *Hard Heads* appears to have had no perceptible influence on the political debate over economic policy. Alas, that is hardly unusual. Economists' influence over economic policy is vastly overrated.

The *Business Week* columns ended when I joined the Clinton administration in January 1993 as a member of the new president's first CEA. When news of my appointment was leaked to the *New York Times*, a front-page story described me as "a prominent mainstream economist," which I clearly was.[26] No one would have described my career to that point as unconventional. I went to Washington with hopes that the Clinton administration would stand for the kinds of hardheaded but soft-hearted policies I had extolled – and they were realized in part.

The Clinton years were good ones for the president's economic team. As the US economy improved and improved, we were lauded as geniuses. I learned a huge amount during the Clinton administration – not about economics, but about politics and government. For example, I saw more clearly than ever the truth of some of the themes expounded in *Hard Heads, Soft Hearts*. Prominently, I experienced firsthand (and frequently) something I had only intellectualized about before: that the most serious problems that beset economic policy rarely stem from weaknesses in economic science (though there certainly are weaknesses). Rather, they almost always stem from failures of political decision makers to heed even the simplest economic logic – and from the public illiteracy that lets them get away with it. This realization strengthened my resolve to "go public."

My stay in the Clinton administration lasted just eighteen months. As I told friends, that's how long the policy phase of any administration lasts. Then it was off to become vice-chairman of the Federal Reserve Board, an economist-dominated organization that actually *makes decisions* rather than just *gives advice*. At the Fed, I learned that the false image that many economists have of the CEA – as the bastion of academia within the government – comes far closer to describing the Fed. You could lose arguments there, of course, especially if you were on the wrong side of Chairman Alan Greenspan (as I sometimes was). But the battles were fought on economic and logical, not political and polemic, grounds. So at least I was armed.

Armed, but not heavily. According to legend, Greenspan and I ("the other Alan") often clashed along traditional hawk-dove lines, with me favoring easier monetary policy. There is a grain of truth there, but only a grain. In fact, our strongest disagreements came over Federal Reserve communication, with me always favoring greater openness, clarity, and disclosure, and him adhering more to time-honored central bank traditions of secrecy and obfuscation. Operationally, of course, Greenspan won every such battle; he was, after all, the boss. But I like to think that I won intellectually. After I left the Fed, I started writing quite a bit about central bank communications.[27] And the Fed, under Greenspan's leadership, moved notably in the direction of greater openness.

BACK TO THE ACADEMY

After a little more than three years in government, I returned to Princeton – thereby demonstrating that some people don't advance in life. But my professional career would never be the same.

Prior to going to Washington, I was "a prominent mainstream economist" with the standard résumé of a successful academic. After my service as vice-chairman of the Federal Reserve Board, I was truly a public person, and the *nonacademic* demands on my time – for conferences, speeches, consulting, and much else – escalated sharply. I appeared frequently in the media, wound up on too many boards and committees, and helped found two entrepreneurial businesses.[28]

There being only twenty-four hours in a day, my presence and profile *inside* academia inevitably receded a bit. But I didn't mind much, for I was not eager to return to the academic warfare I had left behind in 1992. (The armies were still fighting.) Furthermore, I knew that the rejection of Keynesianism had never happened in the real policy world, anyway. So I wasn't missing much by staying out of the intellectual crossfire as macroeconomics lurched from one fad to another without palpable forward progress. I judged that I had earned my purple heart in the 1970s and 1980s.

But my research agenda changed again, dramatically. Even *before* I went into the government, I had grown impatient with papers whose only connections with reality were their titles. After more than three years of total immersion in real-world policy making, my tolerance was all but gone.

Thus began a period of academic apostasy – starting with my first big research project after returning to Princeton, which was finishing a major study of price stickiness that I had started before entering government service. It finally came out as a 1998 book called *Asking About Prices*.[29] Unlike all of my previous research, *Asking About Prices* was neither theoretical nor econometric. Instead, I used a team of Princeton graduate students to *ask* actual price setters questions about their behavior. While interview methodology is routine in most social sciences, it places you well outside the established church in economics. Such work is more likely to earn you studied indifference, or even scorn, than plaudits. (In my case, it was mostly indifference.) Undaunted, I conducted yet another questionnaire study – this time on central bank credibility – in 1998.[30] This work was soon followed by yet another major piece of survey research in which Alan Krueger and I studied public knowledge of and opinions on economic policy issues,[31] a topic I viewed as of the utmost importance.

By the late 1990s, I no longer wanted to write obscure papers that only a handful of specialists would ever read. Been there, done that. Now, I would write about whatever I found interesting and important. If the referees and editors of top academic journals agreed (as seemed unlikely), so much the better. If not, that was okay, too. So I published two books of lectures on aspects of central banking;[32] wrote papers for *Foreign Affairs*, where most of the readers weren't even economists;[33] and even engaged in some experimental research with my colleague John Morgan.[34]

And another new research direction developed: an interest in the phenomenon of offshoring, which was prompted not by anything that was going on in the academy, but rather by my observation *and thinking* about things that were happening in the real world. The offshoring of service-sector jobs looked to be in its infancy, and I thought it was destined to be a big deal. So I began with a speculative but widely read "think piece" in *Foreign Affairs*,[35] precisely the sort of essay that academic economists almost *never* write. Then I had the temerity to use data on job characteristics to make *subjective* judgments on which jobs might be offshorable in the not-too-distant future.[36] Economists are supposed to eschew such subjective judgments. Most recently, collaborating again with Alan Krueger,[37] I engaged in more survey research, using individual-based data to develop three different measures of offshorability.[38] Amazingly, all the guesstimation methods point toward the same conclusion: that roughly a quarter of all US jobs are potentially offshorable, which is enough to matter.

While there was some conventional econometrics in most of these papers, there was virtually no theory. The young economic "theorist" of 1971 had come full circle, taking cues from Yogi and Groucho along the way.

REFLECTIONS ON THE DISCIPLINE OF ECONOMICS

There is a condominium complex for senior citizens in south Florida called "Journey's End." A bone-chilling name, I've always thought, and my journey is not yet over. But my personal intellectual journey has led me to a few conclusions about our discipline. Call it part of my "professional philosophy," if you wish.

One is that the age-old debate over whether economics is or is not too mathematical is a red herring. I don't much care how mathematical economics is now or becomes in the future; modern econometrics, for example, demands a great deal of math. The question should be, instead, whether the mathematics is illuminating previously dark corners or condemning economists to tunnel vision. I fear we have far too much of the latter. One particularly painful example is the way the profession ignored Hyman Minsky's insightful work on credit cycles. No one ever told me about Minsky when I was a student, and I didn't study his work on my own, either, until very recently. Why? There are no equations.

Second, I have come to view the traditional distinction between theory and empirical work as a red herring, too. Instead, I believe the right place to draw the intellectual line places *both* empirical research *and* theory that is *about something* on one side and theory that is *about nothing* on the other. Loose translation: it's the economy, stupid!

Third, I have long believed that substantive questions should dictate the investigative techniques used to study them, rather than the other way around. We economists suffer from chronic physics envy. But ask yourself this: Did Newton and Leibniz invent calculus and then look around for places to apply their newfound toy? Or did they invent calculus to study substantive problems in physics? Too much modern economic research, it seems to me, looks like technique looking for a place to happen.

Fourth, I have come to believe that the profession's implicit ban on "think pieces" – essays with ideas, but perhaps bereft of formal models or regressions – is a mistake. When I read Robert Heilbroner's marvelous *Worldly Philosophers*[39] as a college freshman, it piqued my interest in economics. But who today would call academic economists "worldly," never mind "philosophers"? I am not arguing that *most* economic writing should be free of equations and replete with big think. Perish the thought. But how about just a little – maybe even in the leading scholarly journals?

I finish where I started, with hysteresis. This essay has emphasized how accidents here and there shaped my career, opening some pathways while foreclosing others. And my professional life has not been especially accident-prone; indeed, it has probably been more linear and deterministic than most. Path dependence, I venture to say, is a normal and dominant feature of both personal and professional life. So why won't we let it creep into our models more?

Notes

1. A postjudice is, in some sense, the opposite of a prejudice. It is based on real information, thought, and experience.
2. When I arrived at MIT, I scanned the recent dissertations in the library and concluded that all the best students had written on growth.
3. As I left MIT, Paul Samuelson told me I was the fastest person through the MIT PhD program since Lawrence Klein. I gulped.
4. Alan S. Blinder, *Toward an Economic Theory of Income Distribution* (Cambridge, MA: MIT Press, 1974). My thesis committee was pretty remarkable: Bob Solow, Peter Diamond, and Bob Hall.
5. Alan S. Blinder, "Wage Discrimination: Reduced Form and Structural Estimates," *Journal of Human Resources* (Fall 1973): 436–455. That paper introduced a simple decomposition method that is nowadays called either the "Blinder decomposition" or the "Blinder-Oaxaca decomposition." See Ronald Oaxaca, "Male-Female Wage Differentials in Urban Labor Markets," *International Economic Review* (October 1973): 693–709.
6. Alan S. Blinder, "A Model of Inherited Wealth," *Quarterly Journal of Economics* (November 1973): 608–626.
7. Alan S. Blinder and Yoram Weiss, "Human Capital and Labor Supply: A Synthesis," *Journal of Political Economy* (June 1976): 449–472.
8. Alan S. Blinder et al., *The Economics of Public Finance* (Washington, DC: Brookings Institution, 1974). Fiscal stabilization policy was part of public finance in those ancient days.
9. It is a measure of Bob's legendary graciousness that it was "Blinder and Solow" or, as it was called at the time, "Solow and what's-his-name." See Alan S. Blinder and Robert M. Solow, "Analytical Foundations of Fiscal Policy," in Alan S. Blinder et al., *The Economics of Public Finance* (Washington, DC: Brookings Institution, 1974).
10. Alan S. Blinder and Robert M. Solow, "Does Fiscal Policy Matter? *Journal of Public Economics* (November 1973): 319–337.
11. After numerous mergers and acquisitions, the company is now Cengage Learning.
12. Quoted by Sylvia Nasar, "A Hard Act to Follow? Here Goes," *New York Times*, March 14, 1995.
13. Otto Eckstein, *The Great Recession, with a Postscript on Stagflation* (Amsterdam: North-Holland, 1978); Alan S. Blinder, *Economic Policy and the Great Stagflation* (New York: Academic Press, 1979).
14. Robert E. Lucas, Jr., "Some International Evidence on Output-Inflation Tradeoffs," *American Economic Review* (June 1973): 326–334. Thomas J. Sargent and Neil

Wallace, "'Rational' Expectations, the Optimal Monetary Instrument, and the Optimal Money Supply Rule," *Journal of Political Economy* (April 1975): 241–254.

15 Robert E. Lucas, Jr., "Econometric Policy Evaluation: A Critique," in *The Phillips Curve and Labor Markets, Carnegie-Rochester Conference Series*, no. 1 (1976), 19–46. That famous paper was originally presented to a Carnegie-Rochester conference in April 1973. Lest there be any misunderstanding, I do not blame Lucas one bit for the unproductive period that his "critique" ushered in. He made an insightful and correct point. I consider his "critique" paper one of the most important in modern macroeconomics. He is not to be blamed if his disciples went overboard.

16 Alan S. Blinder, "The Fall and Rise of Keynesian Economics," *Economic Record* (1988): 278.

17 Alan S. Blinder, "Keynes after Lucas," *Eastern Economic Journal* (July–September 1986): 209–216; and "Keynes, Lucas, and Scientific Progress," *American Economic Review* (May 1987): 130–136.

18 Blinder, "Keynes, Lucas, and Scientific Progress."

19 The first CBO report was *Recovery: How Fast and How Far?* (September 1975).

20 In 1978, Lucas and Sargent penned an anti-Keynesian screed called "After Keynesian Macroeconomics" (first published in Federal Reserve Bank of Boston, *After the Phillips Curve*, 1978), which asserted, among other things, that Keynesian predictions were "wildly incorrect and that the doctrine on which they were based is fundamentally flawed." Fightin' words.

21 One of the few exceptions was Louis Maccini. See, e.g., his "An Aggregate Dynamic Model of Short-Run Price and Output Behavior," The *Quarterly Journal of Economics* (May 1976): 177–196.

22 One paper spanned the two: Alan S. Blinder and Stanley Fischer, "Inventories, Rational Expectations, and the Business Cycle," *Journal of Monetary Economics* (November 1981): 277–304.

23 Alan S. Blinder, "It's a Peter Pan Style of Economics," *Boston Globe*, April 10, 1981.

24 Alan S. Blinder, *Hard Heads, Soft Hearts* (Reading, MA: Addison-Wesley, 1987).

25 Ibid., 10.

26 Louis Uchitelle, "Princeton Economist to Be Named to Clinton's Council, Aides Say," *New York Times*, January 4, 1993.

27 See, e.g., parts of chapter 3 of my book *Central Banking in Theory and Practice*; Alan S. Blinder, "Critical Issues for Modern Major Central Bankers," in European Central Bank, *Monetary Policymaking under Uncertainty* (Frankfurt, 2000), 64–74; "Central Bank Transparency and Accountability in the Future," in A. Posen (ed.), *The Future of Monetary Policy* (London: Blackwell, 2002); and chapter 1 of my book *The Quiet Revolution: Central Banking Goes Modern* (New Haven, CT: Yale University Press, 2004). There was more.

28 Promontory Financial Group and Promontory Interfinancial Network. I am still heavily involved with the latter, as its vice-chairman. I often get criticized by hostile readers of my *Wall Street Journal* columns as an egghead who never met a payroll. In fact, our company has met payroll consistently for years.

29 Alan S. Blinder, Elie R. D. Canetti, David E. Lebow, and Jeremy B. Rudd, *Asking About Prices* (New York: Russell Sage Foundation, 1998). Notice the date. The actual interviews ended in March 1992, but my government service had stopped everything in its tracks.

30 Alan S. Blinder, "Central Bank Credibility: Why Do We Care? How Do We Build It?" *American Economic Review* (December 2000): 1421–1431.

31 Alan S. Blinder and Alan B. Krueger, "What Does the Public Know about Economic Policy, and How Does It Know It?" *Brookings Papers on Economic Activity* 1 (2004): 327–387.

32 Alan S. Blinder, *Central Banking in Theory and Practice* (Cambridge, MA: MIT Press, 1998); and *The Quiet Revolution*. Both were from invited lecture series: the Robbins Lectures at the London School of Economics and the Okun Lectures at Yale. So you might say these were accidents, too.

33 Alan S. Blinder, "Is Government Too Political?" *Foreign Affairs* 76, no. 6 (November–December 1997): 115–126; and "Eight Steps to a New Financial Order," *Foreign Affairs* 78, no. 5 (September–October 1999): 50–63.

34 Alan S. Blinder and John Morgan, "Are Two Heads Better than One? Monetary Policy by Committee," *Journal of Money, Credit, and Banking* (October 2005): 789–812; and "Leadership in Groups: A Monetary Policy Experiment," *International Journal of Central Banking* (December 2008): 117–150.

35 Alan S. Blinder, "Offshoring: The Next Industrial Revolution?" *Foreign Affairs* 85 no. 2 (March–April 2006): 113–128.

36 Alan S. Blinder, "How Many U.S. Jobs Might Be Offshorable?" *World Economics* (April–June 2009): 41–78. J. Bradford Jensen and Lori Kletzer, "Measuring Tradable Services and the Task Content of Offshorable Service Jobs" in K. Abraham, J. Spletzer, and M. Harper (eds.), *Labor in the New Economy*, 309–342 (Chicago: University of Chicago Press, 2010), followed a somewhat different methodology and reached different conclusions.

37 Another good lesson for prospective economists is: choose your coauthors well. I have.

38 Alan S. Blinder and Alan B. Krueger, "Alternative Measures of Offshorability: A Survey Approach," *Journal of Labor Economics* 31, no. 2 (April 2013): S97–S128.

39 Robert Heilbroner, *The Worldly Philosophers* (New York: Simon & Schuster, 1953).

2

Social Norms in Economics and in the Economics Profession

Clair Brown

MY FORMATIVE YEARS

I probably became an economist when I was five years old, walking my beloved maid Nazarene to catch her bus.

Skipping along, I said, "I want to be Alice in Wonderland. It's a great movie. You've got to see it."

Nazarene replied, "Clair, I can't go see it."

Puzzled, I asked, "Why not?"

"'Cause it's playing at the whites' theater. They don't allow coloreds in."

Confused, I started noticing many other things that didn't make sense – Nazarene's worn-out sandals, her walking to the back of the bus after she got on, her drinking out of a different water fountain at the grocery store.

Nazarene gave me a good start in life with her loving care, her patience, and her wisdom. She also unknowingly taught me how the world set up rules that were grossly unfair, and yet people followed them as if they were fair and reasonable. Nazarene prepared me to question discrimination against women as well as people of color, and taught me through example not to take injury incurred through discrimination personally. Years later these childhood lessons gave me the courage to go into a profession that was not welcoming to women.

Growing up in Tampa, Florida, provided me with a supportive and safe community, and even today I stay in touch with and see my childhood friends, especially those from my Girl Scout troop. Daily I saw people's generous nature with their families and friends and their mean-spirited behavior toward people "beneath them" at work and in the community. The male boss who was cruel to his African American workers was charming, admirable, and kind in his own social circle. The wives of the men who ran the city – doctors, lawyers, bankers, and business owners – treated their servants as if they had no feelings. These women were charming and gracious in their own circles and spent time doing volunteer work to help "the needy."

Both my parents grew up in Tampa, and my mother felt at home there amid its old-time southern ways. She thought a woman's highest calling was as a wife and mother. Fortunately, my father was a "Roosevelt Democrat" rather than a Dixiecrat. After graduating from Harvard Law School, he had gone to work in the Roosevelt administration until the United States declared war and he joined the military. My dad felt much more at home in Washington, DC, and eventually I understood why he felt like an outsider in Tampa.

Although I was studious in high school, I tried to hide this behind popular activities like being a cheerleader and dating football players. I knew I wanted to go north to college when I graduated from high school in 1964. My goal was to get out of the South. My mother insisted that I attend a girls' school, so after visiting some of the Seven Sisters colleges I decided upon Wellesley. Even though I suffered culture shock, intellectually I came alive. Finally I had challenging professors and access to a wide array of ideas, and I learned to question and think. Because I found math interesting and easy, I became a math major. By my junior year, however, I was finding math removed from social and political problems, and was intrigued by the economic discussions of my friends who were economics majors. I started taking economics courses and quickly became hooked.

Meanwhile I fell in love with a Harvard law student, and we were married by senior year. This allowed me to live in Cambridge and take courses at MIT, and life was much more interesting in Cambridge. After graduation in 1968, my husband accepted a job with a major law firm in DC, and so I found a job as a research assistant at a think tank. The emerging women's movement had not yet had an impact on my thinking. Fortunately this was soon to change. In many ways I was a budding labor economist because I looked at the job structure around me and realized that the only way for a woman to advance was to get a graduate degree. Otherwise she would remain an assistant of some kind to a male boss.

BECOMING AN ECONOMIST

I decided to apply to graduate school in economics, and the University of Maryland had the best economics program in the DC area. For me the most important part of the program turned out to be working with a superlative economist, who happened to be a woman – Professor Barbara Bergmann. Barbara became my teacher and mentor and role model, and her influence has remained with me throughout my career. I was also supported in my studies by Professor Charlie Schultze, who turned me on to policy analysis. Dr. Alice Rivlin at Brookings and Dr. Belle Sawhill at the Urban Institute also mentored me.

The Vietnam War helped women enter the economics field because when the draft lottery began in 1970 and graduate studies no longer provided draft deferment, the universities were scrambling to replace male graduate students who were drafted and others who decided not to apply. Joanne Linnerooth from Carnegie Mellon University and I had been admitted to the University of Maryland, but we were not allowed to work as teaching assistants, positions that were only for male students. Then suddenly this changed when the department had some empty slots. However, we were given a TA office in some attic on the other side of campus because, as the economics chair told us, "Male and female TAs cannot share an office." Joanne and I ignored this and went to the large TA office and asked the male TAs if we could use the two empty desks. "Of course," they replied.

With the women's movement spurred on by the civil rights and anti-war movements, things were slowly starting to improve for women in academe. The Equal Employment Opportunity Act of 1972 provided the Equal Employment Opportunity Commission (EEOC) with litigation authority to enforce Title VII of the Civil Rights Act of 1964. Finally the EEOC had real power, and it began to enforce Title VII by choosing key cases, including looking closely at the University of California, Berkeley and why it had so few female faculty members. This turned out to have a major impact on my career.

As I was working on my dissertation, which would demonstrate that the higher unemployment rate of women than of men was related more to segmentation of labor markets by gender than to women making different choices than men in a well-functioning market,[1] I was nominated by Bergmann and Schultze for a doctoral fellowship at the Brookings Institution and became its first female doctoral fellow. My year at Brookings was intellectually stimulating, and my understanding of how economics is used to make policy grew dramatically. I also came to realize that politics trumped economics in formulating policy. The public-spirited economists who continued to push for specific policies based upon their research needed to have a great deal of patience and fortitude.

In 1972 I confined my job hunt to the DC area because my husband, who was involved in local politics in Virginia, did not want to move. I was interviewing at various federal agencies and local universities when I received a call from Professor Gerard Debreu, who asked me if I would like to apply for a job opening at UC Berkeley.

"Of course, I'll send my packet right away," I replied without hesitation. I could not say no to Debreu and Berkeley, and immediately started getting ready for my first trip across the country. Another Brookings fellow and good friend, Steve Roach, helped me by providing feedback on my job market paper and my seminar presentation. Without his help, I would never have been ready for Berkeley. The trip went extraordinarily well, and I was immediately drawn to Professors Lloyd Ulman and Aaron Gordon, who knew Bergmann and Schultze well. Much to my surprise, I was offered the job. After some soul searching, I knew I would accept. However, my husband was running for Virginia State Assembly, and I wanted to help campaign for him before I left for Berkeley. So I accepted the job but postponed starting until January 1974. My husband won his race, and I packed up my books and bicycle.

CHANGING THE OPPORTUNITIES FOR WOMEN IN ECONOMICS

Being the sole female faculty member in the Economics Department was trying, and I was able to do my research and teach primarily because I was supported by key faculty, especially Professors Ulman, Gordon, George Akerlof, Frank Levy, and Michael Wiseman. The graduate students were supportive as well, and I worked with them, including the few females among them, and the Graduate Admissions Committee to increase the number of female admits. In the beginning, we had to educate the male

faculty on how to judge female applicants. For example, an MIT male graduate with some C grades was admitted, while a woman from Smith with a
stellar record was denied admission. When I asked a colleague about this,
he said, "MIT grads are bright and do well in our program. Women don't
do well in math." I did a comparison of the performance of the male and
female grad students in the Berkeley program to show that women did at
least as well as men. Slowly we made headway.

One of my undergraduate courses, "Women in the Labor Force," had been
created by Professor Myra Strober when she was a lecturer at Berkeley.[2] I
realized that I did not know the legal literature well enough to teach it, and
I asked one of the leading legal scholars on Title VII, Professor Herma Hill
Kay at Boalt Hall, to present the lecture. Professor Kay graciously came, and
her lecture quickly provided the students and me with a broad overview of
and deep insights into discrimination law and practice. I also had the students read "The Story of O" by Rosabeth Kanter, which explains how being
"different," that is, the only female or black in a group, makes the others in
the group see you and treat you as inferior. Kanter's conclusion was that the
only remedy was to hire more women (or blacks). I took this advice seriously and pushed for the department to hire more women. During my second year on the faculty we interviewed a very bright woman from a top-five
university. She made it to short list for fly-outs and was then dropped from
consideration in the faculty meeting when we decided on the final candidate. The reason given was her field: we didn't need another faculty member
in industrial organization. The female candidate was hired by Stanford. The
next year we hired a new faculty member in industrial organization. When
I mentioned that we had decided not to hire someone in this field the year
before, I was told, "We never hire on the basis of field, only on merit."

Discrimination seems to work by our implicitly judging men and women
by different criteria without realizing it. This hiring experience showed me
how my colleagues could discriminate without understanding that their
behavior reflected discriminatory social norms that they accepted and followed without question. I also understood that my department most likely
would not hire another woman, and I decided to take action. I wrote a memo
stating that the Economics Department did not hire a female in industrial
organization one year and then hired a male in that field the next year. I
sent the memo to Professor Kay and asked her for feedback. I followed her
suggestion to send it to the EEOC and sent a copy to my chair.

The chair called me into his office and asked, "Why would you write this
about us? We are nice people." I readily agreed that my colleagues were
nice and added that people discriminate without knowing or intending

to do so. That year the department searched diligently for women to hire, and we hired two female economists, including Laura Tyson. Having two other women on the faculty completely changed the dynamics – Kanter was right.

We teach that every benefit has a cost, plus it is a cold hard fact of life that you don't rock the boat when you are an assistant professor. Having the idealism of youth, I had not considered that my colleagues would be insulted and angered by my memo. After all, I knew they were following social norms and were not doing anything wrong by their standards. I only wanted the standards to change so women could be fairly judged. In the years that followed the EEOC memo, I encountered backlash from some of my colleagues. When I came up for tenure review a few years later, the department was deeply split on my case, and a split vote is a negative vote. I knew my case was controversial and also that I had some strong supporters in the department. The department decided to postpone my vote until the following year and advised me to continue to build my résumé.

I was feeling despondent about the stressful tenure process, which had taken a lot of time. To my surprise, female faculty from across campus contacted me because they knew about my work and thought I should be granted tenure. They formed a support group that provided me with invaluable advice and new energy. The graduate students in economics also actively supported my case and wrote letters for the file about my work with them. What had appeared to be an overwhelming and negative situation now turned positive, and I was able to have a productive year and navigate the system. The following year the department again had a split vote that went forward for campus review, which was positive, and the chancellor accepted it.

Confidentiality is maintained during the tenure process, and so I do not know much about my departmental review or the campus reviews. I do know that without the ongoing help I received from my supporters in the department and the female faculty outside economics, I would not have been able to deal with the process and certainly would not have been granted tenure.

Berkeley economics has always prided itself on having had a female faculty member early in the twentieth century. Professor Jessica Peixotto, known for her studies of household budgets and living standards, held UC Berkeley faculty positions in sociology and social economics from 1903 to 1935. At least four other female faculty members were in social economics, which later became the School of Social Welfare.

Since the mid-1970s Berkeley economics has been a national leader in hiring female faculty and admitting women to the PhD program, and more recently admitting minority PhD students when I led the department's participation in the campus-wide program to find and encourage minority students to join Berkeley's PhD programs. I am proud to be part of our department's progress in becoming more inclusive, and I think that it has supported our creativity as economists.

Having been raised female in the South, I was keenly aware of how social norms affect one's behavior and opportunities. I was lucky to be able to go north for college and to benefit from the civil rights and women's movements as I was coming of age. I realized that one benefit of being a woman in a male world is to understand that discrimination is at work and not to take it personally. This helped me enormously during my early years as an assistant professor.

BALANCING WORK AND FAMILY

Meanwhile I had remarried, to a sociology professor, and had my first son, Daniel, in November 1980. I had put off having children until the time seemed right, when I would have more time to balance work with family life. Slowly I realized that this time would never come, that I would have to find a way to fit children into my life. Economists, being mostly male, did not share child-rearing responsibilities, did not say that they had to rush off to pick up kids from daycare.

One outcome of the national push for gender equality was maternity leave, which was granted at UC Berkeley shortly before I had my baby. When I went to ask my department chair, Bent Hansen, about taking maternity leave, he said, "What I know is that you can have twelve paid weeks off, and the rest of the semester you fulfill your work obligations without having to teach. Frankly I have no idea how to do this, so let's figure it out." I was lucky that he came from a European social democracy and was willing to find a way to make the policy fit our semester schedule.

Having my first child taught me the valuable lesson of saying no. Finally I could evaluate the seemingly endless requests to serve on an administrative committee, or review an article, or write a tenure review, sponsor an undergraduate group, or give a public presentation. Before I had children, I found it hard to say no because each request seemed valid and important to the people involved. Now, however, the opportunity cost was clear – less time with my child. I could evaluate a request quickly and decide whether it was worth accepting.

Although this provided me with a better sense of balance between work and personal life, I never achieved what I think of as a truly balanced life.

My guess is that it doesn't really exist, because being highly educated and goal-oriented, academics push themselves to the extreme. We always have one more question we want to study, one more lecture to polish, one more grad student to help, one more request that seems legitimate. My second marriage ended in divorce, and then I married a biochemist, Richard Katz, and had a second son, Jason. I don't recommend taking three marriages to figure out how to make marriage work, and I feel good about having celebrated my twenty-fifth anniversary.

Having raised two sons together with two dads, I still wonder how I managed the very long hours. I worked before my family woke up, took time off for dinner and kids' homework, and then went back to my own work. We relied upon a community of others – babysitters, preschools, K–12 – and I always thought of raising children as one-third my time, one-third the dads' time, and one-third the time of others, who were an important part of my children's lives.

When my students ask me how I balance work and family, I reply, "I don't know 'how'; I just do it with help from others." Although policies have become more supportive for parents, a sixty-hour work week plus family time is a brutal schedule. Yet I would not give up either the intellectual or parental challenges and rewards. My sons were supportive by being easy and forgiving, and I was lucky. I am a proud and grateful parent. My sons are now independent adults: Daniel works as an attorney in Manhattan and is a musician. Jason works as a software engineer in Silicon Valley and is a long-distance skater and international Scrabble player. I have recently become a grandmother, which I think of as a reward for raising children.

Most academics I know today, both men and women, don't want to give up work or family. Those who want a more balanced life often decide not to work at a university. More than one student has said, "Please don't be disappointed in me, but I am not applying for a job at a research university. I want a more balanced life." I respect this decision and look forward to a time when research universities find ways to be more supportive of family life. Fortunately many young male professors are more involved with child rearing because their wives also have demanding jobs, and my heart smiles when one says, "I have to leave to get my child from daycare."

MY RESEARCH IN LABOR ECONOMICS

Labor economics presents two basic frameworks: an institutional model, where social rule and custom provide the structure upon which market forces play out; and a competitive model, where markets are assumed to clear and provide efficient outcomes. I personally knew the importance of social and political forces in economic life, and I became an institutional labor economist, following in the long line from Veblen to Commons to Ulman. However, the tide had turned, and the Chicago school with its assumption of competitive markets that cleared over time became the dominant school, and institutional economics languished for several decades.

With the supportive environment that UC Berkeley provided for a broad range of methods, I was able to continue my work in institutional labor economics. My early research focused on showing that time and income were not substitutes in many household activities, and demonstrating the far-reaching impact this had on women's use of time, on the constraints faced by one-parent households, and on the constraints faced by unemployed people on unemployment insurance.[3] Concerned about the standard of living, especially of the poor and working class, I was drawn to studying household budgets. Assuming that families based their own sense of well-being on the social norms of their peers and friends, I used a relative income approach, which had been developed by Duesenberry but eclipsed by Friedman's permanent income hypothesis. Following Marshall, I assumed that family expenditures could be divided into basics (necessaries), variety (comforts), and status (luxuries). I naively thought that if I could demonstrate that the rich used their marginal income for status, this would provide a strong argument for progressive taxation. Again my timing was off – during the Reagan years supply-side economics and reduced taxation were in the limelight. I was unable to get funding for the standard-of-living work except from the Institute of Industrial Relations at UC Berkeley, which has been an important source of both intellectual and financial support. Because I also worked on other topics that did get funding to support students, my book on living standards took many years to complete.[4] When it was published in 1994, sociologists paid more attention to it than economists, and I appreciated Veblen's feeling of being neglected by his fellow economists.

As the United States became agitated over the rapid rise of Japanese industry in the 1980s, I began studying the relationship between human resource systems and firm performance in the automobile and communication industries. This required fieldwork, which I had never done before. So, along with Michael Reich and David Stern, my collaborators in this project, I learned how to collect both interview and survey data from firms and workers. We confined our fieldwork to the United States because we did not know Japanese. At the end of the 1980s, we were approached by our former graduate student, Professor Yoshi Nakata, and his Japanese team to do a collaborative study of Japan and the United States.[5] With Japanese teammates, the possibility of doing fieldwork in Japan became a reality, and we jumped at the chance.

Analyzing Japanese industrial relations was challenging, and so we turned to Lloyd Ulman to lend this expertise to our team. Since my arrival at Berkeley, I have never stopped learning from Lloyd, through our joint seminars and continual discussions, about how labor markets work. Lloyd is a natural mentor and teacher, with his real-life examples, four-quadrant graphs, and exactly the right insights without pushing for a certain result. Lloyd has provided me with the wisdom I needed at key times, and he gives his students unconditional support in their work. Once Lloyd told me, "Students do their best work when they are driven by their own questions and methods. All the professor has to do is provide feedback that supports and pushes their research along, even if it is not our style of research."

Being out in the field provided us with a new way of collecting data through observation along with surveys and interviews. This hands-on approach provided a way of verifying whether our interpretations of large data sets made sense and our survey responses were consistent with observed behavior. Eventually in my work with Julia Lane using the Census LEHD data set,[6] we came to believe that rich field data combined with large survey data yield the ideal form of evidence for studying specific economic activities.

After doing fieldwork in the United States and Japan in three industries, I joined the Sloan Competitive Semiconductor Manufacturing Program headed by Dean Dave Hodges and Professor Rob Leachman in engineering. I headed the human resources group, with the goal of studying how the HR system structured worker input into problem solving and process improvements and how workers acquired new knowledge and skills. We designed a detailed survey that included a firm-level questionnaire about the compensation and employment systems, and did extensive interviews with workers to understand how teams functioned and how workers' daily activities contributed to quality, throughput, and cycle time. Working with engineers was a new experience for me, because my earlier work focused on women and less-educated workers. By studying mostly well-educated men, I could ask, "Does education and then a good job allow people to achieve a middle-class life style and leave labor market problems behind?" High-tech labor markets were undergoing a critical restructuring and so this was an opportune time to be studying them. As lifelong employment systems at leading multinational companies broke down and the companies adopted more market-oriented HR systems, engineers faced problems in changing jobs as they aged. Many faced lower earnings and even unemployment.[7]

Once again, institutions mattered – workers now had to take charge of their training and many had to accept inferior jobs as they aged. They could no longer depend on an illustrious career at one company. Now being put out to pasture seemed to be the norm.

Studying semiconductor companies also provided the opportunity to investigate how firms used global activities to gain competitive advantage and to gauge the role of start-ups in creating innovative new technology. I wrote a book with Dr. Greg Linden analyzing eight crises that we had observed the semiconductor industry deal with successfully, because we knew that crises would continue to define industry strategies and outcomes.[8] With this book, I was ready to end my research on semiconductors.

IMPROVING UNDERGRADUATE EDUCATION

In my semiconductor research, I had been spending a lot of time in Asia, especially Japan, and then China and India. Although I had not worked on poverty for many years, seeing global poverty renewed my interest in how I might return to research that helped improve people's lives in less developed countries.

Finding ways to use our talents as economists can take many paths as we get older, and this is part of the reward of being an academic economist who is in continual contact with talented researchers from a broad range of fields. At this point in my career, as I approached the age of sixty, I wanted to spend more time on projects that would help poor people globally and that would not depend on outside grants.

The opportunity to extend my research to work that would have an impact on global poverty occurred by a circuitous route through campus service on undergraduate education. Teaching is one of academics' cherished rewards, even if it is mostly hidden from view or evaluation. We watch our students blossom intellectually and see them develop their critical thinking skills and communication skills as we support their efforts and cheer their accomplishments. I was asked to join and then chair UC Berkeley's campus-wide committee that oversees educational policy, and suddenly I needed to know the latest research on how students learn, how to assess their educational performance, and how to create support and incentives for faculty members to be good teachers. Fortunately UC Berkeley had Christina Maslach, the vice-provost in charge of education and learning, and she taught me as we worked together under Berkeley's shared governance structure. With input from a broad range of faculty, Christina and I structured an undergraduate learning assessment program for the Berkeley campus. Each department developed learning goals for their majors and then set up a way to measure their majors' performance in achieving these goals.[5] We wanted the program to be useful to the departments and the students in evaluating progress without wasting faculty time. To make it efficient, we worked on how departments could embed the assessment in regular assignments, including tests, labs, problem sets, and reports. Meanwhile the move to extend standardized testing to college students similar to testing for K–12 began, and our alternative approach gained attention. I chaired a University of California–wide committee to look at learning assessment for all UC campuses as a means of improving undergraduate education, and after a year of evaluating many methods of assessment, our committee recommended that UC adopt an assessment approach similar to the one being implemented at Berkeley.[10]

TIME FOR GIVING BACK

On the basis of what I had learned doing educational assessment and my ongoing work with social enterprises that were transferring technology to developing nations, I finally had a way to link my research expertise to helping reduce global poverty. These social enterprises needed a simple and cheap way to document outcomes that would be useful in learning about their programs and would also give their funders and investors an assessment of their impact. These organizations operated on tight budgets and wanted to use their limited resources to provide services and save lives. I heard the lament that to scale their projects required impact assessment, and few had the resources or the expertise to undertake a useful impact assessment. The stories I heard sounded familiar to those I had heard when looking at educational assessment – too expensive and not worth the resources. I began a social assessment program called *ReadyMade Impact Assessment* and teamed up with a great group of Berkeley faculty and students. We are in the early stage of developing the prototype based on five pilot projects and using open-source software. Soon we'll have a Web site for you to check out.

I am also working with my husband, Richard, who discovered a natural cure for bladder infections. I help collect and analyze data, and learn firsthand how hard it is to change medical norms – the way that MDs provide care. Although antibiotic resistance has been a top concern at the Centers for Disease Control since 1995, and up to one-fourth of women with urinary tract infections at college clinics have antibiotic-resistant *E. coli*, MDs stay wedded to prescribing antibiotics for UTIs. My own experiences have taught me that changing norms requires working with a group of dedicated and talented people who have patience and perseverance. We are slowly making progress with input from Professor Lee Riley, an MD at UC Berkeley Public Health School, and Dr. Michael McCulloch of the Pine Street Foundation.

Still caring about globalization and US jobs, I teamed up with Tim Sturgeon and Julia Lane to add a module to the 2008 General Social Survey. This led to developing a firm-based survey of the firm's global activities and its US jobs. Funded by the National Science Foundation, the 2010 survey was made publicly available in 2013]] and hopefully provides data to help us understand how firms structure their activities globally and their jobs domestically.

An ongoing frustration for me, as for many economists, has been developing research projects that are both rigorous and relevant. Even before the era of massive computing power, the problem was addressed by Aaron Gordon at his American Economic Association presidential talk.[11] With computerization and access to large data sets, too often economists think that in documenting economic activities, especially if they can cleverly devise treatment and control groups, the issue of relevance is eclipsed by the rigor of statistical analysis used to identify causation. However, the assumptions, which implicitly include institutions and norms, used in setting up the analysis usually prevent generalization of the findings to other situations. The question of relevance cannot be ignored, however, because with the transformation of the financial sector wrought by deregulation combined with information technological change, we are caught unawares by what talented and motivated people will do when presented with new opportunities, such as in the investment banking industry over the past two decades. Economists were caught shorthanded in their ability to predict and then respond to the major recession that occurred in 2007–2008 after the housing bubble burst. A focus on rigor has reduced most economists' ability to analyze the bigger picture. In labor economics, we know that the observed growth in income inequality, especially during the recent period when the financial sector was taking home a large proportion of both profits and compensation, cannot be easily reversed with our traditional policies. We have not been able to provide policy prescriptions to reduce the huge proportion of compensation going to the top 2 percent of earners, while the bottom 40 percent see earnings languish. We have not been able to explain why the link between GDP growth and employment growth seems to have changed for the worse during the recent recovery in 2009–2010. As economists, we have our work cut out for us.

Even when answers are lacking, one of the rewards of being an academic economist has been to work on socially important problems, along with talented (and admirable) students and colleagues. Some of my close friends today were former students of mine, and they provide me with continual inspiration in my work and life. The year I turned sixty-four, I celebrated my birthday at my former student Teresa Ghilarducci's place because I knew her work on pensions is instrumental in making retirement possible.[12] Other former students – Peter Rappoport, who explains the financial sector to me, and Marcia Marley, who organizes projects for the poor and also helps keep the Democrats winning – were there. Another former student, Sandy Jacoby, became my mentor in understanding Eastern philosophy. Melissa Appleyard provides me with renewed energy and feedback on high-tech industries. The list goes on and on, with my gratitude to my students for enriching my life.

We all struggle with key issues – how to use economics to help society, how to keep pushing policies even when being ignored, and how to balance work, family, and community. No one has found the golden path, and yet we have found meaningful paths.

Growing up white in the South, I witnessed nice white people who were also innately racist, although they did not think they were racist and would have been insulted if called racist. Similarly, in my early career, I experienced nice male economists who were innately sexist, although they did not think they were sexist and were insulted when called sexist. Social norms are so embedded in daily life that they are hard for people to observe; they are taken for granted as normal, acceptable behavior. Much of my life, both personal and professional, has involved confronting and seeking to change social norms that result in pain for those disadvantaged by them as well as unspoken and erroneous policy prescriptions that stem from them.

Notes

1 "The Impact of Turnover on Group Unemployment Rates," *Review of Economics and Statistics* 59 (November 1978): 415–426.
2 See Strober's essay in this volume, which describes her discriminatory treatment at UC Berkeley.
3 "The Time-Poor: A New Look at Poverty," *Journal of Human Resources* 21 (Winter 1977): 27–48; "Unemployment: Theory and Policy, 1946–1980," *Industrial Relations* 22 (Spring 1983): 27–48; "The Changing Household: Implications for Devising an Income Support Program," *Public Policy* 26 (Winter 1978): 121–151; "Unemployment Insurance: A Positive Reappraisal," *Industrial Relations* 18 (Winter 1979): 121–151; "Training, Productivity, and Underemployment in Institutional Labor Markets," *International Journal of Manpower* 2 (1993): 47–58.

4 *American Standards of Living, 1918–1988* (Cambridge: Blackwell, 1994).
5 *Work and Pay in the United States and Japan* (with Y. Nakata, M. Reich, and L. Ulman) (New York: Oxford University Press, 1997); "Developing Skills and Pay through Career Ladders: Lessons from Japanese and U.S. Companies" (with Michael Reich), *California Management Review* (Winter 1997): 124–144.
6 *Economic Turbulence: Is a Volatile Economy Good for America?* (with Julia Lane and John Haltiwanger) (Chicago: University of Chicago Press, 2006).
7 "The Impact of Technological Change on Work and Wages" (with Ben Campbell), *Industrial Relations* (Winter 2002); *Chips and Change: How Crisis Reshapes the Semiconductor Industry* (with Greg Linden) (Cambridge, MA: MIT Press, 2009), ch. 6.
8 *Chips and Change.*
9 See the Department of Economics Learning Goals for Majors at UCB: elsa.berkeley. edu/econ/ugrad/ugrad_goals.shtml.
10 www.universityofcalifornia.edu/senate/underreview/HP_Senate_UEETF%20 review%20request.pdf.
11 R. A. Gordon, "Rigor and Relevance in a Changing Institutional Setting," *American Economic Review* 66 (1976): 1–14.
12 Teresa Ghilarducci, *When I'm Sixty-Four: The Plot against Pensions and the Plan to Save Them* (Princeton, NJ: Princeton University Press, 2008).

3

Personal Reflections on My Professional Life

John Y. Campbell

In my middle fifties, and as a father of young adults who are choosing their paths in life, I find myself looking along my own path. I ask myself why I chose it, where it has taken me, and where it will lead next.

HOW I BECAME AN ECONOMIST: ACCIDENTS AND ANCESTORS

Seen from one point of view, my life as an economist is serendipitous, the accidental result of decisions that I made in order to postpone commitments to one career or another. Seen from another point of view, it was no accident that I became a macrofinance economist; perhaps psychological forces have steadily pushed me along a predetermined path.

I grew up in Oxford, England, in an academic family and was fortunate enough to have an intellectually intense education. The private schools I attended, the Dragon School and Winchester College, had their eccentricities but both challenged their students every day.[1] I reached the moment when the English educational system demands that one choose a specialty even earlier than normal, at age fifteen.

Although I was intrigued by natural science, being young and naive I perceived a decision to continue studying science as a commitment to spending my life in a white lab coat, a commitment I was not willing to make. Accordingly I chose to study mathematics, history, French, and – as a last-minute extra – politics and economics.

When I applied to college, I had to choose a specific subject, but I resisted by reading PPE – philosophy, politics, and economics – at Corpus Christi College, Oxford. By making this choice I again avoided specialization. It gave me a strong training in verbal argument and the ability to write in forty-five minutes about any subject with no prior preparation. PPE equipped me to join what the English call the "chattering classes" of journalists, lawyers, politicians, and pundits, but it was not the ideal preparation for a research career.

However, it did make me increasingly interested in economics. After college I still had little idea what to do with my life, but I was intrigued by the possibility of living in the United States. I had US citizenship through my American mother, and I wanted to explore that side of my heritage, which seemed exciting and a little mysterious. At the same time, I hesitated to make an irrevocable commitment to life in another country. Working toward an American PhD seemed an ideal way to spend a few years in the United States while still retaining a natural path back to the United Kingdom. I applied to leading East Coast schools, was offered financial support by Yale, and started the economics PhD program there in the fall of 1979.

My initial interest lay in development economics, but I found little inspiration in that field at Yale. Instead, I came under the magnetic influence of James Tobin, and later on Steve Ross, and finally Bob Shiller, who arrived at Yale in the fall of 1982. The good fortune of meeting these extraordinary scholars led me to specialize in macroeconomics and finance.

What I have written so far is factually correct, but perhaps it is wrong to describe my career choices as a series of accidents and noncommitments. My deeper inclinations were also responsible.

From an early age I admired my father and my two grandfathers and felt a desire to match or exceed their achievements. I am named after my paternal grandfather, John Young Campbell, a gentle, scholarly Presbyterian minister. This J. Y. Campbell taught at Yale Divinity School in the 1920s but returned to parish ministry in Scotland during the Great Depression before finishing his career as a professor at Westminster College, Cambridge. Although the author of a much-cited 1947 article on the meaning of the New

Testament phrase "Son of Man" (an article that can still be found on Google Scholar among my own more worldly contributions), this J. Y. Campbell published little and never completed his magnum opus on St. Paul. I vividly remember my grandmother's distress when, after he suffered a stroke in his nineties, she realized that my grandfather's encyclopedic knowledge was irretrievably lost.

My maternal grandfather, Hans Christian Sonne, was a very different character. A restless Dane, he left home in the Edwardian era to work in the City of London and was one of the first currency speculators during World War I. After the war he moved to New York, became a successful banker, protected his own and his clients' financial interests during the Great Depression, and in later life became deeply concerned with questions of economic policy. He even wrote a children's book on economics, *Enterprise Island*, published in 1948. He was loyal and generous to his family in Denmark, particularly in the difficult period around World War II, and remains a legendary figure in the family two generations later.

Growing up, I found both these men to be intriguing, glamorous figures. I aspired to scholarly renown, but I was also fascinated by H. C. Sonne's forceful personality, entrepreneurial vigor, and worldly success. Looking back, I believe I sought a way to "split the difference," pursuing a hard-headed career that would have a visible impact on the world through the force of ideas.[2]

The energy with which I have aspired to meet this goal has much to do with my parents and my relationship with them. My mother was intelligent, enthusiastic, and giving, and always encouraged my sister and me to pursue learning with high aspirations. She also struggled with anxiety and alcoholism that eventually killed her when I was fourteen. At an early age I felt a responsibility to protect her, and that sense of responsibility has made me the kind of person who reluctantly agrees to be head boy at an English boarding school or department chair in an American university.

My father, who taught American history at Oxford and later at the University of Birmingham, was left to bring up two teenage children on his own. He rose to the occasion, giving us many happy memories, but he lost his professional momentum during the 1970s, writing elegant lectures and copious notes yet publishing little. In reaction I suspect I publish too much, treating even mediocre papers as if they are wounded comrades on the field of battle, never to be abandoned regardless of the cost.

So which of these two accounts is correct? Am I an economist by accident, or was it my destiny to become one? As I look at my professional life I perceive an analogy with the stochastic processes that financial economists use to describe asset prices. The deeper forces determine the long-run trend or drift of the processes, but the random accidents of life generate most of the day-to-day activity. Econometricians use filtering methods to infer the trend from the noisy time series they observe. My attempt to disentangle these two influences on my life is a personal version of such a filtering exercise.

I will make two last observations about my discipline. First, I value the emphasis of economics on underlying forces rather than superficial details. T. S. Eliot memorably wrote that the Elizabethan English playwright John Webster "saw the skull beneath the skin." Economics likewise looks beneath the skin of history to offer deeper insights about human affairs. Second, the universalism of economics appeals to me. Many social sciences increasingly emphasize cross-cultural variation, but economists continue to feel that our discipline goes deep enough to find universal determinants of human behavior – perhaps even determinants of culture itself.[3]

PROFESSIONAL SUCCESS: MENTORS AND MATCHING

An academic career can barely begin, let alone succeed, without the efforts of skilled and dedicated mentors. I was particularly fortunate in the people who played this role for me. At Yale Jim Tobin embodied the wisdom of a mature academic applying a lifetime of research to contemporary policy debates. Steve Ross and Peter Phillips brilliantly taught technique, rigorous analytical thinking, and the particular insights of financial economics and econometrics. Earlier, at Oxford, Andrew Glyn demonstrated how a committed teacher can communicate even ideas he questions or rejects himself.

Most important, though, were the people who showed me what it actually means to do research: to formulate an interesting new question, to develop a strategy for finding the answer, to explore the question from every angle, to test the answer for hidden weaknesses, to present the project to a skeptical audience, and finally to use the answer as a platform for asking another even more interesting question. I had a glimpse of this process in high school, through the exceptional mathematics teaching of John Durran. But at Yale it was the arrival of Bob Shiller that transformed my life. After I had spent eighteen painful months spinning my wheels, Bob's exciting research agenda and his willingness to open it to an enthusiastic but inexperienced student set me on a new and fruitful course.

Later, in my first job at Princeton, other senior economists shared their own research styles with me. Ben Bernanke and Angus Deaton were particularly important at that time. I began to write papers with other young economists such as Greg Mankiw and Pete Kyle, while improving my understanding of econometrics through informal coaching from Whitney Newey.

More recently, I have benefited from the extraordinary quality of the students I teach at Harvard. Lecturing to them about asset pricing and reading their PhD dissertations keep my mind sharp and my knowledge of the field up to date. Two of my books, *The Econometrics of Financial Markets* (with Andrew Lo and Craig MacKinlay, Princeton University Press, 1997) and *Strategic Asset Allocation* (with Luis Viceira, Oxford University Press, 2001), are directly based on my PhD teaching, and I hope to write a third such book soon. My students' able research assistance compensates for my declining technical skills relative to the state of the art. Often, I learn the work of my colleagues indirectly through its influence on students. And by collaborating with students on research papers, I create a team that is much more productive than any of its members could otherwise be.

Teamwork has also been essential to the success of a nonacademic venture, the asset management firm Arrowstreet Capital, LP, which I founded in 1999 with Peter Rathjens (a former PhD student from Princeton) and Bruce Clarke. From the beginning I knew that this enterprise would succeed only if I matched the contributions I could make (within a strict time limit of one day per week) with the energies of full-time investment professionals and the complementary skills of businesspeople. Over time, as the business has grown to employ more than 100 people, including two former colleagues from Harvard, Sam Thompson and Tuomo Vuolteenaho, I have come to appreciate the importance of quality not only in investment research but also in information technology and business disciplines.

All this makes me appreciate the insights of matching models of productivity, such as the "O-rings" model of Michael Kremer, the model of CEO pay by Xavier Gabaix and Augustin Landier, and agglomeration models in urban economics.[4] In these models, output is determined by the quality of a set of inputs, and the marginal product of each input is increasing in the quality of the other inputs. Efficient production requires an elitist matching of the best inputs, and, significantly, it amplifies small quality differences so that those inputs fortunate enough to join the best teams are considerably more productive than others with poorer matches. I am profoundly grateful for the high-quality matches that have shaped my professional life.

What can a young economist learn from this story? To advise a newly minted PhD to "get the best job you can" is not particularly helpful. But beyond this, networking is vitally important for finding compatible partners with whom to discuss ideas and write papers. This was true even in the 1980s, when I started my research career and when long-distance communications were far more primitive than today; how much more so now that one can collaborate with colleagues around the world, and even accelerate research by exploiting time-zone differences to write a paper almost around the clock.

Personal life is outside the scope of this essay, but of course matching is even more important personally than professionally. I met my wife, Susanna Peyton, almost thirty years ago, the only friend I ever met at a graduate student party (but in life, as in academia, quality matters more than quantity). She and I match well for many reasons, but the reason relevant to this essay is that we have complementary strengths. For example, I am an economics professor and she is a master's-prepared nurse; I am good at anticipating and avoiding problems, but when problems inevitably occur Susanna is much better at fixing them. Many academics marry other academics, even colleagues in their own discipline, but for my part I am very happy in a complementary marriage.

I will push this point one stage further. I have learned much about life through my oldest son, Graham, who was born with Down syndrome in 1986. Graham and his friends have taught me that people with developmental disabilities can be remarkably effective at making themselves and others happy. If a family is a team that produces happiness and a sense of shared identity and purpose for its members, you are fortunate indeed to have a person with Down syndrome on your team. When Graham was born, my senior colleague Ben Bernanke told me with characteristically kindly understatement that this was "not the worst thing that could happen." Twenty-five years and three more children later, I have come to understand more fully the wisdom of that remark and how satisfying it is to parent four people, each capable of making a unique contribution.

ASSET PRICING: THE ECONOMICS OF RISK AND TIME

My professional specialty is the field of asset pricing, memorably described by Christian Gollier as *The Economics of Risk and Time* (MIT Press, 2001). Asset pricing models abstract from many issues that are of central importance in other fields of economics – for example, strategic interaction and contracting – to focus on optimal decision making under uncertainty and equilibrium in competitive markets for claims to uncertain future payoffs. In fact, asset pricing economists are among the most active developers and users of decision theory and general equilibrium theory, the latter topic in particular having fallen out of favor among microeconomic theorists.

At the heart of asset pricing theory is the notion that arbitrage opportunities, or riskless profit opportunities, cannot exist. This idea was famously caricatured by Larry Summers as a triviality when he compared financial economists to "ketchup economists," wasting their time studying minor deviations between the prices of ketchup sold in one-quart and two-quart bottles. While the implications of ruling out arbitrage are by no means so trivial in general, my own interests have much more to do with investor attitudes toward *risky* profit opportunities. How great are the equilibrium rewards for taking financial risks? What features of investors' risk attitudes, risk exposures, and beliefs determine those rewards? Instead of "ketchup economics," a student who retains his sense of humor after suffering through my PhD course might call this "the economics of Jensen's inequality."

Another response to Summers is that basic truths can deliver surprisingly powerful insights. One valuable function of economics is to remind us that the real world must respect identities. My most important early work with Robert Shiller began with an accounting identity linking prices, dividends, and returns, sprinkled on some fairy dust by ruling out rational bubbles, and log-linearized to derive implications that I have continued to explore in the ensuing twenty-five years.

It was my privilege to enter the field of asset pricing at the tail end of one revolution, the "rational expectations revolution" of the 1970s, and at the very beginning of another, the "behavioral revolution" that began in the 1980s. Bob Shiller participated in the first and led the second, but when I first met him his behavioral interests were just beginning to emerge. I vividly remember grappling with the material in Tom Sargent's papers and books, the latest papers by Lars Hansen and Ken Singleton, and Bob Hall's classic work on consumption, as well as Shiller's and Eugene Fama's earlier writings on the properties of rational forecasts.

The ideas in this work, that economic theory tells you what should be unpredictable as well as what should be predictable and that rational forecasts have testable properties, have personal as well as professional meaning to me.

The law of iterated expectations states that if your forecasts are rational, you should not be able to predict your own forecast errors or changes in your own future forecasts. For this reason, forecasts should be less volatile than the variables being forecast. In personal life, I aspire to rational self-mastery, which has analogous implications. I try not to make decisions that I can anticipate regretting or enter a state of mind that will predictably change. I try to ensure that my most intense emotions come from experiences rather than the anticipation of those experiences.

Of course, psychologists and behavioral economists have taught us what we know from personal experience: that it is extremely difficult to live up to such an ideal. In fact, the effort is so unnatural that it should be confined to a few areas of life where rationality is most valuable. Homo economicus may be a successful investor, but that will not do him much good if he ends up divorced and estranged from his children.[5] So while my pursuit of rational action is serious, I try not to let it become obsessive.

Behavioral finance has developed enormously in the past twenty-five years, elaborating two main points: that many investors deviate systematically from the prescriptions of traditional decision theory and that attempts by a minority of rational arbitrageurs to exploit this behavior are limited by the capital that those arbitrageurs can deploy. While I am not identified as a behavioral economist, I have spent much of my career reacting in several ways to these important insights.

First, I have explored models of preferences that go beyond the very limited class traditionally considered reasonable by mainstream finance economists. My work with John Cochrane on habit formation is one example, but I also appreciate the usefulness of Epstein-Zin preferences, allowing the coefficient of risk aversion and elasticity of intertemporal substitution to be independent free parameters. Both these preference specifications retain the important property that risk aversion does not vary with long-run movements in wealth, which is necessary to explain the absence of trends in long-run financial time series. Models using these preference specifications are valuable both normatively and as a way to relate the properties of aggregate asset prices to the risk attitudes of long-lived rational investors. Increasingly, I interpret these models not literally as descriptions of a representative agent, but as ways to understand the risk perceptions of important players in a complex economy populated by many different types of investors.

Second, the study of household-level financial decision making forces me to the conclusion that households often behave in ways that are inconsistent with these or any other reasonable specifications of preferences. I believe the right response is to call these behaviors mistakes, to study the circumstances that make them more or less common, and to devise interventions to reduce their incidence. Models of mistakes may be useful but should not be interpreted as stable descriptions of human behavior, comparable to traditional economic models, because people seek – and sometimes find – ways to avoid making mistakes. In 2005 I devoted my presidential address to the American Finance Association to this field of "household finance," which was already flourishing and has become even more active since then.

Third, I agree with behavioral economists that arbitrage is an imperfect mechanism for eliminating anomalies in asset markets. Ironically, though, the finance profession has contributed much more to the elimination of anomalies since it accepted the fact that anomalies exist. Asset pricing economists often devote a portion of their time to asset management companies that trade on patterns documented in the academic literature, and thereby help to eliminate them. The most famous early example, Long-Term Capital Management, traded too aggressively and failed spectacularly, but other firms, including Arrowstreet Capital, continue in this tradition.

I take great pleasure in testing the insights of academic finance in real time, with real money on the line. This activity has given me a keen awareness that predictability of asset returns is hard to exploit. The true meaning of the efficient market hypothesis is not that markets are perfectly efficient at all times but that inefficiencies tend to be transitory, vulnerable to elimination or destabilization by the activities of arbitrageurs, particularly in markets that are liquid enough for large transactions to be accomplished at reasonable cost.

An important, insufficiently appreciated point is that household investment mistakes are important for social welfare whether or not they influence equilibrium asset prices. One can imagine a world in which all stock returns satisfy a classical asset pricing theory such as the capital asset pricing model, yet in which individual investors hold undiversified stock positions or pay excessive fees to mutual fund managers. Such a world could be improved by promoting diversified, low-cost investing even though traditional asset pricing scholars would perceive no alarming anomalies.

ACADEMIC FINANCE: CORRUPT OR CONSTRUCTIVE?

Finance economists have been on the defensive since the global financial crisis began to unfold in 2007. Some of the criticism is absurd. For example, Charles Ferguson's 2010 movie *Inside Job* argues that the economics profession has been corrupted by secret financial ties with the banking industry, and for this reason academic economists kept quiet about the problems they could see developing during the credit boom. This argument ignores some important facts. Economists have a wide variety of outside activities that in general provide helpful insights and experience; these activities have been disclosed on economists' CVs and elsewhere (although not in any standard format, a weakness that should be corrected); economists compete to analyze publicly available data, so even if a few economists were to suppress their misgivings about financial trends, others would fill the gap; and the rewards for correctly predicting financial problems are enormous, providing more than adequate incentives for whistleblowers.

I can only laugh about my own performance in *Inside Job*. At the time of my interview with Charles Ferguson I did not understand that as the incoming chair of the Harvard Economics Department, I had been assigned the role of the evil face of the establishment. I also did not understand that hemming and hawing, even if motivated by the desire to take the time needed to express oneself precisely, looks comically inept when edited with hostile intent. I realized my mistake after sneaking into a showing of the movie with my old friend Jim Poterba, disguised in jeans and a baseball cap. Living in a liberal suburb of Boston with an interest in independent film, I then had to endure the movie's five-week run in my local theater.

Another misguided criticism is that excessive faith in the efficient markets hypothesis caused the financial crisis. While it may be true that some regulators and central bankers were too complacent about rising equity and house prices, the worst problems were caused by financiers who forgot the efficient markets wisdom that an investment opportunity that appears too good to be true actually is. And I have already made the point that academic finance economists were much less attached to the efficient markets hypothesis in the 2000s than they had been in the 1960s or 1970s.

All this said, finance economists do have a responsibility to society, and there are some real lessons to be learned from recent events. One is that we should find ways to speed up our normal deliberate pace of historical analysis. We now have a detailed understanding of problems with mortgage underwriting and credit ratings in 2005 and 2006, but that knowledge would have been much more valuable if it had arrived earlier, albeit with less detail and sophistication. Two ways to achieve this are to involve academics more closely with public-sector data collection efforts and to create more publication outlets like the *Brookings Papers on Economic Activity* for high-quality research focused on current developments.

Finance economists have traditionally been hesitant to address large questions about the structure of the financial industry and financial regulation, but this needs to change. One of the best experiences of my recent professional life was my participation in the Squam Lake Group of financial economists, convened by Ken French. It was astonishing to me that fifteen academics with very different areas of expertise were able to reach consensus on a number of principles of financial reform, in time to publish in 2010

The Squam Lake Report: Fixing the Financial System (Princeton University Press). We were helped by a sense of urgency created by the financial crisis and the Washington debate on financial regulation, but I hope that similar efforts can succeed in the future even when that sense of urgency fades.

Putting all this together, I believe that academic finance economists should not only seek knowledge but also accept the mission (difficult, but hopefully not impossible) of promoting rational financial behavior. If the mission can be accomplished, individuals will benefit directly from the better decisions they take, and society will benefit indirectly from prices that more accurately reflect information about investment opportunities.

Finance economists can fulfill this mission in various ways. We can solve nonstandard investment problems and explain the solutions; we can build investment organizations that invest clients' money on rational principles and drive prices toward efficient levels; we can work as financial educators to improve basic financial literacy; we can try to improve the quality of information provided to consumers; we can help to design easy-to-use investment products that meet real household needs (an activity that might be called "household financial engineering"); and we can give advice on financial regulation to promote financial stability and consumer financial protection. I look forward to contributing to these efforts and enjoy the thought that both my grandfathers would have found them worthwhile.

Notes

1   The Dragon School has many interesting alumni, including among my near contemporaries the writer Pico Iyer, the scientist and entrepreneur Stephen Wolfram, and the actor Hugh Laurie. Iyer has recently written about the school in *Harper's Magazine* (November 2011). Winchester College is an ancient English boarding school founded in 1382, with an intellectual tradition epitomized among its alumni by the physicist Freeman Dyson. When I attended, the living conditions were still somewhat medieval. Central heating was installed only a few years later, after a snowman built in one of the dormitories lasted three days without melting. To explain the experience to American friends, I say, "Hogwarts without the magic," although this does not do justice to the school's own special magic.

2   My goddaughter recently hit the nail on the head by giving me a coffee mug decorated with the cover of the Pelican Books first edition of Susan Stebbins's 1939 *Thinking to Some Purpose*.

3   For this reason I found myself out of sympathy with the treatment of social science in Harvard's most recent reform of its general education curriculum. Standing up to defend a more analytical, universalist emphasis, I provoked criticism from a distinguished colleague, who said, "This is the attitude that got us into Iraq!"

4   Michael Kremer, "The O-Ring Theory of Economic Development," *Quarterly Journal of Economics* 108 (1993): 551–575; Xavier Gabaix and Augustin Landier, "Why Has

CEO Pay Increased So Much?" *Quarterly Journal of Economics* 123 (2008): 49–100. Edward Glaeser, *Triumph of the City* (Harmondsworth, Penguin Press, 2011), gives a popular account of similar ideas in urban economics.

5 In the words of an amusing vodka advertisement, "Your CEO calls you Jack. The Treasury Secretary calls you John. Your kids call you Mr. Phillips." The ad offers a dubious cure: "Find balance. Find Ultimat."

4

Gray Eminence?

Vincent P. Crawford

INTRODUCTION

When the editors invited me to contribute an essay to *Eminent Economists II: Their Life Philosophies*, I found the adjective intimidating. My hesitance grew as I reviewed the list of contributors to the first *Eminent Economists* volume and reread their magnificent, moving essays. I wondered, "Why not *Salient Economists*? That I could live with." My muse (a librarian and sometime bookseller) replied: "Yeah ... just think how many copies *that* would sell!"

My title is an attempt to reduce the gap between expectations and results.[1] But even this reframing of the task left me uncomfortable with the idea of writing about something as self-conscious as a life philosophy. Until recently unaware even of having had one, I doubted my ability to articulate

I owe thanks to Zoë Crawford for her encouragement and valuable advice, both on this essay and over the years. I also owe thanks to Miguel Costa-Gomes, Avinash Dixit, and Nagore Iriberri for their support and good suggestions.

one worth reading about. Besides, didn't those who would be interested already know me well enough to infer what my philosophy must be?

Several factors made me agree to write the essay. First, the invitation came as I finished up a third of a century (literally thirty-three and a third years) at the University of California, San Diego, in preparation for starting a second job at Oxford. That seemed a salient time to summarize what I had learned about my profession. I also had a vivid memory of my colleague Sir Clive Granger, whose 2009 death prevented him from contributing to *Eminent Economists II*, at a UCSD gathering in his honor. He explained the even more ambitious turn his research had lately taken by saying, "Winning a Nobel Prize is one of those things that builds self-confidence." I thought, "What in the world are the *other* things?" When the invitation came I saw that it might be one – one that didn't require anything as difficult as discovering cointegration.

Next, my muse answered my main concern by turning it on its head: "You should do it! You're not very introspective, and you might learn something about yourself" (delivered like a dissertation adviser complimenting a student on a particularly clever choice of research topic). Finally, I discovered that there was a safety net: rereading the first *Eminent Economists* volume suggested that contributors unaware of having a life philosophy, or unable to articulate one, could get by with a professional philosophy.[2] Perhaps data-mining the advice I had been in the habit of giving to students, colleagues, and authors would yield something passable.

This essay never strays far from the net. I start by discussing my research orientation toward game theory and its applications in economics, and how I came by it.[3] By a happy coincidence, my orientation and birth cohort allowed me to participate in not one but two scientific revolutions: the game-theoretic revolution of the 1970s and 1980s and the still-continuing "behavioral" revolution that followed. I next discuss in more detail a representative strand of my work, on strategic communication, whose motivation and development span both revolutions. The openness to evidence and theoretical adaptability this continuing strand required was an important professional lesson. I conclude by trying to distill some other generalizable lessons from my experience in what Tony Hillerman once called "the professor business."

THE ROAD TO GAME THEORY AND ECONOMICS

I came to game theory and then economics by what anyone who has read graduate application essays will see as the normal route: via an early love of mathematics followed by a desire to apply it to something human. I assumed from about age eight that I would find a job in research, without knowing what that meant.[4] I was no clearer about the field than the job description but thought vaguely of something in mathematics, engineering, or natural science.[5]

Until college my love of mathematics was pure, with little thought of application. (I did prefer concrete and visualizable ideas over abstract ones and, perhaps for that reason, discrete over continuous mathematics.) My pre-college formal education did nothing to change this. There was no economics beyond brief, pro forma mentions in civics and history, and no game theory other than the commentaries on military strategy in Caesar and Xenophon.[6]

In my pre-college informal education there was one crucial exception, which greatly expanded my view of what mathematics was for. My parents had the prescience to give me, at age ten, a copy of James R. Newman's wonderful anthology, *The World of Mathematics* (New York: Simon & Schuster, 1956). I devoured all 2,500-plus pages, including Richard B. Braithwaite's article, "Theory of Games as a Tool for the Moral Philosopher."[7] Even without knowing what moral philosophy was, I was surprised and delighted that mathematics could be used to think about human as well as physical phenomena. I do not remember learning much of the substance of game theory from Braithwaite's article, and because I had no easy way to find more to read about game theory, I put it on the back burner. But with hindsight it seems likely that the mere knowledge of the existence of a theory of strategic behavior made me look harder for general principles underlying the behavior patterns I saw "in the wild." I now give several examples, chosen mainly to illustrate principles that later became important in my research.

One of the first organizations I belonged to was the Boy Scouts, a rich source of strategic experience.[8] The most interesting scouting example concerns an orienteering competition, in which one had to take a compass bearing across a field and then follow the bearing to the goal, blindfolded but permitted to look down under the blindfold at the compass. The need to allow us to look at the compass made it easy to cheat, and this was common knowledge. Cheating was in fact so easy that it would have made the contest a boring waste of time. (There was no prize.) I therefore resolved not to cheat, thinking that other scouts would do the same.

I happened to be the first contestant and was pleased to come within a few feet of the goal. Then I watched, amazed, as most of the remaining scouts hit the goal exactly on target. I remained amazed throughout the contest, but the source of my amazement evolved. At first I was amazed at the skill of the scouts who came after me, for it had been quite difficult to come even within a few feet. Then, after the second or third scout hit the goal exactly, I marveled at how obvious it was that they must have cheated. I was next amazed that so few scouts saw how obvious this would be. Finally, I was amazed that it did not occur to any of them to feign small errors.[9] These lessons were driven home to all of us soon afterward, when the scoutmasters promoted me – not otherwise an exceptional scout – to the highest scout office in the troop.

There were two game-theoretic/economic lessons here, which I articulated to myself only much later, when I acquired the required conceptual vocabulary. The first concerns statistical verification of compliance in agency relationships. It is now well understood, though with no help from me. The second and in my view equally important lesson was how difficult people find it to put themselves in others' shoes and how much simpler their models of others are than their models of themselves. This, my first step toward behavioral game theory, plays a leading role in my current research, including the work on strategic communication discussed later in this chapter.

Another especially rich source of strategic experience was competitive sailing, with its clear rules and clearly specified objectives. Here I give four of the most interesting examples.

The first concerns the general principle that when one is ahead in any kind of race, it is beneficial to reduce the variability of changes in the size of one's lead, because (for well-behaved distributions) this increases the probability of still being ahead at the finish. One corollary is obvious: in sports that have deadlines, it is beneficial to stall when ahead.

In sailboat racing the principle has an important but less obvious corollary: when one is ahead, it is beneficial to increase the correlation between shocks to one's own and others' performance, because this reduces the variability of changes in one's lead. Its most common application concerns sailing a windward leg, in which the most important shocks are unpredictable shifts in wind direction. There the way to increase the correlation between one's own and others' shocks is to "cover" that is, to stay on the same side of the course (relative to the direction of the goal) as others do, so that wind shifts, favorable or not, will affect all boats' performances approximately equally. Covering is strategically important in multi-boat races, but it is especially important in two-boat match races like the America's Cup. Dennis Conner taught the non-sailing public how important covering can be when, with a fifty-seven-second lead in *Liberty* at the start of the fifth leg of the last race of the 1983 Cup, he failed to cover and lost the race, and the Cup, to *Australia II*.

This covering principle is more interesting than most because it depends on a rich view of uncertainty. Both stalling and covering have clear analogues in economic competitions. The analogue of stalling is well understood in the literature on patent races. To my knowledge the analogue of covering has not yet been studied, though possibly its practical importance is limited on land.

A second example illustrates the importance of seeing patterns in data when one's understanding is shaped but not dictated by theory. Pop quiz: You are racing in a large fleet, with all of the boats struggling to make progress in a light breeze. They are apparently succeeding, but not by much. Then, suddenly, one boat starts to pull ahead at a small but clearly noticeable rate, just as if it had switched on a tiny, silent engine (not allowed, of course). Soon afterward, another boat starts to pull ahead, at exactly the same rate. What should you do and why?

The (uniquely optimal!) answer is that you should drop your anchor, surreptitiously. The crew of the first boat to pull ahead has figured out that even though they were making progress through the water, the current was strong enough to make them lose ground over the bottom. Anchoring, surreptitiously, stopped that loss while slowing the spread of their insight.

This kind of race, which sailors jokingly call an "anchoring duel," conveys two game-theoretic/economic lessons, which I again failed to articulate to myself until later. The first is the now widely recognized importance of social learning: in some settings we can learn as much from others' responses to experience as from the experience itself. The second lesson is that even with vague knowledge of the structure, attention to data may compel a particular interpretation. (The "smoking gun" here is that the second boat starts to pull ahead at exactly the same rate as the first, which makes alternative explanations of the change in performance highly implausible.)

It seems remarkable that data can be so compelling even when the new interpretation requires expanding the universe of possible models – violating Leonard J. Savage's "small worlds" assumption (*The Foundations of Statistics*, New York: John Wiley and Sons, 1954). A meta-lesson concerns research strategy. The first crew probably learned that they should anchor (long before electronic navigation) by taking a land bearing, something that does not always occur to sailors who are making apparent progress through the closer and much more salient water. That crew (not mine) was disciplined enough to look for disconfirming evidence even when its favored theory seemed to be performing well, a choice that goes against human instinct. The second crew (still not mine) was more alert than most but managed to replace its favored theory by the correct one only when confronted with overwhelming evidence of the cost of holding onto it. Even that takes some discipline, but in an anchoring duel it doesn't take long for the rest of the fleet to adopt and act on a better theory. It is no less important for economists to be intellectually flexible enough to accept disconfirming evidence, but their adjustments often seem to be slower, perhaps because the penalties for being persistently wrong are weaker.

Another sailing example has to do with a tactic that I saw only later, in college. Races start at a specified time, after which the boats may cross a line usually marked by buoys. One of "my" skippers had an unusual starting method, in which he sailed along the "wrong" side of the line, timing it to swing around the buoy at the favored end and cross the line from the correct side, just on time. This would not have worked in equilibrium, because a boat making a nearly perfect orthodox start has the right of way (via the "antibarging" rule) and can legally block a barger like my skipper from starting on time. With my skipper, however, it worked every time, because no one ever anticipated his ploy well enough to block his start.[10] He is now a tax attorney, and I can only imagine the revenue losses caused by his tax avoidance schemes.

This example is intriguing because it depends on deviating from Nash equilibrium to exploit anticipated suboptimal choices by opponents. Robert E. Lee (quoted in Douglas Southall Freeman, *R. E. Lee: A Biography*, New York: Charles Scribner's Sons, 1934) once explained why he had failed to exploit a mistake by the opposing Union general, saying, "It is proper for us to expect [the enemy] to do what he ought to do." Prescient as this half-definition of Nash equilibrium was, I think this was one of few instances in which General Lee was wrong.

A final sailing example, again from college, has to do with the contest between reason and emotion in decision making. Early in a five-race series for the MacMillan Cup, our boat was forced, by another boat fouling us, to foul a third boat. Unlike common law, the rules of sailing make no distinction between voluntary and involuntary violations; or more precisely (much as in the Catholic requirement to avoid "occasions of sin") they treat failure to avoid a situation where one is forced to commit a foul as equally culpable as a freely chosen foul. Thus, we were as sure to be disqualified as the boat that forced us to commit the foul. In discussion after the race, it was noted that we would get one more point if we withdrew voluntarily than if we contested the foul and lost. We decided to contest it anyway, because the foul had not been "our fault" and (though this was unstated) we thought the point was unlikely to decide the series. Unsurprisingly, we lost the hearing and the point. Surprisingly, three days later we lost the Cup, by exactly one point. I would like to think that we all learned to control our emotions better, but I cannot swear to this.

GAME THEORY AND ECONOMICS

I began my formal study of game theory and economics almost simultaneously, when I enrolled at Princeton in 1968. I enrolled in my first economics courses and didn't like them very much, but I greatly enjoyed Paul A. Samuelson's textbook, *Economics: An Introductory Analysis* (7th ed., New York: McGraw-Hill, 1967). I also enrolled in the honors mathematics sequence and learned in the first few weeks – at one of the best places in the world to learn that one doesn't really want to be a pure mathematician – that I needed to look elsewhere for my field of research. I still had no formal instruction in game theory, but I started reading about it more seriously – starting with Anatol Rapoport's *Two-Person Game Theory: The Essential Ideas* (Ann Arbor: University of Michigan Press, 1966) – and also reading more about economics – starting with Samuelson's *Foundations of Economic Analysis* (Cambridge, MA: Harvard University Press, 1947) and John R. Hicks's *Value and Capital* (2d ed., Oxford: Clarendon Press, 1946).

Needing more guidance, I went to Oskar Morgenstern's secretary to make an appointment.[11] I had planned only to make an appointment, and so was dressed normally for me at the time rather than properly. To my chagrin his secretary waved me in to see him immediately, and he (dressed more than well enough for both of us) was very kind. He wrote me a short reading list, which I still have. There were four references: Morton D. Davis, *Game Theory: A Nontechnical Introduction* (New York: Basic Books, 1970); John D. Williams, *The Compleat Strategyst: Being a Primer on the Theory of Games of Strategy* (New York: McGraw-Hill, 1966); R. D. Luce and H. Raiffa, *Games and Decisions: Introduction and Critical Survey* (New York: John Wiley & Sons, 1957); and John von Neumann and Oskar Morgenstern, *Theory of Games and Economic Behavior* (3d ed., Princeton University Press, 1953). The thing I remember most clearly was his advice: "Don't start with my book with von Neumann!" My next stop was the bookstore, and needless to say I didn't follow that part of his advice.

Princeton offered even more than this to a budding game theorist. Despite my fiasco in honors mathematics, there were many mathematics courses a non-genius could take, and I took most of them. I indulged my love of discrete mathematics by taking several courses from Albert W. Tucker. His discussion of his students David Gale and Lloyd S. Shapley's "College Admissions and the Stability of Marriage," *American Mathematical*

Monthly (January 1962): 9–14, and the recognition that their models were markets even though they had no prices, led me a decade later to write my first papers on matching markets.

More importantly, and probably inspired by Rapoport's book, I did part of my Economics Department junior independent work on the (non)convergence of adaptive learning processes to mixed-strategy Nash equilibrium. Later this led to my first published paper, "Learning the Optimal Strategy in a Zero-Sum Game," *Econometrica* (September 1974): 885–891.

Most importantly, a dormitory neighbor in my senior year, having just returned from two (voluntary) years of combat in Vietnam, gave me his copy of Thomas C. Schelling's *The Strategy of Conflict* (Oxford University Press, 1960), saying, "You'll get more out of this than I did." Even without bullet holes, the book looked like it had been in combat, and my neighbor's jungle marginalia often revealed spirited disagreement with Schelling's arguments. *The Strategy of Conflict* was like nothing I had read, and it opened up a new world for me, full of rich analyses of strategic thinking and applications whose realism and institutional detail went far beyond the toy examples I had seen before. If one book can change an intellectual life, that was it for me.[12]

In graduate school at the Massachusetts Institute of Technology I learned a great deal of economics, which was enormously important to my research. I was also allowed to write an entirely game-theoretic dissertation, one with no mention of prices. But what I learned has comparatively little to do with the research I discuss here, so I do not discuss it.

STRATEGIC COMMUNICATION THROUGH TWO SCIENTIFIC REVOLUTIONS

As I said earlier, my birth cohort and orientation toward game theory and its economic applications allowed me to participate in two scientific revolutions. The first was the game-theoretic revolution of the 1970s and 1980s, in which researchers in economics took game theory over from its previous owners in mathematics, used it (mostly noncooperative game theory) to formulate economic models that everyone had assumed were intractable only a few years before, and then used equilibrium to analyze the models. These advances made it possible to do strategic microeconomics with the rigor and clarity that had previously been thought possible only for perfect competition and monopoly. Something that bears emphasis for younger readers is how great an achievement it was just to get the logic of equilibrium analysis of those models right.

My most important contribution to the strategic revolution was the analysis of strategic communication via natural language (now called "cheap talk") in Vincent P. Crawford and Joel Sobel, "Strategic Information Transmission," *Econometrica* (November 1982): 1431–1451. "Cheap talk" refers to communication that has no direct payoff consequences. It can influence players' welfare, but only by influencing decisions that do have direct payoff consequences. Thus, lying involves no personal cost to the liar, as is commonly assumed in economics.

When Sobel and I started thinking about strategic communication, most people – encouraged by Michael Spence's emphasis on the importance of direct signaling costs in "Job Market Signaling," *Quarterly Journal of Economics* (August 1973): 355–374 – assumed that cheap talk could not credibly convey information in equilibrium, as the phrase "talk is cheap" suggests. That intuition is correct in two-person games of pure conflict, for if there were an equilibrium in which cheap talk conveyed information, the receiver's response to the sender's message would make the receiver better off, which would thus make the sender worse off, so that he would prefer to make his message uninformative. Nonetheless, it was clear from Schelling's *Strategy of Conflict* that cheap talk could be very effective in pure coordination games. The difference in cheap talk's effectiveness between the extremes of pure conflict and coordination made me want to know what happens in the mixed-motive games in between.

Sobel and I posed this question in a class of what are now called sender-receiver games, in which the sender observes a one-dimensional piece of private information and sends a message based on it to the receiver, who then takes an action that determines the welfare of both. The receiver cannot commit to a mechanism as in the agency literature. Thus, in a sequential equilibrium he must take an action that is optimal given his beliefs after hearing the message. We assumed that the sender's and receiver's preferences differ in a limited, realistic way, in that a fully informed sender and receiver would both prefer a higher action, the higher the sender's private information, but the sender would always prefer a higher action than the receiver.

Sobel and I characterized the relationships between the sender's observed signal and the receiver's choice of action that are possible in a sequential equilibrium.[13] The key issue is how much information can be transmitted in equilibrium and how the amount is influenced by the difference between the sender's and receiver's preferences.

We showed that all equilibria are "partition equilibria," in which the sender, in effect, partitions the set of states into contiguous groups and tells the receiver only which group his observation lies in. When talk is cheap, in equilibrium the receiver reads the sender's message as meaning "I like what you do when I say this (better than anything I could get you to do by saying something else)." Our analysis showed that, despite the prevailing intuition at the time, if preferences are not too different this reading of the message conveys some useful information.

For any given difference in preferences we showed that there is a range of equilibria, from a "babbling" equilibrium with one partition element to equilibria with more elements that exist if the preference difference is small enough. Under reasonable assumptions there is a most informative equilibrium, which has the most partition elements and gives both sender and receiver the highest ex ante expected payoffs of any equilibrium. As the preference difference decreases, the amount of information transmitted in the most informative equilibrium increases. But unless preferences are identical, even the most informative equilibrium has a coarse partition and so conveys the sender's information only with a certain intentional vagueness. Although both sender and receiver would be better off ex ante if the sender could commit to telling the truth, his inability to so commit makes any equilibrium involve some degree of vagueness.

It was very satisfying to show that cheap talk can convey information when the difference in preferences is not too large and to confirm the intuition that the preference difference limits the amount of information that can be transmitted in equilibrium. But we were disappointed that our analysis shed no light on lying or deception. In equilibrium the receiver's beliefs on hearing the sender's message must be an unbiased (though noisy) estimate of the signal. Thus, in equilibrium the sender's message cannot systematically fool the receiver; it can only add noise to the sender's information.

There are various remedies for this, one of which is explored in Sobel's "A Theory of Credibility," *Review of Economic Studies* (October 1985); 557–573, which explores the equilibrium implications, in repeated play, of the receiver's uncertainty about the sender's motives. But I was also concerned that predictions of senders' and receivers' strategies based on our equilibria seemed to miss systematic patterns in subjects' behavior in experiments. In Hongbin Cai and Joseph Tao-Yi Wang, "Overcommunication in Strategic Information Transmission Games," *Games and Economic Behavior* (July 2006): 7–36, and several prior experiments, senders told the truth more than predicted in any equilibrium ("overcommunication"), and receivers were more credulous than in any equilibrium. Yet despite these deviations, our equilibrium comparative statics prediction, that the closer the sender's and receiver's preferences the more information is transmitted, was strongly confirmed.

How could these results be reconciled with a sensible theory? Having survived the struggle to get the logic of the equilibrium analysis right, I had to adapt, moving from the strategic revolution to a second, "behavioral" revolution. Behavioral game theory alloys the decision-theoretic rationality of traditional game theory with psychologically more realistic models of how people think about others' responses to incentives. The part of the theory I shall discuss here concerns initial responses to games, where people's beliefs about others' responses must come from strategic thinking rather than learning.

Equilibrium can and often is viewed as a model of strategic thinking, but an important experimental regularity is that people's thinking often fails to follow the fixed-point logic that equilibrium usually requires. Instead people seem to follow strategic rules of thumb based on models of others that are systematically simpler than their models of themselves – like my fellow scouts' models. That doesn't mean that people never behave as if in an equilibrium. The evidence suggests that the most common rules of thumb mimic equilibrium in sufficiently simple games, while deviating systematically in some more complex games. Nor does people's aversion to fixed-point logic mean that with enough stationary experience, they cannot converge to equilibrium strategies an analyst would need fixed-point logic to characterize. It only means that fixed-point logic does not *directly* describe people's thinking in their initial responses to games.

A series of experimental analyses with normal-form games, culminating in Miguel Costa-Gomes, Vincent Crawford, and Bruno Broseta, "Cognition and Behavior in Normal-Form Games: An Experimental Study," *Econometrica* (September 2001: 1193–1235, and Costa-Gomes and Crawford, "Cognition and Behavior in Two-Person Guessing Games: An Experimental Study," *American Economic Review* (December 2006): 1737–1768, seeks to identify the most common rules of thumb people use in lieu of equilibrium logic. A robust finding is that many people use "level-k" rules, in which they start by anchoring their beliefs in a naive model of others' instinctive reactions to the game and then massage their beliefs by iterating best responses a small number of times: one, two, or at most three. The resulting level-k models provide an empirically well-supported structural alternative to equilibrium models of strategic thinking.

In "Lying for Strategic Advantage: Rational and Boundedly Rational Misrepresentation of Intentions," *American Economic Review* (March 2003): 133–149, I adapted level-k models to sender-receiver games in which a sender could communicate his intentions about how he would play an underlying two-person zero-sum game. Here, as explained earlier, in any equilibrium the sender's message must be uninformative, and the receiver must ignore it. Yet in real-world games with communication of intentions, we often observe messages that attempt to deceive, and such attempts sometimes succeed. My 2003 paper showed that a level-k model in which people anchor their beliefs in the literal meaning of messages gives a simple explanation of several commonly observed patterns in such settings.

My 2003 analysis is readily adapted to games in which the message concerns private information, as in Crawford and Sobel's analysis, rather than intentions. In such a model our equilibrium-based comparative statics result, that the closer the sender's and receiver's preferences, the more information is transmitted, continues to hold for empirically realistic distributions of level-k players. Earlier I stressed the importance of being open to disconfirming evidence. It is also important to be open to confirming evidence. Building on Cai and Wang's 2006 analysis of a sender-receiver game with one-sided private information as in Crawford and Sobel's analysis, Wang, Michael Spezio, and Colin F. Camerer, "Pinocchio's Pupil: Using Eyetracking and Pupil Dilation to Understand Truth-Telling and Deception in Sender-Receiver Games," *American Economic Review* (June 2010): 984–1007, have now found strong experimental support for such a level-k model. The model gracefully reconciles subjects' tendencies toward over-communication, excessive credulity, and other systematic deviations from equilibrium with the persistent support for Crawford and Sobel's comparative statics prediction.

FURTHER GENERALIZABLE LESSONS

What further lessons might be gleaned from all of this? Here are some simple rules (I take it that I am allowed to advise you to follow rules I haven't always followed myself):

1. Know the literature, but as much as you can, get your ideas from the world.
2. Put your ideas carefully into the context of others' work, giving them all due credit. We stand on the shoulders of giants, and medium-sized and short people too. If you give a clear, accurate summary of how ideas evolved, you will probably get at least your share of the credit anyway.
3. Make 99 percent sure your ideas are right, and then fight for them. Tough-mindedness is particularly necessary for original ideas. One

of my students persisted for a year trying to prove a result I was convinced wasn't true, and I am sorry to say I did not encourage him: quite the contrary. He was right, and the result was worth the year. Even worse, years before that I had proposed a significant generalization of one of my own results to an adviser who immediately conveyed his belief that the generalization wasn't true, saying, "Forget it!" I uncritically took his advice, only to discover years later that my generalization was an easily proved extension of my earlier result.

4. But even when 99 percent sure you are right, listen to others' criticisms and learn from them. And pick your fights: if you fight too often, unless you are very lucky your credibility will suffer.

5. Be kind to your juniors. One Saturday in graduate school I received a reprint in Russian, whose English title and abstract might as well have read "Chapter 2 of Vince Crawford's Dissertation." I phoned one of the two people I knew who spoke Russian, a senior faculty member, and asked if he would translate it for me. He said, "Sure. Come in Monday morning." I said, "But I mean *now*." Without batting an eye, he told me his address. His translation of the first few paragraphs made clear that it wasn't really Chapter 2. I will never forget his generosity. Many years later I had an opportunity to repay part of it by helping him get a difficult paper into shape for publication; but I still think I owe him. Good students are one of the best things about the professor business. The joy of being kind to them should be enough reward, but even if not, they will repay any kindness you show them many times over. (Stephen Jay Gould, *Wonderful Life* [New York: W. W. Norton, 1989, 139–141], has a wonderful passage on the reciprocal relationship between mentors and students.)

6. Be kind to your seniors. They can be fun. Besides, someday you will be a codger yourself.

7. Last but not least: be kind to your contemporaries. This follows from rules 5 and 6 by continuity – or is it convexity?

Notes

1 According to Wikipedia (en.wikipedia.org/wiki/%C3%89minence_grise), "An éminence grise … is a powerful advisor or decision-maker who operates secretly or unofficially. This phrase originally referred to Franois Leclerc du Tremblay, the right-hand man of Cardinal Richelieu. Leclerc was a Capuchin friar who wore grey, or rather brown, robes. Brown or light brown (now called 'beige') was called grey

in that era. The phrase 'His Eminence' is used to describe a Cardinal in the Roman Catholic Church."

2 Indeed, one contributor – a beloved teacher at MIT – seemed to have written about precisely what he pleased, claiming at the end to have forgotten what the assignment was.

3 Academic astrologers might attribute my orientation to having been born "under the star" of John F. Nash, Jr.'s "The Bargaining Problem," *Econometrica* (April 1950): 155–162.

4 I date this from a gift of a toy printing set, which I used to set a stamp that read "Vincent Crawford, Ph.D."

5 All this without clear examples: I learned a lot from my family, but those who worked at jobs closest to mine (engineers) died before they could teach me about their disciplines. So much for the importance of role models.

6 In grade school or high school in the 1960s, game theory was out of the question. In high school there might have been economics, but my Jesuit prep school prided itself on curricular conservatism. I now recognize their allegiance to the *Ratio Studiorum* (en.wikipedia.org/wiki/Ratio_studiorum) as a blessing, because it taught me things I later would have lacked the patience to learn, but virtually nothing I later had to unlearn. It also once allowed me to surprise an educationally traditionalist dinner companion by quipping that I had been educated in the seventeenth century.

7 This I now see was his inaugural lecture as the Knightbridge Professor of Philosophy at the University of Cambridge, originally published in book form (Cambridge University Press, 1955).

8 I experienced another rich source only as a spectator, when my parents, then active in local politics, bridged the gap between the ends of my school day and their work-days by using the spectator's gallery of the Maryland state legislature as a day care center. Perhaps because I was not directly involved, I extracted few if any concrete insights. But watching the legislature in action did give me a feel for the semistruc-tured maneuvers that are more characteristic of politics and economics as practiced than as usually modeled in noncooperative game theory.

9 Years later this lesson was reinforced by the experience of a graduate school class-mate. Fresh out of a British university soon after the end of the colonial era, he worked for an international organization that gave him the task of creating the first national income accounts for a developing country. Quickly realizing that collect-ing accurate data would be difficult, perhaps impossible, he took the "creating" in his task description more literally than his employers intended, generating syn-thetic data by simulating a then-popular growth model. Cleverer than my fellow boy scouts, he added normal errors with modest variance, and his dissimulation has apparently escaped detection.

10 The ploy worked better when others hadn't seen it before, but it worked even when they had. It can be argued that adapting equilibrium to incorporate decision errors, as in quantal response equilibrium, explains its success, but it worked even in top-level races where decision errors were small. He was the US national champion of his class.

11 This did not seem pushy at the time. Although John Nash was a recognized, legend-ary figure on campus, he was not on the faculty and he had not yet recovered to the point where students thought that they could interact with him.

12 I try to repay part of my debt in "Thomas Schelling and the Analysis of Strategic Behavior," in Richard Zeckhauser (ed.), *Strategy and Choice* (Cambridge, MA: MIT Press, 1991).

13 Because cheap talk signals have no direct payoff consequences, equilibrium does not determine the signaling strategies that support these relationships, but the possible relationships are independent of how they are supported.

5

Biochemist to Economist

Paul Davidson

My career as "professional economist" spans more than five decades. Entrance into the economics profession, however, began rather later than usual. I graduated from Brooklyn College in 1950 with majors in chemistry and biology. I never took a course in economics during my undergraduate years.

From 1950 to 1952, I went on to graduate training in biochemistry at the University of Pennsylvania, where I easily completed my courses while working as an instructor in biochemistry at the Medical and Dental Schools of the University of Pennsylvania. I decided to do a PhD thesis on DNA (this was before the discovery of the "double helix"). Although I had enjoyed my teaching duties, I quickly lost interest in biochemical research and withdrew from the program.

Not knowing what I would do for a living, I returned to New York and enrolled at City University of New York in an MBA program to prepare myself for the world of commerce. While there I was required to take a course in the principles of economics. As a biochemist trained in the questions of experimental design and statistical inference, I was appalled by the misuse of empirical data by the leading econometricians of that time.

My master's thesis involved criticizing econometric time series analysis that was being used as a forecasting device. Perhaps it was my biochemistry background and training in the design of experiments that led me to the understanding that most economic theory had little to do with the real world of experience and that the proof of such theory by econometric validation was merely a fanciful falsehood. In this early era of my economic career I recognized that most economic time series were generated by what I would later identify as a nonergodic stochastic process. At that time I tended to emphasize that the problem was the absence of a controlled experimental environment in the production of economic time series data. My biochemical background forced me to reject any analysis of data that was not collected under controlled experimental conditions. It was only years later, when I immersed myself in the rational expectations literature, that I made the obvious connection that in economics uncertainty about the future was associated with nonergodic stochastic processes. My master's thesis concluded that for most macroeconomic problems and analysis, current and past market data could not provide a reliable statistical forecast of future outcomes.

It was when I recognized that the "highly sophisticated" econometric analysis of the time was so misused that I decided that this was a field where I could return to a teaching occupation that I had enjoyed, while making a mark for myself and a contribution to society and the economics profession.

After returning to New York, I was conscripted (during the Korean War) into the US Army. I was properly identified as a scientific and professional person. After my basic military training as an infantryman, I was assigned to an Army biochemical research project. This convinced me that I did not want to become a biochemist.

After completing my military service, I returned to City University to complete my coursework and earn my MBA degree. At graduation I was the first recipient of the Leon Levy Award in finance and investments. (Leon Levy was the prime benefactor in establishing the Levy Institute for Economic Research at Bard College.)

While completing my work for the MBA, I applied to various universities for some form of fellowship remuneration while I went on to study for a PhD in economics. I received offers from MIT, Stanford, Brown, Chicago, and the University of Pennsylvania. Given my "scientific" biochemistry background, I thought I would prefer to go to a more technically oriented school such as MIT. (Had I gone to MIT I would probably have been a student of either Paul Samuelson or Robert Solow.) The University of Pennsylvania, however, made an offer that was more than twice as large as the MIT stipend offer. Consequently, the "invisible hand" of graduate student fellowship money led me to enroll in the graduate economics program at the University of Pennsylvania. There I came under the influence of Sidney Weintraub, who was just completing his masterpiece, *An Approach to the Theory of Income Distribution* (1958), which I found to be an engrossing analysis of what Keynes's general theory was really all about. Consequently, Sidney was the adviser on my doctoral dissertation, entitled *Theories of Relative Shares* (1960). This dissertation explains my early interest in macroeconomics, and especially income distribution.

My first academic job after receiving my PhD was as an assistant professor at Rutgers University. My first published article, "A Clarification of the Ricardian Rent Share" (1959), was in this area of income distribution. Although Weintraub had an important influence on my thinking over the years, we collaborated on only one published paper, "Money as Cause and Effect" (1973), which dealt with the question of exogenous versus endogenous changes in the money supply. In 1978, however, Weintraub and I together founded the *Journal of Post Keynesian Economics*. I have been an editor of this journal ever since 1978.

The connection between inflation, income distribution, and money was only vaguely perceived by Weintraub in those days. His discussion of Keynes's finance motive seemed to me oddly disjointed when combined with Sidney's masterful exposition of the aggregate supply-demand interdependence of Keynes's *General Theory*. It was not until I "cracked the nut" of Keynes's 1937 finance motive analysis addendum to his liquidity theory of money and showed my results to Keynes's biographer, Sir Roy Harrod (who happened to be visiting the University of Pennsylvania at the time), that I got a glimmer of the true role of money in the Keynesian revolution. Harrod was very enthusiastic about my finance motive manuscript and sent it to the editor of the *Oxford Economics Papers* with his recommendation for publication. With characteristic English reserve, Harrod wrote to me from Christ Church on May 27, 1964, indicating that he believed the editor "to be favourably disposed to it."

It was the publication of my "Keynes's Finance Motive" (1965) article that provided me with the confidence to strike out on my own in attempting to explicitly integrate monetary analysis into Keynes's revolutionary general theory. My paper "Money, Portfolio Balance, Capital Accumulation, and Economic Growth" (1968) was written in 1965 and submitted to

Econometrica in March 1966. The paper began with a specific criticism of Tobin's 1965 *Econometrica* money and growth model. My paper presented an alternative approach to money and capital accumulation more in tune with Keynes's *General Theory*. My alternative to Tobin's 1965 accumulation analysis involved utilizing the ratio of the spot market price of capital to the forward market price for capital, that is, the market demand price of existing real capital relative to the cost of producing new capital, as the relevant "invisible hand" ratio directing the entrepreneurial determination of the rate of investment or disinvestment in real capital each period. This spot to forward price of capital ratio is, of course, the equivalent of the famous q-ratio that Tobin was to discover three years later in 1968.

The story of this paper's history from its submission until its publication in *Econometrica* two years later in 1968 may have a moral for fledgling economists. Many months after the paper was submitted, Robert Stoltz, then the editor of *Econometrica*, sent back two referees' reports. Stoltz wrote that "[b]oth referees have found much in the paper of merit, but both feel that it falls short of being publishable in its present form ... [because it] is not precise enough in its analytic content." Stoltz encouragingly indicated that he would be "very willing to consider a revision that would be more analytic in character." Both referees had noted what they perceived as a lack of analytical precision. One referee specifically stated his displeasure at the paper's "essayistic and nonanalytical character."

Although the originally submitted manuscript that the referees believed lacked "precision" used the same supply and demand geometric diagrams as the published paper, the original manuscript was devoid of any algebraic expressions. This absence of algebra was apparently the basis for the referees' characterization of the manuscript as nonanalytical. I revised the paper by merely introducing a simple algebraic equation for each supply and demand relationship in the text just before the verbal description of these relationships and their geometric representations. The result was the addition of a total of fourteen equations. Otherwise, the textual exposition and geometric diagrams remained virtually unchanged.

On April 13, 1967, the editor informed me that this revised version of the manuscript was now apparently precise enough to be accepted for publication. I was overjoyed and expected the editor would follow normal publication protocol and request a rejoinder from Tobin that would be published in the same issue as my paper. I thought a response from such an eminent economist as Tobin – even if his comments were very critical (which I could not conceive as possible) – would be extremely useful for promoting my standing in the economics profession. My paper was finally published in the

April 1968 issue of *Econometrica* without any comment from Tobin. Instead Tobin published a paper announcing his discovery of the q-ratio in a different journal later in the same year.

Although I still believe this *Econometrica* article was one of my best papers, and even though it appeared in a very prestigious journal, it apparently failed to create any stir in the profession. I decided it would be necessary to write a book that would tie all my thoughts on money and employment together in a bundle that could not be overlooked. That book, which was written during my stay at Cambridge University in 1970–1971, was *Money and the Real World* (1972).

My visit to Cambridge was one of the most productive investments of my life. I gained tremendously from the almost daily interactions with Basil Moore (who was also visiting), as well as less frequent, but still fruitful discussions with Nicky Kaldor, Richard Kahn, Michael Posner, and Ken Galbraith (also visiting). Most important was my relationship with Joan Robinson. Joan and I immediately embarked on heated discussions regarding drafts of various chapters of my manuscript of *Money and the Real World.* Joan was clearly unhappy with my arguments regarding the Cambridge post-Keynesian approach. I remember her being particularly distressed by my criticisms of Kaldor's neo-Pasinetti theorem. After a few weeks of such discussions, she finally refused to speak to me further about my work.

Nevertheless, almost every morning when I arrived at my office at the faculty building on Sidgwick Avenue, I would find on my desk a sheet of paper with a question across the top in Joan Robinson's handwriting. Just as she did when she tutored an undergraduate student at Cambridge, Joan was setting me a daily essay to write. I diligently wrote my answer, and when she went up for morning coffee, I would place the paper with my answer to her question on the desk in her office. After lunch I would find my essay paper back on my desk with her easily recognizable scrawl indicating why the various points I had made in my essay were either wrongheaded or just plain wrong.

I learned a tremendous amount from these daily essay exercises – and, although she did not admit it at the time, I believe so did Joan Robinson. For in the years following my visit to Cambridge, I would often receive notes praising published papers of mine. For example, on July 3, 1978, she wrote about my paper "Money and General Equilibrium" (1977), which was published in the French journal *Économie Appliqué* – a journal produced by the Institut des Sciences Mathématiques et Économiques Appliquée, or ISMEA) – "I much enjoyed your piece in ISMEA. I hope you will put the same points where they will be read in the USA." And on September 13, 1978, regarding my paper "Why Money Matters" (1978), which appeared in the inaugural issue of the *Journal of Post Keynesian Economics*, Joan wrote, "I like your piece about 'crowding out.' This ought to settle the matter."

My friendship with Sir John Hicks began after we met at the International Economics Association's conference "The Microfoundations of Macroeconomics" in 1975 at S'Agoro in Spain. Among the variety of invited participants at this conference were neoclassical Keynesians, monetarists, general equilibrium Walrasian theorists, and the emerging group of what was to be called post-Keynesians. All the participants apparently agreed that the conference was a failure. Hicks recognized this in his statement at the concluding meeting that "our discussions had so far not done what we had set out to do. We had met to discuss a rather central issue in economics; but it had been shown that economists were not in a good state to discuss central issues ... we were each shooting off on our own paths, and we were lucky if we could keep in sight even our closest neighbour" (Hicks 1977: 373).

Nevertheless, Hicks told me after he heard my paper, "A Discussion of Leijonhufvud's Social Consequences of Inflation" (1977), that he (Hicks) believed that his views on the microfoundations of macroeconomics were closer to mine than to anyone else's at this conference.

After this conference, Hicks and I started to correspond, and I believe I had some impact on his changing view regarding the importance of the ISLM model. Hicks ultimately rejected the ISLM approach in an article published in the *Journal of Post Keynesian Economics* (Winter 1980–1981). In our continuing correspondence and at several personal meetings at the Athenaeum in London and at his home in Blockley during the 1970s and early 1980s, Sir John provided me with some very useful insights – which, though difficult to specify, no doubt had an influence on my developing thought, especially in regard to time, liquidity, contracts, and expectations.

On February 13, 1983, Hicks wrote to me regarding my paper "Rational Expectations: A Fallacious Foundation for Studying Crucial Decision Making Processes" (1982–1983). Hicks wrote: "I do like it very much. I have never been through that RE [Rational Expectations] literature; you know that I don't have proper access to journals; but I had just enough to be put off by the smell of it. You have now rationalized my suspicions, and have shown me that I have missed my chance, of labeling my own point of view as non-ergodic. One needs a name like that to ram a point home."

My interest in resource economics developed from a brief interlude in my academic career in 1960–1961, when, because of my low salary at Rutgers

University and the financial needs of my growing family, I took a position
(at two and a half times my Rutgers annual salary) as the assistant director
of the Economics Division of the Continental Oil Company (Conoco) in
Houston, Texas. At Conoco, I headed a small group of staff economists who
were primarily involved in providing economic projections and evaluating investment projects for the Management Executive Committee of the
corporation. The experience of participating in the managerial decisions
of a large corporation, even though it was in a staff rather than line position, was invaluable in clarifying in my mind the fundamental flaws of the
neoclassical theory of entrepreneurial expectation formation and decision
making.

My 1963 *American Economic Review* article, "Public Policy Problems
of the Domestic Crude Oil Industry," represents the distillation of analytical arguments that I developed (based on Keynes's "user cost" analysis of
the *General Theory*), while working for Conoco. I used my knowledge of
Keynes to try to affect both the decision making of management at Conoco
and the positions the corporation should take relative to the new economic
policy agenda of President Kennedy. Although I do not believe that I was
very successful in changing Conoco's strategies, I apparently impressed the
president of Conoco sufficiently that he asked me to help write all his public
speeches – which in those days were numerous.

My *American Economic Review* paper regarding the domestic crude oil
industry was well regarded in the profession. Several well-known scholars
in the field, for example, A. F. Kahn, M. Adelman, and R. H. Heflebower,
initiated further correspondence and discussions with me based on my
analysis. Years later, when A. F. Kahn was appointed the US "energy czar"
by President Jimmy Carter, Kahn invited me to his office in the Executive
Office Building for a one-on-one discussion of US energy problems and
policies that I thought the Carter Administration should pursue.

One of these kind people, that is, Kahn, Adelman, or Heflebower – I
never found out which one – recommended my name to Allen Kneese of
Resources for the Future (RFF) as a potential principal investigator of the
demand for water recreational activities. Apparently, Kneese did not believe
in the age-old adage that oil and water do not mix. Kneese and RFF provided
a generous grant for me to do an empirical study of the social value of water
recreational facilities. The results of this study, "The Social Value of Water
Recreational Facilities Resulting from an Improvement in Water Quality
in an Estuary: The Delaware – A Case Study" (1966), was published in an
RFF volume. The success of this initial study brought forth new invitations
to take on additional environmental studies, for example, "An Analysis of

Recreation Use of TVA Lakes" (1968) and "An Exploratory Study to Identify and Measure the Benefits Derived from the Scenic Enhancement of Federal Aid Highways" (1967). A further invitation to undertake a massive empirical study of two national recreation surveys for the US Bureau of Outdoor Recreation resulted in a book entitled *The Demand and Supply for Outdoor Recreation* (1968).

In 1973, with the OPEC embargo and resulting oil price spike, the question of crude oil and energy was again on the nation's mind. Art Okun of the Brookings Institution contacted me and asked me to do an analysis of oil production and consumption and its relevance to President Nixon's Project Independence. At approximately the same time, people at the Ford Foundation's Energy Policy Project requested a study regarding incentives and the oil industry. My study for the Brookings Institution was "Oil: Its Time Allocation and Project Independence" (1974), and that for the Ford Foundation was "The Relations of Economic Rent and Price Incentives to Oil and Gas Supplies" (1975). The conclusion of my empirical and theoretical analysis, as well as my understanding of the oil industry that I gleaned from my work at Conoco, was that the oil price spike the global economy absorbed in the 1970s was not the result of a Malthusian shortage in which the world was quickly running out of fossil fuels. It was the result of a monopolistic cartel flexing its economic muscles with the support of a noncompetitive set of domestic producers that wanted higher crude prices and speculative activity in commodity markets. In the early 1970s, many of the most prestigious "energy" economists claimed the global economy was running out of the exhaustible resource known as crude oil, and their forecasts were that by the beginning of the twenty-first century the market price of crude would be more than $100 (in 1972 dollars) per barrel. The historical evidence has supported the conclusions of my Brookings and Ford Foundation studies rather than the predictions of these prestigious energy economists.

During the 1970s, the "energy problem" was continually on the public's mind. Between 1973 and 1979, I was asked to testify nineteen times before various congressional committees on some aspect of this problem. Unfortunately none of the public policies I suggested for alleviating this energy problem was ever adopted by Congress.

In 1980, I decided that Keynes's *General Theory* analysis had been (wrongly) discussed primarily in a closed-economy context. With the growth of a global economic prospective, I decided Keynes's analysis had to be presented in a clear and unambiguous open-economy context. I applied to the National Science Foundation for a research grant to develop my view of Keynes's analysis in terms of open economies in a global economic market system. Although I received high marks from the outside peer evaluators on my research proposal, one of the inside peer evaluations gave away the reason I was denied a grant. The inside evaluator wrote: "Although Davidson has achieved much success with his published research work, Davidson marches to a different drummer and therefore should get his own research money and not use ours."

Nevertheless, Rutgers gave me a year without any teaching obligation to pursue this open-economy research project. The result was my book *International Money and the Real World* (1982), which provided me with a theoretical base for bringing the principle of effective demand into contact with the real-world economic problems of a globalized economy. This required integrating Keynes's Bretton Woods analysis with his general theory framework, as well as explaining (1) why the Ricardian law of comparative analysis was valid only for industries that extracted minerals or produced a climate-related product but had little importance for modern developed economies in a globalized trading system and (2) why full employment stability for a global economy was not primarily a question of fixed versus flexible exchange rates. For most economists the problem of domestic unemployment was often seen to be solved by reducing a nation's exchange rate so domestic industries appear to be more "competitive" than their foreign competitors – although, if one understands Keynes's general theory, the result will be merely to export your unemployment to those trading partners whose exchange rate has relatively risen and therefore makes their industries "less competitive".

If one understands Keynes's analytical framework, instead of fiddling with exchange rate changes, what is required is changing the rules of the economic game so that the onus of adjusting to persistent deficits in a nation's current account is shifted primarily to the creditor and not the debtor nation. This analysis of Keynes resulted in my proposing a new international financial architecture via an International Monetary Clearing Unit institution (or IMCU). My work on the open globalized economy was summarized in my book *Financial Markets, Money and the Real World* (2002).

By the early 1990s I felt that all the available macroeconomic textbooks had abandoned any semblance of Keynes's theoretical analysis in the *General Theory*. Accordingly I wrote what I hoped would be a widely adopted macroeconomics textbook that would reinstall the correct Keynesian principle of effective demand into macroeconomic textbooks. My book was entitled *Post Keynesian Macroeconomic Theory: A Foundation for Successful Economic Policies for the Twenty-First Century* (1994). I have been disappointed by the unwillingness of even heterodox economists to accept this book as a useful first-step tool to displace the conventional orthodoxy of our professional colleagues. Nevertheless, the international financial crisis that led to the Great Recession that began in 2008 encouraged me to write a second edition to this book (published in 2011) in which I clearly explain how the Keynes–post-Keynesian macroeconomic theory can explain to all with open minds the cause of this international economic collapse and the onset of a great recession, which is still being felt.

Finally, in 2009 I wrote a "trade book" entitled *The Keynes Solution: The Path to Global Economic Prosperity* to educate the intelligent layperson as to the cause of and the Keynesian cure for the economic disaster that has been labeled the Great Recession.

As I look over the fifty-plus years of my professional activities, I recognize that I have not been very successful in encouraging most professional economists to recognize that the fundamental principles espoused by the mainstream elite of our profession are not relevant to the world in which we live. Nevertheless, as I look back on my professional research, I have very few regrets, since I wrote within what I believe was Keynes's true analytical framework that is applicable to the entrepreneurial world in which we live, where the macroeconomic future is uncertain and cannot be simply discovered by statistically and quantitatively analyzing existing market data. The future is created by the decisions of market participants and the political environment in which they live. In such an uncertain world, money contracts are used to organize all production and exchange activities that occur in the marketplace. And the sanctity of the money contract is the essence of the operation of the economic system we call capitalism. Yet the elite of the economic profession continue to exclaim that people never suffer from a money illusion and that the essence of the economic system is real contracts that organize production and exchange.

David Colander has told me that I would have been more successful in the profession if I had been more accommodating of my mainstream professional colleagues by tailoring my brand of post-Keynesian economics to fit their view of economics. I have preferred my attempts to propagate Keynes's revolutionary analysis of our entrepreneurial system rather than bending my knee to their classical theory–based vision of macroeconomic problems of a theoretical economy that has no relationship to the world in which we live. I would rather be right than win acclamation for a beautiful but wrong model of our world. Too many human lives have been ruined by well-employed and highly paid economists providing a rationalization that blames the unemployed for their status and the government for merely exacerbating the poverty experienced by such a large proportion of the population during times of economic distress. My efforts have been directed toward bringing the civilized progressive view of Keynes into the public debate among economists and policy makers.

Winston Churchill once said, "No one pretends that democracy is perfect and all-wise. Indeed it has been said that democracy is the worst form of government except for all those other forms that have been tried from time to time." In a similar vein I have tried to develop Keynes's framework to save the imperfect entrepreneurial economic system we call capitalism. Despite its flaws, capitalism is the best economic system humans have devised to achieve a civilized economic society. I believe that proper economic policy can correct the two major flaws of the existing capitalist system, namely (1) its failure to provide persistent full employment and (2) its arbitrary and inequitable distribution of income and wealth. I hope my professional economic writings someday will help our society come closer to a good, civilized economic community.

REFERENCES

Davidson, P. (1959). "A Clarification of the Ricardian Rent Share," *Canadian Journal of Economics and Political Science* 25.

(1960). *Theories of Relative Shares.* New Brunswick, NJ: Rutgers University Press.

(1963). "Public Policy Problems of the Domestic Crude Oil Industry," *American Economic Review* 53.

(1965). "Keynes's Finance Motive," *Oxford Economic Papers.*

(1966). "The Social Value of Water Recreational Facilities Resulting from an Improvement in Water Quality in an Estuary: The Delaware – A Case Study," in A. V. Kneese and S. C. Smith (eds.), *Water Research.* Baltimore: Johns Hopkins University Press.

(1967). "An Exploratory Study to Identify and Measure the Benefits Derived from the Scenic Enhancement of Federal Aid Highways," *Highway Research Record.*

(1968). "Money, Portfolio Balance, Capital Accumulation, and Growth," *Econometrica* 36.

(1972). *Money and the Real World.* London: Macmillan.

(1977). "A Discussion of Leijonhufvud's Social Consequences of Inflation," in G. C. Harcourt (ed.), *The Microfoundations of Macroeconomics.* London: Macmillan.

(1977). "Money and General Equilibrium," *Économie Appliqué* 4.

(1978). "Why Money Matters," *Journal of Post Keynesian Economics* 1.

(1982). *International Money and the Real World.* London: Macmillan.

(1982–1983). "Rational Expectations: A Fallacious Foundation for Studying Crucial Decision Making Processes," *Journal of Post Keynesian Economics* 5.

(1994). *Post Keynesian Macroeconomic Theory: A Foundation for Successful Economic Policies for the Twenty-first Century.* Cheltenham: Edward Elgar.

(2002). *Financial Markets, Money and the Real World.* Cheltenham: Edward Elgar.

(2009). *The Keynes Solution: The Path to Global Economic Prosperity.* New York: Palgrave/Macmillan.

(2011). *Post Keynesian Macroeconomic Theory: A Foundation for Successful Economic Policies for the Twenty-first Century*, 2d ed. Cheltenham: Edward Elgar.

Davidson P., L. Falk, and H. Lee (Summer 1974). "Oil: Its Time Allocation and Project Independence," *Brookings Papers on Economic Activity.*

(1975). "The Relations of Economic Rent and Price Incentives to Oil and Gas Supplies," in G. M. Brannon (ed.), *Studies in Energy Tax Policy.* Cambridge: Ballinger.

Davidson, P., J. Seneca, and C. Chicetti (1968). *The Demand and Supply for Outdoor Recreation.* Washington, DC: US Government Printing Office.

Davidson, P. and S. Weintraub (1973). "Money as Cause and Effect, *Economic Journal* 83, no. 332: 1117–1132.

Hicks, J. R. (1977). "Summary," in G. C. Harcourt (ed.), *The Microfoundations of Macroeconomics.* London: Macmillan.

(1980–1981). "ISLM: An Explanation," *Journal of Post Keynesian Economics* 3.

Seneca, Joseph J., Paul Davidson, and F. Gerard Adams (November 1968) "An Analysis of Recreational Use of the TVA Lakes," *Land Economics* 44, no. 4: 529–534.

Tobin, J. (1965). "Money and Economic Growth," *Econometrica* 33.

Weintraub, S. (1958). *An Approach to the Theory of Income Distribution.* Philadelphia: Chilton.

6

Puzzles and Paradoxes: A Life in Applied Economics

Angus Deaton

STARTING OUT

My father believed in education, and he liked to measure things. He grew up in a mining village in Yorkshire, between the First and Second World Wars. He was bright and motivated, but the school system was designed not for education but to produce workers for the "pit," and only one child in each cohort was allowed to progress to high school. Not my father, who got in the line to be a miner, then was drafted into the army in 1939 and drafted out again with tuberculosis before war's end. In the easy labor market of those days, he got a job with a firm of civil engineers. The managing partner was impressed by my father's skill with a slide rule and a theodolite, and was prepared to ignore his lack of formal education. My father went to night school at what is now the Heriot-Watt University in Edinburgh, graduating after very many years as a civil engineer. He married my mother, the daughter of a carpenter. She had a great gift for storytelling; it is said that Sir

Walter Scott would walk over from Abbotsford to our house in Bowden to share tales with one of her ancestors. Even so, she did not share her spouse's view of education; she found it hard to see me with a book when I could have been using my hands. But my father was determined that I should be educated properly and set his heart on sending me to Fettes College, a famous public school (in the British sense) in Edinburgh, whose annual fees were well in excess of his salary, even once he became the water supply engineer for the county of Roxburgh in the Scottish borders. Then, and perhaps even now, there were schoolteachers in the Scottish state schools who were prepared to coach a bright kid for a scholarship that would take him away, and to do so in their own time.

So I went to Fettes at thirteen, as one of two scholarship boys in my year – Sir William Fettes had left his fortune to give a public school education to the children of the poor, but there was only this remnant of the intent (and the original endowment) by 1959. Fettes had all of the resources to provide a great education and, in those days, sent most of the graduating class to Oxford or Cambridge, as, for example, did Lawrenceville Academy send many of its graduates to Princeton in the United States. I was one of the Cambridge lot. I played the piano, the pipe organ, and the double bass; I was a pretty good second row forward – which is how I got into Cambridge ("Fitzwilliam needs second row forwards, Mr. Deaton," the senior tutor told me at my interview) – and I was a mathematician of sorts in my spare time. But I had no idea what I wanted to be or to do; the rugby at Cambridge was serious and brutal, and the mathematics was appallingly taught, in huge classes by ancients in mildewed gowns whose sinecures depended only on their never publishing their yellowed notes. I quickly drifted away from both rugby and mathematics, tried to become a philosopher of science, but was refused by my college tutor, and instead adopted a largely pointless student life of cardplaying and drinking. Eventually, my college, losing patience with my aimlessness, told me that I could leave or stop pretending to study mathematics. What to do? "Well, there is only one thing for people like you … economics." I should have preferred to leave but doubted that I could explain to my father, who already felt that I was not making enough of the opportunities that I had and that he had lacked, so I accepted the inevitable and set off for the Marshall Library, where the aimlessness came to a surprised and delighted end.

I found economics much more to my taste than mathematics. I was helped by the little mathematics that I had learned, though it hardly got me through David Champernowne's econometrics course, in which the first (French) edition of Malinvaud was the sole text, or indeed the mathematical economics exam in which Jim Mirrlees set all of the parts of Diamond and Mirrlees that neither he nor Peter had been able to figure out,[1] most of which were ill-posed and insoluble. But lectures at Cambridge were like the books in the Marshall Library, varied, sometimes interesting, but entirely optional, and the important thing was reading and writing essays, which were regularly read and discussed by college-appointed supervisors. I found that the material was interesting – Samuelson's *Principles* was terrific – and I found that I could write, indeed that I could write with clarity and with a good deal of pleasure, a lasting benefit of the one-on-one teaching at Fettes.

That single year of (involuntary) undergraduate economics, reading Modigliani and Brumberg on life-cycle saving, Hahn and Matthews on economic growth, Meade on trade, and Kuznets on patterns of consumption, and summarizing what I'd learned for discussion and criticism, provided a template for learning, thinking, and writing that I have had little reason to revise. I understood that economics was about three things: theory that specified mechanisms and stories about how the world worked and how things might be linked together; evidence that could be interpreted in terms of the theory, or that seemed to contradict it, or was just puzzling; and writing (the importance of which is much understated in economics) that could explain mechanisms in a way that made them compelling or that could draw out the lessons that were learned from the combination of theory and evidence.

The two Modigliani and Brumberg papers – both on the consumption function, one on time series and one on cross-sectional evidence – have always stayed with me. They were written when the topic was in a mess, with dozens of unrelated and incoherent empirical studies. Modigliani and Brumberg provided a rigorous statement of a simple theory of behavior that, with careful statement and manipulation, could provide a unified account of all of the evidence and that provided a framework which has dominated thinking ever since. In recent years, I have come to think of those mechanisms as incomplete, and in some places even wrong, but the principle of the thing has stayed with me, that a good theoretical account must explain *all* of the evidence that we see, in this case cross-sectional patterns of consumption and income, time-series patterns of consumption and income, and then – albeit some years later – international patterns of income and saving. If it doesn't work everywhere, we have no idea what we are talking about, and all is chaos.

Kuznets's work on consumption, and more broadly on modern economic growth, was another early influence that has lasted. This is much less theoretical, more historical, and much more data driven, starting from careful empiricisms and cautious induction, always with great attention to problems of measurement and the quality of the underlying data. Underlying everything is historical measurement, considered and qualified, but leading to generalizations of great scope and subtlety and with significance beyond the topic at hand. Modigliani started from behavior and used it to interpret the evidence, while Kuznets mostly worked the other way round. To me as an undergraduate, and to me now, the order matters not at all. What is important is a coherent behavioral or institutional account that provides broad insight into the present and the past and gives us some hope of predicting the future.

I had studied economics only to escape from mathematics and to complete my degree, but after graduation I needed to work, so I went off to the Bank of England. I think I accepted the job because the interview had been really tough and because the job offer came on paper with a letterhead engraved like a high-denomination bank note. But the institution was in flux, it had traditionally not employed university graduates, and it had no idea what to do with me or the small cohort of graduates who entered with me. So I went back to Cambridge, where I could be with my bride, Mary Ann Burnside, a writer and teacher, born in Topeka and raised in Evanston, who was studying psychology at Cambridge. I was a research assistant on a project measuring national wealth – directed by my college economics tutor, Jack Revell, who felt sorry for me and wanted to help me live in the same town as my wife. So, just as I had drifted into economics as an undergraduate, I drifted into it as a profession, though at the time it was just something to do. Revell soon left Cambridge for a chair in Wales, leaving me funded but without anything much to do. I soon fell in with the Cambridge Growth Project, directed by Richard Stone. The project had begun as what was then known as an "indicative planning model" centered around input-output analysis, though it was being developed into something more like a large-scale Keynesian macroeconomic model, albeit with a lot of industrial and commodity detail. Like my fellow researchers, I was assigned to work on one of the model's components, in my case consumption and demand, though the time commitment was not large, and once again, I was left free to work on anything that seemed interesting.

MENTORS AND A COLLABORATOR

I was soon befriended by Richard Stone, who made it clear to me that I was a kindred spirit or, as he would put it, that "we were on the same side of the movement." I was not at all sure what the movement was, let alone which side we were both on, but I was enormously complimented by being told so, and I knew at once that Dick Stone's was the life that I wanted to lead. Dick was married to Giovanna, née Forli, a glamorous and alluring Italian aristocrat, who had started out as a concert pianist. They lived in a beautiful house with gardens, an extensive library, a Bösendorfer, and spectacularly decorated rooms. Their intellectual and personal lives were inseparable; they worked, they talked, and they entertained. There were many dinner parties, and economists and statisticians from around the world flowed through. And because I was on the same side of the movement, Mary Ann and I were frequently included in the dinner parties, the heady conversations, and the even headier glasses of claret and burgundy from the cellars of Kings'. I had been admitted into Aladdin's cave, surrounded by the gems of a good life.

Stone's work inevitably became the model for my own. During the war, he had worked with James Meade, who had been hired by Maynard Keynes to construct a double-entry bookkeeping system of national accounts, work for which Stone later received a Nobel Prize. By 1970 he was still heavily involved with the United Nations developing international standards for national accounts, but my own interest in measurement, although certainly triggered by Stone, was not to come to the forefront for some years. Instead, I was immediately involved in Stone's work on demand analysis.

In 1954 Stone had introduced and estimated the linear expenditure system, so that, for the first time, a utility function was not just being used to prove theorems or to guide thought, but was the direct target of empirical estimation. When I arrived, researchers on the Growth Project were still trying to estimate the model using Stone's original algorithm, and a quick trip to the engineering library provided a much better, up-to-date set of procedures for estimating nonlinear models, so I set about learning FORTRAN and soon had some well-converged parameter estimates. ("Soon" is a relative term: the computer system accepted "jobs" each evening and returned them, usually with compiler errors, only the next morning.) But as I played with my results, I soon discovered that my new toy had some serious drawbacks. When I used it to calculate income and price elasticities – which were needed for the model – I discovered that the estimated price elasticities from the linear expenditure system were close to being proportional to the income elasticities, a regularity that is supported neither by intuition nor by the theory. It was a terrific idea to use the theory very directly to build an empirical model, but the theory here was doing too much, and the model was not as general as the theory allowed. The solution to these problems was to come through the concept of a *flexible functional form*, proposed by Erwin Diewert in 1973; in my own work, this line of research was to culminate in the "almost ideal demand system" that John Muellbauer and I proposed in 1980 as our own favorite flexible functional form. That model is still very widely used today.

Not long after I joined the Department of Applied Economics, Cambridge University changed its rules so that researchers in the department could obtain a PhD by submitting the research that they were paid to do, a terrific arrangement that suited me perfectly. By the mid-1970s I had a published book on demand systems and a paper on how to run horse races between various then-popular demand systems (which was published in *Econometrica* and was later to win the Econometric Society's first Frisch Medal), and my PhD was duly awarded, but not until I had passed a terrifying oral exam. Cambridge required that oral examiners not be supervisors – not that there was much supervision in those days – and PhD theses, including some subsequently famous ones, were not infrequently failed without the possibility of resubmission.

Around this time, I had been befriended by W. M. (Terence) Gorman, then professor at the London School of Economics, who somehow managed to sniff out and make contact with anyone who was using duality methods. Terence was an outstanding theorist who saw the task of theory as providing models and methods that made life easier for applied analysis – I think the mold for that kind of theorist has been lost. He seemed to know more about everything than anyone else but had a charming if occasionally terrifying way (he was one of my oral examiners) of assuming that it was *you* who knew everything, and if you couldn't understand him, it was because he had expressed himself with insufficient subtlety and sophistication, setting up a divergent cascade of misunderstanding. I wanted to understand two-stage budgeting, and Terence had worked it all out in a paper in *Econometrica*, but I found this incomprehensible. I was determined to get to the bottom of it and locked myself away for a week to think and to figure it out. At the end of the week, I understood no more than at the beginning, though I was a good deal more frustrated. Terence had understood very early on that the dual representation of utility – where utility is expressed not as we had all learned it, as a function of quantities, but as a function of prices and income – allowed an intimate and direct connection between the theory and the data. These methods were spreading quickly at the time, particularly through the work of Dan McFadden. One link with Dan came through John Muellbauer, who had done his PhD with Bob Hall at the University of California, Berkeley, and had learned duality from Bob, who in turn had learned it from Dan.

So when John came back to England, we discovered that we had much in common and knew a lot of things that seemed both tremendously useful and not widely understood. So we wrote *Economics and Consumer Behavior* to explain it all. John and I were ideal complements; he was careful, sometimes even fussy, and with the stronger theoretical bent: he had been publishing rapidly since coming back from California, and he had lots of important, unpublished material on which we could draw. I was less careful, impatient to get on, had a good sense of what was important and what was not, but regularly needed to be pulled back and made to think harder. The book was published in 1980, and thirty years later a remarkable number of copies are still sold. I think of it as a synthesis of Dan McFadden, Terence Gorman, and Richard Stone. It tried to lay out a vision of how theory could be taken directly to the data, and modified or refuted depending on the results, with the whole thing leading up to an integrated view of policy and of welfare economics. Looking back, I realize how naive we were, but I see no reason to modify my view that this is what we would like to achieve, even if the goal is a good deal more elusive that it seemed to be with the confidence of youth.

MOVING WESTWARD, IN STAGES

The early 1970s were a time of university expansion in Britain and a great time to be a young economist. In Cambridge, I often played tennis with Mervyn King – later to be governor of the Bank of England and a member of the Wimbledon Lawn Tennis and Croquet Club – and we would relax on the lawn afterward and work ourselves into a lather over the fact that no one was offering us professorships, professorships that only a few years before were grudgingly handed out to (sometimes long-deserving) aspirants in their late fifties and early sixties. (Most British departments then had only one or two professors.) In the event, neither of us had long to wait, and I accepted the chair of econometrics at Bristol before my thirtieth birthday – rather old in those years. I loved Cambridge but, except for the Bank of England, I had been there since undergraduate days, and a chair meant much more money, which I badly needed. Mary Ann had died of breast cancer in 1975, and I had two children under five: it was time to move on.

It was during my time at Bristol that John Muellbauer and I worked together on our book. The computer facilities at Bristol were terrible – the computer was a mile away, on top of a hill, so that boxes of punched cards had to be lugged up and down. I was told to get a research assistant, which was sensible advice, but I have never really figured out how to use research assistance: for me, the process of data gathering – at first with paper and pencil from books and abstracts – programming, and calculation has always been part of the creative process, and without doing it all, I am unlikely to have the flash of insight that tells me that something doesn't fit, that not only does this model not work, but all such models cannot work. Of course, this process has become much easier over time. Not only are data and computing power constantly and easily at one's fingertips, but it is easy to explore data graphically. The delights and possibilities can be fully appreciated only by someone who spent his or her youth with graph paper, pencils, and erasers.

Given how far it was up the computer hill, I substituted theory for data for a while and wrote papers on optimal taxation, the structure of preferences, and quantity and price index numbers, but I never entirely gave up on applied work. Martin Browning had come to Bristol for his first job, and we worked together on life-cycle labor supply and consumption. This led to some good ideas for combining time series of cross-sectional surveys to generate true panel data, and this remains some of my most cited methodological work.

While still at Cambridge, I had met Orley Ashenfelter at a conference in Urbino, and he invited me to visit Princeton for a year, which I did in 1979 and 1980. A year later, he came to Bristol as a visiting professor, bringing a young Canadian graduate student from Princeton (and subsequent John Bates Clark winner), David Card. Faced with Bristol's hilltop computer and its limitations when you got there, Dave didn't last long and fled back to the United States, only to be denied admission at the border and deported to Canada. The Bristol department was outstanding in those days, with a bevy of future stars, but there were difficulties beyond the computing facilities, especially when Mrs. Thatcher cut the university's budget. This prompted an understandably bitter discussion to decide which "tenured" faculty members were to lose their jobs. The endless penny pinching began to make it very difficult to work.

Compared with Britain, Princeton seemed like a paradise awash in resources, so when I was invited to return on a permanent basis, I gratefully accepted. In spite of an increase in bureaucratization over the years, Princeton remains a wonderful environment in which to work, even after the financial crash of 2008; never in thirty years have I felt that my work was hampered by a shortage of funds. Princeton is close enough to Washington and New York so as not to be isolated from finance and from policy, but sufficiently withdrawn to have an element of the ivory tower and to be insulated from the waves of fashion that sweep all before them in hothouses like

Cambridge, Mass. And it is a terrific university, for both undergraduates and graduates. Both of my children went to Princeton, one as a math major and one as an English major (like many of their cohort, both now work in finance), and the breadth and depth of their experience were much superior to what I had in Cambridge. By the time they graduated, they were immeasurably better educated than I had been at the same age.

Princeton was everything I had hoped for. I taught the first course in econometrics to the incoming PhD students, a class that in my first years had a stellar bunch of young economists, including several superstars in the making. Princeton also attracted outstanding new PhDs as assistant professors, one of whom, John Campbell from Yale, shared an interest in consumption and saving. I remember the two of us happily wandering off to the engineering library to try to find out about the spectral density at zero and how to estimate it.

Alan Blinder and I wrote a Brookings Paper on saving, and as a result of that, I began to think about the time-series properties of consumption and income. I realized, after a lot of agonizing and checking my imperfect understanding of time-series analysis, that one common version of the representative agent permanent income model made no sense. The permanent income hypothesis says that consumption is equal to permanent income defined as the annuity flow on the discounted present value of current and future earnings. The relative smoothness of consumption – the pro-cyclical behavior of the saving ratio – then follows from the fact that permanent income is smoother than actual income. But the time-series people had done a pretty good job of showing that aggregate per capita income was stationary only in differences and that the differenced process was positively autocorrelated. This implies that permanent income is *less smooth* than measured income; growth shocks, far from being canceled out later, are actually signals of even more growth to come. Of course, it is only the representative agent version that has this disturbing property, and one of my students, Steve Pischke, figured out that with a proper account of what consumers can actually know, something like a standard view can be restored. But this work taught me something important, that representative agent models are as dangerous and misleading as they are unrealistic.

DEVELOPING INTERESTS

Before coming to Princeton, I had started thinking about economic development and had spent a summer at the World Bank helping them think about their Living Standards Measurement Surveys, which were just getting under way in the early 1980s. Senior Bank researchers had become concerned about how little was known about poverty and inequality in the poor countries of the world and felt that a household survey program was the answer to a better system of measurement. Arthur Lewis had just retired from Princeton when I arrived but was still around, and he was supportive of my first steps in economic development, even though my approach was so different from his own (for reasons I never quite understood, he always referred to me as "chief"), To the end of his life, he remained bitterly disappointed that the economics profession was so little interested in why most of the people in the world remained so desperately poor and what might be done about it. He felt that his own work had failed to set in motion the professional effort that global poverty required. Another Princeton economist, Mark Gersovitz, who was a great admirer of Arthur's, also became a mentor to me; he generously shared his knowledge of the economics of poor countries, on almost all aspects of which Mark had made important contributions.

My new interest in household surveys turned out to be a lasting one, eventually leading to my 1997 book, *The Analysis of Household Surveys*, which focuses on developing countries and has many examples of useful and interesting things that can be done with such data. It also covers the basics of household survey and design, which had long been dropped from courses in econometrics. Students in economics are rarely taught about how the design of a household survey might be relevant when they come to analyze it, and one of the aims of my book was to fill this gap, as well as to discuss some of the practical issues that arise when standard econometric methods are applied to household surveys, especially from poor countries. I was fortunate that this book coincided with a revival of interest in development economics, especially microeconomic development, as well as with a rapid expansion of the availability of household data from around the world, so that it has been widely used.

The book was published by the World Bank, with which I have continued to work over the years. One of the dangers of being an academic economist is that it is easy to wander off on a trail that becomes narrower and narrower, intellectually exciting perhaps, but of interest to very few. For me, the World Bank has been a constant source of interesting topics that are of substantive importance, at least to some people. Of course, most of the problems that come up are too hard to allow much progress, but occasionally a problem arises where I feel I can do something, even if it is just clarifying a misunderstanding. In this way, talking to people at the Bank has helped keep me grounded as an applied economist.

CONFIRMATIONS AND REFUTATIONS

One of my most fruitful collaborations at Princeton was with Christina Paxson. She had done her PhD at Columbia in labor economics, out of frustration at being unable to study development. So we became development economists together and collaborated on a wide range of topics. We looked at life-cycle saving, showing that it is impossible to argue that the cross-country correlation between saving rates and growth rates comes from the life-cycle story according to which the young, who are saving, are richer over their lifetimes than are the old, who are dissaving. There is just not enough life-cycle saving to account for the size of the relationship.

We also argued that if individuals are independent permanent income consumers, the accumulation of lifetime shocks will cause people's consumption levels to drift apart with age, whether or not their earnings do so. If a high school class reassembles for its twenty-fifth class reunion, the inequality of their standards of living will be much larger than was the case when they graduated. This was one of those nice but too rare cases where a prediction that comes out of the theory, whose empirical validity is unknown in advance, turns out to be confirmed by the data. Of course, there are other possible explanations – for example, that consumption is more closely tied to income than the permanent income theory supposes and that the spread of cohort earnings increases as the cohort ages, because people get different opportunities over life, because they make different use of them, and because these advantages and disadvantages accumulate over time. Yet the key insight is still the same, that outcomes depend (at least in part) on the accumulation of luck, which drives ever expanding inequality of living standards within a fixed group of members as they age. Inequality of wealth is driven by a process that accumulates an accumulating process and grows even more rapidly, another prediction that turns out to be correct.

Chris and I also wrote about household economies of scale and their effect on the consumption of food. Economists have long used per capita income as a measure of welfare – for example, in calculating poverty or inequality – but this can't be quite right. For one thing, the needs of adults and children are not the same. But even when there are no children, household economies of scale imply that larger households are better off than smaller households at the same level of per capita income. Some goods are public goods within the household – housing itself, heat, cooking of meals – and the need for them expands less than proportionately to the number of household members. With the same per capita income, larger households can substitute away from such goods toward more private goods, such as food, especially in poor countries, where food needs are often very far from being met. Yet Chris and I found something very odd, which is that, holding per capita income constant, larger households spend less per member on food. And we see the largest *reduction* in food consumption precisely where we would expect to see the largest *increase*, among households in the poorest countries for whom a large share of additional resources goes to food.

The food and household size puzzle remains largely unresolved, yet it is perhaps linked to another paradox that I have recently investigated with my friend Jean Drèze. (Jean is responsible for almost everything I know about India. He is a scholar and social activist, living without apparent means of support, whose work and writings have had an unparalleled effect on policy.) In India today, which has been and is experiencing historically high rates of economic growth, we see another very strange food-related fact, which is that per capita calorie consumption has been *falling* for the past two decades. This is happening in spite of rising per capita incomes, even among the poor, and in spite of the fact that Indian men, women, and children suffer one of the highest rates of physical malnutrition in the world. Indian adults are among the shortest in the world, and Indian children display higher levels of stunting and wasting than in much poorer places in sub-Saharan Africa. Jean and I suspect, though it is far from proved, that the reduction in calories is a consequence of a reduction in hard physical labor, which is fueled largely by cereal consumption. This contention turns out to be politically sensitive in India, where some argue that the fall in calories is an indication of unmeasured immiserization, driven by the supposed horrors of globalization.

In the mid-1980s, my friend Guy Laroque was spending some time in Princeton, working with my colleague Sanford Grossman. Guy and I had known each other for a decade, and we had jointly organized an Econometric Society meeting in Athens in 1979, I as the econometrician and he as the theorist. Sandy Grossman was always short of time, so that Guy had a lot of free time on his hands during his visits to Princeton – where he would usually stay at my house – so we got to talking about an issue in which I had become interested, which is why primary commodity prices behave as they do. I had been thinking about the economies of sub-Saharan Africa, many of whose macroeconomic policies are dominated by enormous fluctuations in commodity prices. In the mid–nineteenth century, Egypt had become fantastically rich from the high prices of cotton that resulted from the American Civil War and had then gone into receivership with Britain during the subsequent collapse, a story that was repeated (with variations) many times subsequently. Nor were outside authorities very good at advising countries how to deal with the problem. During the 1970s, as the world price of copper collapsed, the World Bank kept increasing its forecasts of future prices, driving countries like Zambia deeper and deeper into difficulty.

Guy and I wrote a number of papers on our findings. There is a theory of speculative commodity demand and storage, first developed by Ronald Gustafson in Chicago in the 1950s and later developed by Joe Stiglitz and David Newbery in the 1970s, and Guy and I turned this into something that could be taken to the data. The theory can help explain at least some of what is in the data – we would have done well if we had been content with calibration to suitably chosen facts – but full estimation told a different story: that there are many aspects of the theory that do not sit well with the facts. This is another of these irritating but common puzzles. We have a long-established theory – whose insights are deep enough that *some* part of them *must* be correct – which is at odds with the evidence and where it is far from obvious what is wrong or how the theory might be amended to give us a better handle on the mechanisms at work.

One thing I try to do is find new implications of old theories, and more specifically some implication that permits a relatively straightforward confrontation between theory and evidence. Ideally, such a prediction can be tested by something very simple, like a cross-tabulation of one variable against another or a straightforward graph, if only one knows what to tabulate or what to graph. This method makes the investigation and manipulation of the theory do the work that is often assigned to econometric method, and it avoids at least some of the econometric controversies that abound when inadequately developed questions are taken to the data. Whenever I have managed to do something like this, I have been better at getting refutations or generating puzzles than at getting interesting confirmations. Indeed, I can remember only two clear cases of the latter. One is the consumption inequality story. The other was in the early 1970s when Britain and other countries were experiencing a burst of high inflation, and I argued that consumers, who are buying goods one at a time, not an index of all goods, have no immediate way of distinguishing unanticipated inflation from relative price increases of the goods they happen to be buying. In consequence, unanticipated inflation will cause a short-run increase in the saving ratio. This was quite contrary to what most people thought would happen, yet it was quickly confirmed, not only in Britain, but in a range of other countries.

There is something very exciting about making a theory-based prediction that is not at all obvious – especially if it seems obviously wrong – but that turns out to be true in the data. Yet what happens after that is by no means ensured, depending among other things on whether other explanations – even if developed ex post – are judged to be as or more convincing. Even refutations, although less elating at first, are usually productive, because they lay the platform for subsequent emendation and redevelopment of the theory, so that there is at least a possibility of progress. Indeed, if the theory is one that is heavily used in our normal thinking about the world, refutations and emendations may be more productive than the confirmation of a new theory that is less deeply embedded in our understanding.

One of my standard ways of finding good research topics – though one that is not easily taught or passed on – is to "play" with models and data until I find something that I don't understand. It is nearly always the case that this lack of understanding, or the sense of a paradox, is only apparent. That two ideas, both of which seem correct, are mutually inconsistent is nearly always because I don't understand one of them. Or if some data don't seem to support the earlier results, it is usually because I have misunderstood the earlier findings or because I have made errors in the calculation (something that is much more common in applied work than is usually recognized). But one time in a hundred, the misunderstanding or paradox is not just mine but is more widespread, and that is gold that is worth the prospecting. I have also learned to trust my instincts about empirical findings that seem to me to be absurd. Either the supporting work is wrong, or there is something I don't understand. One example is my work on the Wilkinson hypothesis, which claims that income inequality acts as pollution in the social atmosphere and undermines the health of all who live there. The evidence in favor of this proposition turned out to be a web of bad data, selective reporting, and wishful thinking, but in showing that, I came to understand much about the insidious effects of inequality more generally, especially of the extreme (and today expanding) inequalities that separate the very rich from the community in which they live.

FOR GOOD MEASURE

Measurement is not much of a focus in economics today. Even the obligatory topic of national income accounts that used to be the first thing encountered in macroeconomics courses is no longer much taught, nor are students exposed to the construction of index numbers. Academic economists spend a lot less time with the creators and producers of data than once was the case, to the detriment of both groups; economists often do not understand the data they work with, and the evolution of national income accounting practice has taken place without much input from academic users. Yet much of what we think we know about the world is dependent on data that may not mean what we think they mean or that are contradicted by other data to which, for no very well developed reason except habit, we give less weight. One example that has much concerned me is the inconsistency between national accounts data and household survey data that are encountered in many countries. Only some of the differences are attributable to differences in definition; others arise from an under-researched mélange of errors in the surveys – misreporting, coverage, or something else – as well as weaknesses in the national accounts data. There is no basis that I can see for the usual view that the national accounts are correct and the survey data are wrong. For example, there is little doubt in my mind that the Indian national accounts overstate Indian growth rates, not through conscious manipulation in any sinister way, but because the whole apparatus is shaky and outdated, and certainly not built to work well in a rapidly growing and changing economy.

India has been a continuous source of fascination. For anyone of my age who grew up in Britain, India was the magic tropical kingdom and (along with Robert Louis Stevenson's South Seas) the perfect imaginary contrast to the dreary gray and cold of Edinburgh. And like all schoolboys of the age, we were brought up on (one-sided) stories of Empire. Years later, India has become the exemplar not of imperial glory, but of global poverty and the hope that economic growth might one day do away with it. My work there has focused on price indexes and on how they affect measures of poverty, and I have worked with the government of India to improve its own poverty measures. Much of this work has been with Jean Drèze; it is a constant challenge to keep up with his skepticism, ground-level knowledge, and technical knowledge of economics.

I have also been involved with the International Comparison Program (ICP), which originated at the University of Pennsylvania in the 1970s and is now run by a global consortium headed by the World Bank. Almost everything we know about the empirics of economic growth, global poverty, and global inequality depends on estimates from the ICP, which is essentially a giant price collection enterprise, gathering millions of price quotes on closely comparable goods from almost all the countries of the world. These prices are turned into a system of price indexes (purchasing power parity indexes) that can be used to convert each country's national accounts into an internationally comparable currency. The technical advisory process for the ICP involves an uncommonly diverse and interesting group of national income accountants, statisticians, and economists, as well as numerous subject specialists – in construction, housing, and so on – who try to solve an infinitude of practical and theoretical problems that underlie the definition of prices, as well as the calculation of index numbers. Alan Heston, who worked with Irving Kravis and Bob Summers on the first ICP in 1978 – covering fewer than a dozen countries – remains active in this process, bringing to it more than forty years of experience, as well as the world's deepest understanding of national accounts and price measurement. Working with him has been an education in itself.

LOOKING BACK, LOOKING FORWARD

One is asked to write an account of this kind only once a certain age has been reached, and while it is certainly good to be asked, there is something of an obituary quality about the enterprise. This makes it seem somehow inappropriate to write about future work, or even about currently unfinished work. Yet I don't feel any differently about my current work than about my past work. In particular, I had the good fortune in recent years to occupy the office next to that of Danny Kahneman, whose knowledge, curiosity, and interest in learning and changing his mind are models for how to prolong a long and distinguished career. Over the past decade or so, he has been working with the Gallup Organization to collect data, in the United States and around the world, on how people evaluate and experience their lives. There are wide-open and important questions of what the various measures of "happiness" really mean and to what extent they can and should be used for policy and welfare economics. I do not know whether a new welfare economics can be built around such measures, but working with Danny on these issues has taught me much, and we are making progress on the difference between life evaluation and hedonic experience and on the distinct ways that each responds to income. The old question of whether money buys happiness turns out to have a complicated answer. As always, working with someone from a different tribe can be immensely frustrating – we can spend an enormous amount of time on what subsequently turn out to be non-issues – as well as immensely rewarding, as when I realize that there are completely different ways of thinking about phenomena about which I had thought my views were long settled.

Age brings mental and physical deterioration, but if the former can be temporarily held at bay, it also brings a perspective from having seen the roundabout go past so many times and from having seen and thought about the earlier incarnations of current enthusiasms. I have been recently writing about the latest wave of randomized controlled trials in social science. These are often useful devices, but they are now being used in what seems to me a nonscientific way, not as a complement to theory, enabling its empirical investigation, but as a substitute for it. I think that this is a problem, not only in economics, but also in medicine, where the randomized trial often rules as the only provider of acceptable evidence, in spite of many thoughtful and sometimes devastating critiques over the years by statisticians, physicians, and philosophers. Indeed, to my way of thinking, the turn to randomized controlled trials, or substitutes like instrumental variables or regression discontinuity designs, is a symptom of a deeper malaise, which is the seemingly ever widening gulf between applied work and theory. It seems a long time since the early 1980s, when econometric and economic theorists as well as applied econometricians saw themselves as working on different parts of what was clearly the same enterprise.

When I was starting out in Cambridge, the Econometric Society played an enormously helpful part in my career and in those of my contemporaries, not just those of us who were econometricians or theorists, but anyone who was doing quantitative applied work. *Econometrica* published a good number of applied papers that were worth emulating, and the society held summer meetings in different European cities every year. Those meetings catered to a "broad church" of economists; they gave us a chance to meet and to be met, and to present papers before a wide audience of European and American economists. In those days – the early 1970s – there were almost none of the networks or networking that are so important today, and of course no Internet, so that getting working papers was very much a hit-and-miss business. So the Econometric Society played a vital role in building European economics. In both North America and Europe, an Econometric Society fellowship was a mark of having become a full member of the profession, usually coming at around the same time as tenure in a good department.

I believe that the Econometric Society still plays something of this role in Europe, but it otherwise seems to have become much less important, at least for applied work. In large part, the Society's earlier European role has been taken by the National Bureau of Economic Research, which, after Marty Feldstein became president, was a central focus for networking in applied economics, with similar organizations appearing later in Europe. Like many in the profession, I owe a great deal to Marty and to the NBER, which has frequently been the venue for trying out new work and new ideas. It was through the NBER, through David Wise's aging program and the entrepreneurship of Richard Suzman at the National Institute on Aging, that I owe my interest in health. In recent years, I have also had a fruitful relationship with the American Economic Association. I had the honor to act as its president in 2009, and over many years of meetings, I was part of the movement to expand the Association's role in publication. This eventually came to fruition with the publication of four new Association journals, all of which have terrific editorial boards and all of which publish excellent papers.

It has been a good time to spend a life in economics. Compared with many others, the profession is remarkably open to talent and remarkably free of the nepotism and patronage that are common in professions in which jobs are scarce. It is also a profession that, deservedly or undeservedly, is very well rewarded. The best gifts of a profession are the people it brings, to talk to, to work with, to be mentored by, and to make friends with. I have been truly fortunate in this respect. Princeton has provided me with extraordinary students, not only in economics, but in the Woodrow Wilson School, which brings master's students with multiple gifts, interests, and experiences; working with them is a constant joy and inspiration. Many of my oldest and best friends, many of them also mentors, have come to me through economics. Through economics too, I met my wife, Anne Case, and our personal and professional lives are almost entirely integrated; Anne is my critic, my colleague and coauthor, and my friend. In many, if not all respects (our lives are faster, more interconnected, and it is much harder to have dinner parties every night without servants) we try to lead the ideal academic lives that I had first glimpsed and admired in Cambridge forty years ago.

Notes

1 Peter Diamond, in this volume, refers to the same incident but notes that he and Jim Mirrlees had not yet begun their collaboration at the time that Mirrlees set the exam. The exam was still close to impossible, if only because reading it took most of the time that was allowed.

7

Succeeding in Economics

Harold Demsetz

The editors of this volume invited me to discuss professional aspects of my life as an economist as part of a series of similar discussions by others. They thought readers might find this of interest and might even benefit from learning how contributors to this series go about their work. My intent here is simply to highlight some aspects of my career that have helped me progress in the profession. What has helped me may not be equally helpful to others, each of us being unique in experience, capability, and interest. Indeed, some conditions that have helped me along have not been of my own making. Each of us, for example, is born at a particular time in a particular place and to a particular set of parents. Although we can influence the views of our parents as we mature, we are powerless to affect time and place of birth. Yet these do influence what we will do and how well we will do it.

The first full year of the Great Depression, 1930, is the date of my birth and the city of Chicago is the place. The decade of the 1930s, of course, began a long period of hard times for a great many families, including mine. Although hard times make success more difficult in ways that are well known, the 1930 birth date made success in academia easier. One advantage of this date was that I became a member of an age cohort that was made smaller by the Depression. When I entered the academic marketplace in 1958, I faced fewer competitors than would have been the case if prior years had been more prosperous. Another advantage was that the GI bill, which offset what would have been the impact of prior Depression years, was still channeling a very large number of World War II and Korean War veterans into college as I sought my first professional teaching position. These consequences of my birth date put me in the academic marketplace when the entering supply of new PhDs was relatively small and the demand for their services was relatively large. Adjusting for quality of training, most graduating PhDs enjoyed an abundance of job offers that lasted for the better part of a decade.

Being born in a large city was also advantageous. The neighborhood of my youth was populated largely by immigrant families from Europe who, though not very knowledgeable about post–high school educational institutions, were self-selected for their willingness and ability to deal with circumstances new to them. College presented such circumstances. The first year of my college education took place at an essentially free nearby public city college, one, as it turned out, attended by an ample number of bright students and serviced by capable teachers who probably would have secured better positions if prior years had been better. The second year of my education was at the Chicago undergraduate division of the University of Illinois, where tuition at the time was about $100 per semester. I also kept the cost of going to college low by living at home with the family on Chicago's West Side.

A large city offers opportunities to pay for an education through part-time work; during summers I drove a Checker cab and during the school year I ushered evenings at the Chicago Civic Opera House. I studied engineering during these two years and, therefore, learned some mathematics. As part of the distribution requirements for the engineering degree, I took a course in economics. This was taught well by an instructor who was then working on his PhD at the University of Chicago. I found economics interesting and enjoyable. The Opera House job helped round out my education in the arts as I pursued work in the engineering program. Financing my education this way had its downsides. Commuting took the better part of three hours a day and so did part-time work. Having been raised as a user of urban transport, I did not fully appreciate the weight of this burden until I continued my education at the Champaign-Urbana campus of the University of Illinois. After a brief tour with the US Army, which made me eligible for GI bill aid, I went on to secure an MBA and PhD from Northwestern University.

I did not consciously engage in the long-run planning of my teaching-research career when I entered the profession, as I had no expectation or intent of making a "mark" in the profession; indeed, I saw college teaching as a comfortable job to which a three-month vacation was attached. As things turned out, I became increasingly interested in economics as I read more of it and taught my classes. I began writing on topics I found especially interesting, and perhaps because of having been raised on Chicago's West Side I experienced little apprehension about going public with my work. As things have turned out, I have never, I say *never*, taken even a month away from work. Economics turned out to be too interesting and idea production too stimulating. Not everyone can find remunerative work that keeps a person busy and satisfied at the same time, but I did. It is difficult, I think, to make a confident judgment about this without first really working on the tasks that a career sets before a person.

Although I have written on many topics, the subject matter of my writings falls mainly into three categories: (1) markets and firms; (2) property rights and externalities; and (3) financial markets and transaction costs. This degree of concentration has worked well for me. It offers a comfortable compromise between interesting targets of opportunity and continuity of knowledge accumulation.

Sources of potential topics to work on are many. Examples of where some of my ideas have come from may be given. One of my earliest publications arose from my studies at Northwestern University while I was working toward my PhD. I had been reading Edward Chamberlin's *Theory of Monopolistic Competition* (1933), a book that had become a mainstay of industrial organization theory during the 1950s. An aspect of the way Chamberlin developed his notion of excess capacity equilibrium puzzled me, and I kept mental note of this. The cost curve he used to describe his excess capacity theorem assumed implicitly – without his taking note of it – that promotional expenditures are held constant while a firm varies its output rate; otherwise how could the demand curve facing the firm remain in the fixed position given to it by Chamberlin? In contrast to this, all costs are allowed to vary optimally in discussions of the cost curve of the perfectly competitive firm. Yet, despite the difference in the implicit definitions of these two cost curves, Chamberlin's notion of excess capacity was based on the supposed deduction that the equilibrium rate of output of the monopolistically competitive firm is less than that which would bring unit cost to its minimum if the market were perfectly competitive; true, but this minimum cost is associated with a very special cost curve, one that holds promotional cost constant. The incompatibility between the two cost curves made me wonder about the equilibrium of a monopolistically competitive firm if full consideration is given to the variation in optimal promotional expenditures that surely would take place as output rate varies. At a later time, but before I had completed my PhD work, I returned to this question. The result was the publication in 1959 of "The Nature of Equilibrium in Monopolistic Competition."[1]

The teaching experience is a second source. An essay titled "Purchasing Monopoly"[2] comes from a mental note I made while teaching graduate students at UCLA. The textbook treatment of the reward to monopoly is calculated as the difference between revenue received by a monopolist and cost incurred by the monopolist. In this calculation, cost is treated as expenditures made to produce the monopolist's profit-maximizing rate of output, and the cost conditions that determine these expenditures are those that would define the supply curve of the competitive industry that would exist if there were no monopoly. This would be correct if monopolizing a market required no special expenditures, as if the monopoly were a gift of nature or of a costless conversion of a competitive industry. While discussing the case, I realized that a "free" monopoly would not ordinarily be the case. Rivals would need to be defeated or purchased, and would-be entrants would need to be bought off. Monopolizing would at least require the payment of Ricardian rents to firms in the competitive industry that was being transformed into a monopoly. These *monopolizing* costs are not incurred by firms in a competitive market. I returned later to examine the issues raised by this realization. The essay that came from this shows, or course, that the return to monopolizing is much less than the return to the receiver of a free gift of monopoly, so the customary measure of monopoly profit exaggerates the true return to the monopolist who, in one way or another, must buy the right to exclude rivals. More than this, the essay also shows that the use of deadweight loss triangles to measure the social loss of monopoly yields a biased estimate.

A third idea source is conversation with colleagues. At a lunch shared with colleagues at the University of Chicago, discussion turned to a report about antitrust that had just been written by a committee headed by Phil Neal, then dean of the University of Chicago Law School. One part of the report endorsed the market concentration doctrine. This well-known doctrine had guided thought about the relationship between market structure and pricing power when I was a young man, and to some extent it still does.

An observation was made by one of my colleagues at this lunch. This was that domestic auto industry profits were comparatively high only because GM's profit was high. Neither Ford nor Chrysler, for example, earned exceptionally high profits. I began investigating whether this observation had generalizing power when I arrived at UCLA in 1971. In the absence of governmentally imposed barriers to entry, market concentration may be expected to arise if scale economies are important or if innovation has resulted in a superior product or way of producing an existing product. Competitive responses to these sources yield not just variation in market structure across industries but also variation in measured industry profit rates. Examined in more detail, market concentration as an outcome of efficient structure is consistent with a correlation between profit rate and market concentration if the correlation is calculated only for the larger and historically more successful firms in the markets being compared, but the efficient structure hypothesis would lead to an expectation of this correlation for middle-sized and smaller firms. The higher profits received by the larger, historically more successful firms is to be attributed to their lower costs or their superior products given that product price is determined by cost at the margin in an industry. In contrast to this explanation, a pure collusion explanation would lead one to expect a positive correlation between profit and market concentration for all size classes of firms; evidence for this is nowhere found in the data.[3]

This example is especially useful in revealing a characteristic of some of my work. I tend to push an argument or a model back to an earlier analytical step than is presently covered by it; rather than take market concentration as a given when evaluating data, I first sought to explain variation in market concentration. This tendency is also illustrated by my article "Toward a Theory of Property Rights."[4] While I was at Chicago, R. H. Coase, who arrived a year after I did, amazed the profession by demonstrating, in the context of the externality problem, that who does (and who does not) possess a right to impose a cost on others is irrelevant to efficient resource allocation. (This result obtains if the transaction cost is zero and if income effects on demands for goods involved in the interaction are unaffected by wealth redistribution.) Coase's work took the private property right system as an "existing" given when making his point. I began to think about moving the problem to a prior step by seeking to understand the emergence of a private right system from a preexisting communal right system. This resulted in a simple efficiency explanation for the rise of private rights (and, under specifiable conditions, also for the persistence of communal rights). I explained how changing conditions brought about by the development of the fur trade in the New World affected ownership of land arrangements among Native Americans in the American Northeast and failed to do in the American Southwest.

One more tendency of mine might be noted. The interesting problems seem to me to be those that begin with the observation of an unexpected practice, organization, or business policy. In attempting to make sense of these, I usually begin by seeking an explanation that reconciles the anomaly with efficient allocation of resources. In the Native American landownership example just mentioned, the problem was to explain why Native Americans of the Northeast came to treat land differently than Native Americans of the Southwest. I found my answer in the different habits of forest animals and animals of the Great Plains. Each landownership arrangement seemed efficient in the context of the animal habits facing Native Americans in the two locations.

The work I choose to do is not heavily armored with math and econometrics. It is focused on empirical and policy problems and on the logic of the theory that bears on these. Cold logic, imagination, and exposition by way of words, simple geometry, and basic statistics are the tools on which I have mainly relied throughout most of my career. I do not feel fully in command of a problem or a resolution of it until I can state both clearly in words and/or geometry. This gives my work a wider audience but probably also limits the nature of the problems on which I choose to work. Not many young economists adopt this working methodology today, and I am not sure it is suitable for an initial job search in today's market. Currently, prospective employers seem to strongly emphasize demonstrable ability in econometrics and mathematics. I suspect that the large degree of specialization across fields of economics explains this, since it is now more difficult to have knowledge of material in the many fields in which the renderer of judgment is not a specialist. Technical tooling offers a substitute, but heavy attention to these tools often hampers discovering the *economist*. Quality of economic thinking is more likely to be revealed by the way the underlying problem to which the tools are applied is conceived and analyzed. Economists in training seem to seek a body of data that is appropriate for the exploitation of technical tools rather than one that is of intrinsic economic interest. Not frequently, but still on occasion, a seminar is given by a young economist who has uncovered such a problem and is now busily engaged in a thorough investigation of it; this person has a good chance of becoming a successful economist.

I do regularly attend workshops in my field, and I recommend this as a method for keeping in touch with the profession, for learning from other attendees, and for exposing others to ideas that may come to your mind. A second method is to become a member of dissertation committees and eventually to become a chair of some of these. This is an effective way to learn one's own strengths and weaknesses as well as those of students. It is the most efficient way to learn about the intellection history of the topic featured in the dissertation. Beyond this, graduate students whose dissertations you chair become well acquainted with your work, ideas, and methods and they carry these to other institutions.

One reason I came to UCLA from Chicago is to have the opportunity to interact with students who were writing their dissertations. My position at Chicago was in the Graduate School of Business, a fine school with fine students and colleagues, but most of these students sought only the MBA degree. Those who went for a PhD wrote dissertations in accounting, marketing, management, and finance; few wrote in economics. Chicago, after all, had a world-class Department of Economics to service students seeking to become economists. In the Economics Department at UCLA, I managed to supervise the dissertations of almost eighty students. Times are different now, I suppose; a few more students in business schools seek a PhD in something called business or managerial economics.

A position in a top business school has an important advantage. This is to encourage work on puzzles involving business and market arrangements and on public policies toward business. Economists in economics departments have a stronger tendency to look within economics itself for the problems they study. The issue is not which of these problem sets is better, but which mixture of them works best for you. My personal development has greatly benefited not only from practicing my discipline in a fine business school and fine economics department, but also from teaching in fine law schools. The topics on which I have written reflect this threefold institutional involvement. I began work in two economics departments, continued in Chicago's Business and Law Schools, and then returned to economics. Along the way, I did my share of consulting on antitrust cases and institution building. Engaged thus, I was not easily bored. It goes without saying that one must publish to succeed in economics within academic institutions. High-quality teaching performance and involvement in academic institutional problems count, but these provide no answer to the question "Is he or she a fine economist?" The quality of one's writings supplies this information.

One may write for different audiences. An economist who is good at writing for one audience may not be equally good for another. I recall George Stigler asking me more than once if I thought Milton Friedman will be most remembered for his scientific work (say, on the consumption function and monetary theory) or for his reformist policy work (as in his *Capitalism and Freedom*). The answer George sought was "Milton's scientific work," but the answer, I think, depends on the audience being asked the question. The Nobel Prize Committee, representing the economics profession, stressed Friedman's professional work, and it may well be that future economists will do so also. But I think a broader "committee" of influential intellectuals might well value his reformist work more. To succeed professionally in your own terms, know your audience. Not many of us are as capable as Friedman was of serving two such different groups so well.

It is extremely important to become associated with the best economists available to you. This usually means appointments at the best universities possible. People think about puzzle resolution in different ways. Only by reading what others write and by engaging in discussion with them can you begin to discover different ways of looking at a problem. You also learn to disagree with your colleagues and to bear their disagreement with you – all in a proper spirit. It does not do you or them much good if you keep your thoughts to yourself. For a month or two I sat quietly, saying nothing, in Chicago's Industrial Organization Workshop. One day, George Stigler, the creator and director of the workshop, leaned over to me and whispered, "You owe it others to make your thoughts known." Except for those few months, I always do. Association with the best also broadens the invitations you will receive to make your thoughts available at other institutions.

I have been able to interact with some very fine economists while learning my trade. Perhaps this reflected an ample share of luck. Perhaps it reflected my ability and willingness to engage. However it came about, this has proved extremely important for my professional progress. Surely other things also matter, but I strongly advise young economists to increase the weight they give to associating with the best possible economists when seeking a position.

My work habits are not atypical. I do not often work into the evening hours, preferring instead to do my professional work during the day in my office at the university. I come to my office almost every weekday, and I hardly ever take off more than a week or two during the calendar year. This remains my pattern even though I am now several years past official retirement. I see myself as a long-distance runner when it comes to work; I read and write regularly during daytime hours through most of the year. Once a work project is completed, I quickly search for another if I do not already have one in inventory. I spend weekends at home with my family, sometimes tending to repair work but always enjoying their company. On several evenings of each week my wife and I take three-mile hill walks. During these walks we sometimes discuss the new work I am doing. Rita is quite good at understanding what I am saying and often senses problems that I have not dealt with. Having a great partner in life makes it much easier to succeed professionally. I have no personal experience with and can only imagine the considerable difficulties that face colleagues whose minds are occupied with problems at home or who do not look forward to closing the office door after a good day's work and returning home.

Notes

1 *Journal of Political Economy* (February 1959, pp. 21–30).
2 In my *Efficiency, Competition, and Public Policy* (Cambridge: Basil Blackwell, 1989).
3 See H. Demsetz, "Industry Structure, Market Rivalry, and Public Policy," *Journal of Law and Economy* (April 1973), and H. Demsetz, "Two Systems of Belief about Monopoly," in H.J. Goldschmid, H. Mann, and F. Weston (eds.), *Industrial Concentration: The New Learning* (Boston: Little, Brown, 1974).
4 *American Economic Review* (May 1967, pp. 347–359).

8

My Research Strategy

Peter Diamond

A key question for any researcher is what to work on. Integral to answering is the method of search for an idea that might become a good paper. This is particularly an issue for many students starting on their theses, particularly after a period without a successful start. When I talk with these students, I spell out multiple ways of getting started that I have used, rather than presenting a dry, abstract list of approaches. Generally, students coming to me are trying to write theory papers, and it is my experience with getting started on theory papers that I relate in this essay.[1]

A key part of that strategic process, and also of the tactics of completing and presenting papers, is trying to figure out how interesting an actual result or a conjectured result might be. My movements across different research areas and between basic applied theory and policy analyses have taught me the ongoing importance of strategic planning. This essay reports my

I am grateful for comments on drafts from Nick Barr, Angus Deaton, Avinash Dixit, Jim Poterba, and Joel Yellin.

memory of how I have proceeded strategically over the past fifty years, both before and after recognizing a need to think directly about these choices.[2] Over time I have become aware of the diversity of research approaches that work at different times and for different people and the uneven quality of advice I have given on this issue.[3] So this is one researcher's story, not one researcher's advice, a potted history from my memory of early conscious and not conscious choices.

I started graduate school at MIT in mathematics in 1960. I was taking both math and economics classes as I tried to choose a field, having majored in math at Yale and also having enjoyed both economics classes (principles, intermediate theory, and general equilibrium, taught by Gerard Debreu from the new *Theory of Value*) and a summer job as a research assistant with Tjalling Koopmans. Koopmans hired me to do math for him. He asked me to provide an example of a function with certain properties. Being lazy, or maybe just preferring more abstract thought, I produced a class of functions rather than grinding out a particular one. I had no more thoughts about my response than that I had done what was asked. But Koopmans found real interest in the class of functions, which I had not considered, and generously made me a coauthor of the 1964 *Econometrica* paper that followed. I have had the same experience on the other side; as a graduate assistant working for me and John Geanakoplos (Saku Aura) did an assigned calculation in a particular way that then led to results that were worthy of publication as a joint note in the *American Economic Review* (AER, 2002). The general message for me fifty years ago, and what I would like to communicate to graduate students, is: think about the interest in what you find (stumble over?). I have sometimes put this to students as thinking about what theorems, if true, would be interesting. I have no algorithm for telling what might be interesting. It seems to be an intuition that is built up from reading and listening to what is well received and what isn't. And reactions to individual papers vary considerably with location, one of the reasons it is important to spend time in several places as a student and a young researcher. I find no point in proving uninteresting theorems, although there can be interest in the methods of proving an uninteresting theorem. That has just not been a part of my set of interests. (I don't find a theorem interesting just because it is hard to prove.)

I liked the MIT economics classes better than the math classes. And I was better at them. I was not interested in pursuing more and more general settings for the same basic theorem, which I took to be the heart of the real variables class I took. So I became an economist. One of my formative experiences as a student was a reading seminar, in the spring of my second year, that Frank Fisher gave to me and my classmate Steve Goldfeld. This was really a search for possible thesis topics. Each week we were assigned something to read, followed by a discussion. The only assignment I remember now was Arrow's *Social Choice*. Frank told us there was a mistake in the proof and to find it. We did. But what mattered was that it highlighted a way to read – always looking for what might be wrong, preferably without losing sight of what is interesting in a paper. I attribute much credit to that seminar for what I have considered a very fruitful way to read.

The first two essays of my thesis came effortlessly. One drew on my work with Koopmans, framing the same infinite horizon choice problem differently in a way that led easily to theorems. That became my job market paper, and it was done, apart from polishing, early in the fall. Right after that, I read the thesis of T. N. Srinivasan, with whom I had shared an office at Cowles and a drive across the country in 1960. I thought of a way to prove an additional theorem in his model and had a second thesis essay done.

At that point I thought finding things to work on was easy. I was in for a nervous-making surprise, as months went by without a glimmer of a good idea for another chapter, an experience repeated, as mentioned below, during my first leave from teaching. Well into the spring, Bob Solow, my supervisor, suggested I read W. E. G. Salter's book on technical change and cost reductions. I recognized that the approach could be turned around into a growth model and managed to complete my third thesis essay just barely in time for a June 1963 degree. Only when googling while drafting this essay did I learn anything about the book other than its being handed to me by Solow: "In 1960 Cambridge University Press published Salter's thesis as *Productivity and Technical Change*. M. M. Postan described it as 'one of the most elegant exercises ... in the theory of investment and innovations to come out of post-war Britain.'"[4] Again, there was a research lesson in how to read – look for analyses that can be transferred, what is sometimes called "intellectual arbitrage."[5] Of course, not all transfers are interesting.

I was interested in theory, both micro and macro, and chose public finance as my other main field. At my first job at Berkeley, I started out teaching all three. It was the yearlong public finance class for economics majors that interested me most. What became a 1965 *AER* paper started out as a lecture in that class, as I tried to understand and convey the central issues in the analysis of the public debt, moving beyond the analyses of Franco Modigliani and James Buchanan. And my starting place in the initial optimal tax papers I wrote with Jim Mirrlees occurred, literally, in the classroom in my first year at MIT, as I lectured on deadweight burdens and had the idea of minimizing them.[6] The process of going from my calculation

of first-order conditions for deadweight burden minimization and derivation of the optimality of aggregate efficiency in a one-consumer economy
to a joint paper with Jim Mirrlees addressing a many-person economy was
relatively quick, as the results, in essentially their final form, were presented
at US and European Econometric Society meetings in 1967.[7]

Not surprisingly, I am not one of the researchers who view the relationship between teaching and research as teaching solely interfering with
research. Rather, as indicated, I have found teaching, at both the undergraduate and graduate levels, to be a prime stimulus to research. No doubt
this is related to how I approach teaching. I have often used preparation and
classroom time as an opportunity to develop my own approach to standard
issues or to push forward topics that strike me as worth more development.
When I prepare a handout, I am looking for a good way to present, which
is often not a summary of some existing paper. With this approach there is
a chance of discovering something new. Some students like this approach –
seeing a piece of a research process. Many find it less satisfactory, and certainly harder to decipher.[8]

Indeed, the least productive research period I had was during my
first leave, in 1965–1966, with very little teaching, at Churchill College,
Cambridge. This was a repeat of the frustrating time I had in the midst
of writing my thesis. Shortly before going to Cambridge, I formulated the
model that became my 1967 *AER* paper on the stock market. This was an
unusual process for me. I wanted to explore the allocation of resources in
models of an economy with uncertainty and without the complete set of
Arrow-Debreu markets. My plan was to write down different allocation
processes until I came to one that would look interesting to explore in detail.
The first one I tried led to the paper. Fruitlessly attempting to find results
beyond the very special assumptions that led to constrained efficiency fed
my frustration, and the very limited amount of teaching threw up no alternative ideas to draw me away.[9] While a teaching load can be so heavy as
to interfere with research, I am very far from viewing the optimal amount
of teaching to be zero, even from the narrow perspective of research, not
counting the pleasures of teaching.

To this point, my research choices were one-off, with no sense of having or needing a strategy. That changed in the early 1970s as I was having
trouble finding things as interesting as what I had done earlier. That led to
two ventures. I started taking classes at Harvard Law School, planning to
write on law and economics, hoping to find some question in that realm
that would be a route to what I was really interested in – the importance
for resource allocation that trades happen in real time rather than in the

all-at-once way of Arrow-Debreu theory. That is, I was hoping that thinking about a concrete legal problem would lead to modeling that captured a real-time process and resulted in insights that would be more generally usable. I was hoping for a modeling approach different from sequential equilibrium, which somehow did not turn me on. I chose taking classes (including sitting exams) rather than just reading, for a couple of reasons. I wanted to experience how lawyers learn to approach issues, to identify how I might start researching differently; I like and believe in the merits of understanding a subject from its foundations; and I like taking classes.[10] While I did write a few papers in law and economics, the topics never yielded insights into the kind of dynamic allocation questions I was hoping to explore, and I moved on. While my work on labor market search equilibrium started with analysis of breach of contract in joint work with Eric Maskin (1979, *Bell Journal*), I don't think there was any significant link to the classroom study of contracts, but who knows what lurked in my subconscious. [11]

My second venture was to agree to serve on a panel headed by Bill Hsiao to examine whether Social Security finances were in as much trouble as was being claimed (Panel on Social Security Financing consulting to US Senate Finance Committee, 1974–1975). They were. This was the start of an interest in both basic theory and policy analysis of national pension systems that continues to this day. I found I liked doing policy. And I found that looking at policy questions fueled the identification of good theory questions to model and analyze. As a public finance economist, I was naturally interested in policy (rather than becoming a public finance economist because I was so interested in policy), although that has reversed. And as a theorist more interested in constructing models to analyze questions than in getting new results from existing models, my taste ran to simplifications that seemed to preserve the important properties and so provide plausibly robust policy insights, an approach that fit with finding questions from involvement in policy discussions. My 1978 *Journal of Public Economics* paper with Jim Mirrlees (and several sequels) on how pension benefits should vary with the age at which they start came directly from wondering about that issue for Social Security as part of my time on the second Hsiao panel (Consultant Panel on Social Security of the Congressional Research Service, 1975–1976). The particular motivating policy question made it natural to consider uncertainties in worker opportunities over time, which was (and is) a valuable question to ponder.

I stop the detailed autobiography here, as later experiences reinforced what I had learned earlier – that there are multiple ways of getting to interesting projects and it is important to have at least one.[12] I cite just two more experiences. Sharing the excitement of Eastern Europe's move from communism to capitalism, I asked Jeff Sachs for an opportunity to join in. He had me write about pension issues in Poland. Some Poles were considering imitating Chile, which led me to study Chilean pension reform and prepared me well for the debate about Social Security privatization that is still going on. Returning to teaching optimal income taxation in the 1990s, after many years of not teaching it, I decided to work out a simple example to help convey the insights from that quite complex literature. Another *AER* paper, in 1998, followed from recognizing the potential in a classroom handout.

Beyond the activities that did lead to research, there are the ideas I chose not to follow up, which I mention here in order to make clear that there are indeed choices. I asked Paul Samuelson for a suggestion for a thesis topic. I am guessing this was the spring of 1962. He suggested that I contrast English and Dutch auctions. Despite having studied game theory in the Math Department at Yale, I did not choose to follow up on this suggestion, being too short-sighted to see why analyzing auctions would be interesting. In the late 1960s, while working on uncertainty, I decided that incomplete markets per se were what I wanted to concentrate on, not the new interest in drawing inferences from prices about asymmetric information. So another huge opportunity went by unexamined.

Teaching, working on policy questions, leaving subjects when diminishing returns appear to have set in, and returning to them with a fresh mind later have all served me well.[13] And there is also the elephant in the room of finding the right people to write joint papers with.

Notes

1 Choosing research topics is only part of how one approaches one's professional life. And how one leads a professional life is only part of how one leads life. I have written about what I thought would be useful and interesting to readers, not about other issues like the importance of taking responsibility and working hard at making one's department and university a good place to be a student and faculty member or the critical importance of being part of and taking care of one's family.

2 This essay is about picking topics. For more discussion of my thinking in writing various papers, see Giuseppe Moscarini and Randall Wright, "An Interview with Peter Diamond," *Macroeconomic Dynamics* 11, no. 4 (2007): 543–565.

3 For example, I remember telling the young Bob Hall that Ricardian equivalence, which he had proved, was not interesting, a view I hold to this day. Bob's memory includes a reference I do not recall, as he emailed me: "Actually, you told me something much more pointed and intelligent: Ricardian equivalence was both well known and wrong. The first from Ned Phelps's 1965 book (*Fiscal Neutrality Toward*

Economic Growth [New York: McGraw-Hill, 1965]), which I dutifully consulted and found you to be right. The second from your own work, fresh at the time, in the OLG framework." Either way, there is no doubt that following my advice greatly reduced Bob's nevertheless very high citation level.

4 adbonline.anu.edu.au/biogs/A160198b.htm.

5 A clear expression of arbitrage at work is the title of my 1972 *AER* paper with Menahem Yaari, "Implications of the Theory of Rationing for Consumer Choice Under Uncertainty."

6 Modeling deadweight burdens in a way that led to this use was another example of a move from classroom preparation to a published paper ("Some Uses of the Expenditure Function in Public Finance," *Journal of Public Economics* [1974], with Dan McFadden).

7 Jim was already thinking about optimal tax before we began collaborating. He had set an optimal tax question on the Economics Tripos in 1967.

8 Since student grading of teachers started, I have never once been judged as highly as my co-teachers, Amy Finkelstein, Jon Gruber, or Jim Poterba.

9 The impressive analyses of Oliver Hart and John Geanakoplos and Herakles Polemarchakis show how hard it was to make progress.

10 I saw this first (post-PhD) when I attended David Freedman's graduate class on stochastic processes early in my time at Berkeley. David lectured on Brownian motion, leaving more general analyses to the teaching assistant. I do some of the same, covering simpler models in class, leaving the general theorems for the TA. I enjoyed the Harvard classes enough to take one a year for four years – property, contracts, torts, and taxation. Of course, the reason for taking taxation from Stanley Surrey was to improve my understanding of public finance, not to strike out in another direction. Years later I took another class there, on financial institutions.

11 The underlying concern was with search equilibrium, and the catalyzing event was reading Dale Mortensen, "Specific Capital, Bargaining, and Labor Turnover," *Bell Journal of Economics* 9, no. 2 (Autumn 1978): 572–586. While search equilibrium does have trade that happens in real time, it was not the sort of model I started out in law school hoping for, and was a natural extension of earlier work on search in the consumer market ("A Model of Price Adjustment," *Journal of Economic Theory*, 3, no. 2 [June 1971]: 156–168. *Journal of Economic Theory*, 1971).

12 On reading this, Nick Barr emailed: "At risk of tautology, there is also the strategy (largely the one I have implicitly adopted) of not having a strategy. A while back I was asked to write a short piece about Bill Phillips for the *Oxford Dictionary of National Biography*. As one of the authors, I got the editor's newsletters, and in one he mused about whether there were a small number of career patterns, just like there are a small number of love stories (boy gets girl, boy doesn't get girl, etc.). He went through a series of possible careers; when he got to the 'unintended career,' I got interested; he quoted Isaiah Berlin, who apparently said, 'I am like a taxi – I have to be hailed.' That rang true. It never occurred to me to work for the World Bank, but they asked me. It never occurred to me to write about pensions in China either. So presumably part of a strategy is the ability to benefit from and enjoy serendipity."

13 Some of my colleagues might object to this conclusion in the absence of natural or controlled experiments.

9

My Philosophy of Economics, Life, and Everything (Not!)

Avinash Dixit

In Douglas Adams's brilliant science fiction parody, *The Hitchhiker's Guide to the Galaxy*,[1] "a race of hyperintelligent pandimensional beings ... built themselves a super computer ... the size of a small city." The single task assigned to this computer, which was named Deep Thought, was to provide "the Answer" to "the ultimate question of Life, the Universe, and Everything." After 7.5 million years of work, it came up with the answer: 42.

I thought of this when the editors asked me to write about "my life philosophy ... interspersed with social philosophical issues, some perspective on the nature of life and of the universe, and the relationship between economics and other disciplines." It took me less than 7.5 million years to come up with the answer: 23.

When the hyperintelligent beings complained, "Is that all you've got to show for seven and a half million years' work?" Deep Thought replied, "I

I thank Steven Levitt, Robert Solow, and Lars Svensson for commenting on the first draft and thereby giving me the benefit of fascinating glimpses into their philosophies.

think the problem ... is that you've never actually known what the question is." My assignment is similarly vague. Deep Thought told the hyperintelligent beings that they should construct an even larger computer to calculate "the Question to the Ultimate Answer." I will not set the editors such a daunting task. I will merely make a few random remarks that may help sharpen the question. They may not, but what do you expect after far less than 7.5 million years' worth of shallow thought, coming from a far-from-super computer who occupies barely two square feet of space?

LIFE OF RESEARCH

The same editors had asked me ten years ago to write about my method of work. The only consistent pattern I could find in my random, unsystematic, and unphilosophical approach was always to work as if my mental age stayed at twenty-three – excited to find so many fascinating unanswered questions lying about and not yet weighed down by the demands of teaching or fearful about the approaching tenure review. The intervening years have not changed my ideas – nor, I hope, my mental age – so instead of repeating myself, I will refer interested readers to that article, "My System of Work (Not!)," for my scattered thoughts about research. [2] Here are a few that have occurred to me since then.

Beyond the Fringe, the British comedy stage revue of the early 1960s, gave us a mock Church of England sermon with a memorable lesson: "Life is like opening a tin of sardines. We're all of us looking for the key. Finally we find the key. We roll back the lid of the sardine-tin of life. The sardines – the riches of life – are in there. We get them out; we enjoy them. But you know, there's always a little piece in the corner you can't get at." This is a pretty good description of the process of research. The initial excitement and anticipation on taking up a problem are followed by a long search for the key; then there is another phase of wonder and joy when the rich solution comes into view, only to be followed by the realization that more remains to be done. But that's OK; that becomes the starting point for the next project. A grook by Piet Hein goes:

> Problems worthy of attack
> Prove their worth by hitting back.
> That's research.

The long "search for the key" phase of research may appear frustrating and daunting to outsiders, but I find it exciting. Why? Because for me, it is the mental equivalent of free-climbing a new rock face, using only hands and feet for the ascent, or even free-climbing solo, without any ropes, pitons, or harnesses to protect one if one falls. When one starts on a research project, one has only the vaguest notion of the best route, or of whether there is a feasible route at all. One has to discover as one goes along where, or even whether, the next hold or ledge can be found. One spends a lot of time feeling one's way, or even hanging by one's fingertips. There is the constant risk of failure. It takes all of one's concentration and focus over a long stretch of time. But the breathtaking view from the top is worth all of that, and over time one finds even the process of climbing beautiful and exhilarating in its own way.[3]

LIFE OF TEACHING

Academics who are serious about research usually regard teaching, especially undergraduate teaching, as a necessary evil, as the activity that puts food on the table, as something to be done at the minimal acceptable level while all of one's mental energy is focused on research. The attitude is neatly captured in the wording of the question job candidates usually ask: "What is the teaching *load* ?" When did you last hear a job candidate ask: "What *opportunities* will I have for teaching and for developing new courses?" If you do interviewing for a top economics department, probably the answer is never.

I have always regarded teaching as a rewarding and even enjoyable part of my work. I must admit this has on the whole been detrimental to my research, but in some respects it has contributed to research.

The mental and physical activities of teaching can be divided into several phases: preparation, delivery, and evaluation. These bring very different kinds of rewards and frustrations.

Preparation includes a search for simpler ways to convey ideas; this for me is the most enjoyable aspect of teaching. It is also the aspect that feeds back most directly on research: if something that was previously hard to understand can be understood and explained more simply, that opens up the route to achieve some understanding of the next level of the problem, which was previously impossibly difficult.

I find another aspect of preparation far less enjoyable, namely the preparation of slick PowerPoint slides or similar visual displays and handouts. Alas, that is becoming a sine qua non. Today's students, who have known nothing but high-quality audio-visual media, will take an immediate and instinctive dislike to a teacher who uses old-fashioned chalkboards or handwritten handouts, and to material that is so presented.[4] That is a pity, because a chain of logical reasoning is much better understood when one sees it evolve step by step, and at the teacher's writing pace on the board, than when it is presented on a slide and slides past at the pace of the clicker. Conversely, reading the narrative portions of a talk from slides becomes soporific. At a minimum, one should keep slides incomplete, summarizing the main points and leaving out details to be supplied during the talk. This preserves some spontaneity in the talk.

Preparation of slides, especially when they are optimally designed and especially when they involve mathematics and graphics, takes a long time and much mental energy. This part of teaching does not feed back on research at all. For me, the only way to extract any enjoyment out of it is to regard the slides as minor works of art and get some creative satisfaction from them.

Delivery of the material, in most of the kind of teaching I do, consists of lectures. For me this is routine without being particularly enjoyable. It does contribute to my main interest, namely the simplification of concepts: I can immediately see whether the audience gets it, and that helps me improve or change the exposition for the next time. Teaching the course a second time is the most enjoyable for the same reason; I can see the success (and, I must admit, occasionally the failure) of the improvements I made after the first time.

Evaluation is the least enjoyable part of teaching for me. Making up problem sets and exams is hard. Ensuring good coverage, balance, and difficulty requires too much effort and contributes very little to improvement of the ideas. However, sometimes it does have a research payoff. While constructing an exam question, I have occasionally realized that it could be developed into a research paper.[5]

Grading exams is sheer agony. Not only is the students' handwriting under time pressure hard to read, but their answers sometimes reveal errors and misunderstandings that make me worry about the quality of my teaching. Thank heaven for graduate student graders.

I must confess that my attitude to teaching reveals a fundamental defect: my primary interest is in the ideas, not the people. There are two kinds of teachers: those who regard their students as customers and those who regard their students as children. I am in the former category. Of course, I value my customers and give them respect, attention, and service to the best of my professional ability. But the teachers who regard students as children give something much more personal: love and nurture. That is why, although I am a good teacher, I can never be a great teacher.

ON ECONOMICS

Oliver Heaviside (for whom the integral of the Dirac delta function is named) said nearly a century ago, "Even Cambridge mathematicians deserve justice."[6] This may have been necessary to say at that time and may have remained necessary a few decades later when G. H. Hardy titled his book *A Mathematician's Apology*. But nowadays mathematicians everywhere are on the crest of a wave. Each abstruse new theorem is hailed as the next breakthrough in cryptography or cryptanalysis. Those who prove long-standing conjectures that the public had never heard of before – Fermat's last theorem, the Poincaré conjecture – become instant celebrities. And movies – *Good Will Hunting, A Beautiful Mind* – show off mathematicians' skill at writing complicated formulas in chalk on window glass.

The mantle of public disdain and ridicule has descended on economists in general, and economic theorists in particular. Natural scientists and humanists alike accuse us of pretense at being scientists. We are supposed to be heartless in the pursuit of efficiency and growth. The public doesn't trust our forecasts and is derisive when they turn out to be wrong. In the wake of the financial and macroeconomic crises of 2008, the game of "blame the economist" has reached new levels of popularity, and even those few media that are usually more knowledgeable about the subject have joined the game.[7] Many of our own agree with our critics. But we, too, deserve justice, and it is high time someone stood up for our rights.

The Internet has many economist joke sites.[8] Here are a few of the jokes, selected because I will use them in my arguments that follow:

1. An economist is someone who sees something working in practice and asks whether it would work in theory.
2. Winston Churchill is supposed to have said, "If you put two economists in a room, you get two opinions, unless one of them is Lord Keynes, in which case you get three opinions."
3. Examination questions in economics are the same every year, but the answers change every few years.
4. Economics is the only field in which two people can get a Nobel Prize for saying exactly the opposite thing.

Let us deconstruct these jokes. Why does anyone care that something worked in practice? To heave a sigh of relief? No; we care because we would like to replicate that success in the future in other situations. But how do we know whether the same thing will work again? The situation might be different. Of course, that doesn't automatically imply the opposite, namely that the same thing won't work; the difference might not be relevant. To help us figure out whether we should try the same thing again, we need to know precisely which features of the original context made the thing work. In other words, we need to understand *cause and effect*; for that we need a *theory*. Far from hanging our heads in shame when we hear that joke, we should hold them high and counter that asking whether something that works in practice also works in theory is exactly the right attitude for any researcher.

The same reasoning applies to economists holding different views. There is legitimate room for differences of judgment about what matters and when. Eternal critical vigilance is the price of progress in any science. As for Keynes, his famous reply, "When the facts change, I change my mind. What do you do, sir?" should settle the matter. And Nobel Prizes for saying exactly opposite things are not a preserve of economics. The 1906 Nobel Prize in physics was awarded to J. J. Thomson for proving that electrons were particles and measuring their mass. The 1929 prize went to Louis-Victor De Broglie for his hypothesis about the wave nature of matter, and the 1937 prize was awarded to G. P. Thomson (J. J.'s son) and Joseph Davisson for measuring the wavelength of electrons from diffraction patterns. Wave–particle duality became an important fundamental idea in physics.

Social scientists and philosophers who are suspicious of physics analogies might prefer to think of such apparent contradictions as a Hegelian dialectic: thesis, antithesis, and synthesis. In economics, traditional Keynesianism with price stickiness and other forms of inertia, on the one hand, and the rational expectations theorists' emphasis on forward-looking behavior, on the other, have similarly merged into a fruitful synthesis in the hands of a new generation of researchers like Michael Woodford.

No, the reality of an economist's perspective is very different from its popular perception. Economics gives us a unique insight into the workings of life, if not of the universe. And this understanding is a source of constant fun and pleasure. A glimpse into this state of mind has become available to the public in some wonderful books like Steve Levitt's *Freakonomics* and Tim Harford's *The Logic of Life*. Let me offer two offbeat examples from my own reading in history and biography; you will see how the economist's perspective sheds interesting new light on facts the writers had observed through other lenses.

James McPherson, in his celebrated history of the Civil War, discusses the Union navy's blockade of the South. Blockade running promised handsome profits, but it also risked seizure of the ship and the cargo. McPherson tells us that "[o]wners could make back their investment in one or two round trips, clearing a profit with every subsequent voyage." However, the chance of capture on any one trip was 1 in 10 in 1861, rising to 1 in 6, and 1 in 3 by 1864.[9] An economist reading this would immediately think, what was the expected profit?

If p is the probability of capture on any one-way trip, the expected number of trips until capture is $1/p$. On each successful trip, suppose the profits are X. Suppose the value of the ship and the goods it contains totals K. On the last trip, the ship is captured and no profits are made. Therefore, in expectation, we have $[(1/p) - 1]$ trips earning X each and one trip losing K. In equilibrium, the ex ante expected profit should be zero, so $K = [(1/p) - 1]X$, or $K = X(1 - p)/p$.

If $p = 1/3$, then $K = 2X$, and the investment is recouped in two one-way trips, that is, in one round trip. For recoupment in two round trips, we need $K = 4X$ and $p = 1/5$, which fits the situation earlier in the war. The smuggling trade not only flourished, but was close to equilibrium![10]

My second example features Alfred E. Smith, the Happy Warrior. He had to leave school and take a job as an assistant bookkeeper in the Fulton Fish Market to support his family. He started at 4 A.M., and his first task was to go up to the market roof with a pair of binoculars to watch for the boats sailing in with their catch. If they were riding high in the water, that indicated a poor catch; therefore, his boss could set prices high. If the boats were riding low, the catch must be good and the prices would be low. Here we have rational expectations and information in markets! Smith always claimed that he held an FFM degree – Fulton Fish Market.[11] Clearly he majored in economics.

Economics is all around you, and it is not the least bit dismal. Learn to recognize it, appreciate it, and enjoy it.[12]

If economics is all around you, then game theory, which has become such an important analytical technique in economics research since the 1970s and which has contributed so many new insights on strategy and information, is all around and within you. Almost everything you do has a strategic aspect, which you ignore at your peril. I don't mean that you should always be trying to outwit, outplay, and outlast everyone you meet. There is always a bigger game beyond the one you are currently playing, and recognizing the long-term benefits of nice behavior is at least as important as seizing opportunities for short-term victories. Mathematical game theorists prove theorems; the rest of us should learn to live game-theoretically. I have attempted to convey in some popular books this approach to the game of life, business, and everything, so I will not spend space and time on it here.[13]

ON OTHER SOCIAL SCIENCES

Once upon a time, all scholars who studied human beings and human societies would have regarded themselves as tillers of the same field; I am not sure it even had a name. A little more than a hundred years ago this broad social science split into more specialized fields: political economy (which then split further into economics and political science), sociology, individual and social psychology, and even certain aspects of evolutionary biology. The process of the split can be seen in two interesting examples. The man who gave his name to the fundamental concept of efficiency in economics, Vilfredo Pareto, was in equal measure a sociologist. However, while today we look up to Alfred Marshall for the breadth of his interest (as exemplified by his famous saying, "Economics is a study of mankind in the ordinary business of life"), he was one of the first to distinguish "economics" from "political economy."

For many years the rift widened and deepened, often degenerating into mutual dislike. Sociologists and political "scientists" disdained economists for their narrow perspective; economists disdained these others for their lack of theoretical and empirical rigor. But in the past two decades we have seen a tendency toward reconciliation. Economists have broadened their perspective to include other-regarding preferences and several forms of behavior that would were once dismissed as irrational and to include the political process squarely in their analysis of economic policy making. Sociologists and political scientists have embraced sophisticated statistical methods that were once the preserve of econometricians. All three have benefited from psychologists' approaches to the design of controlled experiments and field experiments. Game theory, further enriched by behavioral contributions from psychology, has become probably the most frequently used theoretical technique underlying recent research in economics and increasingly in political science, and it is slowly making inroads into sociology.

We should not expect a complete reunification of all the social sciences. Specialization is important for making rapid progress in Kuhn's "normal science" mode. Some form of cohabitation rather than marriage seems optimal. We should hope for a time when practitioners of the different branches will be able to converse reasonably fluently in the language of game theory and statistics, will respect one another's endeavors, and will learn from one another's research.

That should not preclude our making affectionate fun of one another's foibles. I always find it amusing that every paper in sociology finds it necessary to begin with a genuflection to Marx, Durkheim, and Weber, and urge my colleagues in that discipline to forget those dead white males and get on with their own new work. Conversely, they find it amusing that the typical economics paper has no references older than five years. A happy medium that combines respect and irreverence for the past in equal measures surely exists. Perhaps political scientists claim that territory.

ON PHILOSOPHY

Some of my remarks about being unphilosophical and so on must have made you wonder, "What has he got against philosophy?" My answer is: "Nothing. Philosophy is great fun, when discussed at midnight over a glass (or two) of Armagnac. But it is not a fit subject for sober daytime research."[14]

The whole purpose of philosophy is to not find answers to anything; rather, it is to complexify questions to the point where they don't have answers. I am not being unfair; most philosophers would agree. To quote a fictional philosopher, Renée Feuer Himmel, "Philosophy always reminds me of fireworks. One question is shot up and bursts into a splendorous many. Answers? Forget answers. The spectacle is all in the questions."[15] However, I am but a poor utilitarian in my attitude toward research and agree with another fictional character, Morris Zapp: "Any damn fool could think of questions; it was answers that separated the men from the boys. If you couldn't answer your own questions it was either because you hadn't worked on them hard enough or because they weren't real questions."[16]

Once upon a time, all sciences were lumped together into "natural philosophy." Then some of them started to find answers, and therefore either were banished by philosophers or unilaterally declared their independence, to become physics, chemistry, and so on. Economics followed more than a century ago. Other social sciences are increasingly distancing themselves from philosophy, going on to develop serious conceptual frameworks and do serious statistical empirical research, although some of their practitioners still retain a fondness for circular discussions of imponderable questions leading nowhere. I prefer to stay with the unphilosophical dimension of the social sciences.

ENVOI

Fans of Douglas Adams will remember that in the second book in the *Hitchhiker* series, *The Restaurant at the End of the Universe*,[17] his intrepid space explorers Arthur and Ford finally find out the Ultimate Question of

Life, Universe, and Everything. It is "What do you get when you multiply 9 by 6?" Remember that the answer was revealed to be 42 in the first book. But this is not an error; 42 indeed equals 9 times 6: in base 13. Deep Thought is thus telling us that 13 is the basis of Life, the Universe, and Everything. In other words, it is all bad luck.

I think this is an excellent starting point for a life philosophy. If "all bad luck" is the basis of your expectations, everything that happens will come as a pleasant surprise. For me, indeed it all has. A cheerfully pessimistic perspective on Work, Life, the Universe, and Everything has much to recommend it.[18]

Notes

1 Originally published by Harmony Books, 1980; reissues/reprints, Random House, 1997.

2 *American Economist* 38, no. 1 (Spring 1994): 10–16, reprinted in Michael Szenberg (ed.), *Passion and Craft: How Economists Work* (Ann Arbor: University of Michigan Press, 1998).

3 The physical equivalent is brilliantly described in *The Economist*'s obituary of John Bachar, July 18, 2009.

4 I exaggerate. Brilliant teachers like my own teacher Robert Solow and my Princeton colleague Harvey Rosen continue to enthrall students and get rave reviews armed only with a piece of chalk. For Solow, even the occasional squeak of the chalk had a pedagogical use.

5 My paper "Strategic Behavior in Contests," *American Economic Review* 77, no. 5 (December 1987): 891–898, had its origin in an exam question.

6 Quoted in Harold Jeffries and Bertha Swirles, *Methods of Mathematical Physics* (Cambridge: Cambridge University Press, 1950), 228.

7 The cover of the July 18, 2009, issue of *The Economist* shows a tome titled "Modern Economic Theory" melting away, to highlight the magazine's five-page "Briefing" criticizing the work in macroeconomics and finance over the past three or four decades. I must admit that the articles in the "Briefing" are quite well informed.

8 netec.wustl.edu/JokEc.html is quite extensive.

9 James McPherson, *Battle Cry of Freedom: The Civil War Era* (New York: Oxford University Press, 1988), 380.

10 This assumes risk neutrality. That may seem doubtful since the gains and losses were huge. But the business of smuggling would selectively attract the least risk-averse adventurers, so the assumption may not be so bad after all.

11 Jack Beatty, *The Rascal King: The Life and Times of James Michael Curley* (Reading, MA: Addison-Wesley,1992), 254–255.

12 In addition to the books by Levitt and Harford that I mentioned earlier, John McMillan's *Reinventing the Bazaar* (New York: W. W. Norton, 2002) is a personal favorite of mine. It gives a wonderful account of the working and failure of markets around the world. It exemplifies how practical economic thinking can and should be informed by good modern economic theory.

13 Most recently in *The Art of Strategy*, coauthored with Barry Nalebuff (New York: W. W. Norton, 2008).

14 Perhaps I should make an exception for the best of analytical philosophy: that of the early Russell and Quine, among others.

15 Rebecca Goldstein, *The Mind-Body Problem* (New York: Random House, 1983).

16 David Lodge, *Changing Places* (London: Martin Secker & Warburg, 1975).

17 Originally published by Crown Publishers, 1980; reissues/reprints, Random House, 1995.

18 Lars Svensson, who has long experience of free-climbing physical as well as mental rock faces, pointed out that such an attitude may lead one to make overly cautious choices of research topics. I don't think so: not if one enjoys the process for its own sake and lets success come as a pleasant surprise on top of that.

10

Finding a Niche

Barry Eichengreen

Becoming a professor was easier than becoming an economist. Growing up in Berkeley I was surrounded by professors; they dominated my parents' dinner parties, though my mother and father themselves were not academics. The conversation touched on book projects, sabbatical plans, and foreign travel. There was the security of a regular paycheck but, so it seemed, no one resembling a boss.

Growing up in Berkeley had its distinctive aspects. An outing for the socially conscious among my high school classmates was going down to the university and getting tear-gassed. At about this time the high school curriculum compelled one to choose between the natural sciences, social sciences, and humanities tracks. Social sciences were irresistible for someone growing up in this political petri dish. The natural sciences track, in contrast, would have meant more math. Early decisions have long-term consequences.

The University of California, Santa Cruz, where I was an undergraduate, was another child of the 1960s. Intended as an alternative to factory schools like Berkeley, it had no grades, few major and breadth requirements, and little intellectual structure.[1] Students were encouraged to design their own majors. This encouraged healthy disrespect for conventional academic boundaries, something that comes in handy for an economic historian. Santa Cruz also sent me for my junior year to the University of St. Andrews. St. Andrews students met periodically with a tutor to discuss assignments and read papers. My tutor was the Spanish economic historian Geoffrey Parker. In my senior year back at Santa Cruz, the department hired as a visitor a brilliant graduate student from Stanford, Flora Gill, to teach a course in economic history.

Put an undergraduate in an unstructured environment, and he or she will go in one of two directions. One is off the deep end, which for my classmates meant making candles in Ben Lomand. The other is in search of more structure. This is my best explanation for how I ended up in economics. Economics seemed to have more intellectual structure than the other social sciences, all of which, as a good Santa Cruz undergraduate, I sampled. Not that I actually learned much about what economists do, Santa Cruz not being organized to convey such knowledge.

Sometime around the middle of my senior year there was a sparsely attended meeting of students and faculty to discuss life after college. Various possibilities were described. One was, of course, to enroll in more school. A more novel alternative was to look for work. One professor who had spent time in Washington, DC, suggested that it might be possible to apply what one had learned by working as a research assistant in a government agency. When I asked him how to go about this, he seemed genuinely shocked at having a student follow up on his suggestion. "Write my former boss at the US Department of Labor," he suggested. After some weeks, there was no response. Fortunately this member of the faculty had also been a dissertation fellow at the Brookings Institution. There the director of Economic Studies, the prominent tax policy expert Joe Pechman, was losing his research assistant before the end of the academic year and was desperate to find someone who could begin in early April. I was graduating a quarter early and was therefore available off-cycle. I like to think that it was on my intellectual merits that I beat out other candidates for this job, but there is another interpretation.

Joe Pechman was a famously successful example of how to do high-quality policy analysis with a limited background in mathematics. Joe substituted intuition, detailed knowledge of the US tax code, and an ability to write clearly and quickly for technical skills. He also moderated a Friday lunch at which a galaxy of Brookings fellows commented on the events of the day.[2] In 1974–1975 the conversation ranged over the first OPEC oil shock, inflation, and Watergate. If events like those couldn't awaken an interest in policy, it was hard to imagine what could. Brookings also offered its research assistants free time and a library that just happened to include a complete run of the *Journal of Economic History*. And it provided a Good Housekeeping Seal of Approval. Many of Joe's previous research assistants, mostly Swarthmore undergraduates (my position was known colloquially as "the Swarthmore chair"), had gone on to graduate school. Thus, it was possible for an applicant with no grades and limited coursework in economics to be admitted to a PhD program.

I arrived at Yale already knowing that I wanted to concentrate on economic history and international macroeconomics. This is the hardest part of my intellectual journey to explain. Economic history was not done seriously at Santa Cruz. It was not done at all at Brookings. Macroeconomics in the 1970s was still almost entirely a closed-economy affair. And the combination of economic history and international macroeconomics was virtually unknown.[3] To be sure, I had already had chance encounters with Geoff Parker and Flora Gill. Economic history appealed to someone with a healthy disregard for disciplinary boundaries. Much of what I knew about economics at this point I taught myself by reading journals from the Brookings library, and economic history journals were more accessible than most. For its part, international economics appealed to someone whose parents were first-generation Americans and who had been made aware from a relatively early age that the United States was part of a larger world. There was also the example of my closest childhood friend, Jeff Frankel, who had already discovered international economics as a student of Rudi Dornbusch at MIT.

James Tobin and William Parker dominated my Yale experience. Tobin, of course, dominated everyone's Yale experience. His belief that economics could be used to make the world more just and equitable affected everyone around him, including graduate students. My own vaguely Keynesian inclinations and belief that economics and economic history can serve the public interest are inherited to a considerable extent from Jim.

Although Tobin was not a member of my dissertation committee, he encouraged me to apply modern macroeconomic methods to historical problems. Much of Tobin's course in monetary economics was organized as Yale-style portfolio theory versus Chicago-style monetarism with Milton Friedman as doppelganger.[4] But we also read one uncharacteristically sympathetic assessment of Friedman, Tobin's review of Friedman and Schwartz's *Monetary History of the United States*, in which he hailed the book as pathbreaking for its systematic application of macroeconomic theory to historical problems.

The Yale department's economic historian, Bill Parker, could lay claim to being the first "new" economic historian, having drawn the Parker-Klein sample of grain-growing farms from the 1840 census and editing, together with Douglass North, the *Journal of History* when the first articles making explicit use of economic theory were accepted for publication in the 1950s. But Bill was known best for his students, Jan deVries, Joel Mokyr, and Gavin Wright prominent among them.[5] Parker at Yale played much the same role as Alexander Gerschenkron at Harvard.[6] He humanized an increasingly technical economics curriculum. He served as a bridge to the historical literature on economic growth and development. In the wake of *Time on the Cross*, scholarship in economic history was driven by debates over methodology. Is quantification good or bad? Should counterfactuals be explicit? Is there anything left to be learned from the narrative approach? In contrast to many other economic historians, Bill was interested more in substance than methodology. He saw the advantage of picking, choosing, and blending methodologies as appropriate for the question at hand. Once the fervor of the cliometric revolution died down, this was the position to which a more mature subdiscipline gravitated. Bill got there before most, which allowed him to pitch a large tent for students with very different analytical inclinations.

Parker's office was divided into a large library containing pretty much every consequential book in economic history, in which I spent the best part of my graduate student career, and an anteroom barely big enough for a desk and chair, where Bill napped and occasionally dispensed advice. My own ideas were met mainly with grunts and nods. I learned that some graduate students, like some missiles, are self-guiding, while others must be pointed at the target.

When it came to international finance, there was no shortage of role models. There was Carlos Díaz-Alejandro, who had already thought of combining economic history and international economics.[7] There was Paul Krugman, whose spell as a Yale assistant professor coincided with the year I began searching for a dissertation topic.[8] There was Pentti Kouri, the *enfant terrible* who had completed his PhD at MIT in two years. Finally, there was Robert Triffin, whose interests in the historical evolution of the international monetary system were closest to my own. Triffin had written the definitive book on the subject. Actually, he had written it three times.[9] Triffin being on leave for most of my years as a graduate student, I encountered him only once, during the qualifying examination that followed coursework but preceded the dissertation, the format for which was two hours of grilling, half an hour from each of four professors. I was warned that Triffin would probably spend his half hour asking about the Triffin dilemma, as the dynamic instability of a gold-exchange or gold-dollar standard was known. So I studied this issue. Fortunately, Triffin's questions focused entirely on this one subject.

This left only finding a thesis topic. The time-tested approach to this problem, employed by generations of graduate students, is delay. I delayed by taking a master's in history: Yale offered a program where graduate students in history and economics could spend a year taking courses in the other department, permitting them to call themselves card-carrying economic historians. I took courses from Vann Woodward, Harry Miskimin, and John Merriman but ended up no closer to a topic.

I thought I knew what a suitable topic would entail. I wanted to look at a different historical time and place, but I also wanted policy relevance so that what I wrote about would speak to an audience beyond historical specialists. I hoped to draw material from the archives in a language with which I was familiar. The problem should have an international dimension about which I could theorize. The statistical base had to be sufficient to permit econometric analysis. This did not leave many degrees of freedom. I ended up writing on the Great Depression in Britain and specifically on the decision to impose a tariff only after the country abandoned the gold standard in 1931.

Whether the imposition of a tariff under these circumstances was sensible was not obvious. What, after all, could a tariff do for industries suffering from inadequate demand, partly owing to import competition, that currency depreciation could not once sterling was free to float? In early 1931 Keynes had written in favor of a tariff on the grounds that the external constraint had to be relaxed in order for monetary policy to be loosened, but he reversed course once the gold standard was abandoned. In the late 1970s a group of post-Keynesian Cambridge economists around Francis Cripps and Wynne Godley rehabilitated his arguments, suggesting that the UK should impose a general tariff to reconcile expansionary policies with the external constraint. Although sterling had again begun to float, the Cambridge Economic Policy Group argued that it was now real rather than nominal wages that were rigid, the implication being that a tariff could have an effect on relative prices that currency depreciation could not. So, in addition to its historical interest, the topic had points of contact with current policy. With benefit of hindsight I now see that this was not the best way of selecting a dissertation topic. A thesis should be driven by an interesting question, not by a long list of methodological desiderata.[10] Given the number of self-imposed constraints, it is perhaps not surprising that I never managed to develop that dissertation into a book.[11]

I finished my thesis in a fellowship year at Oxford. I read files at the Public Record Office documenting the debate over sterling and the tariff. I visited Lionel Robbins, who recalled having been on the wrong side of his debate with Keynes. Wynne Godley explained his position on the tariff over lunch at King's College. I struck up a relationship with Alec Cairncross, who had studied with Keynes in the 1930s, been in government in both the 1940s and 1960s (two key periods in the evolution of Britain's international monetary relations), and now practiced the kind of economic history to which I aspired.[12] I reestimated my model of the interwar economy at the Oxford computing center. This meant submitting the punch cards, going out for dinner at a Chinese restaurant, and returning a couple of hours later to see if the program had run. The supervisor that the university assigned me turned out to be Nicholas Crafts, the leading UK-based new economic historian. Nick at the time had attracted an exceptional collection of students, including Steve Broadberry, Mary McKinnon, and Mark Thomas. The seminar regularly adjourned to the pub, followed by the inevitable Chinese meal. This was where I acquired the research agenda that sustained me for the next couple of years.

What that dissertation did succeed at was getting me a job. It used enough archival material to convince historians that I had something to say about the context in which policy was made. And it contained a sufficiently up-to-date theoretical model and convincing econometric analysis of the effects to sell the economists. Or maybe it was the archival analysis that convinced the economists and the theory that impressed the historians. The challenge was presenting the archival analysis, theoretical model, and econometric results in a single seminar. The discussion of archival material typically occupied the first half of the presentation. I can remember my Harvard job talk, where after forty-five minutes I turned my back on the audience to write the first equation on the chalkboard. The door clicked and a chair scraped. The new arrival asked, *sotto voce*, "Is he only putting up the first equation *now*?"[13]

Harvard was an exceptional place for an assistant professor of economics. Memories of the mid-1970s, when the department refused tenure to a contingent of radical economists led by Sam Bowles, leading to an embarrassingly public spat, were still raw. The senior members of the department concluded that assistant professors were more trouble than they were worth. The year 1980 was the first time that the department swallowed hard and hired a standard-sized contingent of new PhDs.[14] But we assistant professors, not being entirely trustworthy, were not invited to faculty meetings. This, of course, was a great boon. Freed from administrative responsibilities we had more time for research.[15]

What the Economics Department lacked in collegiality the economic historians more than made up for. Bob Fogel had not participated in the decision to hire me because he was already on his way back to the University of Chicago.[16] But Fogel was supportive of my work and characteristically interested in my opinions about his.[17] From Bob I learned how to sustain a research agenda and organize large projects. His successor, Jeff Williamson, exemplified someone who could formulate questions of interest to economists, execute that research efficiently, and attract students. Then there was David Landes, the eminent historian of technology, who had moved to the Economics Department following a falling out with his colleagues in history. David hosted the after-seminar sherry hour in his office, where one could inspect the latest finds that he had unearthed in Widener Library. David had little patience for cliometrics but could play the game. A favorite pastime was guessing how many seconds into the seminar he would ask the first question. If the speaker's opening line was "In this paper I compare agrarian practice in three English villages," the question, typically put in the first minute, was "why three?"

Peter Temin was a regular participant in the Harvard history seminar and central to the Cambridge economic history scene. Just as one waited each week for the David Landes question, one waited with considerably more patience for the Peter Temin question. Generally this came about two-thirds of the way through the seminar and took the form "Isn't the issue that you are really raising ... ?" followed by a more interesting formulation of the question than the author himself had offered. If the single most important skill a scholar can acquire is figuring out what questions are interesting and how to formulate them, then the little I know about this I learned from Peter.[18]

After four years I had written a series of articles on international aspects of the 1920s and 1930s: on the Bank of England's interest rate policy, on the Bank of France's sterilization of gold, on the collapse of the gold-exchange standard, and on the effects of the devaluation of sterling. These were articles in search of a book, though what form that book should take was not yet clear. My colleague Jeff Sachs, together with Michael Bruno, had just written a book taking an international approach to analyzing another economic slump, that of the late 1970s and early 1980s. At some level our interests were similar, and it seemed inevitable that eventually we would coauthor something. By the time we did, Jeff was already in demand as a money doctor; he was spending most of his time on the plane and phone to Bogotá. We did our talking and writing between midnight and 5 A.M., when his more pressing duties were done. One of us then went home to sleep, while the other got back on the phone.

What we did was a cross-country analysis, in the spirit of Bruno and Sachs, of the effects of going off the gold standard. The data analysis was simple, but cross-country variations (comparisons, for example, of economic recovery in counties that were early and late to abandon the gold standard) allowed for powerful tests of a sort that individual country studies did not.[19] The results convinced me both that the gold standard was central to the Great Depression and that abandoning it had been the key to recovery. This pointed also to a problem of political economy: given the advantages, which should have been obvious to contemporaries, of cutting a country's links with the deflationary gold standard system, what was it about its history and politics that had rendered it more or less likely to take that step?[20]

Finally, the fact that one country's decisions had clearly affected outcomes in others meant that it was important to analyze the operation of the gold standard as a system. Here the question was whether the problem was a global gold shortage as suggested by Robert Mundell or the intrinsic fragility of a gold-exchange standard as Robert Triffin had argued.[21]

A thorough analysis of these issues, their interconnections, and how they played out in different countries required a book-length treatment. My view was and is that books should speak to a broader audience than just academic economists. Journals, with their specialized readership, are the best outlets for formal models and econometric analyses. Books best omit this technical apparatus, since they are potentially accessible to a wider audience.[22] The challenge for the author of a monograph is how to characterize the issue, in this case how policy toward the gold standard shaped the Great Depression and in turn what shaped policy toward the gold standard, in a way that is internally consistent and informed by theory but using words rather than equations. It is to be able to sustain that characterization – to draw that red thread through the various chapters so that they work together to advance a single argument. Keeping the thread unbroken also means that not all aspects of the problem can be addressed in a successful book. It means knowing what to leave out.[23]

Some final examples may serve to illustrate how research agendas develop. In 1990 a friend and colleague, Charles Wyplosz, became coeditor of a new European policy forum, *Economic Policy*, and asked me for an article on historical precursors to a European monetary union, an issue that was then rising rapidly on the policy agenda. Surely there were historical precedents, he suggested, from the Latin Union to the Scandinavian Union and the gold standard from which lessons might be drawn. I concluded that this was not the case. If Europe was going to succeed in creating a monetary union, it would have to establish a true transnational institution (a European central bank) unlike anything that had existed under the Latin Union, the Scandinavian Union, or the gold standard.[24] Doing so would entail significant pooling of national sovereignty, something that was conceivable in contemporary Europe, given the continent's history, but had not been possible in earlier times and places. In turn these observations opened up a set of issues about the connections between monetary, economic, and political integration in Europe that occupied me for more than a decade and resulted ultimately in my book *The European Economy Since 1945* (Princeton University Press, 2007).

Unprecedented is not the same as impossible. I was never among those skeptical Americans who thought a European monetary union was impossible because nothing like it had existed before and because it would never work in North America. Floating exchange rates were not acceptable to Europeans because of their history: the experience of the 1930s caused them to associate floating with Franco-German conflict. The pegged but adjustable rates of the European Monetary System (EMS) had been feasible so long as capital controls were pervasive, but the Single European Act mandated a single market in capital as well as labor and merchandise, eliminating all scope for such controls. A close look at the history of the gold standard served to remind one of the fragility of pegged rates in a world of high capital mobility. This logic left monetary union as the only alternative.

This point was driven home for me by the 1992 crisis in the EMS, whose outbreak happily (speaking from a selfish point of view) coincided with the beginning of a sabbatical year. This was the major financial event of my then-young professional life, when George Soros made $1 billion betting against the Bank of England and the process of European integration seemed to be falling off a cliff.[25] Wyplosz and I abandoned our preexisting research agendas to write the history of the crisis in real time. We surveyed financial market participants: Charles's daughters licked the envelopes in which we mailed our survey forms in these pre-Internet days. "The Unstable EMS" appeared in *Brookings Papers on Economic Activity* in 1993. This was the beginning of the financial crisis industry, or at least of my involvement in it. Charles and I coauthored a series of papers together with my Berkeley colleague Andrew Rose in which we developed measures of currency crises and sought to identify their economic and political correlates.[26] This sideline as financial ambulance chaser and historian of financial crises would come in handy in 2008.

A final episode in the development of my research agenda occurred when I was asked to work as senior policy adviser at the International Monetary Fund. It is my observation that organizations like the Fund (I would also include the World Bank, the regional development banks, and national central banks) quite like having economic historians around. Economic historians are more likely than other economists to actually know something about institutions.[27] They are likely to know which policies are new and novel and which ones have precedents. They are in the business of synthesizing large amounts of material. They tend to be able to convey their thoughts in plain English.

Again the timing was fortuitous from a selfish standpoint. I started at the IMF on July 2, 1998, the same day that Thailand devalued and the Asian crisis erupted, and left a year and a few weeks later on the day that Russia defaulted.[28] I had been hired by the Fund's deputy managing director, Stanley Fischer, but worked for the head of the Research Department, Michael Mussa. Stan and Mike could both lay claim to being the best international macroeconomist of their generation, except for the fact that they were both of the same generation. It is hard to imagine two better exemplars of how to do high-quality policy research.

If the IMF is a rolling deck, then the senior policy adviser is its loose cannon. Members of the hierarchy have an incentive to go along in order to get along, not to mention in order to be promoted. But the senior policy adviser has tenure at his university, where he can return after a year. This allows him to say what he thinks. As a reviewer he is expected to criticize and raise objections to policy memos and in-house research products. Not a bad job if you can get it.[29]

In my case the review function was overtaken by events. No sooner did the Asian crisis erupt than the prime minister of Malaysia, Mahathir bin Mohamed, accused hedge funds of fomenting the crisis and demanded that the IMF investigate. The IMF asked me to investigate, which meant giving me a corporate credit card and a team of PhD economists.[30] We visited the regulators. We visited George Soros in New York. We visited Long-Term Capital Management in Greenwich.[31] We visited Bear Stearns, which booked the majority of the trades for the hedge fund industry. The experience was eye-opening for someone who had studied financial markets exclusively through the lens of theoretical models and historical documents.

The exercise was also not unproblematic. It would have been naive to sit down with the manager of a hedge fund and say, "We're from the IMF, and we'd like to know whether you and your friends colluded in causing the Asian crisis." These people knew who had sent us and were understandably cagey with their answers. At the same time, the fact that many of the fund managers in Manhattan had offices in the World Financial Center and could be found at 5 P.M. on Friday drinking together in the atrium bar did convey a certain amount of information. It impressed one with the importance of collective psychology. It couldn't help but incline one to the view that there existed such a thing as herd behavior in financial markets.

Our report concluded that while a number of important hedge funds had taken positions against Asian currencies, they were far from alone. We learned, for example, that the same investment bank that was advising an Asian government on how to fend off speculation was itself the main speculator taking a position against it. More generally investment banks took many of the same positions as hedge funds, and they were at least as highly leveraged. The Malaysian constituency was not pleased by the conclusions, which appeared to let the hedge funds off the hook. Others criticized us for lumping hedge funds and investment banks together. After the crises of Bear Stearns and Lehman Brothers in 2008, it is hard not to feel vindicated.

In February 1998, six months into the Asian crisis, US Treasury Secretary Robert Rubin made a speech at the Brookings Institution calling for a new international financial architecture. Michel Camdessus, the ambitious French technocrat who headed the IMF, wasn't sure what this new financial architecture might entail, but he was certain that the Fund should be in charge of it. I was commissioned to write a series of papers on the subject.[32] These soon came to be known as "the non-papers," since papers in the Fund have to undergo interdepartmental review before they can be widely circulated and no radical ideas about a new international financial architecture could have ever survived this vetting. The non-papers called for the IMF to take the lead in promulgating standards for securities market regulation, corporate governance, and auditing and accounting practice, and for it then to actively monitor compliance. They called for a greater focus on supervision and regulation of banking systems, banking-sector weaknesses having been at the center of the Asian crisis. They called for the Fund to push its members harder to adopt more flexible exchange rates so that there would be a stronger incentive for banks and corporations to hedge their currency exposures.

Whether these non-papers had any impact on the policy debate is for the reader of this essay to judge.[33] The author, for his part, was characteristically unable to write four extended memos without also seeing the outlines of a book. *Toward a New International Financial Architecture* was published by Fred Bergsten's Institute for International Economics late in 1999, just three months after I returned to academia. Books like this having a relatively short shelf life, time was of the essence. I learned that when an author is prepared to give up his royalties, a publisher can move very fast.[34]

As will be clear to those who have gotten to this point, at some level I feel most comfortable in the historian's world where one tells a story, leavens it with anecdotes, and leaves the reader to draw out the broader implications. But the economist in me yearns for general conclusions about how research agendas are formed.

The most general conclusion is, of course, that there are no general conclusions. There are no universally applicable guidelines for finding a topic, settling on an approach, and moving from one topic to another so that a research question turns into a research program and eventually a body of work. The ideas that engage the researcher's imagination will be shaped by the circumstances in which he or she lives. The 1970s were when the Bretton Woods system of fixed exchange rates gave way to generalized floating; it is not surprising that these events provoked historical research on the historical performance of alternative exchange rate regimes. That the 1990s were a decade of financial instability sparked new research on the history of financial crises. The global credit crisis and recession of 2008–2009 will undoubtedly trigger new research on the Great Depression. The scholar seeking to speak to a broad audience is always on the lookout for events that will resonate with readers. The economic historian is always on the lookout for precedents. These tendencies are healthy if they are kept in reasonable check and do not lead the researcher to leap from topic to topic, a problem with which I am not entirely unfamiliar.

It helps, of course, to have a core question – in my case the role of the gold standard in the Great Depression – substantial enough to sustain one's research for a period of years. If that question is sufficiently rich and suggestive, links to other important questions will suggest themselves. In my case those links ran backward to the classical gold standard of the pre-1914 period, which evidently functioned more smoothly and endured longer than its short-lived interwar successor; the questions thrown up by this contrast are obvious. The links also ran forward from the 1931 financial crisis that shattered the gold standard system to the 1992 crisis that shattered the EMS. They ran from there to the incidence of financial crises, both historically and contemporaneously, and to the possibility that the further progress of European integration, extending to the creation of an economic and monetary union, might repair the fissures in the EMS. This is how my own research agenda grew, unpredictably but not entirely without logic.

If one is lucky, this process will be pushed along by impetus from outside, not just in the form of current events but also in the form of commissions and requests for conference papers. These may come from someone with more detachment and therefore insight into how the researcher's past and future work may link to other issues and who, not incidentally, attaches lower value to the researcher's precious time. The trick, of course, is deciding which commissions to accept – those that require extending one's scholarly range in limited but significant ways – and which ones to reject – those that would force the researcher to move far out of his or her comfort zone and turn into a time sink.[35]

The other problem with commissions, conference papers, and coauthors is that they are too interesting. They make it more difficult to pursue to conclusion the task of answering the big question at the heart of one's research program. Big questions require sustained attention – for an economic historian they require book-length treatment. And a serious book requires effort over a period of years. My own most intellectually productive periods have been when I attempted to write a big book – in 1985–1992 on the gold standard and the Great Depression, in 2000–2007 on the European economy since 1945 – while at the same time pursuing other topics, some old and some new.

The challenge is keeping these different balls in the air, all at the same time. It is devoting much of one's research time and effort to a single topic for a sustained period while also working on other subjects. It may be one month on the book followed by one month on other projects. More likely, there will be less regular alternation. Either way, I like to think that I turned out the best appetizers and side dishes when I also had the main course in the oven.

Notes

1 Factory-like environment notwithstanding, sometimes I think that I would have been better off with an actual college education.
2 The observant reader will note that luncheon and dinner party conversation plays an ongoing role in this essay.
3 One thinks only of Charles Kindleberger and his student Carlos Díaz-Alejandro.
4 This had its disadvantages: where graduate students elsewhere were already being taught about rational expectations, Yalies remained largely ignorant of this development, still fighting as we were a rearguard action against monetarism.

5 I myself didn't have any of these eminences as teaching assistants in Bill's course; instead I had Rick Levin, an excellent section leader who eventually chose to forsake economic history for the presidency of Yale.

6 The comparison would have annoyed him: whenever he heard Gerschenkron's name, Bill would remind the listener that he himself had been a student of Gerschenkron's predecessor, Abbot Peyton Usher.

7 Carlos had organized his *Essays on the Economic History of the Argentine Republic*, published in 1970, around the country's terms of trade.

8 I remember Paul writing equations on the chalkboard of the seminar room in the Cowles Foundation – a model of balance-of-payments crises, a model of imperfect competition and trade – and claiming that he had come up with these ideas over the preceding weekend.

9 *Gold and the Dollar Crisis* (1960), *The Evolution of the International Monetary System: Historical Reappraisal and Future Perspectives* (1964), and *The World Money Maze* (1966).

10 Though the broad area, the economics and history of the Great Depression, was hardly uninteresting – and it has hardly lost salience in light of subsequent events.

11 It also was not accepted for the dissertation session of the Economic History Association, a fact that I happily recount to students when their own dissertations are passed over.

12 This resulted in my first book, *Sterling in Decline: The Devaluations of 1931, 1949 and 1967*, with Alec Cairncross (Oxford: Basil Blackwell, 1983).

13 This was Jeff Sachs, a member of the Society of Fellows, late not for the first time.

14 The others were Jeff Sachs, Andy Abel, and Mark Watson, who all went on to distinguished careers and from whom I learned certain basics of research to which I had not been exposed in New Haven.

15 I was also blessed with an appointment as a faculty research fellow of the National Bureau of Economic Research's International Finance Program. I had to lobby Marty Feldstein, who wasn't entirely sure whether an economic historian qualified for membership in an international finance program (or whether I had the qualifications to function as an NBER research fellow at all). Appointment as a fellow admitted one to the Bureau's summer boot camp in international finance, attended by the field's leading figures, which helped me to develop contacts and credentials as an international economist and learn more methods.

16 Chicago offered more resources for his labor-intensive research.

17 I strongly suspect that he still has his tape recordings of the lunches we had at the Harvard Faculty Club to discuss his work.

18 When he started working on the connections between the gold standard and the Great Depression, I knew I had made a sensible choice.

19 Embarrassingly so. On presenting the paper at the 1984 Cliometrics Conference I was given the "Peter Temin award for drawing the strongest conclusions on the basis of the least data."

20 This problem of political economy, with its answer rooted in history and politics, was important in and of itself. But in addition its answer could be used to solve the identification problem. Technically, the problem was that the decision to abandon the gold standard might affect the course of a country's depression, but the depth

of its depreciation might also affect its decision of whether to abandon the gold standard.

21 It was clear in which direction a Yalie would gravitate.

22 In *Golden Fetters: The Gold Standard and the Great Depression, 1919–1939* (Oxford: Oxford University Press, 1992), I at least succeeded in omitting the technical apparatus, if not always in making the material accessible, or so my wife, who has tried to finish reading the book several times, likes to remind me.

23 But that, of course, is where subsequent research agendas come from.

24 I ended up instead writing for *Economic Policy* an article on the fifty US states as a monetary union, which became part of a rapidly growing literature comparing asymmetric shocks, adjustment through capital and labor mobility, and fiscal self-insurance in the United States and the European Union.

25 Along, perhaps, with the 1987 stock market crash when the Dow declined by 500 points, a very large amount given the levels of the era, in a single day. That was the same day that I gave my undergraduate lecture on the Great Crash in 1929 for the first time. When I gave the lecture again in 1988, the Dow declined by 250 points.

26 I claim credit for having first employed the now-standard indicator of exchange market pressure as a measure of crisis incidence and for the labels now conventionally attached to "first- and second-generation" models of financial crises.

27 In a policy environment pure theory takes one only so far.

28 I leave it to the reader to infer cause and effect.

29 And a positive reflection on an institution, the IMF, that does not always enjoy the best image.

30 Both were firsts for someone whose experience had been limited to academia.

31 Some nine months before its failure. Had we seen that train wreck coming we would have been golden. My report to the Board contained a sentence, reflecting our interviews with regulators, stating that "regulators are confident that hedge funds are prudently managing their risks." This statement was entirely accurate so long as one recalls the first four words, which was not always the case of my subsequent interlocutors.

32 Who better, one might ask, than an economic historian to ruminate on the past and future of the international financial architecture?

33 Camdessus found their conclusions exciting. This agenda implied an expanded role for the IMF, and along with more responsibilities would come a bigger budget and more staff. He proposed convening an "informal lunch" in his private dining room. The informal lunch turned out to involve three dozen department heads, microphones, and a stenographer. The overwhelming reaction was that my ideas were unrealistic. The IMF had always focused on monetary and fiscal policies. To imagine that it could now also focus on the plumbing of financial markets was to misunderstand its role. The Fund had always favored stable exchange rates; to make it an active proponent of greater flexibility was beyond the pale.

34 Even then, not everyone disseminates research like Fred Bergsten. My Berkeley colleague Janet Yellen, who was then chair of Bill Clinton's Council of Economic Advisers, told me about walking into the Oval Office in late 1999 and finding the president with his yellow highlighter and a mysterious black and yellow book.

Seeing that the book was called *Toward a New International Financial Architecture*, she whispered to Robert Rubin, "We'd better get a copy of that and find out what he's reading."

35 The trick, of course, is recognizing which requests are which, something I have never entirely mastered.

11

Become an Economist – See the World

Jeffrey Frankel

CHILDHOOD: THE GOLDEN STATE

I grew up in California in the 1950s and 1960s. I considered myself then entirely a child of that time and place. I have always enjoyed being able to tell people that I was born in San Francisco.

To me, California in that golden age had nothing to do with hedonism. During an era known for psychedelic rock in San Francisco – the late 1960s – I was probably one of the few kids in my high school never to try drugs or even touch alcohol.

California to me seemed the culmination of a linear westward march of civilization throughout history. Here is how it went. The first great civilizations arose in Asia, followed by the Egypt of the pharaohs. Progress had flowed westward ever since: the Greece of classical culture, the Rome of the Senate, the Florence of the Renaissance, the England of the Industrial Revolution, the America of the thirteen founding states, and the legendary pushing westward of the frontier.

In my imagination my parents had participated in the final phase of this logical progression. My mother and father grew up in Detroit and Cleveland, respectively, and met at the University of Chicago, at a time when it was dominated by the great books curriculum.

I puzzled a bit over what the logical next stage would be in this historical progression. The possibility that it would be a leap across the Pacific to East Asia did occur to me, even then. But it seemed more likely that the West Coast was the limit. There were no more frontiers left. After all, the millennium was coming. At age twelve, I made a list of things that could be counted on to occur in my lifetime: the bicentennial (1976), 1984 (as in Orwell's book), the return of Haley's Comet (1986), and the millennium. After that? Nothing. No more known dates.

Such words may sound apocalyptic. But that is not at all what I meant. I viewed my time and place as a pinnacle of human well-being – a limit in the sense of an "absorbing barrier," not in the sense of the end. I knew that few decades of history, and few parts of the world contemporaneously, enjoyed the standard of living that my close nuclear family enjoyed, as my brother and I grew up in a California suburb with the sedate name of Kensington. There was a probabilistic paradox: What were the odds that I, thinking about this, would have been born in such a unique time and place? In retrospect, my thinking was excessively linear and extrapolative. Today, I think far more in terms of cycles. Nevertheless, I had a point at the time. First, I correctly perceived how lucky I was. Second, the statistical paradox is similar to the scientists' puzzle that is still unresolved: Is the origin of life on this particular planet an improbable miracle? Or is that a silly question, because if it hadn't happened, there would be nobody to ask it?

ETHNIC IDENTITY

Of my childhood friends, one requires mention. Barry Eichengreen was my classmate starting in preschool (age three). We were best friends and played chess together every weekend. He went to Hebrew school, so I did know he was Jewish, the lone exception to the secularity of my environment. (My family was Jewish, but I barely knew it.) What can one say about the fact that Barry and I eventually ended up in the same field, international economics, and even on the same Economics Department faculty (UC Berkeley, in the late 1980s and the 1990s), other than "there must have been something in that water in Kensington."

Just to finish off the subject of religion: Every Saturday, my father would conduct my brother and me in what I now recognize as an excellently designed substitute for religious education. We read books like *Myths and Legends of All Lands*. I am not sure whether my father was trying to send the message that the Bible stories stood on the same footing as the Greek myths and the rest of them, but that is the message I got. Personally, I preferred the Greek myths, a taste that my own son has now taken on with enthusiasm. I don't want to offend anyone, but Prometheus seems to me a worthier hero than Moses. At one time I briefly bought the line that monotheism had been a step forward historically in that it brought the end of human sacrifice. But then I discovered that the Greek gods detested human sacrifice (see Tantalus). The lesson of the Abraham and Isaac story, meanwhile, seems to me that any atrocity, including human sacrifice, is justified if you are following orders from a higher authority.

LIBERALISM AND THE VIETNAM WAR

I also felt myself intellectually a child of the Enlightenment. Perhaps I naively thought that everybody was a child of the Enlightenment. I am confused today by what most Americans mean when they say "liberal" and "conservative."[1] But to me, liberal meant the Enlightenment, the American Revolution, and freedom, and conservative meant oppressive hidebound institutions such as monarchies, dictatorships, and religious establishments.

The Vietnam War dragged on throughout my teen years. I, like others, thought it was a huge mistake from the beginning. How could the US military, fighting far from home, hope to prevail over a guerilla army that felt it was fighting for its country's freedom? Yes, the army could clear the Vietnamese out of any given geographic patch of ground. But how did that help transform the country in the way we wanted? Didn't we remember the lessons of the American Revolution? Didn't we understand that we were now the Redcoats? Yes, communism was a bad way to run a country. But the sooner we got out of the way, the sooner the Vietnamese would figure that out for themselves.

Further, Lyndon Johnson had originally misled the country about specifics in order to get us into the war (the Tonkin Gulf Resolution), was repeatedly wildly optimistic about what would be required, and was reluctant to raise taxes to pay the cost. Even after it was clear that the initial goals were not achievable, Richard Nixon came up with new reasons we had to stay in. One of the arguments, as is so often invoked in military interventions, was that to pull out would mean a loss of face and credibility for the United States. It never seems to occur to those who make this argument that we lose much more face and credibility if we stay in, double the stakes yet again, and end up eventually pulling out anyway. It seems to me that the United States repeated all these mistakes more recently in Iraq.

At high school graduation, I gave the valedictorian speech. My subject was the war, though I focused mainly on the importance of opposing it non-violently so as to avoid alienating the undecided middle-American opinion. Some parents walked out. Evidently they were alienated anyway.

I had a college deferment, and later a high draft number (211): I came along late enough that I never had to face being asked to participate in a war to which I was opposed.

EDUCATION

I attended excellent schools growing up in California: first, great public schools, during that shining era when California had the best public education in the world and before tax-cutting fanaticism became the sole guiding economic ideology of a substantial fraction of the electorate; and then a great private – but free – high school in San Francisco, with the Hogwarts-sounding name of Lick-Wilmerding.

When I first went east to begin college at Swarthmore, I would not have expected to major in economics. The reason is simply that I, like many students at that stage, had virtually no idea what economics was about. Today, if I had to define the discipline, I would say something about maximizing objective functions subject to constraints. At age seventeen, I would have said economics was all about money.

Sampling various academic fields, I soon developed a way of viewing them that, in retrospect, only a future economist could dream up. It seemed to me that one could array the disciplines along a continuum, with mathematics at one end, followed by physics, chemistry, and biology, and with philosophy at the other end, preceded by the humanities and then the social sciences. At one pole, mathematics held questions that could be answered with enormous precision but were in themselves of no direct import. The opposite pole, philosophy, consisted of questions that were of the largest possible consequence but could not be answered at all.

How, then, to choose a field in which to specialize after the completion of one's liberal arts education? The objective function that seemed the right one to me was the product of two factors: the importance of the questions in a field, multiplied by the ability to answer them. What use was a field where the questions were of cosmic importance but the ability to answer them, when all was said and done, was zero? At that end of the spectrum, the product of the two factors was zero. But what use was a field where precise answers were possible but of no direct use in my daily life, as either an individual or a public citizen? The product again was zero. What field maximized the product? The one in the center, of course: economics. The questions were important, if not as important as the meaning of the universe. The answers to those questions were substantive, even if not as precise as mathematical theorems.

Within economics, my greatest interests were in international economics, macroeconomics, and econometrics. I originally learned international economics from the first edition of a textbook by Richard Caves and Ron Jones, little dreaming that one day I would be coauthor of the fifth through tenth editions.

I didn't discard other disciplines. Looking back on things I learned in high school and college, I am happiest perhaps recalling some of the unlikely-sounding intellectual connections across fields that we overspecialized modern academics usually do not get to make in our adult professions. Here are a select few that I happen to have made use of at some point or other in my economics career:

- From classics: The Greek myth of Odysseus tying himself to the mast is a versatile metaphor for solutions to the problem of "dynamic inconsistency" in monetary economics and elsewhere.
- From American intellectual history: *The Wizard of Oz* is an allegory for the nineteenth-century gold standard.
- From French literature: Albert Camus describes how a deadly plague (in Oran, Algeria) peaks one day and begins to ebb – after what seems like forever and without any clear evidence that the heroic efforts of the medical workers fighting the contagion in fact made the difference. The description fits well with a modern economic crisis.
- From biology: Although one can "feel the pain" when a gazelle on the savannah or a manufacturing firm in a competitive market meets a brutal end, as a scientist one needs to understand the general equilibrium of the system.
- From chemistry: A form of Le Chatelier's principle was generalized beyond the physical sciences by Paul Samuelson. If you exogenously change one variable in a system (heat of a gas or money supply), the reaction of one of the endogenous variables (the pressure or exchange rate) will be greater if a third endogenous variable (the volume or price level) is held fixed than if it too is allowed to respond.
- From mathematics: Even though most of us cannot name more than three irrational numbers, an easily understood proof reveals that there are in fact more of them than of the (much more familiar) rational numbers. This can be used to illustrate the limits to inductive reasoning in

philosophy, the dangers of sample selection bias in econometrics, the "availability heuristic" bias of psychology, the need for Bayes's theorem in probability, and the problem of "black swans" in the housing market or in antiterrorism policy.

True, as PhD students soon discover, narrow specialization is the only way to complete a dissertation, to get a job teaching in a university economics department, and to get tenure. But I think of those stages as akin to basic training in the army or to thirty-hour shifts in medical residencies. After one has achieved the prize (tenure), one can work on whatever one wants to work on.

MIT

My mentor at Swarthmore had been Bernie Saffran, unparalleled Chiron of economics neophytes and a sterling human being. When he packed me off to MIT for grad school in 1974, it was like d'Artagnan's father in the provinces sending him off to join the King's Musketeers in Paris. He told me of his impression that students in the MIT economics program sorted themselves out by ability pretty quickly, implying that one did not have to be insecure about where one stood after that. Within a few weeks of the beginning of classes at MIT, we all knew that Paul Krugman was the smartest student in our year. I have never felt insecure about that; Bernie was right.

My fields included econometrics, where my professors were Bob Hall and Jerry Hausman, and macroeconomics, where my professors included Franco Modigliani and Robert Solow. The latter two were obvious candidates for Nobel Prizes; they got them ten years later. Paul Samuelson, who was one of my micro theory teachers, had already gotten his.

I knew from the start that my primary interests were international. Jagdish Bhagwati, another of my mentors, was my international trade professor. But at that time, the macro and finance side of international economics seemed more exciting than the trade side. Exchange rates had begun to float in 1973; four years later we had enough monthly data to run regressions; capital flows, inflation, and unemployment were all unusually high in the mid-1970s; and the rational expectations revolution was remaking macro-economic theory from the ground up.

During my first year at MIT, I studied international finance with Charlie Kindleberger, a scholar and a gentleman. But in my second year, a young new professor arrived, named Rudiger Dornbusch. I have been pleased to be sometimes known as Rudi's first student.

Rudi and Stan Fischer taught open-economy macro together. Ken Rogoff, Maury Obstfeld, and Ben Bernanke were among those in the year behind me. Some of our contemporaries two miles away at Harvard, including Jeff Sachs and Larry Summers, came down to audit the class. As Ken wrote not long ago, regarding Rudi's habit of cold-calling students with impossible questions, "I would venture that Dornbusch's international finance course at MIT is the answer to the trivia question 'When was the last time these guys were completely humiliated in public?'"[2]

I would give anything to have a videotape of one of those classes, especially one relevant to balance-of-payments crises in developing countries. Later, during the period of the emerging market crashes in the 1990s, Sachs strongly attacked the management of the crises by the US Treasury (where Summers was calling most of the shots, as undersecretary) and the International Monetary Fund (where Fischer was calling most of the shots, as deputy managing director). Newspaper readers must have wondered what the story was behind this conflict, in terms either of schools of thought or of personal conflict.[3] It is interesting to recall, then, that meetings of the Dornbusch-Fischer course in the mid-1970s included, in one room, the following dramatis personae: two students who were to become two of the most important country policy makers presiding, for all their brilliance, over the run-ups to the first and last of the 1990s crises, respectively (Pedro Aspe, finance minister of Mexico in 1994, and Domingo Cavallo, economy minister of Argentina in 1991–1996 and 2001); perhaps the most important hands-on fashioners of the response in Washington (Summers at the Treasury and Fischer at the IMF); and three of the most important outside kibitzers (Dornbusch, an unwelcome augur of the Mexican peso crisis; Sachs, the most sweepingly critical of austerity programs; and Krugman, less critical). There were no big doctrinal disputes or personal animosities to speak of, either in the 1970s or in the 1990s – just different interpretations of what should be done in difficult situations.

Stan and Rudi, my main mentors, were the most popular duo for advising theses in those years at MIT. Neither one ever needed to spend any of the twenty-four hours in a day on sleep, so far as I am aware. Stan always seemed able to find time to read any paper that one of his students sent him and return it rapidly with perfect comments. Rudi would call students up at night to invite them to meet a visiting economist for cappuccino in the North End.

One day, in his office, Rudi tried out the idea of exchange rate overshooting on me and asked what I thought. I was appropriately flattered but told him that I would have to think it over first. The next day I came back and told him I thought it was a good idea.

MIT at this point was, I think, establishing the template that a thesis could be "three essays on X." My X was exchange rates. My central essay was later described by somebody as the first empirical implementation of Dornbusch overshooting. I guess that is a fair description. Certainly I remember that Rudi gave my paper its title ("On the Mark"), without first consulting me, when he signed me up for a job market seminar at the University of Chicago.

THE RESEARCH OF A JUNIOR PROFESSOR

One could also say, in broad perspective, that much of my early research took off from the overshooting theory and then went off in varied directions. Some papers dealt with one or the other of the two key building blocks of the model: uncovered interest parity in the short run and purchasing power parity in the long run. (Overshooting is a consequence of the combination of slow adjustment of prices in goods markets and instantaneous adjustment of asset markets.) Other papers transplanted the insights from the foreign exchange market either to the determination of the interest rate term structure or to the determination of prices of agricultural and mineral commodities. The latter application was the more successful. Just as even a stopped clock is right twice a day, the prediction that an increase in real interest rates should cause a decrease in real prices of oil, gold, and other commodities struck some as right on target in the early 1980s, and the reverse prediction seemed right on target in 2008 and 2011.

A few of my early papers were theoretical. But I soon discovered that, for the most part, my empirical papers sold much better. In some cases, coming up with a new data set took almost as much work as writing the paper. That perhaps applies to my papers coauthored with Charles Engel or Gikas Hardouvelis that used weekly money supply announcements relative to market expectations for "event studies"; my work with Ken Froot that used survey data to study expectations in the foreign exchange market; and my research coauthored with Kathryn Dominguez that used previously confidential daily data to study the effectiveness of intervention in the foreign exchange market. As even this early list shows, I have always been blessed with excellent PhD students and other young colleagues with whom I have collaborated.

I believe that the returns in knowledge from adding to the data set and performing some simple statistical test are greater than the marginal benefit of running the same old overstudied data – such as the standard macro variables for the G-5 countries – through some pointlessly more sophisticated theory or econometric technique. In the 1980s, it became fashionable to claim that the real exchange rate followed a random walk, because statistical tests were unable to reject that null hypothesis at conventional significance levels. (Analogous claims were made about all sorts of variables in macroeconomics and finance.) But these tests were typically run on a few decades of data. I argued that one would not expect such limited data sets to offer enough power to reject the random walk even if mean reversion were the right answer. Economists had forgotten the lesson from introductory econometrics: failure to reject the null hypothesis does not entitle you to assert that the null hypothesis is necessarily true. More provocatively (in "Zen and the Art of Modern Macroeconometrics"), I alleged that economists had subtly redefined the rules for a specific reason: it was too hard in macroeconomics to find statistically significant relationships. It is much easier to fail to find significant relationships. It hardly takes any work at all. But the affirmation "my research supports the hypothesis that the exchange rate follows a random walk" sounds much more respectable and publishable than "I have been studying exchange rates statistically for a year and have absolutely nothing to say about what makes them move."

If one is in pursuit of the right answer, one needs to cast the net wider, to encompass a century-long time series or a panel of countries. On a priori grounds, that is how much data it should take before the test will have the requisite power. Sure enough, when one did that, one could reject a random walk in the real exchange rate and find mean reversion.

Many have taken to using the "black swan problem" to mean a highly unlikely event, as the subprime mortgage crisis of 2007–2008 is interpreted to have been. The way I would prefer to define it is as an event that is considered to be virtually impossible by those whose frame of reference is limited in time span and geographical area, but that is well within the probability distribution for those whose data set includes other countries and other centuries (or those who make appropriate use of a priori theory, as with those irrational numbers). Analysts don't cast the net widely enough. They can't imagine that terrorists might inflict mass casualties by bringing down some buildings (New York, 2001) or that housing prices might fall in dollar terms (United States, 2007) or that an advanced economy might suffer a loss of confidence in its debt (Greece, 2010). "I haven't observed such a thing in the past, so it won't happen in the future." These things had happened before, but mostly in times and places far away.

What do "black swans" have to do with it? An Englishman in the nineteenth century who encountered a black swan for the first time might have considered it a "7-standard deviation event," even though one could have learned of the existence of black swans from ornithology books.[4]

A VOYEUR IN POLITICS

I spent many hot summers in the nation's capital, usually at the Federal Reserve Board, the IMF, or the Institute for International Economics. Those visits were highly rewarding, but strictly research-oriented. Then, in 1983, Martin Feldstein asked me to work for him at the Council of Economic Advisers (CEA). It was the Reagan administration, of which I was not especially fond. But one reason I happily took the job was the opportunity to work with Feldstein. There was extra prestige, at least in retrospect, from the fact that the position I was filling had been held during the preceding year by both Paul Krugman and Larry Summers. (I was single, worked very long hours in those days, and was happy to fill in for two.)

Surprising as this often is to outsiders, the CEA is a rather technocratic, nonpolitical outfit. Making one's best forecast of the trade deficit and the growth rate is the same in either a Republican or a Democratic administration. Trying to explain the virtues of free trade in an interagency meeting is the same in either case. Putting into a presidential speech an explanation as to why a skeptical Congress must approve a quota increase for the IMF is the same.

My best Zelig story dates from November 4, 1983. At that point I did not yet have clearance to enter the White House proper, as opposed to the Old Executive Office Building next door, which housed the CEA office. Nevertheless, through a chain of coincidences, I found myself in the Oval Office for half an hour with President Reagan and his top cabinet members.[5] Chitchat focused on the casualties of the recent Grenada invasion and the bombing of the Marine barracks in Beirut. Nobody asked me who I was, because they assumed that, if I was there, they should already know who I was. Eventually, I figured out that I was at the wrong meeting and left.

During this period, Feldstein popularized the notion of the twin deficits: that the then-new large US trade deficit was the result of a large budget deficit. The analysis was an implicit rebuke to those who had foolishly predicted that the tax cuts enacted in 1981 would lead to smaller budget deficits and higher national saving, rather than the reverse. Others in the White House and the Treasury rejected our forecast in the 1984 Economic Report of the President that the trade deficit would continue to rise, let alone our diagnosis as to why. It made front page headlines when Secretary Regan responded to a question in congressional testimony by confirming that, so far as he was concerned, the ERP could be thrown in the trash. I couldn't have been more pleased. (Our forecast proved right on target the next year.)[6]

THE BUREAU

With Feldstein, my array of mentors was pretty much complete. After his term on the CEA, Feldstein returned to Harvard and the presidency of the National Bureau of Economic Research, with which I became increasingly involved. Later, he decided to divide the NBER's International Studies Program into a trade half and an international finance and macroeconomics (IFM) half. Our forged-in-fire relationship was perhaps one reason he asked me to be the director of the IFM program. This position has helped me ever since to keep my fingers on the pulse of what is the hottest new research in the field and who are the young researchers doing it.

The position also made me a member of the NBER Business Cycle Dating Committee (BCDC), which officially declares the starting dates and ending dates of US recessions. I came on board at the beginning of what turned out to be the longest period of economic expansion in American history (1992–2000). So for nine years I could joke that I was on the best sort of scholarly committee: one that never had any reason to meet. But then came the recession of 2001. We dated the peak of the preceding expansion – that is, the beginning of the 2001 recession – as coming in March of that year, and the trough – the end of the recession – in November.

Part of the job of being on the BCDC is being good-natured when observers react to our announcement of a business cycle dating point by questioning the need for the Committee, housed at a nongovernment research organization, the NBER. Most of the teasing takes one of two (mutually inconsistent) lines of argument. One is that everybody knows that a recession is defined as two consecutive quarters of negative GDP growth; so who needs the more complicated and less easily quantified procedures of the BCDC? The other line of argument is that "everybody has known for a long time" that the country has been in a recession, so it is ridiculous for the Committee to announce it so much after the fact.[7] One rebuttal to both of these criticisms is that the relevant economic statistics come out with lags, are subject to major revisions, and often give signals that conflict with each other. Official GDP fell in the first and third quarters of 2001 but *rose* in the intervening second quarter. So if we had followed the simple two-consecutive-quarters rule of thumb, then we would not have found a recession at all. (We factored in other indicators, including job loss, to reach our judgment.)

At the time when we announced that the 2008 recession had begun with a peak toward the end of 2007, the government estimates still reported that the official GDP measure of output was actually higher in both the first and second quarters of 2008 than the last quarter of 2007. (We again based our call on other indicators, such as job loss and the national income measure of output.) Much later, the Commerce Department revised its statistics, as it always does. The current estimates reassuringly show that GDP was in fact lower in both of the first two quarters of 2008 than in the last quarter of 2007. Even though our announcement of the beginning of the recession was greeted as long overdue when we made it, we would have had to wait another year and a half to get that crucial revision from the Commerce Department. Dating the ends of recessions is even tougher.

Incidentally, some Americans vaguely think that the terrorist attacks of September 11 caused the 2001 recession or the disappearance of the budget surplus that President Bush had inherited in January of that year. Of course, both were in fact well under way before.[8] But I don't blame Bush for the 2001 recession.[9] It usually takes awhile before a new president's actions have an effect on current conditions, whether for good or ill.

UC BERKELEY

I joined the faculty of the Economics Department of the University of California at Berkeley – just a few miles from where I grew up – in 1979. I spent most of the 1980s and 1990s there. I loved walking to work, down the hill, along rose-lined paths and past redwood trees. I grew to enjoy teaching classes of 200 or 300 students.

When I first arrived, the Economics Department happened to be unusually short of faculty members who were close to me in either age or field. But eventually I was joined by Barry Eichengreen, Maury Obstfeld, Ken Rogoff, David Romer, and Christy Romer, who were close colleagues in both the personal and professional senses. And Andy Rose at the Business School. One of my few regrets in life arises from the circumstance that after they all came, and just as the Economics Department had been restored to its status as one of the top half dozen in the national rankings, I left to move east. Since the year I left, others in the Berkeley department have reaped an avalanche of Nobel Prizes and Clark Medals. My mixed feelings about having left derive not from that, but from having left behind good friends and colleagues – and the landscape of my native state. I miss the redwood, live oak, and bay trees; the mountains; and the view of San Francisco Bay. No matter how lost you get in the Berkeley hills, you always know which way is west.

MEMBER OF THE COUNCIL

In 1996 Joe Stiglitz, who was chairman of President Clinton's Council of Economic Advisers, asked if I was interested in being a member of the Council. This is a political appointment – not a staff job like I had had at the CEA thirteen years earlier. Thus, it requires nomination by the president and confirmation by the Senate. The procedures for clearance and confirmation are among the many processes in Washington that are thoroughly broken. I don't think the public understands how many top positions in policy making are empty at any given moment, usually for the silliest of reasons. The Senate did not give me a hard time, in large part because we were in the midst of the strongest expansion in US history. I was sworn in by Vice President Al Gore a mere eight months after taking up residence.

There are three members of the Council. The chair is overall in charge. The other two members divide up responsibility for issue areas. I had international economics, macroeconomics, and a few areas of microeconomic policy.

The main role of the CEA is presenting to the president and to others in the government, through the "interagency process," what, in its view, the field of economics has to say about the policy issues that need to be decided at the time. A hundred policy issues arise every month. The Council does not have any built-in constituencies, in the way that the Agriculture Department has farmers, the Commerce Department business, and the Labor Department workers. Thus, its influence is only as big or as small as the president or others choose to value its advice. Where most agencies have many "line responsibilities" – things that won't get done if the agency doesn't do them – the CEA has only a few. On an annual basis, the CEA writes the Economic Report of the President. On a daily basis, it writes confidential evening memos to the president explaining the official economic statistics that are to be released early the following morning. President Clinton got our memos on an almost daily basis, so great was his thirst for facts and figures. I know that some other presidents have been much less interested in such details.

We also had something called the Weekly Economic Briefing of the President. As soon as I arrived, I was struck by how the WEB went into detail, such as explaining conflicting scholarly studies regarding the success of a school voucher program in Milwaukee. I was sure that this was more than the president needed to know. But I had not yet learned how different this president was from the one I had worked for in the 1980s. The next week, Clinton cited the conflicting evidence over the Milwaukee experiment in a campaign debate on national TV. After that, we kept the facts, figures, charts, and analysis flowing.

One "line responsibility" of the CEA is to lead the process, twice a year, of forecasting the rate of economic growth and the other key macroeconomic variables that feed into the making of the federal budget. The Treasury and the Office of Management and Budget are the other two agencies that participate in the "troika." I was fortunate to be there during a period when the economy repeatedly surprised all observers with good news on all fronts. It was a little embarrassing that the economists in the administration kept underforecasting economic growth. And unemployment, which macroeconomists had long said probably could not go below 5 percent without pushing up inflation, did so in 1997 and eventually went even below 4 percent. Every time we sat down to prepare a new forecast, some of the participants wanted to rely on the historical statistical relationships, while others argued that there had been a fundamental shift in the parameters due, in particular, to information technology. At the time, the latter sort of thinking was called the "new economy." Now it is called the "Internet boom" or even the "Internet bubble" – though it is important to realize that the economic performance was genuine and originally based on fundamentals,[10] even if the stock market got carried away by dot-com-mania, as it clearly did.

My approach was "Bayesian": every six months, if the growth rate had again remained above traditional estimates of "potential" and the unemployment rate had again remained below traditional estimates of the "nonaccelerating inflation rate of unemployment," with no signs of inflation, we would again adjust our estimates of those parameters just a little. But we would not throw in the towel and jump the estimates discretely. I told the staff that the year in which the government adjusted its estimates sharply in the optimistic direction would be the year that the stock market crashed and the economy entered recession. In the event, that is precisely what happened after we left. I am convinced that the grossly overoptimistic forecasts made by the government in January 2001, not just for the short term but for the long term as well, were a major reason President Bush was able to convince the public that the budget surpluses he had inherited not only would continue in the future, but would be so large that they warranted huge long-term tax cuts.

Two issues took up more of my time while I was on the Council than did any other. One was the emerging market crises that hit East Asia in 1997 and Russia in 1998. The other was the Kyoto Protocol on Global Climate Change, which was negotiated in November 1997. The first involved issues that were familiar to me. The parallels to the international debt crisis that began in 1982 were greater than most observers realized. The second issue was unfamiliar to me and required a lot of hurried studying up, followed by a hundred interagency meetings.

It is one of the ironies of working in government that one can sometimes find far more room to influence policy in an area where one knows nothing than in areas where one is putatively a world expert. While I, like most economists, was leery of the high economic costs if greenhouse gas emissions were to be cut very suddenly, I eventually became committed to the Kyoto Protocol.[11] I thought that its design – particularly the provisions for international trade in emissions permits and for trading off among the six greenhouse gases – offered the best hope for addressing the environmental goal in an economically efficient way. The Protocol left a lot out, to be sure. The three biggest gaps that remain to be filled are full participation by all countries, a mechanism for setting emission targets well into the future, and some reason to expect countries to comply with their commitments. These are issues that I have done research on over the years subsequently.

HARVARD

I left the CEA in 1999. Rather than returning to Berkeley, I accepted a job offer from Harvard University's Kennedy School of Government. Ten years earlier I had been leery of moving from an economics department to a school of public policy. One obvious reason for the move in 1999 was that, by that stage in my career, I had developed some interest in participating in the public policy debate, which would be easier to do from Harvard Kennedy School than from the West Coast. Another reason is that I no longer thought I would be giving up much to get these benefits: I could continue to collaborate on research with Andy Rose via email and could have lunch with all the excellent economists in the vicinity just as easily at the Kennedy School as at Berkeley. To name only four of those who are located intellectually in international economics and physically in my building: Ricardo Hausmann, Robert Lawrence, Dani Rodrik, and Carmen Reinhart. But an advantage of the Kennedy School is that it is in fact easy to partake from the elusive grail of interdisciplinary communication, for example at the faculty lunch seminar. Further, being a senior professor at Harvard is a charmed status.

At Berkeley, I had taught undergraduates and PhD students, as one would do in any economics department. I still have both kinds of students at Harvard, but most of my students at the Kennedy School are master's students, who are in between. I like teaching these classes. In an economics department, there is a wide artificial gap between teaching undergraduates and teaching PhD students. On the one hand, undergraduates like to hear about the real world, but there is a limit on how far you can go in terms of theory (though Harvard undergraduates, whom I teach in a course cross-listed in the Economics Department, are very smart). On the other hand, PhD students can do the math, but you are doing them a disservice if you talk about the real world and thereby give them the impression that if they do the same they will be able to write a thesis or get an academic job. The classes I now teach at Harvard Kennedy School are the best of both worlds, for me. I can mix theory and the real world.

I have always made sure that I lived within walking distance of my place of employment. I live in Cambridge and either walk or bicycle to work, often noting when I pass over the spot near Harvard Square where George Washington took command of the Continental Army in 1775. My son's elementary school is seven blocks from our home. I enjoy walking him to school.

MORE RESEARCH

One of several big benefits of achieving tenure, and then full professorship, is that one can choose to work on whatever seems most interesting rather than whatever is most likely to demonstrate technical prowess and be published in the top journals. For me, this freedom included branching out in terms of subject matter, beyond the study of exchange rates and international financial markets. First I ventured into other parts of macroeconomics, including, for example, the coordination of monetary and fiscal policy when different policy makers believe in different models. Then I ventured into other parts of international economics, including, for example, the circumstances under which the "trade-creating" advantages of regional free-trade areas outweigh the "trade-diverting" disadvantages.

During the second half of my research career (so far), I have ventured further afield still, into questions such as why some countries are able to achieve higher incomes than others and whether trade is bad for the environment.

Pontificating about big-think issues such as globalization has its role to play, if one wants to communicate with nonspecialists or even to influence the public debate. But, as any academic knows, one doesn't get articles published in refereed journals by writing judicious surveys of the literature or offering policy recommendations. One must, rather, contribute some incremental new methodological innovation, whether theoretical or econometric. (Preferably the outcome is to show why some other author is wrong, but one should at a minimum fill a supposed glaring gap in the literature.)

A single econometric idea underlies a number of my journal articles over the past decade, even though they appear in different subfields of economics. It has to do with geography. I have been fascinated by geography my whole life, since before I got interested in economics in college.[12] Although this must be a reason for my decision to specialize in international economics thirty years ago, at that time international economics had virtually nothing to do with geography. I am talking about all the standard theories of international economics that sought to predict, say, the trade patterns or growth rates of countries, and that dealt with the set of actual real countries when it came to empirical analysis, and yet featured no role for such fundamental geographic variables as distance, landlockedness, language, or historical relationships. Rather, countries were disembodied points that lacked any spatial coordinates and possessed only capital stocks, labor forces, productivity levels, money supplies, and a few other variables.

This has all changed over the past thirty years. Geography has entered international economics.

Okay, so what was my idea? Perhaps the most ubiquitous and intractable obstacle plaguing all of empirical economics, especially macroeconomics, is the problem of causality. We observe that countries that engage in more international trade tend to benefit from higher incomes. But does trade cause growth or does growth cause trade? "Correlation need not imply causality."

In a 1999 article, David Romer and I used the gravity model of bilateral trade to try to solve the causality question. Newton's theory of gravity says that the attraction between two bodies is proportionate to the product of their sizes and inversely related to the physical distance between them. The gravity theory of trade says that trade between two countries (or provinces) is proportionate to their sizes and inversely related to the economic distance between them. Size can be measured by population.

Economic distance can be measured by geographic distance and other variables to capture transport costs, linguistic and political barriers, and so forth. The gravity model predicts bilateral trade quite well.[13] We used the gravity model, first, to come up with an exogenous predictor of each country's overall level of trade and then to test whether economic growth, other things equal, had blessed those countries that were geographically well situated for trade versus those that were remote, landlocked, or otherwise encumbered. The answer was yes. We now felt better able to claim that, in the case of trade and growth, the relationship was indeed causal. A "point estimate" is that the difference between a hypothetical country with no trade (say, Burma) and one where exports plus imports totals 200 percent of GDP (say, Singapore) is by itself worth an 80 percent increase in income over twenty years.

I have used the geographic determinants of trade to address the causality problem in many other areas as well. "The Endogeneity of the Optimum Currency Area Criteria," with Andy Rose, demonstrated that higher trade between a pair of countries leads to more synchronized business cycles. Another paper with Andy showed that international trade is good for some measures of environmental quality, such as local air pollution, but not others, such as greenhouse gas emissions. A paper with Eduardo Cavallo established that countries that are more open to international trade were less likely to suffer severe financial crises.

BECOME AN ECONOMIST AND SEE THE WORLD

My career has afforded me the luxury of indulging my geographic interests in a more tangible way as well. International economics does not, like the field of development economics, oblige one to spend time in countries without reliable running water and electricity, at least not for more than a few weeks at a time. But I have been able to travel widely, always on somebody else's nickel. I have visited seventy countries so far. Some institution in the host country pays. Most trips are simply for conferences, but sometimes they are for teaching, sometimes research, sometimes consulting.

It all started at the midpoint of my graduate studies at MIT. In 1976 Dick Eckaus and our other professors packed five of us – Krugman, three other classmates, and me – off to Portugal for a summer. I remember thinking on the plane going over, "What do we know about advising a government?" The man we were to work for, José da Silva Lopes, governor of the central bank, apparently thought the same thing when we arrived in Lisbon and he saw how young we were. Eventually we proved, both to ourselves and to our host country, that we had something to offer after all.

One story from that first experience at advising long ago stands me in good stead every year when I need to explain to my students the concept of "seignorage." We were living in hotels. At the end of the first month, we had to pay the bill. But for bureaucratic reasons, the wire transfers we were expecting had not yet come through. We apologetically explained our problem to the governor. Responding "no problem," he summoned an aide, who took us to the basement where the printing presses were turning out the national currency. They counted out enough escudos to tide each of us over. I don't know if the Bank of Portugal ran the printing presses for an extra few seconds that day; if so, it was truly seignorage.

More of the important conferences take place in the United States and Western Europe than in the rest of the world. But the rest of the world is in some sense more interesting. The other places where I have become most involved (in the superficial way that we jet-setting international economists are accustomed to) include Japan, Korea, China, central Europe, Latin America, South Africa, and Mauritius. One benefit of having had what is by now a long line of students – first at Berkeley and now at Harvard – is that one finds them years later all over the world, often in important positions of responsibility. It can make the trips especially interesting.

FAMILY

Just as this manuscript was finalized, I got married to Kathy Moon, a smart and beautiful professor, who teaches political science at Wellesley College, not far away. By coincidence she, like I, was born in San Francisco. She is of Korean descent and an expert on Asian-American relations. Perhaps, as occurred to me half a century ago in California, the next big leap is indeed to Asia.

Notes

1 "Republican and Democratic Presidents Have Switched Economic Policies," *Milken Institute Review* 5, no. 1 (2003): 18–25.
2 "Dornbusch's Overshooting Model after Twenty-Five Years," International Monetary Fund's Second Annual Research Conference Mundell-Fleming Lecture, *IMF Staff Papers*, vol. 49 (2002).
3 At the same time, at least one critic had wild conspiracy theories along the lines that Sachs had once been seen at a meeting with Summers and Fischer and that this elite

cabal must have plotted the deliberate downfall of Russia and Asia. Needless to say, the conspiracy theory at one extreme is even more misguided than the inference of personal animosity at the other extreme.

4 Black swans had been discovered in Australia in 1697.

5 I followed Don Regan, then the secretary of the treasury, into the White House because I thought he was going to the same meeting I was. The Secret Service assumed that I was his aide, even though I was not trying to make it look that way. Intimidated, they neglected to ask for identification.

6 I reviewed the history of what CEA chairs have done over the years when they find themselves at odds with the White House, in "What an Economic Adviser Can Do When He Disagrees with the President," *Challenge* 46, no.3 (May/June 2003): 29–52.

7 We did not announce the March 2001 peak until eight months later. We did not announce the December 2007 peak until twelve months later. We are even slower at announcing the ends of recessions. nber.nber.org/cycles/main.html.

8 In 2004 there was some White House pressure to move the starting date of the recession from the first quarter of the Bush administration to the last quarter of the Clinton administration. The NBER Business Cycle Dating Committee decided not to make such a revision, based on an objective consideration of the data. (I have never heard any member of the Committee raise any political consideration, at that time, before, or since.) The episode is one illustration of the benefits of having institutions such as the NBER BCDC independent and thereby protected from political influence. The federal statistics-collecting agencies – in particular, the Bureau of Economic Analysis in the Commerce Department and the Bureau of Labor Statistics in the Labor Department – are also thoroughly insulated against political interference, contrary to casual and irresponsible inferences made by many commentators over the years.

9 I *do* blame Bush for the severity of the 2007–2009 recession, incidentally, and did before it arrived: "Rather it's the next recession that is going to be his fault. I don't know when that will be. But when it comes, we are not going to have the ability to use fiscal policy, to cut taxes, the way they did in 2001 [because the inherited deficit will already be too high]"; "A Debate on the Deficit," *Challenge* 47, no. 6 (November 2004): 22–23.

10 The expansion of the 1990s was led by growth in private-sector demand and employment, whereas the expansions of the 1960s, 1970s, and 1980s had been led by fiscal expansion on the part of the federal government, as was the decade of the 2000s.

11 At least I became committed to the Clinton-Gore version: although President Clinton signed the treaty, he said that he would not submit it to the Senate for ratification unless and until developing countries took on commitments that were qualitatively similar in nature to those agreed upon by industrialized countries. "You're Getting Warmer: The Most Feasible Path for Addressing Global Climate Change Does Run Through Kyoto," in J. Maxwell and R. Reuveny (eds.), *Trade and Environment: Theory and Policy in the Context of EU Enlargement and Transition Economies* (Cheltenham: Edward Elgar, 2005).

12 It all started with a fascination with maps. My lifelong mode of doodling has been to draw maps freehand. I have never gotten around to patenting my special "Styrofoam cup" projection: I draw a map of the world around the sides of a coffee cup. (It is

superior to the Mercator projection in that the greater land masses in the Northern Hemisphere are neatly accommodated by the tapered shape of the Styrofoam cup.)

13 In the mid-1990s I had already used it to estimate what were usual geographic patterns of trade in order to evaluate questions such as whether trade was unusually concentrated inside the East Asia region or in regional trade blocs generally (e.g., *Regional Trading Blocs* [Washington, D.C.: Institute for International Economics, 1997], coauthored with Shang-Jin Wei and Ernesto Stein).

12

Practitioner of the Dismal Science? Who, Me?
Couldn't Be!!

Richard B. Freeman

Why did I become a labor economist concerned with the institutions that affect the lives of workers and the organization of work when I could have been an investment banker, McKinsey consultant, used-car salesman, or even a theorist working out the truths of the Invisible Hand on a blackboard in some dark office?

When I was in grade school, I did not dream of becoming an economist. I doubt that any kid does. I was more enthralled with literature – ah, to write the great American novel – or with managing a stable of villainous professional wrestlers à la the Grand Wizard, Lou Albano, or Classie Freddie Blassie. Those would be fun careers. Economics? Didn't someone call that the dismal science? Who wants to be dismal?

There is an answer to the why economics? question that would please the Invisible Hand. This is that at age seventeen I calculated the expected present value of lifetime earnings from economics and other plausible careers and, taking account of my preferences for work activities, money, and risk, picked the career most likely to produce the highest utility. The Hand would be even happier if I told you that I had carefully weighed my abilities and interests – strong but not Putnam Prize–level math abilities, strong but not Chekhov-level writing abilities, strong but not Nelson Mandela–level social concerns – against the payoffs to those abilities/interests in different professions and determined that economics was the best fit.

At some level, Invisible Hand explanations of career choice work as a good first approximation for many of us. In a sample of thousands of young persons choosing careers, I almost surely would be in the set of those who fit economics and not in the set of those who fit pro wrestling (save as a manager or script writer). But I am also sure that many in the suitable-for-economics set chose other occupations – law, literature, investment banking, sociology, and so on. Economic models of individual outcomes invariably have huge residuals that tell us that they miss much about what determines individual choices and payoffs.

The economics of education, for example, lives on the fact that education raises earnings. But regressions of ln earnings on formal education, however measured, explain less than 5 percent of the variance in ln earnings. Within each education group, there is a huge dispersion of earnings among observationally equivalent people that dwarfs the variance across the groups. Economics majors from Harvard of the same age, gender, and race and with similar grades, for instance, will have very different earnings ten or twenty years later. One may end up a six-digit earner while another struggles to keep up with the bills.

In physical science, it is irrelevant which rapidly moving atom interacts with neighboring atoms to equilibrate the level of heat in some closed space or which molecules interact with other molecules to form a chemical compound. The atoms and molecules are identical. But our genes and environment make humans heterogeneous, and we invariably ponder the unique factors or accidents that lead us down one path over another. Unless the cosmologists' hypothesized multiverse is true, there is no way to test any story of how idiosyncratic events affect long-term outcomes, and even then it would require traveling to other universes, Dr. Who style. The most we can do is tell a consistent, believable story about why we got to where we are.

What set me up to choose economics was Isaac Asimov's *Foundation* series of science fiction books.[1] The first volume of the series laid out the key proposition that, Hari Seldon[2] be praised, it was possible to construct a science of history. Equations based on verified knowledge could predict the flow of history – at least up to the point where uncertainty allowed the heroes of the series to gain better outcomes for humanity through their brave deeds. The second volume taught the reader that economics dominated military power in determining history. The Foundation expanded through its trading practices. Free trade helped it survive the efforts of the mighty Empire to crush it.

I read the *Foundation* series in junior high school when I caught the learning bug and spent every free moment devouring any 50-cent paperback on whatever caught my fancy – history, literature, science fiction, Greek culture, religion, philosophy, psychology, astronomy, jazz, mathematics, whatever. It was a mad effort to learn all there was to know about anything and everything. There were no interesting economics books in paperback[3] to compete with George Gamow or Edith Hamilton, with Asimov and the other science fiction stars, or with Euripides and Sophocles and the *Bhagavad Gita* or Chekhov or Scott Fitzgerald. So my first appreciation of social science and the power of economics came from the *Foundation* series. My guess is that most junior high school devotees of science fiction are entranced by the speculative physical science and go on to careers as inventors, engineers, or scientists. What I took away was the notion that the aggregation of individual actions rather than the decisions of kings and queens determined the flow of history and that it was possible at least in the far-off future to write down equations that would predict how those actions determined the flow of history. Wow!

In college, I quickly learned that history was not a science; that sociology explored fascinating problems with no clear conceptual framework; and that while experiments made psychology a science, its focus on the individual offered no insight into how behavior aggregated to produce historical change. By contrast, economics had the logical structure of science and dealt with micro and aggregate behavior in ways that could illuminate the dynamics of historical development. To understand the broad sweep of history, one had to begin with economics, or so it seemed to me. I bet that Hari Seldon studied economics before writing down the dynamic general equilibrium equations that underlay the *Foundation* series.

Still, there were aspects of economics that troubled me. Economics lacked the verifiable facts and invariant relations that characterized experimental sciences. It relied too much on abstract principles and too little on careful investigation of actual behavior for my taste. The applied calculus of price theory as presented in undergraduate micro theory seemed far removed from business reality. If all that was required to run a successful business was to differentiate profits functions, why were managers so highly paid? If they did more than that, why were we not taught what they did? When I posed these questions after one particularly tiresome class, the answer that there was a gap between theory and reality did not sit well with me. Science is supposed to fit reality. Why didn't economists start filling in the reality instead of fussing with indifference curves and tangent lines and, even worse, Edgeworth-Bowley boxes? Wouldn't it be better to learn the calculus stuff fast and spend the rest of the time trying to understand the real world?

In grad school I read Samuelson's *Foundations* and loved it. That was the way to teach economic theory. But I wanted more from economics than the mathematics of optimization. I wanted economics to answer the big Hari Seldon questions. What leads some societies to succeed and others to fail? Can a society organized around the interactions of ordinary folk (the Foundation) defeat a totalitarian juggernaut run from on high (the Empire)? That was a real issue in the 1960s and 1970s when the Soviet economy seemed to grow faster than the US economy (few realized how inefficient the Soviet system was or that the service sector rather than heavy manufacturing was the economic future). By allocating resources through central planning, the Soviets had developed an advanced military technology that risked blowing us all up.

One of the supposed advantages of the Soviet system was that the state could order young people to go into engineering and science and work on projects the state deemed in the national interest, while the United States let immature young people like me freely choose careers of lesser import, such as economics. Did this mean that the Soviets would ultimately surpass us? Or was the market analysis right that allowing individuals to choose careers freely gave better outcomes? The issue of whether enough young Americans study science and engineering to maintain the country's technological and economic success has resurfaced several times since then. In the mid-2000s it produced a spate of reports calling for more science and engineering, of which the National Academy of Sciences' *Gathering Storm* attracted most attention.[4] What I didn't know when I was choosing a career was that the National Science Foundation counts economics as a genuine science. But before that goes to your head, fellow followers of the Invisible Hand, the NSF counts sociology also!

In grad school, I looked for the branch of economics that would best help me address the "really big" questions. Initially, economic development seemed to fit the bill. If you understood why country A grows and country B does not, you would be on the way to fulfilling the Hari Seldon vision. If, as a byproduct, that meant great trips to exciting places where you would meet exotic women and learn things that were not chalk marks on a blackboard, so much the better. I arrived at Harvard with the vague idea of using

Bellman dynamic programming and Markov chains to develop a Seldon-esque growth model, but in my first year I took Simon Kuznets's course in development and – squash! – realized how little I knew and how silly it was to try to model something about which you knew little. There were presumably many things that determined whether a country managed to attain a successful development path like Korea or floundered like most developing countries, but there was not much hard knowledge about what those things were. The balanced growth models that were the rage at the time were too far removed from the evidence to be useful. Kuznets bemoaned in class that he could not understand why theorists built such models when the essence of development was unbalanced growth. Kuznets was a great antidote to theory without evidence.

What I took away from this experience was that the "big questions" were too hard to attack directly. One had to come at them from a base of real knowledge, which meant from applied microeconomics, where data related to actual behavior in market settings. If the interactions of millions of people determined the future, then we should study the behavior of those people – how they responded to economic stimuli and how their responses generated new stimuli. Labor economics came closest to trying to do this. It sought to understand the behavior of workers and firms inductively from observation and data rather than deductively from maximizing models. As a bonus, it dealt with unions and social movements that could affect society and the flow of history outside of economic markets. I decided that the road to understanding development and the big questions of history ran through labor.

My undergraduate professor at Dartmouth, Martin Segal, a refugee from the Nazi conquest of Poland, had primed me toward labor. Segal's great gift was thinking about economic behavior. Instead of belaboring income and substitution effects or ways to identify parameters in regression models, he continually asked, What behavior do you think generated that empirical regularity? Does that behavior make sense to you? Long before behavioral economics burst on the scene, this had a big impact on my thinking.

At Harvard, John Dunlop focused more on how institutions acted in the labor market. He held economic analysis against a twofold sieve: first, its consistency with data and, second, whether it squared with what practitioners said about their behavior. Dunlop wanted graduate students to find their topics from the world. When I came into his office with the start of a thesis – a critical assessment of what the literature said on career choice issues – he made as if to tear it up. "OK, now that you've got that literature review BS out of your system, how about doing something real? Think your own thoughts. Get some data. Find something new. Research reality, not old economics papers." Having spent two years reading economics literature ad nauseum for my generals, the idea of analyzing new data to find something new about the world sounded good.

What cemented my choosing labor was Gary Becker's *Human Capital*.[5] Before the human capital revolution, labor economics was largely descriptive and institutional, more concerned with explaining why economics fell short than with making economics work. Reading *Human Capital* showed that it did not have to be that way. The book treated labor decisions from the perspective of rational choice and sought price-theoretic explanations of facts that made price theory a live tool in ways that my undergraduate price theory course had failed to do. Becker had a big vision – not quite like Hari Seldon's but in the Seldon spirit – that microeconomic thinking offered insight into all sorts of behavior – from going to school to allocating time among multiple activities to marriage, fertility, interest group politics, crime – topics that had previously been owned by sociology or demography or political science. This had an empowering and liberating impact on what labor economists could do. It legitimized the range of topics on which I would work in ensuing years.

The human capital optimizing view of labor markets does not explain as much of actual behavior as I and I imagine many others hoped it would do. Behavioral economics, experimental economics, and, most recently, neuroeconomics have shown that optimizing rationality is not always the dominant factor in what we do, even in narrow economic decisions. But even so, the profits constraint that determines whether firms survive or not and that limits what consumers can buy enforces something close to efficient Invisible Hand outcomes even when firms and people make decisions irrationally, for instance by random choice (Becker, again!).[6] The implication is that market models based on rational optimization are the natural starting point for any empirical investigation in labor or economics more broadly. They give the first term in a Taylor series expansion around reality. If the data reject that perspective, then it is up to us to modify the theory and extend the approximation to more terms. If it turns out that some other form of behavior is the first term in the approximation, you still cannot ignore the neoclassical economics, for it will surely be the second or third term.

My thesis was on career choice, with a special focus on science and engineering. I was struck by the paucity of evidence for what I took to be one of the main propositions of the human capital model – that investments in career skills by young persons responded substantially to the returns to those skills. Running ln earnings equations and interpreting the coefficients on years of schooling as returns to schooling, as was prevalent in the literature, did not directly test supply or demand behavior. I felt I had some insights into career choice, having recently been in that game myself, and I knew that I could go beyond introspection and survey other students about what they knew and were thinking as they made their choices. Last but not least, studying career choice would allow me to determine if an economy where young persons made choices freely could compete in science and engineering with a society where central planners determined how many students went into what fields. A well-identified estimate of the elasticity of the supply of students to different fields would go a long way to resolving the larger question.

Examining data on the fields of study chosen by students, I discovered that first-year enrollments in engineering fluctuated with starting salaries reported by college placement offices. When starting salaries went up, the proportion of students choosing engineering went up. When four to five years later students from a large entering class graduated with engineering degrees, the large number of graduates drove salaries down. The fluctuations in the data suggested a classic cobweb cycle. Ted Schultz warned me that all I really had with engineers was one cycle driven in large part by the post-*Sputnik* increase in demand for engineers. Maybe, he suggested, half-joking, I should wait a decade or so for some more observations before I called this. With more data, there was also the potential of building a more sophisticated model. But whereas a tenured professor like Schultz could wait for another cycle or so, a new PhD couldn't, so I proceeded to publish my thesis work.[7]

What made me confident that I had the basic story right – that supply was quite elastic to economic opportunity – was that my survey of students showed that they were reasonably informed about pay and employment opportunities, paid attention to salaries on the margin, knew something about the life-cycle pattern of earnings in different fields, and so on. Yoram Ben-Porath suggested that I probe the link between starting salaries and expected lifetime earnings and the relevance of rational expectations to the cycles in a more structured model. Perhaps I should have followed his advice, but I didn't. Discovering the basic patterns and finding a simple parsimonious story was great fun. I was uneasy about pushing weak data too far into a particular framework. What I did instead was to carry the analysis to other fields where one's major was closely linked to one's occupation, such as physics, and was reassured to find that supply looked elastic in enough areas that the pattern was not a fluke.[8]

Since then I have worked on a host of labor issues – from unions to crime to modes of compensation to labor standards to discrimination to labor–management relations to welfare states, and so on – and have studied labor markets in Asia (Korea, Australia, China, Japan, Sri Lanka), Europe (Sweden, Ireland, Germany, the UK, Spain, Norway, Poland), Latin America (Argentina, Dominican Republic, Venezuela, Colombia, Peru, Chile), and Africa (South Africa). Recently, I have returned to studying the science and engineering workforce, though now in the context of globalization and with greater attention to the demand side of the market, as I will describe later. Someone looking at my portfolio of topics might wonder if I was a mad hatter, caught up with wanderlust, a jet-setter seeking thrills in world hot spots, a secret agent for the CIA or MI5, or a fugitive from the police. Every once in a while I get suspicious looks from immigration officials at airports, but I just say professor of economics and that establishes that I am harmless. (If they only knew the trouble we can cause, at least when we are defunct!)

Let me explain what motivated some of the topics and mode of research.

The second area on which I worked in depth was economic differences between blacks and whites. What grabbed my attention was that just as economists were modeling discriminatory differences as an equilibrium process resulting from statistical discrimination or from the Becker model of how fixed prejudicial tastes produced segregation or income differences in competitive markets, young blacks were making unprecedented gains in earnings and occupational status. The sudden rise in relative black incomes after the 1964 Civil Rights Act could not possibly have resulted from gradual changes in tastes or in statistical discrimination. Shades of Kuznets, why were theorists modeling equilibrium when the data pointed to change? Examining Current Population Survey and Census figures on black and white earnings and occupational attainment, I found that the post-1964 gains occurred largely among young college-educated workers and were greatest in the South. Visiting the historically black colleges, most of whose graduates had gone into teaching and public service, I learned that before the Act virtually no US corporation recruited at those colleges, whereas after the Act, corporations came to recruit in droves. In response, students were shifting rapidly from teaching and social work into business majors. My interpretation was that the change in the law was driving demand along an elastic supply curve.[9]

That the Civil Rights Act was the main exogenous factor raising demand was controversial. Some analysts argued that the late 1960s boom caused the shift in demand. Others said that the increased salaries for new graduates reflected their choosing high-wage/low-investment jobs. Others argued that the gains in wages reflected increased welfare rolls, which reduced the supply of black workers. Many on the left objected to my optimistic reading of the decline in discriminatory income differences: Why did I stress that the glass was half full when it was half empty? My response was that it was filling up from all empty before.

If government actions were important in reducing discrimination, perhaps government actions had also been important in maintaining black-white differences in the years following Emancipation. Examining the historical data, I found that government actions – the discriminatory behavior of southern states – had played a huge role in preventing black Americans from advancing in the labor market for decades. I read Horace Mann Bond and histories of southern states that documented the discriminatory policies and legal and illegal efforts to prevent blacks from investing in skills and advancing in the job market. One of the biggest mistakes of my career was that, wanting and failing to develop a purely economic theory of why poor whites aligned with wealthy whites rather than with poor blacks in Reconstruction days, when both seemed possible, I never brought that historical work to completion.

Ensuing studies have confirmed the view that government policy sparked the increased demand for black workers. Where I was wrong was to think that the rise in black incomes was going to continue smoothly to equalize incomes with whites save for differences in background factors, which invariably would take a long time to work out. While black college graduates were advancing into better jobs, young, less educated black men were having greater problems in the job market.[10] An increasing number were involved in crime and ended up spending years incarcerated. My interest in the economics of crime came from realizing that crime was a major part of the poverty problem facing black Americans. The United States could not cure poverty unless it cured the crime problem and conversely. Curing crime, in turn, required that we understand the supply behavior of young black men living in the inner city. So how did they go about making their career decisions?

To find out I developed the Inner City Youth Survey of the National Bureau of Economic Research, which focused on illuminating how young inner-city men saw the risks and rewards of crime compared with the opportunities, or lack thereof, of employment and earnings in the legitimate economy.[11] One of the lessons of studying youth crime is that the line between legitimate work and crime is porous. Youths shift back and forth depending on opportunities. Later I realized also that excluding the huge proportion of young American men in jail or prison from measures of joblessness exaggerated the success of the US job market compared with European job markets in providing gainful employment. This pleased Brussels but not Washington.

Perhaps my best-known work has been on unions. But for much of my career I stayed away from unions and other traditional labor issues such as minimum wages and hours worked. I was new wave, not old stuff; I studied the market for physicists or postdocs, not for machinists or automobile workers (strangely, the United Automobile Workers has organized more postdocs and graduate students than any other union). I had good reason to stay away from unions. My thesis adviser, John Dunlop, knew more about them than anyone else. In the 1940s he had modeled unions as optimizing organizations with little success.[12] He spent much of his ensuing career accumulating knowledge about particular unions, employers, and markets to be able to make labor relations work better in the country. At Chicago, my mentor on the senior faculty was Gregg Lewis, who took the Kuznets approach to unionism – measuring union wage effects with a skill and care that are a model for labor economists to this day. Milton Friedman interpreted the estimated union wage effects as implying that unions increased inequality by creating differences among similar workers.

I had no intention of working this terrain until, preparing a paper for an American Economic Association session on Albert Hirschman's *Exit, Voice, and Loyalty*,[13] an idea came into my head about how to use the exit–voice dichotomy to study unions and turn Hirschman's analysis from a broad framework for thinking about political versus market responses to problems into a testable model of behavior. Unions were collective voice. This meant they should reduce quits via the exit–voice trade-off and should provide information to firms about worker preferences that would affect many parts of the labor contract, which in turn would lead firms to change their labor practices. Unions were institutions that affected the entire workplace, not just pay.[14]

Suddenly there seemed to be lots of things to study about unions with newly available large computerized data sets on workers and establishments. Ensuing work by me and others at Harvard and the NBER quantified the impacts of unions in the private sector on economic outcomes such as the composition of compensation, the dispersion of pay within firms, productivity, profits, age or experience earnings profiles, layoffs, and capital–labor substitution, and extended the analysis of the union wage effect to examine how it varied with the union share of a market. In 1984, after five or so years of working this topic, I summarized (with James Medoff) the findings in

What do Unions Do? – a book that owes much to the editor of Basic Books, Martin Kessler, who kept pushing for clarity and social significance.[15] The bottom line of quantifying the "two faces of unionism" – voice and monopoly – was a relatively favorable assessment of unions: the voice impact of the institution had greater social effects than the monopoly impact. Unions reduced inequality by compressing wages within workplaces and by shrinking the pay gap between white-collar and managerial workers and production workers. Unions raised savings through negotiated pension programs, and so on.

Fast-forward twenty years. In the early 2000s Bruce Kauffman and James Bennett invited a large coterie of labor researchers to a twenty-year retrospective assessment of the findings of *What Do Unions Do?* or *WDUD*, as they referred to it. After writing the book I had stayed away from further investigating what unions did in the private sector. I worked on unions in the public sector, where they operated in a very different economic environment, on union developments in other countries, and on the continued decline of union density.[16] I did not want to play Ibsen's Master Builder in defending the book against scholarly work from the next generation of researchers. Nor did I want to fall into the cognitive dissonance trap of trying to spin new evidence as if it confirmed the book when it really didn't. It was up to others, less intimately involved with the work and more dispassionate, to judge whether its findings did or did not stand up over time.

The twenty-year review was one of the scarier times of my professional career. I had paid enough attention to ensuing work to know that there was no devastating repudiation of *WDUD*, but maybe when all the experts came together it was going to be "run for cover/hide your head" time. I was nervous at the session on the book and as the papers appeared in one edition after another of the *Journal of Labor Research* over a two-year period. I worried that the *DUD* in the acronym might be a harbinger of what the twenty-year retrospective would conclude. Let me be clear, this was not some *Festschrift* nonsense. The reviews were hard-nosed analyses by researchers who with the passage of time had more evidence, improved econometric techniques, and more knowledge on which to draw than had gone into the book. Some researchers viewed unions less favorably than I did and disagreed with the conclusion that voice effects dominated monopoly effects. At the minimum, they would find any flaws that they could. I was sufficiently frazzled that my paper at the event "What Do Unions Do? The 2004 M-Brane Stringtwister Edition" must be the only economics paper where string theory and Calibi-Yau space play a major role, though not as a geometry for general equilibrium but as a place in the multiverse to hide if I had to face being wrong, wrong, wrong.

When all was said and done, the assessors were critical but fair and the scary event turned out to be more confirmatory of the work than I had imagined beforehand. The general consensus of the reviews, now a published book far larger than the original,[17] was that *WDUD* got most things right. The last chapter had highlighted the ongoing decline in union density, a topic on which I continued to work, and that was what generated the most controversy. Arguments over why union density had been falling in the private sector aside, Barry Hirsch made the comment that struck me as the most telling: "Freeman and Medoff got right what unions did when there were still unions to do it." With just 7.5 percent of private-sector workers organized in 2007 (compared with some 40 percent organized in the mid-1950s and 20 percent in the 1970s), most labor specialists have come to believe that unions are history and that studies of unions are an exercise in paleontology or pathology.

I disagree with that view. I disagree because a larger proportion of the US workforce today says it wants unions or some other worker-based organization to represent them than ever before. The Workplace Representation and Participation survey that I conducted with Joel Rogers in the mid-1990s and ensuing surveys document this desire and delineate the types of organizations that workers want as well as surveys can.[18] Some workers want traditional collective bargaining. Others want committees to meet and discuss workplace issues with management. Confirming the hunger for representation revealed in the surveys, as of 2008 some 2 million workers had joined the AFL-CIO's non–collective bargaining affiliate organization, Working America, even though it does not help workers at their workplace. They joined in the hope that this organization could influence the direction of labor practices and policies in the country.

In a free market, it is hard to believe that the desire for representation will go unmet ad infinitum. At the same time, strong management opposition to collective bargaining makes it hard to imagine that the labor relations system that developed under the Depression era National Labor Relations Act can deliver what workers want. Something will have to give.

Pondering this problem and studying innovative union responses to the Internet and modern information technology suggest that workers need a new union form. In the early 2000s, Rogers and I laid out the framework for such a form, which we labeled open-source unionism.[19] The open-source vision is of a union movement that is more voice than monopoly, that relies on local community support more than strikes to pressure employers, and that delivers services to workers inexpensively over the Internet. To see such a new union form grow and fill the gap between workers' desire for representation and what they have would give me an incredible high, but so far only Working America has managed to sign up large numbers of workers into anything that approaches a new organizational form, and it is unclear what it will do with and for them. As a tenured professor, I can follow Ted Schultz's suggestion years ago and wait and see, but as age creeps up, I can't wait too long. Come on, guys, innovate, make open-source unionism work.

During the two decades between *WDUD* and the retrospective on *WDUD*, my interest in labor institutions shifted from the United States to the rest of the world. I realized that calling the book *What Do Unions Do?* was misleading, for the book examined what unions did in the United States while ignoring the rest of the world. Looking at labor markets in other countries made it clear that one could not study unions in isolation. They were part of the institutional framework that differentiated European Union countries from the United States. The key question for analysis mimicked the question that drove work on US unions: What did labor institutions do to national economic outcomes – in particular, to what extent, if at all, did they explain the lower dispersion of earnings and incomes in the European Union than in the United States and the higher employment rates in the United States than in the European Union.

I was uneasy about generalizing from institutional differences to differences in economic outcomes. In graduate school, Dunlop had told the story of Cantillon's cock (which I believe he learned from John Hicks). Every morning the cock awakens moments before sunrise and does what nature has programmed it to do: let out a mighty "cock-a-doodle-doo." Observing the time sequence of cause and effect, the cock concludes that crowing induces the sun to rise. So too, warned Dunlop, might union leaders, business, and government officials believe that what they say or do determines economic success when in fact market forces are at work. To find out what impact institutions have on economic outcomes requires that we measure the extent to which institutional rules are enforced or implemented and then quantify their effects, one outcome at a time, using the best empirical tools at our disposal.

Comparisons of aggregate outcomes among countries with different levels of collective bargaining coverage and broad indicators of labor market regulations offer one way to gain some insight into what labor institutions do, but no labor economist puts much faith in such aggregated data. Measures of institutions across countries are weak, there are many unmeasured factors and possible interactions of institutions, and there are few data points in most cross-country analyses. A preferable way to learn about how institutions affect outcomes is through microeconomic analysis of individuals or firms, comparing those affected by particular institutions and those not affected, ideally with some form of difference in difference model. Realizing that there were far too many countries and institutions for me to master, I organized the NBER Comparative Labor Project and called for help from my colleagues. We produced five NBER volumes with detailed studies by dozens of researchers focused on differences between US and EU labor markets.[20] The project leaders summarized the findings in their volumes in *Working Under Different Rules*.[21] The NBER labor group has also compared US and Canadian labor markets, studied the welfare state in Sweden, examined the British economy in the 2000s, and investigated youth labor markets in diverse advanced countries.[22] The work highlights the payoff from teamwork and collaboration in research, both among NBER researchers and with researchers in other countries. I would extend Newton's famous statement about "standing on the shoulders of giants" to include the shoulders of our colleagues and peers. We see farther because we are part of a collective cooperative (and competitive) research enterprise.

The diverse empirical studies in the Comparative Labor Market Program notwithstanding, I realized that if I was to truly grasp how European labor institutions operated, I had to get some firsthand experience and observation of those institutions. I made that case to Harvard and convinced the university to allow me to spend the better part of five years in Europe, where I worked at the Centre of Economic Performance at the London School of Economics and interacted frequently with business, labor, and government people and economists throughout the Continent on labor practices and issues. Paris today. Northern Italy tomorrow. Stockholm next week. Then Copenhagen and Amsterdam. Nice work if you can get it. Locales aside, talking with decision makers taught me a lot about country labor practices and operating procedures. How else could I have truly come to appreciate that a social partner is not someone you spin around the dance floor but a union organization or employer federation that participates in determining policies? Advanced Europe is Hirschman's voice mechanism writ large.

The major conclusion that I draw from this work is that labor institutions have a first-order effect in compressing the distribution of earnings but only modest and difficult-to-discern second-order impacts on economic efficiency. It may be that there is more Coase-style efficient bargaining in the world than labor economists have generally realized. But until we have a detailed analysis of the bargaining process and understand how the Europeans do their social dialoguing, that is just an interpretation.

Another promising way to research the impact of institutions on economic outcomes is, seemingly paradoxically, to forget about countries and study companies. For this the United States is particularly valuable because, absent centralized collective bargaining and strong labor regulations, US firms organize work and compensate employees in very different ways, with possible consequences for economic performance and worker well-being. The vastly greater number of firms than countries and greater possibility of finding pseudo-experimental variation in practices across firms than among countries also argued for analyses of labor institutions at the level of firms. My work here, with Doug Kruse and Joseph Blasi, focused on "shared capitalist" modes of compensation – those that link worker pay to company or group performance – and associated methods of devolving some work decisions from management to workers. For years, Kruse and Blasi had studied employee-owned and profit-sharing firms, which most economists, myself included, viewed as occupying an interesting but a not very important niche in the economy (think plywood producers in the Pacific Northwest, a few high-tech start-ups in Silicon Valley, and of course the famous Lincoln Electric). The predominant theory of the firm held that basic economic forces dictated that management retain residual control of assets and decisions and that group incentive systems would fail due to the free-rider problem arising from the fact that workers gain only a modest fraction of the rewards of their effort.

But could it be that Kruse and Blasi were studying a more important phenomenon than the rest of us recognized? In 2000, I set up an NBER project with Kruse and Blasi to find out. We added questions about shared capitalism to the General Social Survey and found that nearly half of the US workforce received part of their pay as group incentive. Shared capitalism in the United States was rarely full employee ownership à la the Mondragon conglomerate in the Basque Country or pure profit sharing, but it was part of the mix of compensation in many firms. Assisted by the managements of some large multinationals and some smaller enterprises, we conducted a largely Web-based survey of more than 40,000 workers covered by different plans and found that worker co-monitoring was an important force in fighting the incentive to free-ride. Workers covered by group incentive pay were more likely to act against shirkers than workers paid in other ways. We also found that shared capitalism gave better outcomes for workers and firms when management combined it with complementary labor policies and practices, which might reflect some underlying latent variable such as the corporate culture that business folk and business school profs sometimes invoked to explain differences in corporate performances.[23]

My great failure in these investigations of institutions across countries and firms has been in combining what I learned into a broad theoretic framework for understanding the interface between institutions and markets. Sometimes I think that I have learned too much about specific institutions to see how they fit together into a single theory. Good theories often come from knowing just enough to see the forest but not the trees. Alfred Russell Wallace knew less about biological variation than Darwin but was first off the gun with the theory of evolution, which galvanized Darwin to put some of his knowledge into *On the Origin of Species*. Coming to biology after earning a history degree, Robert Trivers developed his analyses of reciprocal altruism and parent–child conflict without the knowledge of senior specialists in evolutionary theory. If my memory deteriorates with age, perhaps I will forget enough to see the forest of market and institutional forces taken together.

But at other times I think that what analysis of institutions needs is more and different knowledge – knowledge of advanced mathematics to help guide thinking from the particulars of institutions to a deeper abstract structure. But what math might do the trick – algebraic geometry? representation theory? nonequilibrium statistical mechanics? functional analysis? combinatrics? partial differential equations? Calibi-Yau space and differential geometry? Come on, theorists in dark rooms with blackboards and mathematicians seeking new fields to conquer, try some abstractions with economic institutions. We need them.

One other topic that has attracted my attention and that of virtually every economist concerned with real economic problems: like taxes and death, you cannot escape globalization. My work on globalization has focused on three issues. The first is global labor standards, which I have approached from the perspective of consumer choice – the willingness of consumers to pay more for goods made under good conditions than bad conditions – rather than from the view, favored by some trade economists, that standards are protectionism in disguise. My work with Kimberly Elliot demonstrates further that, contrary to the fear of many on the left that globalization forces firms to reduce standards, globalization and labor standards are complementary rather than antithetical developments.[24] What makes the market for standards unique is that the entrepreneurs are human rights activists who galvanize consumer sentiment to pressure firms to improve conditions to avoid losing sales.

The second issue, which has become common wisdom in discussions of globalization and labor, is that globalization's big impact on labor around the world began when China, India, and the former Soviet bloc (all of which had previously operated as autarkies) joined the global capitalist system in the 1990s. These countries brought lots of low-skilled labor and little useful capital to the world economy, which effectively doubled the size of the global workforce. The ensuing reduction in the capital/labor ratio underlies, I claimed, most of the impacts of globalization on labor: the shift in bargaining power toward capital, the changing patterns of trade and foreign direct investment, and the offshoring of work. This is a case of seeing the forest because you haven't studied the trees.

The third issue, which occupies my research today, has a Hari Seldon quality to it. This is the impact of the spread of university education and knowledge around the world on economic development and in particular on the growth of useful knowledge. Technologists such as Ray Kurzweil argue that the increased power of computers will accelerate our control over nature, producing a "singularity" in history.[25] Without gainsaying the gigabytes of computing power, I stress the growing number of science and engineering specialists around the world. With more highly educated science and engineering specialists today than in all previous times taken together, connected through the Internet and, yes, with access to powerful computers, we have the potential for a singularity-type explosion of useful knowledge that could go a long way to solving the great problems we face in the areas of climate change, energy, pressures on natural resources (water, food, minerals, metals), disease and illness, and so on.

Turning that potential into reality is an economics problem of the first magnitude in allocating and managing human resources. Given the uncertainty of research, the political economy of the allocation of budgets, and problems in evaluating the benefits of public goods like knowledge, decision makers have no easy maximize-the-net-benefit function to guide them, and can and have made some costly mistakes. Between 1998 and 2003 the United States doubled the budget for the National Institutes of Health and then proceeded to cut the budget in real terms, which created a crisis in the careers of many of the new researchers induced into biomedical research during the boom period and potentially penalized the risky and transformative research that scientists believe is in short supply. Working with the science policy community has convinced me that economics can contribute substantially to helping decision makers in the government and in firms make better decisions about funding and deploying the great brainpower at humanity's disposal for solving the world's great problems.

So what does all this work add up to – a bang or a whimper? It has not yielded a theory of history based on scientific verities. Hari Seldon still lives far in the future. I like to think that it has provided partial answers to some manageable questions and clues to the big questions. But even if it only produces partial answers and clues, economics research does not end with a whimper. What economists learn and say – the way we think about problems – can and does influence human affairs. And as economics continues to become more empirical and scientific and less dependent on theory without evidence, it will almost surely become more important. Today we have more ways to find how the world works – from lab and field experiments to behavioral economics to the simulations of computational economics to the brain scans of neuroeconomics to econometric methodology to administrative and survey data on thousands of firms and hundreds of thousands of workers in dozens of countries, longitudinal as well as cross-sectional – that was unimaginable when I was a graduate student. The next decade of research looks to be so much fun and promising and productive that I envy the newest generation of researchers. I wish I could start anew with you.

Samuel Beckett ends *The Unnamable* with "Where I am I don't know, I'll never know, in the silence you don't know, you must go on, I can't go on, I'll go on." Economists don't know the answers to Hari Seldon future-of-history questions. Perhaps we'll never know them. But moving toward answers through smaller manageable questions, creating and analyzing data, interacting with the practitioners in the world whose behavior we study (workers, union leaders, business leaders, scientists, engineers, whoever) is not dismal science. No way. It is fun – more fun, as best I can tell, than making money as an investment banker, McKinsey consultant, or used-car salesman, or even than theorizing on a blackboard in some dark office. And it is more important. With apologies to Beckett, I feel more strongly than when I began that we can and will break the silence of not knowing. I intend to go on searching for answers to the questions that seem important. I hope you will do the same. May your new research and mine illuminate important social phenomena and justify all that fun to the world.

Notes

1 For a detailed discussion of the series see en.wikipedia.org/wiki/The_Foundation_Series.
2 en.wikipedia.org/wiki/Hari-Seldon.
3 There was one paperback nominally on economics, by George Soule, who was actually a technologist.

4 National Academy of Sciences, National Academy of Engineers, and Institute of Medicine of the National Academies, *Rising above the Gathering Storm: Energizing and Employing America for a Brighter Economic Future – Committee on Prospering in the Global Economy of the 21st Century* (Washington, DC: National Academies Press, 2007). My response to the furor over the number of science and engineering graduates is given in Richard Freeman, "Investing in the Best and Brightest: Increased Fellowship Support for American Scientists and Engineers," www.brookings.edu/papers/2006/12technology_freeman.aspx.

5 This is currently in its third edition. Gary Stanley Becker, *Human Capital: A Theoretical and Empirical Analysis, with Special Reference to Education* (Chicago: University of Chicago Press, 1993).

6 Gary Becker, "Irrational Behavior and Economic Theory," *Journal of Political Economy* 70, no. 1 (February 1962): 1–13.

7 Richard Freeman, *The Market for College Trained Manpower* (Cambridge, MA: Harvard University Press, 1971); "A Cobweb Model of the Supply and Starting Salary of New Engineers," *Industrial Labor Relations Review* 29, no. 2 (January 1976): 236–248.

8 Richard Freeman, "Supply and Salary Adjustments to the Changing Science Manpower Market: Physics, 1948–1975," *American Economic Review* 65, no. 1 (March 1975): 27–39; "Employment Opportunities in the Doctorate Manpower Market," *Industrial Labor Relations Review* 33, no. 2 (January 1980); "Legal Cobwebs: A Recursive Model of the Market for Lawyers," *Review of Economics and Statistics* 57, no. 2 (May 1975): 171–179.

9 Richard Freeman, "Changes in the Labor Market for Black Americans," *Brookings Papers*, Summer 1973; "Decline of Labor Market Discrimination and Economic Analysis," *American Economic Review* 63, no. 2 (May 1973): 280–286; *The Black Elite: The New Market for Highly Educated Black Americans* (New York: McGraw-Hill, 1976).

10 Richard Freeman and John Bound, "What Went Wrong? The Erosion of the Relative Earnings and Employment among Young Black Men in the 1980s," *Quarterly Journal of Economics* 107, no. 1 (February 1992): 201–232.

11 In Harry Holzer (ed.), *The Black Youth Employment Crisis*, NBER Conference Volume (Chicago: University of Chicago Press, 1986); "Why Do So Many Young American Men Commit Crimes and What Might We Do About It?" *Journal of Economic Perspectives* 10, no. 1 (Winter 1996): 25–42; "Crime and the Employment of Disadvantaged Youths", in George Peterson and Wayne Vroman (eds.), *Urban Labor Markets and Job Opportunity* (Washington, DC: Urban Institute Press, 1992).

12 John Dunlop, *Wage Determination Under Trade Unions* (New York: Macmillan, 1944).

13 Albert O. Hirschman, *Exit, Voice, and Loyalty: Responses to Decline in Firms, Organizations, and States* (Cambridge, MA: Harvard University Press, 1970).

14 Richard Freeman, "Individual Mobility and Union Voice in the Labor Market," *American Economic Review* 66, no. 2 (May 1976): 361–368.

15 Richard B. Freeman and James L. Medoff, *What Do Unions Do?* (New York: Basic Books, 1984).

16 On the public sector: Richard B. Freeman and Casey Ichniowski (eds.), *When Public Sector Workers Unionize* (Chicago: University of Chicago Press for NBER, 1988);

"Unionism Comes to the Public Sector," *Journal of Economic Literature* 24, no. 1 (March 1986): 41–86; "Contraction and Expansion: The Divergence of Private and Public Sector Unionism in the United States," *Journal of Economic Perspectives* 2, no. 2 (Spring 1988), 63–68. On unions outside the United States: "The Impact of Industrial Relations Legislation on British Union Density," with Jeffrey Pelletier, *British Journal of Industrial Relations* 28, no. 2 (July 1990): 141–164, Crumbling Pillar? Declining Union Density in Japan," with Marcus Rebick, *Journal of the Japanese and International Economies* (1990): 578–605; "The Changing Status of Unionism Around the World," in Wei-Chiao Huang (ed.), *Organized Labor at the Crossroads* (Kalamazoo, MI: Upjohn Institute for Employment Research, 1989); "Unionism in the U.S. and Other OECD Countries," with David G. Blanchflower, *Industrial Relations* 31, no. 1 (Winter 1992): 56–79. On the decline of unions: "Why Are Unions Faring Poorly in NLRB Representation Elections?" in Tom Kochan (ed.), *Challenges and Choices Facing American Labor* (Cambridge, MA: MIT Press, 1985); "The Effect of the Union Wage Differential on Management Opposition and Union Organizing Success," *American Economic Review: AEA Papers and Proceedings* 76, no. 2 (May 1986): 92–96; "Employer Behavior in the Face of Union Organizing Drives," with Morris Kleiner, *Industrial and Labor Relations Review* 43, no. 4 (April 1990): 351–365.

17 James T. Bennett and Bruce E. Kaufman (eds.), *What Do Unions Do? A Twenty-Year Perspective* (Piscataway, NJ: Transaction, 2007).

18 Richard Barry Freeman and Joel Rogers, *What Workers Want* (Ithaca, NY: Cornell University Press, 1999; 2d ed. 2006).

19 Richard B. Freeman and J. Rogers, "Open Source Unionism: Beyond Exclusive Collective Bargaining," *WorkingUSA: The Journal of Labor and Society* 6, no. 2; (2002): "A Proposal to American Labor." *The Nation*, June 6, 2002, available on the Web in various places, including the Web site of the International Workers of the World, or "Wobblies," famous in US labor history.

20 These volumes are David Card and Richard B. Freeman (eds.), *Small Differences That Matter: Labor Markets and Income Maintenance in Canada and the United States* (Chicago, IL: The University of Chicago Press, 1993); Rebecca M. Blank (ed.), *Social Protection vs. Economic Flexibility: Is There a Tradeoff?* (Chicago, IL: The University of Chicago Press, 1994); Lisa M. Lynch (ed.), *Training and the Private Sector: International Comparisons* (Chicago, IL: The University of Chicago Press, 1994); Joel Rogers and Wolfang Streeck (eds.), *Works Councils Consultation, Representation, and Cooperation in Industrial Relations*, (Chicago, IL.: The University of Chicago Press, 1995); Richard B. Freeman and Lawrence F. Katz (eds.), *Differences and Changes in Wage Structures* (Chicago, IL: The University of Chicago Press, 1995).

21 Richard Freeman (ed.), *Working Under Different Rules* (New York: Russell Sage Foundation, 1994).

22 Richard B. Freeman, Robert H. Topel, and Birgitta Swedenborg (eds.), *The Welfare State in Transition: Reforming the Swedish Model* (1997); David G. Blanchflower and Richard B. Freeman (eds.), *Youth Employment and Joblessness in Advanced Countries* (2000); David Card, Richard Blundell, and Richard B. Freeman, *Seeking a Premier Economy: The Economic Effects of British Economic Reforms, 1980–2000* (2004); Edward P. Lazear and Kathryn L. Shaw, *The Structure of Wages: An International Comparison* (2008); Richard B. Freeman, Birgitta Swedenborg, Robert H. Topel (eds.), *Reforming the Welfare State: Recovery and Beyond in Sweden* (2010).

23 The research for this appeared inj NBER working papers, and in *Shared Capitalism at Work: Employee Ownership, Profit and Gain Sharing, and Broad-based Stock Options* (University of Chicago Press for NBER, 2010). In 2013 we published *The Citizens Share: Putting Ownership Back into Democracy* (Yale University Press, 2013), Which links this work to the ideas of the founders of the United States.

24 Kimberly Ann Elliott and Richard B. Freeman, *Can Labor Standards Improve Under Globalization?* (Washington, DC: Peterson Institute for International Economics, 2003).

25 en.wikipedia.org/wiki/Technological_singularity.

13

One Job, Four Careers

Benjamin M. Friedman

Most people spend the greater part of their working lives carrying out more or less the same activity but from time to time face the inconvenience of changing jobs. I've had the opposite experience. As I write this essay, I am beginning my fortieth year in the same job: economics professor at Harvard. But from time to time I've shifted the focus of my work to such an extent that the new path feels, in many ways, like a new career – not just different questions to consider but different starting presumptions, a different set of relevant institutions, different background literature, and a different cast of characters whose contributions and judgment matter.

To be sure, all this is a matter of perspective. To some – perhaps to most people not engaged in an academic or research enterprise – what has seemed to me like a series of career changes may well appear far more seamless. After all, I've continued throughout to write books and articles about economics and to teach economics to both graduate students and undergraduates at my university. Isn't that all really the same thing? From my perspective, no it isn't. To me, these transitions increasingly have had the feeling of career changes. To the question of what it's like to have "done the same thing" for so many years, my reaction is that I wouldn't know; I haven't.

FINANCIAL MARKETS AND MONETARY POLICY

Taking an active research interest in monetary policy came naturally to me. I had become an economist because I was attracted by the field's focus on macroeconomic policy, and I was optimistic about the possibilities for a combination of cogent theory, carefully derived empirical evidence, and detailed knowledge of economic and financial institutions to improve macroeconomic outcomes. During graduate school years, I had gotten a good feel for what the Federal Reserve System did and how it went about it: one summer spent in the Research Department at the Federal Reserve Bank of New York, two summers at the Federal Reserve Board, an ongoing assignment as an adviser to the president of the Federal Reserve Bank of Boston, and a special assignment to the staff of an ad hoc subcommittee of the Federal Open Market Committee. After I finished my graduate studies, I had spent two summers and the year in between at a New York investment banking firm, learning about the bond market. By the time I started on my professional research agenda, I was ready to think about the day's questions pertaining to monetary policy.

It is embarrassing for monetary economists and macroeconomists today to acknowledge how many of the issues that were at the center of professional debate decades ago are still high on the field's agenda: To what extent, and through what behavioral channels, do the central bank's policy actions affect nonfinancial economic activity? Does monetary policy affect prices merely via its effect on demand and supply conditions in the markets for goods and services, and for labor and other factors of production, or is there some more direct effect? Should the central bank's policy objectives reflect only prices (or their rate of change) or also real economic outcomes like output (or its rate of change) and employment? What is the right balance between discretionary and rule-based policy making? It is often difficult to say whether such central questions remain unresolved because objective circumstances change over time, so that one decade's answers need not be determinative for future periods, or because the methods economists use to analyze them are simply not up to the task. (A third, more troubling reason may be that such questions, seemingly about substantive economics, carry political implications – indeed, a substantive question may in effect be a proxy for some unstated political debate – on which the interests of the parties concerned are prior, and therefore impervious, to economic argument and evidence.)

One question that has mostly disappeared from the profession's agenda, however, is whether the central bank should formulate and carry out its monetary policy as if its objective were to achieve a stated growth rate for some specified aggregate measure of "money." This question too was the focus of enormous debate and attention at the time I began my professional career, and in retrospect it is no surprise that much of my early work addressed it. The work I did advanced two, only partially related ideas. First, the conditions required to render monetary targeting a useful way to conduct monetary policy (conditions that others had largely worked out before I came on the scene) seemed to me, on the evidence, unlikely to be satisfied in the United States, or in many other countries either. I therefore argued against this practice, then in its ascendency at the US Federal Reserve System but already riding high in countries like Germany and the United Kingdom. Put most simply, the argument was (and still is) that using any one variable like the money stock as an intermediate target variable constrained the central bank to disregard information that might usefully bear on policy decisions but did not happen to be embodied in that particular observable measure.

But second, if the central bank *were* to conduct policy in terms of a target for some quantity measure drawn from the financial arena, both theory and the available empirical evidence (again, for the United States and many other countries too) seemed to me to present just as strong a case for targeting credit – that is, a measure of the public's liabilities and drawn from the asset side of the balance sheet of banks and other lenders – as for money. In part, this finding merely strengthened the first argument: How could a central bank single out some monetary aggregate to target if there is just as good a case not merely for other monetary aggregates but for credit aggregates too? In part, however, it was meant to be constructive in its own terms. Since central banks, including the Federal Reserve, appeared to be comfortable in simultaneously pursuing multiple targets, why restrict those targets to various measures of *money*? From the perspective of the use of such targets as a way of organizing the flow of incoming information ("information variables," as many of us called them), using a monetary target *and* a credit target appeared, again on the evidence, a more comprehensive and therefore more efficient way of doing so than having two monetary targets. In 1979 the Federal Reserve began setting a range for a credit measure, specifically using the one I had emphasized in my empirical work (the outstanding debt of all nonfinancial obligors), along with ranges for several monetary aggregates.

In the end, monetary targeting pretty well disappeared from most central banks' monetary policies. In the United States, the Federal Reserve abandoned its narrow money target in 1987 and then "downgraded" its broad money target in 1993. The Bank of Japan, the Bank of England, the Bank of Canada, and the Swedish Riksbank all followed suit. The Swiss National Bank held to one monetary target or another (initially monetary base but then a broad monetary aggregate) longer than most of the others, but by 1999 it too abandoned the practice. As of this writing the European Central Bank continues to include a "monetary pillar" as one of the two research disciplines it employs to guide monetary policy, but whether this practice as stated actually matters remains a matter of controversy and a focus of research. (An ungenerous interpretation is that when the ECB first started operations, policy makers were eager to announce a "monetary pillar" as a rhetorical way of claiming the mantle of the German Bundesbank, and once having publicly begun on that footing the Bank then found itself unable to abandon the idea, at least not openly.) As Milton Friedman famously put it, not long before he died, "The use of money as a target has not been a success."

In place of a monetary target, many central banks around the world – but none of the "big three," in the United States, Europe, and Japan – have moved to an inflation target. I've been a critic here too, in this case not so much of the concept as of how inflation targeting is mostly put into practice. The concept is clear enough. For reasons that Tinbergen explained long ago, if the central bank has only one "instrument variable" at its disposal, then no matter how many "target variables" it seeks to influence, in the absence of some degeneracy any one of them will be sufficient to describe the entire intended policy trajectory; and since the theoretical basis for a long-run effect of monetary policy on real outcomes is dubious at best, for purposes of looking more than a short horizon ahead it makes sense for that one target variable to be from the price, rather than the real, side of the economy. In practice, however, many central banks have used inflation targeting as a rhetorical device for avoiding any open discussion of their real objectives at all, in effect hoping that the public, whose expectations they are trying to influence, will lose sight of the fact that monetary policy even has real objectives. My criticism of inflation targeting as practiced has emphasized the resulting sacrifice of transparency in policy making (which is ironic, since inflation targeting, as originally proposed, was supposed to *enhance* transparency) and ultimately, therefore, the loss of central banks' accountability and political legitimacy as well. But by the time most of the central banks that have adopted inflation targeting did so, the center of my research agenda had moved elsewhere.

FISCAL POLICY, DEFICITS AND DEBT

The time I had spent working in the bond market, just after finishing my education, had shown me in some detail the process by which the issuers of securities (which, given corporate finance patterns in the United States in those days, meant mostly bonds) found buyers for them. It also made me aware that bond investors can and regularly do substitute one kind of bond for another in their portfolios. And it made me keenly aware that most bond investors have limited portfolios to deploy. Buying one bond, therefore, means not buying some other one. The underwriting firm for which I worked was in the business of competing for space, in its sell-side customers' portfolios, for its buy-side clients' securities.

All this may have been a matter best left to finance professors when I saw it at first hand in the early 1970s, but by a decade later the principle at issue suddenly loomed large in the macroeconomic policy context in the United States. Then, as now, the US government rarely balanced its budget. But the deficits the government ran then were mostly small, and they mostly occurred at times of economic weakness; they came about not so much because the government was nimble enough to time discretionary policy actions to combat the business cycle as simply because a weak economy meant shrunken tax collections and a bulge in cyclically sensitive expenditures like unemployment benefits. As of 1980 the largest deficit the federal government had run since World War II was 4.6 percent of the US gross national product, and that was in 1976, immediately following what was until that time the deepest and most protracted economic downturn since the war.

The 1980s were different. The Reagan policy, combining tax cuts, a defense build-up, and no cuts whatever in the largest nondefense programs like Social Security and Medicare, led to deficits that peaked at 6 percent of GDP in 1983, again immediately following a severe business recession, but then averaged 5 percent of GDP over the next three years running – well after the economy had returned to full employment. In parallel, under this policy the government's outstanding debt, which had declined irregularly from more than one dollar of debt for every dollar of the US GDP at the end of World War II to just 26 cents per dollar of GDP by 1980, was rising continuously: the first, and to date the only, such increase in American history during peacetime and with the economy at full employment. By 1987 the debt ratio was back up to 40 cents per dollar. By the time the first President Bush left office, it was 49 cents. Compared with the size of the economy, the government's debt nearly doubled. (On a nominal basis, over those twelve years the debt more than quadrupled.)

Not only did this extraordinary fiscal phenomenon arrest the attention of macroeconomists and the public at large, it also bore straightforward relationships to several lines of research on which I had been working. The key point was that, with Paul Volcker now heading the Federal Reserve, and with the anti-inflationary monetary policy he introduced fully supported by President Reagan (though not by some high-ranking members of his administration), the deficits of the 1980s were not going to be monetized by the central bank.

A few years earlier, prompted by what had then seemed a very large deficit in the wake of the 1973–1975 recession, I had thought some about the consequences of bond-financed deficits at a time of *un*used economic resources. The question that interested me was not the direct effect of government spending or tax cuts but rather the financial effect created by the need to fund the resulting deficit by selling bonds to the public – something I had watched at close hand not long before. The analytical approach that seemed natural to me was one that Tobin had developed a decade or so earlier: the government's increased supply of bonds would take up space in investors' portfolios, with consequences not just for bond yields but, in a financial market general equilibrium setting, for the market-clearing returns on all securities investors held. The question that emerged as most interesting to me from that particular line of work was whether the required return on equity capital would rise along with the deficit-induced rise in bond interest rates or fall in response to the enlargement of investors' portfolios and their demand for diversification. Since firms' willingness and ability to invest depend on a cost of capital that embodies not just bond rates but the required return on equity, the question bore directly on the consequences of government deficits for fixed investment.

A second, closely related line of research that I undertook in the early 1980s focused on financial quantities rather than returns. From work I had done together with colleagues at the Federal Reserve Board, I had become aware that although there were large changes over time in the amounts, compared with GDP, of different kinds of securities outstanding, the total amount of debt issued by all nonfinancial borrowers had remained fairly steady compared with GDP for quite some time (a regularity that did not survive the financial innovation and consequent leveraging boom that the

United States underwent some years later). The implication was again consistent with the intuition I had absorbed while working in the bond market more than a decade earlier: if investors bought more of one kind of security, in the end they were likely to buy less of something else. In the case at hand, greater purchases of government bonds would mean fewer purchases of corporate bonds, and hence less financing for firms unless they shifted in a very large way to issuing equity. Once again, the matter bore fairly directly on prospects for fixed investment.

What made these issues of central importance was that, unlike in the past, the fiscal policy of the Reagan (and subsequently Bush I) era produced large deficits even in a fully employed economy. Hence the direct effects of enlarged spending and reduced taxes, which normally took center stage in discussions of this subject, were unlikely to be at work except in a very transient way. By contrast, the *financial* consequences of issuing bonds to fund the deficit, normally a sideshow in discussions of the subject, were now the main event.

Prompted by these two lines of research – together with the fact that, contrary to frequently expressed expectations by some of its advocates, the policy did not change even as the economy regained and then maintained full employment – once the main outlines of the Reagan policy became clear I took the better part of a year away from my usual program of academic research to write a book for a broad readership that was published with the title *Day of Reckoning.* (The title, suggested by my editor at Random House, referred to a speech by Mr. Reagan stating that *if the country continued on the fiscal path that existed before he became president* it would eventually face a day of reckoning. The title was meant to be ironic, in that what had put the country on the path to a fiscal "day of reckoning" was instead *Mr. Reagan's* new policy.) The book's main argument was that continued large government deficits, even in a fully employed economy, would lead to shrunken investment or enlarged foreign borrowing or both. In the event, the "both" turned out to be right. US business fixed investment as a share of GDP declined to a record low for the post–World War II period, and net foreign investment turned negative – so much so that by the end of the 1980s the United States became a net debtor country for the first time since World War I.

THE MORAL DIMENSION OF MACROECONOMIC POLICY

A few years after the Reagan-Bush policy that had prompted me to write *Day of Reckoning* ended, as I was preparing to teach one of my usual courses on policy-oriented macroeconomics I thought I might usefully give a lecture or two at the beginning on why improved macroeconomic performance, and therefore effective macroeconomic policy, was an important subject in the first place. In lower-income countries, increases in per capita income translated pretty directly into longer life expectancy, reduced morbidity, lower rates of infant mortality and adult malnutrition, and improvement in other basic human conditions. But the evidence showed that these relationships mostly play themselves out by the time an economy reaches, say, half the per capita income of the United States. Moreover, substantial evidence of a different kind cast doubt on the idea that in the more advanced economies rising average income levels over time, within any given country, translated into rising average levels of happiness (in psychologists' vocabulary, subjective well-being).

Why, then, for a high-income economy like the United States in the final years of the twentieth century was it important to use macroeconomic policy tools to best advantage? To put the question in terms of the two traditional areas of inquiry within macroeconomics – business cycles and growth – why was it important to maintain production in the short and medium run as close as possible to its existing stable-price frontier? Since recessions typically amounted to no more than a few percentage points' dip in aggregate production, lasting only a year or two, why was preventing them, or mitigating them once they happened, such a high priority? And why did it matter, over longer periods, that the economy's frontier of per capita production continue to move outward? With incomes already so high, not just compared with elsewhere in the world but especially compared with historical experience, what difference did it make whether per capita expansion over the next generation was 3 percent per annum (which for the United States would be hailed as an achievement) or only 1 percent per annum (which would be a disappointment)? Answers that would be obvious for an economy with far lower average incomes simply were not persuasive for the United States.

I assumed that I would easily find some adequate statements on the subject that I could assign students in the first week of a macroeconomic policy course – most likely from Tobin or Okun or Solow, or, if not, perhaps from Samuelson or Boulding or any of the other great lights who had thought about the fundamental underpinnings of macroeconomics. To my surprise, and frustration, I found little to assign. Rather than drop the idea of adding these few introductory lectures, I tried thinking through on my own what I might say.

The result was a line of research that ended up occupying a substantial part of my attention over nearly the next decade and that eventually led to my 2005 book, *The Moral Consequences of Economic Growth*. The conclusion I reached was that continued advances in incomes and living standards are indeed important, but not for their material value per se. Rather, sustained improvement in material living standards, broadly shared through the citizenry, provide the basis for a society to advance also along other dimensions to which Western thinking, at least since the Enlightenment of the eighteenth century, has attached positive moral value: openness of opportunity, tolerance, fairness and even a sense of generosity toward the disadvantaged, and commitment to democracy. Conversely, a society in which most citizens see their living standards stagnate, and lose confidence that progress in their material lives will resume any time soon, not only is unlikely to make further progress along any of these moral dimensions of its existence but, all too often, will experience rigidification and retrenchment, in some cases with disastrous consequences for its own people and perhaps for other countries too.

The model I conceived to underlie this relationship, based on work by Duesenberry, Easterlin, and others on the "relative income" idea, as well as on work by numerous economists on how "habit formation" affects preferences, posited that individuals derive utility not exclusively (in the limit, not at all) from the absolute level of their consumption but from their consumption relative to two benchmarks, for each of which we have a great deal of supporting evidence: people gain satisfaction from living better than they, or their families, have lived in the past; and they also gain satisfaction from living better than other people with whom they compare themselves. Under the assumption that these two sources of satisfaction are substitutes, in the familiar demand-theoretic sense that doing well on either one reduces the urgency attached to doing well on the other (a standard example would be coffee and tea), the implication of broadly shared economic growth – meaning living conditions systematically better than in the relevant past, for the broad bulk of the population – is a blunting of the kind of socially competitive inclinations that so often underlie intolerance and a lack of generosity. Significantly, in this model what primarily matters is the *change* in living standards, not the level per se.

The main argumentation of the book I wrote, however, was empirical. Conceiving a model of preferences to explain the relationship between rising material living standards and progress in the various moral dimensions of a society's existence that I had in mind (using "moral" in a self-consciously eighteenth-century sense) was fairly straight forward. Documenting these relationships was more challenging.

The empirical strategy I chose for this purpose was to match up economic history – in the simplest terms, whether most of a country's population was enjoying improving incomes and living standards or suffering stagnation or perhaps even decline, at any given time – with the corresponding political and social history. Like most economists, I knew something of economic history (I never worked in the field, but I've always found the subject extremely interesting), and purely as a layman I had read fairly broadly, although certainly not deeply, in American and European history. (In this latter respect I have the sense of being a product of the era in which I was educated; my impression is that most students today don't do that.) By the time I finished the project, more than a fourth of the book I wrote was my account of how alternating eras of robust growth and stagnation in the US economic experience since the Civil War lined up with periods in which racial and religious prejudice and xenophobia either ebbed or waned, in which the country moved either forward or back in providing education and other opportunities for its young people and either jobs or other relief for its disadvantaged adults, and in which American democratic institutions either broadened and strengthened or not. Nearly another fourth carried out parallel but more limited exercises for Britain since the Napoleonic Wars, for France since the establishment of the Third Republic, and for Germany since the unification of the Empire.

Fortunately for this effort, over the years a legion of economic historians has constructed rich sets of data on the rate of economic growth, and to some extent also the distribution of the fruits of that growth, in the countries in which I was primarily interested. The economic historians have also amply explored the forces accounting for this growth or for the stagnation when there was no growth. All this material was there for me to use as I needed it. The harder part was to decide what elements of the social and political histories of these countries were most relevant and to learn what I needed to know from across such a broad range of intellectual territory involving hundreds of individual issues – in the United States, for example, the anti-British and anti-Semitic overtones of the populists' campaign for free silver in the 1890s, the resurgence of the Ku Klux Klan in the 1920s, the civil rights movement of the 1950s and 1960s, and then the push-back against affirmative action in the 1970s and 1980s; but also the repression of the suffragettes under Asquith in pre–World War I Britain, the Boulangists (1880s) and Poujadists (1950s) in France, and of course the rise of Nazism in Germany, along with many, many others – each with its own well-developed scholarly literature.

Learning what I needed to know was a major challenge. But one of the great advantages of living in a university community is the abundance of knowledgeable colleagues inhabiting an astonishing array of disciplines, and I found mine at Harvard more than willing to guide me through many of these issues to which scholars in some cases devote entire careers. To gauge how economic growth, or stagnation, was affecting a society I ended up examining not only the social and political histories of these four countries but their *belles lettres* too, on the ground that yet another way of knowing what was on people's minds, in eras for which no opinion survey data exist, is to examine what they were reading. I did not actually abandon economics to become a social or political historian (although one of my favorite colleagues, looking over the syllabus for the course I taught to help me think through some of the issues this project involved, remarked that he thought it must be a fascinating course but couldn't understand why it had an Economics number in the Harvard catalog). But in many ways what I was doing did feel like a new career.

What I argued in *The Moral Consequences of Economic Growth* was that although there are exceptions – including some prominent and very intriguing ones, like the experience of the 1930s depression in the United States – most of the time it is true that rising living standards, sustained over significant periods of time and widely shared across the citizenry, foster advances in tolerance and fairness and democracy, while economic stagnation mostly blocks such positive tendencies and frequently sets the stage for adverse developments. Given the focus on the *change* in living standards, not the absolute level, as the driving force in these movements, I drew two broader conclusions from these findings. First, many countries in the developing world will not have to wait until they achieve living standards on a par with those in today's industrialized world before they can evolve functioning liberal democracies; what matters for this purpose is that they maintain broadly shared growth. And second, no matter how rich an industrial or postindustrial country becomes, its democratic freedoms nonetheless remain at risk if living standards for the majority of its citizens stagnate. It follows from both points that today's familiar popular discussion that pits economic growth *against* society's moral concerns, as if there were an inherent conflict between them, presents a false choice. Concern for a society's moral character should be a reason for advocating economic growth, not resisting it, and therefore for seeking out policies to promote growth rather than opposing them.

Another of my Harvard colleagues with whom I discussed in some detail the hypothesis I was advancing about the close connection between economic growth and moral progress, a European scholar a decade and a half older than I, remarked that only an American – and at that, only an American of my generation – would write a book expressing such an optimistic perspective. I don't know if he was right, but if so I gladly accept the identification.

THE RELIGIOUS ORIGINS OF MODERN ECONOMICS

My work on *The Moral Consequences of Economic Growth* also led me to take an interest in history of a different kind. To begin, I wanted to gain a better understanding of what the Enlightenment thinkers who taught Western society the value of these democratic freedoms had in mind. I also became aware that over time, going back much farther than the eighteenth century, Western attitudes toward progress more generally had evolved in interesting ways. I had explored some of these connections in two chapters of my 2005 book, but that was all. It was enough, however, to draw my interest – I remain, after all, an economist – to a different question: Where (in the sense of intellectual origins) did our modern economics come from? The Enlightenment gave us more than just an appreciation for liberal democracy. Adam Smith and his contemporaries were a part of that era too, and economics as the intellectual discipline we have had ever since is also very much a product of the Enlightenment.

Most economists are at least partly familiar with the origins of our discipline as a "moral science." Adam Smith's academic appointment was as professor of moral philosophy, and not only his earlier *Theory of Moral Sentiments* but the *Wealth of Nations* too reflects it. But the research I had done in the course of writing *The Moral Consequences of Economic Growth* had also made me aware of the important role that religious thinking so often plays, influencing attitudes and intellectual approaches toward subjects ranging from secular progress to business ethics. I wondered, therefore, whether matters not just moral but religious (in the traditional sense) might also have played a role in the all-important transition in thinking, in the eighteenth century, that gave us economics as we now know it.

The project on which I am now working seeks to show that the transition in thinking about what we now call "economics" – the transition that we rightly associate with such figures as Mandeville, Hutcheson, Hume, and above all Adam Smith – was significantly shaped by what were then new and highly controversial lines of thought within the English-speaking

Protestant world. Further, I posit that this at-the-origins influence of religious thinking on modern economic thinking established resonances that then persisted, albeit in evolving form as the economic context shifted, right through the nineteenth and twentieth centuries. And although we do not talk of them – indeed, for the most part we are not conscious of them – these lasting resonances, especially in North America but throughout the Western world, continue to shape our current-day discussion of economic issues and our debates over questions of economic policy. Critics sometimes complain that belief in free markets, not just by economists but among ordinary citizens too, is a form of religion. I think there is something to the idea: not in the way the critics mean, but in a deeper, more historically grounded sense.

I am well aware that the idea of a central religious influence on Adam Smith's thinking, or on that of many of his contemporaries, will initially strike many knowledgeable readers as implausible on its face. Smith's great friend David Hume was, notoriously, an avowed atheist and an outspoken opponent of organized religion. (Because of Hume's well-known views on religion, he was never able to secure a university professorship.) Smith, as far as one can tell, was at best a deist of the sort Americans would mostly identify with Thomas Jefferson. There is little evidence of Smith's active religious participation, much less religious enthusiasm. My argument in this project is most certainly *not* that these were religiously dedicated men who self-consciously brought their theological commitments to bear on their economic thinking.

Rather, I start from the fact that Smith and his contemporaries lived at a time when religion was both more pervasive and more central than anything we know in today's Western world. And, crucially, intellectual life was more integrated then. Not only were the sciences and humanities (to use today's language) normally discussed in the same circles and mostly by the same individuals, but theology too was part of the ongoing discussion. Smith, Hume, and the other early creators of economics as we know it, therefore, were continually exposed to what were then fresh debates about new lines of theological thinking. My hypothesis is that what they heard and read and discussed influenced the economics they produced, just as the ideas of today's economists are visibly shaped by what they learn from physics ("gravity" models of trade) or biology (models of contagion in a financial crisis) or demography (migration models of technology transfer). Schumpeter called this kind of influence on the intellectual process "preanalytic vision": what is on people's minds – what they know and how they perceive the world – before they even begin to explore a specific subject in any systematic way. Einstein famously wrote about his "weltbild" (literally translated, "world picture").

The key insight that gave rise to modern economics – the idea that we know as Adam Smith's "invisible hand" (even though Smith's use of the phrase, only once in the *Theory of Moral Sentiments* and once again in the *Wealth of Nations*, was neither original nor so specific) – was that behavior motivated merely by individuals' self-interest can, and under the right conditions will, lead to beneficial outcomes not merely for the individuals concerned but for others as well. My hypothesis is that the preanalytic vision that gave rise to this line of thinking was shaped not merely by Mandeville's and Hume's and Smith's observations of the mercantile activity going on around them but by the intense debate, then playing out in England and Scotland, over core religious ideas such as human depravity and predestination. In particular, I argue that the erosion of these beliefs, in favor of a more benign view of the human character and a universalist interpretation of individuals' prospects for salvation (with a key role for human agency in affecting that determination), helped create the preanalytic vision that made these thinkers' more optimistic assessment of the implications of self-interested behavior possible.

I think this idea – if true – is significant in two respects. First, it changes our view of the historical process by which Western thinking produced "economics." The conventional account is that the Smithian revolution and the subsequent development of economics as an intellectual discipline were part of the familiar process of secular modernization, in the sense of a historic turn in thinking away from a God-centered universe toward what we now broadly call humanism. Realizing also that the Smithian revolution grew partly out of new ideas in *theology* and that the *religious* debates of that day shaped it – not because that is what Smith and others consciously intended, but because the theological debates of their time fundamentally altered how they thought about human nature and the most basic underpinnings of everyday human interaction – puts a very different gloss on the matter. So does understanding the ways in which the evolution of economic thinking during the nineteenth and twentieth centuries continued to reflect this initial religious influence.

Second, understanding this from-the-bottom-up connection between economic thinking and key strands of religious thinking (the ones at issue in the debates of Smith's time) helps explain a wide variety of other puzzling phenomena, now and in the past: Why is there, today, an "Anglo-Saxon model" of how to organize an economy and run economic policy, and why do so many people, in countries otherwise very similar to ours, reject it?

Why do most Americans, when asked to name the two US presidents since World War II who were most opposed to taxes and government regulation, give the same answer as when they are asked which two presidents were most identified with the Evangelical churches (to both questions, Ronald Reagan and George W. Bush)? Why do so many Americans who have no chance whatever of inheriting money from a taxable estate passionately advocate abolishing "death taxes"? (For an American male, the probability of being a beneficiary of a taxable estate is smaller than the probability of being 6' 9" tall; for a female, 6' 3".) At a more philosophical level, why are economists, policy makers, and the general public in most Western countries all so resistant to explanations of either individual or economy-wide outcomes in which initial conditions – a person's childhood family circumstances or a nation's resource endowments or its long-inherited social institutions – determine such matters as who becomes rich and who remains poor or which countries can govern themselves effectively and which will become "failed states"? I argue that understanding the historical link between religious thinking and economic thinking helps to explain these and other currents underlying today's debate over essential issues of economic policy, including in particular questions revolving around the efficacy and appropriate role of markets and, in parallel, the role of government in our society.

Just as my work on *The Moral Consequences of Economic Growth* did not make me a social or political historian, my ongoing work on this project has not made me an intellectual historian. And it won't. I remain an economist. But it once again feels like a new career nonetheless.

Is moving from one "career" to another in this way a good thing to do? It's hard to say. Everyone knows that scientific progress depends on specialization. The point is especially familiar to economists. In the very first sentence of the *Wealth of Nations*, Adam Smith pointed to "division of labor" – in our vocabulary, specialization in production – as the key to superior productivity.

But in his own work Smith hardly stuck to a narrow specialization. Both the *Theory of Moral Sentiments* and the *Wealth of Nations* were part of a much broader attempt to construct what he and his colleagues conceived as a "science of man." Both books are replete with analyses of individuals' motivations and psychological states and the ways in which what we now think of as economic activity, carried out in social settings, enables them to lead satisfying lives or not. The *Wealth of Nations* is also very much a book about politics, including not just what we think of as economic policy issues but also Britain's foreign policy of the day. Smith also wrote – and wrote interestingly – on topics ranging from astronomy and physics to music, dance, and poetry. At the time of his death he was working on what he intended to be a major work spanning all of the "imitative arts."

Indeed, in the same book that opened with the famous paean to the productive advantages of division of labor, Smith went on to deplore the effect of excessive specialization on the individuals subjected to it. Farther on in the *Wealth of Nations*, Smith wrote that a worker assigned to repeat the same few tasks again and again became "stupid and ignorant" and suffered "torpor of his mind." Smith was especially worried about the effect of excessive division of labor on people's moral character. Such a person, he wrote, became "not only incapable of relishing or bearing a part in any rational conversation, but of conceiving any generous, noble, or tender sentiment, and consequently of forming any just judgment concerning many even of the ordinary duties of private life. Of the great and extensive interests of his country he is altogether incapable of judging."

Do we think Smith is referring to his successors of two-plus centuries later – today's economists? If so, I hope I've escaped the trap.

14

My Life and Research Strategy

John Hull

It is an honor to be invited to contribute to this volume. Indeed, I am somewhat overawed when I look at the list of other academics who are contributing. There can be no question that my career path has been different from theirs. I did not get my PhD from a top school, and my research has tended to be influenced as much by practitioners as by other academics. My research strategy (and life philosophy) may therefore be an outlier, but I hope it will nevertheless be of interest to readers.

MY BACKGROUND

My undergraduate degree was in math at Cambridge University in England. The Mathematical Tripos lasted three years. The courses in the first two years (Parts IA and IB of the Tripos) were compulsory. In the third year (Part II of the Tripos), students specialized in pure or applied math. I chose pure math simply because I enjoyed it. At the time I made this choice, I had no firm ideas about a future career. (Of course, applied math would have been somewhat more useful given the way my career actually developed.)

I was offered the chance to stay on at Cambridge and do Part III of the Mathematical Tripos and (assuming I fared well in that) a PhD, but I decided I wanted to apply my skills in the outside world. In those days, mathematicians, physicists, engineers, and the like had not made their mark on the financial sector, and there were relatively few career opportunities outside of teaching that involved math. I liked probability theory and toyed with the idea of becoming an actuary. I liked number theory and considered joining GCHQ (the British government's code-breaking unit). In the end, I decided to do a master's degree in operational research at Lancaster University. Operational research was a relatively new discipline, and Lancaster was considered the best place in the UK to study it.

When I graduated from Lancaster, I again rejected the opportunity to stay on and do a PhD. Instead, I accepted a job as a corporate planning analyst at a large UK footwear retailer, which had 2,000 outlets and was based in Leicester. I got involved in helping to fine-tune the software that determined which shoes were stocked in which sizes in which retail outlets. I was also involved to some extent in strategic decisions concerned with determining which outlets should be closed and where new outlets should be opened.

After two years I was, by chance, offered a job as a senior research officer on a project concerned with decision theory at London Business School. I was not unhappy with my career in the private sector, but the project sounded interesting and the offer came at a time when I wanted to move to London for personal reasons. I therefore accepted the offer and moved back into the academic world. (Arguably, therefore, my career in academia started largely by chance.) I did some teaching at LBS, found that I enjoyed it (although at the time I was not very good at it), and moved to the School of Management at Cranfield Institute of Technology (now Cranfield University), where I decided it was time to get a PhD. My position at Cranfield was lecturer (equivalent to assistant professor), but in reality I was part PhD student and part instructor. This arrangement may seem strange to many people, but it was not uncommon in UK universities at the time.[1]

At first, I was in the management science area at Cranfield. One day, out of the blue, I was offered the chance to switch from management science to finance and accounting. (In many British universities, finance and accounting constitute a single area.) I accepted without hesitation, as my PhD research was at the interface of management science and finance. Switching areas is unusual, if not impossible, at most business schools. I will always be grateful to David Myddelton, who headed up the finance and accounting area at Cranfield and was sufficiently open-minded to give me the chance to rebrand myself.

I finally finished my PhD and accepted a one-year visiting position at the University of British Columbia's Business School, teaching management accounting and corporate finance.[2] At the end of my year at UBC, I returned to Cranfield expecting to stay there. But halfway through the next year I got a call from Peter Lusztig, who was dean of the Business School at UBC, inviting me to visit UBC again the following year. I managed (with difficulty) to persuade Cranfield to let me take another unpaid leave of absence and spent another year at UBC (again teaching management accounting and corporate finance).

My two years at UBC gave me the opportunity to attend many excellent research workshops and fill in some of the gaps in my knowledge of the finance literature. During the second year I spent at UBC, I started to think about the possibility of getting a permanent position in North America. I did not go on the job market in the usual way (and this may well have been a mistake), but a few Canadian schools had heard about me through the grapevine and invited me to present a paper. I was offered tenure-stream positions at Simon Fraser and York University, as well as UBC. I chose York University in Toronto for two reasons. First, I would be teaching only finance. (The move to York completed my rebranding. I was in "finance," not "management science" or "finance and accounting."). Second, I liked the idea of working in a financial center, as my research had an applied focus.

MATH EDUCATION

Before saying more about the development of my research interests, I would like to digress a little on the subject of math education. Math skills have been really important to me in my research, and readers may be surprised to learn that I consider that the most important part of my math education was in high school, not in university.

I received my high school education in the UK in the 1960s at an excellent school, Bradford Grammar School. The British high school system required students who wanted to go to university to specialize to a far greater extent than the current North American high school system. As early as age twelve, students selected three subjects for specialization. These were the subjects in which they would take exams, known as A-levels, at the age of seventeen. After flirting with classics (which would have led me to take Latin, Greek, and ancient history at A-level), I chose math, higher math, and physics as my three subjects.[3] This meant that before I left high school I was doing advanced calculus, solving fairly complicated differential equations, wrestling with some quite difficult applied math problems in fields such as mechanics and fluid dynamics, and so on.

I firmly believe that it is important for students who will follow quantitative careers to take relatively advanced courses in math at a young age. First-year university is too late for this. At university you can learn math skills well enough to pass exams. But if they are to be internalized so that they can be used for problems encountered in later life, the skills must be acquired at a young age. This may not be true for other disciplines, but I firmly believe that it is true for math.

It is no coincidence that PhD students in quantitative disciplines (including finance and economics) in North America have in most cases attended high school outside of North America. Typically, these students come from the Far East, India, Eastern Europe, Denmark, and so on, where the level of specialization in high school is quite different from that in North America. It is not just university PhD programs that find it necessary to recruit from abroad. When banks and companies such as Microsoft look for people for quant jobs, they often end up hiring individuals who were born outside North America.

The United States and Canada appear to have a policy of importing people for jobs that require quant skills. I am not saying this has worked badly. Indeed, in many respects, it has worked very well. But we have not been developing the math skills of the students who go through our high school systems as much as we might.[4] Math skills are becoming increasingly important in many walks of life. Importing quant talent might not be the best strategy for us to follow going forward. As India, China, and other countries offer more opportunities, their students may become less inclined to emigrate to North America. Furthermore, there is a trend in the United States toward making the immigration of highly qualified individuals more difficult.

GETTING STARTED IN DERIVATIVES

When I joined York University in 1981, I hardly knew what an option was. However, within a year, I did write a paper with a colleague, Nahum Biger, on the valuation of currency options.[5] This led to an invitation in 1984 from the Royal Bank of Canada to give a one-day seminar to its currency options traders. (By this time Nahum had moved to Israel.) The traders were based in New York, London, and Toronto and were in Toronto for three days of meetings. I accepted the invitation to give the seminar on the first of the three days, but then realized I didn't know enough about currency options to fill a whole day! I explained my problem to Alan White, who had just joined York University. We agreed to make it a joint presentation and to include Monte Carlo simulation results on the performance of delta hedging. Very quickly, Alan developed the necessary software.

We presented the simulation results at the seminar. The results showed that delta hedging worked quite well, but the participants at the seminar were skeptical. One very sharp member of the group told us the results were unrealistic because we were assuming that volatility was constant, whereas in reality volatility moved around a lot. We argued (incorrectly) that delta hedging would work well when volatility was stochastic, provided that the latest information on volatility was used in the calculation of delta. (Remember, this was 1984 and we were new to the field.) We agreed to settle the issue by modifying our Monte Carlo simulation software so that it incorporated a stochastic volatility and sending in the results before the group left at the end of the three days of meetings. Of course, when we modified the program, we found that the person who made the comment during the seminar was right and we were totally wrong. The extra source of uncertainty, volatility, resulted in delta hedging working far less well than it had in our original Monte Carlo simulations.

At the time of the Royal Bank presentation, neither Alan nor I regarded derivatives as our main area of research. However, that one comment at the seminar changed the focus of our research. It led to several years of joint research on stochastic volatility (and indirectly to many more years of joint research on other derivatives topics). In the mid-1980s, we looked at the impact of stochastic volatility on both the pricing of options and the hedging of options. A hedging paper, which arose in a very direct way out of the Royal Bank seminar, is Hull and White (1987a). The main pricing paper was Hull and White (1987b), which we are proud to note is the tenth most cited paper published by the *Journal of Finance*.

Doing research on stochastic volatility was a great way to learn about the theoretical underpinnings of derivatives pricing, and asset pricing in general. When volatility is stochastic, a derivatives price depends on two stochastic variables: the asset price and its volatility. One is the price of a traded security, while the other is not. As a result, if you know how to price a call option on an asset when volatility is stochastic, you are in good shape to price almost any other derivative. I can remember spending a lot of time in the mid-1980s pouring over papers such as Cox, Ingersoll, and Ross (1985).

A PARTNERSHIP

Alan White and I both moved from York University to the University of Toronto in 1988. After finishing our stochastic volatility research, we moved on to do research in areas such as numerical procedures for valuing derivatives, the pricing of interest rate derivatives, methods for calculating value at risk, the impact of counterparty credit risk on derivatives pricing, the pricing of employee stock options, the valuation of credit derivatives, and lessons from the credit crisis.

We have now been working together for almost thirty years. It must be one of the longest-running partnerships in the history of academia (and hopefully it still has a few years to go). It has worked well. We both understand the derivatives pricing and risk management literature in the same way. That means that we often can "talk in shorthand" to each other when discussing research issues. This is usually very efficient. When I talk to another researcher, I find that it can take a much longer time for the communication to be effective.

Being a researcher can be a lonely existence. Working with someone who has the same perspectives as oneself on research and on the academic world in general certainly improves the quality of one's life. How should a researcher choose coauthors? What are the characteristics of someone who is likely to be a good research collaborator? These are tough questions. I think you know a good research collaborator when you find one, but it is hard to list what his or her characteristics should be in advance.[6] Peter Diamond describes the choice of coauthors as "the elephant in the room" in his essay in this volume.

MY BOOKS

I am probably best known for my book *Options, Futures, and Other Derivatives*.[7] This arose from lecture notes I prepared when teaching an elective course in options to MBAs at York University in the 1980s. At the time, many people working in the Toronto financial community were very interested in learning about the new science of pricing and hedging derivatives. As a result, a number of people from downtown audited my course. They and the MBA students in my classes provided me with a lot of valuable feedback, and the lecture notes were converted into a book in 1988 (at about the time Alan and I moved to University of Toronto).

I am often asked why Alan is not a coauthor on the book, given that almost everything else I have written on derivatives has been coauthored with him. I do not remember exactly how this happened. The book was based on my lecture notes and, as I recall, Alan was involved in other projects when I worked on converting the lecture notes into a book. But I do remember that Alan was kind enough to read my manuscript and give me many detailed comments.[8] Another person who provided valuable feedback on that first manuscript was Eduardo Schwartz.

Only in my wildest dreams could I have hoped for the book to be the success it has been. The first edition was about 300 pages (with a fairly small page size and big typeface) and its sales were modest. With successive editions, the book grew in both its size and its sales. The eighth edition is more than 800 pages long, and I have lost count of the number of foreign language translations. One of the unusual features of the book is that it sells equally well in the practitioner and college markets.

Writing textbooks is often regarded as a waste of time because it takes time away from research. Certainly, it is a very time-consuming process. I now have three books, each of which goes into a new edition every three years, and so every year I have to produce a new edition of one of the books.[9] I do most of the work in the summer while spending time with my family at our lakeside cottage.

I like to think of my books as more than just textbooks because they are read by both academics and practitioners. Also, *Options, Futures, and Other Derivatives* has been quite influential. It has been quoted by regulators and cited in court decisions.[10] One of my proudest moments was in 1997 when it was mentioned in the press release announcing the Nobel Prize of Robert Merton and Myron Scholes.[11]

Is writing books a waste of time? My own personal experience is that it can complement research quite well. Derivatives and risk management are fast-changing disciplines. I find that my books help to keep me up to date. They also force me to structure my thinking of the disciplines in a logical way. For example, the material I wrote on counterparty credit risk for *Risk Management and Financial Institutions*[12] led indirectly to research on wrong-way risk with Alan White.[13]

RESEARCH IDEAS

Alan and I have always had close links with practitioners. We speak regularly at academic/practitioner conferences and are in regular email contact with practitioners on a range of topics concerned with derivatives and risk management. Many of our ideas for research have come from, and continue to come from, these interactions.

I have already described how our research on stochastic volatility started with a comment by an employee of the Royal Bank of Canada at an in-house seminar. There are many similar examples. One result of our approach to research is that the research has tended to mirror the concerns of the market. As the interest rate derivative market was growing in the 1990s, our research focused on the valuation of caps, swaptions, and other interest rate derivatives. This led to what is referred to as the Hull-White interest rate model.[14] Once the model and its analytic results had been developed, we spent a lot of time developing trinomial tree numerical procedures for Hull-White and other one-factor interest rate models. During the 2000–2010 period, as the credit derivatives market grew rapidly, we focused on the valuation of products such as credit default swaps and collateralized debt obligations and developed the implied copula approach. When accounting standards for employee stock options were changing in 2003, we researched the valuation of employee stock options. When value at risk was becoming established as the risk measure of choice (at least by regulators) in the 1990s, we researched ways of improving estimates. Our long-standing interest in quantifying counterparty credit risk in derivatives arises in part from discussions on this that we have had with risk managers and regulators over the years.

My research strategy would not, of course, work in all areas of finance and economics. Derivatives research is different from much other research in that derivatives practitioners and derivatives academics are, to a large extent, interested in solving the same problems and answering the same questions. Other academics who work in derivatives would have no difficulty following my strategy (indeed, many of them do so), and the strategy can probably be used to some extent by those who work in investments or macroeconomics. However, my colleagues in corporate finance might well have quite a bit of difficulty relating to the research strategy I have outlined.

Academic researchers tend to get their ideas for research by going to workshops, talking to other academics, reading academic journals, and attending academic conferences. These are important activities. But going to a practitioner or academic/practitioner conference from time to time can be useful. All it takes is one really good idea to come from attending a two-day conference for it to be time well spent. Trade journals are also a sometimes underestimated source of research ideas.

THE ROLE OF LUCK

Looking back on my career to date, it seems as though a number of chance events have shaped my professional activities. The job at London

Business School, which led to my move back to academia, happened by chance; my move from the UK to Canada happened by chance; my derivatives research with Alan started by chance; and so on. Was I just lucky to end up where I am, doing something I enjoy and am reasonably good at?

There can be no question that luck plays an important part in anyone's life. But we should not underestimate the importance of education, industriousness, perseverance, pragmatism, searching for opportunities, and taking full advantage of opportunities when they present themselves. If the opportunities I accepted had not arisen, others would have. Hopefully I would have been sensible enough to take full advantage of them. To quote Denzel Washington:

> Luck is where opportunity meets preparation,

and Thomas Jefferson:

> I'm a great believer in luck, and I find the harder I work the more I have of it.

Luck tends to happen more often when we are doing what we enjoy. My favorite quote of all is from Steve Jobs's commencement speech at Stanford in 2005. I think it applies to the choices we researchers make:

> You've got to find what you love. And that is as true for your work as it is for your lovers. Your work is going to fill a large part of your life, and the only way to be truly satisfied is to do what you believe is great work. And the only way to do great work is to love what you do. If you haven't found it yet, keep looking. Don't settle. As with all matters of the heart, you'll know when you find it. And, like any great relationship, it just gets better and better as the years roll on. So keep looking until you find it. Don't settle.

REFERENCES

Biger, N. and J. C. Hull (1983). "Valuation of Currency Options," *Financial Management* 12, no. 1: 24–28.

Cox, J. C., J. E. Ingersoll, and S. A. Ross (1985). "An Intertemporal General Equilibrium Model of Asset Prices," *Econometrica* 53: 363–384.

Hull, J. C. (2014). *Fundamentals of Futures and Options Markets*, 8th ed. Upper Saddle River, NJ: Pearson.

(2012a). *Options, Futures, and Other Derivatives*, 8th ed. Upper Saddle River, NJ: Pearson.

(2012b). *Risk Management and Financial Institutions*, 3rd ed. Hoboken, NJ: John Wiley and Sons.

Hull, J. C. and A. White (1987a). "Hedging the Risks from Writing Foreign Currency Options," *Journal of International Money and Finance* 6, no. 2: 131–152.

(1987b). "The Pricing of Options on Assets with Stochastic Volatilities," *Journal of Finance* 42, no. 2: 281–300.

(1990). "Pricing Interest-Rate Derivative Securities", *Review of Financial Studies* 3, no. 4: 573–592.

(2012). "CVA and Wrong-Way Risk," *Financial Analysts Journal* 68, no. 5: 58–69.

Notes

1 I would not recommend the arrangement. I have always regretted not doing a traditional North American PhD in finance.

2 I was interviewed for this position by Michael Brennan, who was visiting the UK at the time. He probably had some reservations about my knowledge of the finance literature, but he was very courteous and was kind enough to recommend me for the job.

3 I was actually in the classics stream for three years. The move to science and math was a good move because I was not particularly good at classics.

4 Apart from the lack of specialization in high school, another problem in North America is that it is not considered "cool" by teenagers to be good at math.

5 See Biger and Hull (1983).

6 Perhaps choosing a coauthor is like choosing a spouse in this respect.

7 See Hull (2012a).

8 Alan has also done most of the development work on DerivaGem, the widely used software that accompanies my books.

9 The books are *Options, Futures and Other Derivatives*; *Risk Management and Financial Institutions*; and *Fundamentals of Futures and Options Markets*. The last-named book, Hull (2014), is sometimes referred to as "Baby Hull" because it covers some of the same ground as *Options, Futures and Other Derivatives*, but in a gentler way.

10 Unbelievable though it sounds, I have even been asked by derivatives professionals at banks to include particular things in the book because it will make it easier for them to be approved internally.

11 See www.nobelprize.org/nobel_prizes/economics/laureates/1997/press.html.

12 See Hull (2012b).

13 See Hull and White (2012).

14 See Hull and White (1990).

15

How I Ended Up Being a Multifaceted Economist and the Mentors I Have Had

Michael D. Intriligator

As is clear from my title, professor of economics, political science, and public policy at UCLA, I ended up being a multifaceted economist, working not only in economics per se but also in international relations as part of my involvement in political science and public policy issues. Even within economics itself, while most economists work in one or two fields, I work in many, including:

1. Economic theory and mathematical economics
2. Econometrics
3. Health economics
4. Reform of the Russian economy
5. Strategy and arms control

In this essay I would like to explain how this happened, starting from the beginning when I was an undergraduate student at MIT, majoring in mathematics. As I started the junior- and senior-level courses in mathematics, I felt that the material was too abstract, and I was looking for something that was tangible and more connected to the real world. I took a course on twentieth-century economists taught by Elspeth Huxley Rostow, and it was this course that convinced me to become an economist. The course included a few lectures by Elspeth's husband, Walt W. Rostow, at that time professor of economics at MIT and later to become national security adviser to President Lyndon B. Johnson during the Vietnam War. (They both ended up at the LBJ School of the University of Texas, Austin, and I saw them there many years later when visiting James Galbraith while Elspeth was the dean of the school.)

As part of this course Elspeth had us read Roy Harrod's *Life of Keynes*, and this book changed my life. Keynes was involved in so many interesting activities: reformulating economic theory in his 1935 classic, *The General Theory of Employment, Interest, and Money*, creating the World Bank and the International Monetary Fund at the Bretton Woods conference, starting the Arts Council of Great Britain, being part of the Bloomsbury Group, making a huge fortune for King's College, Cambridge, as its bursar, marrying a Russian ballerina, and much more. As I read this book I decided to become an economist, with Keynes as my role model or mentor, the first of many.

I graduated from MIT in 1959 and went to Yale on a Woodrow Wilson Fellowship to study for a PhD in economics. There I had the opportunity to take courses from Jacob Marschak, James Tobin, and Tjalling Koopmans, among other eminent economists. I loved the economics and Yale but missed Cambridge, so I returned to MIT to complete my PhD. There I worked with Robert Solow and Paul Samuelson, who also became important role models for me. I particularly admired Solow's work in that it encompassed both economic theory and empirical research. He chaired my doctoral committee, and in my dissertation I attempted to integrate his separate work on disembodied and embodied technical change, involving both economic theory and econometrics.

I spent the summer before completing my PhD in the Economics Department of the RAND Corporation in Santa Monica, California. There I became a colleague and friend of Daniel Ellsberg, and we had long conversations about strategy and arms control. As a result of these conversations I started to work in this field, initially by developing a dynamic model of a missile war that provided an extension of Ellsberg's article in the *American Economic Review* about strategic choices in a nuclear war. Dan also became an important role model and mentor for me, and he continued to fill that role much later in his revelation of the Pentagon Papers, a very brave act in my view, both then and now.

After that summer I returned to MIT and completed my doctorate, married Devrie, and took my first and basically only job at UCLA, all in 1963. Devrie is an astrophysicist and space scientist, and I like to note when meeting new people that we reverse the usual stereotype of the husband in the physical sciences and the wife in the social sciences. I also arranged to stay on at RAND as a resident consultant, where I continued my work in strategy and arms control and other areas. I enjoyed having two offices, two sets of colleagues, and two different issue areas to work on that I re-created after leaving RAND by becoming a senior fellow of the Milken Institute in Santa Monica.

At UCLA I became a colleague and friend of Jacob (Jascha) Marschak, who had been my teacher at Yale and who had moved to UCLA a few years before me. He asked me to speak for the Interdisciplinary Colloquium on Mathematics in the Behavioral Sciences that he had started and invited me to join its Advisory Committee. Jascha was also a mentor to me about economics and the behavioral sciences in general, introducing me to other such sciences as a regular at the Colloquium. He had set up the Colloquium to break down the artificial barriers between university departments so scholars could communicate across departmental lines. When he died in July 1977, we had an emergency meeting of the Advisory Committee in which we decided to continue the Colloquium and name it the Jacob Marschak Interdisciplinary Colloquium on Mathematics in the Behavioral Sciences, and I became its director. We continued it as Jascha had run it, meeting alternative Fridays and covering all the behavioral sciences. After a few years, at a meeting of the Advisory Committee, one of our members, Marvin Hoffenberg, an economist in the UCLA Political Science Department, proposed we have an annual Marschak Memorial Lecture and we have added that, with the following as our speakers (the asterisks signify Nobel laureates):

1979–1980, Tjalling C. Koopmans *
1980–1981, Kenneth J. Arrow *
1981–1982, Lawrence R. Klein *
1982–1983, Herbert Simon *
1983–1984, Roy Radner
1984–1985, Paul A. Samuelson *
1985–1986, James Tobin *
1986–1987, Robert M. Solow *
1987–1988, Franco Modigliani *
1988–1989, Leonid Hurwicz *

1989–1990, Allen Newell
1990–1991, Murray Gell-Mann *
1991–1992, Wassily Leontief *
1992–1993, Anatol Rapoport
1993–1994, Francis Crick *
1994–1995, Gary S. Becker *
1995–1996, Harry Markowitz *
1996–1997, Marvin Minsky
1997–1998, Thomas C. Schelling *
1998–1999, James March
1999–2000, Edward Feigenbaum
2000–2001, E. O. Wilson
2001–2002, David Baltimore *
2002–2003, Jared Diamond
2003–2004, Daniel Kahneman *
2004–2005, Gerald Edelman *
2005–2006, Daniel L. McFadden *
2006–2007, Roald Hoffmann *
2007–2008, Vernon Smith *
2008–2009, Freeman Dyson
2009–2010, Frances Arnold
2010–2011, James Heckman *

The early speakers were all economists closely associated with Jascha, and then we broadened the lecture to include distinguished scientists from other fields, including many Nobel laureates. Now I run the Marschak Colloquium with my colleague in public policy, Mark Kleiman.

My work in economic theory began with my dissertation but expanded substantially as a result of teaching courses in this subject and writing my first book, *Mathematical Optimization and Economic Theory*. My review of the literature made me appreciate enormously the work of Kenneth Arrow, who wrote many of the seminal papers and reviews in various areas of the subject. When the North-Holland Publishing Company approached me about editing the *Handbook of Mathematical Economics* I responded that it was an excellent idea, but I didn't want to do it alone and suggested that the ideal coeditor for this handbook would be Ken Arrow. I had met Ken on my sabbatical at Stanford and approached him about editing this book together, and we did so. The book was a success, and the publisher invited us to edit a book series, Handbooks in Economics, which we have been editing for many years. The series, now published by Elsevier, covers many of the traditional fields of economics and also includes some newer ones. In the process of editing this series with Ken, I've learned much about economics and other areas from him, and he is one of my most important mentors.

My work in econometrics also began with my dissertation and continued with my second book, *Econometric Models, Techniques, and Applications*, published by Prentice-Hall. In addition, I edited the first three volumes of the *Handbook of Econometrics* with Zvi Griliches, another mentor. This was the second handbook in the Handbooks in Economics series, and we have brought out several later volumes of this handbook edited by very distinguished econometricians, Robert Engle, Daniel L. McFadden, James Heckman, and Edward Leamer.

My work in health economics started with my participation in the University of Southern California Human Resources Research Center, which led to several articles and a book on the US health care system. I later worked with Dr. Eric Fonkalsrud, the former chief of pediatric surgery at UCLA on reforming the health care system in the United States through a process of expansion of the Medicare program, starting by bringing pre-school children and pregnant women into the program and then gradually and predictably expanding the program so that everyone is in Medicare. He is another mentor.

My work on Russia stems from my many trips to that country to participate in conferences or visit several research institutes. Russian coauthors and colleagues influenced my work there. They included Vitalii I. Goldanski, who was the director of the Semenyov Institute of Chemical Physics and whom I met while attending the Pugwash Conferences, where he led the Soviet delegation. We wrote a paper entitled "U.S.-Soviet Relations: From Confrontation to Cooperation Through Verificational Deterrence," and he was another mentor. I also was inspired by working with Vladimir (Volodya) I. Keilis-Borok on several papers on prediction of the economy and of crime rates, and he was yet another mentor. I have also been a visiting professor at the Moscow School of Economics and taught a short course on economic theory there, using my book *Mathematical Optimization and Economic Theory* at the invitation of my friend and colleague, academician Alexander (Sasha) Nekipelov, the director (dean) of MSE.

My work on strategy and arms control began with my conversations with Dan Ellsberg at RAND in 1962 and continues with my recent work on nuclear proliferation and on terrorism. Many of my publications in this area are joint ones with Dagobert L. (Bob) Brito at Rice University. In fact, I have published more papers with Bob than with anyone else, and they are on a variety of topics, most involving strategy, security, and arms control issues.

Several people have asked Bob or me why some of our papers are authored by "Brito and Intriligator," while others are authored by "Intriligator and Brito." Bob and I have an agreement that the person who initiated the study and authored the first draft would be the first author. In the past few years I have been teaching an interdisciplinary honors course on terrorism at UCLA with two colleagues, Dr. Peter Katona of the UCLA Medical School and Robert Spich of the UCLA Anderson School of Management. Peter Katona and I have edited two books on terrorism jointly with John Sullivan of the Los Angeles County Sheriff's Department.

I am grateful to all the people I have worked with over the years on a wide range of topics. I have learned much from all of them and very much appreciate their guidance and inspiration.

16

Searching for My Personal Philosophy

Peter B. Kenen

When I was invited to contribute to this volume, I had to ask myself whether I had a personal philosophy. I had never given the matter much thought. I had therefore to recall the events and circumstances that led me to where I am today.

HOW I BECAME AN ECONOMIST

I come from a family that was avidly interested in world affairs. My earliest memories include the voices of Franklin Roosevelt, Winston Churchill, and Adolph Hitler's interpreter ("Der Führer says …"). I even recall being taken by my father to hear Eduard Benes and Fiorello LaGuardia denounce the Munich Agreement. My father, a journalist, was one of the founders of the American Newspaper Guild and an active Zionist. He was one of the Jewish leaders who attended the San Francisco Conference, concerned to protect the interests of the Jewish community in Palestine, and he was later a member of Israel's first delegation to the United Nations, which may be why I became very interested in the work of that organization. During my college years, in fact, I obtained accreditation as a UN correspondent for Columbia University's student-run radio station and a network of other such stations.

When I arrived at Morningside Heights in 1950 to start my freshman year at Columbia, I had no intention of becoming an academic, let alone an economist. I didn't even know what economists did. In my first two years of college, moreover, my efforts were devoted largely to Columbia's celebrated courses in the humanities and in contemporary civilization (and I taught the latter when I returned as a faculty member). The faculty of the college included some of the nation's leading intellectuals, such as Lionel Trilling, Richard Hofstadter, and Fritz Stern, and I came to know them well when I returned as a faculty member. (During the Columbia student uprising in 1968, I joined them and others in a self-appointed caucus that met at Fritz Stern's apartment and thus called itself the Stern Gang, although we were neither terrorists nor counterterrorists but merely concerned to counsel against attempts by other faculty members to mediate between the students' leaders and the university administration.)

In my last two undergraduate years at Columbia, I divided my time between courses in politics and economics, and it was not until my senior year that I decided to go on to graduate work in economics. For a long time, I had thought of joining the United Nations Secretariat, which was my main reason for taking undergraduate courses in economics. I even wrote an inordinately long senior seminar paper on India's five-year plan. I changed my mind, however, however, when Senator Joseph McCarthy extended his search for hidden Communists to US members of the UN Secretariat, and I was then uncertain about what I would do with the rest of my life. I did not yet contemplate an academic career. Had I known, moreover, that economics would become as mathematical as it is today, I doubt that I would have chosen to do graduate work in economics. My only formal training in mathematics was a yearlong course in analytic geometric and differential calculus, which I took to satisfy Columbia's math/science requirement. (One day, my instructor, Samuel Eilenberg, a distinguished mathematician, asked me whether I planned to be a math major. When I said, "No, sir," he said, "Thank God." What mathematical competence I acquired thereafter I owe to a noncredit course for graduate students at Harvard, which was, by present standards, fairly elementary.)

In those days, however, it was possible to rely largely on diagrams rather than equations, and that is what I did in my early papers on the theory of international trade. It soon became clear to me, however, that I could most readily make way professionally by focusing on international monetary economics, a less math-intensive subject, rather than trade theory, and that is what I have done for most of my career.

My decision to contemplate an academic career began to take shape when I was urged by my faculty adviser to apply for a Woodrow Wilson Fellowship, and that is what I did, choosing economics rather than political science because economics appeared to offer a broader range of career opportunities. Woodrow Wilson fellows, however, were asked to give serious thought to a teaching career, and I did that too, deciding early in my first year as a Harvard graduate student that I would indeed become an academic. Nevertheless, I had modest expectations. When I proposed to my wife, I warned her that we were likely to wind up at a midlevel institution and that I would never earn more than $10,000 a year. But she had more faith in me, believing that I might make $15,000.

At Harvard, I was fortunate to take courses with Wassily Leontief, Gottfried Haberler, and Alvin Hansen, and I went on to write my dissertation at the London School of Economics, where I had the good fortune to participate in seminars led by Lionel Robbins and James Meade and to meet another American student, Richard Cooper (whose age I can always calculate because he owned a 1934 Ford that was just as old as he was then).

My first published papers did in fact deal with trade theory (Kenen 1957, 1959), and I wrote another later (Kenen 1965), inspired by the pioneering work on human capital done by my Columbia colleagues Gary Becker and Jacob Mincer. Yet I wrote my dissertation on a monetary matter. Written at the London School of Economics under the supervision of Alan Day and Richard Sayers, it dealt with monetary policy and the British balance of payments. (I recall to this day my first encounter with Sayers, to whom I had submitted a draft chapter. It was, he said, "not bad," and I was crestfallen. But Alan Day restored my confidence by assuring me that this was high praise indeed coming from Sayers.) To my genuine surprise and gratification, the dissertation won the Wells Prize and was subsequently published by Harvard University Press (Kenen 1960). My work since then has focused mainly on international monetary matters, although my own favorite paper is the 1965 article previously cited, "Nature, Capital, and Trade."[1] As for my favorite books, the first is *Asset Markets, Exchange Rates, and Economic Integration* (1980), coauthored with Polly Reynolds Allen, and the other is *Economic and Monetary Union in Europe* (1995), reflecting work I did at the Bank of England as Houblon-Norman fellow, during the run-up to the Maastricht Summit that adopted the plan for European monetary union. The book was based on memoranda I wrote when I was co-opted to participate in the work of the Bank's staff committee that was monitoring the preparations for the Maastricht Summit. Because I was party to those deliberations, I felt bound to submit the manuscript of the book to the Bank's senior official concerned with the issues involved. His only request was that I refer to Britain's opt-out as an opt-in, a suggestion I declined to adopt.

FROM COLUMBIA TO PRINCETON

When I returned to the United States from the LSE, I faced a choice between teaching positions at Harvard and Columbia. Although I already knew that instructors at Columbia were rarely promoted and taught only undergraduates in Columbia College, I chose Columbia, partly out of loyalty to my alma mater and partly because my wife preferred New York to Cambridge. I know now, however, that I had been offered the position at Columbia with the expectation that I would indeed teach graduate courses eventually. Nor could I have foreseen the untimely death of Ragnar Nurkse, which created an immediate need for someone to staff the yearlong graduate course in international economics – both the trade side and the monetary side – and I would be asked to teach those courses.

I remained at Columbia for some fifteen years, serving briefly as department chairman and, in my last two years, as university provost following the student uprising in the spring of 1968. During the student demonstrations, I divided my time between Columbia and my home in New Jersey, where I had been nominated to run for election to New Jersey's delegation to the Chicago Democratic Convention, pledged to the candidacy of Eugene McCarthy, my one quest for elective office. I won and went to Chicago, where I was among the delegates who led a march to the convention hall on the night of Hubert Humphrey's acceptance speech. I was duly arrested and spent a few hours as a guest in one of Mayor Daley's jail cells. I was later found guilty of being a "pedestrian obstructing traffic" and paid a small fine. But when I sent letters to the federal agencies with which I held security clearances, informing them of my arrest, the head of one agency replied with a handwritten answer: "Right on!"

Having spent so many years at Columbia as a student, faculty member, and administrator, I decided that it was time for a change, and I accepted Princeton's offer to hold the Walker Professorship in Economics and International Finance.

My years at Princeton have been very rewarding. Upon the retirement of Fritz Machlup, I became director of the International Finance Section, which published essays and studies in international finance, although that was a misnomer, given present-day usage, as they were in fact monographs on international monetary economics. I taught the graduate courses in international economics and an undergraduate course in that same subject. I was fortunate, moreover, in being asked to join the so-called Bellagio Group of international economists and senior government officials concerned with international monetary matters. It was led then by Fritz Machlup, Robert Triffin, and William Fellner but included among its younger members Richard Cooper and Robert Mundell. We met twice yearly for more than a decade, disbanding only after the collapse of the effort to reform the international monetary system following the advent of floating exchange rates and the failure of an official body, the Committee of Twenty, to agree on a plan for comprehensive reform. (Years later, I was asked to revive and lead a second incarnation of the Bellagio Group, which comprises academics and officials and meets once each year. It is now led by Barry Eichengreen.) I was also a founding member of the Group of Thirty, comprising officials, academics, and bankers, which has been a remarkably productive endeavor.

Only once in my career was I strongly tempted to leave the academic world. That was when Jacques de Larosière, managing director of the International Monetary Fund, asked me to become director of the Research Department and economic counselor at the Fund, a position previously held for many years by Edward Bernstein. In those days, however, this was deemed to be a career appointment, not what it is now, a short-term appointment, and I was reluctant to give up teaching and the freedom to undertake research on subjects of my choosing. I am fortunate, however, that Jacques forgave me, and I cherish our long friendship.

WHAT I BELIEVE

On most matters, I continue to hold the values and views I acquired long ago, reflecting in part my upbringing. I am a liberal in the American sense, believing that government can be and often is an agent of beneficial change and that equality of opportunity should be a paramount aim of public policy, whether it is the opportunity to obtain a first-rate education or affordable health care. I favor the public financing of electoral campaigns or, at least, strict limits on political contributions, because I do not believe that private wealth should confer political power. I am nevertheless aware of the practical problems involved, including the risk that public financing could perpetuate the dominance of well-established political movements. I also doubt that there is any way to regulate or limit the political activities of private-sector entities, including businesses and labor unions, without impairing the protection of free speech afforded by the US Constitution.

In short, I have throughout my life worried about the consequences of granting unconstrained freedom to individuals and institutions that can do great harm to others. That is why I believe in speed limits for drivers and proxies for speed limits to constrain the activities of firms, especially financial institutions, that can do much harm to so many. As I write, many governments are engaged in fashioning the equivalent of speed limits for large financial institutions, and I welcome those efforts, although I acknowledge that those constraints may have adverse effects on nonfinancial institutions, especially new and novel ones, by limiting their access to credit.

I likewise favor strict limits on the emission of air pollution, even though they may raise the cost of producing electricity. Those emissions threaten the livelihoods and even the lives of millions of people, let alone generations not yet born. In short, I believe that governments have an obligation to intervene whenever private-sector practices have adverse consequences for groups of individuals or whole nations. Nevertheless, I prefer the use of taxes rather than outright prohibitions on economic activities that can have damaging effects on others. Returning to the example I gave before, I favor constraints on the overall level of damaging emissions combined with an economically efficient regime to distribute the costs of those constraints, such as a cap-and-trade regime. I strongly favor free trade, not only because it promotes a globally efficient allocation of economic activity, the conventional case for international specialization, but because it fosters competition among firms that would otherwise have much market power in their own countries.

I readily acknowledge that the choice among various ways to limit externalities and market power has nontrivial political dimensions, which is one reason I prefer democracies to benevolent dictatorships. Democratic governments can and do make errors of omission and commission, but they can be voted out of office by those they govern. I do not have blind faith in the democratic process. Although one-person, one-vote is, in my view, the best of political systems, I also know that money talks, as does the fear of the unknown, especially in an era of mass communication, when voters are bombarded with half-truths and outright lies. I may be unduly influenced, however, by the current political environment in the United States, where lies about the birthplace of President Obama and about the inclusion in health-care reform of provisions creating "death panels" have poisoned political discourse.

In light of what I have already written, readers will surely understand why I reject one fad – the evaluation of economic policies solely in terms of their effects on so-called economic freedom (see, e.g., Grubel 2009). Because we rightly limit the freedom of individuals and firms to engage in activities injurious to others, so too must we favor public policies that have the incidental effect of limiting the unconstrained exercise of property rights. Grubel may truly believe that "market economies eliminate recessions without deliberate government intervention." They do so, he says, through automatic stabilizers involving financial markets and government budgets, and he goes on to explain how those stabilizers work. Whether he and others are right or wrong about the power of those automatic stabilizers, there is surely reason to question the speed with which they would operate, as well as their distributional effects.

Going further, I question the case for relying entirely on the capacity of "economic freedom" to maintain or achieve economic stability, when weighed against the human cost of the untrammeled exercise of "economic freedom," even if it could be trusted to do that eventually. There may be reason to question the quality of the particular policies adopted by the Obama administration to combat the effects of the financial crisis and the ensuing deep recession.

But to elevate "economic freedom" to something intrinsically precious and efficacious that should never be abridged is, in my view, to trample on more fundamental rights – the right to secure employment or, at the very least, compensatory payments to those who lose their jobs, as well as the right of everyone injured through no fault of their own to adequate relief from the hardships of a deep economic downturn. Property rights cannot come before the fundamental human right to a reasonable degree of economic security.

Like most economists, I favor free trade, not merely because it is conducive to efficient specialization within individual countries, but also because it enlarges the market in which national firms must compete and thus promotes competition within every national market. Carried to its logical conclusion, however, this Smithian argument for free trade implies that governments are morally bound to provide effective forms of adjustment assistance to those who are displaced by all sorts of economic changes, especially changes in trade policy that firms and workers cannot readily anticipate. These should include educational opportunities and temporary income support for those who lose their livelihood because of abrupt trade policy changes, which differ qualitatively from the more gradual dislocation that results from technological change and other economic innovations.

MY AUDIENCE

As an international economist, I know that my main audience is not the voting public so much as it is the groups of officials and politicians responsible for making decisions that do not always impinge directly on the lives of their countries' citizens. This is especially true of decisions involving the form and functioning of the international monetary system. In fact, the policy makers themselves don't always give enough thought to the long-term effects of their decisions. Many of those decisions, more-over, seem remote from the day-to-day concerns of the public at large, even from the usual concerns of most legislators. Households don't think about exchange rates unless they are planning a trip abroad, and legislators don't think about the monetary system until they are asked to appropriate taxpayers' money to finance some innovation, such as one I will mention shortly.

I have also learned that bureaucrats, policy makers, and legislators alike are nationalists at heart. They apply a parochial cost-benefit calculus to any proposed change in the international economic system – if indeed it is a system rather than an accretion of incremental changes such as those agreed upon at recent economic summits. Yet that is understandable, precisely because they are elected or appointed by their own countries' citizens or their citizens' representatives and should be accountable to them, not to the entire community of nations. Furthermore, they are rarely confronted by systemically important innovations that directly affect their national economies and their citizens' lives, and when those rare occasions arise, they do not always have sufficient imagination, let alone time, to contemplate the long-term implications. That is or ought to be the task of those who devote their careers to those matters.

Throughout my career, I have tried to help, whether by research and writing or serving as a consultant to a policy maker. I have, indeed, served as a consultant to officials at the US Treasury, going back to the Kennedy administration, and have found that to be very fruitful from my own stand-point. It has helped me to learn how policy is made and compelled me to think through questions that had not occurred to me before. At my retirement dinner at Princeton, Jeffrey Schafer, a former undersecretary of the treasury, paid me a high compliment. "Peter," he said, "was the perfect consultant. He asked what was on my mind rather than telling me what was on his mind." But I hope that I have done much more during my professional career – that I have spoken firmly about matters that were on my mind, hoping that my students, among others, would ask themselves what was really on their minds. That is what my best teachers did for me and what I have tried to do for my students.

I confess, however, that I have sometimes been too hard on my students. Determined to help them write clearly whatever the subject at issue, I have marked up their papers with copious comments in red ink. One of them came to me waving a paper that was very good but marred by my red pen. "Look," he said, "arterial bleeding." *Mea culpa.*

HOW I WORK

In his contribution to the first volume of *Eminent Economists*, Paul Samuelson told us that he is never short of interesting questions. I have envied him for that and, indeed, much else. I have sometimes run out of new questions to ask and have then returned to subjects I took up earlier in my career.

As I write this, for instance, I am drafting a paper on the creation of a so-called substitution account lodged within the International Monetary Fund into which foreign official holders of US dollars could deposit some of them for claims denominated in special drawing rights (SDRs), the Fund's own quasi-currency. The proposal was first made in the late 1970s and rejected by the US Treasury, because the United States would have been obliged to make deficiency payments to the IMF whenever the dollar value of the SDR fell below what it was when the dollars were deposited. It is therefore important to know what history can tell us about the evolution of the relevant interest rates and the dollar value of the SDR and to assess their impact on the solvency of the substitution account.

To this end, I once ran a voluminous set of simulations aimed at assessing the potential cost to the United States of a substitution account, using various hypothetical paths of the key variables, especially the dollar value of the SDR, and I am now engaged in a similar exercise, because the governor of China's central bank has revived the idea. There is an understandable reluctance on the part of US policy makers to entertain an idea of this sort, as they cannot predict with confidence the potential cost of the proposal. Equally important, however, they cannot predict with confidence the future course of China's policy regarding the currency composition of its huge reserves.

This simulation exercise is entertaining, like most of the projects I have undertaken. Indeed, I have rarely undertaken a project that did not promise to answer a question that interested me, whether it was theoretical or empirical, or something bearing on current or prospective policy issues. I don't yet know what I will do when I have completed the project I have just described but know that I will not be idle for long. Like Mr. Micawber, I firmly believe that "something will turn up."

REFERENCES

Grubel, Herbert (2009). "The Effects of American Recession: Fighting Policies on Economic Freedom," in *Economic Freedom of the World, 2009 Annual Report* (Economic Freedom Network), 31–47.

Kenen, P. B. (1957). "On the Geometry of Welfare Economics: A Suggested Diagrammatic Treatment of Some Basic Propositions," *Quarterly Journal of Economics* 71, no. 3: 426–447.

(1959). "Distribution, Demand, and Equilibrium in International Trade: A Diagrammatic Analysis," *Kyklos* 12, no. 4: 629–638.

(1960). *British Monetary Policy and the Balance of Payments, 1951–1957.* Cambridge, MA: Harvard University Press.

(1965). "Nature, Capital, and Trade," *Journal of Political Economy* 73, no. 5: 437–460.

(1969). "The Theory of Optimum Currency Areas: An Eclectic View," in R. A. Mundell and A. K. Swoboda (eds.), *Monetary Problems of the International Economy.* Chicago: University of Chicago Press, 41–60.

(1995). *Economic and Monetary Union in Europe: Moving Beyond Maastricht.* Cambridge: Cambridge University Press.

Kenen, P. B. and P. R. Allen (1980). *Asset Markets, Exchange Rates, and Economic Integration.* Cambridge: Cambridge University Press.

Notes

1 My most frequently cited paper, "The Theory of Optimum Currency Areas: An Eclectic View," was merely an amendment to Robert Mundell's seminal work on that subject, in which I suggested that a country with a well-diversified domestic economy was perhaps the best candidate for membership in a monetary union, because domestic diversification would facilitate equilibrating movements of labor and capital in response to external shocks. It gained prominence, however, only when it was cited, along with work by Ronald McKinnon, when Mundell was awarded the Nobel Prize in economic science.

17

Learning about the Evolving International Economy

Anne O. Krueger

Two pre-PhD influences were relevant to my interests as an economist. First, my parents immigrated to the United States from Australia shortly before I was born, and the household was keenly oriented to news from overseas, especially during World War II and in the immediate postwar period. I vividly remember the radio announcement of the German invasion of Poland, Australian flyers staying with us en route to or from the Battle of Britain, and many other events, even though I was only five when World War II began. Later, the postwar reconstruction, the Marshall Plan, Indian independence (and the assassination of Gandhi), the founding of the Bretton Woods institutions, and other developments were a source of excitement and interest.

Second, some of the most interesting of my fellow graduate students were those from developing countries, especially India. From hours of discussion, I learned much about the issues as they were perceived at that time: disguised unemployment, Arthur Lewis's perfectly elastic labor supply, "export pessimism" with the perceived need for import substitution, "structural inflation," and so on.

During my undergraduate years at Oberlin College, my focus was on law and hence I did not initially decide on a specific major. At various times, I was majoring, or thinking of majoring, in political science, sociology, and other fields, and it was not until my senior year that my economics major was declared. I liked economics courses, although I initially took them because I thought one had to understand economics in order to understand law and politics. The undergraduate economics major was rigorous by the standards of the day, and when the question of what I would do after graduating arose, financing was an issue, and I was able to get a (small) fellowship to graduate school in economics (and, of course, nothing for law). So economics it was – at the University of Wisconsin.

Although those discussions about the challenges of development were of most interest to me in graduate school, I majored in "economic theory" and took international economics as my second field. I did so, although my interests were clearly applied, partly because I regarded theory as the tool that could be used for all my interests. International economics in those days was almost everywhere taught as a full-year course covering both international trade and "balance-of-payments" theory, as it was then called. Of course, I took econometrics, but it was not at that time very challenging. Like almost everyone else then, I felt equipped for statistical analysis but was skeptical of its usefulness for many problems. Much of my skepticism has been subsequently voided with advances in econometric technique, although I did not keep up with them and would fear to attempt econometric analysis now.

In 1959, I was fortunate to get an assistant professorship at the University of Minnesota, which turned out to be an ideal place for me. The department was very strong in theory and almost all its members ascribed to the view that good theory was important for underpinning analysis of any applied problem – a perspective I hold to this day. It was also a very collegial department, and the senior faculty members were all approachable. After four years there, I was promoted with tenure; my publications to that time were almost all models with little empirical content.

By the summer of 1965, I felt that I could afford to take some time to follow my interests, and I accepted an offer to serve as a consultant to the US Agency for International Development (USAID). At that time USAID was seeking economists to do research related to the trade policy problems of developing countries. I was asked to write a paper on trade policy for developing countries.[1] After I submitted a draft in mid-July in which I focused on the incentives created by high levels of protection and overvalued exchange rates, I was told that I should choose a country of interest to USAID (either Colombia or Turkey), visit that country, and apply what I had written.

I chose Turkey, partly because the other economist who was also working on trade issues preferred Colombia, partly because I didn't speak Spanish, and partly because Turkey seemed the more interesting. It was a fortunate choice: I made many friends in Turkey over the years and have maintained my interest in the country.

I arrived in Ankara early in August 1965 and was met at the airport by a USAID official, who told me that everyone was out of town but that a military attaché would take me to lunch the following day. He also said that the Turkish economists in government whom I had hoped to meet were either on holiday or too busy to see me. After some thought, I decided that the only strategy open to me was to use the good offices of the embassy for introductions to the US consulates in Izmir and Istanbul and, through them, ask individual businessmen about their experiences with exporting and importing. I left Ankara very shortly. The consulates were helpful in providing introductions, and all of the Turks who were approached were delighted to discuss their experience with the trade regime. Many introduced me to still other businessmen and remained friends, as well as sources of understanding of the trade regime, for many years.

Contrasted with my dismal experience in Ankara, Izmir and Istanbul were absorbing, and I learned a lot about how the foreign trade and exchange control regime actually worked. Enough data were available to calculate what I called domestic resource costs (Krueger 1966), and many anecdotal reports were suggestive of side effects of the trade and payments regime that I had not really considered, nor had I seen them discussed in the literature. Even more amazingly, the next time I went to Turkey[2] (in 1967, at the behest of Ernest Sturc, then head of the International Monetary Fund Policy Review Department)[3], I met many of the Turks who were economic policy makers in the government whom I had hoped to meet in 1965, all of whom had asked to see me! They wanted me to tell them what was happening on the basis of my discussions in Izmir and Istanbul.

I learned many important lessons from my times in Turkey.[4] First, I realized that it was not sufficient to hear government officials' (even good economists') accounts of the system, both because those subject to it would not necessarily reveal much to government officials and, equally important, because one then had nothing useful to exchange in discussions with those officials. My impressions and data on the effects of the system were of interest to those in government, who were therefore willing to share with me (although I kept the identity of those providing information confidential). Second, I learned a lot about the many and varied ways in which people responded to the incentives created by government regulations, especially in the trade and payments regime. These included not only the predictable smuggling and over- and underinvoicing, but also phenomena such as the "exportation" of shiploads of stones, which were then dumped overboard (to collect export subsidies), the misgrading of commodities such as tobacco (tobacco inspectors were bribed by farmers to overstate the quality of tobacco),[5] the wasteful stockpiling of spare parts and even entire machines in order to be able to produce should a crucial part or machine malfunction or import licenses be delayed or unavailable,[6] and many, many more. Third, as I continued to undertake research on Turkish trade and exchange rate policy, I learned the value of following the course of events in a country; one not only understood some of the history of policy and why it was what it was, but also learned how change could come about.

From my experiences in Turkey and later in India, I held and still hold strongly two propositions that underpinned my work on development. The first is that poverty is degrading and an unnecessary waste of human and other resources and that virtually all, including the poor, benefit over the medium and long run from more rapid economic growth.[7] This is confirmed by statistics of life expectancy, literacy, nutritional standards, infant mortality, and more, all of which have improved markedly in countries whose rates of growth of real per capita income have risen.[8] While it is possible, and desirable, for policies to be put in place to help the poor within an overall development strategy, those policies cannot and should not be at the expense of growth, as more rapid growth holds out greater hope for more in the longer run.[9] The second proposition is that enough (if not all) people will respond to relative rewards so that political and social objectives need to be sought through measures that create incentives for behavior consistent with those objectives. For example, a greater gap between the official exchange rate and the black market rate will almost certainly lead to more behavior, both legal and illegal, to arbitrage at least to some extent the differential with significant economic costs. Similarly, jobs for life in a bureaucracy greatly reduce incentives for employees to expend effort in their work. When the rewards for receiving patronage from a politician are greater or more certain than those from cutting costs, businessmen will allocate their resources to influencing the politicians. When government jobs require university degrees and pay substantially more than those in the private sector, a queue will form of unemployed graduates applying and reapplying for government jobs, with waiting times of several years in many cases. And so on.

Although my focus was on Turkey, my earlier interest in India was rekindled with an invitation from USAID to go there in 1968 to examine the trade regime in much the same way I had done in Turkey. There were, of course, significant differences between India and Turkey, but there were also great similarities. I chose to undertake a microeconomic study, finding the suppliers of auto parts and relying on assemblers to enable me to determine what international prices of the same parts and components might be. I was fortunate to get the support of Hindustan Motors and was able to interview and get data from more than fifty suppliers of parts. These suppliers kindly spent hours providing me with data (including, in some cases, data from the three sets of books they kept – that for the taxman, that for the public, and that for purposes of management).[10]

At that time, it was held that corruption entailed transfer payments and did not have real resource costs. That seemed clearly inconsistent with the evidence of behavior in Turkey and in India and also with the very high payoffs for those who could find their way around the regulations encompassed in the trade and payments regime. That line of thinking led to the "Political Economy of the Rent-Seeking Society" (Krueger 1974b), in which I set up a simple model of rent seeking in a two-good economy in which imports were quantitatively restrained by licensing and workers from the other two goods sectors were drawn into the rent-seeking activity of acquiring import licenses and earning the import premium when they were successful, so that there were significant real economic costs to quantitative restrictions. I illustrated these costs with a number of other phenomena as well – regulations requiring urban wages well above rural earnings, resulting in open urban unemployment (the model of Harris and Todaro 1970), rate of return regulation of utilities with incentives for capital intensity, and more.

At conferences on trade and exchange problems in developing countries, I heard more and more similar stories from other countries with similar trade regimes and also talked with economists interested in the same set of phenomena. This resulted in the project that Jagdish Bhagwati and I led, Foreign Trade Regimes and Economic Development, under the auspices of the National Bureau of Economic Research. We asked economists familiar with individual countries to analyze the trade and payments regimes in their countries after we had written an analytical framework in which we posed questions about the regimes and their effects.

To the great surprise of participants, and even somewhat to ourselves, many of the same phenomena were reported across the ten countries covered in the project. Moreover, South Korea – one of the countries covered – had undertaken remarkably serious reforms in the late 1950s and early 1960s, after having had one of the most restrictive and distortive trade and payments regimes in the world in the 1950s. The authors of the Korean study, Frank, Kim, and Westphal (1975), documented how the Korean economy and its prospects had been transformed.

The results of the project came out in the late 1970s, with a book for each but one of the countries and two "synthesis" volumes, one by Bhagwati and one by me. The volumes on the individual countries, the synthesis volumes, and several other important research papers[11] were among several factors that led many policy makers and economists to rethink some of their earlier conclusions about the costs and benefits of import substitution policies and the likely benefits of a policy change. Since the 1980s, most developing countries have removed most of their quantitative restrictions, moved to more realistic exchange rates, and greatly lowered their tariffs. While there is still considerable protection in many developing countries, there are few instances of the extremes of the 1960s, when it was not unusual to find tariffs in the hundreds of percentage points and prohibitions of imports of many protected items.

At about the time the volumes were going to press, I was fortunate enough to be invited to South Korea, first to participate in a project sponsored by the Korea Development Institute (KDI) in 1974 and then in the late 1970s to work on a joint Harvard-KDI project on the first twenty-five years of Korean development, 1948–1973. For the latter project I was asked to examine the history of South Korea's trade and payments over that period. That was a learning experience very different from those in India and Turkey. The economy was growing at a rate of about 10 percent annually. The entire government was focused on economic achievements, using export performance as a metric. That was successful at that time because the Korean economy had been so distorted that exports had been 3 percent of GDP while imports had been 13 percent![12] It was probably not wrong, at least for a while, for policy makers to hold a virtual export theory of value. Exports were growing at an average annual rate of more than 40 percent, with imports growing a much slower 30 percent. The savings and investment rates were both rising dramatically with higher incomes.[13]

There was no comparison between the economic performances of Turkey (whose growth rate had been below 5 percent in the 1970s) and India (whose rate of growth was between 3 and 4 percent during those years) with that of Korea, especially since Korean economic performance had appeared to be worse than Turkey's in the 1950s and not markedly better than India's in that same decade. That the change in Korea's growth, which had been sluggish in the 1950s despite the opportunities that postwar reconstruction provided, came about at the same time as reforms took hold was telling, and Korea's continued success disproved much of the "export pessimism" that had prevailed in so many countries in earlier years.

The experience of the countries in the Bhagwati-Krueger project, combined with the more in-depth experience in Turkey and India and the evidence of the benefits resulting from policy reform in Korea, convinced me that the benefits of an open-trade regime, while certainly including those in the traditional comparative advantage analysis, went far beyond that. An open-trade regime constrained economic policy makers in ways that an inner-oriented trade regime did not. It gave policy makers an objective way of estimating and enabling rewards for the performance of individual firms, so that entrepreneurs could no longer claim efficiency and productivity they did not in fact have. An open-trade regime also provided competition for domestic producers, which was important even for relatively large developing countries. For success, an open-trade regime had to be supported at least by adequate infrastructure and a reasonably stable and predictable set of macroeconomic policies.

Although I learned a great deal about South Korean reforms and the huge contrast between the policies of the 1950s and later years, the first country in which I saw and followed firsthand the effects of economic policy reform was Turkey in 1980–1981. After a severe foreign exchange crisis,[14] quantitative restrictions on imports were almost entirely removed, the exchange rate was allowed to float, tariffs were greatly lowered, the financial market was significantly freed, the regime governing state economic enterprises was rationalized, and almost all restrictions on foreign exchange for current account purposes were dismantled. These reforms enabled Turkish growth rates (and integration with the international economy) to increase markedly in the early 1980s at a time when there was a worldwide recession and most other developing countries were experiencing slowdowns. Turkish exports also boomed, and with that, the disrepute in which Turkish businessmen had been held evaporated. That, in turn, gave policy makers more latitude for promulgating economic policies conducive to further growth. Unfortunately, there was little attention to the underlying fiscal deficits, and macroeconomic balances reemerged as a major issue later in the decade.[15]

I was on the faculty of the University of Minnesota for twenty-three years. It was a good time for the department, which was collegial and was gaining increasing recognition. Teaching was rewarding, as the students were highly motivated and interested in learning how to apply the (excellent) theory and econometrics that they had learned. I always enjoyed, and learned a lot, from teaching. Although I later taught elsewhere, the Minnesota years probably gave me more satisfaction in terms of interaction with graduate students than did later teaching. Some of my close friends today were students at Minnesota in those years. I never understood those who spoke of "teaching versus research." My research on trade and development fed directly into my teaching, and teaching enabled me to sharpen ideas and meaningfully formulate many of the phenomena I had confronted in the "real world."

I continued to focus on trade and economic policy reform issues, especially with respect to developing countries, in the early 1980s. But in 1982 I accepted an offer to become the vice president for economics and research at the World Bank. Until then, either my experience had been academic or I had served as a policy adviser. The World Bank challenge was new and different: here was a large international organization with very diverse membership. Learning the ways of an organization was itself a major challenge, contrasted with the freedom I had had to do my own research.[16] There was a considerable degree of culture shock.

Moreover, while I had thought the costs of import substitution policies were high in India, Turkey, and South Korea (in the 1950s), I had not had any significant exposure to countries whose policies were even more egregious – particularly those in sub-Saharan Africa. Nor had I had much exposure to those whose support of these policies was based on an ideology that blamed the West and colonialism for all economic problems and regarded World Bank support as part of a "neocolonial plot."[17]

The World Bank had done much effective project support lending for infrastructure and related activities. However, it had also supported government activities in areas such as tourism and steel, which in most countries had been the traditional preserve of the private sector. The Bank was also less critical of exchange control regimes and other government interventionist policies than I tended to be. I had never thought that "ideology" was the basis for economists' judgments but found myself accused of being "ideological" when questioning price controls, import licensing regimes, and so on.

Over the four and a half years I was there, the Bank's focus shifted toward providing a framework for private economic activity, and that shift has continued since.[18] Because many of the developing countries had been oil importers, they had experienced severe difficulties when oil prices rose in 1973 and 1979. The Bank's response, to support policy reform through structural adjustment lending, was probably appropriate, but there was much learning to be done.

Since the 1980s the Bank has generally continued to move toward what I would judge to be a more appropriate focus for support of development and poverty reduction. Some of the Bank's current initiatives, including its evaluations in *Doing Business* and similar publications, are extremely valuable and have a significant impact. In my judgment their importance is not yet fully appreciated.

With the difficulties of oil importers and heavily indebted countries (because of the worldwide recession of the early 1980s and the high real interest rates at that time) and the challenges of structural adjustment lending, my interest in economic policy reforms increased, and there was a lot to learn. I recall vividly one team from an African country that had convinced us all that they recognized the error of their ways and were serious about policy reform. They had been in Washington, in the final negotiations of a structural adjustment loan, when they informed us that a special session of parliament had been called and that they had to return to the capital. After several weeks when they had not come back to Washington, it became evident that the commodity prices of their two major exports were rising significantly. We heard no more about economic policy reforms – for me, a major lesson! It was several years before the economy's difficulties again became so acute that reforms were finally undertaken.

As head of research at the World Bank, I thought a lot about the role of research in an operating institution. There are obvious conflicts, as the operational staff believes that their work is important and the basis on which the institution is judged, while the researchers are convinced that their work is important (and should be published in academic journals without necessarily being relevant to the institution's issues). Aligning incentives so that researchers would be encouraged to focus on the issues arising in the Bank's operations seemed to me to be the solution.[19] I believed, and believe, that the research of the Bank (and the IMF) is vitally important in enabling lessons learned in some parts of the world to be used elsewhere at lower cost than would be required if people had to learn these lessons for themselves. Comparative research can shed light on a large number of questions, but it is difficult for individual researchers to carry out. Researchers can also fulfill a number of other vital functions, acting as a resource for operations staff members who need to acquaint themselves with the latest thinking on relevant problems, informing the wider policy and academic community of challenging issues, and serving as a two-way conduit between the Bank (or IMF) and the academic research community.

At the same time, I learned that someone wanting to kill a proposal would very often suggest "the need for further study" prior to taking action. While sometimes further research is called for before action is taken, failure to act is itself a policy decision and many decisions must be made in a timely way based on the best available thinking at the time. As a researcher, it seemed to me strange at first, but in the Bank I often had to oppose those who wanted more research prior to deciding on any action. The role of research is in part to anticipate and analyze issues that may arise (including results of earlier policies) and to formulate clearer frameworks for policy going forward, but policy makers must decide on the basis of the best available evidence.

When I left the World Bank at the end of 1986, I moved to Duke University, greatly saddened by cutting ties with Minnesota. I thought I should spend some time undertaking research on developed countries' economic policies, given how much I had spent criticizing and pushing reforms for low-income countries. I decided that US sugar policy was an appropriate initial target.

Over the next year, frustration mounted as my efforts to understand the sugar program in the United States seemed unsuccessful. Later on, I realized that the program was purposely complex, as the lack of transparency helped shield it from public criticism. But as I learned more about the sugar program and its evolution, I recognized that many of the same political forces that drove inappropriate economic policies in low-income countries were at work in the United States and that I had been naive in thinking otherwise.[20] Among other telling clues was the fact that the sugar growers themselves no longer supported the program: they had lost too much market to corn growers. Meanwhile, corn growers were adamantly opposed to any effort to dismantle the sugar program![21] It seemed obvious that once the sugar program had been put in place in the 1930s, it was extremely difficult to eliminate or even cut back, but equally obvious that the sugar program of the 1980s would never have been enacted had it not already been there. The sugar program initially had been used to support Cuba (in the 1930s and again after World War II); then it was changed to punish Cuba and reward friendly countries (after Castro came to power in 1959), then again to support domestic producers of beet sugar and for other purposes. The purpose of the program changed, but the program continued. By the 1980s, almost all the consequences of the program were "unintended" and certainly not consistent with the original intentions.

I returned to my focus on trade issues more generally (the US sugar program being one small part). I did a monograph for Brookings (Krueger 1993) on US trade policy. I thought I knew a fair amount about it but even so was surprised at the extent to which there was protection (especially in antidumping and countervailing duty procedures) and the divergence between the official claim that the United States supported free trade and actual practices.

I was initially an interested bystander in the Canada-US free-trade negotiations but became somewhat involved when Mexico proposed to make it a three-way preferential trade agreement (PTA). Instinctively I viewed PTAs as protectionist and unnecessary in an open multilateral trading system. But on learning more, instinct became strongly aligned with evidence. Rules of origin proved to be a means by which an apparent freeing of trade in fact protected domestic producers, as for example when the Mexican agreement set a sufficiently high rule of origin that the Japanese could no longer assemble cars with Japanese parts in Mexico and export to the United States, thus protecting US parts producers and assemblers.[22]

In 1993, I was invited to join the Stanford Economics Department and did so that September. Focus on trade issues continued. I was enthusiastic about the new World Trade Organization (WTO), believing that as an international organization it could achieve more than had been the case before it had that status. I organized a conference that brought together many of those interested in the world trading system and produced a series of papers out of which came a volume examining the prospects for the WTO in its various aspects. With the NAFTA, there were also many questions about the ways in which PTAs might (or might not) be consistent with an open multilateral trading system. An early discovery was the potential for protectionist pressures in PTAs, and several papers on rules of origin were one result (Krueger 2001, which appeared as an NBER working paper in 1992, was the first).

So the early and middle 1990s were for me a period of continuing focus primarily on economic policy reform, trade policy, and trade issues.[23] I did, however, in 1997 agree to become the founding director of the Stanford Center for International Development (SCID).[24] During the following several years I was busy establishing the Center. Initially, the most successful component was the establishment of an India research program, under which research was undertaken and an annual volume was published and a conference held. Several of the conferences were very influential in moving the Indian economic policy reform agenda forward.[25] In addition, I was able to persuade Nicholas Hope of the World Bank (who had, among other important assignments, recently been the World Bank's director of its China Department) to come to Stanford and become deputy director of the Center. In addition to tasks associated with the Center as a whole, Nick took responsibility for developing a research program on China[26] and is now director of the Center.

That all came to an abrupt halt in 2001, when I was approached to become the first deputy managing director[27] of the IMF. I agreed to a five-year term starting in September 2001. The timing was good in the sense that I had completed the various projects I had undertaken with regard to trade policy and the Center seemed to have sufficient momentum to continue its growth. The timing was poor, however, in that Turkey and Argentina, two important countries, were in crisis, and at the same time the attack on September 11, 2001, took place within days of my joining the Fund. Worse yet, the managing director had left for Europe before that awful day, and I was acting managing director at the time.[28] However, within a few days, it was possible to arrange for transport for the managing director to return, and my attention turned to learning the job and the plights of Argentina and Turkey.

My earlier work in Turkey enabled me to catch up quickly with the IMF program (which I had in any event been following from Stanford) already in place. I had in the early 1980s spent some time in Argentina when there were earlier reform attempts, and so had followed with great interest the reforms of the early 1990s, including the currency board, privatizations, and deregulation. Thus, while I was not as conversant with Argentine economic issues as with Turkey's, I at least had some basis. Moreover, the Argentine difficulties were simpler in their origins than were the Turkish.[29] The quasi-currency board had kept the Argentina peso pegged to the US dollar while fiscal excesses were mounting, since the Argentine provinces could in effect borrow to finance their activities without a hard budget constraint. As borrowing continued over time and as the current account deficit of Argentina cumulated, a crisis was in the making unless major steps were quickly taken to right the situation. That did not happen, and the Argentines chose to default on their obligations, abandon the currency board peg, and "pesify" the banks' obligations at 3 pesos per US dollar while "pesifying" their assets at 1 peso per dollar. The result, of course, was that the banks were all insolvent and had to be recapitalized. But for most of these activities, the Fund was a bystander.

In part because the Argentines chose a very unusual set of policies to address their problems, relations between the Fund and Argentina were difficult for at least the first two years of my tenure at the Fund, and they remained cool even after Argentina made an early repayment of its outstanding obligations to the Fund. Argentina rebounded from a recession (which had started in 1996 and resulted in a drop of about 20 percent in real GDP in the ensuing five years), in part because of the removal of debt servicing obligations, in part because uncertainty was removed with the abandonment of the fixed exchange rate, in part because there was so much excess capacity, and in part because commodity prices rose sharply. Involvement with the Argentines was one of the least satisfactory aspects of my tenure at the Fund. Although Argentine real GDP rose considerably, it was and is by no means clear that the underlying problems have been addressed.

Far more satisfactory were the outcomes for Turkey and Brazil. By mid-2001, Turkey had a very high ratio of debt to GDP (120 percent) and high inflation (which had peaked at a little more than 100 percent), and many of the banks were insolvent. A Fund program had begun in 1999 based on a nominal anchor exchange rate to bring down inflation, but by mid-2001 a further program was needed and the nominal anchor abandoned. But even that was not enough, and in December the first Turkish program in which I had a significant role was begun. Given the extreme difficulties facing the Turkish economy, the program was very risky, but the alternative was certain default and a banking crisis with attendant economic chaos and falling real GDP. The Turkish government committed to serious reforms in banking regulation and supervision, a primary surplus of 6 percent of GDP, and a number of other difficult, but necessary measures.[30]

For the next two years, despite considerable difficulties faced by the government in carrying out its commitments and anxiety as to whether measures would achieve their desired objectives, it was satisfying to witness growth resuming, inflation falling to single digits for the first time in almost forty years, and the debt/GDP ratio dropping sharply. For the next several years, Turkey sustained a high rate of growth. Even with the financial crisis of 2007–2009, Turkey resumed growth in 2010, and inflation has remained relatively low. To be sure, there are still challenges (including a large current account deficit), but real per capita income is twice what it was a decade ago, and debt at around 40 percent of GDP is significantly lower than that of most Western European countries.

The story in Brazil was different. Brazil had had a major economic crisis in 1999[31] and had entered into a Fund program early in 2000. The program had been more or less on target until early in 2002 (although there had been some earlier modifications), but with an election scheduled for October, spreads on Brazilian sovereign debt began rising. One of the candidates had for years been a major political figure and had advocated highly expansionary macroeconomic policies. As he, Lula, began gaining in the polls, a sell-off of Brazilian bonds intensified. By July the spreads had mounted and a full-blown crisis was developing. But the finance minister, Pedro Malan, and the governor of the central bank, Arminio Fraga, worked quickly with

Fund staff to develop a program and managed to persuade all three major presidential candidates to announce that they would support it. The Fund lent $30 billion – at that time the largest loan ever – to Brazil. With the commitment of the three candidates and those financial resources, market pressures eased. After President Lula was inaugurated, the authorities adhered to the program, and economic recovery began rapidly. Brazil's inflation rate fell gradually, growth of real GDP accelerated, and the Brazilian debt/GDP ratio fell. Hence, the Brazilian program made it possible to avert a crisis, and that in turn no doubt led to higher real incomes subsequently than would otherwise have been the case.

In addition to Fund work on individual countries (both surveillance and programs), there were many ongoing discussions of Fund policy. The one that attracted the most attention focused on sovereign debt. It had long struck me that the absence of any international insolvency mechanism (analogous to bankruptcy procedures for private creditors within a country) induced policy makers to struggle with heavy debt burdens for longer, and with higher than necessary costs, before facing up to them. The issue had arisen in the mid-1990s, and there had been a proposal for collective action clauses (CACs) in sovereign debt bonds (to avoid the problem of holdout creditors). There had been no action on the CAC proposal.

But there were and are several problems associated with high and unsustainable debt levels. The first is that policy makers are tempted to, and do, defer confronting their creditors for as long as they possibly can. The period during which there are delays is costly, in that real GDP is falling and countries are often rolling over existing debt and borrowing additional funds on ever more unfavorable terms. From the viewpoint of existing creditors, there are also issues, as the extension of new loans (by the IMF and other official agencies) dilutes the value of their holdings (especially when, as is usually the case, the official agencies have preferred creditor status). In addition to being costly for the country, the period of delay is a period during which public credit is being supplied and private creditors are enabled to exit.

There are also a number of other problems, but only one other need be mentioned here. That is, in some efforts at rescheduling, "vulture funds" have purchased outstanding sovereign debt at a highly discounted price and then held out for repayment at par to enable debt restructuring.[32]

In the fall of 2001, the Fund proposed a sovereign debt restructuring mechanism, under which a country faced with a truly unsustainable debt burden could seek a stay on any court action while getting an international court's judgment on restructuring. The issues involved were many and difficult.[33] Suffice it to say that the private financial sector opposed the proposal (presumably believing that there would be more restructurings and that more debt would be written down), several middle-income debtor countries opposed the proposal on the grounds that they thought they would have to pay higher interest rates on their bonds floated internationally, and the proposal was finally rejected. The international community did, in its stead, endorse the inclusion of CACs in sovereign bonds, which now is fairly standard. CACs at least reduce the risk of vulture funds precluding a restructuring agreement.

There were, of course, many other challenging issues that arose while I was at the Fund. But the ones I've described give an idea of the scope of the problems that were faced, even though the international economy was generally growing so rapidly that many observers maintained that the Fund had become "irrelevant."[34] However, the Fund was anxious about the "global imbalances" that were increasing with large US fiscal and current account deficits (despite the evidence that there was little or no output gap) and large Chinese, other East Asian, and oil exporters' current account surpluses. An effort was made, termed "multilateral consultations," to bring the large surplus and deficit countries together to confront the issue. The six participants all agreed that the situation was unsustainable, but surplus and deficit countries each insisted that the other side should take remedial action. Nothing was achieved.

I left the Fund when my five-year term ended in August 2006. It had been a challenging and an exhausting time. The financial crisis broke in the spring of 2007, and of course perception of the Fund's relevance has increased greatly since then, both in supporting countries attempting to cope with sovereign debt issues and with the recognition that global imbalances are still there and will likely mount as recovery proceeds. But while I still watch events with keen interest, I am no longer a participant. The issues that arose while I was at the Fund, however, are challenging and I continue to focus on various aspects of economic policy reform programs.

In hindsight, it is almost astonishing how much thought and policy on trade and development have changed since the 1950s. Then, export pessimism (that developing countries could not develop competitive manufacturing industries), import substitution policies, even government ownership of new industries, and much more were regarded as underpinnings of development policy. The experience of countries such as South Korea (and now many others) and research (on outcomes of the earlier policies as well as much more) have contributed to the remarkable acceleration of growth and higher living standards of most developing countries.

While many questions remain, the change that has occurred over the past half-century provides hope that research and analysis can enable further improvements in economic policies and performance.

REFERENCES

Bates, Robert H. and Anne O. Krueger (1993). *Political and Economic Interactions in Economic Policy Reform.* Oxford: Basil Blackwell.

Bhagwati, Jagdish (1978). *Foreign Trade Regimes and Economic Development: Anatomy and Consequences of Exchange Control Regimes.* Cambridge, MA: Ballinger for the National Bureau of Economic Research

Frank, Charles R., Jr., Kim Kwan Suk, and Larry E. Westphal (1975). *Foreign Trade Regimes and Economic Development: Korea.* New York: Columbia University Press for the National Bureau of Economic Research.

Harris, John R. and Michael P. Todaro (1970). "Migration, Unemployment and Development: A Two-Sector Analysis," *American Economic Review* 60 (March): 126–142.

International Monetary Fund (2003). "Report of the Managing Director to the International Monetary and Financial Committee on a Statutory Sovereign Debt Restructuring Mechanism." April 8.

Krueger, Anne O. (1961). "Export Prospects and Economic Growth: India. A Comment," *Economic Journal* 71 (June): 436–442.

(1966). "Some Economic Costs of Exchange Control: The Turkish Case," *Journal of Political Economy* (October).

(1974a). *Foreign Trade Regimes and Economic Development: Turkey.* New York: Columbia University Press for the National Bureau of Economic Research.

(1974b). "The Political Economy of the Rent-Seeking Society," *American Economic Review* 64, no. 3: 291–303.

(1975). *The Benefits and Costs of Import Substitution in India: A Microeconomic Study.* Minneapolis: University of Minnesota Press.

(1978). *Foreign Trade Regimes and Economic Development: Liberalization Attempts and Consequences.* Cambridge, MA: Ballinger Publishing Company for the National Bureau of Economic Research.

(1990). "The Political Economy of Controls: American Sugar," in Deepak Lal and Maurice Scott (eds.), *Public Policy and Economic Development: Essays in Honour of Ian Little.* Oxford: Clarendon Press.

(1992). *Economic Policy Reform in Developing Countries.* Oxford: Basil Blackwell.

(1993). *Economic Policies at Cross-Purposes: The United States and Developing Countries.* Washington, DC: Brookings Institution.

(2001). "Free Trade Agreements as Protectionist Devices: Rules of Origin," in James R. Melvin, James Moore, and Raymond Riezman (eds.), *Trade, Theory and Econometrics: Essays in Honor of John S. Chipman*, 91–102 London: Routledge.

ed. (2002a). *Economic Policy Reforms and the Indian Economy.* Chicago: University of Chicago Press.

(2002b). *A New Approach to Sovereign Debt Restructuring.* Washington, DC: International Monetary Fund. April.

(2011). "Economic Policy Reforms in Turkey and Brazil," in Anne O. Krueger, *Struggling with Success*, ch. 8 Singapore: World Scientific.

Krueger, Anne O. and Okan Aktan (1992). *Swimming Against the Tide: Turkish Trade Reforms in the 1980s*. San Francisco: ICS Press.

Krueger, Anne O. and Rosalinda Quintanilla (1992). *Private Sector Perspectives on the Mexican-U.S. Free Trade Agreement*. Garza Barcia, N.L. Mexico: Instituto Quantum.

Little, Ian, Tibor Scitovsky, and Maurice Scott (1970). *Industry and Trade in Some Developing Countries*. Oxford: Oxford University Press for the OECD Development Center.

Notes

1 I had earlier published several papers on India's balance-of-payments difficulties. The only one to appear in a refereed journal was a note in the *Economic Journal* (Krueger 1961) in which I argued that the failure of Indian exports to grow was in significant part a result of the strong incentives for producing goods for the domestic market. While I enjoyed writing these papers, I did not think that they could count toward promotion (and suspect I was probably right).

2 I also met again with some of the people I had interviewed in 1965. I was able to stay in touch with many of them until the early 1980s, and learned a great deal about how they coped and maintained flexibility in response to huge swings in economic policy and macroeconomic conditions. During the period from 1965 to 1980, there were three major IMF programs, at least the same number of balance-of-payments crises, and inflation rates ranging up to 60 percent. Macroeconomic instability persisted until 2001, but the reforms of the early 1980s paved the way for a much smoother functioning of the trade and payments regime. The major remaining economic policy problem was macroeconomic instability. See more discussion of Turkey from the years I was at the IMF.

3 Sturc had a PhD from the University of Chicago and had been the Czech delegate to the Bretton Woods Conference during World War II. He was interested in Turkey, had wonderful stories about the Conference, and was a major figure in negotiating the 1967 British devaluation. When I saw him in the summer of 1967 after returning from Turkey, he had just returned from negotiating the British devaluation and, among other things, said that he recalled Keynes's toast at Bretton Woods: "Here is to no more competitive devaluations." Sturc commented, "Little did I dream that I would spend the rest of my life persuading countries to devalue."

4 I visited Turkey at least once a year, often for several months, after 1967 until the early 1980s, when I went to the World Bank. In the 1990s, I again spent much time there. Early in the decade, Okan Aktan and I (Krueger and Aktan 1992) wrote a monograph on the Turkish economic reforms of the 1980s, their aftermath, and the macroeconomic dangers. Later in the decade, I worked with the Turkish Treasury producing a paper on the probable macroeconomic effects of Turkish entry into customs union (in manufactures only) with the European Union. When I joined the IMF in 2001, Turkey was in the midst of a macroeconomic crisis and was one of my major concerns during my five-year tenure at the Fund (as described later in this essay).

5 The proportion of the tobacco crop graded "top quality" jumped from a relatively small fraction to more than 90 percent once the inspection system was started. On university entrance exams, the highest average grades were scored by those who indicated that they wanted to become tobacco inspectors.

6 My favorite example came from India, where small-tractor imports were prohibited but large-tractor imports were permitted. The cost of small engines (produced in India) for small tractors was very high; after several years, a customs inspector discovered that the large tractor he was inspecting had, in addition to its own engine, twenty small engines for the smaller tractors! The practice of smuggling small engines in as extra engines in large tractors had apparently been going on for years.

7 Not all will agree, but in my view economic growth also generates the resources with which societal problems such as those with the environment can be more effectively tackled; in addition, as people escape from poverty, their demands for a better environment and other public goods also increase, thus enabling the government to address these issues more readily. But I am also convinced that satisfactory growth rates cannot be sustained unless more and more people are healthy and educated and that the so-called social sector is vital to economic growth.

8 When I was first learning about India, life expectancy for men was thirty-two years and that for women twenty-eight. Today, life expectancy is well above sixty for both sexes.

9 Many policies, such as those increasing educational opportunities and quality, are important for accelerating growth as well as for helping the poor. Indeed, some of the discussion of a growth–poverty reduction trade-off seems to me to imply more of a trade-off than is really there if policies for growth are followed.

10 The outcome of that project was a book called *The Benefits and Costs of Import Substitution in India: A Microeconomic Study* (Krueger 1975).

11 Probably the most notable of the others was that led by Ian Little, Tibor Scitovsky, and Maurice Scott (1970) for the OECD on industrialization policies in developing countries. The work of Bela Balassa was also influential.

12 Foreign aid had financed the imbalance.

13 The national savings rate had been zero in 1960; by the mid-1980s, it was more than 35 percent. Lending by foreign banks of about 10 percent of GDP made possible an investment rate much above the savings rate in the 1960s and early 1970s.

14 In the winter of 1979–1980, dislocations were so severe that Turkey (which has no oil reserves to speak of) could import very little petroleum (or anything else). I had lunch in parliament on a January day when all of us kept our coats and scarves on and the food was cold by the time it reached the tables.

15 Fiscal deficits of up to 13 percent of GDP had been incurred prior to the reforms, largely because of losses of state economic enterprises. After 1980, state economic enterprise losses were sharply reduced, but spending on infrastructure and other government activities increased to offset most of the reductions in the fiscal deficit.

16 I was surprised, when I went to the IMF in 2001, that I did not experience a challenge to the same extent in adjusting to the organization. I attribute that to the earlier experience at the World Bank, although the two organizations are very different.

17 Now, when I hear policy makers blaming external circumstances for their difficulties, I am reasonably certain that economic performance will not improve. While it is certainly true that external factors can make things easier or harder, some of the

most successful developing countries have been those without "good luck." In my first years at the Bank, however, I do not believe I had an adequate response to the argument.

18 I recall a meeting of the Loan Committee to consider a proposed loan to an African country (I have forgotten which) for reforming the import licensing regime. License issuances were to be differentiated between consumer and producer goods, between intermediate and final goods, and so on. I asked who would decide and how one could tell the purposes for which a car or pickup truck would be used, when either would be an intermediate good (used in a business) or a final good, and so on. The project was sent to be reconsidered, but first there was stunned silence, as these questions seemed not to have been asked before.

19 To increase incentives for Bank-relevant research, the *World Bank Research Observer* and *World Bank Economic Review* were begun to give researchers an outlet for top-quality results on those issues. There was considerable opposition to starting them at the time, but they have continued to be published to this day.

20 It was and is true, however, that the magnitude and extent of distortions in the United States and most other industrial countries are generally far less than in low-income countries.

21 High-fructose corn syrup (HFCS) had by the late 1980s replaced sugar in all soft drinks in the United States, and in many other products as well. Sugar's world price fluctuated between 5 and 10 cents, while the support price in the United States was more than 20 cents a pound. It was estimated that at any sugar price above 16 cents, HFCS was the cheaper for sweetening purposes in products where it could serve as a substitute.

22 There were also concerns with the exchange rate, which had been used as a "nominal anchor" to attempt to reduce inflation, thus leading to currency overvaluation (see Krueger and Quintanilla 1992). I supported the Mexican entry into NAFTA, believing that it would benefit Mexico considerably and would provide some, but small, economic benefits to the United States while improving relations with Mexico.

23 See Krueger (1992).

24 The initial name was the Stanford Center for Research on Economic Development and Policy Reform. The name was changed after I left Stanford to its current one after I moved to Washington, and I shall refer to it as SCID here. As the WTO conference volume was already under way, the conference was held and the volume published under SCID auspices.

25 See, e.g., Krueger (2002a).

26 There was a promising start to a Latin American research program when José Antonio González joined the Center to organize one. Several conferences were held (and volumes published), and the program began well, but it did not achieve critical minimum mass before he left for the Mexican Hacienda.

27 The title is confusing. Initially there was a managing director (the chief executive) of the IMF and one deputy managing director. But when the workload became heavy, two additional deputy managing directors were appointed. As the name implies, the first deputy managing director is in the number two position in the IMF and serves as acting managing director when the managing director is gone. I was also acting managing director for several months after the managing director, Horst Kohler, resigned until Rodrigo de Rato became managing director.

28 On September 11, it was believed that six airplanes were flying toward targets, and for a while there was concern that one of the planes not yet located might be aiming for the IMF. The building was evacuated.

29 Turkey's difficulties centered on an overvalued currency (as a nominal anchor exchange rate policy had failed to tame inflation as rapidly as anticipated), fiscal deficits, and major difficulties in the banking system.

30 Some of these measures were essential for achieving the primary surplus target. Among the important ones was the freeing of the Turkish lira to float.

31 The authorities had adopted a nominal anchor exchange rate earlier in the decade, and inflationary pressures were not consistent with maintenance of the exchange rate, as fiscal and monetary policy were both laxer than had been anticipated.

32 See Krueger (2002b) for more details on this and other aspects of the proposal. It is not clear that vulture funds harm creditors, as those funds presumably support a smaller discount on bonds when there are questions about sustainability than would otherwise arise.

33 See International Monetary Fund (2003) for an elaboration of the proposal.

34 It was tempting to respond that the Fund was irrelevant in the same way that a fire department would be irrelevant if there were no fires for a period of time.

18

Confessions of a Wellesley FEM

Helen F. Ladd

I enrolled in my first economics course in 1963, my freshman year at Wellesley College, which was then, and still is, only for women. On the first day of class, my thirty freshman classmates and I eagerly awaited the arrival of our teacher. When she entered the classroom, she immediately announced that, as the chair of the department, she got to choose which section to teach, and she chose ours. Her intent was to share with us her excitement about the field and to send a signal that economics was very much an appropriate field for women. The teacher was Carolyn Shaw Bell, who later founded the American Economic Association's Committee on the Status of Women in the Economics Profession. That first course inspired me to join the ranks of Wellesley FEMs – her term for female economics majors. Little did I understand at the time the intellectual opportunities that were then opening up for me.

This chapter was first written in 2010.

MY LIFE HISTORY

I was raised as a provincial New Englander. My parents, all my grand-parents, and many of my great-grandparents lived in New England, with most of them spending much of their lives in the Boston area. The men in the family all went to Harvard College, and my mother and two of my aunts went to Wellesley College in a Boston suburb. It was clear to me that Boston was the center of the universe, and for men a Harvard degree was the key to a successful life. When I was ready for college, the choice was obvious. I applied early decision to Wellesley, without considering any other place. Later when I was ready for graduate school, I applied only to Harvard.

My decision to enroll in an economics course during my first term was almost as inevitable as my decision to go to Wellesley. I was simply following in the footsteps of my mother, who had majored in economics at Wellesley in the early 1940s (but who, like many of the women of her generation, subsequently became a stay-at-home mom and, like her own mother, was an avid golfer). The analytical rigor and policy relevance of that first course appealed to me. I took thirteen more economics courses, which I supplemented with a solid set of math courses and a few political science courses, before I graduated in 1967.

For many years, Wellesley boasted the highest proportion of female economics majors of any college or university in the country (and may still, for all I know) and was the only undergraduate institution to hold a reception at the annual American Economic Association meetings. Moreover, during her long career at Wellesley, Carolyn Shaw Bell successfully shepherded many of us into top graduate programs and many others into economics-related fields after graduation. Her success in encouraging Wellesley women to pursue economics was no mean feat given the male orientation of the discipline. She did it by displaying great confidence in all of us, inviting us to dinners at her house with visiting speakers and economists from nearby universities, including Harvard and MIT, and developing a supportive net-work of former FEMs. The network was impressive. She kept in close touch with all of us once we graduated and encouraged us to write long letters describing our experiences with work or graduate programs for use by current FEMs deciding on next steps and career paths. One such letter was particularly relevant to me during my senior year. It was from an earlier FEM who had gone on to obtain a degree at the London School of Economics and inspired me to open my eyes to the broader world and to consider the possibility of spending a year in London.

I had made a small step toward ending my Boston provincialism the summer before my senior year by going to Washington as an economics intern (arranged by the Wellesley Economics Department) at the Office of the Comptroller of the Currency, where I worked in the Research Department on issues related to bank mergers. After my first visit to the Virginia countryside, which I described with great enthusiasm in a letter to my Bostonian grandmother (a lovely, strong woman who was blind for the final thirty years of her life), I received a clear warning not to forget that Boston was where I belonged. Fortunately, though, my boss encouraged me to think about the Fulbright program, with which he was familiar because his wife had had a Fulbright to Germany a few years earlier. Returning to Wellesley in the fall, I successfully applied for a Fulbright graduate fellowship and used it to enroll in the MSc program at the London School of Economics (LSE) the following year. My decision to go to LSE greatly pleased Carolyn Shaw Bell, who had earned her own PhD there. True to form, she sent me off with letters of introduction to some of her former (by then retired) professors.

That year in London was pivotal. For the first time, I had an opportunity to step back and recognize how narrow my own world had been – not that this world had been bad. Indeed, my childhood had been wonderful, with opportunities to excel in tennis, sailing, and golf; access to a first-class education at a private high school and then Wellesley College; and an intact family with three siblings. Although we were not wealthy (my father was an insurance salesman), we lived well in Hingham, a suburb of Boston, and benefited from my parents' commitment to education. My father had traveled extensively as a naval officer during the Second World War, but my mother had never been out of the country. My parents were both Republicans, were active in the Unitarian Church, and were engaged in town politics and other community activities. I was fully rooted, and that felt good and natural.

Imagine my confusion when upon meeting David Morawetz, a new classmate in London who has since become a lifelong friend, I asked the obvious first question – "Where do you live?" – and he replied that he did not know. How could someone not know where he lived? His parents were Czech, he had grown up in Australia, he was then living in England and his parents had moved to Israel, and he was not sure where he would end up. In fact, he went on to get a PhD in development economics at MIT, married a Swiss woman, worked in Bolivia, received tenure in economics at Boston University, and then returned to Australia, no longer as an economist but rather as a counseling psychologist. Clearly there was more to life than what

I had experienced by excelling in school and in sports; there was a wide world to explore.

The London School of Economics was an intellectual treat. Arriving there with an interest in monetary economics, I found myself buffeted by the monetarist approach of Harry Johnson, who at that time had appointments at both the University of Chicago and LSE and was teaching the required macro course, and the institutional approach of Richard Sayers, who in 1959 had authored the Radcliffe Report on the British monetary system and was teaching the monetary course. As strongly as Harry Johnson trumpeted the importance of the money supply as the basis for monetary policy, Richard Sayers focused on the central role of the interest rate. Although I suspect that they did not discuss their differences much with each other, I found it exhilarating to be engaging them each with the ideas of the other, both inside and outside of class. Added to that was the lively national discussion and debate about the role of the British pound as a reserve currency. I still vividly recall Harry Johnson's lecture to the graduate students explaining why it would not be appropriate for the British to change the value of the pound, only to have the pound be devalued by almost 15 percent two days later. Big things were happening all around me. It was exciting to be in London and to be studying economics.

In those years, the London School had a reputation for student unrest, and I must admit I was looking forward to a bit of protest activity after the peace and relative complacency of Wellesley. As it turned out, I was between years – there were student strikes the year before I arrived, and LSE was shut down for a while the year after I was there. Nonetheless, there were ample reasons for my political views to evolve beyond the conservative views of my parents. Although I had arrived in the early fall thinking Richard Nixon would make a good US president, my new English and American friends soon forced me to rethink that view. Later that year the deaths of Martin Luther King and Robert Kennedy had a big impact on us all regardless of our nationality. Living in London, interacting with classmates from all over the British Commonwealth, and traveling during vacations to many other parts of Europe was as much a part of my education that year as my study of economics.

Much as I might have wanted to remain in London at the end of that year, the original logic of my life led me back to New England and to marriage to my high school sweetheart (yes, a Harvard graduate) who was halfway through a two-year business degree at Dartmouth's Tuck School of Business. That meant that I would be living in Hanover, New Hampshire, for a year before we would return to Boston, where I hoped to start my PhD in economics. Not being sure how to spend that year, I had written to the Dartmouth Economics Department the previous fall offering my services as a research assistant, or possibly as a teacher. The department kept my name on file and when the unexpected departure of the chair opened up a one-year position, they contacted me in London in March to ask if I would be interested in being a visiting lecturer during the 1968–1969 school year. That offer was quite remarkable given that I was one year out of Wellesley, would have only a master's degree when I started, was not enrolled in a PhD program, was a female who would be teaching in all-male college, and no one in the department had met me.

The job offer came, I am convinced, because of the strong recommendation letters from my Wellesley professors and, in particular, from Carolyn Shaw Bell. When asked about my teaching experience, she informed them that I had been in a senior seminar under her supervision, one component of which involved running small discussion sessions for the introductory economics course, and she assured them that, of course, I could handle a regular teaching load. It probably also helped that my husband-to-be was concentrating in marketing. Together they clearly did an effective job of promoting me – at least to the Economics Department. The dean of the college was a tougher sell. What in the world was the Economics Department thinking? Given its need for another faculty member, however, he finally relented and let the department offer me the position, but only for the first trimester, with the option of extending it to the rest of the year conditional on my performance. Fortunately, Wellesley had done a superb job of modeling good economics teaching, and with some hard work I passed the fall term test with flying colors and was permitted to teach for the full year, and in fact taught an extra course when another faculty member became ill. Despite Carolyn Shaw Bell's confidence in me, I had started the year not fully convinced I would be a good teacher, but by the end of the year I realized not only how much I enjoyed teaching but also that I could, with effort, be quite good at it.

The following fall, I entered Harvard's PhD program in economics. For reasons I never understood, the entering class that year was large – close to fifty students overall, including five females, which was as many women as in the four surrounding classes combined. Despite my prior interest in monetary theory, I soon came to appreciate Harvard's strength in public finance, which at the time was being taught by the father of modern public finance, Richard Musgrave, and by the younger and more empirically oriented Martin Feldstein. Their differing perspectives – with Musgrave having more faith in government than Feldstein, who was more concerned with tax distortions – provided yet another fertile environment for a budding economist. Although both served as advisers for my dissertation on local public finance, my strongest intellectual and personal debt is to Richard Musgrave.[1] Until his death in 2007 at age ninety-six, Richard was a lifelong mentor and friend.

By the end of July 1974 I had my PhD and two little boys – Ethan, two years old, and Haven, a newborn. A month later I started as an assistant professor in the Economics Department at Wellesley. That position made sense for me given that I was constrained by my husband's job and inclination to the Boston area and that my mother-in-law, who lived near Wellesley, was willing to take care of the boys one day a week. On that day, I would drop off both boys, teach one class, return to her house at lunchtime to nurse the baby, and then return to Wellesley to teach a second class. Every evening I was exhausted, a fact that makes me strongly supportive of the maternity leaves that most academic institutions now provide. I was fortunate, though, in finding a wonderful middle-aged woman who came to my house for many years, initially three days and later five days a week, to take care of the boys. As a result of her high-quality care and love for the boys, I never experienced the guilt and conflict that many other equally ambitious women of my generation felt about leaving children at home.

Also helping me make the transition to my life as a full-time academic and mother was the fact that the National Tax Association–Tax Institute of America selected my thesis as the outstanding dissertation of 1974. I was notified of the award during the summer before I started teaching at Wellesley and at a time when I was beginning to have a few doubts about my decision to proceed directly into a full-time job. The external validation was huge. The combination of knowing that my research was respected by the profession and the offer of a publication in the *National Tax Journal* spurred me on during that first fall of teaching when I was perpetually tired.

The Wellesley Economics Department was very good to me, but within a few years I was ready to move on to bigger challenges. With some encouragement, I applied for a position in Harvard's City and Regional Planning Department, which the urban economist John Kain was in the process of revitalizing, but not without some serious trepidation about abandoning an economics department for a professional program. My concern was that I might lose my integrity as an economist, which by then was a central part of my identity. To his credit, John Kain invited me to try it out for a term before I made a final decision. So after a trial term at Harvard and a final term at Wellesley, I joined the City and Regional Planning Department in Harvard's Design School in the fall of 1977. My main responsibility was to work with two other newly recruited young faculty members – John Yinger and Howard Bloom – to develop core courses on state and local public finance and quantitative methods for students earning a master's degree in planning. Three years later, Derek Bok, the president of Harvard, took the program out of the Design School and merged it into Harvard's Kennedy School of Government in recognition of the fact that we had in fact morphed into a program on urban public policy.

Moving to the Kennedy School had both advantages and disadvantages. On the plus side, it was a much bigger program with extensive resources and wonderful opportunities for me to grow professionally, of which I took full advantage. I learned the techniques of teaching policy cases (techniques that are essential for engaging professional students, but also, I have found, for teaching undergraduates as well) and benefited from an impressive array of colleagues. In addition, I successfully applied for and received various research grants, including a Bunting Fellowship for a year at the Radcliffe Institute.

On the negative side, the move to the Kennedy School represented a significant change in work environment. Most of the faculty members at the City and Regional Planning Department were young and untenured, four of us were women, and we had been given a lot of responsibility for the development and operation of the revitalized program. In contrast, many of the Kennedy School faculty members were quite senior, and virtually all were men who were, to say the least, not unambiguously pleased to have us thrust upon them. The biggest downside was that, despite the implied promises by Derek Bok at the time of the merger, the opportunities for tenured positions in the Kennedy School for those of us interested in urban policy were essentially nonexistent. That was because tenure in the Kennedy School required a funded chair, and there were none in our area. Some of us, myself included, were fortunate in being reappointed to additional four-year terms as untenured associate professors (which are typically untenured positions at Harvard, although they are tenured elsewhere) but were dutifully warned that there would be no opportunities for tenure and that most likely we would not be further evaluated. The fact that there were no tenured women on the Kennedy School faculty at that time strengthened my argument to the dean that he should identify a chair for which I, as the most senior of the women who had been part of the merger, could compete and, hence, be evaluated. He ultimately relented and let me compete for a chair in financial management, which was a stretch given that my main expertise was in state and local public finance, not financial management. To no one's surprise, including my own, I was not given the chair.

Meanwhile Duke University had already offered me a senior position. In 1986, I moved to Duke as a tenured full professor of public policy studies, with a secondary appointment in economics, in what has since become the Sanford School of Public Policy. From a professional and career perspective that move has been positive in every way. At the time I arrived, Duke was a young and energetic university in the process of moving from being a strong regional undergraduate institution to one of the top universities in the country and now, increasingly, in the world. In addition, it boasted a group of active senior female faculty members who were working with the administration to make Duke a welcoming place for women. In 1993, much to my delight, the university hired as president Nannerl Keohane, the former president of Wellesley College.

My years at Harvard had made me fully comfortable being an economist in a policy program (and Duke offered a large undergraduate major, as well as the more typical professional master's programs). In particular, I derived great pleasure from convincing my often skeptical master's students of the power and usefulness of economics while at the same time making sure they understood its limitations. The year after I arrived, I was invited to direct the master's program in public policy, which I then did, with a few breaks for academic leaves, for fourteen years. For one three-year period, I also served as the associate director of what was then called the Sanford Institute. Overall, the move to Duke provided the professional balance that I was seeking; I was teaching strong students in a department that put a high value on teaching, I had ample opportunities for research, and my administrative responsibilities gave me some control over the quality of my work environment without being too much of a burden.

The only downside of the move to Duke was personal. During my final year at Harvard, my marriage had begun to fall apart and I ended up moving to North Carolina with only my younger son, the older one choosing to stay in the Boston area for his high school years. That split was terribly painful for me. Despite my professional successes both as a teacher and as a researcher by that point, the failure of my marriage and the breakup of my family were major blows to my self-image as a professional woman who had successfully balanced career and family. It took me several years to recover from this jolt to my self-esteem, and not until 1993 did I finally get divorced. During those personally difficult early years at Duke, I was grateful to my colleagues for their friendship and support and to my two sons for their understanding. But my life felt unbalanced. In 1997 the situation changed dramatically for the better with my marriage to Edward B. (Ted) Fiske, a former education editor at the *New York Times*, author of the *Fiske Guide to Colleges*, and an education writer for international organizations such as UNESCO. Between us, we now have four children and nine grandchildren. In addition we have written three books together and several articles, but that takes me ahead of my story.

STATE AND LOCAL PUBLIC FINANCE: MY FIRST TWENTY YEARS OF RESEARCH

As a graduate student at Harvard in the early 1970s, I soon became fully engaged in the field of public finance, took courses, and actively participated in the public finance seminar run by Richard Musgrave and Martin Feldstein.[2] Although most of the research discussed in that seminar focused on national taxes and spending, some productive new work on subnational governments was beginning to emerge.

One strand of work was inspired by Charles Tiebout's seminal 1956 article (originally presented at a seminar Musgrave had been running at the University of Michigan), in which he argues that, under certain conditions, a system of local governments will generate an efficient provision of local public services.[3] During the late 1960s and early 1970s, scholars at Princeton, including Wallace Oates, were making the model more realistic by incorporating the main features of actual property taxes and by empirically testing its implications for voting with one's feet.[4] The second strand was the innovative research by Peter Mieszkowski that, by focusing on the observation that the property tax was a tax on wealth, would alter how economists would view the incidence of the property tax.[5] The third strand was the empirical modeling of local government expenditures in the context of median voter models that appeared in two empirical papers in the *American Economic Review* in 1972 and 1973.[6] In the policy arena, the importance of better modeling of the local expenditure decision was highlighted by the 1971 *Serrano v. Priest* court case in California that challenged the use of the property tax as a revenue source for schools.

Given my evolving interest in pursuing applied, policy-oriented research based on a strong conceptual foundation, I found the new work on local government appealing and full of potential. My dissertation topic emerged quite directly from a chapter that Richard Musgrave invited me to write during my third year on the local property tax for a volume he was editing.[7] In the process of writing that chapter, I soon came to appreciate one of the major features related to the analysis of local taxes: it is extremely difficult, and often not desirable, to separate the analysis of the tax side from the expenditure side of the budget. That insight served as the basis for my dissertation, *Local*

Public Expenditures and the Composition of the Property Tax Base (1974) and
for much of my research for the following twenty years.

As I started my career, I had no overall research plan and, in the early
years, worried that I might run out of interesting research topics. In fact
that turned out not to be a problem. One project naturally led to another or
opened up new or related lines of inquiry or opportunities.

Emerging directly from one part of my dissertation was the question of
how to measure the fiscal capacity of local governments. In my thesis, I had
developed a behavioral approach in which the commercial, industrial, and
residential components of the local property tax base contributed differ-
entially to a community's revenue- raising capacity. In the following years,
I teamed with other scholars, including John Yinger, Andrew Reschovsky,
Katharine Bradbury, and Ronald Ferguson, to develop a more refined
approach to measuring local revenue-raising capacity and augmented it
with new regression-based models of the spending side to develop broader
measures of local fiscal capacity.

Our approach found favor with Massachusetts policy makers, and a modified version was used as the central component of an equalizing state aid
program for the state's 351 cities and towns.[8] We were then recruited by a
Minnesota legislative commission to rethink that state's approach to aiding
its cities. In contrast to Massachusetts, Minnesota did not implement the
approach, but there is little doubt that our report, and the various memos
on which it was based, had a significant impact on the nature of subsequent
discussion about state aid to local governments in that state. My interest in
the conceptual and technical challenges of measuring local fiscal disparities
reflected my normative view that higher levels of government should try
to make more equitable the ability of lower-level jurisdictions to meet the
expenditure needs of their residents. In a subsequent paper, John Yinger
and I spelled out the normative arguments for intergovernmental aid, playing close attention to the equity objectives of the donor government.[9]

He and I took the basic approach to measuring capacity a big step further
with the publication of our book *America's Ailing Cities: Fiscal Health and
the Design of Urban Policy* (1989, updated 1991).[10] In the book we calculated
for each of the country's eighty-six largest cities both potential and actual
measures of fiscal capacity in order to distinguish the role of state policies –
such as the assignment of specific expenditure or tax responsibilities to
their cities as well as state aid – from the role of economic and demographic
changes that were putting pressure on cities during the 1970s and 1980s.
Concluding that the fiscal health of America's big cities had worsened since
1972, we called for new state and federal urban policies that would direct
assistance to the neediest cities.

One useful characteristic of policy-oriented research is that there is no shortage of topics to explore. For example, President Reagan's changes in fiscal federalism in the early 1980s provided grist for a paper entitled "Which Level of Government Should Assist the Poor?" and another one on how the states responded to cutbacks in federal aid to cities.[11] Later, the 1986 changes in the federal tax code, which generated windfall gains of income tax revenues in some states whose income tax laws were linked to the federal law, produced a natural experiment for a new and different empirical test of one of the central puzzles in subnational public finance, namely the "flypaper effect." That effect refers to the observation, confirmed in my study, that money tends to stick where it first hits, a finding that is inconsistent with the standard predictions of the median voter model of local government behavior.[12]

The most interesting local public finance issue to arise during the period was the tax limitation movement, which catapulted to national attention in 1978 with the passage of California's Proposition 13, a voter initiative that significantly rolled back local property taxes in that state. Efforts to limit property taxes were not new – indeed, I had already published a paper on such measures in 1978[13] – but the severity of the California initiative sent shock waves across the country. Correctly anticipating a similarly successful vote on a comparable 1980 tax limitation measure in Massachusetts (called Proposition 2 1/1), my Kennedy School sociology colleague Julie Wilson and I obtained funding to survey voters shortly after the vote to determine who supported the tax limitation measure and why. Such survey-based analysis was important because, unlike legislation, voter initiatives do not have a legislative history from which policy makers can infer intent. Teaming up with a sociologist made sense not only because of my own weaknesses in the area of survey research, but also because, as an economist, I would not have been sufficiently attuned to the importance of voters' perceptions about local taxes and spending and their expectations of how the state would respond should the initiative pass. Interactions between those perceptions and expectations turned out to be critical to our conclusion that voters apparently supported the limitation with the expectation that gains in efficiency would make it possible to lower taxes with little or no adverse impact on the public services they enjoyed. The insights from our analyses were directly relevant to state policy makers as well as to the literature on local public finance, where models of local government spending left little room for a statewide referendum to reduce taxes and spending. In related work I teamed with Katherine Bradbury of the Federal Reserve of Boston to examine the effects of the limitation on local taxes and spending, as well as with Nicolaus Tideman to edit a volume on tax and expenditure limitations.[14]

Not all of my research was driven by immediate policy issues. At other times I took the initiative to engage in larger projects of more general conceptual and long-term policy interest. During a yearlong leave from Duke in 1989–1990 at the Lincoln Institute of Land Policy in Cambridge, Massachusetts (which I arranged in order to spend more time with my older son before he left the Boston area for college), I wrote a series of conceptual and empirical articles on the relationship between local economic growth and local spending based on a panel of all large US counties in 1978 and 1985 (chosen to be at the same point of the economic cycle). That work naturally led to a more broadly based book inspired by the land value ideas of Henry George in which I examined the relationship between the two major functions of local government in the United States: the power to tax and the power to regulate land use.[15] Based on much of my own research and that of other public finance experts, the book reviews and challenges many elements of the conventional wisdom in the fields of urban public finance and planning. For example, it challenges the views that a land tax does not distort land use decisions, that the property tax is regressive, and that high-density development puts a lesser burden on spending and taxes than does development that is more spread out.

By the early 1990s, my publications and other professional activities had established my reputation within the field of state and local public finance, and I served as the president of the National Tax Association for the 1993–1994 year. Later I was invited to publish a book of my collected essays, entitled *The Challenge of Fiscal Disparities for State and Local Governments*.[16] It was time, however, for me to move on to a new area of research. Some of the topics that I had written about ten years earlier, such as which level of government should finance income support programs, were returning to the policy agenda, and I was not sure I had anything more to say about them. In addition, national economic growth along with a concomitant rise in tax revenues had relieved much of the fiscal pressures state and local governments had been experiencing during the previous two decades, thereby reducing general policy interest in their fiscal problems.

EDUCATION POLICY RESEARCH: MID-1990S TO THE PRESENT

With education being a major expenditure function of state and local governments, school finance has always been on my radar screen and I had published a number of papers on the topic. Changes in the broader field of education, however, meant that it no longer made sense to study school finance as a subject distinct from the broader field of education policy. These changes included the top-down standards-based reform efforts, the goal of which was to generate ambitious gains in student achievement, and the bottom-up efforts to improve education by promoting more parental choice of schools and school autonomy. Moreover, the education policy discussion itself was raising a number of issues about which economists potentially had something to contribute. Such issues required an understanding of the production function for education, how incentives work, the design of accountability systems, the potential for competition to improve educational efficiency, the distributional aspects of parental choice, and the operation of teacher labor markets.

A sabbatical leave from Duke in 1994–1995 made it possible for me to spend a year at the Brookings Institution in Washington as a visiting fellow and to start doing research in the field of education policy. I chose to spend the year investing in new knowledge about education policy by organizing a conference out of which emerged my edited volume, *Holding Schools Accountable: Performance-Based Reform in Education*.[17] That brought me in close contact with the broader education research community and established me as a solid contributor to the field and opened up a multitude of new research opportunities.

Partly because of my work on that volume, I was invited in 1996 to co-chair a National Research Council committee on school finance that was specifically charged to take a broader view of school finance than had traditionally been the case. The committee was composed of a multidisciplinary group of scholars and practitioners, and the three-year project culminated in two books, the main one being *Making Money Matter: Financing America's Schools*.[18] As the more academic of the two co-chairs I ended up taking most responsibility for the books and, as required by National Academy of Science guidelines, bringing the group to consensus. Chairing that committee was one of the most challenging, but also one of the most rewarding activities of my career. Right from the beginning there were major disputes between the economists and the others regarding standards of evidence and how much we knew or did not know in each of the relevant sub-areas, with the economists paying far more attention to whether the effects were causal than the others members of the committee.

Near the end, the process nearly fell apart as some members (mainly, but not exclusively, the economists) pushed hard to recommend a publicly funded large school voucher experiment, while others adamantly opposed that recommendation and threatened not to sign the report if it was included. Despite being an economist, I was not a fan of the recommendation on two grounds. One was my general skepticism about school vouchers, which led to my concern that such a school voucher experiment would, at best, generate answers to partial equilibrium questions, such as whether the students who made use of the voucher would achieve at higher levels, while shedding no light on what I viewed as the more important general equilibrium questions, such as how a large-scale voucher program would affect the public school system over time. The second was my fear that such a recommendation would detract attention from the broader analysis and recommendations in the volume. After some sleepless nights and a few tense meetings, I finally succeeded in gaining consensus by including the voucher recommendation as only one of three proposed experiments in urban education. In addition to the voucher experiment, we proposed experiments related to the building of teacher capacity and different forms of incentive systems, including alternative ways of compensating teachers. Nonetheless, as I had feared, much of the public commentary on our report centered on our proposal for a voucher experiment.

My general skepticism about vouchers, about which I later wrote in a 2002 article in the *Journal of Economic Perspectives*,[19] had arisen from the five months I had spent in New Zealand in 1998 doing research on that country's experience with parental choice of school, self-governing schools, and competition. That experience, which overlapped in time with the National Research Council study, was the first effort in what has become a wonderful collaboration with my husband in which we examined education reforms in various countries around the world. Given the global marketplace of ideas in education reform, we were convinced there were lessons the United States could learn from the experiences of other countries. The challenge was to find natural experiments in the form of large, bold reforms for which we could examine the general equilibrium effects over time. With its dramatic policy shift toward school autonomy and parental choice in the 1989–1991 period, New Zealand proved a worthy first case study, and, with the support of a Fulbright grant for lecturing and research, Ted and I spent the first five months of 1998 in that country working on our first coauthored book.[20] Four years later we repeated the experience with another Fulbright grant to South Africa, where we looked at that country's effort to fashion a racially equitable education system out of the ashes of apartheid.[21] Most recently we spent the spring of 2009 in the Netherlands examining the Dutch system of weighted student funding.

Our approach has been the same in all three countries. Drawing on his skills as a seasoned reporter, Ted spends a lot of time in schools finding out what is happening on the ground; with my skills as an applied policy analyst, I spend time collecting and analyzing data; and together we peruse public documents and interview policy makers. The result in each case has been a far more richly textured, comprehensive, and useful analysis than I could have produced with my economics training alone. Any initial concerns I might have had about writing a book with my new husband were quickly dispelled. Our skills were clearly complementary, and the writing turned out to be a smooth process with the text benefiting from intensive discussion about the framework and conclusions as well as detailed editing by each of us on the initial drafts of the other. Within the context of those projects, there was no need to make trade-offs between professional and personal activities – they were one and the same as we searched for information and developed our hypotheses, whether in discussion with others, arguing about what the data said, or brainstorming over a beer as we downloaded our respective findings or insights from the day's activities. The only rule we had to impose early on was no discussion of book-related topics after 10:00 P.M.

The first book that emerged from that collaboration – one on school choice and competition in New Zealand – is one of the most gratifying of my many research projects over the years. By transferring full operating authority to individual schools and giving parents the freedom to choose schools for their children, New Zealand created what might be described as a whole country of charter schools (albeit charter schools that were converted from traditional public schools) or as a quasi-voucher system. By the standards of some economists, our book, *When Schools Compete: A Cautionary Tale*, may fall short because the absence of test score data (other than from the school leaving exam for fifteen-year-olds) kept us from answering with any precision the main question often asked by economists these days: Did the move to choice and competition raise test scores? Other economists have criticized the book on the ground that it cannot shed much light on an ideal model of school choice and competition because New Zealand did not implement the model in its ideal form. Nonetheless, the boldness of the reform effort and the fact that we were able to observe how the policy was playing out over time generated a range of insights that have proved remarkably useful in understanding related reform efforts in the United States, whether they involve self-governing schools, additional parental choice of schools within the public system, charter schools, or voucher programs.

The New Zealand experience clearly demonstrates, for example, how unchecked parental choice generates pressures for polarization of student enrollment by ethnicity and socioeconomic status. In addition, it highlights a major downside of competition in the education context, namely that some schools inevitably end up as losers, in the sense that they lose not only students but also resources. Because schooling is compulsory and other schools are typically reluctant to accept their students, it is often not easy for such schools – referred to in the New Zealand context as downwardly spiraling schools – to be shut down. Further, our analysis showed how systems of parental choice tend to privilege the interests of a single group of stakeholders, namely those of current parents, unless specific counteractions are taken. Perhaps most important is our finding that governance changes alone are not able to solve the educational problems of schools serving large proportions of disadvantaged students. Despite the fact that the New Zealand reform effort removed bureaucratic barriers and provided clear incentives for schools to perform well, the schools at the bottom of the performance distribution were not successful largely because they ended up with greater concentrations of educationally disadvantaged students and fewer qualified teachers than before the reform.

The US emphasis on the testing of all students, a policy that began in many southern states well before the federal 2001 No Child Left Behind Act required annual testing of all students in grades 3 through 8 in all states, opened up for me quite a different line of research, one that was heavily dependent on massive amounts of good data. In the early 2000s, with funding from the Spencer Foundation, I worked with other researchers at Duke and the University of North Carolina on a memorandum of understanding with the North Carolina Department of Public Instruction to establish an education research data center. That center, housed at Duke, receives the administrative data from the state, cleans it, adds encrypted identifiers so that students can be matched over time, and makes the data available to researchers in North Carolina and elsewhere. Those rich administrative data, including test scores for all students, as well as detailed information on teachers and schools in the state of North Carolina over time, have provided the foundation for a highly productive and rewarding collaboration with two of my economist colleagues in Duke's policy school, Charles Clotfelter and Jacob Vigdor.

With additional funding from the Spencer Foundation, the team of Clotfelter, Ladd, and Vigdor was off and running, first with a series of papers on the segregation of students within and across schools, followed by a series of papers on various aspects of teacher policy. That put us in the right position at the right time to become part of the Center for Longitudinal Analysis in Education Research (CALDER), a research center funded by the US Department of Education operated through the Urban Institute with

Duke and four other universities as partners. For the past four years, funding through CALDER has allowed us to continue our research on teachers and teacher policy, student segregation, and racial and ethnic achievement gaps, and to broaden it in various ways, for example, to the effects of home access to computers or to high-speed Internet access on math and reading test scores. Most recently, the three of us have expanded our research into community colleges as part of a larger project financed by the Smith-Richardson Foundation on educational outcomes other than test scores.

Where I go from here in terms of research is not clear. As I noted earlier, I have no overall research plan. Instead, each research project typically opens up opportunities for new ones, albeit typically with some advance planning along the way to make sure I am in a position to seize those opportunities. My interest in doing policy-relevant research means that the topics I investigate are inevitably determined, at least in part, by the policy environment and that my research methods are heavily empirical. At the same time, most of my research projects have built on prior ones, are overlapping, and represent an ongoing search for more complete understanding –whether through broadening the perspective or deepening the analysis – of the policy issues I view as important.

As I write this, I am also involved with a range of other professional and policy activities. I am currently president-elect of the national Association for Public Policy and Management and co-chair of the Campaign for a Broader, Bolder Approach to Education Policy (bold.approach.org). The purpose of this campaign is to replace the current policy emphasis on punitive test-based approaches to accountability with a broader approach that expands beyond improving schools to addressing non-school factors that affect student learning. I suspect that this activity will inspire me to pursue new research projects examining some of those factors.

MY LIFE AND WORK PHILOSOPHY

As I have described, I started out strongly rooted in New England but have branched out far beyond my childhood dreams in terms of worldly experience and political orientation. I have now lived for extended periods in four different countries outside the United States, have traveled extensively to various parts of the world, and am happily ensconced in the southern state of North Carolina. Starting with the initial leftward shift in my political orientation during my year at the London School of Economics in the late 1960s, I have become increasingly concerned about income and wealth inequalities, poverty, and the challenges facing disadvantaged children and families. My move to North Carolina in 1986 – a mere twenty years or so after the civil rights movement – raised my awareness of the damaging legacy of racial injustice. My sensitivity to that issue was dramatically reinforced by the six months my husband and I spent in South Africa in 2002 doing research on the terrible legacy of the colonial and apartheid periods for the education of black and colored people in that country.

At the same time I have managed to hold onto the things that have always been important to me, including my ties to New England (we typically spend six weeks in New England each summer) and a commitment to family (through time with children and grandchildren in New England each summer, as well as visits to London and Amsterdam, where some of them live). I have also maintained a commitment to the New England–based religion of Unitarianism of my parents, but in its newer, broader form of Unitarian-Universalism. This noncreedal liberal religion is an affirmation of my view that no religion has a monopoly on wisdom and that the purpose of one's spiritual life is the continual search for wisdom, not the attainment of some ultimate truth.

With respect to my professional life, my philosophy is simple: it is to enjoy what I do, to work hard to do it as well as I can, and to make my research meaningful by focusing on policy-related issues consistent with my values. My approach in every area has always been to set my goals high, to work hard to meet them, but to lower them when I find they are unattainable. Such an approach to work has helped me maintain a healthy balance between my competitive drive to excel and my emotional well-being.

I have also strived to maintain a healthy balance between the various components of my professional life. I enjoy all aspects of my job: teaching, doing research, influencing policy, and (in moderation) taking on administrative tasks. I feel fortunate to have ended up as an applied economist in a policy school that suits me perfectly – one in which good teaching is highly valued, in which research opportunities abound, and in which I can have an impact on public policy both indirectly through the training of students and directly through my writing and involvement in the policy arena. The teaching of professional master's students who are pursuing careers in the public sector has been particularly rewarding for me, perhaps in part because it has been a way for me to carry on the spirit of my mentor, Richard Musgrave. He viewed government as essential to a healthy society and devoted much of his academic writing to the challenge of making it operate more efficiently and equitably. It gives me pleasure to pass some of his values and ideas on to my students and, in the process, to make them more effective public servants. Among the most satisfying of my accomplishments over the years are the three teaching awards I have received. The first was given to me by the Kennedy School master's students the year Harvard denied me tenure, and the other two were awarded by Duke for the teaching and mentoring of graduate students.

With respect to administrative work, my other mentor, Carolyn Shaw Bell, gave me some excellent advice early in my career when I was teaching at Wellesley. She pulled me aside one day and cautioned me with respect to administrative duties. The strategy she recommended – and the one that has worked superbly throughout my career – is to take on one significant administrative position each year and then to use that position as an excuse to turn down most other administrative tasks that would otherwise eat into time for research and teaching. Fortunately, I have found the main administrative jobs I have had at Duke, namely running the master's program, being associate director, and serving on the executive committee of the university faculty, not only enjoyable but also rewarding.

Turning to the balance between efficiency and other values in my teaching and research, I typically put more emphasis on equity considerations than do many of my colleagues. In my teaching, I do that in part by the order of the topics. Thus, in a microeconomics course, whether for professional master's students or undergraduates, I send a clear signal that distributional issues are an integral part of the course by placing a number of topics, such as information on the distribution of income and wealth and the design of income support programs or equalizing intergovernmental aid programs, early in the term, rather than waiting to the end of the course, as is typically the case in microeconomics textbooks when those topics are addressed at all. In addition, I continually emphasize that, however important efficiency may be as an economic concept, it is only one of many values of interest to policy makers. Consequently, I do not permit my students to confuse "efficient" with "optimal." Within the context of economics case discussions in which students are asked to make policy recommendations, I push them to make clear and to defend their value judgments, and to be quite explicit about how their value judgments help them make the often difficult trade-offs that emerge from their economic analysis. Finally, I am not afraid to model my own liberal values but am careful to clarify that no student need share my values to receive a high grade in the course.

I pursue a similar approach with my research. In this case, my liberal values are reflected in my choice of research topics. For example, my work on the fiscal problems of US cities was motivated largely by my concern about the low-income residents in declining cities. Once it became clear that the federal government was not going to direct significant aid to those cities, I investigated the literature on the potential for place-based strategies such as enterprise zones to help such residents.[22] Despite my hopes, I was forced to conclude that even if the tax breaks in the enterprise zones succeeded in attracting or creating new jobs, the existing low-income residents were unlikely to benefit because they lacked the skills needed to compete for the new jobs. That conclusion, in turn, was one of the considerations that generated my interest in education policy research and, within that field, in the careful, and often critical, analysis of policies that have been proposed as ways to improve education for disadvantaged students. The large role of values in influencing my research topics notwithstanding, I set high standards for the quality of my work and am careful to avoid having them influence my analysis and conclusions.

Finally, the reader has undoubtedly noticed that over the years I have worked with a large number of coauthors. In fact, a perusal of my résumé will uncover many more than the ones I have mentioned by name in this essay. Although I have also written many sole-authored articles and books, I have particularly enjoyed working with other researchers, whether they be junior or senior, economist or noneconomist. They have brought out the best in me and helped me be far more productive than I would have been working on my own. To all my collaborators, I am extremely grateful.

Notes

1 See his essay "Social Science, Ethics, and the Role of the Public Sector," in Michael Szenberg (ed.), *Eminent Economists: Their Life Philosophies* (Cambridge: Cambridge University Press, 1992).

2 This section draws heavily on the introduction to Helen F. Ladd, *The Challenge of Fiscal Disparities for State and Local Governments: The Selected Essays of Helen F. Ladd* (Cheltenham: Edward Elgar, 1999).

3 Charles M. Tiebout, "A Pure Theory of Local Expenditures," *Journal of Political Economy* 64 (October 1956): 416–424.

4 Wallace H. Oates, "The Effects of Property Taxes and Local Public Spending on Property Values: An Empirical Study of Tax Capitalization and the Tiebout Hypothesis," *Journal of Political Economy* 64 (October 1969): 416–424.

5 Peter Mieszkowski, "The Property Tax: An Excise Tax or a Profits Tax?" *Journal of Public Economics* 1, no. 1 (April 1972): 73–96.

6 T. C. Bergstrom and R. P. Goodman, "Private Demands for Public Goods," *American Economic Review* 63, no. 3 (June 1973): 280–297; T. E. Borcherding and R. T. Deacon, "The Demand for the Services of Non-Federal Governments," *American Economic Review* 62, no. 5 (December 1972): 891–901.

7 Helen F. Ladd, "The Role of the Property Tax: A Reassessment," in R. A. Musgrave (ed.), *Broad Based Taxes: New Options and Sources* (Baltimore: Johns Hopkins Press, Committee for Economic Development, 1973).

8 The approach is described in Katherine L. Bradbury, Helen F. Ladd, Mark Perrault, Andrew Reschovsky, and John Yinger, "State Aid to Offset Fiscal Disparities Across Communities," *National Tax Journal* 37, no. 2 (June 1984): 151–170.

9 Helen F. Ladd and John M. Yinger, "The Case for Equalizing Aid," *National Tax Journal* 47, no. 1 (March 1994): 211–224.

10 Baltimore: Johns Hopkins University Press.

11 Fred C. Doolittle and Helen F. Ladd, "Which Level of Government Should Assist the Poor?" *National Tax Journal* 35, no. 3 (September 1982): 322–336; Helen F. Ladd, "The State Aid Decision: Changes in State Aid to Local Governments, 1982–87," *National Tax Journal* 44, no. 4, pt. 2 (December 1991): 477–496.

12 Helen F. Ladd, "State Responses to the TRA86 Revenue Windfalls: A New Test of the Flypaper Effect," *Journal of Policy Analysis and Management* 12, no. 1 (Winter 1993): 82–103.

13 Helen F. Ladd, "An Economic Evaluation of State Limitations on Local Taxing and Spending Powers," *National Tax Journal* 31, no. 1 (March 1993): 1–18.

14 Katherine L. Bradbury, Helen F. Ladd, and Claire Christopherson, "Proposition 2 1/2: Initial Impacts, Part I" and "Proposition 2 1/2: Initial Impacts: Part II," *New England Economic Review* (January/February, March/April 1982); Helen F. Ladd and Nicolaus Tideman (eds.), *Tax and Expenditure Limitations* (Washington, DC: Urban Institute, 1981).

15 Helen F. Ladd (primary author), *Local Government Tax and Land Use Policy in the U.S.: Understanding the Links* (Cheltenham: Edward Elgar, 1998).

16 See note 1.

17 Washington, DC: Brookings Institution Press, 1996.

18 Washington, DC: National Academy of Sciences, 1999.

19 Helen F. Ladd, "School Vouchers: A Critical View," *Journal of Economic Perspectives* (November 2002).

20 Edward B. Fiske and Helen F. Ladd, *When Schools Compete: A Cautionary Tale* (Washington DC: Brookings Institution, 2000).

21 We published that research in Edward B. Fiske and Helen F. Ladd, *Elusive Equity: Education Reform in Post-Apartheid South Africa* (Washington, DC: Brookings Institution, 2004).

22 Helen F. Ladd, "Spatially Targeted Economic Development Strategies: Do They Work?" *Cityscape: A Journal of Policy Development and Research* 1, no. 1 (August 1994): 193–218.

19

God, Ants, and Thomas Bayes

Harry M. Markowitz

The editors of this volume have invited me to present here my personal philosophy. But I cannot distinguish between my personal philosophy and my theoretical philosophy. As I explained in my autobiography (Markowitz 1990), when I was in high school I read science at a nontechnical level, like the *ABC of Relativity*, and the original writings of great philosophers. In particular, I was struck by David Hume's (1776) argument that even though I release a ball a thousand times and, in every instant, it falls to the floor, that does not prove that it will necessarily fall to the floor the thousand-and-first time. In other words, even though Newton's law of gravity worked in thousands of instances, that did not prove that it would never fail – such as in explaining the orbit of Mercury! Essentially, my philosophical interest in high school lay in the question "What do we know and how do we know it?"

When I entered the Economics Department at the University of Chicago I was naturally drawn to the economics of uncertainty. In particular, the work of Leonard J. Savage (1954) – building on that of von Neumann and

Morgenstern (1944) – presented, to me among many others, a convincing axiomatic argument that, in acting under uncertainty, one should maximize expected utility using probability beliefs where objective probabilities are not known. It is a corollary of the latter conclusion that, as information accumulates, one should shift one's beliefs according to Bayes's rule, reviewed later in this essay. (Hume, too, said that one should attach probabilities to beliefs but did not specify that Bayes's rule should be used in response to growing evidence for or against various hypotheses.)

In a sense, Savage finesses the question of "What do we know and how do we know it?" Instead he answers the question of how we should *act* in the face of uncertainty. Since everything is uncertain – everything, that is, except possibly mathematical relationships – the L. J. Savage solution is a prescription for all action.[1]

This does not mean that I do a mathematical calculation to decide which DVD to choose when it is my turn to pick out one for my wife's and my nightly movie watching. However, when I think reflectively about questions of expected utility, personal probability, and actual action, I ask myself if, and in what manner, my various actions are consistent or not with my beliefs.

If it is true (as Ralph Waldo Emerson said) that "foolish consistency is the hobgoblin of little minds," then my mind must be exceedingly small. It is a fetish of mine to not have a theory I hold in one context be inconsistent with a theory I hold in another context. Furthermore, I make a living by giving advice. In particular, I advise on how one should allocate funds among investments. It is essential to me to understand whether my advice is consistent with my beliefs. I am not saying that I have reconciled all my beliefs and hypotheses. But one of my objectives is to try to do so.

By and large I find that the attempt to reconcile apparently conflicting beliefs is a driving force for pondering and, sometimes, for discovery. After all, "it is the exception that *tests* the rule."[2] For example, since I believe in maximizing expected utility (using probability beliefs where objective probabilities are not known), then how dare I recommend the use of the mean and variance of return in choosing portfolios of securities? I did not think about this issue prior to writing my 1952 article but gave it serious thought while writing my 1959 book. I concluded that, for many utility functions, if probability distributions are not too spread out, then a quadratic approximation fits quite well. In that case the mean-variance approximation to expected utility is quite good – *no matter what the shape of the distribution*. In particular, for Daniel Bernoulli's (1738) logarithmic utility function

$$U = \log(1 + \textit{return}) \tag{1}$$

a distribution of returns mostly between a 30 percent loss and a 40 percent gain on the portfolio-as-a-whole, and never too close to a 100 percent loss, ensures a close approximation between expected utility and a certain function of only mean and variance (see Markowitz 1959: ch. 6).

I was questioned on this during a visit to Hebrew University. Someone asked how I justified mean-variance analysis when utility functions are not quadratic nor probability distributions Gaussian. I cited the arguments in my 1959 book on quadratic approximations – as distinguished from quadratic utility functions. Marshall Sarnat said, "Let's test Harry's theory. Let's get lots of utility functions and returns on portfolios, and see if one can approximate expected utility from mean and variance." The details of how this should be done were worked out by Haim Levy and me, and published as Levy and Markowitz (1979). We concluded that, except for some rather strange utility functions that were subject to "pathological risk aversion," mean-variance approximations to expected utility are quite robust (see also Markowitz, Reid, and Tew 1989).

In the following sections I will not discuss the application of mean-variance analysis to investment decisions, or operations research techniques I have developed for other practical decision problems (Markowitz 2009). Rather, I will review Bayesianism as put forth by L. J. Savage; tell you how I know I am a Bayesian; and apply Bayesianism to philosophical questions such as: Is there a God and, if so, what is He or She or It like?

WHAT IS A BAYESIAN?

Bayes's (1763) rule, published posthumously, is named after Thomas Bayes (1702–1761). As an example of the use of Bayes's rule, suppose that a ball – either red or black – is to be drawn from one of two urns. Suppose that, in advance, there is a probability of 3/4 that the ball will be drawn from urn A and 1/4 that it will be drawn from urn B. Suppose that four out of five balls in urn A are red, whereas two out of five balls in B are red. Suppose that a red ball is drawn in fact. What is the probability, given this information, that the ball was drawn from urn A?

Bayes's rule is based on the following calculation: There are three out of four chances that urn A was chosen and, if urn A was chosen, then there are four out of five chances that the red ball would appear. Therefore, there was a

$$\frac{3}{4}\frac{4}{5} = \frac{12}{20}$$

chance that a red ball would be drawn from urn A. There similarly was a

$$\frac{1}{4}\frac{2}{5} = \frac{2}{20}$$

chance that a red ball would be drawn from urn B. The remaining probability – six out of twenty – is the probability that a black ball would be drawn. Given that a red ball is drawn, there are twelve out of fourteen (not out of twenty) chances that it came from urn A and two out of fourteen that it came from urn B. Thus, the probability that the ball was drawn from urn A, given that a red ball was drawn, is 12/14 (= 6/7). Thus, the calculation

$$\frac{12}{20} / \left(\frac{12}{20} + \frac{2}{20} \right) = \frac{12}{14}$$

yields the probability that the ball came from the first urn.

The general case, expressed algebraically, is that

$$P(h_i|O) = \frac{P(h_i) \cdot L(O|h_i)}{\sum_{j=1}^{n} P(h_j) \cdot L(O|h_j)}, \tag{2}$$

where $P(h_i)$ is the *prior* probability of hypothesis h_i (before the observation), $L(O|h_i)$ is the probability (or "likelihood") of getting observation O if the hypothesis h_i is true, $P(h_i|O)$ is the *posterior* probability of the hypothesis given the observation (and similarly for j, of course), and n is the number of hypotheses (assumed here to be finite). This calculation is known as Bayes's rule.

One is not referred to as a Bayesian because one applies Bayes's rule to the type of situation that Thomas Bayes analyzed. Rather, one is referred to as a Bayesian if one believes that action should be based on "probability beliefs" when objective probabilities are not known and that one should update these beliefs according to Bayes's rule as evidence accumulates. This view was held, and vigorously defended, by Bruno de Finetti (1937) but was not widely held by statisticians until the publication of Savage (1954).

Savage used an "axiomatic approach" to argue his case. He took certain rules about "rational decision making" as axiomatic and deduced personal probability and Bayes's rules from these. A simplified version of these axioms is presented in Markowitz (1959). The simplification comes, in part, because I assumed that there are only a finite number of possible hypotheses that might be true (where this number could be in the billions or trillions) and only a finite number of possible outcomes that can occur from any experiment or any one lifetime.

Another reason the Markowitz (1959) axiom system could be simpler is that Savage excludes any consideration of objective probability, whereas I assumed that the decision maker can rank alternatives that involve the possibility of objective probabilities. This does not mean that I assume that there are true random-number-generating devices in fact – only that hypotheses can be stated and considered involving such devices. An example would be the hypothesis that the logarithm of the ratio of some market index on day $t + 1$ to that on day t is normally distributed. I will not repeat the Savage or Markowitz arguments here or the thrusts of those who disagree and the parries of those of us who defend Bayesianism. The Savage and Markowitz citations – and whatever citations they (and Google) have in turn – can speak for themselves. Rather, I would like to explore the implications of Bayesianism for certain philosophical questions. In particular, I start with the following question.

HOW DO I KNOW I AM A BAYESIAN?

In his "Meditations," Descartes (1641) asked himself, "What do I know with certainty?" He said that what seems to him solid may be an illusion, his memories might be in error, or he might be dreaming. He decided that he knew this much at least: "I think, therefore I am." I go through the same exercise as Descartes, trying to clear my mind of other matters. When I reflectively pose questions like:

Is there a God?
Assuming there is a God, what is He or She or It like?
Will it rain tomorrow?

I always ask myself: What is the evidence pro and con? What is the likelihood that the evidence would be observed if this or that hypothesis were true? In other words, when I ask myself deep philosophical questions such as Descartes asked – or, in principle, when I ask questions of a more immediate practical sort – I answer (more or less) in terms of Bayes's rule. I conclude, therefore, that whatever else I am, "I am a Bayesian."

Note that I do not start by asking what my priors are and then do a Bayes's rule calculation. Rather, I consider what my views are on the subject; ask what is the evidence that supports my views and what would tend to contradict them; and consider how strongly I hold views on this particular subject and what alternate views seem nearly as plausible. In short, I seem to form my opinions (usually implicitly) *more or less* in accord with Bayes's rule.

"GOD DID IT" AND OTHER DIFFUSE HYPOTHESES

In the following discussion, an observation is essentially the same as it was for Descartes: it is the totality of sensations I (you) have now, including memories of what I (you) read many years ago about the definition of π, the history of the American Revolution, and what I (you) recall – that is, think I (you) remember – about what the Bible says that God said to Moses. If I were truly a Leonard J. Savage RDM (rational decision maker) I would hold many hypotheses – perhaps an infinity of them – in my head simultaneously and would shift my beliefs from their prior values, before this instant, to posterior values according to Bayes's rule. Clearly this is not a human capability. All I can do is humbly try to emulate my idol L. J. Savage's RDM.

In particular, let us try to think through the shifts in belief that an RDM would make on the question "Does God exist?" The probability an RDM would attach to the compound hypothesis that God (or gods) exists is the sum of the probabilities that a God (or gods) like this or that exist. (We will assume that, as in Markowitz 1959, there are only a finite number of hypotheses about the world. This allows us to use finite sums rather than Lesbegue integrals and not worry about integrability.)

We divide hypotheses about God into two classes: those that assert that God did it (or the gods did it) equally surely no matter what occurs and those that admit that some observations are more likely than others even if there is a God (or gods). If there are a very large number (n) of possible observations, then the likelihood of getting observation O given the hypothesis H_G, that "no matter what happens God did it," is

$$L(O|H_G) = 1/n. \tag{3}$$

Then, according to Equation (2), for a Bayesian the probability that H_G is true given the observation is

$$P(H_G|O) = \frac{P(H_G)/n}{\sum_{i=1}^{n} P(H_i)L(O|H_i)}$$

Suppose that H_a is an alternative hypothesis which does not imply that all observations are equally likely. In particular, suppose that H_a implies that the probability of O is $1/m$, which is substantially greater than $1/n$ Then the ratio of posterior belief in H_G to that of H_a is

$$\frac{P(H_G|O)}{P(H_a|O)} = \frac{1/n}{1/m} = \frac{m}{n}. \tag{4}$$

Thus, if $1/m \gg 1/n$, because $n \gg m$, belief shifts substantially against H_G in favor of H_a. In short, no matter what is observed, the hypothesis that "whatever happens God did it" loses probability massively in favor of any hypothesis that sticks its neck out and is not contradicted. Belief similarly shifts against any other "diffuse hypothesis" that considers all possible observations equally likely.

Another class of hypotheses is that some specific hypothesis is true, like H_{GN}, Newton's (law) of universal gravity and, in addition, God decreed that the world should be so. Since the hypothesis H_{NN} of Newton's law of gravity and *no* God, implies the same likelihood for every observation as does H_{GN} (Newton's law of gravity and God decreed it so), no observation can shift belief between H_{NN} and H_{GN}. The pair of hypotheses "H_{NN} or H_{GN}" will gain or lose probability depending on what is observed, but the split between them will not change.

For example, consider the really implausible tale that scientists tell, that prior to about 14 billion years ago there was absolutely nothing: neither space, nor time, nor Einstein's space-time, as well as no matter and no energy. Then, out of literally nowhere, an infinitely dense, infinitesimal spark of world appeared and expanded to today's entire universe. Further, as of this moment, it seems that the universe will continue to expand – at an ever increasing rate – forever. Since this increasing rate of expansion is inconsistent with the known laws of the universe (including either Newton's or Einstein's theory of gravity) there must be "dark energy" (in addition to an already postulated invisible "dark matter").

Concerning the hypothesis that God created the world (not in six human days a few thousand years ago, but) about 14 billion years ago versus the hypothesis that there is no God (or gods) and nothing existed prior to some 14 billion years ago: Since I can see no verifiable implication to shift beliefs between them, I am free to believe whatever I fancy. In fact, I do not find either hypothesis very appealing. I prefer to believe that the world did not start 14 billion years ago; that the singularity at the start of the Big Bang was preceded by a so-called Big Crunch, when the world contracted to a singularity before expanding from the same singularity; that, despite its current apparent accelerating expansion, the expanding universe will eventually begin to contract and end again in another Big Crunch – to end one cycle and begin another. Since God (or something) *does* seem to play dice, contrary to Einstein's conjecture, the next time will not be the same as this time, which was not the same as the previous time.

A MOSTLY NICER HYPOTHESIS

The following is another hypothesis about the genesis of the world. At first I spun this yarn because it portrayed a rather pleasant picture. After I thought about it a bit, I decided that it was arguably more plausible than the standard cosmologist's story (15 billion years ago there was nothing – no space, no time, no stuff) as well as the *literal* creationist story. The evidence, admittedly, is circumstantial, and my probabilities have shifted toward this hypothesis very little as compared with their shift toward the hypothesis "Huge living things existed millions of years ago" that took place when I first saw the skeletons of a brontosaurus and a *Tyrannosaurus rex*.

The Bible says God created man in His image. But clearly man created God in man's image. For example, when man was a shepherd he wrote, "God is my shepherd." So I will assume that God is like me, but supersized. The most God-like activity in which I currently engage is the building (with Bruce Jacobs and Ken Levy) of the JLMSim market simulator (see Jacobs, Levy, and Markowitz 2005).

JLMSim contains various types of entities such as investors, traders, portfolio analysts, and statisticians. Individuals of these types estimate means, variances, and covariances of various securities; generate efficient frontiers from these estimates; use the efficient frontiers for reoptimization; place orders with traders who execute them; and so on. The objective in building JLMSim is for the economic agents inside the computer to act "just like people" (we have created them in our image) and to see if their interactions produce markets such as we see in fact.

My proposal concerning the creation of the world that we see about us (including you and me) is that it is a simulation programmed by a superior being whom I will call "Yang H." As the investors in JLMSim are to me, so I am to Yang H. (Thus, my hypothesis does indeed imply that Yang H created man in Yang H's image.)

This hypothesis has certain implications. The first is that Yang H is not omniscient. If he were, he would not have to run a program to see if a certain set of hypotheses imply Yang-like behavior; he could think through the implications of any such hypothesis. A second implication is that 14 billion years for Yang H is like a computer run (maybe an overnight run) for us.

Since the capabilities of Yang H are limited (although tremendously superior to ours), I will refer to him in lowercase, as "he" rather than "He." Since I cannot conceive of a world in which the researcher has no one "at home" to whom to explain his latest theories and observations, I assume that Yang H has a Yin B, whom I assume is a "she." I also assume that there are other YinYang-lings in YinYang Land.

The physics of YinYang Land is quite different from that of the world in which you and I live. In particular, since 14 billion years in our world is a feasible computer run in their world, it is not plausible for signals to propagate there no faster than the speed of light here. Perhaps the speed of light in our world is determined by the speed of Yang H's computer, and the granularity of our world, as expressed by Planck's constant, is determined by the arithmetic of Yang H's PC.

Clearly the quantum (i.e., discrete) nature of various fundamental phenomena in our world (such as the location and spin of an electron within an atom) helps Yang H represent, for example, the state of the electron within his digital computer. Also, the Pauli exclusion principle – that no two electrons in an atom can have the same quantum numbers (e.g., two can have all other numbers the same if they have different spins, but not if they have the same spins) – helps Yang H represent the state of the entire ensemble of electrons within an atom. It might seem unnecessary for Yang H to use such programming conveniences, but perhaps our world is a very large simulation, even for *his* PC, and is pushing the state of the art.[3]

One problem for any deistic hypothesis is: Why does evil exist? If our world is a miniature of YinYang Land, then the YinYangs too must be subject to a struggle between good and evil. Perhaps they have their Hitler or Stalin, or they have a fallen angel like our devil, or good guys and bad guys, as in our Hollywood westerns, Darth Vadar in *Star Wars*, and He Who Must Not Be Mentioned in the *Harry Potter* series.

It may be objected that the investors in JLMSim do not *feel* fear and greed as real investors do. But Yang H's simulation is more "realistic" than that of my colleagues and me, because he is a much better programmer than we are and has a better PC. In *his* simulation, that is, *our* world, greed and fear occur naturally, by natural selection, so that we will seek to secure the food, territory, and sex we need for our species to survive and will cautiously avoid our predators and enemies.

The preceding paragraph discusses an objection one might have to my YinYang hypothesis. Now let us consider major alternatives. I do not believe that a literal interpretation of the Bible is sufficiently plausible to need comment. But what about the notion that God is a benevolent, omnipotent being for whom a day may be hundreds of millions of years for a human. My problem with this kind of hypothesis is that I cannot see how such a being would permit rape, torture, and genocide. The explanation that He will make it all right in the end, at the sounding of the last trumpet, seems to me lame.

As to a completely humanistic explanation, without hypothesizing any transhuman being, William James (1902), in his *Varieties of Religious Experience*, describes overwhelming flashes of insight and ecstasy that have come to humans with a great variety of religious beliefs. Explanations for these observations are (1) that they are some unusual psychological aberration into which people sometimes stumble or (2) that they are a reward for getting close to some transcendental truth (e.g., that Yang H programmed into us to encourage us to try to understand YinYangs). My problem with the first explanation is: What was the survival value of this aberration? What good was such a capability to an erect great ape?

DO HUMANS HAVE A SIXTH SENSE?

Except for the remote possibility mentioned in note 3, I do not see how to test the hypothesis that this world is a simulation run programmed by a superior being. I now turn to another matter that most find "way out," at least at first, but that is based on observing nature and can be easily subjected to experimental verification.

By and large I assign low probabilities to the existence of objects, forces, and events that some call supernatural. Not only do I think it unlikely that the sun stood still – that is, the earth stopped rotating about its axis without anyone feeling an enormous deceleration – I also don't believe in the Loch Ness monster and assign a low probability to the existence of Big Foot.

Nor did I give much credence to reports by perfectly sane and sensible friends and acquaintances of mine who reported that, under extraordinary circumstances, they had received a message from someone near and dear, that the transmitting party was in great trouble, or that the person had just died or was about to die. The reason I did not believe that these happenings were more than coincidence was that I could not see any mechanism – any sequence of natural events – that explained them.

Then, when we had a temporary ant problem in our kitchen, it struck me how the ants must know where food is and that the same mechanism must work as well for other species. In order to take advantage of the presence of people, who sometimes leave almost invisible ant yummies on kitchen counters, ants had to evolve rapidly to exploit the opportunities presented to them by humans. If you think that natural selection cannot adapt a population to a new situation that fast recall how, starting with a wolf, the Pekingese and the Great Dane were produced by human selection. The only difference is that the selection process in one case depended on some human taste for cuddliness or massive size while, in the other case, it was (for the ants) a matter of life or death.

One capability ants now have is to sense the presence of ant-supportive food and send the appropriate number of ants to it. An appropriate number might be one or two ants for very small pieces of food, whereas the proper response in other cases may be to send great squads.

How does the ant know where ant-supportive food is located? I will use, as data, the response of ants in my kitchen. I think it is particularly instructive to consider ant response to an after-dinner situation. I cite the following facts in this regard: First, the ants do not live in our house; they live in the grass or underground at least thirty or forty feet away. They do not seem to be constantly exploring every part of the house that might contain food. While we do on occasion see one or two isolated ants wandering on the kitchen counter, and this is sometimes interpreted as ant scouts getting ready to alert the entire pack if food is found, we do not find similar ants in any other place where food might possibly be found. For example, how do they know that we don't snack in the living room? We didn't find ants wandering about there.

So what signal alerts a few or many ants to the presence of ant-supportive food? We know that this signal travels no faster than the speed of light. Given the distances involved, the latter may be considered instantaneous. The response by ants to the presence of food is conceivably "instantaneous," in fact, since the time that elapses between the food being left on the counter and the arrival of the ants is consistent with the tiny ants, with their tiny legs, starting out immediately upon the presence of food.

The signal is clearly not human-visible electromagnetic waves, since nothing glows when I turn off the lights in the kitchen. Nor is it sound that transmits the signal, since the little piece of food just lies there very quietly. Nor, I contend, is it smell that signals the ants, for sometimes the food particles are extremely small and the house presents an effective barrier to odor. Consider the stockyard smell in Chicago, where I lived when I was a child. If the wind was blowing in the wrong direction you smelled the stockyard, distinctly. But you had to step outside of the house on the north side of Chicago to be reminded that there were meatpacking plants on the south side. Ants have to eat even if the wind is blowing from the ant colony to the house. It seems hard to believe that a tiny morsel that I can hardly see generates enough odor that it passes through the walls of the house and, in spite of the wind, makes its way to the ants. (Think of Native Americans keeping on the leeward side of the herd when hunting bison long ago.)

The ants clearly must rely on some signal that can pass through walls. As we observe when we listen to the radios in our houses, what passes through walls easily is radio waves, that is, *low-frequency* electromagnetic waves. It may seem absurd that ants can see low-frequency radio waves. (I say "see" since the eye is said to see human-visible electromagnetic waves.) There is no particular reason that the longer, less energetic part of the spectrum should not be used by various species. It should be easier to work with these than the more energetic human-visible light whose upper limit approaches frequencies that cause sunburn and mutations. The less energetic waves seem quite friendly in comparison. Humans usually do not find them useful, because humans live aboveground and have to worry about things a few dozen yards away that might eat them. Radio waves are not as useful as waves in the human-visible range because they do not as clearly resolve the fine details of objects that humans might eat or that might eat humans.

Low-frequency radiation is given off in great profusion by objects even when they are not visible to humans. In particular, bodies must be relatively hot in order to radiate visible light (think "hot poker"), whereas much less energy is required to emit low-frequency photons (think infrared goggles). Ants presumably use higher-energy parts of the electromagnetic spectrum when appropriate, namely when they are aboveground and are coming within sight of food or when feet walk near them. But our concern now is not how ants respond in the world where we can see them, but how they find their way from underground to our kitchen as quickly as they do. The only signal I can think of that can penetrate walls and reach ants underground is low-frequency electromagnetic (radio) waves.

OTHER SPECIES

Other users of radio waves include silverfish and roaches that live inside houses or apartment buildings and can find their way to food in the dark. Also, since the US Army has developed a capability of seeing at night using the infrared part of the electromagnetic spectrum, it is absurd to assume that thousands of years of natural selection would not develop a similar capability in owls.

I will further argue that radio waves are used by dogs, elephants, and human beings. I have heard and read many stories of humans knowing immediately when another human dies. Since I did not know of any mechanism for this, I assumed that it was sheer accident. I now understand the method, and the motive.

All things radiate electromagnetic waves in the low-energy region. The radiation is especially effective if, as with radio stations, the radiator and/or the recipient uses an antenna. Antennae do not necessarily look like such. For example, the instructions for a radio I own say that the cord used to transmit electricity from the wall socket to the radio is also the antenna that receives radio signals.

Ants seem to have obvious antennae on the top of their heads – like the "rabbit ears" on an old television set. Perhaps humans also have an antenna, namely their spinal cord (similar to the electrical cord on the aforementioned radio). Such would also be the case, then, for all vertebrates, animals with backbones. But not all vertebrates are observed communicating when one of their members dies. This pertains to motive, whereas the cord pertains to method. The motive requires a strong attachment like a herd of elephants waiting for an elder elephant to die somewhere where they cannot see, a dog waiting for word of the fate of its master even though it is not allowed in the room where the master lies dying, or a human who will be very moved upon learning of the death of someone near and dear.

It may be objected that the universe is filled with countless bodies radiating low-frequency electromagnetic waves. How is it possible for one being to pick out the waves that emanate from some other specific being? And what particular signal does a dying person transmit?

True, the world is filled with radio waves. Nevertheless, my radio is able to distinguish waves that come from one station as opposed to another station. As to the message the dying person broadcasts: the only message is that the dying person stopped radiating. The entity that receives the information that a beloved has stopped radiating must have some ability to distinguish the spectrum of a specific person from that of all others. But this entity has been very close to the beloved and thus can recognize, subconsciously, the beloved's peculiar electromagnetic pattern. The fact that this is subconscious rather than conscious reinforces the notion that the capability exists in pre-human species.

I propose, therefore, that higher mammals have motive and method to use electromagnetic waves in the low-energy range for purposes that are sufficiently important and are not covered by other signals. This is a testable hypothesis, not for humans with dying loved ones, of course, but for ants. It requires two experimental setups: one in which smells and wandering ants can get through but radiation cannot (think lead barriers staggered so that ants can find their way through this maze, but there is no-line-of-sight radiation possible) versus a similar maze (maybe made of plaster boards) where radio waves are not impeded.

If the ants find their treats in the latter maze but not the former, that should shift beliefs toward the use of radio waves, at least by ants. But if the experiment shifts beliefs substantially concerning ants, it should shift them at least a little for dogs, elephants, and humans.

THE GOLDEN RULE

Philosophy is concerned with "What is right and wrong?" as well as "What do we know and how do we know it?" Answers to the former question are often deduced from first principles. The most famous such first principle is "Do unto others as you would have others do unto you."

While this rule sounds plausible and comes to us from high authority, it has a problem. If the one who is being advised is a masochist, then he or she would like to be treated sadistically. We would not want that person to act sadistically unto others. Nor does the rule work universally if we switch it around to "Do unto others as they wish to be done unto." If the person to be done unto is an egomaniac who wants all to bow down to him or her, don't do it. My proposal for a golden rule is this:

> Live so that when you die those who know you will say, "I am saddened to see him [or her] go, but he [or she] lived a good life."

The recently deceased Peter Bernstein (of Bernstein 1996) is a perfect example.

REFERENCES

Bayes, T. R. (1763). "An Essay Towards Solving a Problem in the Doctrine of Chances," *Philosophical Transactions of the Royal Society of London* 53: 370. (Reprinted in *Biometrika* **45** [1958]: 293–295.)

Bernoulli, Daniel (1738). *"Specimen theoriae novae de mensura sortis.* Exposition of a New Theory on the Measurement of Risk" (English translation by Louise Sommer), *Econometrica* 22 (1954): 23–36. (Originally published in *Communications of the Academy of Science Imp. Petropolitanae* 5 [1738]: 175–192).

Bernstein, Peter L. (1996). *Against the Gods: The Remarkable Story of Risk.* New York: John Wiley and Sons.

De Finetti, B. (1937). "Sur la condition d'equivalence partille, Colloque Geneve 1937," in *Actualites Scientifiques et Industrielles,* no. 739. Paris: Hermann, 1938.

Descartes, R. (1641). *Meditationes de prima philosophia, in qua Dei existential et animae immortalitas demonstrtur. Meditations on First Philosophy,* translated by John Cottingham. Cambridge: Cambridge University Press, 1996.

Gödel, K. (1931). "Uber Formal unentscheidbare Sätze der Principia Mathematica und verwandter Systeme, I." *Monatshefte für Mathematik und Physik* 38: 173–198. (Reprinted in Jean van Heijenoort, *A Source Book in Mathematical Logic, 1879–1931*. Cambridge, MA: Harvard University Press, 1967, pp. 596–616.)

Hume, D. (1776). *A Treatise of Human Nature*. Glasgow: William Collins Sons, 1962.

Jacobs, Bruce I., Kenneth N. Levy, and Harry M. Markowitz, "Portfolio Optimization with Factors, Scenarios, and Realistic Short Positions," by *Operations Research*, 53, no. 4, July/August 2005, pp. 586–599.

James, William (1902). *The Varieties of Religious Experience: A Study in Human Nature*. New York: Modern Library.

Levy, H. and H. M. Markowitz (1979). "Approximating Expected Utility by a Function of Mean and Variance," *American Economic Review* 69, no. 3 (June): 308–317.

Markowitz, H. M. (1952). "Portfolio Selection," *Journal of Finance* 7, no. 1 (March): 77–91.

(1959). *Portfolio Selection: Efficient Diversification of Investments*. New York: John Wiley & Sons; New Haven, CT: Yale University Press, 1970; 2d ed. Oxford: Basil Blackwell, 1991.

(1990). Harry M. Markowitz Biography. In *The Nobel Prizes Yearbook*, 291–294. Stockholm: Nobel Foundation.

(2009). *Harry Markowitz: Selected Works*. Hackensack, NJ: World Scientific.

Markowitz, H. M., D. W. Reid, and B. V. Tew (1989). "The Value of a Blank Check," *Journal of Portfolio Management* (Summer): 82–91.

Savage, L. J. [1954] (1972). *The Foundations of Statistics*. 2d rev. ed. Dover, New York.

Von Neumann, J. and O. Morgenstern (1944). *Theory of Games and Economic Behavior*, Princeton, NJ: Princeton University Press; 3d ed. (1953).

Notes

1 I say that mathematical theorems are *possibly* known with certainty, for two reasons. First, Gödel (1931) shows that any logical system, that is strong enough to include or prove the rules of integer arithmetic cannot prove itself consistent. Second, for any believed proposition there is some probability that there is a bug in its proof. Hume's advice on this matter is to keep proofs short.

2 One usually says, "The exception pro*v*es the rule" and then one explains that "proves" really means "tests." But the original meaning was not the latter; rather it was that the exception defines the rule. For example, a sign in a dorm saying "No loud noises after 10 P.M." implies that loud noises are permitted before 10 P.M. But the idea that the exception tests the rule deserves to have a saying of its own. For example, when the orbit of Uranus seemed to be an exception to Newton's law of gravity, astronomers looked for a new planet and found Neptune, confirming Newton's law. However, Mercury's failure to obey the Newtonian "law" confirmed Einstein's rethinking of the nature of gravity.

3 It is not necessary that YinYang Land have a three-dimensional space or a four-dimensional space-time. It does seem to me that YinYang Land space-time must be some kind of metric space whose points are partially ordered by before-after-ness (BA-ness): think "event horizon." The mechanics of YinYang Land may be "classical"

or "quantum." The randomness in our own world may be due to Yang H's deterministic but highly sophisticated random-number generator. In this case, Einstein was right: the apparent randomness of our world is due to a deeper deterministic process. This then is a testable hypothesis or, more precisely, has testable variants. Suppose that some observable, apparently random process is in fact generated by a known pseudo-random-number generator, carried on with a large number of decimal places. Then it will have a nonrandom pattern, perhaps discernible sooner than it can be seen that the whole stream is repeating itself. Our cryptographers and numerical analysts could look for such.

If YinYang people are three-dimensional like us, but we are both embedded in a four-dimensional space (5D space-time), then Yang H could be close but still invisible to us. Think of a two-dimensional playing card held perpendicular to one's line of vision. Then Yang H's output screen would have to be parallel to his space rather than ours.

20

The Path of a Monetary Economist

Frederic S. Mishkin

In this essay, I outline the path that I have taken as a monetary economist. As befits this volume, my discussion is necessarily very personal (hopefully not too self-indulgent), and it also illustrates my personal philosophy of economics and how it developed over my career. Let me start by describing why I became an economist in the first place, and then I will move on to my research, teaching, and role as a policy maker.

WHY I BECAME AN ECONOMIST

The path to becoming an economist starts as early as I remember. I was a pretty nerdy child and I was destined for academia. From the time I was six,

The views expressed here are my own and are not necessarily those of Columbia University or the National Bureau of Economic Research. Disclosure of my outside compensated activities can be found on my website at http://www0.gsb.columbia.edu/faculty/fmishkin/ OUTSIDEACTIVITIES.pdf.

my parents and siblings sometimes referred to me as the "little professor," not just because I was studious, with my face always in a book, but also because I was a "space cadet" who often was off in another world. Although this appellation was to some extent a criticism that my social skills were not of the highest order, I never took offense. Indeed, I was proud to be a nerd. When my eldest sister, whom I love dearly, came home for Thanksgiving from her freshman year at college at a small teacher's college in Boston, she told us about going to a mixer with boys from MIT and described them as "creeps" (the word used for "nerds" at the time, which was in the early 1960s). She then turned to me and said, "Just like you." Again, I didn't take offense at all. Indeed, I took it as a compliment because I wanted to be just like them and go to MIT, which I did six years later.

My first love was science. I couldn't get enough of it and loved to think about how things worked. With the launch of *Sputnik* in the late 1950s and the space race, schools and the media took a greater interest in science. My favorite TV show was *Mr. Wizard*, in which Don Herbert conducted all these fantastic science experiments with a group of kids. At first, I wanted to be an astronomer, but living in New York City meant that I could rarely see the stars, so I dropped that idea and thought I might become a physicist.

My father, whom I still miss every day, played a key role in turning my academic interests toward economics. The central event in his life was the Great Depression. He started college at CCNY (City College of New York) in 1929 as a full-time student. My grandfather owned an army-navy store in New York City, and as my father told it, one of his big items was silk shirts, which he sold to working men. But with the Crash of 1929, which my grandfather said "served those rich bastards right," the working men no longer bought silk shirts and his store went broke. My father then had to quit day school and continued his education at night, taking a full-time job during the day to support his family. Through his hard work, he got his CPA and became an accountant. He would always regale me with stories about the Great Depression – like the time he was waiting outside an office to apply for an accounting job, and all the discussion was about what salary to ask for. If I remember correctly, everyone agreed to ask for $12 a week, but when he got into the interview, my father asked for $15. When the interviewer asked him why he was asking for $15 rather than $12, my father answered that he was worth $15, but the others weren't worth $12. He did get the job, but shortly thereafter the firm folded and he was out looking for work again.

I loved the stories my father told about his struggles during the Great Depression, and they created the lifelong fascination that I had with this period of history. My interest in understanding why the Great Depression occurred was a major factor in my becoming an economist. Interestingly, although my father fought in Europe during World War II, he never talked about it, even though I would have loved to have heard his war stories. (Movies about World War II were immensely popular when I was a kid and I just loved them. To this day, I still love to read military history.) Only when I was an adult did he ever talk about the war.

The other way that my father influenced my decision to become an economist was intentional on his part. He told me later that he knew that I wanted to be a scholar. (Indeed, the trajectory for my family is a classic one for Jews who emigrated to the United States: poor peddler to successful businessman to scholar. My grandfather came to the United States from Russia at the beginning of the twentieth century and initially earned a living as a peddler, selling door to door. My father, who grew up pretty poor, became a very successful businessman, and I then became the scholar.) Although my father encouraged my scholarly tendencies, particularly by recognizing my intellectual capabilities and talking to me as if I were his intellectual equal when I reached eleven years old, he had doubts that the life of a scientist would be a good one. Hence, when I was twelve, he exposed me to technical analysis of the stock market, where you looked for patterns in stock prices, like ones called "head and shoulders," which supposedly would tell you where stock prices would head in the future. These were the days without computers, so we would chart stock prices by hand, look for these patterns, and then make investments. He gave me 1 percent of the profits to heighten my interest. His idea was that this exercise, which involved some mathematics and reading books about the stock market, would steer my intellectual interests to the real world. Indeed, when I was older and was thinking about going to graduate school, he told me that he was happy I wanted to be scholar, but he would be very upset if I became an "egghead."

My father's influence worked even though the technical analysis we studied is now perceived as pretty much nonsense. I applied early decision to MIT because it not only had great science programs but also had a world-renowned economics department. I will never forget how excited and proud my father was when my acceptance letter arrived, because although he was able to go to college, he did not have an opportunity to go to a top school; he could only afford to go to CCNY, which was completely free.

I started MIT in 1969 and I just loved it. Everyone was serious about learning, and being a nerd was just fine because everyone else was too. In addition, it turned out that nerds could have a lot of fun, although in a pretty nerdy way. When I came to MIT, I planned to be a double major in physics and economics. Interestingly, my first course in economics, on economic principles, was pretty bad. My teacher was a graduate student whose English was poor and he was a pretty terrible teacher. However, I sensed that I liked the field. One of the great things about MIT, which is still true, is that undergraduates are given great encouragement to work with the faculty on research. Indeed, I don't think there is any top research university that has more undergraduates percentage-wise who do research with faculty than MIT. At the end of my freshman year, I started work with Dick Eckaus on a project on education's effects on economic development. The project never panned out, but I was hooked. I had found my calling. I realized that there was no other academic discipline that combined analytic rigor with analysis of the real world, which I had been encouraged by my father to value highly. I dropped the idea of doing a physics major (although I did take five semesters of physics) and became an economics major at the beginning of my sophomore year.

My interest in understanding what caused the Great Depression meant that I was far more interested in macroeconomics than microeconomics. (I use the term "macroeconomics" interchangeably with "monetary economics" throughout this essay, although monetary economics has a greater focus on monetary policy.) This was even truer after I took my first macro course from Bob Solow in the fall of 1970. Bob is one of my heroes. Not only is he a great scholar, as his Nobel Prize attests, but he is a great teacher and one of the funniest men alive. (He is famous for commenting on one of Milton Friedman's papers by saying, "All Milton Friedman ever thinks about is the money supply. All I ever think about is sex. But I try to keep sex out of my papers.") Bob is also one of the nicest human beings I have ever encountered. He was incredibly generous of his time with students like me, not only reading and commenting on my terrible undergraduate thesis, but also arranging for me to go to Oxford University for my junior year abroad, even when Oxford did not have such a program. The bottom line is that Bob's course inspired me and I knew I was destined to be a macro/monetary economist.

After spending a year at Oxford, where Avinash Dixit, whose essay also appears in this volume, was my tutor, I started the PhD program at MIT while I was still a senior because I still had some coursework to finish for my BS. I then officially started the PhD program in 1973, having already completed the first-year courses.

I was very lucky to start the PhD program right after Stan Fischer arrived at MIT. He was another truly great teacher, who was completely revamping his research because the rational expectations revolution had revealed that the old way of thinking about conducting policy analysis was incorrect. Bob

Lucas had presented his "Econometric Policy Evaluation: A Critique" paper, which became known as the Lucas critique, at the Carnegie-Rochester conference in 1973 (it wasn't published until 1976), and Stan immediately recognized that there was a paradigm shift in macro/monetary economics. Stan brought rational expectations to MIT, but from a more Keynesian perspective, not buying fully into the flexible-price, market-clearing perspective that Lucas incorporated into his models.

I also was exposed to longtime faculty member Franco Modigliani, who though an often unclear lecturer, was a truly inspiring teacher because of his tremendous enthusiasm for the subject of macroeconomics. Rudi Dornbusch came to MIT shortly after Stan, and he along with Stan and Franco eventually made up my thesis committee. All three of these extraordinary people (sadly, both Franco and Rudi are deceased) not only brought a love of economics into the classroom, but also were extremely interested in macroeconomic policy, with Stan later entering the policy world as chief economist of the World Bank, the first deputy managing director of the International Monetary Fund, and recently the governor of the Bank of Israel.

Working with them cemented the philosophical underpinning of my research program: economic research should not be directed at getting published in top journals to enhance your reputation, but rather should be conducted to help design policies that would make the world a better place.

Three other faculty members in the MIT Economics Department had a major impact on my future research. Paul Joskow, who took me on as a research assistant early in my PhD studies, taught me a lot about how to do empirical research, and our work together resulted in a coauthored piece which is the only paper I have ever written that has nothing to do with macroeconomics, focusing on the fuel choice of electric utilities (Joskow and Mishkin 1977). Peter Temin and Charlie Kindleberger taught me about the importance of economic history, which could provide new data sets to understand not only the past, but also current economic phenomenon. Their teaching and my reading of Friedman and Schwartz's (1963) *A Monetary History of the United States*, discussed later, led me to another philosophical principle behind my research: looking at past economic history not only is a legitimate research activity, but can be extremely informative about current policy issues.

RESEARCH

My research career in monetary economics began with my PhD thesis. I was greatly impressed by Friedman and Schwartz's *A Monetary History*.

Indeed, when I took my first course from Stan Fischer, Stan told the class that if you wanted to be a serious monetary economist, you had to read Friedman and Schwartz before you went to bed every night. Being a dutiful student, I did exactly that. Before Friedman and Schwartz's classic work, the majority of the economics profession had come to the view that monetary policy was not that important in business cycle episodes. There was a view that since interest rates were so low during the contraction phase of the Great Depression and monetary policy was easy, monetary policy could not have been an important factor in triggering the Great Depression. Friedman and Schwartz's book changed all that. It demonstrated that monetary policy was not easy in the contraction phase of the Great Depression, but rather quite the opposite, because the contraction in the money supply was the largest in US history. In addition it pointed out that there were episodes of monetary contractions that look pretty exogenous because they were caused by bank panics or arbitrary decisions to raise reserve requirements, as in 1937–1938, and these were then followed by declines in economic activity.

Friedman and Schwartz's book and other monetarist evidence led to a rethinking of the role of money in the economy. It stimulated the search for new transmission mechanisms to explain how monetary policy would affect aggregate economic activity. A leader in this research was my teacher Franco Modigliani, who with others built the Keynesian MIT-Penn-SSRC (MPS) macroeconometric model, which embedded many new transmission mechanisms of monetary policy. Nevertheless, the MPS model did not display nearly as strong a role for monetary policy in business cycle fluctuations as monetarist research suggested. I believed that monetary policy was far more important than Keynesian macroeconometric models suggested at the time, and so there had to be other transmission mechanisms of monetary policy that had not yet been discovered. I now knew what I wanted to work on for my thesis.

One challenge for PhD students starting their thesis is that they have read a lot of journal articles that give the false impression that empirical research is very linear. Successful empirical articles typically start by outlining a theoretical model and then test it. It all seems so straightforward. It shouldn't be very hard to do. However, when PhD students start to think about research projects for their thesis, they find it very difficult to come up with a model that is testable. The natural reaction is for these students to think that they are not very smart and they begin to doubt their ability to do original research. They don't recognize that research is highly nonlinear. Empirical research often starts with a messy idea that morphs into a theoretical model, but the idea that led to the model is often not actually mentioned in the published article.

One of my favorite examples of this that I saw firsthand is Bob Hall's famous paper, "Stochastic Implications of the Life Cycle–Permanent Income Hypothesis: Theory and Evidence" (Hall 1978). The paper lays out a simple Euler equation model of the permanent income/life cycle theory of consumption which shows that consumption should essentially be a random walk, and then presents empirical tests of this hypothesis. I heard Bob give this paper at Northwestern University in its very early stages and it started with a very different premise. His basic insight was that the permanent income theory is based on the idea that consumption is forward-looking, just like a stock price, and therefore it should have similar random-walk behavior, which he then tested. Bob was criticized at the seminar because the paper did not have a model, so Bob rewrote it with the model that you now see. His brilliant idea was not a model, which came afterward, but the insight that consumption is like a stock price.

My thesis came in a similar nonlinear way. I had been beating my head against the wall trying to find effects of the quantity of money on consumer durable expenditure, because I sensed that this was a natural place where monetary policy should matter. I was getting nowhere and was worried that maybe I didn't have what it takes to be a successful researcher. Then I was sitting on an airplane staring out the window on the way to my parents' house for the Thanksgiving holiday in the fall of 1974. I suddenly had the idea that households' balance sheets could be a way that monetary policy could affect consumer durable expenditure if consumer durables were highly illiquid. That is, if they couldn't be turned into cash readily when a household experienced financial distress, households would buy them only when their balance sheets were strong and so the probability of financial distress was low. I then did some empirical analysis which revealed that the ratio of households' assets to their liabilities was strongly correlated with consumer durable expenditure. From that point on, my thesis practically wrote itself and I finished it by September 1975. (Because I still had a National Science Foundation Fellowship with full support, I didn't defend my thesis until May 1976, with my last semester at MIT devoted to a photography course and a course on music in the romantic period.) Of course, in the paper "Illiquidity, Consumer Durable Expenditure, and Monetary Policy" (Mishkin 1976), I started by laying out a simple theoretical model to show how illiquidity of consumer durables implied balance-sheet effects on durables expenditure. However, I developed this model only after my thesis adviser, Stan Fischer, berated me for not having a model in the initial draft of the research that I showed him. This experience provided me with another philosophical principle that has guided me in my research: you never know where your research ideas are going to come from. Staring out into space can often be a very productive research activity.

(Note that this philosophical principle can get you into trouble. When my wife and I were first married, she once came home and saw me lying on a couch in my underwear. She told me that if I was going to lie around, at least I could help clean up the house. I replied that I was working, which indeed I was, thinking hard about a research project. To this day, she doesn't believe me.)

One of the papers that came out of my thesis, "The Household Balance-Sheet and the Great Depression" (Mishkin 1978), deeply affected my philosophy of doing economics. In it I applied the ideas in my thesis to the Great Depression period and argued that the deterioration in household balance sheets at the onset of the Great Depression was a major factor in the decline in economic activity afterward. As I mentioned earlier, one of my motivations for becoming an economist was to understand why the Great Depression occurred, and I also believed that economic history is an important testing ground for hypotheses. I thought the paper was one of my best and I still think so, but when I sent it out to journals, I got really awful referees' reports. The problem was that the limited data for the period allowed me to construct only a small number of data points to examine the hypothesis. Thus, there weren't enough degrees of freedom to conduct any econometric analysis and so reviewers did not think the paper was worth publishing. They even made snide remarks that I was not a serious economist if I conducted analysis like this. However, I believed then and believe now that if a research question is important enough, and the source of the Great Depression surely is in that category, it is still worth doing research on that question even if you cannot use the techniques you would like to because of data inadequacies. Too often, economists focus on narrow questions because the data are available and avoid bigger, more important questions when the data are not available. Nonetheless, I did not get discouraged and showed the paper to Peter Temin, who was very enthusiastic about it and told me to submit it to the *Journal of Economic History*, where it was accepted almost immediately and then published in 1978. Economic historians are used to data limitations and to their credit are willing to examine big questions even if the data are not all that good. The only person to cite the paper for years was Peter Temin, but eventually Ben Bernanke picked it up in his famous paper, "Non-Monetary Effects of the Financial Crisis in the Propagation of the Great Depression" (Bernanke 1983), and after that it was cited as an important paper in the literature on financial factors and the Great Depression (see the survey by Calomiris 1993)

This episode taught me another important philosophical lesson about research: don't worry about having an impact immediately with any individual piece of research. The gestation period of ideas can be incredibly long. You never know which of your papers will have an impact and how long it will take for them to do so. If you think a research project is worth doing, then just do it. Patience is an important virtue for an academic economist.

I started my first job as an assistant professor in the Economics Department at the University of Chicago. I wanted to learn all I could about the new paradigm in monetary economics, rational expectations. However, I really did not fit in at the department because although I accepted rational expectations as the right starting place for any analysis in monetary economics, I still was a Keynesian at heart since I did not believe that prices were particularly flexible or that markets always cleared. I would have been classified as a new Keynesian, but at that time this term didn't exist.

I continued to do applied research because I still wanted to understand how monetary policy affected the economy, but I was developing some new econometric techniques to do so. This resulted in my work on testing rational expectations models, initially stemming from my work on whether anticipated monetary policy matters for business cycle fluctuations (Mishkin 1982). I eventually produced a series of papers testing rational expectations macro models, which resulted in my book *A Rational Expectations Approach to Macroeconometrics: Testing Policy Ineffectiveness and Efficient Markets Models* (Mishkin 1983). My father made the most wonderful comment when I sent him the book, which was my first. Although he told me he was very proud, not only could he not understand anything inside the book, but he couldn't understand any word in the title. Amazingly, this book is still in print today, almost thirty years later. However, it is by no means a best seller. I get a royalty check every couple of years for $25 or so.

My quest to understand how monetary policy affects the economy led me to focus my econometric work on interest rates. I would characterize my philosophical approach to this research by saying that I was in the business of beating the data with a rubber hose (in this case, econometric analysis) until it squealed and revealed all that it could. It was not that I was watching too many spy movies or that I had a latent enjoyment of torture, but rather I believed that only by putting data through a whole battery of econometric tests can we get some sense of what the data are trying to tell us. This empirical research on interest rates started with the use of rational expectations techniques to provide measures of real interest rates and test hypotheses about how real interest rates move over time and with other variables. I then explored the information in the term structure of nominal interest rates and what it could tell us about the path of future inflation.

My continuing intellectual interest in economic history and my view that it can help us think about current policy issues led me to another new line of research that has proved to be both tremendously exciting for me and very productive. The burgeoning literature on asymmetric information, which started with George Akerlof's famous, and eventually Nobel Prize–winning, paper on the lemons problem (Akerlof 1970), was providing a framework for understanding financial crises and their impact on economic activity. I started to think about financial crises and was then given an opportunity to write about them when, in 1990, Glenn Hubbard invited me to write a paper for a National Bureau of Economic Research conference on financial crises. This paper, "Asymmetric Information and Financial Crises: A Historical Perspective" (Mishkin 1991), provided a framework for understanding the sequence of events in financial crises, which I then applied to more than ten historical case studies in the United States, starting with the panic of 1857 and including the panic of 1907 and the Great Depression, and then more recent crises, the Penn Central bankruptcy in 1970 and the 1987 stock market crash. For me, this research had elements of "sex, drugs, and rock and roll" because there were so many wonderful stories of bad behavior and even dirty-sounding words like "defalcation," which actually is a term for committing fraud. In addition, I now felt that I was converging on a goal that had motivated me to become an academic economist in the first place: understanding why episodes like the Great Depression occurred and how they could be prevented.

The study of financial crises became even sexier when the Mexican "tequila" crisis hit in December 1994, which Michelle Cadmessus, managing director of the International Monetary Fund, referred to as the first financial crisis of the twenty-first century. It displayed the twin-crisis phenomenon in which there was a currency crisis, with the peso plummeting in value, that occurred simultaneously with a financial crisis. At the time, I had just started working at the Federal Reserve Bank of New York as the director of research in the fall of 1994 (more on that later), and my boss, Bill McDonough, the president of the bank, kept on asking me questions about the Mexican currency and financial crisis. Unfortunately, up until that time, I was pretty parochial and had conducted little research on foreign economies, having done just a few studies using foreign data, but always from advanced economies. I had never thought about emerging market countries at all and indeed had never even traveled in one. This limited my ability to understand what was happening in Mexico and give sensible answers to my boss's questions, so in early 1995 I arranged a trip to visit the Bank of Mexico and particularly Augustín Carstens, who was its chief economist and hence my counterpart there. (Augustín is now the governor of the Bank of Mexico.) He invited me to give a seminar on my research on financial crises in the United States, hoping that it might be relevant to Mexico's current situation. In my presentation, I mentioned the debt-deflation phenomenon in the US Great Depression in which the fall in the price level led to a rise in the value of firms' liabilities and a decline in firms' net worth, and this deterioration in firms' balance sheets then sharply increased asymmetric information problems in credit markets and caused a collapse of the economy. Augustín then pointed out that the debt-deflation phenomenon did not apply to emerging market economies like Mexico's because their credit markets were fundamentally different from those in advanced economies. In contrast to advanced economies, in which debt is typically long term and denominated in domestic currency, debt in places like Mexico was extremely short term (with interest rates often adjusted daily) and was typically denominated in foreign currency like US dollars. The lightbulb went off in my head and I now understood what was happening in Mexico. The different structure of debt in Mexico meant that something like the debt-deflation phenomenon was taking place, but instead the mechanism was a collapse of the value of the domestic currency, which raised the value of the foreign currency–denominated debt, so that just as in a debt deflation, firms' balance sheets deteriorated, which led to a collapse of the economy. I actually started bringing this idea into my talk and was in effect writing a new paper on the fly in the seminar room. Again this illustrates the point that you never know where your research ideas will come from and what will be the source of that "Aha" moment.

The paper that resulted, "Understanding Financial Crises: A Developing Country Perspective" (Mishkin 1996), was presented at the World Bank's Annual World Bank Conference on Development Economics. This research led me to think harder about financial development in emerging market economies and how it could go wrong. After writing a number of papers in this area over the years, I finally put these ideas together in my book *The Next Great Globalization: How Disadvantaged Nations Can Harness Their Financial Systems to Get Rich* (Mishkin 2006).

In addition, my work on financial crises and thinking about how to prevent them resulted in my writing numerous papers over the years on financial regulation and the role of central banks and international organizations like the IMF in making financial systems more stable and less prone to blowing up. One of the most interesting collaborations in this research area occurred just after the Lehman Brothers' bankruptcy in the fall of 2008, when the global financial crisis was at its peak. Ken French and Matt Slaughter, both of Dartmouth's Tuck Business School, organized a meeting of a group of fifteen prominent policy and financial economists (including eight of the nine most recent presidents of the American Finance Association) at a beautiful venue in New Hampshire, Squam Lake, to think about what reforms of the financial system would be needed to make financial crises of the type we were experiencing less likely and less damaging. We formed the Squam Lake Working Group on Financial Reform, which produced a number of white papers on the following topics: a systemic regulator for the financial system; a new information infrastructure; retirement savings; capital requirements; hybrid securities to recapitalize distressed financial firms; resolution options for systemically important financial institutions; credit default swaps, clearinghouses, and exchanges; and prime brokers, derivative dealers, and runs. The results of this work was a book entitled *The Squam Lake Report: Fixing the Financial System* (French et al, 2010).

The opportunity to bounce ideas off of colleagues while doing a joint research project is one reason that collaboration is so useful in producing high-quality research. However, I was never involved in a research project with so many participants. In this case, the collaboration was quite extraordinary. Usually when this many academics get together, there is a competition to show who is the smartest guy in the room. However, in this case, this did not happen at all. Maybe it was because Ken and Matt chose the participants so carefully, or possibly it was because the gravity of the crisis and the importance of the project encouraged good behavior. The result was a fabulous interaction with really top minds that produced not only an excellent piece of work, but research that seemed to have an impact on the policy debate in Washington and subsequent legislation.

My belief that economic history and case studies are a useful way to learn about how to conduct policy led me down another path of research and an important collaboration that was to be extremely productive. Ben Bernanke and I had some contact in graduate school even though he was three years behind me because we had the same thesis supervisor, Stan Fischer. Over the years we often crossed paths at academic and policy conferences and became friends. In 1992 we decided to write a paper on monetary policy strategy for the National Bureau of Economic Research Macro Annual, a major conference that the NBER ran annually. The paper, "Central Bank Behavior and the Strategy of Monetary Policy: Observations from Six Industrialized Countries" (Bernanke and Mishkin 1992), was a pure case study analysis of how monetary policy was conducted in the United States, Canada, the United Kingdom, Germany, Switzerland, and Japan from 1973 to 1991. Our presentation at the Macro Annual conference was probably the most disappointing of my career. The discussion focused almost entirely on whether case studies were a legitimate way to do research in monetary economics, and very little was said about the actual content of the paper. Having other academics ignore the content of your work is one of the most depressing experiences an academic can ever have. Nonetheless, both Ben and I continued to feel that case study work was essential for understanding how best to conduct monetary policy. Having the strength of our convictions and both being tenured at top universities, myself at Columbia and Ben at Princeton, meant that we would work on whatever we felt was important. This led to a collaboration that resulted in one of my most successful areas of research.

When I went to the Federal Reserve Bank of New York as the director of research in the fall of 1994, I had both the resources and the incentive to continue research on monetary policy strategy, because this research would be especially valuable to my boss, the president of the New York Fed. Several other central banks, beginning with New Zealand and the Bank of Canada, had adopted a new strategy for the conduct of monetary policy, which has become known as inflation targeting. This strategy, which has become increasingly popular over the years, involves five elements: (1) public announcement of medium-term numerical objectives (targets) for inflation; (2) an institutional commitment to price stability as the primary, long-run goal of monetary policy and a commitment to achieving the inflation goal; (3) an information-inclusive approach in which many variables (not just monetary aggregates) are used in making decisions about monetary policy; (4) increased transparency of the monetary policy strategy through communication with the public and the markets about the plans and objectives of monetary policy makers; and (5) increased accountability of the central bank for attaining its inflation objectives. Despite the negative reaction to our NBER Macro Annual paper, my plan was to produce an even more in depth case study analysis of this new approach to monetary policy strategy. I announced to my staff that I planned to do a major research project along these lines, and Adam Posen, a recently minted Harvard PhD who had just started in my research group when I arrived, came to see me and asked if he could participate in the project. I was looking for someone on my staff just like him who was entrepreneurial and hungry to work on a project like this, so I immediately told him he was onboard. (Adam has had a very successful policy career. After leaving the New York Fed, he went to the Petersen Institute for International Economics, eventually rising to the position of president, and served as a member of the Monetary Policy Committee of the Bank of England.) I then called Ben and asked him if he wanted to become part of the project, and he immediately said yes. He also was not deterred by the negative reaction to our case study work in the Macro Annual paper. He recommended that one of his students, Thomas Laubach, work on the project and our team was set.

We started work on this project over the next two and a half years. In 1997 we published the first two articles that came out of this research. In the first article, "Inflation Targeting: A New Framework for Monetary Policy?" (Bernanke and Mishkin 1997), we laid out the rationale for inflation targeting and argued that the rules versus discretion debate in the academic literature, which viewed these as two mutually exclusive alternatives, was not quite correct. Instead we argued that flexible inflation targeting can be characterized as "constrained discretion" in which policy makers pursue rulelike policies that are targeted on achieving long-run goals but respond in the short run with discretion to changes in economic circumstances. It allows monetary policy makers to respond to shocks on a day-to-day basis but constrains their policies to be consistent with the long-run objective of stabilizing inflation in the long run. The benefits of such a strategy are that it retains price stability as the primary, long-run objective of monetary policy and keeps long-run inflation expectations stable, which helps reduce both the variability of inflation and output fluctuations, thereby improving economic performance and making monetary policy more efficient. To our knowledge, we were the first to coin the expression "constrained discretion," and it has since become a standard way of characterizing inflation targeting regimes.

The second article, "Inflation Targeting: Lessons from Four Countries," was coauthored with Adam Posen and took up an entire issue of the August 1997 *Economic Policy Review*, the flagship research publication of the Federal Reserve Bank of New York. This article contained case studies of the monetary policy strategy of four countries, three of which were early inflation targeters – New Zealand, Canada, and the United Kingdom – and one of which, Germany, had a monetary targeting strategy with many elements of later inflation targeting regimes. This article was a precursor of our book coauthored with Ben Bernanke, Thomas Laubach, and Adam Posen, *Inflation Targeting: Lessons from the International Experience* (Bernanke et al. 1999). This book not only contained the four case studies in my paper with Adam Posen, but contained case studies of four other inflation targeting countries – Australia, Israel, Spain, and Sweden– and one other monetary targeter, Switzerland. It also included some empirical analysis of the inflation targeting experience in those countries, assessing how successful this new monetary strategy had been.

The research project that culminated in our book and many other research papers I have written on monetary policy strategy over the years, even to this day (see Mishkin 2011), is one of my proudest accomplishments because it seemed to have a major impact on the practice of central banking. I was paid one of the best compliments I have ever received at the August 1999 Federal Reserve Bank of Kansas City's Jackson Hole Conference, which always has the who's who of the central banking world attending every year. The president of the Central Bank of Brazil, Arminio Fraga, came up to me at the conference and told me that he wanted to meet me because he found our book so helpful when he was designing the inflation targeting regime for Brazil in the first half of 1999. Indeed, the inflation targeting regime in Brazil has been deemed a great success; Arminio Fraga is considered to have been one of the most successful central bankers in the developing world and is called the Alan Greenspan of Latin America in his entry in Wikipedia. (In the interests of full disclosure: Arminio has become a very good friend and, starting in 2011, I became a consultant to his hedge fund, Gavea Investimentos.)

As I mentioned earlier, I became an economist because I hoped that my research would make a positive difference in the world, and here was confirmation that my work had made a difference. As my son, Matt, who has a wonderful sense of humor, would have put it, "It don't get no better than this."

TEACHING

Another element of my philosophy that has had a major influence on my career is that I have never felt it is enough to develop new ideas; they have to be disseminated. This includes not only getting ideas out to academic peers, which occurs through publishing in academic venues like professional journals, but also disseminating them to a much wider audience. This is where teaching comes in.

Teaching has always been one of my favorite activities as an economist. Besides experiencing the joy of disseminating ideas, I guess I also like to be a showman and the center of attention. My wife, Sally, often teases me by saying that I love to teach because I like to have a captive audience, since no one listens to me at home.

I first started teaching as a PhD student at MIT even though I was not required to teach because I had received a National Science Foundation scholarship that not only paid all my tuition, but gave me a stipend that allowed me to live a decent student life. Nonetheless, in my last year as a graduate student I asked to be a teaching assistant and was given my own section of an undergraduate intermediate macroeconomics class to teach. I loved teaching then and still do. I also find that teaching helps your research because it makes you think about what questions are the most interesting to you and your students. Once you have thought about these questions, research projects often immediately spring to mind.

My love of teaching has led me into the world of textbook publishing. When I was a faculty member of the University of Chicago's Economics Department, one of my regular courses was an undergraduate class in money and banking. Unfortunately, I found that I couldn't teach using any of the textbooks for this course. They were very old fashioned in terms of their discussion of monetary theory and principally just discussed numerous facts about the financial system without an economic framework for thinking about them. I therefore taught completely from my own notes and was frustrated that I didn't have a good textbook for students to read. I knew that if I were to keep teaching this course, I would have to write my own book. However, that would have to wait until I had tenure.

In the academic year 1982–1983, I went on the job market because I knew I could not stay permanently at the University of Chicago, where I didn't really fit in. I had tenure offers from a number of schools, but the most attractive was a full professorship at the Graduate School of Business of Columbia University, which is where I have been happily ever since. Once this was settled, I began talking to college textbook publishers about writing a money and banking textbook. Just before leaving Chicago for Columbia, I signed with Little Brown, which had two extraordinary editors: Will Ethridge, my acquisition editor, who eventually became the president of Pearson Higher Education, and Jane Tufts, the head development editor. I was driven by the philosophy that a truly successful textbook for this market had to be one that brought the latest economic research into the undergraduate and MBA classrooms, but at a level that these students could understand, without all the technical apparatus that appears in professional journals. This meant that my book was going to be really innovative, and I was willing to take a lot of risks. For example, my book was the first in the money and banking field to include material on modern monetary theory such as rational expectations. Will Ethridge shared my vision. Indeed, we often found that the money and banking teachers who we surveyed were not amenable to my including this innovative material in the book, which I felt was essential to properly teach money and banking. I told Will that the reason they were not supportive was that they had never heard of teaching money and banking in this way, but they would like it once they had been exposed to it. Will supported my decisions and encouraged me to write the book that I felt needed to be written.

Once I arrived at Columbia in the fall of 1983, I started working on the book. Because my development editor, Jane Tufts, was working on another project, over the next six months I wrote initial drafts for more than half the book. I thought that writing a textbook wasn't so hard, and I expected to finish it in record time. But then Jane started reading my chapters. When the first one came back from her, I was in for a shock. Almost everything was crossed out, with large sections redlined with comments that she had no idea what I was talking about and students wouldn't either. I called Will and asked him if Jane ate raw meat for breakfast. On the other hand, I knew that she was dead right, so I also told Will that he should tell her to keep eating that meat and continue to ruthlessly push me to make the book better. I now realized how hard it was going to be to write this textbook. Working with Jane was like taking Textbook Writing 101. I was lucky to work with one of the best in the business and she taught me to sweat the details. This principle was one I had understood was essential to research, but I now realized that it is just as important for writing textbooks, particularly for the revisions that you do every three years. (Jane has many top textbooks to her credit, including both of Greg Mankiw's highly successful macroeconomics and principles of economics textbooks and the macroeconomics textbook by Andy Abel and Ben Bernanke.)

I wrote at least four or five drafts of every chapter, and combined with the hours I devoted to my teaching and research over the next year and a half, the time I spent working was more than a hundred hours a week. Indeed, to keep up this work pace, I cut my sleep back from eight and a half hours a night to four and a half, by sleeping in two shifts, three hours at night and then a one and a half hours during a daytime nap. However, because I could control my time, I never missed reading to my son in bed every night before he went to sleep. This was the hardest work I had ever done in my life, but luckily I was in my early thirties and so had the stamina to do it.

The result of this brutal pace was that my textbook, *The Economics of Money, Banking and Financial Markets*, was published in the summer of 1985 (Mishkin 1986). Within the first year of its publication, not only did it become the number one selling book in the money and banking market, but sales were higher than had ever been achieved in this market. I have been told that what happened was extremely unusual because the most successful textbooks generally require several editions to become the number one book in their market. My book did this in its first year of publication.

Over the years, I have continually tried to improve the textbook, and it is now in its tenth edition, with more than 1 million students having learned money and banking using my book. In every edition, I have tried to add innovative material. For example, the first two editions had a pretty conventional discussion of financial institutions, which was mostly descriptive and which I hated to teach. However, the research on financial crises that I started in 1990 gave me a framework for thinking about how asymmetric information affected financial structure and could lead to financial crises. Hence, starting with the third edition, published in the summer of 1991, I was able to provide an economic analysis of financial structure and financial crises, which meant that the teaching of financial institutions now could be very exciting. In the wake of the recent worldwide financial crisis, the ninth edition, published in the summer of 2009, greatly expanded the discussion of financial crises, with an entire chapter on this topic.

I became increasingly dissatisfied with the monetary theory part of the book, which is based on an ISLM and traditional aggregate demand and supply analysis. This framework is increasingly out of touch with what has been happening in modern monetary theory and practice. In the traditional framework, monetary policy is conducted by changing the money supply, but this bears no reality to the way monetary policy is actually conducted, which involves changes in a policy interest rate like the federal funds rate (or, since 2007, nonconventional policy measures involving the central bank's balance sheet to affect the spreads between different interest rates). Also the traditional framework focuses on the price level rather than the inflation rate, while it is the inflation rate that monetary policy makers are trying to keep under control. Furthermore, financial frictions are not a feature of traditional aggregate demand and supply analysis, and yet these have played such a prominent role in economic fluctuations in recent years because of the financial crisis. I knew that I had to revise this part of the textbook and realized that the best way to do that was to write an entirely new textbook, *Macroeconomics: Policy and Practice*, (Mishkin 2012). With that done, I rewrote the entire monetary theory part of my money and banking textbook in the tenth edition, which was published in January 2012.

POLICY MAKING

My research and teaching have always focused on policy issues. I became an economist because I believed that economics could help us design policies that would make the world a better place. I had always hoped that I could apply my research expertise to real-world policy problems. I got my chance to enter the policy makers' world when in the spring of 1994 the new president of the Federal Reserve Bank of New York, William McDonough, decided that he needed to improve the Research Department at the bank. He approached me about becoming an executive vice president and director of research. The timing was propitious because, at forty-three, I was going through a bit of a midlife crisis. I needed a change at the time because I felt that my research program had become a little stale. When I met with Bill, I told him that if he hired me I was going to have to break a lot of dishes because the Research Department needed a complete makeover. Although it had a lot of resources with around fifty PhD economists and a staff of well over a hundred, it was one of the weakest research departments in the Federal Reserve System. Bill told me that if I didn't want to break dishes he wouldn't want to hire me; he offered me the job the next day.

I couldn't start work immediately because I had made an arrangement to work at the Research Department of the Reserve Bank of Australia from May through August, because my wife thought it would be great for the family to live in a foreign country for four months. Because that time of year was the late fall and winter in Australia, my son and daughter went to school in Sydney, which was an experience that broadened their horizons. (My son, Matt, who was twelve, could give hysterical renditions of Banjo Patterson's poems, while my daughter, Laura, who was six, took on a complete Aussie accent.) Not only did the family have a wonderful time because Sydney is a delightful place to live, but I got to understand how a research department functioned. I became very close to Steve Grenville, who was the assistant governor in charge of the research function, and our sometimes heated debates about how to run a research department helped me hit the ground running when I started as the research director at the New York Fed in September.

The president of the Federal Reserve Bank of New York had taken a big risk with me because, although I had a strong research record, I had never been involved in any managerial position, not even in academia, having been able to avoid any administrative position like department head. However, it is amazing what you learn from your parents without knowing it. As I mentioned earlier, my father was a businessman who had a factory with about a hundred employees in Manhattan at 85 Tenth Avenue. (Surprising to most people now is that New York City had more than 1 million manufacturing jobs in the 1950s, almost all of which are gone. My dad's factory is now the location of one of the fanciest restaurants in New York,

Del Posto. How that neighborhood has changed!) Besides charting stocks with me, he would often discuss his business with me, and from the age of sixteen I worked in the factory during the summers until I went to graduate school. All of this rubbed off. I found that I had actually had undergone a course in how to manage, but didn't know it.

The first thing I did when I arrived at the New York Fed was to interview all the people in my department so I could come up with a new management structure. The Research Department was incredibly hierarchical, with seven layers of management. In addition, most of the staff wrote long memos that no one in the rest of the bank ever read. After two months, I came up with a management plan that reduced the layers of management from seven to two. I then put in a new group of department heads, some of whom had lower official positions than members of their department, including one person who was not an officer of the bank and thus had to get one of the officers in her unit to sign authorizations for her because that was required by the bank rules. (She was very successful in her new position and was made an officer within a year and so no longer had this problem.)

Economics teaches us that incentives are a powerful motivator. I was to put this principle into practice by instituting a number of measures to increase incentives for more entrepreneurial research activities, but ones that would be relevant to the bank's mission.

First, I dramatically changed the role of department heads. Instead of a top-down approach to research in which department heads would tell staff what research to work on, I introduced an approach whereby staff members were encouraged to come up with their own research agenda and would be given a significant amount of time to work on their own research projects.

Second, I beefed up our annual evaluation procedures, which were considered to be among the laxest in the bank, so that department heads would give their staffers a very honest appraisal of their work over the past year and this would have a major effect on their salary increase. In addition, department heads were directed to consult other groups outside of research to assess the quality of work that the staff had done for that group, and this assessment was to be part of the evaluation. These two measures meant that staff members would have a chance to work on their own ideas but would have strong incentives to improve the quality of output because they would be highly accountable for their own work.

Third, no research staff member was allowed to spend all of his or her time doing purely academic research. All were assigned some practical research duties for the bank. Being exposed to practical research relevant to the bank would naturally get them to think about research questions that would guide their academic research and make it more relevant to the bank.

Fourth, I established a rule that if a memo was written and I or someone else outside of research did not find that it provided useful information, then the memo should never have been written in the first place. I did this to free up the staff to do research because when I arrived they were engaged in writing hundreds of memos that no one in the bank was reading. This rule had a remarkable effect. Within several months, the number of memos shrunk by more than 80 percent, so that if staff members wanted to spend up to 50 percent of their time on their own research projects, they could.

Fifth, we went to a merit-based salary regime in which the dispersion of salary increases rose dramatically so that good performance resulted in large salary increases, while weaker staffers received only minimal or no increases.

Sixth, briefings of the president and senior management of the bank, which occurred before every Federal Open Market Committee (FOMC) meeting, was no longer a top-down affair. Staffers at any level could propose a briefing, and there was a competition of ideas discussed by all of the department heads to determine which briefings would take place. (We even had one briefing by a research assistant, who I thought was going to pass out when he stood in front of the senior management in the bank's regal boardroom. However, he very quickly got his footing and gave an excellent briefing.) The effect on our briefings was electrifying. Within several months, they moved from being dull affairs to ones that the president and the senior management of the bank greatly looked forward to.

I also wanted to increase our department's visibility and exposure to outside academic economists. I created a visitor program of academic economists whom I asked to come to the bank on Fridays, and this included local notables such as Chris Sims, Mike Woodford, Mark Gertler, and Ben Bernanke. This group not only interacted with the staff, but also served as an advisory board to me on my measures to improve the quality of the Research Department. I also instituted another visitor program in which the staff at any level could invite an academic from anywhere in the country to visit for one week. The only proviso that I insisted on was that whoever invited the academic had to make sure that the visitor was looked after and had a great time at the bank. Not only would these visitors provide valuable interaction with the staff that would improve the quality of the research environment, but they would now be natural salespeople for the research group when we were recruiting new PhDs.

The outcome of these measures was that the research group at the New York Fed became a happening place. Its effectiveness in providing policy advice to the president and senior management of the bank increased dramatically, while research output that was published in outside professional journals increased by an order of magnitude. The research group's reputation in both academia and the policy world shot up, with the New York Fed's research operation becoming one of the most prominent in the system.

I also got to see the policy-making process firsthand, although not as a decision maker but rather as an adviser to the president of the bank. The president of the New York Fed has a particularly powerful position in the Federal Reserve System. The New York Fed has the largest staff of any of the Federal Reserve banks and is second in size only to the Board of Governors, which is headquartered in Washington; not only that, its job is to interact with all the top financial firms and market participants on Wall Street. The information the New York Fed acquires from its Wall Street contacts plays a critical role in monetary policy decisions, and thus the president of the New York Fed typically turns out to be one of the most influential policy makers that votes on the FOMC. When I was at the New York Fed, the president of the bank, Bill McDonough, would be in close contact with the chairman before every FOMC meeting and would help Greenspan think about what policy he would advocate at the upcoming meeting. Furthermore, during the coffee break after the initial go around, during which all the participants would outline their views on the economy, Bill would meet with the chairman and vice-chairman to talk about where the committee was leaning, after which Greenspan would start the next part of the meeting by outlining his policy views and proposing the wording of the directive.

I had input into this policy process because before every FOMC meeting I would meet with the president of the bank, sometimes multiple times, to discuss policy alternatives, usually with Peter Fisher, who was the executive vice president in charge of the markets group, which monitored developments in financial markets and conducted both foreign exchange and open-market operations. Not only did these meetings give me access to the policy process firsthand, but I also got to intimately understand the decision process better at the FOMC because I frequently knew before the meeting what outcome Greenspan wanted at the meeting since he had discussed this with my boss beforehand. Hence, I had an insider's view and could see how Greenspan would get the committee to move where he wanted it to, which he was an absolute master at. I also learned a tremendous amount from Peter Fisher, whom I was very close to at the bank. Peter is a Harvard-trained lawyer with a deep understanding of markets. We would meet at least once a week to discuss our thinking about policy and what advice we would give to the president. This helped me see that policy not only has to be well grounded in economic analysis, but also has to be attuned to the psychology of the markets. Getting the desired reaction of the markets to a policy action is critical to getting the desired outcome for the ultimate objectives of monetary policy: low inflation and unemployment.

Another result of my experience at the New York Fed was that it reinvigorated my research program. As I mentioned earlier, I went to the New York Fed because my research was getting a little stale and I needed a change. I thought I would enjoy the challenge of an entirely new activity, managing more than a hundred people, but what I didn't expect was how much it would stimulate my research. When you are advising on policy, you are continually bombarded with questions that you have never thought about before. Not only that, but the stakes are high because the answers you give can make a real difference. As a result you start to think pretty hard about these questions, and that naturally stimulates your research. I have already mentioned two examples of my policy work leading to a major research project: my research on financial crises in emerging market economies and my work on monetary policy strategy and inflation targeting. Indeed, over the three-year period in which I worked at the New York Fed, I produced seventeen articles in professional journals and books, along with the *Inflation Targeting* book mentioned earlier. Doing a policy job was just what the doctor ordered to get my research charged up again. Policy work does not always lead to increased research output since it is so time-consuming, but in my case it certainly did, both because I was in such a stimulating atmosphere and because I knew that I always wanted to go back to academia.

My time at the New York Fed was incredibly exciting, but it was exhausting. I was in effect doing two full-time jobs: managing a large research group and conducting my own research, if anything at an accelerated pace. I again was working very long hours, which was getting harder to do because I was now in my forties. In addition, managing people and dealing with the politics of a corporate bureaucracy were extremely stressful. I initially planned to spend two years at the New York Fed because Columbia University allows professors who are working in policy jobs two years of leave. However, I recognized that I needed one more year to consolidate the changes I was making in the research group so that it would continue to be successful after I left. Hence, when the president of the bank told me that he had already talked to the president of the university and a third year of leave could be arranged (which I didn't even know was possible), I stayed on for the third year. At the end of the third year, the president of the bank tried to convince me to stay by asking me why I wanted to go back to having a crappy, small office at the university. I responded that in academia, having a nice office means you are an administrator, and who wants to do administration? The reality was that I have always loved being a professor because it is my calling and I was happy to return.

Then in 2006, I received another opportunity to return to the policy world, but at a higher level. In May 2006, I was contacted by the White House to see if I was interested in becoming a member (governor) of the Board of Governors of the Federal Reserve System. At first I wasn't sure because it would mean living apart from my wife, who is a chemistry teacher at a high school for emotionally disturbed teenagers in New York and so could not move with me to Washington. She knew I loved to do policy work and told me that this was a once-in-a-lifetime opportunity and so I should take the job if it was offered. Within a week, I was told to come to Washington and met people from the White House and my friend Ben Bernanke, who was now the chairman of the Fed and obviously instrumental in my being approached for the job. Indeed, Ben, whose personality is not one that lends itself to leaning on people, told me that as a friend I had to take the job. He really didn't have to twist my arm very hard, and I passed the test with the White House people because by the end of my visit to Washington, indicated they would put my name before the Senate.

The appointment process was very fast, with my FBI background check taking about six weeks and my confirmation vote in the Senate occurring in July. Indeed, this process was unusually quick, instead of being the grueling process that typically occurs where politics can even block exceptional appointments, as in the foiled appointment to my seat at the Board of Governors of Peter Diamond, whose recent Nobel Prize did not deter senators from stating that he was unqualified for the job. The rapidity of the appointment process actually created a problem because, before being approached for the Board job, I had started to work on a project for the Swedish parliament, the Riksdag, to evaluate Swedish monetary policy and its inflation targeting regime over the period from 1995 to 2005, and I wouldn't be able to finish it until the end of the summer. Work for a foreign government, even if purely technocratic, would not be allowed if I was a governor of the Federal Reserve, but I was told that this would not be a problem because the appointment process would certainly take that long. However, the quick Senate confirmation was a surprise, and under the law you have to begin serving your term within two weeks of confirmation. Luckily, it turned out that confirmation required not just the Senate vote, but also a signature by the president of the United States, so the problem was solved by the president not signing the confirmation order until late August. I then finished the final report for the Riksdag (Giavazzi and Mishkin 2006) over the Labor Day weekend and was sworn in as a governor the day after Labor Day.

My first eleven months at the Board were not terribly exciting. I had already attended FOMC meetings when I was at the Federal Reserve Bank of New York from 1994 to 1997, and so the process was not new to me. I did, however, have an actual seat at the huge table in the boardroom and was now a decision maker rather than just an adviser who sat on a bench behind the table. Shortly before I became a governor, the Federal Reserve had stopped raising the federal funds rate at the June FOMC meeting. The economy was chugging along with inflation under control and so the Fed was in a wait-and-see mode with monetary policy on hold. Not surprisingly, discussion of monetary policy at the FOMC was pretty straightforward.

The most interesting policy issue being discussed at the Federal Reserve in my first year there was the Fed's communication strategy. Chairman Bernanke had set up a subcommittee in the fall of 2006 to discuss this issue. Our research together on this topic had led us to be strong advocates of a flexible form of inflation targeting and I was hoping that the committee would head in this direction. However, the innate inertia of a large policy committee like the FOMC meant that progress in this direction was frustratingly slow. A substantial fraction of the governors and bank presidents did not understand that announcing an inflation objective would help anchor inflation expectations and give more coherence to monetary policy. There also was a concern that Congress would be upset if the Fed announced an inflation objective. The discussion at FOMC meetings was incredibly frustrating. After one such meeting, I said to the vice-chairman, Don Kohn, that the meeting "was worse than a faculty meeting." He replied, "Maybe so, but at least this meeting is more important."

Finally in November 2007, after a year of deliberations, the decision was made to introduce only a minor tweak in our communication strategy, a lengthening of the horizon for the published projections of FOMC participants from two years to three of inflation and other variables under appropriate policy. This was a great disappointment to me because I was unable to get my ideas into practice. However, as part of a team, you often have to just suck it up. Indeed, after discussions with Ben, whose heart was in the right place, I agreed not to push for an inflation targeting regime in my public speeches because I might be seen by outsiders as a stalking horse for the chairman. It was only after I had announced my resignation from the Board that I started giving speeches that advocated that the Federal Reserve adopt an explicit, numerical inflation objective, a so-called mandate-consistent inflation rate and I outlined a road map for how the Federal Reserve could get to a flexible inflation targeting regime. (Over the next three and a half years, the Fed moved to an inflation targeting regime very much along the path I had suggested, finally announcing an explicit numerical inflation objective of 2 percent in January 2012.)

On August 7, 2007, everything changed. The global financial crisis started when a French bank, BNP Paribas, suspended redemption of shares held in some of its money market funds, and the interbank lending markets began to seize up. I would never have predicted that my research on financial crises would have such tremendous real-world relevance for policy making at the Federal Reserve. As mentioned earlier, I had done a lot of research on past financial crises in the United States and more recent financial crises in emerging market economies. However, I couldn't imagine that a full-blown financial crisis could happen in advanced countries like the United States. Obviously, I and most of the economics profession had got it wrong.

Nonetheless, the research that people like Ben Bernanke and myself had done on financial crises proved invaluable in this period. Because of my past research, I became one of the strongest advocates in the FOMC of aggressive action to stem the crisis. At an emergency FOMC meeting on August 10, the committee decided that more liquidity needed to be provided to the banking system and that the discount rate should be dropped by 50 basis points (0.50 percentage point). At the meeting, I asked why we weren't dropping the discount rate by more, which was eventually done later. It was clear that many of the FOMC participants who had not studied or read the research on financial crises did not see how dangerous the evolving situation would become. At the FOMC meeting on December 11, 2007, I argued that the Federal Reserve was not going far enough with a cut of 25 basis points in the federal funds rate target. I felt so strongly that I wanted to dissent from the FOMC's decision. However, in discussions with the chairman shortly before the meeting, I realized that if I dissented, I would damage his credibility because governors rarely dissent and the markets might interpret my doing so as a lack of confidence in his leadership. Thus, I expressed my view in the meeting that the cut of 25 basis points was inadequate and that I felt so strongly about this that normally I would have dissented from the FOMC decision, but I was not going to do so because of possible misinterpretation by the markets. To his credit, within two weeks of the FOMC decision, Ben came to me and told me that I had been right. Indeed, in a public speech that I gave on January 11, 2008, I advocated that central banks needed to get ahead of the curve as part of a risk management approach to the conduct of monetary policy when faced with a major financial disruption of the type we were experiencing. Then on January 22 and 30, the FOMC did get more aggressive and made two cuts in the federal funds rate of 75 and 50 basis points.

One of my objectives when I went to the Board of Governors was to see if I could help improve the research environment there, as I had done at the Federal Reserve Bank of New York ten years earlier. I asked for and was assigned the position of chairman of the Board's Committee on Economic Affairs, which is the committee that oversees the research operation at the Board. I interviewed a large number of the research staff members, just as I had done at the Federal Reserve Bank of New York and produced a document for the Board that made a number of suggestions for improving the research operation of the Board staff. Although some of these recommendations were followed – for example, allowing the Board to sponsor noncitizens for US citizenship, which helped us be competitive with US universities that already did this and so could attract the best foreigners to their faculties – I found progress to be frustratingly slow. For example, one recommendation was to streamline the two major FOMC documents, the green and blue books, to make them more readable and to reduce overlap, so that less time would be required to produce them. This recommendation was eventually implemented, with the green and blue books combined into one book, now known as the teal book (teal being a combination of blue and green), but not until four years after the recommendation was made, well after I had left the Board. Although I had been told by some staffers that I had instituted more reforms than any other chair of the Committee on Economic Affairs, getting the research operation at the Board to be more efficient and research friendly was like pulling teeth. Because of its structure, with a permanent staff but rotating board members, the Board of Governors is necessarily far more bureaucratic than the Federal Reserve Banks. Thus, getting change implemented was far more difficult than it was when I was an executive at the Federal Reserve Bank of New York.

I had always planned to spend only two years on the Board because, as mentioned earlier, this was the allowable leave under Columbia University's policy, and so when my leave ended I decided to return to academia. I might have stayed one more year, as I had when I was at the Federal Reserve Bank of New York, by requesting a special exemption from the two-year-leave policy, but the Office of Government Ethics had a rule that prevented me from working on the revision of my money and banking textbook while in a government position. I did ask for a slight easing of this rule to allow me to work on the book on my own time if I delayed publication, so that it would not be published until after I had left the Board, but they were unwilling to grant this. It was time for me to go home.

It is very common for academics who fill high-level government positions to have a hard time when they reenter academia. As a high-level government official, you have a luxurious office (mine at the Board was huge, had a gorgeous view of the mall, and had a private bathroom) and you are often treated as royalty. In contrast, as a professor you sit in a cramped office and your colleagues show you no deference. In addition, your work does not give you instant gratification because it does not have an immediate impact on the world. However, another of my philosophical principles is that ideas really matter and are every bit as important as making policy decisions. It's just that you have to have patience, because ideas often take a very long time to make a difference. I personally found the transition back to academia to be extremely easy. I left the Board on August 31, 2008, and started teaching the day after Labor Day. It was great to be back.

SOME CONCLUDING THOUGHTS ON MY PHILOSOPHY OF LIFE AND RESEARCH

Let me conclude by stating three general philosophical principles that have been central to my life. The first is that passion is everything. By passion, I mean both enthusiasm and deep caring. If you have passion for your work, you are far more likely to be successful because you will always go that extra mile. I have been blessed with finding a career that has been my passion. To paraphrase Mel Brooks playing Louis XIV in his movie *History of the World, Part II*, "It's good to be a professor." Indeed, I am always amazed that I am paid to do something that I love so much, and this includes both research and teaching economics. Similarly, if you have passion in your marriage (and this is not sex, by the way), it will be a good marriage because your deep caring for the your spouse will carry you through the bad times.

The second principle is that you should always keep learning. Economics is a field where there are no clear-cut answers and so there is something new to learn every day. If you keep learning, you stay young. I never want to completely grow up and I still feel – and, to the consternation of my wife, sometimes act – like a twenty-five-year-old, although my body is falling apart. My eagerness to learn means that I am never bored, and this encourages me to continually come up with something new in my research, teaching, and policy work.

The final philosophical principle, but one that has nothing to do with economics, is one that my wife, Sally, has drilled into me: your job will never love you back. Although my career has been very important to me, my wife has made sure that I make time for my family and am always around when I'm needed. A wonderful aspect of being a professor is that you have almost complete control of your time. The only time I absolutely have to be somewhere is when I teach, but this takes up only slightly more than a hundred hours a year. Thus, even when you are working you can make the time to be there for the family. Indeed, one of the deals I made with my wife early on is that she be willing to let me pursue my work, even sometimes when it takes me away from home, but that if my work is interfering with the family, she has veto power over my activities. Adhering to the principle that my job will never love me back, but having a profession that gives me control over my time, has meant that I have been blessed with both a fulfilling career and a wonderful family life.

REFERENCES

Akerlof, George (1970). "The Market for Lemons," *Quarterly Journal of Economics* 84 (August): 488–500.

Bernanke, Ben S. (1983). "Non-Monetary Effects of the Financial Crisis in the Propagation of the Great Depression," *American Economic Review* 73, no. 3 (June): 257–276.

Bernanke, Ben S., Thomas Laubach, Frederic S. Mishkin, and Adam S. Posen (1999). *Inflation Targeting: Lessons from the International Experience.* Princeton, NJ: Princeton University Press.

Bernanke, Ben S. and Frederic S. Mishkin (1992). "Central Bank Behavior and the Strategy of Monetary Policy: Observations from Six Industrialized Countries," *NBER Macroeconomics Annual,* 183–228.

(1997). "Inflation Targeting: A New Framework for Monetary Policy?" *Journal of Economic Perspectives* 11, no. 2 (Spring): 97–116.

Calomiris, Charles W. (1993). "Financial Factors and the Great Depression," *Journal of Economic Perspectives* (Spring): 61–85.

French, Kenneth, et al. (2010). *The Squam Lake Report: Fixing the Financial System.* Princeton, NJ: Princeton University Press.

Friedman, Milton and Anna Jacobson Schwartz (1963). *A Monetary History of the United States, 1867–1960.* Princeton, NJ: Princeton University Press.

Giavazzi, Francesco and Frederic S. Mishkin (2006). *An Evaluation of Swedish Monetary Policy Between 1995 and 2005.* Stockholm: Sveriges Riksdag.

Hall, Robert E. (1978). "Stochastic Implications of the Life Cycle–Permanent Income Hypothesis: Theory and Evidence," *Journal of Political Economy* 86, no. 6 (December): 971–987.

Joskow, Paul and Frederic S. Mishkin (1977). "Electric Utility Fuel Choice Behavior in the United States," *International Economic Review* 18, no. 3 (October): 719–736.

Lucas, Robert E., Jr. (1976). "Econometric Policy Evaluation: A Critique," *Carnegie Rochester Conference Series on Public Policy* 1: 19–46.

Mishkin, Frederic S. (1976). "Illiquidity, Consumer Durable Expenditure, and Monetary Policy," *American Economic Review* 66, no. 4 (September): 642–654.

(1978). "The Household Balance-Sheet and the Great Depression," *Journal of Economic History* 38 (December): 918–937.

(1982). "Does Anticipated Monetary Policy Matter? An Econometric Investigation," *Journal of Political Economy* 90 (February): 21–51.

(1983). *A Rational Expectations Approach to Macroeconometrics: Testing Policy Ineffectiveness and Efficient Markets Models.* Chicago: University of Chicago Press.

(1986). *The Economics of Money, Banking and Financial Markets.* Boston: Little Brown.

(1991). "Asymmetric Information and Financial Crises: A Historical Perspective," in R. Glenn Hubbard (ed.), *Financial Markets and Financial Crises*, 69–108. Chicago: University of Chicago Press.

(1996). "Understanding Financial Crises: A Developing Country Perspective," in Michael Bruno and Boris Pleskovic (eds.), *Annual World Bank Conference on Development Economics, 1996*, 29–62. Washington, DC: World Bank.

(2006). *The Next Great Globalization: How Disadvantaged Nations Can Harness Their Financial Systems to Get Rich.* Princeton, NJ: Princeton University Press.

(2011). "Monetary Policy Strategy: Lessons from the Crisis," in Marek Jarocinski, Frank Smets, and Christian Thimann (eds.), *Monetary Policy Revisited: Lessons from the Crisis*, Sixth ECB Central Banking Conference, 67–118. Frankfurt: European Central Bank.

(2012). *Macroeconomics: Policy and Practice.* Boston: Addison-Wesley.

Mishkin, Frederic S. and Adam S. Posen (1997). "Inflation Targeting: Lessons from Four Countries," Federal Reserve Bank of New York, *Economic Policy Review* 3, no. 3 (August): 9–110.

21

Learning from the Field

Elinor Ostrom

Let me first extend my thanks to Michael Szenberg and his colleagues for inviting me to contribute a chapter to this distinguished volume. It has given me an opportunity to rethink some of the foundations of my own work.

While many of the economists who have contributed to this volume began their academic journeys in high school or college, mine did not begin until I was a graduate student at UCLA in the early 1960s. As a poor kid born in the Depression (1933), my early years were focused primarily on survival. We were fortunate to have a relatively large backyard in our home in Los Angeles, where we had a variety of fruit trees and room to plant a vegetable garden. As a kid, I learned how to garden and also how to preserve fruits by standing over a hot stove to can them. Now I must confess that the long, hot August days that I spent canning peaches and apricots are not my favorite memories of my childhood, but I certainly learned a lot about the household economics of a poor family – long before I studied these problems in developing countries.

Since neither of my parents had more than a high school education, I received no encouragement to obtain a college degree. My mother, in fact, strongly discouraged any thought of college. Fortunately, she had transferred me to Beverly Hills High School from the Los Angeles school system, and 90 percent of my high school classmates planned to go to college. Consequently, I wanted to go to college just to "keep up" with my friends. I entered UCLA in 1951. When asked by a counselor what major I wanted to adopt, I responded "debate," as I had really enjoyed and learned a lot from debating in high school. The counselor somewhat indignantly told me there was no such major in college. The counselor then noted my major as education, as this was the only major that the counselor thought was appropriate for a girl at that time. Girls who received good grades in college (as I had done in high school) could find a job teaching grammar school or high school, but the counselor did not know of any other opportunities for girls with a BA degree in the early 1950s.

My most pressing need was to find part-time work to support myself in college. Fortunately, I was able to combine teaching swimming during the summers (I had been on a swim team in high school) with a variety of part-time jobs in the library and in local stores. Given UCLA's low tuition fees in that era, I was able to graduate from college without any debt by working twenty-five to thirty hours a week. After taking an interesting political science course in my first semester, I became a political science major, not because of job opportunities but because of enjoyment of the class. I also took a variety of economics classes for enjoyment, and I received good grades in both. I was asked to become a grader for freshman economics courses during the last year and a half of my undergrad program.

After graduation in 1954, I married my high school steady date and moved to the Boston area to help finance his training at Harvard Law School. After an extensive job search, I spent my first year in a clerical job, since very few positions were available in those days to a young woman with a college degree. Then, I stubbornly talked my way into a position as the assistant personnel manager for the home office of Godfrey Lowell Cabot located in downtown Boston. As the first woman in a professional position for the firm, I worked hard and was quite pleased that I was successful in opening up the staff to the possibility of a greater variety of religious, gender, and racial characteristics among employees than when I joined, while also receiving strong recommendation letters for the future. After returning to Los Angeles, I was surprised when my husband took a position with a private business corporation rather than a law firm. Over the next few years, our paths continued to go in different directions, and we decided on a divorce before having children.

My experience in personnel administration in Boston enabled me to obtain a good professional position as a personnel analyst at UCLA, and I began taking courses leading to an MPA degree in personnel management. I really enjoyed the content of my initial graduate courses in political science and economics, and I did well. I began to dream about entering a PhD program in economics or political science. Because of the lack of mathematics in my undergraduate program (due to the counseling I had received as an undergraduate), the UCLA Economics Department rapidly turned down my application but encouraged me to take an outside minor in economics if I was accepted by the Political Science Department. Some political science faculty members strongly objected to the admission of women to their doctoral program, but I was admitted in the fall of 1960 and began to dig into an exciting interdisciplinary program. I was very fortunate that several faculty members in economics and political science, including Jack Hirshleifer, Vincent Ostrom, and Charles Tiebout, were engaged in active research programs on the organization of governance in metropolitan areas and the governance of the water industry in California (Hirshleifer, DeHaven, and Milliman 1960; V. Ostrom, Tiebout, and Warren 1961; see also Bain 1959).

Their early work challenged the notion that order in the public sector stemmed only from central direction. Instead of prejudging the performance of complex organizations in metropolitan areas, Ostrom, Tiebout, and Warren proposed, for example, that the multiplicity of local jurisdictions in a metropolitan area be conceived as a "polycentric political system."

> "Polycentric" connotes many centers of decision-making which are formally independent of each other.... To the extent that they take each other into account in competitive relationships, enter into various contractual and cooperative undertakings or have recourse to central mechanisms to resolve conflicts, the various political jurisdictions in a metropolitan area may function in a coherent manner with consistent and predictable patterns of interacting behavior. To the extent that this is so, they may be said to function as a system. (V. Ostrom, Tiebout, and Warren 1961: 831)

This brought a different perspective to the study of governance. Instead of presuming the existence of only two kinds of order – the market and the government – they concluded that order could be achieved in *public industries* where large, medium, and small governmental and nongovernmental enterprises engage in both competitive and cooperative relationships.

PUBLIC ENTREPRENEURSHIP

In a research seminar organized by Vincent Ostrom on the water industry in southern California, each graduate student was assigned one groundwater basin underlying Los Angeles County or the adjacent Orange County and asked to gather and analyze data regarding how water producers were coping with or ignoring growing overdrafts. I was assigned West Coast Basin, which underlay the coast from approximately the Los Angeles International Airport south to the Palos Verdes peninsula. Water production had expanded during the war years of the early 1940s. By 1945 there were approximately 350 groundwater producers composed of public water utilities and private water companies, oil companies, industrial producers, and 250 nonindustrial groundwater pumpers, many of which produced vegetables and fruit for the Los Angeles market.

In 1945 the West Basin Water Association was formed to provide an arena where the multiple issues of groundwater overdraft and saltwater intrusion could be discussed on a regular basis. In 1961, when I started my study – not knowing at that time that I would continue to study West Basin for my doctoral dissertation – the leaders of the West Basin Water Association invited me to attend their regular meetings and to examine their extensive archives. The problems faced in West Basin were substantial and complicated, involving the major overdraft of the basin and substantial disagreements regarding how to arrive at agreed-upon water rights, how to gain sufficient and accurate information about the underground structure and flow of water into the basin, and how to create and sustain new enterprises.

After my first-semester report on the developments I observed in West Basin, I realized that the resource problems of West Basin represented a variety of classic problems that I was reading about in the literature. I was studying the work on entrepreneurship by Joseph Schumpeter (1936) and Frank Knight (1921), as well as Ciriacy-Wantrup's (1952) work on the economics of resource conservation, Musgrave's (1959) work on public finance, and Buchanan and Tullock's (1962) analysis of constitutional choice at multiple levels. I was witnessing forms of public entrepreneurship that would be hard to match if one were studying elected public officials representing state or federal agencies with limited access to relevant records or the officials themselves.

Fortunately, I began my study sixteen years after the initial formation of the West Basin Water Association, and I had full access to all of its correspondence and records. Therefore, I was able to obtain detailed records of many of the concrete actions that the local leaders had already adopted to overcome the threat of losing a valuable natural resource – a groundwater basin – through overuse and saltwater intrusion. I could hear and read about years of head-on conflict that was slowly resolved in the shadow of an equity court jurisdiction by an agreement negotiated by a committee of attorneys and engineers that was finally agreed to by more than 80 percent of those pumping water from the basin. Further, these public entrepreneurs invented several physical structures to create a barrier against further saltwater intrusion and means of using reclaimed fresh water to replenish the supply of water in the basin. I do not want to go into further detail here, but interested readers can find more in Ostrom (1990: ch. 4), Blomquist (1992), and Blomquist and Ostrom (2008).

What were the major lessons I learned from my dissertation research that have influenced my academic career in the more than fifty years since I defended?

First, I recognized how difficult it is to find economically efficient allocations for what I now know are common-pool resources.

Second, I witnessed the incredible amount of time and energy that some participants facing a tough public problem are willing to devote to achieving solutions that reflect long-term gains to their own entity and are relatively fair to the interests of others.

Third, I learned about large-scale government facilities – such as equity jurisprudence in a state court system, the creation of special districts, and national agencies (such as the US Geological Survey) that can provide rigorous scientific information about local unknowns (such as the hidden underground boundaries of a groundwater basin) that increase the capabilities of locals to solve tough problems.

Fourth, I learned about the operational advantages of polycentric systems (V. Ostrom, Tiebout, and Warren 1961), which were under considerable development and discussion at UCLA, for helping solve public problems that did not conform to any of the boundaries of core public and private actors involved. I also learned that involving multiple agencies in coping with a complex problem was not automatically chaotic in nature. Rather, some combination of agencies potentially enabled citizens, private industry, and local, regional, state, and national public agencies to work together to bring diverse knowledge and capabilities to bear on difficult problems.

Fifth, I learned the advantage of drawing on multiple disciplines for the study of complex public problems.

Sixth, I learned the importance of patience and persistence. The public entrepreneurs of West Basin spent the better part of two decades working out the system of public and private industry that was basically in place by 1965. Further studies backed up my initial findings. Blomquist (1992) studied eight groundwater basins in southern California that documented further progress in West Basin (but not uniformly across all eight basins he studied). Brian Steed (2010) has examined the achievements fifty years later and found that the groundwater conditions of West Basin have continued to improve significantly over time.

After completing my dissertation (1965), I learned that the basic theory of "collective *in*action" propounded by Mancur Olson (1965) and the "tragedy of the commons" articulated by Garrett Hardin (1968) were both correct in pointing to the difficulty of solving collective-action problems. I had, however, substantial evidence that it was *not impossible* for those involved to solve these challenging problems if allowed to engage in public entrepreneurship.

STUDYING SCALE OF PUBLIC ORGANIZATION TO PROVIDE PUBLIC GOODS

For the next phase of my work, the work of Vincent Ostrom (1999) on polycentricity and that of Herbert Simon (1957a, 1957b, 1978) on public administration and ways of thinking about human choice were both foundational. Both Ostrom and Simon stressed the lack of well-developed and tested theory related to the provision of public goods and services by governmental agencies in urban areas. Both stressed the essential complexity of governmental relationships in urban areas and criticized the many public administration scholars (e.g., Gulick 1957; Friesema 1966; Hawley and Zimmer 1970; Wood 1961) who propounded the untested theory that concentrating governance in a single hierarchical unit in a metropolitan area was the most efficient way to organize the provision of public services.

On the basis of this untested theory, public administration scholars strongly recommended massive consolidation of urban government units. The basic textbook on urban governance during the second half of the nineteenth century recommended that "as far as possible in each major urban area *there should be only one local government*.... Furthermore, the *administration should be organized as a single integrated system* upon the hierarchical principle, tapering upward and culminating a single chief executive officer" (Anderson and Weidner 1950: 609–610; emphasis in original; see also Committee for Economic Development 1970).

Simon strongly criticized the repeated calls for reform without a sound theory or careful field research to test that theory. In his treatise *Administrative*

Behavior, he asked what steps research should take to improve our understanding of diverse governance arrangements:

> First, it must develop adequate case studies of existing administrative situations. It will do well to initiate these on a small scale – dealing in minute detail with organizational units of moderate size. Only in this way can superficiality be avoided.
>
> Second, techniques must be developed and improved for measuring the success of particular administrative arrangements.... The only procedure of evaluation that can possibly be valid is the comparison of alternative administrative schemes in terms of their objective results. (Simon 1957a: 247)

In the early 1970s, I had an opportunity to take Simon's advice seriously. After a period of administrative responsibility as the graduate adviser for the Department of Political Science during the Vietnam era, where the administrative load was very large, I had my first opportunity to teach a yearlong graduate seminar. I chose to focus on the challenge of developing better theory and empirical methods for understanding the incentives generated by diverse ways of organizing the production of diverse urban goods and how this affected outcomes. Fortunately, Roger Parks, Gordon Whitaker, Dennis Smith, and several other advanced graduate students joined in an initial effort to understand how police were organized and performed. Without a research grant, it was challenging to think about how structure and performance could be studied effectively, but Roger Parks came up with an excellent idea, and my spring undergraduate seminar involved students who wanted to participate in a real research project.

In the nearby Indianapolis metropolitan area, there were three small, independent police departments located immediately adjacent to the city of Indianapolis. The neighborhoods inside Indianapolis were quite similar to the neighborhoods served by these small departments. From reading extensively on the causes of crime, we had come to a basic understanding that the level of crime in an area was a function of both the socioeconomic status of the neighborhood and how local government and police services were organized and provided. The location of these neighborhoods side-by-side provided an opportunity to take Simon's advice to compare "alternative administrative schemes in terms of their objective results" by designing a small, "most-similar systems" comparative case study of how the size of a police department affected crime rates, citizen evaluations and willingness to call on the police, police response times, internal work patterns in the different departments, and other measures of performance.

When we drew our initial frame for doing a random sample of households to be interviewed, we were very concerned that we draw boundaries in such a way that we selected neighborhoods inside the city of Indianapolis that were very similar to those being serviced by the three independent departments. Consequently, after working with census block data, we took students, who were not at all familiar with Indianapolis, there for a day. We drove them through the independent communities and crossed into Indianapolis without mentioning that we had crossed boundaries. After we had gone back and forth several times, we asked the students if they had noticed any obvious change in the basic structure of the neighborhoods they were observing, and they had not. We also conducted statistics analyses, after we had finished our interviews, to ascertain whether the social and economic structure of the respondents sampled in the independent communities was similar to that of the three Indianapolis neighborhoods. We were relieved to find that very few differences existed in the socioeconomic characteristics of the respondents in the survey data (see E. Ostrom et al. 1973).

On the other hand, there were major statistical differences in regard to basic data related to police performance. We found that the citizens living in the small, independent communities had a statistically significant lower victimization rate, a greater willingness to report victimization when it occurred, faster and more extensive police follow-up, and higher evaluations of promptness, police–citizen relations, and general evaluations of the job being done by their police department (E. Ostrom et al. 1973). Research conducted two decades later demonstrates that the relationships found in Indianapolis in the 1970s were still valid twenty-five years later (Parks 1999).

This first study of the impact of police organization was replicated in relatively similar neighborhoods in Grand Rapids, Michigan, by Samir IsHak (1972) and in the Nashville–Davidson County metropolitan areas by Bruce Rogers and C. McCurdy Lipsey (1974). Then we conducted a closely related study of two poor black communities with their own police departments and three similar black communities located within the city of Chicago and served by that city's large police department (E. Ostrom and Whitaker 1974). We found that the allocations of resources to the two types of neighborhoods were extremely different in that more than fourteen times as many resources were devoted to police services in the city of Chicago neighborhoods as in either of the two small, independent communities. The major difference in allocated resources, however, did *not* increase the service levels received by black citizens in the city of Chicago.

With our increased confidence in our findings and ability now to obtain research grants to conduct broader studies, we decided to do a major study of policing in the St. Louis metropolitan area. The residents of the city of St. Louis were served by a very large department with more than 2,000 officers. Two-thirds of the ninety-three independently incorporated cities had their own police departments, ranging from one with only part-time officials to one with seventy-six full-time officers (E. Ostrom 1976). We again utilized a most-similar systems research design to generate a design matrix that included three strata of neighborhood wealth and racial characteristics served by police departments that ranged from very small to the St. Louis Department with more than 2,000 officers. We conducted citizen surveys, interviewed officers serving these neighborhoods, rode with officers as observers, and recorded data obtained from official police records and reports to their citizens.

We found that the size of a police department was positively and significantly related to the victimization rate within a neighborhood and citizens' sense that crime was increasing. Size was negatively related to (1) the percentage of citizens assisted, (2) the percentage of citizens indicating that police responded "very rapidly" in their neighborhood, (3) the percentage of citizens rating the job being done by their police as "outstanding," (4) the percentage of citizens strongly agreeing with the statement that "police are honest," and (5) the percentage of citizens strongly agreeing that "police treat all citizens equally" (E. Ostrom and Parks 1973).

Our findings strongly negated the presumption that the size of police departments was positively related to performance across this series of studies. However, we received considerable criticism when we presented papers at professional meetings about our reliance on survey data, rather than official crime data, as measures of performance. There was substantial skepticism that citizens would be able to provide accurate data about police department performance. Some scholars urged us to use official crime statistics rather than survey data, even though multiple scholars who had examined police service delivery and quality of service had challenged the notion that police were measured well by crime data. Obviously, one problem that many scholars pointed out is that aspects of the neighborhood itself affected crime rates, but this is why we very carefully matched neighborhoods before examining the impact of differently organized police departments.

This skepticism about citizen capacity to measure performance led us to conduct a very careful "measurement study" (E. Ostrom et al. 1975). We studied a variety of ways of measuring street lighting and developed a method for taking measurements of street brightness using a light meter. We then developed two methods for measuring road roughness. One was a "roughometer" that we dragged behind a car in order to produce a graph of the smoothness to roughness of a neighborhood street. The second was a way of sampling urban streets and observing how smooth they were and whether there were potholes and, if there were, measuring their depth. Then we did a random sample of citizens on each street sampled and asked questions regarding their estimates of road roughness and brightness of street lighting. Findings from this study showed us that citizens accurately reported the road roughness in front of their homes. Their evaluation of street lighting turned out to be less accurate, but lighting experts later explained that the color of the street lighting affects what citizens see as contrasted with our physical measurements. The experts concluded that the citizen evaluations were relatively accurate, given the diversity of colors of street lighting in the neighborhoods we studied.

Our growing sense that citizens could give us reasonable evaluations of public services was also reinforced by our efforts to obtain good data about how police were organized internally. In most of the departments studied, we drew a random sample of officers' beats and rode with the officers for an eight-hour shift. This gave us an excellent opportunity to see if there were differences in the knowledge of the police officers and the way that police related to neighborhoods served. We did observe differences. When we rode in police cars assigned to small- to medium-sized departments, officers would spend time on our first observation, telling us about the background of the neighborhood and showing us where particularly safe neighborhoods were located and where there were problematic areas in which they kept a careful watch. On our first observation in a large police department, on the other hand, officers would frequently apologize for not knowing the neighborhood they were patrolling very well since they had to rotate every twenty-eight days. These rotation shifts represented an attempt by large departments to deal with threats of corruption, but our citizen surveys revealed that there was a higher level of police corruption in the large jurisdictions than in the small (Parks 1984).

STUDYING POLICE INDUSTRY STRUCTURE AND PERFORMANCE

In our studies of the effect of the size of a police department on performance, we shared the skepticism of Vincent Ostrom, Charles Tiebout, and Herbert Simon regarding the naive theory advanced in public administration regarding the advantages of hierarchical organization for the production of public goods. We also followed Simon's (1957a) advice to conduct careful case studies of existing administrative structure, as well as his skepticism about the performance of public hierarchies. As previously discussed, we started with a carefully designed but small study of police organization and performance for six very similar neighborhoods served by one large and three small police departments. We found that the presumptions made by the Committee for Economic Development (1970, 1972) and many scholars that larger departments would produce better services were not supported in Indianapolis. Nor were they supported in Grand Rapids, Nashville, or Chicago, with similar designs but different types of neighborhoods, or in our large study of diversely organized departments and neighborhoods in St. Louis.

While we were able to publish our results in reputable journals, not much attention was paid to our surprising findings by national commissions or public administration scholars. Major reports were still recommending the consolidation of most police agencies serving urban areas into metropolitan-wide departments (National Advisory Commission on Criminal Justice Standards and Goals 1973). Two observations tended to dominate the thinking of scholars who assumed that hierarchy was the best way to organize public-service delivery. First, it was noted that small- to medium-sized police departments rarely had their own crime laboratories. Because few studies were made of the day-to-day administrative life of police departments, the presumption was made that police serving smaller communities did not have access to *any* criminal laboratories to conduct blood tests and analyze other crime investigation data. Second, it was observed that many different agencies engaged in traffic patrol in a single metropolitan area. The assumption drawn from this observation was that the distribution of this service was chaotic and thus of low quality.

Given the theoretical tradition that focused on public-service industries among those active in the early development of the Workshop in Political Theory and Policy Analysis at Indiana University, we thought it would be important to do a careful, large-scale study of the structure and performance of the police service industry in metropolitan areas. This would require the development of a new approach to the study of police *industry* rather than the study of individual police *organizations*. Further, we needed to develop completely new research instruments to measure the structure of the police industry accurately in multiple metropolitan areas so that we could assess how structure affected performance. We spent time studying the research strategies and methods of those studying private-service firms and industries (Caves 1964; Williamson 1964, 1967; Robinson 1958; Bain 1959; McKean 1964; Margolis 1964) but realized we could not use exactly the same methods developed to assess the structure and flow of private-good industries.

We had to invest heavily in a new analytical approach to characterize direct and intermediate police services. *Direct services*, such as general area patrol, traffic regulation and patrol, and various types of investigatory services, are produced directly by police for citizens. *Intermediate services* are required in the production of direct services and include radio communications, detention, training, and crime laboratory analyses. We identified six characteristics of local collective goods as they combine with institutional arrangements to affect performance in providing or producing direct and intermediate police services. On the production side, these were (1) economies of scale in production, (2) co-production, and (3) measurability. On the provision side, these were (1) the size and location of the group of individuals who jointly consume a service, (2) the diversity of preferences about service styles and levels, and (3) the degree of choice that citizens have concerning their consumption of a service.

Economies and Diseconomies of Scale

Economies of scale occur when the average costs of production decrease with increases in the amount of the good being produced. Many intermediate police services are capital intensive, and economies of scale are reached in large production units. Average costs of crime laboratory analysis, for example, tend to fall over an extended range of output. Initial capital expenditures involved in purchasing equipment are large. Highly trained personnel are needed to run analyses. Training of new police officers can also involve substantial economies of scale. When training is conducted in an "academy," substantial investments must be made in a building and a staff so that training a large number of recruits will be less expensive (per recruit) than training only a small number. Radio communications also involve the purchase of relatively expensive equipment and the likelihood of economies of scale.

In contrast, direct services are highly labor intensive. Between 85 and 90 percent of the costs of direct services relate to personnel or variable expenses, such as gasoline. Serving a larger jurisdiction may increase average costs rather than reducing them for most direct services. In regard to the investigation of infrequent events, such as homicides, one might expect that specialized units serving a large area might process a sufficient number of cases to enhance skills at production.

Co-production of Police Services by Citizens

Physical goods can be produced independently of the inputs of those who eventually may consume them. However, the production of all services involves some input by the consumers being served (Parks et al. 1981). If students, for example, do not participate actively in their own education, input resources devoted to education have little effect on results achieved. Students are essential co-producers of education. In regard to safety in a community, citizens are important co-producers. They provide the "public eyes" that may prevent criminal activities or alert the police to problems. Without the active help of citizens giving information and being willing to serve as witnesses in court, police are less effective in solving crimes or in building cases that can be prosecuted in court. Citizens can prevent many types of criminal activities by taking precautionary efforts of many kinds.

Co-production of direct police services by citizens is likely to be more intensive in small collective consumption units where citizens perceive themselves to have a stake in preserving the peace and safety of their neighborhoods and view the police as providing valuable services to assist in those efforts. Officers serving in small police departments should also be more oriented to encouraging citizens to help in the co-production of direct services. In regard to intermediate services, citizens are not normally involved as co-producers, but the direct and indirect-service producers themselves may be involved in co-production activities.

Measurability

Satisfactory measures of direct police services are difficult to obtain. Conceptually, the outputs of direct services are "states of affairs" improved to some degree by the efforts of police. Thus, the output of general area patrol is the extent to which it is safer to walk on the streets or keep valuable possessions because of the efforts of police.

One can never directly measure the output of direct services, as it requires reference to a counterfactual situation: the state of affairs that would have existed in the absence of police services. Measurement must rely on either statistical inference or proxy measures. Reliable statistical inference would require that we *know* the set of factors that cause crime and could accurately predict the level of crime that would occur without any police services. Such knowledge is not available. Police and citizens alike tend to rely on three types of proxy measures: (1) resource inputs, (2) activity levels, and (3) crime rates.

Indicators of *resource inputs* include the total budget or expenditures and the number of employees. These provide information only about the resources available to produce services and give no information on the level or quality of output. While many social scientists have presumed that output is linearly associated with resource inputs, our own studies made us skeptical about this assumption. Indicators of *activity levels* include number of miles driven, number of tickets issued, number of calls answered, number of arrests, and number of crimes solved. These are "closer" to what we mean by the output of police, but are still proxy measures and are largely under the control of the producer. A police department can increase its "output" by increasing the number of people arrested or the number of traffic tickets issued. In other words, police can arrest more drunks on Saturday night and increase their "productivity." Whether that reflects an increase in "output" is highly questionable.

Crime rates, the third type of proxy measures, are trace data that survive a long series of transformations under the control of many different actors. Some information is lost at each transformation, and systematic distortion can occur at each step. For example, police can record information so that a lesser crime is coded when they want to reduce serious crime, while increasing the "seriousness" of the offense when they want to produce a local "crime wave." Since budgetary allocations are frequently increased after a local crime wave has occurred, internal incentives exist within departments to bias data recordation so as to produce the given results.

The difficulties of developing reliable and valid quantitative measures of direct services output make it advantageous to organize both the production and the provision of direct police services in relatively small units. The police chief of a very large department is a captive of the statistical reports on activities and crime rates that he receives. He cannot have a good "feel" for what is happening on the street, as he is too far removed by status and physical barriers. On the other hand, the police chief of a small department, who actively patrols and observes his officers on a day-to-day basis, is better able to monitor performance. Police chiefs of small departments are *not* entirely dependent upon statistics to estimate the quality of police work. In medium-sized departments, the chain of command is quite shallow, and police chiefs still have a relatively accurate picture of what is happening on the street. Thus, police chiefs of small- to medium-sized departments can monitor internal performance on the basis of more detailed and accurate information than police chiefs of larger departments.

On the provision side, local public officials representing a large community cannot know firsthand what is happening in many different locations.

They are also captives of the statistical information they receive. Thus, they have difficulty articulating demands related to the real performance of officers on the street. In a small community, mayors and local councils have a chance to observe the activities of their local police on a day-to-day basis and are able to specify far more precisely what they want and what they do not want in their community.

While measurement problems are severe in regard to direct services, intermediate services are easier to measure. Many private-sector "for-profit" firms sell equivalent types of services, such as telephone answering services, laboratory services, and training services. Since meaningful records of such services can be kept, a direct-service producer may easily arrange for intermediate services with alternative producers of those services.

Size and Location of the Group of Individuals Jointly Consuming a Service

Only a relatively small group of citizens simultaneously consumes the benefits of most direct services. Those who receive the protection of a police car on patrol, for example, live in small and concentrated areas. Traffic patrol and accident investigation on major freeway systems, however, serve a larger community of individuals, some of whom live and work in a particular metropolitan area and some of whom are traveling between more distant locations. Most intermediate services may jointly affect a relatively large group.

Diversity of Preferences

Citizens' preferences vary substantially in regard to the level and type of police services. In poor neighborhoods where the streets are extensively used for recreational purposes, citizens strongly prefer a sense of public order that involves an extensive use of sidewalks and streets for outdoor activities. The same level of noise and commotion would be viewed negatively in a wealthy neighborhood where citizens have a strong preference that police maintain quiet and peaceful streets.

When exclusion is of low cost to the supplier, as with private goods, preferences for the amount and quantity of a good are revealed as a result of many quid pro quo transactions. Producers learn about preferences through consumers' willingness to pay for various goods offered for sale. Where exclusion is difficult, designing mechanisms that honestly reflect beneficiaries' preferences and their willingness to pay is difficult and complex, regardless of whether the providing unit is organized in the public or the private sphere. In very small groups, those affected are usually able to discuss their preferences and constraints on a face-to-face basis and to reach a rough consensus. In larger groups, decisions about provision are apt to be made through mechanisms such as voting or the delegation of authority to public officials. The extensive literature on voting systems demonstrates how difficult it is to translate individual preferences into collective choices that adequately reflect individual views (Arrow 1951; Shepsle 1979; Buchanan and Tullock 1962). The problem of preference aggregation is intensified when individuals with radically different preferences are combined into one collective consumption unit. Consequently, smaller provision units with a greater homogeneity of preferences reduce some of the difficulties of arriving at collective decisions (Bish 1971).

Degree of Choice That Citizens Have Concerning Consumption of a Service

Citizens have extremely little choice about whether to consume most direct police services. The existence of a particular style of patrolling in a neighborhood, for example, makes it difficult for those living in the neighborhood to avoid being affected unless they physically move from the neighborhood. When aggressive patrol techniques are utilized and individuals are frequently stopped and frisked, all families living in the neighborhood are forced to consume this type of order. Any in-person protest to the officers on patrol may result in physical harm. From the consumers' point of view, living in a small jurisdiction where the voices of individual citizens may carry greater weight is an important institutional factor offsetting to some extent the degree of coercion imposed upon local residents. Citizens can articulate more effectively preferences about how their neighborhoods should be served. More effective voice is particularly important for poorer families who cannot easily move and who are thus more exposed to threats of coercion either from those who offend against the law or from those who serve as police officers.

In regard to intermediate services, citizens are not the actors who can exercise direct choice in any case. It is producers of direct services who may be able to exercise some degree of choice. Choice depends upon the availability of alternative suppliers. If a police department has its own radio transmitter and is tied into other networks, it can exercise some degree of choice concerning its use of alternative facilities.

Measuring Industry Structure

Drawing on work related to the structure of private industry, we developed a method for recording how police were organized in a metropolitan area by using police service matrices. For each of the direct and intermediate services observed in a metropolitan area, we recorded the producers as columns in the matrix. Then we recorded the consumption units, such as local city governments, as rows in the matrix. For each direct or intermediate service, we could then assess whether there was any duplication of services whereby one producing agency (columns) served more than one provision agency (rows). This enabled us to array metropolitan areas into those that were more consolidated, where there were fewer producers for the population served, as compared with those that were more "fragmented," meaning there were a larger number of distinct organized consuming units for any particular service in question. We developed a relative *fragmentation* measure by dividing the absolute fragmentation by the population of the metropolitan area.

We also developed a measure for *multiplicity*. The absolute measure was the number of producers for a particular service, while two relative measures were obtained by dividing the absolute number by the number of consuming units for that service as well as dividing it by population size. We measured *duplication* by examining the matrix to determine when two or more consuming units regularly received a service from more than one producer.

We carried out our study of police industry structure in a random sample of eighty metropolitan areas (E. Ostrom, Parks, and Whitaker 1978). We identified a total of 1,159 direct-service producers. Most of these agencies produced general area patrol, traffic patrol, accident investigation, and burglary investigation services. In regard to intermediate services, we found that 70 percent of the direct-service producers also produced their own radio communications, but only a small proportion of any of the direct-service producers produced the other intermediate services such as crime labs or entry-level training. However, in *all* eighty metropolitan areas, indirect services were made available to *all* direct-service producers, contrary to the assertions of those proposing major consolidation of police departments. Our findings regarding the structure and performance of police industry in these eighty metropolitan areas substantially challenged the presumptions made by many scholars.

Our measures of performance included the allocation of police personnel to on-the-street assignments and the relative efficiency of agencies in producing response capacity and solving crime. For each of the eighty metropolitan areas, we calculated the number of producers of each type of service (multiplicity) and the proportion of the population being served by the largest producer of each type of service (dominance). Metropolitan areas with low scores in regard to multiplicity and high scores in regard to dominance come closest to approximating the "consolidated" model so frequently recommended by consolidation proponents. Metropolitan areas with high scores in regard to multiplicity and low scores in regard to dominance came closest to approximating the "fragmented" metropolitan areas criticized by these same proponents.

We found a distinct difference in the availability of sworn officers to engage in patrol activities in the metropolitan areas depending upon the industry structure. While more officers per capita were employed in the most consolidated areas, a lower percentage of these officers were actually assigned to patrol divisions in these metropolitan areas. One-third more officers were required in the most consolidated metropolitan areas to place the *same* number of officers on patrol as compared with the least consolidated metropolitan areas. Citizens living in the most fragmented metropolitan areas received more police presence on the streets for their tax expenditures than did citizens living in the most consolidated areas (Parks 1985).

THE UNDERLYING PHILOSOPHY OF MY WORK

In this essay, I have focused on my early career rather than the research carried on over the past forty years. The philosophical foundation of my research program was well established by the early 1980s, even though I have ventured forth on a rich program of research focusing on how institutions affect incentives related to common-pool resources (E. Ostrom 1990; E. Ostrom, Gardner, and Walker 1994; Poteete, Janssen, and Ostrom 2010). The most important theoretical foundation has continued to be the theory of polycentricity initially developed by V. Ostrom, Tiebout, and Warren (1961) and V. Ostrom (1999), as well as Herbert Simon's (1957b, 1978) theory of bounded rationality and his stress on the importance of field research. I have also been deeply enriched by important studies in public choice (Brennan and Buchanan 1985; Buchanan 1968; Buchanan and Tullock 1962) and the new institutional economics tradition (North 1978, 1990, 2005). The extensive field research conducted early in my career generated findings contrary to the presumption that when the market is not an efficient solution to a problem, hierarchy is the only other viable solution.

Basically, I believe that solving problems related to the long-term sustainability of common-pool resources and the efficient provision of public goods is difficult but not impossible. Further, the theoretical presumption that public officials in hierarchical governments are most likely to find efficient and fair solutions does not have an empirical foundation. Imposing policies based on a faulty theory can generate substantial problems.

Instead of using different models for citizens and public officials, I prefer to think of all individuals in most situations as facing incomplete information but having the capacity to learn over time if they continue their interactions. Further, individuals can learn norms regarding what they should, should not, or may do in particular situations given the actions of others in that situation. Individuals also acquire diverse preferences for outcomes (both positive and negative) to be achieved by others. Thus, instead of expecting to find narrow utility-maximizing individuals in most settings, I expect to find a mixture of types of individuals. In repeated social dilemmas that generate relatively accurate information about the actions that other individuals have taken in the past and that facilitate communication, I expect to find that many individuals adopt strategies that improve their own and other persons' outcomes, but not necessarily the outcomes of all participants. An important factor affecting individual orientations to benefits for self and others is whether those involved are able to change the structure of frequent encounters so as to increase the likelihood of jointly positive outcomes. Thus, the possibilities of public entrepreneurship have continued to fascinate me throughout my career.

It is indeed important to build a stronger theoretical foundation for understanding public economies at local community, metropolitan, national, and international levels. But to do so requires a behavioral theory of human behavior and a rigorous, but more complex analysis of the diverse contexts that affect the initial incentives of participants, information that participants obtain about a situation over time, and their capacity to adapt to changes in that environment (these ideas are developed in greater depth in E. Ostrom 2010; Poteete, Janssen, and Ostrom 2010).

REFERENCES

Anderson, William and Edward Weidner (1950). *American City Government*. New York: Henry Holt.

Arrow, Kenneth J. (1951). *Social Choice and Individual Values*. New York: John Wiley.

Bain, Joe S. (1959). *Industrial Organization*. New York: John Wiley.

Bish, Robert (1971). *The Public Economy of Metropolitan Areas*. Chicago: Markham.

Blomquist, William (1992). *Dividing the Waters: Governing Groundwater in Southern California*. San Francisco: ICS Press.

Blomquist, William and Elinor Ostrom (2008). "Deliberation, Learning, and Institutional Change: The Evolution of Institutions in Judicial Settings," *Constitutional Political Economy* 19, no. 3: 180–202.

Brennan, Geoffrey and James Buchanan (1985). *The Reason of Rules: Constitutional Political Economy*. New York: Cambridge University Press.

Buchanan, James M. (1968). *The Demand and Supply of Public Goods*. Chicago: Rand McNally.

Buchanan, James M. and Gordon Tullock (1962). *The Calculus of Consent*. Ann Arbor: University of Michigan Press.

Caves, Richard (1964). *American Industry: Structure, Conduct, Performance*. Englewood Cliffs, NJ: Prentice-Hall.

Ciriacy-Wantrup, Siegfried V. (1952). *Resource Conservation, Economics, and Policies*. Berkeley: University of California Press.

Committee for Economic Development (1970). *Reshaping Government in Metropolitan Areas*. New York: Committee for Economic Development.

 (1972). *Reducing Crime and Assuring Justice*. New York: Committee for Economic Development.

Friesema, H. Paul (1966). "The Metropolis and the Maze of Local Government," *Urban Affairs Quarterly* 2: 68–90.

Gulick, Luther (1957). "Metropolitan Organization," *Annals of the American Academy of Political and Social Sciences* 314: 57–65.

Hardin, Garrett (1968). "The Tragedy of the Commons," *Science* 162, no. 3859: 1243–1248.

Hawley, Amos H. and Basil G. Zimmer (1970). *The Metropolitan Community: Its People and Government*. Beverly Hills, CA: Sage.

Hirshleifer, Jack, James C. DeHaven, and Jerome Milliman (1960). *Water Supply: Economics, Technology and Policy*. Chicago: University of Chicago Press.

IsHak, Samir (1972). "Consumers' Perception of Police Performance: Consolidation vs. Deconcentration – The Case of Grand Rapids, Michigan Metropolitan Area." PhD dissertation, Indiana University.

Knight, Frank H. (1921). *Risk, Uncertainty, and Profit*. Boston: Houghton Mifflin.

Margolis, Julius (1964). "The Structure of Government and Public Investment." *American Economic Review* 54 (May): 236–342.

McKean, Roland N. (1964). "Divergences between Institution and Total Costs within Government," *American Economic Review* 54 (May): 243–249.

Musgrave, Richard. 1959. *The Theory of Public Finance: A Study in Public Economy*. New York: McGraw-Hill.

National Advisory Commission on Criminal Justice Standards and Goals (1973). *Report on Police*. Washington, DC: US Government Printing Office.

North, Douglass C. (1978). "Structure and Performance: The Task of Economic History," *Journal of Economic Literature* 16: 963–978.

 (1990). *Institutions, Institutional Change and Economic Performance*. New York: Cambridge University Press.

 (2005). *Understanding the Process of Institutional Change*. Princeton, NJ: Princeton University Press.

Olson, Mancur (1965). *The Logic of Collective Action: Public Goods and the Theory of Groups*. Cambridge, MA: Harvard University Press.

Ostrom, Elinor (1965). "Public Entrepreneurship: A Case Study in Ground Water Basin Management." PhD dissertation, University of California, Los Angeles.

— (1976). "Size and Performance in a Federal System," *Publius* 6, no. 2: 33–73.

— (1990). *Governing the Commons: The Evolution of Institutions for Collective Action.* New York: Cambridge University Press.

— (2010). "Beyond Markets and States: Polycentric Governance of Complex Economic Systems," *American Economic Review* 100, no. 3 (June): 641–672.

Ostrom, Elinor, William H. Baugh, Richard Guarasci, Roger B. Parks, and Gordon P. Whitaker (1973). *Community Organization and the Provision of Police Services.* Beverly Hills, CA: Sage.

Ostrom, Elinor, Roy Gardner, and James Walker (1994). *Rules, Games, and Common Pool Resources.* Ann Arbor: University of Michigan Press.

Ostrom, Elinor, and Roger B. Parks (1973). "Suburban Police Departments: Too Many and Too Small?" in Louis H. Masotti and Jeffrey K. Hadden (eds.), *The Urbanization of the Suburbs*, 367–402. Beverly Hills, CA: Sage.

Ostrom, Elinor, Roger B. Parks, et al. (1975). "Measuring Urban Street Conditions," in *Measuring Urban Services: A Multi-Mode Approach*, pamphlet 2, Portfolio of Professional Papers on Measuring Urban Services (Measures Project). Bloomington: Indiana University, Workshop in Political Theory and Policy Analysis.

Ostrom, Elinor, Roger B. Parks, and Gordon Whitaker (1978). *Patterns of Metropolitan Policing*. Cambridge, MA: Ballinger.

Ostrom, Elinor and Gordon P. Whitaker (1974). "Community Control and Governmental Responsiveness: The Case of Police in Black Neighborhoods," in Willis Hawley and David Rogers (eds.), *Improving the Quality of Urban Management*, 303–334. Beverly Hills, CA: Sage.

Ostrom, Vincent (1999). "Polycentricity" (parts 1 and 2), in Michael McGinnis (ed.), *Polycentricity and Local Public Economies: Readings from the Workshop in Political Theory and Policy Analysis*, 52–74, 119–138. Ann Arbor: University of Michigan Press.

Ostrom, Vincent, Charles M. Tiebout, and Robert Warren (1961). "The Organization of Government in Metropolitan Areas: A Theoretical Inquiry," *American Political Science Review* 55, no. 4: 831–842.

Parks, Roger B. (1984). "Linking Subjective and Objective Measures of Performance," in Gordon P. Whitaker (ed.), *Understanding Police Agency Performance*, 148–159. Washington, DC: US Department of Justice, National Institute of Justice.

— (1985). "Metropolitan Structure and Systemic Performance: The Case of Police Service Delivery," in Kenneth Hanf and Theo A. J. Toonen (eds.), *Policy Implementation in Federal and Unitary Systems*, 161–191. Dordrecht: Martinus Nijhoff.

— (1999). "Do We Really Want to Consolidate Urban Areas? [It's Like Déjà Vu All Over Again]," in Michael McGinnis (ed.), *Polycentricity and Local Public Economies: Readings from the Workshop in Political Theory and Policy Analysis*, 349–351. Ann Arbor: University of Michigan Press.

Parks, Roger B., Paula Baker, Larry Kiser, Ronald J. Oakerson, Elinor Ostrom, Vincent Ostrom, Stephen L. Percy, Martha Vandivort, Gordon P. Whitaker, and Rick

Wilson (1981). "Consumers as Coproducers of Public Services: Some Economic and Institutional Considerations," *Policy Studies Journal* 9, no. 7: 1001–1011.

Poteete, Amy, Marco Janssen, and Elinor Ostrom (2010). *Working Together: Collective Action, the Commons, and Multiple Methods in Practice*. Princeton, NJ: Princeton University Press.

Robinson, E. A. G. (1958). *The Structure of Competitive Industry*. Chicago: University of Chicago Press.

Rogers, Bruce D. and C. McCurdy Lipsey. 1974. "Metropolitan Report: Citizen Evaluations of Performance in Nashville–Davidson County, Tennessee," *Publius* 4, no. 4: 19–34.

Schumpeter, Joseph A. (1936). *The Theory of Economic Development*, trans. Redvers Opie. Cambridge, MA: Harvard University Press.

Shepsle, Kenneth A. (1979). "Institutional Arrangements and Equilibrium in Multidimensional Voting Models," *American Journal of Political Science* 23, no. 1: 27–59.

Simon, Herbert A. (1957a). *Administrative Behavior: A Study of Decision-Making Processes in Administrative Organization*. New York: Free Press.

(1957b). *Models of Man, Social and Rational*. New York: John Wiley.

(1978). "Rationality as Process and as Product of Thought," *American Economic Review* 68, no. 2: 1–17.

Steed, Brian C. (2010). "Natural Forces, Human Choices: An Over Time Study of Responses to Biophysical and Human Induced Disturbance in Los Angeles, California Groundwater Governance." PhD dissertation, Indiana University.

Williamson, Oliver E. (1964). *The Economics of Discretionary Behavior: Managerial Objectives in a Theory of the Firm*. Englewood Cliffs, NJ: Prentice-Hall.

(1967). "Hierarchical Control and Optimum Firm Size," *Journal of Political Economy* 75, no. 2: 123–138.

Wood, Robert C. (1961). *1400 Governments*. Garden City, NJ: Doubleday, Anchor Books.

22

Order in and through Disorder: The Invisible Hand as a Turbulent Regulator

Anwar Shaikh

ORIGINS AND EARLY INFLUENCES

I was born in 1945 in Karachi, Pakistan, two years before the partition of India. My early years were spent in Karachi, but after my father joined the Pakistani Foreign Service in 1948, I also lived in Ankara, Washington, DC, New York, Lagos, Kuala Lumpur, and Kuwait. I received a BSE from Princeton University in 1965, worked for two years in Kuwait (as an engineer and as a teacher of social science and physics), and returned to the United States to study at Columbia University, from which I received my PhD in economics in 1973. In 1972 I joined the Economics Department at the Graduate Faculty of the New School for Social Research, where I am presently employed.

My mother was a Christian from the south of India, and my father was a Muslim from the north. Both were educated and well read, and believed in social and gender equality. My father was an articulate speaker with a wry sense of humor, and my mother a gifted teacher with an ear for language. They made sure that my sister, brother, and I were very well schooled and taught us the importance of self-reliance. I spent my early years in an apartment building occupied largely by various members of my father's extended family, ranging from grandparents to toddlers. My favorite grand-aunt was English. Once my parents began to travel on various postings, I moved from country to country and school to school. I am told that at the age of six I briefly attended a French school in Ankara but was somewhat handicapped by the fact that I did not speak a word of French. A transfer to a one-room schoolhouse run by an Englishwoman solved that problem. When I was in Catholic secondary school in Karachi my best friend was Zoroastrian, in high school in Washington, DC, my best friend was Chinese American, and in Stuyvesant and Princeton my best friends were Jewish. I did not actually notice any of this at the time. It seemed normal.

After I graduated from Princeton in 1965, I went to Kuwait to live with my parents. I worked first as a clerk in a bank, then as an engineer in the full heat of Kuwaiti summer. This latter activity proved unwise, and one morning I woke up with "desert blindness." While I was recovering in a darkened room, I received an inquiry from the Kuwait-American School: Would I be willing to teach math, physics, and social studies to secondary and high school students? I said yes. And so it was, at the age of nineteen, that I found my calling (thereby following in the footsteps of my mother). Mr. Ebert, the extraordinary principal of the school, let me reinvent the curriculum in each of my courses. For physics and math this was not so hard, but in social studies the previous text, sanctioned by the John Birch Society, proved somewhat limited. I was forced to improvise by relying on articles and pamphlets on social subjects, sometimes found in the dusty recesses of local bookstores. Nonetheless, my classes were very well received. When I went on to graduate school in New York in the late 1960s, I lived in Harlem for some time, teaching math and social science at a newly formed school called Harlem Prep. The school had been set up through a coalition between local educators and dedicated nuns of the Catholic Church in order to work with minority students and dropouts deemed unreachable by the public school system. In the math department, headed by a gifted African American teacher called Gaywood McGuire, we were able take students from essentially zero to first-year calculus.

In my peregrinations I was fortunate to have several outstanding teachers. In Ankara at the age of six I attended the previously mentioned one-room school, in which I was given the opportunity to study at any level that

I could handle. I came to love learning, and I advanced rapidly. As a result, when I returned to Pakistan at the age of eight I was much younger than my classmates. It was at St. Patrick's School in Karachi that I had to learn to stand up to bullying. Bullies, I discovered, are mostly bluff. Still, in later years I found it useful to supplement my acquired skills by studying judo and karate.

When my parents were posted to the United States in 1958, the school counselors in Washington, DC, wisely decided that I was too young for high school and placed me in eighth grade instead. It was there that I encountered Mr. Green, who completely changed my attitude toward algebra. He was a wonderful teacher and was quick to provide positive feedback (which often took the form of candy tossed across the room). I retain a deep fondness for algebra and for sweets. When my parents moved once again, this time to New York, I was placed in Stuyvesant High School. The school is nationally renowned for its advanced science and math curriculum. However, it was in the advanced shop class that I met one of my best teachers. Under the extraordinary tutelage of Mr. Howard Natter, each one of us built our own six-foot reflector telescope from scratch, cutting and machining all parts (even the screws) and grinding the mirror to the appropriate shape and glassy smoothness. His practical lessons in engineering were supplemented with lectures on physics and astronomy. It is my recollection that a subsequent set of students was taught to build a particle accelerator. I learned from him that practice has to be guided by theory, and theory tempered by practice.

Gary Becker was a brilliant teacher, and his advanced microeconomics course in graduate school at Columbia University taught me what orthodox microeconomics was all about. I have never forgotten his presentation of his article "Irrational Behavior and Economic Theory" (Becker 1962), in which he demonstrated that major empirical patterns of microeconomic behavior can be derived without any reference to so-called rational choice. I remember excitedly going after the lecture to Low Library in order to sketch out an extended version of that type of argument. Thirty-five years later I managed to write up this material for a forthcoming book and link it to a discussion of emergent properties grounded in what the physicist (and Nobel laureate) Robert Laughlin calls the "robust insensitivity" of empirical macro patterns to the particularities of micro behaviors (Laughlin 2005). In a course taught in the Business School at Columbia I was exposed to Robert Heilbroner's elegant and exciting account of the history of Western economic thought. I was even more fortunate to subsequently become Bob's colleague in 1972 at the New School, where I now teach a course on this subject myself. At

Columbia I was also privileged to attend extremely illuminating lectures on Sraffian economics given by Luigi Pasinetti when he was a visiting professor at Columbia in 1971. Heilbroner led me to Smith, Ricardo, Marx, and Keynes, and Pasinetti to Sraffa. These have been major influences on my work ever since.

SOCIAL VALUES AND SOCIAL SCIENCE

My political awakening began at Princeton in the early 1960s. I heard Martin Luther King speak at a general forum and Malcolm X speak at a small seminar in the Islamic Studies Department. I also heard the governor of Mississippi, Ross R. Barnett, inform us that many a civilization had been destroyed by miscegenation (I recall that he cited ancient Egypt as an example). Governor Barnett had been invited by a coalition of Southern students who felt underrepresented in the discourse. I can still picture them, replete with Confederate insignia and flags, filling the first two rows of the hall.

At Columbia in the late 1960s I encountered various factions of the American Left, and in Harlem I encountered the Black Panthers and the Black Muslims (Malcolm X had been assassinated by then). And, of course, I was at the same time studying microeconomics, mathematical economics, international trade, and monetary theory. I joined the Columbia Occupation in 1968, going into Fayerweather Hall still clutching my copy of Patinkin's classic text on money. I was forced to leave it behind in the subsequent chaotic evacuation but was able to quickly buy another one from an obliging fellow student. The subject remains an abiding interest. While at Columbia I wrote to Joan Robinson and brashly asked her if she would be willing to speak to the Economics Department. On receiving an affirmative response, I excitedly rushed to tell the department chair. To my astonishment, the department originally declined to invite her but, after some pressure from students, finally acceded. When the time came, she strode into the room, resplendent in a coat given to her by Mao, having just come from conversations with Fidel. She proceeded to say sharply critical things about aggregate production functions and the marginal productivity theory of distribution. The hall was full of students. But a mandatory department meeting just happened to have been scheduled at the same time, and only two faculty members from the Economics Department attended her talk. They spent their time during the discussion period attempting to defend standard theory.

Joan Robinson's visit had quite an impact on me. On a small note, it led to my expulsion from the local chapter of the Union for Radical Political

Economics, which I had helped start, on the grounds of "bourgeois deviationism." The issue was that I had gone to the airport to meet Joan rather than attend a scheduled meeting. My censure only deepened my revealed preference. More important, while Joan was on campus, she asked me to "look into" the apparent empirical support for aggregate production functions. My wise and gifted supervisor, Ron Findlay, gave me time and space to work on this as my first seminar paper, which in turn became my first journal publication, in the *Review of Economics Statistics* in 1974. I argued there that the apparent strength of fitted production functions was a statistical artifact generated by the fact that labor, capital, wage rates, and profit rates are tied together through the accounting identity that the value of output must equal the sum of wages and profits. I illustrated my argument with a fictitious set of data points whose arrangement spelled "Humbug" (Shaikh 1974). This was ferociously attacked in print, but my request to respond was denied. Still, my argument continued to percolate through the heterodox literature and was even accorded the status of a separate entry in the original *New Palgrave* in 1987. According to one academic citation index, the phrase "Humbug production function" has now been cited 2,196 times.

My interest in economics can be traced back to my time in Kuwait, where I came to wonder why there were so many poor people in such a fabulously rich country. The same question came up in New York as I shuttled between the poverty of Harlem and the privilege of Columbia. I had been told that the answer lay in economics, yet as I attended my classes and studied my textbooks I grew more and more disenchanted with what was being presented. My life history had convinced me that presumptions about what is normal or desirable vary greatly across cultures. It was in this light that I approached the assumptions of orthodox economics, and I found them wanting. It seemed to me the standard model did not describe how people or businesses actually behave, and the argument that assumptions do not matter struck me as an evasion. Nor was I persuaded by the claim that the standard model represented some kind of ideal. Why should it be ideal for economic agents to be concerned only with the things they can acquire, in supreme indifference to direct interactions among themselves? Why should social interactions be relegated to the status of "externalities" to be discussed, *sotto voce*, at the very end of the lessons? Such an approach struck me as a narrow cultural prejudice even within the Western tradition. Becker taught me that many different kinds of behavior can produce the same market patterns. I could think of no sensible intellectual reason, then, for adhering to the particular assumptions of "rational" choice or "perfect" competition.

On the other hand, I found myself equally unhappy with the notion of "imperfect" competition. The great discrepancy between actual business behavior and the model of perfect competition could have led to the conclusion that the latter was an inadequate representation of real competition. It led instead to the rejection of competition itself. In this way, perfect competition ended up being retained as a social ideal, as a benchmark for all real processes, and as a theoretical point of departure for models of imperfect competition. These in turn were often ad hoc and inconsistent with each other. My rejection of imperfect competition put me at odds not only with the post-Keynesian tradition, but also with the vast bulk of modern Marxian economics, but not with Marx.

I should say that my objections have never been to the use of mathematics, econometrics, or other tools of our trade. These can be powerful when used appropriately, and I have myself relied on linear algebra, nonlinear differential equations, agent-based simulation, and most recently the stochastic tools of econophysics. Nor am I opposed to abstraction. But it seems to me that there is a difference between abstraction, which seeks to get to the essentials of some actual process, and idealization, which seeks to raise it to the sky. My foremost concern was always with the overall "vision" of economics and with its applications to the real world. Such considerations led me to turn to Smith, Ricardo, Marx, P. S. Andrews, Harrod, and Sraffa for theory, and to reams of data ranging from national accounts and input-output tables to income distributions by nation, gender, and race. At long last, I am in the process of writing up my investigations in a book under review at Oxford University Press.

I was fortunate at the Economics Department of the New School for Social Research to have the space to work on an alternative approach to competition and macrodynamics, to be mentored by Adolph Lowe and Robert Heilbroner, and receive critical feedback from knowledgeable and literate colleagues and graduate students. I was equally fortunate to get the unstinting support of Dimitri Papadimitriou and the Levy Economics Institute of Bard College, and more recently Rob Johnson of the Institute for New Economic Thinking (INET), at several crucial points in my intellectual development. It was at the Levy Institute that I also met Wynne Godley, who became a mentor on macroeconomics, a coauthor, and a lifelong friend. He is greatly missed.

MY VISION AND WORK

The economic history of the developed capitalist world appears to be one of almost constant progress: inexorable growth, rising standards of living, rising productivity, ever-improving health, well-being, and welfare. Seen from afar, it is the system's order that stands out. Yet the closer one looks, the more one encounters individuals wandering along entangled paths, propelled by obscure motivations toward some dimly imagined ends. Information, misinformation, and disinformation hold equal sway. Ignorance is as purposeful as knowledge. Private and public spheres are entwined throughout, as are wealth and poverty, development and under-development, conquest and cooperation. And everywhere there appears a characteristic unevenness: across localities, regions, and nations, and across time, in the form of booms, busts, and breakdowns. Seen close, it is the system's disorder that is most striking. Neoclassical economics seizes on the order and recasts it as a consequence of the supreme optimality of the mar-ket. Heterodox economics, most notably Keynesian and post-Keynesian economics, generally takes the opposite tack. It emphasizes the inefficien-cies, inequalities, and imbalances generated by the system. Most of modern economics operates on a continuum between these two competing visions.

My own understanding of the operations of the invisible hand, derived from the classicals, is different. The capitalist economic system generates powerful ordered patterns that transcend historical and regional partic-ularities. The forces that shape these patterns are neither steely rails nor mere constellations of circumstance. They are, rather, moving limits whose gradients define what is easy and what is difficult at any moment of time. In this way they channel the temporal paths of key economic variables. Indeed, these shaping forces are themselves the results of certain imma-nent imperatives, such as "gain-seeking behavior," that dominate the capi-talist social form in all of its historical expressions. Agency and law coexist within a multidimensional structure of influences. But this structure is itself deeply hierarchical, with some forces (such as the profit motive) dominat-ing others.

From this point of view, systemic patterns are generated in and through continual fluctuations: disorder is the operative mechanism of order. To attempt to theoretically separate order from disorder, or even to merely emphasize one over the other, is to lose sight of their intrinsic unity, and hence of the very factors that endow the system with its deep patterns. In this sense, order is not synonymous with optimality, nor is disorder syn-onymous with chaos. Order-in-and-through-disorder is a brute force that tramples both expectations and preferences. This is precisely the source of the system's vigor, whether or not one likes the outcome.

It is, of course, necessary to identify particular mechanisms through which order and disorder operate in given circumstances. The great virtue of the classical approach, in my opinion, is that it is able to derive a large variety of phenomena from a very small set of coherent operative principles that give rise to forces which make actual outcomes gravitate around their ever-moving centers of gravity. This is the system's mode of *turbulent regulation*, whose characteristic expression is *pattern recurrence*. The theoretical and empirical applications of these two notions are woven into the structure of my work.

Turbulent regulation and recurrence apply to the system's various gravitational tendencies. Of these, the first set consists of those that channel the actual movements of commodity prices, profit rates, wage rates, interest rates, equity prices, and exchange rates. Equalizing tendencies driven by the restless search for monetary advantage reduce the very differentials that motivate them while at the same time giving rise to new differences. For example, equalization processes make individual wage and profit rates gravitate around the corresponding averages, which are themselves affected by the processes and by other factors. These are familiar notions in economics, but the point here is that there is a big difference between gravitation around an ever-moving balance point and equilibrium-as-a-state-of-rest. To study the properties of balance points, as the classicals do with natural prices or Marx does with balanced reproduction, is not to assume that these points exist as such. On the contrary, the relevant variables are generally away from this point and hit it only as they pass through from one side to the other. Among other things, this implies that one cannot assume that agents make their decisions as if they are in equilibrium.

The principle of turbulent regulation has its roots in the method of Smith, Ricardo, and Marx, for whom economic "laws" are dominant regulative principles that exert themselves in and through various countertendencies. The theory of real competition has similar roots in the economics canon, but also in the work of P. W. S. Andrews and Roy Harrod, two prominent members of the Oxford Economic Research Group. Elements can also be found in the business literature, most notably in the work of Michael Porter. A characteristic feature of this vision is that *competitive* firms necessarily engage in price-cutting and cost-cutting behavior, that technical and labor conditions vary across firms, and that only the firms with the best generally available conditions of production (best practice) have their profit rates equalized with those of similar firms in other industries. The resulting patterns closely resemble those found in business studies and in the literature on imperfect competition. Yet they represent the outcomes of price and profit rate equalizing competition, not "imperfect" competition. I have spent a great deal of time over the years developing and testing the theory of real competition.

The second set of gravitational tendencies arises from the system's *turbulent macrodynamics*. This gives rise to its characteristic expansionary processes, with its waves of growth and slowdown, persistent unemployment, and periodic bouts of inflation. Once again, it is the profit motive that is the dominant factor in the regulation of production, investment, economic growth, employment, business cycles, and inflation. The emphasis on growth also has roots in the classical tradition, as well as in the works of Harrod and Joan Robinson. The latter two share an emphasis on growth as the normal state but disagree on its determinants. For a given technology, Harrod believes that growth is driven by exogenously given savings rates,[1] while Robinson (like Keynes) argues that it is the profitability of investment that drives growth,[2] In the Pasinetti-Kaldor extension of Harrod, profitability adapts to growth, while in Robinson's argument, it is the other way around. I take the classical-Keynesian-Robinsonian path here. But because the classical starting point accords a central role to production, the end result is characteristically different. Supply is neither the imperial force of neoclassical economics nor the ghostly presence of Keynesian and Kaleckian economics. Supply and demand are coequals here, and as always, profit is pulling the strings.

I have focused so far on my life experiences as they have influenced my vision of economics. In what follows, I would like to illustrate some of the applications of my general approach.

At a methodological level, I have focused on the fact that gravitation of actual outcomes around their balance points (fundamentals) is generally mediated by expectations. In my earlier work, I focused on nonlinear dynamics as a means of formalizing such processes, inspired by earlier work by Kaldor and Goodwin. More recently, I realized that George Soros's theory of reflectivity, which emerges from his considerable experience in the world of finance, provides a more general framework for the interactions of these three variables. Soros advances three general theses: expectations affect actual outcomes, actual outcomes can affect fundamentals, and expectations are in turn influenced by the discrepancies between outcomes and fundamentals. The end result is a process in which actual variables oscillate turbulently around their gravitational values. Expectations can induce *extended disequilibrium* cycles in which a boom eventually gives way to a bust (Soros 2009: 50–75, 105–106). Because expectations can affect fundamentals, the gravitational centers are path dependent. Hence, the future is not a stochastic reflection of the past, so that the overall system is nonergodic (Davidson 1991). The existence of extended disequilibrium processes invalidates the efficient market hypothesis, and the dependence of fundamentals on actual outcomes invalidates the notion of rational expectations. Last, it is important to recognize that although expectations can influence actual outcomes, they cannot simply create a reality that validates them. On the contrary, gravitational centers continue to act as regulators of actual outcomes, which is precisely why booms eventually give way to busts (Soros 2009: 40–44, 50–58, 75, 216–222). Such patterns are consistent with the empirical evidence and with classical ideas on turbulent equilibration, but they invalidate notions such as rational expectations and the efficient market hypothesis. By tracing the elements of Soros's theory, I showed that it can be formalized in a simple and general manner that gives rise to testable propositions (Shaikh 2010).

Profit rate equalization is a central concept in all theories of competition. In the classical view of competition, profit rate equalization is conceived as a dynamic and turbulent process involving ceaseless fluctuations around a moving center of gravity. New conditions of production are constantly entering the battle of competition as older ones fall away. This perpetual fray gives rise to profit rates that generally differ across methods and firms. I have long argued that what is relevant to competition is the profit rate on the best-practice conditions of production, because their profitability is the relevant gauge for new investment. This led me to develop an approximation to the profit rate on recent investment in the form of an incremental rate of profit, defined as the ratio of the change in gross profits to the previous period's gross investment (Shaikh 1998). In a more recent paper I examine average and incremental rates of profit from 1970 to 1990 in eight manufacturing subsectors, each aggregated across eight major OECD countries; in subsectors of US manufacturing from 1979 to 1990; and in thirty US industries from 1987 to 2005. Average rates of profit were found to cluster around a common mean, but many remained persistently above or below that benchmark. By contrast, incremental rates of profit consistently moved back and forth across their common mean, as would be expected from the classical theory of the turbulent equalization of actual profit rates (Shaikh 2008). It should be said that an incremental rate of return, with its erratic path and boisterous interactions, is very different from the genteel marginal rate portrayed in standard theory.

I applied the same approach to the financial market. All theories of competition expect that rates of return are equalized between sectors, for instance between the corporate sector and the stock market. Orthodox economics builds the expectation of exact equalization into its theory of stock prices, through various versions of the discounted cash flow model. Yet this model performs so badly at an empirical level that economists such as Robert Shiller have concluded that financial markets are driven largely by irrational expectations, fads, and fancies – not just in periods of bubbles, but in general. Shiller shows that the average rate of return in the equity market and the average profit rate in the corporate sector differ considerably in their levels, volatilities, and trends. This is the empirical foundation for his well-known thesis that equity markets exhibit "irrational exuberance" (Shiller 1989, 2001). I argued on theoretical grounds that competition serves to equalize returns on new investment, not average rates of return. This is significant, because industrial capital stocks are of varying efficiencies and vintages, whereas all equities in a given corporation are the same regardless of the date of their issue. My own calculations using Shiller's data (which he had generously provided to me) showed that the incremental rates of return in the stock market and the corporate sector are extremely similar: both are highly turbulent, yet they have virtually the same mean and variance, and even move together most of the time except for specific and limited bubble periods, as in the 1990s. From a classical perspective, the combination of the incremental rate of return and Soros's concept of reflexivity with its notion of a moving center of gravity provides a far better explanation of stock prices than does Shiller's "irrational exuberance" (Shaikh 1998, 2010).

Another strand of my work involves the explanation of growth. Along Harrod's warranted path, long-term growth is driven by the savings rate (thrift). But in Solow's influential growth model, thrift has no effect on the long-run rate of growth, which is instead driven largely by exogenous technical change. The endogenous growth theory of Frankel and Romer therefore makes technical change internal to accumulation in a very particular manner, precisely in order to reinstate thrift as the driver of capital growth. I observe that there is a striking discrepancy between micro- and macroeconomic reasoning in all three approaches. All sides agree on the notion that individual investment (capital expansion) is driven by its expected profitability, and yet all sides conclude that in the long run aggregate capital expansion is driven by something totally different. I argue that this break is neither theoretically necessary nor empirically plausible. The key to reconciling the microeconomic understanding and the macroeconomic results lies in recognizing that the business savings (retained earnings) are crucially linked to business investment: both are internal to any given firm, so they cannot be taken as independent. In a path-dependent nonergodic world, it is not possible to link the two through the usual calculus of all-seeing optimization. I show that that it is mathematically sufficient if the business savings rate responds (in any degree) to the gap between total savings and investment. This makes the overall savings rate endogenous, and then it is possible to reconcile profit-driven growth as in Keynes and post-Keynesian economics with roughly normal levels of long-run capacity utilization as in Harrod (Shaikh 2009). The further implications for the analysis of multiplier effects, particularly for those arising from deficit spending by the state, will be addressed in my forthcoming book.

I have also developed an approach to inflation that derives from the classical link between growth and profitability. Marx, Leontief, and von Neumann established that the profit rate provides the upper limit to the sustainable growth rate of the economy even when there are no input (including labor) constraints. From this perspective, I argue that the *ratio* of the growth rate to the profit rate provides an index of the degree of utilization of an economy's growth potential. In contrast to conventional measures of unemployment or capacity utilization, my measure of the utilization of growth potential works quite well in explaining actual episodes of inflation in OECD countries, including the infamous "stagflation" of the 1970s and 1980s (Shaikh 1999). This work is being extended to cover inflation and episodes of hyperinflation in countries like Argentina and Brazil.

Finally, and perhaps most controversially, I have long argued that the theory of comparative costs is fundamentally incorrect on both theoretical and empirical grounds. The theory of international trade is actually a subset of the general theory of competition. In a capitalist world, free international trade is conducted by *businesses*. Domestic exporters sell to foreign importers, who in turn sell to their residents, while domestic importers buy from foreign exporters and sell to us. At each step in the chain, it is profit that motivates the business decision. Comparative cost theory rests on the proposition that a trade surplus will drive up the real price of the country's currency, which in turn will reduce the surplus, until at some point both the balance of trade and the balance of payments are automatically reduced to zero. A trade deficit would have the opposite initial effect, leading to the same conclusion. In Ricardo's original derivation, the nominal exchange rate is fixed, so imbalances generate money inflows and outflows that raise or lower national price levels, thereby moving the real exchange rate in the opposite direction – until the trade balance is zero and the terms of trade lie between comparative cost limits. In the case of flexible exchange rates, the money flows move the nominal exchange rate to the same ultimate point. In either case, it is the real exchange rate that adjusts automatically. Both Marx and Harrod make a compelling counterargument: money inflows increase liquidity and lower interest rates, while money outflows have the opposite effects. Neither of these substantially alters the trade balance. Instead, they induce short-term capital flows, which bring overall payments into balance by covering the persistent trade deficits (Harrod 1957: 90–96, 112–116, 130–138). My own extension has been to show both theoretically and empirically that international terms of trade are, in the end, relative prices regulated by relative real costs. Thus, international competition operates in much the same way as national competition, rewarding cost advantages and punishing cost disadvantages (Shaikh 2007; Shaikh and Antonopoulos 2012).

My work has generally focused on understanding and explaining fundamental patterns in the developed world. This is not due to a lack of interest in economic policy or in economic development. On the former front, I worked for several years with Wynne Godley and Dimitri Papadimitriou on the macroeconomic model of the Levy Institute of Bard College, helping put out a biannual macroeconomic report on the patterns and prospects of the US economy. On the latter front, I have always believed that an analysis of the developed world is an essential foundation for an adequate understanding of economic policy and economic development.

Finally, I have always believed that economics must be a moral science. Today, in the midst of a global great depression, the International Labor Organization reports that income inequality has actually worsened, that there are more than 900 million working people in the world living below the US$2 poverty line, that there are 1.52 billion workers in vulnerable employment, and that young people are nearly three times as likely to be unemployed as are adults. Moral and ethical differences affect the goals to which we subscribe, and theoretical differences affect the prescriptions we offer. One important task is to make these differences explicit and to confront their implications. There is no such thing as a value-free or socially neutral economics.

REFERENCES

Becker, Gary S. (1962). "Irrational Behavior and Economic Theory," *Journal of Political Economy* 70: 1–13.

Davidson, Paul (1991). "Is Probability Theory Relevant for Uncertainty? A Post Keynesian Perspective," *Journal of Economic Perspectives* 5, no. 1: 129–143.

Harrod, Roy F. (1957). *International Economics*. Chicago: University of Chicago Press.

Laughlin, Robert B. (2005). *A Different Universe: Reinventing Physics from the Bottom Down*. New York: Basic Books.

Sardoni, Claudio (1987). *Marx and Keynes on Economic Recession: The Theory of Unemployment and Effective Demand*. New York: New York University Press.

Shaikh, Anwar (1974). "Laws of Production and Laws of Algebra: The Humbug Production Function," *Review of Economics and Statistics* 61, no. 1: 115–120.

(1998). "The Stock Market and the Corporate Sector: A Profit-Based Approach," in M. Sawyer, P. Arestis, and G. Palma (eds.), *Fetschrift for Geoffrey Harcourt*, 389–404. London: Routledge & Kegan Paul.

(1999). "Explaining Inflation and Unemployment: An Alternative to Neoliberal Economic Theory," in A. Vachlou (ed.), *Contemporary Economic Theory*, 89–105. London: MacMillan.

(2007). "Globalization and the Myth of Free Trade," in A. Shaikh (ed.), *Globalization and the Myth of Free Trade*, 50–68. London: Routledge.

(2008). "Competition and Industrial Rates of Return," in P. Arestis and J. Eatwell (eds.), *Issues in Economic Development and Globalisation, Festschrift in Honor of Ajit Singh*, 167–194. Houndmills: Palgrave MacMillan.

(2009). "Economic Policy in a Growth Context: A Classical Synthesis of Keynes and Harrod," *Metroeconomica* 60, no. 3: 455–494.

(2010). "Reflexivity, Path-Dependence and Disequilibrium Dynamics," *Journal of Post Keynesian Economics* 33, no. 1: 3–16.

Shaikh, Anwar and Rania Antonopoulos (2012). "Explaining Long-Term Exchange Rate Behavior in the United States and Japan," in J. Moudud, C. Bina, and P. L. Mason (eds.), *Alternative Theories of Competition: Challenges to the Orthodoxy*. Abingdon: Routledge.

Shiller, Robert J. (1989). "Comovements in Stock Prices and Comovements in Dividends," *Journal of Finance* 44, no. 3: 719–729.

(2001). *Irrational Exuberance*. Princeton, NJ: Princeton University Press.

Soros, George (2009). *The Crash of 2008 and What It Means*. New York: Public Affairs.

Notes

1 Differentiating saving rates by income class (wages and profits, for instance, as in Kaldor and Pasinetti) allows changes in the distribution of income to modify the aggregate savings rate. Even so, it is the assumed fixity of class savings rates that leads to the result that the distribution of income (the profit/wage ratio) must adapt to make the actual growth rate conform to the natural rate of growth.

2 Keynes also notes that it is profitability, not demand, which drives production itself. "An entrepreneur is interested, not in the amount of the product, but in the amount of money which will fall to his share. He will increase his output if by so doing he expects to increase his money profit, even though this profit represents a smaller quantity of product than before" (Sardoni 1987: 75).

23

The Education of an Economist

Jeremy J. Siegel

It has always been important for me to understand what motivates individuals to do what they do and formulate a "big picture" of how the world
works. In this essay I describe the events that have impacted my life and
were important for formulating my philosophy. My philosophy is no "fixed
star." I know that no one, including myself, holds the key to the "Truth,"
and, to paraphrase John Maynard Keynes, I am quite willing to change my
mind when the facts so dictate. In short, at the same time I am teaching, I
am learning; we are all educators who are constantly being educated.

EARLY LIFE

My mother, an intellectual who was well read in philosophy, anthropology,
and sociology, named me "Jeremy" (an extremely uncommon name for
American boys at that time), after Jeremy Bentham, the early-nineteenth-
century British philosopher, whom she greatly admired.[1] Bentham was a
progressive thinker, arguing against slavery and for women's rights, and a

utilitarian who believed that law should be structured to maximize society's "pleasures" and minimize its "pains." Bentham was also a believer in free markets.

My own philosophy is not far from Bentham's: I am a moderate libertarian, a believer in a legal structure that maintains law and order, establishes property rights, and maximizes individual freedom. Although I believe in free markets, my own study of history convinces me that there exists an important role for the government in stabilizing economic activity.

It would be nice to say that I became an economist to find the right system to achieve these ends. But I became an economist for less worthy reasons. First, I was always fascinated with the stock market and believed that the study of economics would provide me with a better understanding of what moves markets. Second, to echo the words of Paul Samuelson in the first volume of *Eminent Economists*, I became an economist because I was good at it. My mind was analytical, I sought to maximize my own and later my family's well-being, and I easily grasped economic concepts, such as equilibrium and markets. Since I knew from my early teenage years that I loved to teach, I knew I wanted to work at an academic institution.

EARLY UPBRINGING

I was raised in a home where my mother was an avid and vocal (but not card-carrying) communist, while my father was conservative but nonpolitical.[2] My grandparents came from Europe, and my paternal grandfather was a carpenter from Austria-Hungry who came directly to Chicago at the end of the nineteenth century to help rebuild the city after the Great Chicago Fire of 1871. He eventually founded Siegel Lumber Company, which he and his four sons ran for almost seventy years but which none of his grandchildren carried on. My grandfather's skills at woodworking passed on to my brother, a wood turner and an inventor who holds patents on woodworking tools. In a remarkable coincidence, Jeremy Bentham's brother, Samuel, was also an inventor who was also awarded patents on woodworking tools by the British Patent Office in 1791 and 1793.

My mother came from a much poorer family than my father and was intensely intellectual, earning a master's degree and almost a PhD in anthropology from Northwestern University. It was there that she met a staunchly pro-communist professor who influenced her political thinking for many years to come.

My mother's political orientation had a profound impact on my life. When I was in seventh grade she had me tutored in the Russian language, because she said that when the Russians took over America (this was right after the Russians launched *Sputnik*), it would be to my great advantage to know Russian. During my sophomore year in high school she took my brother and me on an extensive trip to the Soviet Union, making a special tour of the University of Moscow, where she wanted me to enroll.

She also believed that it was the Russians, not the Americans, who were responsible for defeating Nazi Germany. I recall that when we visited the site of the Battle of Stalingrad, she picked up a piece of shrapnel left during World War II. Holding it up to us, she proclaimed how thankful we should be to the Russians, for had they lost, we too would have died under Nazi rule.[3]

Although both my parents were Jewish, because of my mother's communist beliefs, neither my brother nor I had any religious training at all. Yet my mother was aware of and deeply distressed by the plight the Jews under Nazi Germany. We traveled around the world, but Germany and Spain (when Franco was living) were strictly off-limits.

But I found neither the Soviet Union nor communism alluring, and I enrolled in Columbia University in the fall of 1963 at the age of seventeen. Being next to the world's largest financial markets was a much greater thrill than being near the Kremlin. And even though I strongly disagreed with my mother's political views, the experience of being exposed at an early age to politics and travel gave me an invaluable perspective on political and economic issues that would interest me for the rest of my life.

EARLY INTERESTS IN THE STOCK MARKET

The stock market had held a fascination for me since I was very young. When I studied the history of the market, I was captivated by the Great Crash of 1929–1932. The topic I chose in my speech class during my sophomore year of high school was "The Great Stock Crash and Great Depression." I had read John Kenneth Galbraith's *The Great Stock Crash, 1929* and wanted to present to the class the drama of the market, accompanied by graphs of the plunging Dow-Jones averages. It is striking how that experience, teaching financial markets, foreshadowed my professional life.

I sought out information from those who lived through the crash. I asked my maternal grandmother, my only living grandparent, whether she remembered anything about the market crisis. She said that her family was too poor to own stocks, but she remembered one day in October 1929 walking down the steps of her apartment building and hearing her neighbor sobbing uncontrollably on the landing. She asked her what had happened, and she responded that the market had crashed and that she and her husband had lost everything.

That conversation stuck in my mind. Why had the market crashed? What caused the Great Depression? Was there anything that government could have done to prevent such a disaster? Could it happen again?

Despite my interest in the market and the economy, there was no way that I could answer those questions until I took an economics class. To my knowledge, economics was not taught in any high school at that time; it was not even a first-year college course. I entered Columbia as a mathematics major and did not take my first economics course until I was a junior.

Paul Samuelson claimed that he "was born as an economist on January 2, 1932," when he attended his first college lecture on Thomas Malthus, by Frank Knight at the University of Chicago. I don't recall the exact date, but my first economics class at Columbia in September 1965, taught by Professor Peter Kenen (a contributor to this volume), similarly changed my life. Although I found myself in a huge lecture hall with more than 300 other students, after two weeks I was completely captivated by the subject matter and knew that I would become an economist.

Kenen introduced a Keynesian framework for understanding the business cycle and the Great Depression. He integrated the concepts of aggregate demand and liquidity preference together into what he called the "4 quadrant diagram," a forerunner of the "ISLM" analysis, which at that time was taught only in more advanced classes. I took as many economics courses as I could in my last three semesters at Columbia and cherry-picked the math classes that would be useful for graduate school. I graduated from Columbia with a double major in economics and mathematics.

During my undergraduate years I retained a keen interest in the stock market. After my Friday morning classes I often took the subway down to Wall Street to watch the closing of the New York Stock Exchange. In those days the visitors' gallery was open to anyone, and I would enter the gallery around 3:00 P.M. to watch the last half hour of trading.

My senior thesis at Columbia was an analysis of whether short selling was a major factor driving down stock prices during the Depression, as many critics had contended. I found no significant correlation and concluded that the restrictions on short selling put in place during the 1930s (particularly the uptick rules) were not supported by the data.

Despite my aversion to communism, in my early years at Columbia I had no strong political leanings. But that wouldn't last long as the war in Vietnam and the military draft threatened students. I was decidedly against the war, but also against the left-wing politics of the large majority of student protesters. I believed that the military draft was an affront to personal freedom, and I was impressed with the arguments that Professor Milton Friedman of the University of Chicago raised against conscription.

It was during my senior year that I read Friedman's *Capitalism and Freedom* and his ideas lit up my brain. I realized that libertarianism was the best description of my political philosophy.

I have often wondered why I didn't follow my mother's path to the political left. Perhaps because I saw my father, a small businessman, struggle long hours but ultimately fail to keep his father's business going. Perhaps because I didn't see "exploited workers" or greedy capitalists: in the 1950s the workers in the auto and steel industries were earning the most generous wage and benefit packages.

But I also saw America as a place where immigrants who felt discriminated against in their homeland could come to earn a living, raise their families, and enjoy political, religious, and economic freedom. I never thought that government "knew best" or was more efficient than the private sector. I felt that Adam Smith's "invisible hand" of competition did a much better job of allocating resources and maximizing welfare than any government bureaucrat. Most of these ideas still remain at the core of my political philosophy.

GRADUATE SCHOOL: MASSACHUSETTS INSTITUTE OF TECHNOLOGY

Given my political orientation, the University of Chicago would have seemed the logical choice for graduate study. But I was set on the Massachusetts Institute of Technology, which was reputed to be the best school for those with good economics and mathematical skills.

And MIT did not disappoint me. First-semester macroeconomics was taught by Professor Evsey Domar (a contributor to the first volume *Eminent Economist*), who lectured on Don Patinkin's *Money, Interest, and Prices*.[4] Professor Robert Solow, a superb teacher (also in the first volume of *Eminent Economists*), taught us neoclassical growth theory. Franco Modigliani taught the empirical macroeconomics course, since he was heavily involved in developing a large econometric model of the macroeconomy. Paul Samuelson taught us advanced monetary theory, substituting on short notice after the untimely death of Professor Miguel Sidrauski.

Samuelson was a remarkable man, and I regard him as the greatest theoretical economist of the twentieth century, and arguably of all time. Well into his nineties, he called or wrote me if he had a comment on something I wrote. He reminded me, in response to a free-trade op-ed piece I wrote for the *Wall Street Journal*, that technological progress in one country, such as India, may make its trading partners, such as the United States, worse off. He called to discuss my "noisy market hypothesis," which I introduced as an alternative to the efficient market hypothesis that was the foundation of the finance literature.

A topic that fascinated me in graduate school was hyperinflation, and the article that attracted my attention was "Monetary Dynamics of Hyperinflation" by Phillip Cagan. Cagan adapted this article from his doctoral dissertation, written under the tutelage of Milton Friedman. The article not only determined the maximum amount of seignorage that a government could obtain through the inflationary process, but also derived the stability conditions of a monetary economic with inflationary expectations.

Cagan's analysis was not only relevant to hyperinflation. In the late 1960s, inflation had risen to levels the United States had not seen since the late 1940s, when price controls were removed following the Second World War. The monetarists from the University of Chicago and the Federal Reserve of St. Louis were blaming inflation on the excessive growth of the money supply. In his presidential address to the American Economic Association in 1967, Milton Friedman asserted that once inflationary expectations were taken into account, there was no long-term trade-off between inflation and unemployment. The profession was filled with controversy, and I wondered whether the feedback of inflation to inflationary expectations could destabilize the economy.

I tried to put all these ideas together in my doctoral dissertation, "Stability of a Monetary Economy with Inflationary Expectations." I generalized the Cagan model and derived the stability conditions for a flexible-price Patinkin model with Friedman's expectations-enhanced Phillips curve. I was honored to have Samuelson, Solow, and Modigliani as my three thesis advisers. Samuelson was awarded the Nobel Prize in economics the year after I began my graduate studies, and Solow and Modigliani won the award after I received my PhD.

Although monetary theory was my primary interest, I was also very interested in the foreign exchange market. During my graduate school years, the Bretton Woods system of fixed international exchange was in its death throes. I was a staunch believer in floating exchange rates and found Milton Friedman's arguments for such a system, put forth in his small volume, *The Case for Flexible Exchange Rates*, very convincing. I recall having long arguments with Professor Charles Kindleberger, a staunch supporter of the fixed rate system, when I took his graduate class on international economics at MIT.

I also closely followed the forward exchange markets to seek clues as to the probability of future exchange rate changes. Much foreign exchange rate analysis had been done under the simplifying assumption of risk neutrality, so that the mean, or expected value, of the exchange rate became a very important variable for investors.

But because of a statistical property called "Jensen's inequality," the expected value of, say, the dollar–pound exchange rate, important for American investors, could not be equal to one over the expected value of the pound–dollar exchange rate, relevant to British investors. It therefore appeared that risk-neutral investors on each side of the Atlantic could not simultaneously arbitrage the dollar–pound exchange rate to its expected value.

I wrote this "conundrum" up as a side note in a broader paper entitled "Risk, Interest Rates, and the Forward Exchange," which was accepted by the *Quarterly Journal of Economics*. The body of the paper, which explained how expectations of the dollar–pound exchange rate changed over time was mostly ignored, but the "conundrum" drew a large response. It was dubbed the "Siegel paradox" and became one of the best-known paradoxes in the economics literature. Mark Kritzman, in his book *Puzzles in Finance*, named it one of six major conundrums in finance.

Of all my published academic articles, this one, my first, probably has the most citations. Certainly I found it an honor to have a paradox named after me, but the irony is that the paradox was not the central issue of the article. For years I received correspondence from around the world on possible solutions to this paradox but never pursued further research in this area.[5]

UNIVERSITY OF CHICAGO

After MIT, I was anxious to be a colleague of Milton Friedman at the University of Chicago, and I was fortunate to be offered a position at Chicago's Graduate School of Business. The intellectual atmosphere at Chicago was intense and my teaching load was heavy.[6] I regularly attended Friedman's Money Workshop and developed a friendship with Merton Miller, with whom I used to go out to dinner after we had completed our evening teaching responsibilities at the downtown campus of the Business School.

Although Samuelson dazzled me with his brilliance, it was clearly Milton Friedman who had the most influence on my thinking.[7] I believe he was the most influential economist of the second half of the twentieth century, with

Keynes having the most influence in the first. His *Monetary History of the United States*, and particularly the chapter entitled "The Great Contraction," had a great impact on my thinking.

I found his hypothesis that the failure of the Fed to back up financial institutions was the major cause of the Great Depression compelling. This does not mean that I dismissed other factors influencing aggregate demand; indeed, all the models I have worked with have Keynesian short-run components. Yet I believe that the collapse of the banking system, the loss of deposits, and the subsequent deflation plunged the economy into a much deeper hole than would have occurred had the banking system been saved.

LONG-RUN ECONOMIC DATA

I have always been fascinated with long-term economic data. Perhaps my most significant work during my four years at the University of Chicago was a joint paper I published with my life-long friend Robert Shiller in the *Journal of Political Economy* called "The Gibson Paradox and Historical Movements in Real Interest Rates."[8] I plumbed Sidney Homer's great volume, *Interest Rates*, for historical interest rates on British government bonds going back to the eighteenth century. I wanted to test Irving Fisher's assumption that changing investors' expectations of inflation explained the surprising correlation between the price level of commodities and the long-term interest rate, which was known as the Gibson paradox.

I formed what I called the "ex post rational" interest rate on consols, defined as the nominal rate that would prevail if individuals knew exactly the future path of prices. The ex post rational interest rate series had a strong negative correlation with the actual interest rate. This implied that if Fisher's explanation was correct, bond holders not only had no ability to forecast inflation but made large systematic errors in their forecasts.

Bob Shiller took the idea of "ex post rational" series and applied it to stock prices. In theory stock prices are supposed to be the present value of dividends, but Bob showed that stock prices were far too volatile to be explained by fluctuations in dividends and gave birth to the entire "excess volatility" literature. This was the work that the Nobel Committee cited when they awarded him the Nobel Prize in Economic Sciences in 2013.

POLITICS AT CHICAGO

When I started MIT, student demonstrations against the Vietnam War were reaching a crescendo. Fortunately, I had graduated from Columbia before students occupied key buildings, effectively shutting down the university. MIT, as one can imagine, was politically far less active.

As most students shifted further to the left, my libertarian leanings grew, and at MIT I found myself joining the editorial board of a weekly libertarian paper called *Ergo*. I wrote editorials on the military draft, the prohibition of drugs and gambling, free markets, and politics.

When members of the University of Chicago community learned that I was a libertarian columnist in Cambridge, I was besieged with offers to join libertarian groups at the university. But my time was too short. The Gates Commission had recommended instituting a volunteer army, and President Nixon had agreed to this; floating exchange rates had become a reality. So a number of my major political causes were already implemented.

THE WHARTON SCHOOL

In the fall of 1975 I received a call from Professor Anthony Santomero from the Wharton School, whom I had met at a previous conference, inviting me to join him on the faculty of the Finance Department. I consented, and in July 1976 I moved into the Society Hill area of center city Philadelphia, where I have lived ever since. Tony also introduced me to a woman whom I married two years later.

Certainly my life would have been very different if Tony had never called me. This highlights the large role that chance plays in our lives. Milton Friedman told me that when he and his wife, Rose, chose the title *Two Lucky People* for their autobiography, they faced strong opposition from their publisher. But he and Rose prevailed because they believe their life was filled with good fortune.

But luck had little to do with Friedman's success. Given his brilliance, it would not be long before opportunities came his way that showcased his many talents. I believe you can set yourself up for good outcomes. Those who get the "lucky breaks" are often those who have prepared the best and practiced the most.

Beginning in 1984 I regularly traveled to New York to teach in JPMorgan's Finance Program, where I developed a markets-oriented approach to macroeconomics. When I was asked by Wharton's Finance Department the following year to redesign the macroeconomics course for MBAs, I liberally borrowed from the material I developed for JPMorgan.

At Wharton, unlike Chicago, I taught both graduates and undergraduates. The undergraduates were extraordinary, and the honors classes I taught contained the best students I had ever had. Although the MBA students were excellent, they were less interested in macroeconomic theory and more curious about how economic and political developments impacted the stock, bond, and foreign exchange markets. As a result, my markets-oriented approach to macroeconomics proved very popular.

This did not mean that I taught only current events in my course. I believe that students must understand the "big picture" before they can do any analysis. The model I taught was a flexible price ISLM model, patterned after what I learned from Don Patinkin and used in my doctoral dissertation.

From my work at JPMorgan I became quite adept at manipulating Bloomberg financial data. I loaded the Bloomberg software onto my laptop and customized the screen to exhibit selected stock indexes, interest rates, exchange rates, and commodity prices, which were continuously displayed to the class. I could then show how these variables reacted immediately after economic data or central bank statements were released.

The course proved very popular and was regularly oversubscribed. I increased my class size to about 120 and allowed selected undergraduates to enroll alongside the MBAs. I spent the first twenty to thirty minutes of the class reviewing market developments and explaining them in the context of the macro theory that I taught. These "market commentaries" became popular, and I allowed second-year students to stand at the back of the class for these updates. In recent years my market commentaries were digitally recorded and made available to students on the Wharton Internet.

I have always experienced a great deal of satisfaction from teaching, and during my [JJS: 42] years in academia I have taught more than 10,000 students. It is most gratifying when former students come up to me, stating, "Professor Siegel, you don't remember me, but back in [some year] I took your course and it was among the most enjoyable and valuable course that I took at Wharton [or Chicago]." A number of my students told me that they decided to pursue a career in the financial markets as a result of my course.

RESEARCH AT WHARTON

In my early years at Wharton I continued to work on macroeconomic models and monetary policy. But that changed in 1989 when my colleague Marshall Blume said that the New York Stock Exchange, which was approaching its two hundredth anniversary in 1992, wanted him to write a history of the capital markets. Marshall said that although I had not written much on the markets, he knew I had a strong interest and wanted to know whether I would join him in this project.

I jumped at the opportunity. Professor William Schwert from the University of Rochester had published a stock price series from 1802 onward, and I knew from the work of Bob Shiller that the Cowles Foundation had published a stock return series from 1871. Using Sidney Homer's *Interest Rates* (the same book I used for British consols rates), I obtained interest rate data and, by splicing together commodity price data, I developed a series for inflation. With these variables I could compute a series of total real returns for each class of financial asset: stocks, short- and long-term bonds, gold, and the dollar from 1802 onward.

When I plotted these data on a semilogarithmic scale the results were striking. The annual real returns on stocks, although very volatile in the short run, closely adhered to a long-term trend line whose slope was between 6.5 and 7.0 percent per year. This real returns for stocks subsequently became known as "Siegel's Constant."[9] The real returns on bonds were more stable in the short run, but their long-term returns were less certain.

The ability of long-term economic series to adhere to a trend line has always fascinated me. As a graduate student at MIT, I purchased a Department of Commerce publication entitled *Long-Term Economic Growth, 1860–1965*. One graph in that volume struck me: the GDP of Germany from 1870 forward. The terrible impact of World Wars I and II on output was readily visible. But if you were to construct a trend line using only the data from 1870 to 1914 and then extended it to 1965, the year the book was published, you would have exactly hit the actual German GDP.

This was remarkable. If you gave GDP data to a German economist on the eve of World War I and asked him to predict output fifty years later, the simple extrapolation would give him the right answer. The world wars, which killed millions of Germans and destroyed almost their entire capital stock, had no impact on their long-term GDP. The economy displayed amazing healing power. In a similar vein I found that World Wars I and II and the Great Depression, which impacted stock prices drastically in the short run, did not influence their long-term returns.

I published my data in the *Financial Analysts Journal*, and the article was awarded the Graham and Dodd Scroll for one of the best five articles published in 1992. I received words of encouragement from my colleagues, especially Bob Shiller, to publish a book about my results.

STOCKS FOR THE LONG RUN

From this research, *Stocks for the Long Run* was born. For the first time I could indulge myself in writing a book on the subject I loved most: what moves the stock market and how macroeconomic events impact stock returns.

In the early phase of my academic career, the thought of writing a book would have been daunting. But the development of the personal computer made all the difference. Some authors are able to type a first draft that is almost a completed manuscript. But I cannot. I must frequently write and rewrite sentences until they say what I mean. Before word processing, this was an extraordinarily time-consuming and arduous process. But the advent of the personal computer energized my writing. With a word processor, I could shift and rewrite sentences easily.[10]

This did not mean that good writing was a breeze. I remember reading my first draft of *Stocks for the Long Run* and thinking how dull my prose was. Academics are often stuck in a turgid writing style, patterned after the style required in academic journals, where every statement must be footnoted and every opinion must be hedged. I forced myself out of that mold and the experience was liberating. I later learned that both Milton Friedman and John Kenneth Galbraith went through the same struggle of transforming their academic writings into a readable form that would capture the interest of the nonprofessional, yet informed reader.

Stocks for the Long Run came out in May 1994, in the middle of the 1991–2000 bull market. It quickly garnered good reviews in *Barron's*, *Business Week*, and other periodicals. One of the reasons for the success of the book was that the claim that stocks were not as risky as bonds for long-term investors now had a sound empirical basis. I was particularly pleased that my book was used as a textbook by a number of colleagues, particularly by Burton Malkiel, whose book, *A Random Walk Down Wall Street*, I often recommended to students.

The research in *Stocks for the Long Run* led to many speaking engagements, and I traveled to scores of cities in the United States and abroad to present my findings. I tolerated the travel well, making sure that I had a laptop on which to do work on planes or during delays. I especially enjoyed the dinners after the presentations, where I could relax over food and wine and trade ideas with key analysts in the private sector about the market and the economy. My international travel expanded when the Wharton Global Alumni network began to hold meetings abroad. My wife and two sons often joined me on the international trips or at other times when we could get away.

The second edition of *Stocks for the Long Run* came out to strong sales in 1998. But as the decade wore on, I became uneasy about the surge in technology and especially Internet stocks. In April 1999, at the behest of the *Wall Street Journal*, I wrote an article detailing the overvaluation of these stocks entitled "Are Internet Stocks Overvalued? Are They Ever." Nearly a year later the *Journal* again asked me to write about the meteoric rise in the price of large tech stocks. Out of this came my most widely known op-ed piece, which appeared in March 2000, entitled "Big Cap Tech Stocks are a Sucker's Bet." For many years afterward, investors came up to me, often with that clipped article, stating either that I had saved them a lot of money or that they *wished* they had followed my advice.

THE SUBPRIME CRISIS

Calling the top of the market turned out to be mixed blessing. I felt very uncomfortable with the "guru" appellation that the media had bestowed on me, since predicting when bubbles will break is pure luck. Indeed, I did not foresee the next bear market, sparked by the subprime crisis. I knew there was excessive real estate speculation and that a lot of bad mortgages were written, but I calculated the total value of those mortgages to be less than the wealth lost during the technology meltdown seven years earlier, so if many of them went sour, that wouldn't have a major impact on the economy.

What I did not realize was that huge sums of these mortgages and other real estate assets were held by major commercial and investment banks on borrowed money. When the real estate market collapsed, the decline in the real estate assets overwhelmed the capital structure of key financial institutions and led to the demise of Bear Stearns, Lehman Brothers, AIG, and others.

I remember sitting in my office watching my Bloomberg screen on that fateful week of September 15, 2008. On Monday Lehman filed for bankruptcy and Bank of America bought Merrill Lynch, on Tuesday markets collapsed and a panicked Fed rescued AIG, and on Wednesday the Reserve Primary money market fund halted withdrawals and broke below a dollar.

These events led investors to flee in panic from all assets except Treasury securities. For the first time in my life I saw the Treasury bill rates plunge toward zero, and I feared for the viability of our financial institutions. When Fed Chairman Bernanke stood behind the banks and money market deposits later that week, I knew he was acting on the knowledge he had gained through the same studies of the Great Depression that I had read as a graduate student.

The crisis greatly increased student interest in my macroeconomics class. The macroeconomic model that I used proved extremely relevant in explaining what was happening. The credit shock and loss in real estate and stock market wealth caused aggregate demand to plummet, and the financial crisis caused a tremendous increase in the demand for reserves. The Federal Reserve responded properly by supplying those reserves and preventing deflation. I felt that had Milton Friedman been alive, he would have approved the Fed's generous liquidity provisions and backstops to bank deposits and money market funds.

The credit crisis and the resulting recession did, however, strain the thesis of *Stocks for the Long Run*. The crisis caused a second major bear market just seven years after the bursting of the tech bubble; by March 2009 stocks fell to thirteen-year lows. On Monday, March 9, the day the market hit its low, Gene Epstein, economist for *Barron's* who had been in contact with me over the past few months, wrote a bullish cover story entitled "Case Closed: Stocks Work." The article featured my picture and my research on why this was now an excellent time to buy stocks.

But the media continued to focus on those who had predicted the decline. Although I felt confident that over time stocks would once again prove to be the best asset class for investors, I could not deny the pain of those who had held onto stocks during this dreadful period.

Even though I believed strongly in the importance of free markets and the signals that market prices provided, I was never a blind devotee of the efficient market hypothesis. In fact my experience with the tech bubble convinced me that market prices could be wrong for an extended period of time. And I was impressed with the empirical work that showed that "value stocks," those stocks with relatively low prices relative to fundamentals such as earnings and dividends, systemically outperformed "growth stocks." In *The Future for Investors* I discussed the "growth trap" and how investors generally overpay for "growth stocks."[11]

FAMILY, POLITICS, AND (A LITTLE) FREE TIME

When I began studying economics I felt for sure that I would marry an economist. After all, what could be more valuable than talking over your ideas with someone over the dinner table. But I didn't marry an economist, and I believe I am much better off. When I met my wife, she was director of speech pathology at the Children's Hospital of Philadelphia. After our first son was born she went into private practice, specializing in improving the communications skills of autistic children. In order to discuss my work with Ellen I had to be able to distill my ideas down to their essence, a skill that proved very valuable for lecturing to nonprofessional audiences. I recall something that Professor Samuelson had said when I was a graduate student: you do not really understand a concept until you can explain it to your wife over the dinner table. He failed to mention that *his* wife has a PhD in economics!

My political orientation changed little during my years at Wharton. The fall of communism bolstered my conviction that socialist economies would fall far short of those that enjoyed free markets. The tremendous surge in economic activity when China and India liberalized their economies further supported my beliefs. In 2005 I wrote my second book, *The Future for Investors*, which showed how the growth in emerging markets could offset the aging in developed economies.

In 2000 I signed on to be a principal economic adviser to Arizona Senator John McCain in his bid for the Republican presidential nomination. I traveled with him to the primary states Michigan and New Hampshire but had to drop out of the campaign in the spring semester because of my heavy teaching responsibilities. I had great respect for the man, but I declined McCain's offer to join his 2008 campaign because I disagreed with his position on Iraq. I remained noninterventionist in foreign affairs except where I thought the interests of the United States were vitally involved, the same position that I held when I opposed the Vietnam War three decades earlier.

When I finished the fourth edition of *Stocks for the Long Run* in 2008, I vowed that I would spend more time playing duplicate bridge, a game I took up shortly after I finished my degree at MIT but had let lapse in the intervening years. I was fascinated with bridge's unique application of logic, probability, and communications (in bidding) and shared Warren Buffett's enthusiasm for the game. In fact, when I invited Buffett to come to Wharton to give a talk in 1999 (the first time he had returned to the campus since he dropped out more than fifty years earlier), we spent the first thirty minutes talking about how the game had enriched our lives.

FINAL WORDS

In developing a philosophy of how the world works, I constantly compare what I see against what I believe and am willing to change my mind when I see contrary evidence. The events that have unfolded in recent years have supported my fundamental conception of how the world works. Free financial markets are still the best way to achieve economic success, but they must be tempered by a monetary backstop to ensure the smooth functioning of the financial system.

I have experienced great satisfaction in my career by not only trying to figure out how our economy works, but teaching it to others. As I stated at the outset of this essay, the world is far too complex for us to understand everything. We build on what others have accomplished and hope that we can add a little more, enriching ourselves and others in the process.

REFERENCES

Department of Commerce (1966), *Long-Term Economic Growth, 1860–1965* Washington, DC: US Census Bureau.

Friedman, Milton (1953). "The Case for Flexible Exchange Rates," in *Essays in Positive Economics*, 157–203. Chicago: University of Chicago Press.

(1962). *Capitalism and Freedom*. Chicago: University of Chicago Press.

Friedman, Milton and Anna J. Schwartz (1963). *A Monetary History of the United States: 1867–1960*. NBER Studies in business cycles no. 12. Princeton: Princeton University Press, reprinted as *The Great Contraction, 1929–1933*. Princeton: N.J. Princeton University Press, 1965.

Galbraith, John Kenneth (1954). *The Great Crash, 1929*. Pelican.

Homer, Sidney (1963). *The History of Interest Rates*. New York: John Wiley.

Kritzman, Mark (2000), *Puzzles in Finance: Six Practical Problems and Their Remarkable Solutions*. New York: Wiley Investment.

Malkiel, Burton (1973), *A Random Walk Down Wall Street*. New York: W. W. Norton.

Patinkin, Don (1956) *Money, Interest, and Prices*, 2d ed. (1st ed. 1956). Evanston (Illinois): Row, Peterson and Company.

Siegel, Jeremy (1972). "Risk, Interest Rates, and the Forward Exchange," *Quarterly Journal of Economics* 86, no. 2 (May): 303–309; "Reply," *Quarterly Journal of Economics* 89, no. 1 (February 1975): 173–175.

(1992). "The Equity Premium, Stock and Bond Returns Since 1802," *Financial Analysts Journal* 48, no. 1 (January/February): 28–38; winner of the 1992 Graham and Dodd Scroll Award.

(2005). *The Future for Investors: Why the Tried and the True Triumph over the Bold and the New*. New York: Crown Business, Random House.

(2008). *Stocks for the Long Run: The Definitive Guide to Financial Market Returns and Long-Term Investment Strategies*, 4th ed. New York: McGraw-Hill.

Siegel, Jeremy and Robert Shiller (1977). "The Gibson Paradox and Historical Movements in Real Interest Rates," *Journal of Political Economy* 85, no. 5 (October): 891–907.

Notes

1 Although Jeremy has become an extremely popular name in the past twenty years in the United States, I had never met anyone born in the United States with my name until I was nearly forty years old.

2 My mother's economic views were not very Benthamite!

3 I have that piece of shrapnel to this day, as the Russians, despite tight border controls, allowed us to take it out of the country.

4 We called the book "The White Bible" because of the color of its cover.

5 The solution involves looking at consumption bundles of actual goods rather than an "index" of purchasing power, which is what money does.

6 In those days the standard teaching load was six quarter courses per year.

7 In my second book, *The Future for Investors*, my dedication read, "To Paul Samuelson, my teacher, and Milton Friedman, my mentor, colleague, and friend."

8 Bob Shiller and I met the first week we arrived at MIT in the fall of 1967 and developed a friendship that persists to this day. Our families often vacationed together either in the Poconos or at the New Jersey shore when our children were young.

9 The name was first applied by the British economists Andrew Smithers and Stephen Wright in their 2000 book, *Valuing Wall Street*.

10 I was an extremely fast touch typist. Typing was a required course in seventh grade in my public elementary school, and I often claim it was the most valuable course I took prior to high school. Ranked second in my class, I maintained good accuracy at sixty to sixty-five words per minute.

11 At the same time, I became senior investment strategy adviser to WisdomTree Investments, which issues exchange traded funds (ETFs), many based on fundamentally weighted indexes.

24

Faith, Science, and Religion

Vernon L. Smith

Science has outgrown the "modern mistake" of discounting invisible realities.

Houston Smith, The Soul of Christianity (2005: 41)

INTRODUCTION: WHAT IS FAITH?

Faith in invisible realities, once considered the exclusive province of religion, has pervaded physics since Newton, has created a counterintuitive new reality since Einstein, and was at the core of how Adam Smith viewed both human sociality in *The Theory of Moral Sentiments* (1759; hereafter

I am grateful to the editors of this volume, who have encouraged me beyond my original intention to revisit and revise my "Postscript on Faith in Science and Religion," written for *Discovery – A Memoir* (Smith 2008), melding it with my thoughts on experimental economics and the Great Recession, and thus meeting their charge to include "some perspective on the nature of life and of the universe."

TMS) and national economies in *The Wealth of Nations* (1776; hereafter WN). The story I will tell of invisible realities from Newton though the Scottish Enlightenment to the Great Recession is the story of the physical world, then human social and economic systems, all subject to unannounced but discoverable rules of order.

But what is faith and how might it be relevant to science, economics, and religion? I propose to build upon a positive New Testament definition. It is expressed in the inimitable style of the anonymous learned author of Hebrews (11.1): "Now faith is the substance of things hoped for the evidence of things not seen." The meaning expressed here, I believe, applies just as appropriately to science as to religion. My elaboration will be dispersed throughout the essay: briefly, for now, the idea is that, in science, theory provides the substance of hope; evidence is always indirect and in this sense is not seen.[1]

Let me preface my explorations, however, with some autobiographical background. My early exposure to religion was powerfully conditioned by the prevailing materialist-agnostic interpretation represented by the ascension of science at the time. My mother and her father, both skeptics, had been attracted to Unitarianism before I was born. Although Unitarians had a very strong naturalistic and scientific bent, this was the fashionable face of reason that was always tempered and qualified by an inner private experience emanating from deep secular and Judaic-Christian sources of poetic inspiration.

Although materialism breaths with vigor in the rhetoric of scientists and other intellectuals today, I think the truth-seeking processes of science have undermined this belief system, making it obsolete. Truth seeking is, of course, one of the guiding principles of Christian theology, as well as of science, as in John (8.32): "And ye shall know the truth, and the truth shall make you free." Hence, I see no inherent conflict between science and religion. Each can be at peace one with the other, although I am far from predicting that they will be.

Public debates are polarized on the issue of design versus a naturalistic rule-governed order, particularly as it affects public education, much controlled from top-down bureaucratic directives to which all are expected to conform and therefore destined to generate heated controversy. Each side in this controversy fears that some child somewhere will have her mind permanently corrupted by not being properly indoctrinated in its version of what it passionately considers to be the "truth."

In my day, by written parental consent, public school pupils attended a weekly local church Bible school for a couple of hours – at my school, when

I was in the third or fourth grade, it was every Thursday. Separation of state and religion did not mean that such voluntary contacts were prohibited. My mother approved, but only after asking me if I wanted to attend. The fact that, as a lefty, she heartily approved of Clarence Darrow's 1925 "Monkey Trial" defense of Scopes for teaching evolution in Tennessee did not mean that she would intervene in my decision in order to impose her views. After an elapse of time my mother asked how I liked Bible school, and I replied, "Fine." She asked why, and I replied that I liked all those stories about God and Jesus. I was comparing them with my early reading of the classic tales of Grimm, Anderson, and, my favorite, *Tal* (1929) by Paul Fenimore Cooper, great-grandson of the acclaimed wilderness novelist, James Fenimore Cooper.

My mother was not a believer, but neither was she threatened by believers; in retrospect I often think that this was her most precious gift to me. Ultimately, I came to understand that people comfortable in their own search for meaning live well with those whose search leads to different outcomes.

FAITH AND PHYSICS

Returning to my thought trail, the basic materialist faith was that physical science would determine the ultimate reductionist elements from which matter was built, and in that discovery humankind would come to understand our universe at a depth that would subvert and replace any need for appealing to some spiritual or mystical entity to comprehend human existence. In the meantime we may as well suspend traditional religious values in anticipation of that liberating day of salvation!

This materialist expectation was implicit in my naive childhood belief that everything was knowable, once you became an adult. I had yet to learn that along with the answer to any question came a host of deeper questions created by the answer. This state of our knowledge is illustrated by the observation that in any epoch a child can force you to the outer limits of knowledge by asking why three times in a row following each of your attempts to answer. When you do economics experiments, unanswered questions arise in the pursuit of every topic, but you stop long enough to write about the answers, leaving the new questions for their day in the sun.

In my view this materialist conception of the universe started to unravel with two of Einstein's four famous 1905 papers: one on the special theory of relativity (actually entitled "On the Electrodynamics of Moving Bodies"), the other on the photoelectric effect. One of the implications of the first was the equivalence of matter and energy (the equation was actually derived in another of Einstein's 1905 papers), leading to a revolutionary understanding of classical physics as well as to practical nuclear engineering; it also led to his 1916 general theory of relativity, which reinterpreted our concept of gravity, space, and time, later forming the cosmological basis for an expanding universe in which time started with the Big Bang of creation and also accounting for the black holes of collapsed stars, where (local) time ends.

Einstein's second 1905 paper established that energy came in discrete packets that were governed by uncertainty; this paper, cited when he won the Nobel Prize in 1921, jump-started the field of quantum mechanics. As Einstein put it in 1905, "[W]hen a light ray is spreading from a point, the energy is not distributed continuously over ever-increasing spaces, but consists of a finite number of energy quanta that are localized in space, move without dividing, and can be absorbed or generated only as a whole." The new breakthrough quantum physics would later be discovered to imply an ethereal reality of "spooky action at a distance" that troubled Einstein, as it collided with his far more intuitive modifications of classical physics. The trouble continued with increasing experimental support for quantum physics down to the present. He saw quantum physics as only provisionally correct until the theory had been modified and become more "complete," but the substance of this hoped-for rescue has receded ever further from view, much as has the materialist expectation mentioned earlier.

In 1929 Hubble's observations revealed that the stars and galaxies of the universe are expanding in all directions at velocities that increase in proportion to their distance from us. The most prominent implication was that our space-time universe had a single region of origin. Originally, the idea had been proposed by Lemaître in the year of my birth (1927), but in 1949 the astronomer Fred Hoyle dubbed it appropriately "the Big Bang," a label that stuck. For perhaps thirty years after Hubble's observations, scientists were resistant to the idea that all matter and energy in the universe must have once emanated from a particular historical region in space-time: mathematicians called it a "singularity," massive compared with the singularities sprinkled in all directions throughout the universe like Swiss cheese and associated with local imploded stars, or black holes.

Why this resistance? I think it emanates from the Newtonian idea that the universe had always existed, which seemed psychologically more comforting and natural – no beginning, no end. If there was a beginning, then science – the search for truth in physical phenomena – had to face up to the psychologically overwhelming fact that before the beginning there was nothing: no matter, no energy, no space, no time, just a monstrously pervasive *nothing*! I am using "nothing" here in the sense of classical and relativistic physics, not necessarily in the sense of quantum physics, which I will come to later. But if the universe had always existed, then it seemed that there was room aplenty for Einstein's impersonal God, the deism of natural rules, order, and beauty, to say nothing of agnosticism and atheism.

Our Judaic-Christian ancestors had understood their world in terms of Genesis (1.2). Before creation there "was a formless void and darkness covered the face of the deep," while in our day, the time of the Big Bang, we have come to understand our world, technically, as originating at a massive singularity at which the equations that chart everything from stars and dark matter to particles have no finite solution when extrapolated backward in time.

The ancient question of human existence, "Why is there something rather than nothing?" could be avoided if this *something* that we observe everywhere was thought to have always been – in direct contradiction to Genesis and to Hebrews (11.3), where it is stated that "[t]hrough faith we understand that the worlds were framed by the word of God, so that things which are seen were not made of things which do appear." But the new question for science, implicit in the Big Bang theory, "Why was there nothing that became something?" seemed to deepen the state of our ignorance and mystery. This is because the *mystery of origins is beyond any conceivable science* and the whole apparatus of hypothesis testing. Creation – that is, the beginning – could be located in history and, backward in time, the limiting state of equations that have again and again proved to have enormous experimental and astrophysical predictive power when they were used to locate events in our observable world of space-time, energy, and matter.

At its best, these developments, and those in quantum physics, can only be described as embarrassing for classical materialism. That the materialist rhetoric is little changed tells you how deep its belief system penetrated.

Also beyond science is a personal experience shared by all humans, the sense of awe and mystery of existence. For me this experience must count as an observation even if it is incommensurate with our rhetorical vision of the objective tests of science.[2]

Materialism ignored, denied, or marginalized any references to experiences of awe and mystery. Kahlil Gibran may have had such dismissals at heart in his book *The Madman* (1918): "[W]e heard a voice crying, 'This is the sea. This is the deep sea. This is the vast and mighty sea.' And when we reached the voice it was a man whose back was turned to the sea, and at his ear he held a shell, listening to its murmur. And my soul said, 'Let us pass on. He is the realist who turns his back on the whole he cannot grasp and busies himself with a fragment.'"

What spooked Einstein about quantum theory was that two quantum particles could interact instantaneously no matter where they were located. In experiments in Switzerland, such particles are studied at a separation of 18 kilometers (*Nature*, August 14, 2008). Thus, if one particle is perturbed, there is an instantaneous synchronous effect on the other. This seemed to violate special relativity by allowing physics to embrace speeds greater than that of light. The best verbal description that could be mustered was the concept that two such particles are "entangled" – the term introduced by Schrödinger in 1935 – a phenomenon subsequently found over and over again to be consistent with indirect experimental observations. But let me here emphasize that all perception, and all scientific observations, are indirect and are therefore necessarily the "evidence of things not seen," as in Hebrews (11.1).

So, even if quantum theory is "incomplete" and due to be improved upon, scientists now harbor the faith that quantum-spooky interconnectedness will be retained. Indeed, what does it mean to say that two entangled particles are subject to simultaneous effects independent of their distance from each other? It actually means that the time required by any postulated signal passing between the two particles is below the detection limit of (classical) instruments. The Swiss measurements showed that any supposed signal passing between entangled particles must be traveling at least 10,000 times the speed of light!

Earlier I used the phrase "objective tests of science," which carries the ring of "reality" but is a rhetorical distraction. "Reality," when penetrated by new, deeper instrumental probes, is never what it seems, and no one was a greater champion of this principle than Einstein. For example, he used the term "ponderable matter" in contrasting elements of classical physics with his new space-time physics. His general relativity theory created a counter-intuitive space that curved back on itself in a four-dimensional space-time continuum, its analogue being the infinite number of great circle (distance-minimizing) paths through a point on a sphere. Incredibly, as he and others would show, that space curvature allows for the theoretical possibility of "wormholes" through which various points in space are accessibly connected by shortcuts that, if traversable, do not violate special relativity but simply bypass it. In particular, gravity is not instantaneous, but is mediated by a finite signal that, through the warping of space-time, travels only at the speed of light. Keep in mind that we are talking of theory some of the implications of which have survived experimental tests, at least where observations could be brought to bear on certain of its predictions, beginning with the eclipse experiments by Eddington in 1919.

Contemporary theorists have learned to take such incredibility at equation, if not face, value. After all, in less than a hundred years after the special theory and the photoelectric effect we encountered engineering miracles like atomic energy and lasers that are manifestations of the new relativity and quantum mechanical theories. So we should not shoot from the hip in rejecting wormholes, entangled objects, and teleportation as the stuff only of science fiction. Indeed, teleportation in the sense of information transfer has been achieved in atoms and molecules, and seems likely to be achieved soon in elementary life forms. At quantum levels if you have copied all the information in an object, you have teleported that object. As with atomic energy and lasers, the challenge of teleporting a more complex object is in the engineering, not the principle. These fairytale-like stories are now serious physics, at least for some, within the framework of contemporary science.

The point I want to emphasize is that science is about physical and biological mechanisms; about discovering how things work; about engineering; about theories that describe and can predict observations that we experience entirely through instruments. It is the instruments of science that supply us with the indirect "evidence of things not seen." They can be likened to Plato's Allegory of the Cave, in which reality can be experienced only as shadows on a cave wall – what casts the shadows is always beyond our direct experience, though not beyond faith, the imagination that we call "theory." An experimental physicist says that he measures the "spin" of an electron – a mathematical concept – whereas the engineering reality is that he records certain anomalies on a screen and has used the theory to calculate their implication and help him locate it, calling it a measurement. Carl Anderson discovered the positron, but in reality merely photographed a streak (caused by its energy) in a cloud chamber, which was an implication or predictable consequence of the theory. Instruments are classical physics machines. Science keeps getting better exponentially in this instrumental task, on a scale beyond anything that could be believed possible in 1905, let alone at the beginning of the Christian era. That success easily breeds the belief and even the pretense of deeper understanding than is justified.

In science we observe nothing directly, only indirectly through instruments that record the secondary effects implied by conceptual models of objects – particles, waves, energy – whose postulated existence in the theories that fulfill our hopes is not violated by our indirect observations. But you cannot derive the existence of those objects and the richness of the theory from the sparse indirect effects and measurements we record – theory is resolutely committed to being underdetermined by observation, the gap always an unexplained mystery. You can only do the reverse: deduce from those constructed objects and models their implications for what we can expect to observe. The constructs come from unidentified flights of the imagination, from scientific intuition comprehended mathematically. That undergirding substance, the theory, the hope that drives imagination, is something you accept on faith, whose origin is itself beyond science, its believability reinforced by the occasional tests that one is lucky and ingenious enough to perform, until that faith is disturbed by contrary observations or a more comprehensive construct able to account for new shadows that we can experience.

Hence, what is inescapable is the dependence of science on faith, as in Hebrews. The conceptual and theoretical constructs of science constitute the "substance of things hoped for" whose evidential support depends on instruments that record the "evidence of things not seen." Einstein once said, "It is theory which first determines what can be observed."

This unseen reality of theory brings an operating understanding of how our world works and enables us to accomplish engineering miracles by trial, error, tinkering, and adjustment. But science cannot identify, nor can it disprove, *purpose*. Some prominent scientists and philosophers have claimed – somewhat intemperately, it seems – that science shows that there is no purpose in the universe. But failing to find something does not allow one to conclude therefore that it does not exist. *The lack of observable evidence for purpose does not constitute evidence for the absence of purpose.* Religions everywhere have sought to comprehend a universal purposeful human experience: a longing born of high yearnings that come welling and surging in, that do indeed come from a mystic ocean on whose rim no foot has trod.

The ancients confounded their mystical experience and religious faith with explanations of everyday events. Science has invaded that everyday world of explanation and created marvels out of the new understanding of how things work. That success should not, however, be extrapolated arbitrarily beyond the bounds of what science is capable of investigating.

I want to close this half of the essay by returning to my claim that our sense of awe and mystery should count as an observation consistent with the religious faith of our fathers. Our experience of that sense (emanating from that we call "Spirit"),[3] like shadows on the cave wall, is the evidence of things not seen. In religious inquiry, people have compared notes on that experience and thereby given it an intersubjective commonality – controversial to be sure, but so is the interpretation of theory and observation in science. When confronted by new observations, scientists ask each other, "Do you see what I see?" The answers are often controversial for extended periods but, in time, the discussion may settle on provisional agreement – a temporary equilibrium.

INVISIBLE REALITIES IN ECONOMICS

The leading Scottish Enlightenment figures, such as David Hume, Adam Smith, and Adam Ferguson, were all inspired by the fundamental idea that the social and economic order that they observed everywhere around them was "the result of human action but not the execution of human design" (Ferguson 1767: 102). I think a good case can be made that their program was a consequence of the intellectual influence of Isaac Newton, their immediate intellectual forebear,[4] who had astonished the scholarly world by accounting for our natural physical environment using only a handful of rules invisible to human awareness but bringing order to humans' sensible experience. The Newtonians predicted the appearance of a certain comet in 1758. This is referenced by Adam Smith in his "History of Astronomy," which was published posthumously in 1795 but had been written sometime before 1758, as is indicated by Smith himself when he records, "His [Newton's] followers have, from his principles, ventured even to predict the returns of several of them [comets], particularly of one which is to make its appearance in 1758" (Smith 1795: 103). Then, explaining in a footnote: "It must be observed, that the whole of this Essay was written previous to the date here mentioned; and that the return of the comet happened agreeably to the prediction." Smith is referring to Halley's Comet, which has returned on schedule about every seventy-six years since 1758.

Imagine, if you will, that this prediction and its confirmation must have been a truly mind-bending experience for those living in the mid–eighteenth century. Newton's modeling of invisible reality provided an orderly account of observations from the physical world. The Scottish Enlightenment search was on for the emergent rules underlying the observed socioeconomic order – except that Newton had applied reason to modeling nature's physical order, whereas the socioeconomic order could not have resulted from the "execution of human design." Now reason would be used to understand how such rules might have arisen.

Economics, in the form imputed to it by Adam Smith, began with the proposition that wealth creation in the emerging national economies of the time had been the unintended consequence of a single process axiom:

"the propensity to truck, barter and exchange one thing for another" (WN, 25). This axiom of commercial sociality generated market prices, whose existence facilitated the discovery, through a slow and gradual process, of those forms of specialization ("division of labor") that individuals found it was in their own interest to choose. From the perspective of experimental economics, Adam Smith's process axiom was central to the finding that naive subjects are quickly able to discover, through trial-and-error adjustment, the abstract equilibrium of supply and demand, although that equilibrium was entirely unknown to the subjects.[5] The invisible hand metaphor was right on, although it is so often maligned by many who never read WN, never heard of TMS, and had not a clue as to Smith's scientific program.

The formal equilibrium underlying the experiments had not been part of Smith's thinking: its comprehensive articulation, based on subjective utility theory, had to await the passage of nearly 100 years in the person of W. S. Jevons (1871). Jevons, however, failed to benefit from Smith's comprehension of an invisible reality of specialization and wealth creation that ordinary people, characterized by his market process axiom, could discover. Indeed, Jevons – a rational constructivist – believed the opposite: "A market, then, is theoretically perfect only when all traders have perfect knowledge of the conditions of supply and demand, and the consequent ratio of exchange" (Jevons 1871: 87). Jevons needed perfect knowledge for his model, but his traders in the world, armed with Smith's axiom, did not. What the experiments reveal is that traders need have knowledge only of their own private values (costs), not that of others and of the entire supply and demand. Over time subject traders in experiments tend to converge stochastically to a shrinking neighborhood of the price that equates supply and demand. Unfortunately, Jevons's important contribution to the concept of market equilibrium displaced rather than supplemented Smith's concept of a market exploration process. Indeed, the profession is still weak in its capacity to model discovery processes, while expanding to the ends of the economic earth the things that we model as a static, inert Nash equilibrium.

But for Smith's axiom to perform its miracle, civil society also needed the rights of property – people must play the game of trade, not steal, if the game is to do the world's work.[6] He said little, however, on this subject in WN; for example, "Every man, as long as he does not violate the laws of justice, is left perfectly free to pursue his *own interest* his *own* way" [Emphasis added] (WN, 687). He said little of it in WN because he already had said much about the origin of property in TMS:

Among equals each individual is naturally, and *antecedent to the institution of civil government*, regarded as having a right both to defend himself from injuries, and to exact a certain degree of punishment for those which have been done to him." (TMS, 80; emphasis added)

As the greater and more irreparable the evil that is done, the resentment of the sufferer runs naturally the higher; so does likewise the sympathetic indignation of the spectator. (TMS, 83–84)

The most sacred laws of justice, therefore, those whose violation seems to call loudest for vengeance and punishment, are the laws which guard the life and person of our neighbour; the next are those which guard his property and possessions; and last of all come those which guard what ... is due to him from the promises of others. (TMS, 84)

The reason broken promises (contract violation) carry smaller punishments than robbery – unlike the latter, the former are not criminal – is that Smith thoroughly understood the asymmetry between losses and gains in human behavior,[7] affirmed more than two centuries later by the experiments of Kahneman and Tversky (1979).[8] Smith argued that robbery deprives us of that which we have already obtained, while contract violation only frustrates our expectation of gain (TMS, 84).

Although markets are central to understanding the sources of wealth creation and their high-efficiency performance was affirmed in laboratory experiments beginning in the 1960s, I want to make clear that the market miracle image was significantly qualified in Smith's WN, as it was in the laboratory in the 1980s. For twenty years I had thought and believed that the supply and demand experiments, and the many variations that followed, probably illustrated how well *all* markets function. But as it turned out not all markets are born equal.

In the early 1980s there entered into research the idea that it would be interesting to study a simple transparent asset environment, one in which people would have complete information on the fundamental dividend value of share assets. The objective was to develop a baseline in which people, trading over a fifteen-period horizon, would confirm "rational expectations theory" by trading at fundamental value which declined over the horizon as fewer dividend draws from the distribution remained from time *t* to the end. The program plan then called for seeing if we could create bubbles by manipulating/controlling the information given subjects by the experimenter. Well, the baseline, the anchor for this grand research scheme of "best-laid plans," didn't come close to converging as quickly as had the earlier supply and demand markets: right off the starting blocks we had enormous, enigmatic bubbles on the way to equilibrium (Smith et al. 1988). Our first idea was to squelch the bubbles by a heavy-handed instructional treatment in which we would remind everyone at the end of each period, over and over again down to the last period, what the declining dividend holding value of a share would be in the next period. That did not work, as the new experiments made it clear that subjects were doing what they wanted to do and it had nothing to do with any initial and repeatedly updated notion of true fundamental value that we informed them about.

While we found that markets consisting of individuals who were twice previously experienced finally converged, they reliably generated substantial bubbles on the way to that fundamental rational expectations equilibrium. Although baffling at first, the results were replicated with widely different groups of traders – college students, small-business owners, corporate-business executives, and over-the-counter stock traders in Chicago – and by skeptical new experimenters.

Initially, we had been skeptical about our own findings and did not believe them, but the phenomena turned out to be at the hard core of human behavior. Twenty-five years of experimental research on asset market bubbles showed clearly that under a wide variety of treatments, asset prices initially deviate substantially from those predicted by the rational expectations market model (see Postrel 2008, who reports her interview with Charles Noussair, a prominent contributor to the experimental asset market literature). Our explanation was that in accordance with the theory people ultimately came to have rational expectations of equilibrium, but it was an *experiential learning process*, not an inference from economic logic (the flaw presumed by theory) applied by the individual to herself and others based on given information: "What we learn from the particular experiments reported here is that a common dividend, and common knowledge thereof is insufficient to induce common expectations.... With experience, and its lessons in trial-and-error learning, expectations tend ultimately to converge and yield an REM (Rational Expectations Muth) equilibrium"[9] (Smith et al. 1988: 1148).

Looking back over fifty years, in the first twenty-five years we had to overcome the shock that laboratory markets, like those of daily consumer life, proved the "wisdom of crowds" and converged very quickly (in minutes) where people are informed only of their private individual values or their private costs, and items bought are consumed, with that process replicated over time. Then we had to adapt to the shock that asset markets were a case in which that wisdom failed decisively in the absence of three to four hours of experience in three repeat sessions.

An invisible equilibrating reality existed in these asset markets, but it took longer than we had come to believe was necessary. I will claim that the Great Recession was and is still subject to the same unanticipated slow process of equilibrium restoration.

What eventually dawned clear was the key difference in the two kinds of markets: the prospect of resale in asset markets, with no immediate end-point consumption. There are no bubble troubles in markets where the items exchanged *are not re-traded later*, but rather are produced, purchased, consumed, and disappear and this process is repeated over and over and people learn it unmindfully like they learn spoken language. In the national economy these properties predominate in the composition of total output: some 75 percent of the private gross domestic product consists of nondurable goods that are bought to consume (hamburgers), not re-trade, and services, in which delivery by specialist producers is synonymous with consumption (haircuts). But houses and securities are routinely re-traded, unlike hamburgers, maintenance repairs, haircuts, commercial airline seats, and all manner of consumer services. Moreover, people are strongly specialized as either buyers or sellers of perishable goods and services. When you or I investigate the hamburger or haircut market, we already know that we will be buyers for immediate consumption – sellers have the same personal knowledge as specialized producers. But securities and houses are routinely re-traded. With securities on any given day an investor may be a seller or a buyer and must decide on the basis of market information. Similarly, house owners may over the course of their lives sometimes be buyers and sometimes sellers, depending on price information generated in the market. Both securities and houses are bought with the knowledge that the purchase is not final, that resale is always an option. These differences help to account for why all markets are not born equal – why some may be bubble prone, and others never.

The crisis in 2007–2008 brought home to me the relevance of these two kinds of market experiments – demand and supply for nondurables versus asset markets – to shedding light on the crash and the subsequent recession. There was no instability problem in the ordinary markets of daily life. It was housing that was the trouble – a big-time bubble – leveraged by low (or zero and even negative) down payments, easy loan money, and financial wizardry (mortgage-backed securities "insured" by derivatives). People easily can get caught up in self-sustaining expectations of rising asset prices in the lab and – if only occasionally –in rising housing prices in the world, and both are sustained longer if there is a lot of liquidity, but ultimately they must end in long-run rational expectations style equilibrium!

The long housing price run-up after 1997 engendered the sense that prices would continue to rise; here is an example:

Cassano agreed to meet with all the big Wall Street firms … to investigate how a bunch of shaky loans could be transformed into AAA-rated bonds … with Park and a few others, Cassano set out on a series of meetings with Morgan Stanley, Goldman Sachs, and the rest.… "They all said the same thing," says one of the traders present. "They'd go back to historical real-estate prices over 60 years and say they had never fallen all at once." (Michael Lewis, *Vanity Fair*, July 2009)

These were not the blindsided economic experts, but the practitioners on the firing line who were failing to reexamine what they thought they knew and finding justifications that protected the state of their presumed knowledge from invisible and surreptitious realities.

A feature of national housing bubbles not studied in the experiments, however, is the asymmetry between the upswing and the downswing in its impact on household and bank balance sheets. Consumption demand and the supply of credit are broadly buoyed by expectations on the upside with new debt incurred at rising price levels. On the downside, expectations and existing asset prices adjust freely, while mortgage debt outstanding is fixed ratchet-like as housing prices fall against fixed loan obligations. Households (22 percent of them as of 2011) get stuck in the black hole of a negative equity loop, and far more are in a gray hole not much above water. Since the banks hold the mortgages, the banks are stuck in the same negative equity loop. The effect is the same on both: households are reluctant to spend, and banks are reluctant to lend, and the economy awaits the resulting painful process of deleveraging.

The balance sheet damage wrought by the crash of the credit-fueled house bubble is why monetary policy is so ineffective – now and in the Great Depression. Calling such ineffectiveness the "liquidity trap" is merely providing a name for the ineffectiveness that is experienced; the name helps us not a whit to understand why it occurs. It is caused by the black hole of household/bank negative balance sheet equity.

Moreover, the mainsprings of the Great Recession were not unique to it. Steven Gjerstad and I were surprised, even dismayed, to discover that we were observing a very old story, going back at least ninety years (Gjerstad and Smith 2009a, 2009b, 2010). For example, let's compare the Great Recession with the Depression:

Housing construction expenditures started increasing in 1998, briefly flattened out in 2001–2002, and rose sharply to a peak in early 2006. Remarkably, at their 2006 peak housing expenditures were 79 percent higher than when the recession began in Q4, 2007, but then proceeded to fall another 60 percent by Q2, 2009.

These data are just a rerun of comparable movements in new housing expenditures before and during the Depression, when the investment boom in housing was shorter-lived than in the recent run-up: starting in 1922 it rose to twin peaks in 1925 and 1926, when expenditures stood almost 60 percent above their 1929 level. By 1933 new housing expenditures had cratered to more than 85 percent below their 1929 level.

The seventy-nine years from 1929 to 2008 are bounded on each end by downturns arising from similar housing-financial market collapses, with twelve recessions in between. In eleven of these fourteen downturns, the percent decline in housing and in consumer durables expenditure occurred earlier and exceeded in magnitude the percent decline in every other major component of GDP. Thus, consumer durable goods expenditures sometimes join housing in leading recession downturns, but in the Great Recession, durables as well as firms' fixed investment declined in coincidence with GDP; most likely this was due to the outsized collapse of the housing mortgage market and the banks, taking everybody – consumers, producers, and policy makers – by surprise.[10]

In addition to their role in leading most downturns, housing expenditures lead in every recovery. It is not an exaggeration to say that if there is no recovery in housing, there is no recovery in the economy (Gjerstad and Smith 2010). The current weak recovery may qualify as a technical exception. As of 2011, the housing recovery had not occurred in spite of federal tax subsidies to new home buyers or programs designed to refinance mortgages at lower rates and stretch payment terms to allow people to stay in their homes.

These programs were well intentioned, but more artificial kiting of the demand for housing – the original driver of the problem – surely cannot suddenly now be the solution. House prices relative to other prices have been driven far too high by credit expansion, not by the ordinary money income growth reflected in other prices. The adjustment needed to rejuvenate housing demand is for house prices to be restored to levels in line with current income; artificially propping up the price of a house stock bloated by borrowing from future housing demand with mortgage credit is the wrong policy for a return to sustainability.

From this brief economic history it is evident that "business cycle" is a misnomer in economic parlance; pure and simple, it's a "consumer housing-durables cycle" driven by volatility in consumer expenditures, aided and abetted by fickle private and politicized credit terms. The rest of the real economy then does its level best to adapt to these dynamic surges.

The problem of economic instability arises from episodes of housing expansion financed not by rising incomes, but by an unsustainable inflow of credit to home buyers. From 2000 to 2005 the ratio of median home price to median family income rose by 30 percent (4 to 5.2), and according to the National Association of Realtors (2006), 45 percent of first-time home buyers in 2005 paid no money down! As Adam Smith put it:

> [B]eing the managers rather of other people's money than of their own, it cannot well be expected, that they should watch over it with the same anxious vigilance with which ... [they] frequently watch over their own. (WN, vol. II, 741)

An important puzzle is why stock market crashes like the dot-com crash leave the banking system and economy whole, while a bursting housing bubble can devastate both The answer informs us of the critical role of houses in household and bank balance sheets during recessions.

The dot-com stock market crash, December 1999 to September 2002, wiped out approximately $10 trillion in market value, but the financial system was unscathed. When Gjerstad and I wrote our *Wall Street Journal* article of April 6, 2009, we noted that by mid-2007 the value of homes had declined by only about $3 trillion, but the financial system had been devastated, ultimately requiring the largest Fed intervention in history. This difference in impact is not due to a discrepancy in sector size: housing and all listed public securities each accounted for about one-third of all US wealth.

This contrast reiterates an important lesson from the 1920s and 1930s. Whenever stock bubbles burst, the combination of tough margin requirements and callable loans serves well to confine the damage to investors and speculators; but when housing prices decline, mortgages extended to home buyers with inadequate cash buffers (strict minimum down payment and amortization rules) threaten the banking system and the economy. In housing markets, when banks lend long against inadequate asset collateral, and home buyers borrow long against uncertain wage income, it is hazardous not only for individual borrowers and lenders, but – through interdependent leverage in the banking system – for the innocent and profligate alike.

Beginning in 1928 and culminating in 1934, we fashioned the right rules for containing the fallout from stock bubbles and never deviated from those rules; soon thereafter we found, then ultimately lost, the correct set of mortgage market rules. Why?

Significantly, the housing boom in the 1920s was fueled by credit. Although savings and loan associations had long amortized practically all mortgage loans and were the major source of housing finance, in commercial banks and insurance companies the practice of balloon repayment of all or part of the original loan accounted for more than 85 percent of their mortgage lending from 1925 to 1929. The wave of mortgage foreclosures in 1930–1934 did little to change these conventions, as political pressures (much like today) overwhelmingly sought to prevent foreclosures and allow people to stay in the homes they had hoped to own.[11] This tide of debtor and political resistance to tightened standards had changed by 1935–1939, when banks and insurance companies were amortizing 70 percent or more of their mortgage loans. As noted in an important 1956 monograph by the National Bureau of Economic Research:

> [T]he change during the last two decades is … one from unamortized and partially amortized mortgage loans to regular, periodic amortization calculated to retire the loan in full during its term. Much of this change came during the late thirties when the adoption of fully amortized loans in HOLC and FHA operations increased the popularity of this type of mortgage. (Glebler et al. 1956: 232)

High mortgage standards for both public and private home finance remained the norm for decades but began to erode in the 1990s with the growing political consensus – and widespread private financial accommodation – that US society should be more aggressive in mortgage lending to low- to middle-income families.

The political reasons for the differential treatment of stock and house purchase loans are transparent: there is no political constituency for enabling those of modest means to improve their lot by investing in stocks, as has existed for those who buy homes. Tough margin rules have not and will not prevent stock market crashes, but they have demonstrably controlled collateral damage to the banks and the economy. Laxity in mortgage standards can and has brought great unintended harm, even to those it was hoped would be made to prosper; righting the rules will be difficult if blame is sought in men rather than in property right constraints on the excesses that all must agree to live by. As Adam Smith understood, it's a problem of too much of "other people's money."

From 1997 through 2006 the median national price of homes rose 85 percent faster than the consumer price index. Restoring that equilibrium will require either a further decline in home prices or an increase in other prices. But the Fed's massive expansion of excess reserves – on the order of a trillion dollars – has yet to produce any wage inflation and therefore has had little impact on the general price level. Gradually, with a slowly rising CPI, and perhaps further declines in home prices, this equilibrium will be restored.

But a further decline in home prices exacerbates the negative equity loop that has entrapped the banks and households. Restoring these stressed balance sheets requires home mortgage principal to fall to the current market price level of houses – ever so gradually that deleveraging is happening as people use current income to pay down their mortgages. A faster solution is for banks to renegotiate loans, lowering the loan principal; this is much more important than stretching the term of loans and lowering interest for any given reduction in monthly payments. Banks are reluctant to recognize these true losses; instead they resist mark-to-market accounting standards, show phantom profits, and stretch the losses into the future.

Public and private policy is unlikely to address both the relative home price disequilibrium and the need to restore damaged household and bank balance sheets. The stimulus spending by the two most recent administrations addressed neither of these core problems, and the economy continues to be stuck.

Houston Smith's invisible realities, from their origins in religion to science – physical and social – have always been at the core of human attempts to understand their world. Faith has often led to false understandings in the light of the evidence, the dim shadows on the cave wall of the reality we perceive, and launched new searches. But the wisdom in Hebrews and its prior traditions define the thread connecting all those searches.

REFERENCES

Cooper, Paul F. (1929). *Tal*. Cynthia, KY: Purple House, 2001.

Ferguson, Adam (1767). *An Essay on the History of Civil Society*. Middlesex: Echo Library, 2007.

Gibran, Kahlil (1918). *The Madman*. Mineola, NY: Dover, 2002.

Gjerstad, S. and V. Smith (2009a). "From Bubble to Depression?" *Wall Street Journal*, April 6.

(2009b). "Monetary Policy, Credit Extension and Housing Bubbles, 2008 and 1929," *Critical Review* 21: 260–300.

(2010). "Household Expenditure Cycles and Economic Cycles, 1920–2010." Chapman University, Working paper 2010-02.

Glebler, Leo, D. Blank, and L. Winnick (1956). *Capital Formation in Residential Real Estate: Trends and Prospects*. Princeton, NJ: Princeton University Press.

Jevons, W. S. (1871). *The Theory of Political Economy*. Online Library of Liberty. London: Macmillan (1888, 3d ed. used).

Kahneman, D. and A. Tversky (1979). "Prospect Theory: An Analysis of Decision Under Risk," *Economtrica* 47: 263–91.

Kimbrough, E., V. Smith, and B. Wilson (2008). "Historical Property Rights, Sociality, and the Emergence of Impersonal Exchange in Long-distance Trade," *American Economic Review* 98: 1009–39.

Kirchler, M., J. Huber, and T. Stockl (2012). "Thar She Bursts: A Critical Investigation of Bubble Experiments," *American Economic Review* 102: 865–83.

Kohn, Donald L. (2009). "Monetary Policy and Asset Prices Revisited," *Cato Journal* 29: 31–44, no. 1 (Winter).

Lewis, Michael (2009). *Vanity Fair*, July.

Postrel, V. (2008). "Pop Psychology: Why Asset Bubbles Are a Part of the Human Condition That Regulation Can't Cure," *Atlantic Magazine*, December.

Smith, Adam (1759). *The Theory of Moral Sentiments*. Indianapolis: Liberty Fund, 1976.

(1776). *The Wealth of Nations*. Indianapolis: Liberty Fund, 1981.

(1795). "History of Astronomy," in *Essays on Philosophical Subjects*. Indianapolis: Liberty Fund, 1982.

Smith, Houston (2005). *The Soul of Christianity*. San Francisco: Harper.

Smith, Vernon L. (1991). *Papers in Experimental Economics*. Cambridge: Cambridge University Press.

(2008). *Discovery – A Memoir*. Bloomington, IN: Authorhouse.

Smith, V., G. Suchanek, and A. Williams (1988), "Bubbles, Crashes and Endogenous Expectations in Experimental Spot Asset Markets," *Econometrica* (September) 56: 119–51.

Notes

1 The quote from Hebrews and any to follow are from the King James edition. But other translations, if in my view less poetic, support this interpretation. In the New International edition, we have: "Now faith is being sure of what we hope for and certain of what we do not see" (Hebrews 11.1)

2 That power to inspire awe is magically expressed in Carruth's moving lines:

> Like tides on a crescent sea beach,
> When the moon is new and thin,
> Into our hearts high yearnings
> Come welling and surging in,
> Come from the mystic ocean,
> Whose rim no foot has trod,
> Some of us call it Longing,
> And others call it God.

3 Skeptics, as is their wont, press for an explanation of "Spirit." I am always reminded of one of James Thurber's cartoons. A client is sitting at a table with a Medium, who is staring into a crystal ball. The caption: "I can't get in touch with your uncle, but there's a horse here that wants to say hello."

4 David Hume was born in 1711, Adam Smith and Adam Ferguson in 1723; Isaac Newton died in 1727.

5 See Smith (1991: Part I) for many of the early papers on equilibrium discovery in repeat-trade supply and demand markets organized under various exchange institutions.

6 For experiments motivated by the proposition that exchange, specialization, and property rights must be discovered simultaneously, see Kimbrough et al. (2008).

7 Smith's formal statement of this asymmetry is in TMS, paragraph VI.i.6, p. 213.

8 Unlike Kahneman and Tversky, Smith would not have seen the loss-gain asymmetry as irrational any more than he saw deviations from the pursuit of self-interest as irrational. He wrote rather of one's "own interest," which required each person to "humble the arrogance of his self-love, and bring it down to something which other men can go along with" (TMS, 83).

9 Recent experiments report treatments showing that instructions and context (shares in a depleting gold mine) can substitute for experience in inducing trading prices that on average track declining fundamental value Kirchler et al., 2012).

10 Maybe it was because my parents lost their Kansas farm to the bank in 1934 that I found the financial and economic collapse in 2007–2008 so riveting (Smith 2008). Much more compelling, I think, was the stunning inability of the experts to anticipate its approach, recognize its arrival, or believe in and accept its severity. Observing the absence of subsequent expert confessions of this human frailty, any exceptions deserve to be recognized. Here is a refreshing example by the Fed's number 2, Donald Kohn, who retired in 2010: "Although I was concerned about the potential fallout from a collapse of the housing market, I think that it is fair to say that these costs have turned out to be much greater than I and many other observers imagined. In particular … the degree to which such a decline would create difficulties for homeowners, and, most important, the vulnerability of the broader financial system to these events" (Kohn 2009: 33).

11 The bank's foreclosure on my parents farm in 1934 would have included their house in Wichita, via recourse, but that prospect had been avoided earlier by its having been deeded to my mother's father.

25

My Studies in International Economics

Robert M. Stern

INTRODUCTION

In what follows, I first review some of the major influences that shaped my early years. I then relate the subsequent developments in my professional career, including my research orientation, chief publications, collaborative relationships, and long-standing involvement in undergraduate and graduate teaching and supervision.

THE EARLY YEARS

Growing up for the most part in Brookline, Massachusetts, I had the benefit of a first-class education in the local public schools. I remember in particular Ms. Fitzgerald and Ms. Frame, my seventh- and eighth-grade English teachers at the Edward Devotion primary school, for their instruction and care in imparting the main elements of written expression to me and my fellow students. It was then that I first really learned how to write and the need for clarity and conciseness in written expression. I have carried forward these lessons and have found great satisfaction in my own professional writing and the writing of my students.

I later attended Brookline High School, which at the time had an outstanding coterie of devoted and effective teachers. I liked and continued to benefit from my English teachers, but the greatest impressions and influences that I experienced were in the study of French with Ms. Perrin and in Spanish with Ms. Placido. I wanted to emulate their methods of language teaching and thought at the time that teaching was what I wanted to do.

In 1944, after graduating from high school, I enrolled as an undergraduate at the University of California, Berkeley, having chosen to apply there on a recommendation of a brother who had been enrolled. When I entered UC Berkeley, I declared romance languages, Spanish in particular, as my major. My Spanish from high school was good enough that I could enroll as a freshman in upper-division Spanish courses. To further my background, I also enrolled in college-level Latin and Portuguese. As I progressed, as part of my major, the more advanced courses were in Spanish literature and philosophy, which I found to be rather demanding and difficult. I then decided to reevaluate my long-run goal and switched my major to economics and business administration. This switch was motivated in part by parental influence, since my father, who ran a wholesale meatpacking business in Boston, let it be known that he would very much like for me to join the business.

My switch in majors was in 1946, which was after World War II had ended and veterans were returning to school in large numbers. Although the classes were now fairly large, I recalled that I especially enjoyed the courses in business cycles taught by Robert A. Gordon, labor economics by Clark Kerr, and money and banking by Ira Cross. I also took courses in accounting and auditing, and it was these courses that led to me to take a civilian job after graduation in 1948 as an auditor with the 8th Army Central Exchange in occupied Japan. This gave me an opportunity to travel, which I had always wanted to do, and to gain experience in working in a large organization. During my time in Japan, I was able to travel considerably, conducting audits of post exchanges on different military bases. I later became the head accountant at the main post exchange in Tokyo, which involved supervising a large staff of American and Japanese employees and preparing the periodic financial statements that were required. I took away from this experience that I could handle administrative responsibilities as well as the responsibilities of working with large amounts of financial data and preparation of detailed financial reports. These skills served me well subsequently.

Following my stay in Japan, I enrolled in the MBA program at the University of Chicago. While I concentrated on the study of marketing and accounting, I found that I was most interested in the courses with economic content, in particular industrial organization. During my time at Chicago and given my family involvement in the meatpacking business, I was able to make arrangements to visit some of the local slaughterhouses and get a firsthand impression of this phase of the business. The slaughterhouses were by no means very pleasant places to visit or to work at, or in which to see how the cattle and hogs were being processed. Indeed, I felt that the writing of Upton Sinclair about the industry was not an exaggeration of the conditions in the slaughterhouses of Chicago. My time in Chicago convinced me that I did not want to follow in my father's footsteps in the meatpacking industry and that I wanted to pursue a career in teaching and in economics in particular.

I decided, therefore, to apply for PhD study in economics and chose Columbia University, largely because George Stigler was on the Columbia faculty and I was interested in specializing in industrial organization. Before entering Columbia in 1954, I taught economics and accounting at Union College, a small liberal arts institution in Schenectady, New York. This was a worthwhile experience and reinforced my intention to pursue a teaching career. My PhD coursework was interesting and demanding. I took price theory with William Vickrey, monetary economics with James Angell, macro with Albert Hart, public finance with Carl Shoup, industrial organization and the history of thought with George Stigler, statistics with F. C. Mills, and international economics and international capital movements with Ragnar Nurkse. Of all these courses, those taught by Nurkse were for me by far the best and most interesting. After completing the PhD oral examinations, I decided to write my doctoral dissertation under Nurkse's guidance. This got me started on a long career in the field of international trade and finance.

During my coursework, I had become interested in international commodity problems and sought Nurkse's assistance in developing a dissertation proposal. I remember vividly how we discussed different topics and his suggestion that I might write on issues of US agricultural surplus disposal and trade policies. He guided me along in our periodic meetings, and he was of great help in reading and commenting on my research. It is to his credit that I was able subsequently to publish five papers based on my dissertation.[1] I continued to work on international commodity problems after

completing my PhD, focusing especially on measuring the price responsiveness of primary commodity producers in a variety of settings, including
rice and jute in India, Egyptian cotton, West African cocoa, and Malayan
natural rubber. Thereafter, I concentrated on empirical research in international trade, beginning with a study of the Ricardian model of comparative
advantage, using American and British data on trade and wages and productivity that built upon material covered in Nurkse's course. My research
interests over the past decades have spanned both international trade and
international finance, which is something that I can attribute to Nurkse's
influence, since his own research and publications similarly spanned both
aspects of international economics.

On a more personal note, I had occasion in late 1958 to assist Nurkse in
Geneva in compiling historical data on international capital flows in connection with the preparation of his Wicksell Lectures on trade and development, which he delivered in Stockholm in April 1959, shortly before his
untimely death. At the time, I was a Fulbright scholar studying econometrics in Rotterdam with Henri Theil. When Nurkse asked if I could come to
Geneva for a couple of weeks to work with him, I welcomed the opportunity. During my stay in Geneva, we met each day to discuss my data collection and how it would fit into the preparation of his lectures. I look back on
this experience with nostalgia and warmth as one of the high points of my
academic career.

After Nurkse died, James Tobin of Yale University, who was on leave in
Geneva and was a close friend of Nurkse, called me in Rotterdam and asked
if I would be able to come to Geneva to help Mrs. Nurkse organize her husband's papers. This was a sad occasion, needless to say, and I was glad to
be of assistance to Mrs. Nurkse in a time of need. It turned out later that I
was able to work with Gottfried Haberler of Harvard University and a close
friend and associate of Nurkse going back to his time in Vienna and in the
League of Nations Secretariat, in assembling Nurkse's collected papers and
publishing them in 1961 as a Harvard Economic Study entitled *Equilibrium
and Growth in the World Economy: Economic Essays by Ragnar Nurkse*. This
was the first edited volume that I published and that later motivated me to
publish many other edited volumes individually and jointly, the last count
being twenty-nine volumes as of 2011–2012.

In August 2007, I was invited to present a paper to a conference in Tallinn,
Estonia, to mark the hundredth anniversary of Nurkse's birth and the issu-
ance by the Estonian government of a postage stamp with his portrait in his
honor. This was a wonderful occasion, in which Nurkse's son, Dennis, at the
time poet laureate of Brooklyn, and I were the only ones present who had

had close contact with Nurkse. This conference gave me the opportunity to visit the house in which Nurkse was born and to celebrate publicly his life and accomplishments and to express my sincere appreciation for the role that he played in my professional development.

QUANTITATIVE INTERNATIONAL ECONOMICS AND DOING TRADE THEORY WITH NUMBERS

In my Fulbright year at the Netherlands School of Economics, I had close contact with Henri Theil. He supervised my work on an econometric study of distributed lags, which was later published jointly. To do this work required using a Monroe hand-cranked calculator for several weeks and calculating a seemingly endless number of correlation coefficients and analyzing their distributive patterns. It is interesting in the present computer age to look back to see how far we have come computationally in a half-century.

Following my Fulbright year in the Netherlands, I received an appointment as an assistant professor of economics in the college at Columbia University. In 1959–1961, I taught a course in international trade and one in contemporary civilization, which was a social science and humanities course required for undergraduates. I entered the PhD job market in 1960–1961 and succeeded in obtaining an appointment as an assistant professor of economics at the University of Michigan beginning in 1961–1962. Wolfgang Stolper had been teaching at Michigan for several years, and he decided to change his field of specialization from international trade to economic development, thus creating the opening that I filled. Needless to say, I was delighted with this opportunity, which has served me well and enabled me to pursue my teaching and research for nearly the subsequent fifty years.

In my beginning years, I taught the PhD courses in international trade theory and international finance, served on some dissertation committees, and continued my research on international commodity issues. I also published two conceptual papers with Elliott Zupnick, a longtime friend from Columbia days, on the theory and measurement of the elasticity of substitution in international trade and on the analysis of devaluation in a three-country world. Further, I published an empirical paper entitled "The U.S. Tariff and the Efficiency of the U.S. Economy" in the May 1964 *American Economic Review, Papers and Proce*edings. As far as I know, this was one of the first published papers on the measurement of welfare effects of US tariffs.

Around this same time, I became interested in the subject of export-led growth, which a number of countries were experiencing. Italy was one such country, and I decided to undertake research on its growth experience. With the assistance of a Ford Foundation Faculty Fellowship, I was able to spend the 1964–1965 academic year in the Research Department of the Banca d'Italia in Rome. It was a very enriching experience to interact with the research staff and to get advice on pertinent modeling and econometric issues and pertinent data. I had close contact in particular with Antonio Fazio, who was a young researcher at the Banca d'Italia and had spent a year studying at MIT. I was grateful to Antonio for our many conversations and for his feedback on my research. As many people may know, Antonio later became governor of the Banca d'Italia and served effectively, until he was accused in 2004–2005 of using his influence to resist foreign interest in an Italian bank. He resigned from his position at the end of 2005 and was subsequently convicted in the Italian justice system. He was sentenced in May 2011 to four years in jail for market rigging and ordered to pay a 1.4 million euro fine. It is difficult for me to reconcile his downfall with the person I had come to know well and respected in years gone by. In any event, I published an English-language version of a book on Italy's export-led growth in 1967 and an Italian-language version in 1968.

Following my return from Italy in 1965, I turned my attention more directly to quantitative issues in international economics. In this connection, I enlisted the services of Ed Leamer, who was a PhD student at Michigan in the late 1960s, specializing in econometrics and international economics. This resulted in the preparation of a coauthored volume, *Quantitative International Economics*, which was published in 1970 and covered such topics as measuring price and income elasticities in international trade, the gravity model, and constant-market share analysis. This was a kind of pioneering effort at the time, and it is an especial tribute to Ed Leamer's knowledge and skills with econometric methods and data analysis, which he has continued to apply throughout his subsequent academic career.

At around this same time, I turned my attention to writing a book, *The Balance of Payments: Theory and Economic Policy*, which drew on my teaching of the PhD-level course in international finance at Michigan. Harry Johnson, with whom I had some contact, suggested that I undertake this book, and he offered some very helpful comments at the time. The book was structured in terms of the Keynesian ISLM model and was published by Aldine in 1973.[2] It sold reasonably well for a few years until it was superseded by the movement to flexible exchange rates and the monetary approach to the balance of payments, which I had not covered systematically in my book.

During the 1969–1970 academic year, the Michigan Economics Department was given authorization to recruit a new PhD specializing in international economics. It was then that Alan Deardorff was hired. He was completing his PhD at Cornell University and had worked especially with Jaroslav Vanek. On the basis of his excellent theoretical work on trade and growth, he was offered a position and joined the Economics Department in the fall of 1970. I subsequently had occasion to give him feedback on his writings on topics that were new to me and that he was preparing for journal submission. After a short time, I proposed that we might work together on some research that would draw upon his modeling skills in conjunction with my own empirical and policy orientation. Thus began a collaboration and close association between us that has continued for about forty years.

It turned out that not only was Alan a truly accomplished trade theorist, he also quickly mastered issues of data and policy application and analysis. In particular, in 1972–1973, the US Bureau of International Labor Affairs (ILAB) put out a request for proposals for studies of the trade and employment effects of tariffs and other trade policies and for the effects of multilateral trade liberalization. We decided to focus on the latter topic and to address it by means of a computational general equilibrium model, following work that was being done at the time in economic development studies. In the event, our modeling proposal was turned down. We decided nonetheless to continue with the modeling work and to embark on the construction of a data set covering the trade, output, employment, and pertinent elasticities for the major industrialized and developing countries. It was this joint effort that led to the development of what we were to call the Michigan computational general equilibrium (CGE) model of world production and trade.

Once the computer code and data were in place, we tried various modeling experiments involving trade liberalization. The challenge then was to study and interpret the computational results. In the early stages, it appeared that some results were counterintuitive or much larger than seemed reasonable. What we did then was to go back to the theoretical structure of the model as well as the data to determine what was wrong and to make theoretical and data changes that yielded what we thought were more reasonable results of trade liberalization. We thus became deeply involved at the time in doing what we called "trade theory with numbers." We proceeded to publish a series of papers beginning in 1977 in which we used the Michigan model for a variety of issues involving the effects of policy changes on trade and employment for the major industrialized and developing countries.

In the course of work with the Michigan model, we maintained contact with ILAB and the Office of the US Trade Representative (USTR). This led to our being commissioned by the US Senate Finance Committee, which was responsible for monitoring and evaluating the US negotiating position in the Tokyo Round of Multilateral Negotiations. For this purpose, it was necessary to obtain access to the tariff offers of the United States and those of its major trading partners that had been tabled in the negotiations. We had to obtain official clearance to gain access to the tariff offers. When we first ran the model and sent the detailed sectoral results on trade and employment to the Senate Finance Committee and the USTR, we were informed that the USTR objected to our results. We could not find any errors, however.

On further investigation, it turned out that the USTR had not provided the most up-to-date data on the tariff offers that had been tabled. It was only after the Senate Finance Committee threatened to subpoena the latest tariff offers that the USTR provided the requisite data. Our computational results were that the sectoral trade and employment and aggregate economic welfare effects of the proposed reciprocal tariff offers were comparatively small in both absolute and relative terms for the United States. These results were comparable to those that we had obtained previously in running hypothetical tariff reductions. Our task then was to meet with pertinent staff members in Washington to explain our modeling methodology and results, which was not always an easy task. In any event, we were informed by the staff of the Finance Committee that they found our study and results useful in countering the claims, especially of US organized labor, that the Tokyo Round negotiations would lead to significant displacement of US workers. Our study was published by the US Government Printing Office in 1979.

During the 1980s, we used the Michigan model to analyze a variety of issues, including the effects of changes in exchange rates, domestic tax/subsidies and tariffs, input-output technologies, and the structure of protection. We also used the model, in collaboration with Bob Staiger, to analyze the role of US and Japanese factor endowments and factor contents in the context of the Heckscher-Ohlin trade model. Further, we carried out some modeling studies of international trade in armaments in the late 1980s and early 1990s.

Around the mid-1980s, Drusilla Brown began working on a new version of the Michigan model that embodied developments in the "new trade theory," which included the representation of monopolistic competition and product differentiation in manufacturing and services firms, economies of scale, and product variety, as well as new data and parameters. This new version of the Michigan model was first applied by Drusilla and me to the US-Canadian Free Trade Agreement that became operative in the late 1980s. Then, in the early 1990s, we enlisted Alan Deardorff to work with us in applying the model to analysis of the North American Free Trade Agreement (NAFTA) that was being negotiated. We were commissioned by the US National Commission on Employment Policy to use the model to analyze the economic effects of NAFTA and to calculate the size and patterns of US employment disruption and wage losses, as well as the budgetary implications of adjustment assistance for displaced workers. Once again, our modeling results suggested small absolute and relative changes in US trade and employment and small budgetary needs for adjustment assistance. Our results were thus a far cry from the "giant sucking sound" that Ross Perot was predicting about NAFTA during the 1992 presidential campaign.

In the years that followed, we expanded the database of the Michigan model to include sectoral estimates of services barriers. This was important insofar as these barriers, which included domestic regulations, yielded much larger welfare gains than merchandise trade liberalization, because the services barriers were considerably higher than the tariffs on merchandise trade. We also had occasion to use the Michigan model to do a series of studies of bilateral and regional preferential trading arrangements (PTAs) for the United States and partner countries and to compare these results with the effects of multilateral liberalization. The computational results of these PTAs were again small in absolute and relative terms for the United States but somewhat larger particularly for the partner developing countries. There was some evidence of trade diversion, but it was not substantial. A message in this research was that the potential benefits of multilateral trade liberalization were estimated to be many times greater than the benefits of the preferential arrangements.

With the new century, Alan Deardorff and Drusilla Brown were turning their attention to other topics of research, and I had occasion to enlist the collaboration of Kozo Kiyota, a young Japanese economist who had obtained financing to work on modeling issues with me in residence at the University of Michigan. We concentrated especially on updating the database of the Michigan model and using it to analyze a variety of PTAs, especially for the United States and Japan, with results that generally paralleled those found in the earlier modeling work mentioned.

SOCIAL QUESTIONS

Beginning in the mid-1990s, my research interests were shifting toward social questions and issues of economic relations between the United States and Japan. In a 1996 paper, Drusilla Brown, Alan Deardorff, and I explored the theoretical aspects of trade and labor standards, and we later did a paper on child labor. I also published some papers on my own, one of which was awarded first prize of $10,000 in October 1998 in an essay contest on the topic "Labor Standards and Income Distribution and Their Relation to Trade," sponsored by the Institute for the Integration of Latin America and the Caribbean. In 2000 Deardorff and I published an edited conference volume, *Social Dimensions of U.S. Trade Policies*. In 2007 Drusilla Brown and I published an edited volume, *The WTO and Labor and Employment*. Our most recent collaboration was a 2011 conference paper, "Labor Standards and Human Rights: Implications for International Trade and Investment," jointly authored by Brown, Deardorff, and myself.

FOREIGN LECTURING AND MODELING PROJECTS

In my capacity as the general editor of a University of Michigan Press series entitled Studies in International Economics, I had occasion to publish a book by Andrew G. Brown, *Reluctant Partners: A History of Multilateral Trade Cooperation, 1850–2000*. Brown was a retired UN staff economist, living in Wellfleet on Cape Cod, where I had a summer home. We began meeting regularly in the summers and found a lot of interests in common, which we later pursued in a number of joint papers on issues of fairness in the global trading system, global market integration and national sovereignty, and trade agreements and international labor standards. We [still] maintained close contact and corresponded frequently on developments in the international economy, until his death in 2012. Foreign Lecturing and Modeling Projects

As already mentioned, I was a Fulbright scholar in the Netherlands in 1958–1959 studying econometrics and had a Ford Foundation Faculty Fellowship at the Banca d'Italia in 1964–1965 to do research on Italian export-led growth. I later had a series of grants from the US State Department to lecture in Japan (1973, 1977, 1985), Surinam and Barbados (1977), India (1980, 1990), Spain (1990), Hong Kong (1985), Indonesia (1985, 1990), Turkey (1985), Sri Lanka (1990), and Malaysia (1995). I lectured mostly on issues of trade liberalization and computational modeling.

In the course of my visits to India, I established contact with the National Council for Applied Economic Research (NCAER) in New Delhi and gave a presentation on the Michigan model. This led to collaboration with the

NCAER staff to develop a version of the Michigan model for the Indian economy that could be used to study the economic impact of the process of liberalization that began in the early 1990s. We published a book in 1998, *The Impact of Trade and Domestic Policy Reforms in India: A CGE Modeling Approach*, coauthored by Alan Deardorff and myself together with Rajesh Chadha and Sanjib Pohit of the NCAER staff. The India model has continued to be used under Chadha's direction to provide computational estimates of India's trade and related policies.

In the mid-1990s, we were commissioned by the United Nations Development Programme to do a modeling study of a free-trade agreement (FTA) between the European Union and Tunisia. The Tunisian Ministry of Foreign Affairs was particularly concerned about whether the FTA would engender a significant inflow of foreign direct investment (FDI) from the EU. We adapted the Michigan model to incorporate FDI and found, to the disappointment of the Ministry, that our model suggested only relatively small FDI inflows. Some concern was expressed about the accuracy of our modeling results. Nonetheless, it turned out, following the implementation of the FTA, that the FDI inflows did not materialize as had been hoped.

In 2007, I traveled to Ethiopia on two occasions as a member of a World Bank team to study the Ethiopian financial sector in connection with Ethiopia's application to join the World Trade Organization (WTO). Since the Ethiopian financial sector was primarily under government regulation and operation, the main issue was the extent to which Ethiopia would have to liberalize its financial sector in the course of the WTO accession process. The study that I directed, jointly with Kozo Kiyota and Barbara Peitsch, attempted to measure the potential benefits of financial liberalization to Ethiopia using proprietary data and making comparisons with the liberalization experiences of other developing countries. But, in the end, the results and recommendations of our study were resisted by the pertinent government agencies even though we had received support in meetings with a number of Ethiopian private-sector firms. Needless to say, this was a humbling experience in showing the political constraints on economic analysis and policy recommendations.

In retrospect, I learned a great deal from the contacts and experiences in my foreign travels, lecturing, and projects.

ECONOMIC RELATIONS BETWEEN THE UNITED STATES AND JAPAN

My Michigan colleague Gary Saxonhouse and I obtained a series of grants beginning in 2000 from the Japan Foundation Center for Global Partnership and carried out a program of research and book publications subsequently, involving both US and Japanese scholars on issues and options for United States–Japan trade policies, Japan's economic recovery and the lost decade, and newly evolving patterns of international trade. Saxonhouse was one of the leading world scholars on the Japanese economy. His remarkable accomplishments and influence were cut short by his untimely death in November 2006, following a battle with leukemia. In his honor, I edited two volumes of his selected papers together with Hugh Patrick and Gavin Wright entitled *The Japanese Economy in Retrospect*, which was published in 2010.

UNDERGRADUATE AND GRADUATE TEACHING AND SUPERVISION

For many years, I taught both undergraduate and graduate courses in international trade and international finance and helped to organize the graduate research seminar in international economics. I also taught a junior-year honors seminar for a number of years. I didn't find the undergraduate teaching particularly satisfying because of the large class enrollments and limited personal contacts with the students. An exception was the junior honors seminar, which brought together the best economics majors in a small group setting that made it possible to read and discuss in depth a variety of interesting economics articles and books and to provide writing opportunities for the students. Similarly, the graduate courses and the research seminars were also very stimulating and provided valuable learning opportunities both for the students and for myself. The weekly meetings of the research seminar were devoted to presentations of papers by faculty members and invited speakers, as well as presentations of graduate students' dissertations in process.

As previously mentioned, I have always looked back to my Columbia University days when I would meet regularly with Ragnar Nurkse to get feedback on my dissertation in progress. This experience motivated me to play a proactive role with the Michigan graduate students at the dissertation stage to give them feedback on the content and, if needed, the rewriting of their chapters. In my nearly five decades at Michigan, I served as chairman or as a member of eighty economics dissertation committees on topics in international trade and finance.

LOOKING BACK

As I reflect over years past, I consider myself truly fortunate for the working relationships that I developed. I am especially grateful to Ragnar Nurkse for his guidance and personal interest in my graduate student research. Some of the other individuals who supported and encouraged my work in the early years included Elliot Zupnick and Harry Johnson. During my career at the University of Michigan, my work with Ed Leamer was a high point in the late 1960s. Thereafter, I received endless benefits in my collaborative work with Alan Deardorff, and later with Drusilla Brown, Kozo Kiyota, and Andrew Brown.[3] These relationships greatly enhanced my understanding of international trade and finance and contributed directly to my numerous individual and jointly authored publications. This is true also of my relationships with the many students whom I taught and supervised. I owe a great deal, furthermore, to Judith Jackson for her devoted and able assistance for more than three decades with manuscript preparation, conference organizing, and course materials. She has been indispensable in keeping the Michigan research engine going.

I was honored in 1994 that some of my former students, Ed Leamer, J. David Richardson, Peter Hooper, and Keith Maskus, organized a *Festschrift* for me. While a *Festschrift* is an occasion to pay compliments to the honoree, I think it may be fitting nonetheless to refer to some of what the late Bob Baldwin said in his keynote speech at the *Festschrift* concerning what he thought were my signal accomplishments and influences:

> The important point about Bob's research is not so much the particular topics on which he has written but the general approach that he has taken. From the beginning, Bob got it right. Somehow he realized that the period in which his career would take place was the age of empirical economics. I don't know just what the status of the computer was at the time he began his career, but he started right out by testing various hypotheses empirically. It is apparent that he appreciated early the importance of applying sophisticated statistical techniques to gain important empirical insights. This appreciation of applying sophisticated econometrics and utilizing the new computer technology to analyze important empirical and public policy issues is what, in my mind, uniquely characterizes his career. Further, he has passed this approach on to his students. Empirical work in trade is widely followed today, but let me point out that, in the 1960s and 1970s, it was not. In their book on *Quantitative International Economics*, Bob Stern and Ed Leamer were way ahead of the rest of us in appreciating what was unique about research in the modern era. Theory is still important, but I am convinced that historians will look back and characterize this period as one in which empirical economics came of age and began to dominate the discipline.

> A major accomplishment of Bob's research career has been the Michigan computable general equilibrium (CGE) model, which he developed along with Alan Deardorff. This is easily the most important CGE model with international economics and has had tremendous influence, not only in academic

economics, but also in the policymaking field. For every major international economic policy in recent years, this model has been very important in influencing what economists and policymakers think about the economic impact of the policy. One additional benefit from the model is that it has encouraged its developers to think even more deeply about trade policies and the various institutions dealing with these policies. In my view, Stern and Deardorff have gone beyond being outstanding empirical economists and are now also wise in the ways of trade policy in a real-world setting.

Now let me move away from Bob's accomplishments through his writing and discuss another important feature of his career, namely, his ability to attract an extraordinarily talented group of graduate students. He has done this consistently over the years. One can look at the students of other trade economists, not just contemporary ones, but leading trade economists over the years, to realize how extraordinary his accomplishment is. So what is the secret of his success in attracting top-notch graduate students? Well, after talking to several of them, I think I've figured it out. Bob has followed what I would call the big-time football model in building up his teams of outstanding graduate students – a model he must have become familiar with over his many years here at Michigan.

How has Michigan managed to build up and maintain consistently an outstanding football team? The first point to make is that its coaches don't get their players just by waiting for them to walk in and express interest in playing. The coaches go out and recruit their players. And that is what Bob seems to do. He identifies the top graduate students, not just those who have wandered into trade but those in other fields (Ed Leamer was recruited from econometrics) and goes after them to write theses in the trade area. But how is successful recruitment done? Well, first of all you've got to have some scholarships to attract your recruits. And this is where the Stern-Deardorff research organization comes into play. These two guys have used Bob's MBA knowledge to put together a highly efficient, smooth research operation that must be the envy of many private research firms. They put out first-rate research proposals involving funding for graduate students that seem to be better than the rest of us can do. I know this from personal experience in competing against them for research funds. And they have found places to tap for research funds that I have never heard of. Thus, they always seem to have the funds to offer research assistantships to the top graduate students that they go after.

But, successful recruiting is much more than just having attractive scholarships. A key question in the mind of a recruit is whether the particular team he joins will be useful in helping him get into the pros after he or she completes his or her college career. And Bob is especially helpful on this point. First, while they are on the team, he makes sure that their names get around to the pros. Part of the funds he raises are used for the series of working papers that come out of the Research Seminar on International Economics. So a graduate student knows that if he gives a good paper in the Seminar, it will be sent around to all the major academics and non-academics in the field. Secondly, a prospective recruit sees that Bob often write papers jointly with his students so they can rely on his name to help them get published early on after they leave. Third, Bob also uses the funds he raises to hold a large number of conferences for which he is able to attract the top people. He invites his former students to give papers at these conferences, so they get further exposure.

So is it any wonder that Bob has been so successful in attracting outstanding graduate students? He has built a big-time research organization that not only recruits but ensures that members of the team get the best opportunity to make the top professional ranks after they leave. None of the rest of us has come close to operating such an organization as the Michigan research machine. (www-personal.umich.edu/~rmstern/baldwin.htm)

I am, of course, grateful to Bob Baldwin for these remarks on my behalf, since he has captured my inner motivations, goals, and accomplishments.

Notes

1 Details on my various publications noted here and in what follows can be found on my curriculum vitae: fordschool.umich.edu/faculty/Robert_Stern.
2 One never knows how useful or influential one's publications may be. But Marina Whitman, my longtime colleague at Michigan, has written in her essay in this volume how my book influenced her thinking and teaching: "By a stroke of luck, I found a useful organizing framework in Bob Stern's just-published (1973) book, *The Balance of Payments*. To me, at least, his approach was revolutionary, and far more realistic than the one I had absorbed in graduate school and had incorporated into my own teaching ever since. Rather than analyzing international economic interactions using what was essentially a closed-economy model with the current account tacked on, adding the term $(X - M)$ to the definition of national income, Stern outlined a full-fledged model of an open economy, incorporating as endogenous shifts in both the current and capital accounts. Rather than defining balance-of-payments equilibrium in terms of a zero balance on current account, as I had absorbed from Kindleberger, he defined it as zero net flows of "accommodating transactions" or balancing items, that is, short-term flows of official capital and movements of international reserves. Finally, he incorporated into what was effectively a graduate-level textbook Mundell's two-instrument solution to achieving both internal and external balance under different exchange rate systems. Eureka!"
3 I had occasion, together with Drusilla Brown and Bob Staiger, to organize a *Festschrift* for Alan Deardorff that was held at the University of Michigan in October 2009 to mark his sixty-fifth birthday. I have edited the *Festschrift* proceedings, which include reflections by many leading trade economists on Alan's contributions and reprints of his significant individual and jointly authored publications in a book published in 2011. My 2009 book, *Globalization and International Trade Policies*, contains many of my collaborative and jointly authored papers.

26

Sailing into the Wind

Myra H. Strober

When I was growing up, my father was in constant fear of losing his job. He worked as a salesman in the clothing industry in New York for a small firm that bought cloth from textile mills and sold it to manufacturers of men's suits, and firms such as his closed frequently. Unemployment was a recurrent topic at dinners in my family, not only possible unemployment for my dad, but also the Great Depression and the suffering faced by my parents' siblings and friends during those years. The topic intrigued me. How could we make sure that everyone who wanted to work had a job? How did people who wanted jobs get matched (or fail to get matched) with people who needed workers?

When I learned in high school about the School of Industrial and Labor Relations (ILR) at Cornell University, their interdisciplinary curriculum seemed to have been designed with precisely my questions in mind. But my parents were opposed to my applying to Cornell. They wanted me to continue to live at home and attend Brooklyn College, tuition-free and just down the street. My father had not finished college at all and my mother had completed City College of New York over seven years of night school, while she worked as a secretary during the day. To them, the fact that I could go to college full time and not have to work was pure luxury. What more could I possibly want?

I pulled out all the stops with my parents. To get into Brooklyn College, one had to have at least an 85 GPA. I knew I could maintain an 85 without ever opening another book, and I told my father that if he and my mother didn't let me apply to colleges outside of New York City, that was just what I would do. Horrified that I might stop reading books for two years, my father convinced my mother that I should be allowed to apply to out-of-town colleges and try to win a scholarship.

ILR had very few women students, but my application was successful. And because it was a New York state school, tuition was free for New York residents. In addition, I won a scholarship and agreed to work fifteen hours a week. But my parents made it clear that if my dad lost his job, I would have to return to Brooklyn.

SCHOOL DAYS

My favorite course freshman year was what we fondly called "Bus Riding 101." Every week we took a daylong trip to a different work site – a coal mine, a steel mill, an IBM factory, a pajama factory, and so on. We interviewed representatives from management and labor and toured the workplaces. At the coal mine, the school had to get special permission from the United Mine Workers to allow the women in our group to go underground, something that was generally considered bad luck by the miners. After each visit, we wrote a comprehensive paper on significant issues in that industry and workplace.

Years later, in a course I taught in labor relations at the Stanford Business School, I was leading a discussion of a case from a chemical factory in which a worker had filed a grievance with his union because he was denied the right to go to the bathroom. One of the students, annoyed with having to talk about the case, said he felt it dealt with matters too trivial to warrant his attention. Something clicked for me. "How many of you have ever been inside a factory?" I asked the sixty students. Not a single hand went up. I dismissed the class and arranged for our own Bus Riding 101, a trip to an automobile assembly plant in nearby Fremont. When we returned to the case afterward, the students had a quite different take on it, more fully appreciating the role of a grievance procedure in helping to humanize an otherwise harsh workplace. I have often thought that not only MBA students but also doctoral students in economics should have a course in which they visit workplaces. It might lend some reality, and perhaps empathy, to their views on workers and their daily challenges.

In the fall of my senior year at Cornell, the dean of ILR called me in to tell me that several faculty members had recommended me for a Woodrow Wilson Fellowship. Did I intend to get a doctorate, he asked? I told him I didn't, that I planned to be a high school social studies teacher. By and large, that was what women interested in social and economic questions did in the late 1950s. But when I discussed the matter with my husband-to-be, he had a different view. "Why not teach in college instead of high school?" was his way of looking at it.

The idea of spending the next four years studying was exceedingly appealing, and having no idea that teaching at a college or university was a completely different career than teaching in high school, I went back to the dean and told him I would like to get a doctorate. "In what field will you apply?" he asked. Hmmm, what field, indeed? The two possible candidates were history and economics. I had taken substantial coursework in both. But history seemed too large an area of study. I had no understanding that historians specialize by region, time period, and type of history, and I never talked with any of my history professors about possible graduate work. I talked only with M. Gardner Clark, an economist from whom I had taken two courses. He was encouraging but thought that I might need to take an MA first, since I had not majored in economics.

I was given a fellowship by Tufts University to do an MA in economics and got the training in micro and macro theory there that I had not received at Cornell. Then, since my fiancé was a medical student in Boston, I applied to Harvard and MIT for the PhD. My interview at Harvard was short.

"Are you normal?" the eminent macroeconomist asked me.

"What do you mean?"

"Do you want to get married and have children?"

"Yes, I'm engaged to be married, and eventually I want to have children."

"Well, then," he said, standing to end the conversation, "why would you want to get a PhD?"

My interview at MIT was more positive, and I wasn't surprised when several months later I got a thin envelope from Harvard but an acceptance, which included a fellowship, from MIT.

When I began MIT in the fall of 1964, my first class was a small labor seminar in which I was the only woman.

"I think you are in the wrong room," Professor Charles Meyers said to me as he sat down to begin the class.

"No, I don't think so," I said. "I'm Myra Strober."

"Oh," he smiled. "You're Myra Strober. Welcome."

The message was clear. In general, women were not acceptable in the class, but I was. I tried to puzzle it out. Somehow I was an honorary man.

But I wasn't a man, and I was starved for female companionship. There were no women professors, no women undergraduates, and only a handful of women economics graduate students (one or two in each PhD cohort). The women secretaries and administrators saw me as odd. My only real female companion at school was the janitress, a lively Irish woman with seven children. We met and chatted regularly midmorning while she cleaned the ladies' room.

In my third year at MIT, I became pregnant. Every morning I promised myself that that day I would announce my pregnancy. But every evening I came home having failed to do so. How could an honorary man say she was pregnant? Eventually, of course, my status revealed itself. I had given a talk on my thesis proposal, and when I was finished, Professor Abraham Siegel came up and shook my hand.

"I see you're pregnant," he said straightforwardly. "Congratulations."

I didn't fully appreciate Siegel's attitude until years later, when I saw male colleagues and thesis advisers berate newly pregnant women colleagues and graduate students in male-dominated fields: "You could have been a star, and now look what you've gone and done."

LAUNCHING

In the fall of 1967, when my son was six weeks old, I began my first teaching job as a lecturer in the Economics Department at the University of Maryland. I would have preferred to stay another year at MIT to finish my thesis, but my husband was required to serve in the military (during the Vietnam War, all physicians had to serve in the military), and he had arranged to do his service at the National Institutes of Health in Bethesda. So in early 1967, five months pregnant but not yet "showing," I went on the job market, confining my search to the Washington, DC, area.

I spent my first year at Maryland preparing courses in labor economics and macroeconomics. In my second year I worked to complete my doctoral dissertation comparing wage structures in manufacturing industries across fifty-three countries. Completing a thesis in absentia is never easy, and during the time I was writing I appreciated a call from Charles

Meyers asking how I was doing and telling me that my thesis committee was looking forward to my manuscript. I also had support from my very first woman colleague, Barbara Bergmann, who was a professor of economics at Maryland.

When I finished the dissertation in the summer of 1969, I was promoted to assistant professor. Then, shortly thereafter, in early November, I gave birth to my second child. There was no such thing as maternity leave and I taught until the day she was born. Robert Knight, a fellow labor economist, kindly offered to teach my classes for three weeks after the birth, and I was back teaching after Thanksgiving. Fortunately, I'd had an easy pregnancy and birth, and my daughter was an easy baby, but taking off only three weeks was enormously stressful.

I knew that at the end of my third year at Maryland our family would have to move again so my husband could complete his medical residency. It never occurred to either of us to go on the job market at the same time and find a city where both of us had attractive jobs. The tacit compact among couples in our generation was that the husband's career came first and the wife followed. My husband had accepted a residency at Stanford. Now it was up to me to find a job in the Bay Area.

In those days, jobs were not always posted, and junior faculty were often hired merely on the say-so of respected colleagues. So almost a year before we were to move to Stanford, I asked my thesis advisers if they knew Mel Reder, the senior faculty member in labor economics at Stanford. They didn't. But they knew Lloyd Ulman at Berkeley, and at the Allied Social Sciences Association (ASSA) meetings in New York, about two months after my daughter was born, I interviewed with Ulman for an assistant professor position in labor economics. Several months later, he called to offer me the position, but as a lecturer, not an assistant professor. I had no other choices. I had been turned down for assistant professor positions at three other institutions near Stanford. I accepted the position as a lecturer at Berkeley.

When I got to Berkeley in the fall of 1970, I saw that two classmates from my PhD program at MIT, Tu Jarvis and Richard Sutch, were faculty colleagues. But they were assistant professors. I made an appointment to discuss this with George Break, chair of the Economics Department.

"Why am I a lecturer, while Tu and Richard are assistant professors?" I asked.

"It's because you live in Palo Alto," he responded.

I always say I became a feminist on the Bay Bridge. As I drove across it, from Berkeley to San Francisco after my meeting with Break, the truth hit me: My position as a lecturer had nothing to do with living in Palo Alto. It had to do with being a woman. There was not a single woman in the regular faculty ranks in the Economics Department at Berkeley. When I got home, I called Break's office to make a follow-up appointment.

"He's busy," his secretary told me. "He says he can't see you for three weeks."

During the time I was waiting for Break to see me again, I learned that the last woman who had been tenured in the Economics Department at Berkeley had been hired more than forty years earlier. I also discovered that most women faculty members at Berkeley across all departments were lecturers and that Berkeley had been part of a sex discrimination complaint filed the previous spring by the Women's Equity Action League. A few weeks into the fall quarter, investigators arrived from the U.S. Labor Department to look into sex discrimination on Berkeley's faculty.

During those weeks I also read all the literature on women and work in the Stanford library. It wasn't a difficult project. The materials were sparse. But I was excited by what I read. Suddenly I had a whole new research area.

When I had my second meeting with Break. I asked the same question I'd asked before and said I would appreciate an honest answer.

"You're a lecturer because you're a mom of two children under the age of three. We don't know what's going to happen to you."

"Happen to me? I'm not asking you to *give* me tenure. I'm asking you to put me on the tenure track so that I can work to get tenure."

"No," he said. "I could never sell that to the department."

Fortunately for me, the wind shifted at Berkeley after the Labor Department poked around for a year, and the following year I did get an assistant professor offer from Berkeley. But I also got one from the Graduate School of Business (GSB) at Stanford. Stanford was nervous about the HEW investigations at Berkeley, and not only did they hire me and Francine Gordon (a social psychologist) as the first women ever on the faculty of the GSB, they also hired their first women faculty members ever in the Law School and the School of Engineering.

STANFORD: THE GRADUATE SCHOOL OF BUSINESS AND THE CENTER FOR RESEARCH ON WOMEN

Together, Gordon and I represented slightly more than 2 percent of the GSB faculty – ninety men and us. At Stanford as a whole, women were approximately 7 percent of the total faculty and 4 percent of its tenured faculty. I say "approximately" because in 1972 Stanford had yet to officially count its women faculty members. It was not until 1974 that the first official count took place.

My initiation at the GSB was disturbing. Just a few weeks after I started, the chair of the economics group, Lee Bach, asked me to give a seminar. My talk was on the research I was doing on the economics of childcare, and I began by making the argument that good childcare produces numerous external benefits and that there is a powerful economic case for government subsidization of childcare, much like the argument for the subsidization of education. But before I could go any further than this introduction, my colleagues, fifteen conservative male professors of economics and finance, jumped in. Didn't I understand, they asked over and over, that government intervention was something to be avoided and that adding yet another category of intervention, especially one that interfered with something so private as the raising of young children, was surely a dreadful idea? Their disapproval was heated. Bach, who chaired the session, did nothing to stop their interruption. Mercifully, after fifty minutes, we adjourned.

President Nixon had the same views as my colleagues. The previous year, when Congress sent him a bill designed to create a childcare system with federal funding, he vetoed it. Such legislation would weaken the family, he said. To this day, Congress has yet to pass a childcare bill.

After my talk, one of my economics colleagues took me aside and solicitously advised me to stop doing work on topics such as women's employment and childcare.

I didn't follow his advice. I couldn't. I was fired up about the economics of childcare, the effects of women's earnings on family spending patterns, the value of unpaid labor in the home, and most of all occupational segregation – the fact that some occupations were predominantly female while others, the more lucrative ones, were predominantly male. These guys are not paying me enough for me to sell my soul, I thought. If I'm going to be an academic, I'm going to work on the topics I care about.

Stanford wanted to publicize the fact that it had hired its first women faculty members in business, law, and engineering, and just before the quarter started, the university's public relations office had taken us up to San Francisco for a press conference. As a result, the *Stanford Daily* as well as the local papers noted not only that the Stanford Business School had women faculty members for the first time, but that one of them, namely me, was doing research on, of all things, women.

Shortly thereafter three Stanford students visited me independently. They all asked the same question: Would I help them start a research center on women at Stanford? Initially, I declined. "Assistant professors don't start research centers," I told them. But as my alienation at the Business School increased, I changed my mind. Some of the senior male faculty had begun to fuss at Gordon and me in an unpleasant way because now that the school had two women faculty members they would have to move their annual faculty retreat from its usual venue, an all-male club. I also had male students in my macro theory class tell me that they intended to switch sections. They weren't paying all that money for tuition, they said, to be taught by a woman. And then, reflecting their own alienation, all five women in the second-year class, who represented a mere 1.5 percent of the MBA students, made a slide show titled "What's a Nice Girl Like You Doing in a Place Like This?"

I decided I *would* create a center for research on women. I recruited senior faculty from across the university, men as well as women, and also got the backing of the president and provost. I began an interdisciplinary weekly lecture series, held meetings to develop themes for the center, and wrote a proposal to the Ford Foundation. When Ford funded the proposal, the university officially created the Center for Research on Women (CROW) with me at its helm. There are now more than 100 centers for research on women in the United States, but in 1974 the ones at Stanford and Wellesley College were the first. CROW, now endowed as the Michelle R. Clayman Institute for Research on Gender, will soon celebrate its fortieth anniversary. It remains one of my proudest accomplishments.

CROW gave me the colleagues I didn't have at the GSB. We started what we called the CROW group, a group of faculty from all over the university interested in scholarship and research on women – Carol Jacklin and Eleanor Maccoby from psychology, Diane Middlebrook from English, Estelle Freedman from history, Shelly Rosaldo and Jane Collier from anthropology, and I, an economist. There was so little scholarly literature on women at that time that each of us could tell the others about the work in our fields in just a few lectures. It seems impossible all these years later, with the veritable flood of scholarship that ensued, but in those days, at the end of one year of meetings, each of us was familiar with the totality of literature in the fields we represented.

The intellectual and personal friendships forged in the CROW group led to interdisciplinary courses. Psychologist Jacklin, literary scholar Ann Mellor, and I taught a course in feminist theory for undergraduates. Later, Middlebrook and I taught a course on women's choices, where I got a chance to teach economics from novels – the economics of slavery from *Beloved*, the economics of marriage markets from *Pride and Prejudice*, and the economic effects of World War I on women's employment in France from Collette's book, *Cheri, and the End of Cheri.*

The CROW group also gave birth to the interdisciplinary women's studies teaching program at Stanford and later to success in a competition run by the University of Chicago Press to edit *Signs*, the foremost journal in women's studies. With Barbara Gelpi as the editor and many of us in the original CROW group serving as associate editors, we had five heady years as we tried to wrap our minds around a field that was growing geometrically all over the world. Our most valiant efforts were trying to understand French feminist literary theory.

My own research in those years was mostly on occupational segregation. Why was it that certain occupations were dominated by men and others by women? How come occupations that were largely male in some countries were largely female in others? And when occupations switched their gender designation, why and how did that occur? My main research project on this last question was with historian David Tyack in the School of Education to examine how and why teaching became a woman's occupation in the United States in the nineteenth century.

I also looked at differences in saving and spending patterns between dual-earner and single-earner husband-wife families and forged close working relationships with two junior faculty members at the GSB, Bill Dunkelberg in economics and Charles Weinberg in marketing. Bill helped me learn to work with large data sets from the University of Michigan, and Charles and I coauthored an article on expenditure patterns. Another collaborator at the GSB was the dean, Arjay Miller, who supported Gordon and me to put on the first national conference ever on women in management. Miller had been president of the Ford Motor Company before he became dean, and he assured us that he would get his friends and colleagues, male executives from major corporations, to attend. The conference discussed strategies for bringing women into management and argued that corporate top managers needn't wait for their companies to be sued before they took action to hire and promote women into powerful positions.[1]

STANFORD'S SCHOOL OF EDUCATION

In 1978 the GSB turned me down for tenure. I had two strikes against me. I was a woman and I studied women's issues. But fortunately for me, Tyack, my collaborator on the research project on the feminization of teaching, brought my vitae to the attention of the dean of the Stanford University School of Education (SUSE). The SUSE faculty voted to form a review committee to seek outside letters about my work, and within a few months, they voted to offer me a tenured associate professorship. But the appointment ran into a snag. The University Advisory Board said it was confused. How could someone be turned down for tenure in one school and then be voted tenure a few months later in another? They denied the promotion.

That summer, SUSE's dean retired. When the new dean took up his post, he decided to start my whole tenure and promotion process all over again. As a result, I came up for tenure three times in eighteen months. But the third time the stars were aligned.

Joining the SUSE faculty proved to be one of the best decisions I ever made. I finally had senior colleagues who understood and supported my work and students who worked on a variety of fascinating subjects. I was free to use an interdisciplinary approach to questions I found important (including using qualitative methods) and did not need to confine my publications to economics journals.

However, a few years after my tenure came through, my marriage began to fall apart. Although my husband had initially been extremely encouraging about my teaching in college, he now said he would prefer that I devote full-time attention to our family. I could not do that. I could not imagine my life without teaching and research. Besides, I had worked hard to achieve a tenured position. I was not about to give it up. Within a year or so, we divorced.

TEACHING

One of the courses I taught at SUSE was the economics of education, and because the MA and PhD students in the class had a wide variety of backgrounds, and few knew much economics, I ran a parallel course in elementary economic analysis. After several years, I noticed a pattern. At the conclusion of the second or third class of the quarter, two types of students would come up to me at the end of class to ask a question. The first group had been undergraduates in literature, history, languages, or one of the soft social sciences. They maintained that they understood basic microeconomics concepts when I explained things "in words" but were lost when I put up graphs or, worse, equations. Was it okay if they understood economics only in words? The second group had the mirror question: They had majored in math, engineering, or one of the hard sciences. Why, they asked, did I spend so much time "talking" when everything was so clear once I put up the graphs, and especially the equations? Was it okay if they just understood the graphs and equations and not the words?

I asked one of my cognitive psychology colleagues, James Greeno, how I could design an experiment that would help me understand the students' patterns of thinking and understanding. He suggested I design a simple economics problem and ask my teaching assistant to videotape small groups of students from the class talking to one another about the problem and then graphing the solution. I put the following problem to them: Suppose there is a severe shortage of science teachers in San Jose. Using a supply and demand diagram to represent the labor market for science teachers, show what you think would happen in the short run and long run if the school board were to raise the salary of science teachers by 10 percent above and beyond the salary increase for other teachers. I was shocked when I saw the videotapes. Although these bright students could answer essay questions I posed to them on exams, they could not use economic reasoning to talk to one another and collectively graph the lessening of a shortage resulting from a salary increase. When I showed the videotapes to faculty teaching introductory economics to undergraduates at Stanford, they wanted to do the same experiment with groups of their students. The results for the undergraduates were the same as those for my graduate students.

I wrote two papers about this videotaping exercise[2] and concluded that unless students could use verbal reasoning *and* graph a solution, they really did not understand economic analysis. I also changed my teaching of basic economics. I stopped lecturing and started asking frequent questions as I presented concepts, attempting to make sure that students understood each new idea before I went on to the next. I covered less material, but got improved understanding.

In 1992 Stanford's provost asked me to chair a committee on the recruitment and retention of women faculty members. By then, women were 16 percent of the Stanford faculty, a doubling of the percentage since 1974, but nonetheless low as compared with our peer institutions.[3] My committee gathered data and interviewed junior faculty. Our report found several problems: an absence of a culture of support for junior faculty (male as well as female), lack of support for combining an academic career with family life, and persistent male/female salary differentials. We made sixteen recommendations for change. In response, the provost created a mentoring system for junior faculty and appointed a vice-provost to assist women who wished to redress salary inequities. Many women received substantial salary adjustments, and a process was put into place to have deans and the provost examine gender differences in faculty salaries on an ongoing basis.

Stanford is a better place for women today than when I came. In 2009–2010, 26 percent of the faculty was female. The university has also made important changes with regard to parental leave and stopping the tenure clock for new parents. And there are several on-site childcare programs and a junior faculty childcare assistance program.

Nonetheless, there is much for the next generation to do. In science, engineering, and, I must say, economics, there remains a dearth of women faculty. Also, salary differences by gender continue to reappear, as some male faculty members get large raises to prevent them from accepting offers at other universities. (Women less frequently seek or receive such outside offers, since they are so often members of a two-career couple.)

About ten years after I chaired the provost's committee, I began a new affiliation with the Stanford Business School, and for several years served as director of the joint MA program between the GSB and SUSE. I also began teaching two sections of what has become an exceedingly popular course at the GSB, "Work and Family." Even after officially retiring from Stanford, I continue to teach the course; 40 percent of its students are now men. And at the time of my retirement, the women students' organization at the GSB, Women in Management, honored me for my pioneering work for women at the Business School. Sometimes, life has a way of righting itself.

WOULD I DO IT AGAIN?

I recently told my eleven-year old granddaughter that I had finished the book I'd been working on, *Interdisciplinary Conversations: Challenging Habits of Thought*, and that it would soon be published.[4] The book is a study of six interdisciplinary faculty seminars at three research universities and examines why the conversations were so difficult and what factors helped them to succeed. She asked if the book would make me famous or rich, and when I said I doubted it would, she asked me why I had spent ten years writing it. How difficult it is to explain the joys of scholarship, the freedom to choose a puzzle and carefully solve it, collecting materials and data, slowly developing a theoretical framework, and then meticulously writing it all out so that colleagues can understand, critique, and build upon it.

I have enjoyed academic life – investigating how and why discrimination, gender segregation, and traditional family roles affect women's earnings and employment, bringing feminist analysis into economics, and probing the cognitive and cultural processes that make interdisciplinarity so difficult. I have also taken pleasure in understanding students' difficulties in learning economics and how best to overcome them. But perhaps most of all, I have enjoyed being prominent among those who fought vigorously to enable women to enter and flourish as faculty members at colleges and

universities. While my sojourn has often been rocky, I have had the opportunity to be part of a movement that has markedly changed the world. Some
of the gender bias that encumbered my own path is still out there, but it is
now more muted, and the voices that call "foul" in response are now men's
as well as women's.

I consider myself lucky. Fortunately, my father never lost his job. Yet
my family's frequent conversations about unemployment and other economic issues propelled me into a field whose questions still fascinate me.
Interestingly, my younger sister, Alice Amsden, also became an economist.
I have been privileged to live in a place of astonishing physical beauty
and superb climate and have been blessed with outstanding students, colleagues, friends, and family, especially my second husband, Jay Jackman.
I have also had the freedom to teach, study, and write where my interests
take me. Despite the fact that many of my women students say they would
never want to do what I have done, that it is just too hard to raise a family
and succeed in a Research I University, I'd do it again in a flash. I love the
high that comes from sailing into the wind. And I love the taste of victory
when the wind finally shifts.

Notes

1 Gordon and I edited a book based on the conference presentations: *Bringing Women
   into Management* (New York: McGraw-Hill, 1975).
2 Myra H. Strober and Allen Cook, "Economics, Lies, and Videotapes," *Journal of
   Economic Education*, Spring 1992 and Myra H. Strober, Kasi Fuller, and Allen
   Cook, "Making and Correcting Errors in Economic Analyses: An Examination of
   Videotapes," *Journal of Economic Education*, Summer 1997.
3 Stanford University, "Final Report of the Provost's Committee on the Recruitment
   and Retention of Women Faculty." A summary of the report can be found at news.
   stanford.edu/pr/93/931130Arc3027.html (accessed July 14, 2010). The interested
   reader can download the full report by typing Stanford University and the title of
   the report into Google.
4 Myra H. Strober, *Interdisciplinary Conversations: Challenging Habits of Thought*
   (Stanford: Stanford University Press, 2010).

27

My Life and Work Philosophy

Hal R. Varian

I was born in Wooster, Ohio, a small Midwestern town about fifty miles south of Cleveland. My brother and I grew up on an apple orchard owned by my father and grandfather. In many respects I had an idyllic childhood – I remember long summer days of playing among the apple trees and lying on the hillside watching the shapes form in the clouds. However, despite the appeals of this pastoral life, I always felt trapped on the orchard. There was a whole wide world out there beyond Wooster, Ohio, that I was missing out on.

I was an avid reader, especially of science and science fiction, and spent virtually every Saturday morning at the library picking out the next week's set of books. When I was about twelve I joined some mail-order book clubs. One of the initial three offerings was Isaac Asimov's *Foundation Trilogy*,

The material up until I became dean at Berkeley is a modified version of the biographical essay that appeared in Varian (2000), a volume of my collected works. I have also drawn on some material from Varian (1995, 2001, 2005).

which was a series of novels revolving around the predictions of a "psycho-historian" who created an elaborate mathematical model of the Galactic Empire. The idea that one could construct mathematical models of human behavior made a big impression on me; perhaps this is why I eventually became an economist. (It appears that both Paul Krugman and Newt Gingrich were also inspired by Asimov's book; see Dowd 2011; Krugman 2000.)

My mother always professed surprise at my career choice. She says that she was sure I would become a scientist. I kept explaining that economics *is* a science, but I don't think I ever convinced her.

In 1957 the Russians shot *Sputnik* into orbit, an event that was to have a great impact on my life. The perceived lag in US education prompted the National Defense Education Act, which provided scholarship and loans without which I would have probably been unable to pay for college.

I did very well in grade school and high school. In the summer of 1964, I was chosen to attend a National Science Foundation Summer Science camp at Ohio University. I spent about six weeks there, previewing college life. Among other things I learned to program in Fortran II on an IBM 1620. We had to feed an entire box of punched cards into the computer just to load the compiler, with my own puny little eighty-card program stuck at the end.

My science project was to estimate the angular distribution of cosmic rays, and by the end of the summer, I actually succeeded in writing the curve-fitting program and analyzing the data. The fall of my senior year I applied to MIT, since I was convinced that it was the best place for science. I had never visited the campus – indeed, I had barely been out of Wooster – yet I was supremely confident that this was the right choice.

MIT

I entered MIT in the fall of 1965, very much the typical smug freshman who had always been at the top of his class. At one orientation meeting, the leader asked how many of us had at least one perfect score on our college entrance exams. I proudly raised my hand ... and then noticed that virtually all of my classmates also had their hands up. The lesson was clear – I wasn't in Wooster anymore!

I had a great time in college. I did reasonably well in my classes, maintaining a B average and making the dean's list for a few semesters. But I also went through the standard experience of a small-town boy discovering life in the big city. I suppose I could have studied more and done better, but I would have missed a lot of other experiences.

During the summer of 1966, I got a programming job writing assembly language code for a Univac 1108. This was incredibly tedious – if I was lucky, I was able to run two jobs a day. At the end of the summer, both my boss and I were leaving the company. He called me aside and told me to take all the comment cards out of my deck. "But then," I said, "no one will be able to figure out what we did." "Exactly," he replied. "If they want to make any changes they'll have to hire us back as consultants!" Since then I have always insisted that my own programmers write liberal comments in their code.

While at MIT I was still inspired by the vision of mathematical modeling of human behavior, but I wasn't sure what subject dealt with that: I looked into psychology, operations research, and, finally, economics. In my sophomore year I took intermediate microeconomics from Joe Stiglitz and decided this was the subject for me.

MIT is known as a technical university, but it has a remarkably good set of courses in the arts and humanities. I took music, art, philosophy, and several other such courses, all of which I enjoyed very much. One semester I was president of the MIT Student Art Association.

During my senior year, I took the first-year graduate course in micro theory, taught by Bob Bishop. I didn't do all that well, mostly because I was distracted by extracurricular activities, but this didn't discourage me. My senior thesis adviser was Duncan Foley, who apparently saw potential in me and encouraged me to go to Berkeley. I dutifully followed his advice.

BERKELEY

I was admitted to Berkeley and vividly remember sending in my letter of acceptance one day in the spring of 1969. After dropping the letter in the mailbox, I picked up the student newspaper, only to see that the top news story of the day involved helicopters gassing students in Sproul Plaza! I contemplated retrieving my admissions letter but figured that the tear gas would dissipate by the time I arrived.

I got a summer job at Berkeley doing computer programming for the Center for Real Estate and Urban Economics and drove west with some friends in June 1969. Berkeley in the early seventies was a remarkable place. Something new was happening every day. I look back now and ask how we all could have been so silly, but at the time it was an exciting experience. Despite the temptation to describe the entire range of what was *really* going on, I will devote my attention solely to my academic development during this period.

When the term started, the admitted class was required to take an advanced placement exam for the graduate micro sequence. Having taken the equivalent course at MIT, I easily passed the placement exam and so created a hole in my schedule. The graduate adviser, George Akerloff, encouraged me to take an advanced micro course from Dan McFadden and suggested I "take something" in the Mathematics Department.

Somehow I discovered that John Kelley was teaching a three-quarter course in general topology, function spaces, and measure theory. I had no idea what these topics were, but I had heard that Kelley was an excellent teacher, so I signed up for the courses. This turned out to be one of the great intellectual experiences of my life. This is ironic, since if I had understood clearly what I was getting into, I would have realized the subjects were much too advanced for me.

Berkeley had the best Mathematics Department in the world, and all of the other students had been top math undergraduates. I, on the other hand, had taken only the three required math courses at MIT and never had taken a "real" math course involving proofs. Nevertheless, I persevered, and by the end of the term I was doing as well as the best students in the class. It was only much later that I learned that topology was a generalization of real analysis, which one is supposed to study first!

I went on to take several other math courses at Berkeley and eventually accumulated enough credits for a master's degree. Despite this accomplishment, I have never considered myself a very good mathematician. My main shortcoming is that I am too sloppy and not careful enough in my proofs. Luckily, peer review has caught most of my really egregious errors.

McFadden's course in micro theory was also a very nice course, but I have to say that I didn't really appreciate its importance at the time. During this year I took a course from a philosopher, Hubert Dreyfus, on existential philosophy, which had a big influence on me. During subsequent terms I took several philosophy courses on Heidegger, Kierkegaard, Wittgenstein, and various analytic philosophers.

This period in my life was intensely exciting – I was taking courses in economics, mathematics, statistics, and philosophy, as well as enjoying the pleasures of the Bay Area. Looking back, I wonder how I had the energy for it all.

Tom Rothenberg encouraged me to apply for an NSF Fellowship, which I received and which relieved me of financial worries for the next three years. I had a stipend of $10,000 a year, my rent was $50 per month, a good dinner cost $3, and I could take any course I wanted at one of the best universities in the world. What a life!

At the beginning of my fourth year, I attended a seminar by Menachem Yaari, who talked about a theory of "fairness." Interestingly, the particular formalization of fairness that he described was first proposed by my former undergraduate adviser, Duncan Foley. I found the concept intriguing and ended up writing my thesis on it.

BACK TO MIT

I went on the job market in the spring of 1973 and was invited to speak at a number of schools, including Minnesota, Michigan, Harvard, Penn, and MIT. I received an offer at MIT, which then had the best Economics Department in the country. Clearly, that was the job to take.

I was asked to teach one of the four core micro courses. Bob Bishop taught the first course, on Marshallian economics. Marty Weitzman taught the second on activity analysis. I taught the third on duality, and Paul Samuelson taught the fourth. The students referred to these courses as "curves, vectors, sets, and jokes." This is a bit unfair to Samuelson, who rarely told jokes narrowly defined but seemed to have a never-ending supply of amusing anecdotes.

My course, "sets," was supposed to be "Berkeley economics," which meant duality, general equilibrium, and other topics that had been developed in the 1970s by Dan McFadden, Gerard Debreu, Erwin Diewert, and other Berkeley researchers. The trouble was that there was no textbook to teach from. There were a few advanced journal articles, but these were inaccessible to beginning students. Bob Hall gave me twenty pages of lecture notes he had written, and I also had the fifty or so pages of notes written by Dan McFadden and Sid Winter for the course I had taken at Berkeley.

I wrote up some more notes myself, trying to make this material more accessible to the students. This had the side effect of making it more accessible to me. As is commonly observed, teaching is the best method for learning.

MIT had just purchased one of the first word processors, an IBM desk-sized computer that stored each page on a magnetic card. I had the operator enter my notes on that machine because I realized they were going to be revised frequently. One defect of this system was that it didn't handle Greek characters, which is why the first edition of *Microeconomic Analysis* had no Greek.

Each time I taught the course, the notes got bigger. One day Don Lamm, an acquisitions editor from W. W. Norton, was visiting my office. He asked the obligatory question: "Are you working on any books?"

"Of course not," I replied. "That would be a foolish way to spend time as an assistant professor."

"What's that pile of paper over there?" Don asked.

"Oh," I said, "that's just class notes."

"Well," said Lamm, "that's close enough for me." He left the office with the notes and sent me a book contract a month later.

I continued to do some work in economic theories of equity and a little bit of mathematical economics, but in the early 1970s the most exciting intellectual work at MIT was in macroeconomics, and I found myself gravitating to that area. I was particularly interested in "disequilibrium theory," a way of approaching macro that has since fallen into disrepute – unjustly so, in my opinion. Perhaps the increased interest in "depression economics" will rekindle work on disequilibrium economics.

During this time I taught undergraduate courses in statistics, mathematical economics, and macroeconomics. These were great teaching assignments, because they compelled me to actually learn this material. I had some tremendous students while at MIT. Paul Krugman, Olivier Blanchard, and Jeff Frankel were among the graduate students I taught there. I also taught mathematical economics to Carl Shapiro and Larry Summers, as well as supervising their senior theses.

In the spring of 1975, I got offers from both Berkeley and Stanford to come visit for a year. It was, and is, a common recruiting tactic for schools like these to invite young assistant professors to visit. The invitees were paid comparatively little, and it gave the schools a chance to look them over to see if they wanted to make a preemptive offer when tenure time came.

The University of Michigan also called me in the fall of 1996, inviting me out for a "job talk." I enjoyed the visit to Ann Arbor but didn't take the "job" part all that seriously.

I spent the winter of 1977 at Stanford and the spring at Berkeley. During this time I worked on the manuscript of *Microeconomic Analysis*. Carl Shapiro was also at Berkeley as a first-year student in mathematics, and I hired him as research assistant for the book. I like to think that this experience had something to do with his deciding to pursue economics as a profession.

MICHIGAN

During the spring of 1977 I received an offer from Michigan as a full professor, with a salary double what I was making at MIT. It meant that I would move directly from assistant to full professor less than four years out of grad school. This opportunity was too attractive to turn down, so I moved to Ann Arbor that summer.

At Michigan I became interested in industrial organization and public finance and wrote my papers "A Model of Sales" and "Redistributive Taxation as Social Insurance." I formed a long and fruitful collaboration and friendship with Ted Bergstrom, from whom I have learned much over the years.

In early 1979, I was chosen as a Guggenheim fellow and decided to spend the year at Oxford, at the invitation of Jim Mirrlees, whom I had met at MIT. This was a wonderful year. I spent about six weeks in the summer with a Eurail pass exploring the capitals of Europe, also finding time to teach courses in Stockholm and Helsinki.

I lived "in college" at Nuffield, which meant I didn't have to worry about mundane details of life and spent nearly all my time on research. This is where I wrote most of my papers on "nonparametric methods," which, being rather mathematical, required more sustained concentration than most work. I couldn't have done nearly as much in this area in a less sequestered environment.

I returned to Michigan in the summer of 1980. At this time Michigan was a pretty backward place, compared with the East and West Coast schools, and we struggled to convince the administration to modernize the Economics Department.

In the mid-1980s I was able to attract Roger Gordon and Michelle White, who made a huge difference in the intellectual life of the department. In the late 1980s I helped bring Ken Binmore to Ann Arbor, and he added a much-needed capability in game theory.

Around 1986 I decided to write a textbook on intermediate microeconomics. I had several motivations. By this time, my graduate text had become the standard, and people kept asking me what their students should read to prepare them for the graduate book. I was also quite unhappy with the existing books, which were becoming more and more dumbed down. I vividly remember the event that got me to actually start writing: I had to prepare a midterm exam for my course and, looking through the textbook I had used, I found it hard to think of anything substantive that the students had learned.

It was something of a painful experience writing the book, since the students were quite critical of the slightest error or ambiguity, but their criticisms ultimately produced a better product. My colleague Ted Bergstrom collaborated with me on the workbook, which turned out to be a great success. I can say that in all due modesty since most of the best material in the workbook came from Ted.

This book has gone on to be translated into at least a dozen languages and is used around the world. I recently finished the eighth edition, and it seems to be going strong, despite the very competitive market in this area.

COMPUTERS

During the 1980s I also spent a lot of time with microcomputers. I had bought an IBM PC back in 1981, shortly after it first came out, and continued to upgrade to each new model. I helped to organize a users' group in Ann Arbor and spent a lot of time hacking. There was a serious side to all this – I was using computation much more in my research – but, I have to say, that was more an excuse than a motivation.

In the early 1990s, one of my colleagues asked me a difficult question: "Who pays for my email? You're an economist and a computer geek, so you should know." I had to admit there was some logic in his view, so I set out to find the answer.

At that time the main US Internet backbone, the NSFNET, was managed in Ann Arbor, so the resources were close by. I teamed up with my colleague Jeff MacKie-Mason, and a few months later we wrote our paper "The Economics of the Internet." This paper was the first that married my interest in computers with my interest in economics. As I learned more and more about digital technology, I saw that there were a huge number of fascinating economic questions waiting to be answered, and I spent more and more time thinking and writing about pricing information, intellectual property, and other similar topics.

One paper I published during that time was "Mechanism Design for Computerized Agents." This was presented in the Usenix Workshop on Electronic Commerce, July 11–12, 1995, in New York. The basic point of the paper was that economic mechanism design was highly relevant to computer science, since it gave a systematic way to incorporate incentives into distributed algorithms. There was nothing much original from an economic point of view, but this was one of the first papers to describe economic mechanism design to a computer science audience. This field subsequently became a hot area in computational theory. It is a beautiful example of how interdisciplinary work can be both intellectually exciting and highly relevant.

BACK TO BERKELEY

In 1993 the president of the University of Michigan did a very strange thing: he appointed Dan Atkins, the associate dean of engineering, to be the new dean of the Library School. This seemingly inexplicable appointment was prescient: within the year it had become clear that the management of digital information was going to require a whole new profession, which combined traditional library skills with skills in information technology.

Dan wanted to create a new interdisciplinary degree program within the Library School to deal with information management, and he asked me to serve on the committee organizing this new school. Sometime during this period I received a letter from Berkeley inviting me to apply to be dean of a similar school that was being established there. I tossed the letter in the wastebasket, as I had done with previous offers to be dean here and there, but then thought that I should take a look at what Berkeley was doing. I read the proposal for the new school at Berkeley and was very impressed – this was just what we were trying to do at Michigan, only the thinking at Berkeley was much farther along. One thing led to another, and before I knew it I was dean of the new school at Berkeley.

When I went to my first Council of Deans meeting at Berkeley, I introduced myself by saying, "I am Berkeley's newest dean, but I have no faculty and no students." One of them responded, "Why ruin a good thing?" I must say that during my time as dean I thought of that remark often.

The School of Information Management and Systems (as it was then called) was a successor to the Library School at Berkeley, and I must say that I did not always see eye to eye with the faculty, students, and alumni of that organization. But as time went on, it became clear that "information management" was a compelling vision for the new school.

One of my colleagues from computer science correctly noted that, for a chair, there is hiring and there is everything else. Luckily for me, the first person I hired, Pamela Samuelson, was named a MacArthur fellow a few months after she joined the school. Pam is a law school professor who specialized in intellectual property and what was then becoming known as cyberlaw. She did exactly the sort of interdisciplinary work that the school was designed to foster, and the recognition for her work from MacArthur did a lot for the standing of the school on campus.

Subsequently, I hired specialists in computer security, human–computer interfaces, communications networks, databases, regional development, and other areas. The faculty all had interests in technology and social science, which fit very well with the rise of the Internet that occurred about that time.

I remember that time as a very busy period – there is a lot to be done when you build a brand new school. But at the same time, it was a very exciting time.

In 1993 the National Science Foundation started a major digital libraries initiative (Varian 1995) and funded six universities to work in this area.
Berkeley was one of the recipients, and a lot of great work came out of this
initiative. Inktomi, an early Web search company, was initially created as
part of the Berkeley program, while Google was inspired by the Stanford
program. The vision that motivated the NSF research program has largely
come to pass. Nowadays virtually everyone in the developed world has
access to a phenomenal amount of information online.

As Herbert Simon once said, "A wealth of information creates a poverty
of attention." The challenge we all face now is how to collect, search, manage, and understand all that information.

Information Rules

Late in 2007 Carl Shapiro and I began to talk about writing a book on the
economics of information technology. We started writing in the summer of
1998. Writing with Carl was a great pleasure. We would each take responsibility for a chapter, then take turns lobbing it back and forth. With each
volley, the chapter got better, and by the fall of 1997 we had something we
could send out to readers.

The interest level was very high, as everyone was trying to figure out
what was going on in the "new economy." There was a lot of loose talk about
how "the Internet changes everything," "the business cycle is dead," and
other bits of nonsense. Our message was the antithesis to all that posturing:
"Technology changes; economic laws do not."

I have to admit that we thought about putting a different spin on things.
Two of the major themes of our book – lock-in and network effects – had
been developed in the past ten to twenty years. That could still count as
"new economics." But we decided that even if the analysis was relatively
"new," the phenomena were quite "old," so emphasizing the durable principles seemed to be a better strategy to us. We were also pretty convinced
that the hype surrounding the Internet would eventually dissipate, and we
wanted to be left standing when it all blew over.

Having a one-sentence summary of the book turned out to be a great
idea. People always ask, "What is your book about?" Giving them a suc-
cinct and provocative answer was more useful than I ever could have
imagined.

When the book, *Information Rules*, was finally published in November
1999, I was convinced that we had missed the peak of Internet-mania.
Things couldn't get any crazier than they were then, I thought. Luckily for

us, I was dead wrong. From today's perspective, 1998 was the beginning, not the end, of the Internet's impact on the economic and social spheres.

The book became a big success, and I began to get invitations to speak at various events. Initially, I was flattered to be getting all this attention, and following the conventional academic model I spoke for free. After a while, this got to be pretty tiring. One time I fell asleep and dreamed that I was lecturing to a group of Silicon Valley executives about network effects. I woke up and by gosh I was!

All right, it didn't go quite that far, but almost. My brother (who had a heating and cooling business) provided me with some great advice. "Hal," he said, "always bid on a job. If you've got little work, bid low, and if you've got a lot of work, bid high. But always bid."

So I starting pricing my services according to my supply, and things went a lot better. It is ironic that my brother had to explain simple economics to me, but that's the way it goes. Oh, and I also learned to always get bids from at least four home improvement contractors in subsequent remodeling projects.

By 2000 I had become a full-fledged pundit, at least with respect to Internet economics. In the spring of 2000, the *New York Times* asked me to write a monthly column and I enthusiastically agreed to do it. This was a great learning experience for me.

They say that in Washington nothing gets noticed unless it can fit on a bumper sticker. In business, nothing gets noticed unless it can fit on a one-page memo. And in academia nothing gets noticed unless it can fit into sixty pages of single-spaced text, along with twenty or thirty pages of appendixes. Well, my *New York Times* column was 1,000 words. This was constraining at first, but I eventually learned how to write essays of this length. Today, I find it hard to write longer pieces.

A great thing about the job was that I could write about pretty much anything I wanted to explore. Sometimes it was about some interesting economic research. Other times it was about what economics had to say about current events. And sometimes it was about my own pet interests.

Russell Baker's collection of columns, *There's a Country in My Cellar*, has a great introduction in which he describes his experience in writing a column:

> Notified that I was now free to write three columns a week about almost any subject on earth, I was exultant. After fifteen years of living under reporters' constraints, I was at last free to disgorge the entire content of my brain.
>
> Somewhere between the third and fourth weeks, having written fewer than a dozen columns, I made a terrifying discovery: I had now disgorged the entire content of my brain, yet another column was due at once. (11)

I never quite experienced Russell Baker's terror, but I have an inkling of what it feels like.

GOOGLE

Sometime in the late 1990s I met Eric Schmidt at a Berkeley computer science social event. He had been a PhD student there and dropped by occasionally to see his old teachers and friends. A that time, he was chief technology officer at Sun and spending a lot of time thinking about economic and policy issues. I told him that I was writing a book on "Internet economics," and he was very intrigued. I sent him the manuscript, and later on he got back to me with several thoughts. When the book came out, he gave us a very flattering jacket quote. We also had blurbs from Andy Grove, CEO of Intel, Scott Cook, CEO of Intuit, and Jeff Bezos, CEO of Amazon, which made for a pretty impressive group of endorsers.

The term for a dean at Berkeley is five years. I re-upped in 2000 but told them that I was unlikely to serve out a full second term. By 2002 I was pretty tired of the job and wanted to do something different.

In January 2002, I ran into Eric at the World Economic Forum meeting in New York. He told me that he had moved to a cute little start-up in Silicon Valley called "Google." "Why don't you come visit us?" he suggested.

I drove down in April 2002 and spent a day with the group. I must have said something right, because they invited me to consult with them. I figured why not? It would make for some good stories if nothing else. When asked how much they should pay me, I said, "Don't worry about it, just give me a few options or something." That turned out to be the smartest financial decision I ever made in my life. But I'm getting ahead of myself.

I asked Eric what he wanted me to work on, and he said, "Why don't you take a look at this ad auction? I think it might make us a little money." As it turned out, that was a vast understatement! My first attempt to model the Google ad auction involved extending the classical single-item Bayesian analysis to multiple items. This worked naturally but didn't seem to have useful empirical properties. I then hit on the idea of looking at the Nash equilibrium, which ended up giving a nice, simple theory that also had empirical consequences.

This work was done in the summer of 2002, but since it was a consulting project for Google it remained under wraps. I presented the basic results at a Federal Trade Commission symposium on online auctions held in October 2005. I also gave a talk on the Google auction analysis in Paul Milgrom's class at Stanford. Michael Schwartz (then at Berkeley) attended that talk. We met beforehand for coffee, and I discovered that he and his coauthors were working on the same problem and had come up with a similar model. I asked Google whether I could publish my analysis, and, after review, they said, "OK." The paper came out in the *International Journal of Industrial Organization*, where it won a Best Paper of the Year award and is still the most cited paper published in that journal. The Edelman-Ostovsky-Schwartz paper came out the same year in the *American Economic Review*.

The analysis of online ad auctions has subsequently became a central part of algorithmic mechanism design, and literally hundreds of papers have been spawned by this work.

I finished up my initial work on the Google ad auction in the summer of 2002. Sometime during that summer someone asked me, "Can you help us forecast query growth?"

I said, "How do you do it now?"

She answered, "We select the column of daily queries in Excel and click 'forecast.'"

I said, "I think we can do better than that."

The first thing I tried to do was reproduce the Excel forecasts, which turned out to be harder than I anticipated. I finally discovered that Excel's option for "exponential growth" was actually "geometric growth." Things got easier after that.

It turned out that fairly simple ARIMA models did a pretty good job of forecasting queries and revenue several months in advance. Later on my models were refined and improved, but the basic logic is still used at Google.

At about the same time, another Google group asked me how to estimate the lifetime value of an advertiser in order to figure out how to spend to acquire additional advertisers. This required estimating the survival models, so I started digging into that literature as well.

At the time, I didn't really know that much about time series or survival modeling, but at least I knew they existed. It was fun to learn new things, particularly when the data and applications were readily at hand. This has been one of the most exciting things about working at Google: there is a continual stream of new problems coming along and thus a continual opportunity to learn.

I had so much fun at Google in 2002 that I asked if I could continue to consult for them on a one-day-a-week basis. Google was amenable, so that's what I did. Mostly I did statistical/econometric work but from a very practical perspective. I also continued to do some work on auction design, some of which was eventually published.

In 2004 Google decided to go public. Larry and Sergey wanted to use an auction for the IPO and asked me to do the "due diligence" on the auction design. As it happened, there had been about 200 IPO auctions around the world so there was a literature to draw on. I think that we managed to avoid some of the largest potential problems, but there were still some minor glitches along the way. After the IPO wrapped up in August 2004, the question I faced was "What now?"

I went on half-time at Berkeley and increased my consulting at Google. The company grew much more rapidly after the IPO, and by 2007 there were very substantial demands on my time. I decided then to shift to full time at Google and start hiring a team. The team consisted of statisticians, econometricians, operations researchers, and other "quants."

Google is, in many ways, an ideal environment for people who like to work with data. The computing and data access environment is superb and there are plenty of smart people to interact with. And, as I mentioned earlier, there is no shortage of interesting problems.

People often ask me, "What does an economist do at Google?" My response is, "I try to answer the questions that management will ask next month." Sometimes this involves internal business questions, sometimes it has to do with the industry, and sometimes it involves policy questions.

May 2012 was my tenth anniversary at Google, and I have to say I've had a great time. Having several careers as an economic theorist, an academic administrator, and a business economist has been an exciting experience. I've been very lucky.

HOW I WORK

A wise man once said, "If you enjoy your job, you will never have to work a day in your life." Clearly, he never served as a university administrator, but despite that exception, it is a good maxim: Make sure you enjoy what you do. If you don't, you are doing something wrong.

I have outlined some detailed advice about how to build economic models elsewhere (Varian 1995), so I will summarize that here and add a few new points.

1. *Look for ideas outside of journals.* The most important and influential papers are those that start with observations of real-world phenomena.
2. *Talk to knowledgeable people.* People who are intimately familiar with practice in a given area are very helpful. Of course, remember they are describing how things look only from their vantage point, not necessarily from the viewpoint of the system as a whole.

3. *Don't look at the literature too soon.* Of course, you should (eventually) do a thorough literature review, but it can be helpful to spend a few weeks working on the problem on your own – you might have an insight that no one else has had.

4. *Ask the four basic questions.* When you are trying to model some behavior, ask yourself: Who are the people making the choices? What are the constraints they face? How do they interact? What adjusts if the choices aren't mutually consistent?

5. *Work an example.* Start with an example, not a model. Once you thoroughly understand your example you can generalize it to a model.

6. *Keep it simple.* Follow the KISS principle: keep it simple, stupid. Write down the simplest possible example you can think of, and see if it still exhibits some interesting behavior. If it does, then make it even simpler. One practical tip: instead of writing down some general choice model, look at a choice between two alternatives. The math is a lot simpler.

7. *Generalize your model.* Once you have a simple model that you understand clearly, generalize. This is where you finally get to use all those techniques you learned in graduate school. Iterate back and forth between the simple examples and the general model.

8. *Do a literature search.* Now you can read the literature and see what others have said about the problem you are examining.

9. *Give a seminar.* The most important thing about giving a seminar is to start at the beginning. Most students give a seminar after they have spent months and months working on a topic, so they end up completely immersed in the subject. When they give a seminar, they will assume the audience knows almost as much as they do, and so they start in the middle of the story. Instead, assume the audience knows nothing and start at the beginning. Working out that first example you came up with is a good place to start. Pay attention to your audience, particularly what they find obvious and what they find difficult.

10. *Write a paper.* Based on your seminar experience, write up a paper. The two points mentioned earlier – keep it simple and start at the beginning – are critically important for the paper. Avoid stilted academic prose and the passive voice. Keep your writing lively; nobody is forced to read your papers.

I think that these are all useful points to keep in mind when doing economic modeling. I try to follow them myself, though, to be honest, I don't always succeed.

During the ten years I have been at Google, I have spent a lot of time doing empirical work, so I have additional thoughts that could be helpful there.

1. *Know your data.* Know how your data were generated. If this involved survey questions, you should know the wording of every question. If the data were seasonally adjusted, you should know how. If the data were categorized, you should know what the categories mean.
2. *Examine your data.* Examine the data carefully, and pay special attention to outliers. Many conventional statistical techniques are very sensitive to outliers, so you need to be especially vigilant about this problem.
3. *Use a holdout.* If you have plenty of data, estimate your model on only part of your data and examine the fit on the other part. Also consider using cross-validation where you repeatedly draw a training sample from your data, estimate, and then examine the fit on the other part of your data. (Cross-validation is widely used in machine learning, a subject that is well worth studying.)
4. *Plots are your friend.* You should create a lot of plots, to help you both understand the data and communicate your understanding to others. Read some books on statistical graphics for ideas.
5. *Don't confuse statistical significance and practical significance.* This is an old maxim, but it is still important. When you find some seemingly interesting effect, make sure you understand how large it is in practice.
6. *Consider model averaging.* Try several different models and see if they tell a consistent story. If you are doing some sort of simple forecasting, it is generally the case that model averaging is better than using a single model. This is frustrating from a scientific perspective but very important in practice.
7. *Make sure your results can be replicated.* Once you've reached a satisfactory conclusion, you should start over from scratch and document every step in your analysis so that other people can replicate it.

CONCLUSION

This essay has ended up much longer than I had planned, but I hope that it contains some useful advice. I'm not sure that I would encourage anyone to try to emulate my career, but I have to say I have enjoyed it.

REFERENCES

Baker, Russell (1990). *There's a Country in My Cellar*. New York: William Morrow.

Dowd, Maureen (2011). "Honeymoons in Space," *New York Times*, December 13, 2011; www.nytimes.com/2011/12/14/opinion/dowd-honeymoons-in-space.html.

Krugman, Paul (2000). "Incidents from My Career," Technical report. Cambridge, MA: MIT; web.mit.edu/krugman/www/incidents.html.

Varian, Hal R. (1995). "How to Build an Economic Model in Your Spare Time," in Michael Szenberg (ed.), *Passion and Craft, How Economists Work*. Ann Arbor: University of Michigan Press. Also published in "How to Build an Economic Model in your Spare Time," *The American Economist* 41, no. 2 (Fall, 1997): 3–10

(2000). *Variants in Economic Theory: Selected Papers of Hal R. Varian*. Cheltenham: Edward Elgar; www.e-elgar.co.uk/action.lasso?-database=ElgarTitles.fp3 -layout=Website-response=Selection.html CDM+SerialNo=1033-search.

(2001). "What I've Learned about Writing Economics," *Journal of Economic Methodology* 8, no. 1: 129–132.

(2005). "How to Make a Scene," *Journal of Economic Education*, Taylor and Francis Journals, vol. 35, no. 4 (October): 383–390.

Varian, Hal R. and Carl Shapiro (1999). *Information Rules*, Harvard Business School Press, Boston.

28

Scaling Fortress Economics

Michelle J. White

My philosophy of economics has mainly involved how to get into and stay in the field. This essay gives some reminiscences of the bad old days and what it was like to be among the first women in academic economics.

Many economists have interesting stories about how and why they went into the field. Mine is that I was an undergraduate at Harvard during the 1960s. I didn't have a scholarship, so my parents were paying all the costs. While they were happy that I was at Harvard and ungrudging about the expense, they really wanted me to be able to support myself after I graduated. This could be by getting married at graduation or by getting a good job. I grew up in the "civil service suburbs" of Washington, DC, so a good job was defined as a government job with a professional rating. My parents pressured me to major in a field in which professional jobs were available

I am grateful to the Cheung Kong Graduate School of Business in Beijing, where I was an adjunct professor while writing this essay, and to Elyce Rotella for helpful feedback and some historical corrections.

to applicants with only a bachelor's degree. These fields included all the sciences, plus economics. At Harvard, students decide on a major field at the end of their freshman year. On entering college, I was planning to major in chemistry but quickly changed my mind. I thought about history, but it wasn't on the list. So I signed up to major in economics even though I had never taken an economics course, simply because it was the only social science on the federal government's list.

In those days, women students at Harvard were tolerated rather than welcomed, with their numbers limited to one-fifth of the student body. They were banned from most Harvard facilities and confined to inferior substitutes. In class, female students were thought to work harder but to be inevitably inferior to the best males. When I started taking economics classes, women students were even rarer and I was often the only one. This was good for my social life but isolated me from my female classmates. It was the beginning of my long experience of being one of very few women in a mainly male field. There were no female faculty members in economics or any female teaching assistants. But the lack of female instructors didn't make economics very different from other fields at the time.

My first exposure to economics research was writing my senior thesis, which was a study of the Teamsters' Union local in Boston. A family friend gave me an introduction to the head of the Boston local. He was flattered that a Harvard student was interested in the union, took me out to dinner so other union officials wouldn't hear what he said, and told me almost more than I wanted to know – including hints about unsolved crimes on the waterfront. He also gave me access to the local's records. My thesis discussed how union officials decided which firms to unionize and the factors that made unionization campaigns more likely to succeed. When I say that I discussed these issues, I mean words and tables, not regressions or statistical tests. I thought I did a great job but got rather tepid feedback from my adviser and the other readers.

Many of my female friends in college were a year ahead of me, and their experiences in making post-college plans were discouraging. One wanted to go to medical school, but applying required an interview and, at the interview, women applicants were asked whether they planned to have children. If they said yes, their applications were rejected because they would stay home to take care of their children and their medical training would be wasted. If they said no, their applications were rejected because they were weird and shouldn't become doctors. Another friend started a PhD program in history but found that women students were encouraged to drop out after a year or two, because there were no jobs for them if they finished their PhDs. Many of my classmates got married at graduation and went wherever their husbands' plans took them. Others took jobs that amounted to glorified secretarial positions. The message was that it was fine for women to do well in college, but academic achievement didn't open up any post-graduation opportunities.

I didn't think much about this at the time; it was just the way things were. Also, I was badly bitten by the travel bug and wanted to go everywhere. During my first summer after graduation, I got a grant to work for a Harvard research project in Tunisia. (I almost didn't get there because of the outbreak of the 1967 Arab-Israeli War. But fortunately for me, the war was quick.) The project was studying how new techniques in agriculture diffused among farmers who were illiterate. My part of the project was to examine the operations of the local agricultural cooperative that exported the farmers' main crop, which was oranges. My main challenge was to conduct interviews in French, which I hadn't studied since high school. It helped that I lived with a group of French-speaking students from the Tunisian agricultural university who were conducting the project's interviews with farmers. The students initially thought that I was very standoffish, but it took some time before I could understand and speak well enough to interact comfortably with them. The main conclusion of my study was that the cooperative was the farmers' worst enemy: it paid farmers based on the number of oranges they produced and therefore encouraged them to grow lots of small oranges. But prices in Europe were much higher for large oranges than small ones, so the cooperative should have been encouraging farmers to prune their trees and produce fewer, larger oranges. I couldn't explain why a farmer-owned organization didn't do a better job of representing farmers' interests.

I spent the next year in London, studying for a master's degree in economic history at the London School of Economics during the day and going to the opera and the theater at night. I didn't like the economic history program, which placed too much emphasis on collecting data from historical documents at the (cold!) public records office and too little on using economics to analyze it. I thought the best thing about the LSE was its proximity to Covent Garden, where I indulged heavily in cheap tickets. The following year, by then married to Lawrence White, I ventured further afield when we both took jobs in Pakistan working for the Harvard Development Advisory Service (DAS). This organization placed economists in the planning commissions of developing countries, to advise them on what government policies would encourage economic growth. Larry had just received his PhD in economics and his job was as a development adviser. My job was as a research assistant to the development advisers. The DAS offered me a job only when I started exploring the possibility of working for the US Agency for International Development in Pakistan. The director didn't like the idea of one spouse working for the Pakistanis while the other worked for the Americans.

In Pakistan, I studied the taxing and spending of Pakistani cities. The main local revenue source consisted of import taxes levied on food and anything else that entered cities from outside. These taxes were startlingly regressive. They also discouraged long-distance trade, since the taxes were paid when goods entered a city and generally not refunded when the goods left. On the expenditure side, cities were responsible for providing schools, water, and sanitation, but in fact they provided these services to only a few. Indoor water connections, for example, were provided in well-off neighborhoods, but poor neighborhoods lacked even public water taps. I wondered whether the favoritism shown to the wealthy reflected the fact that top local officials were appointed by the central government rather than elected.

Living in Pakistan made me conscious of how rules and customs that are accepted and unquestioned in one culture could be completely different in other cultures. Some of these differences seemed completely arbitrary. In the United States, alcohol was legal, but drugs like marijuana and hashish were banned, while in Pakistan, alcohol was illegal, but drugs were accepted. Pakistanis didn't eat pork because of the Islamic prohibition, and they also followed the Hindu prohibition and didn't eat beef. But other differences were more pernicious, such as *purdah* – the custom of keeping women at home to prevent them from being seen by men who are not their relatives. In the Pakistan government office complex where I worked, there were thousands of government employees, but I never saw another woman. Not only were all of the professionals men, but the secretaries, the cleaning staff, and the people who brought tea were also all men. In the bazaar, all the shopkeepers and all the customers were men; few women were on the streets at all. When I made the mistake of going into the old part of the city wearing a dress with bare legs below the knees, people threw stones at my legs. (I quickly acquired a new wardrobe!) Even wealthy and educated Pakistani women were in "semi-purdah." They went out of their houses, but only in cars driven by male relatives, and they shopped only in stores frequented by women like themselves. Although sex discrimination in the United States barred women from many occupations and seemed both inefficient and inequitable, it was far less restrictive than purdah.

I had planned to spend a year and a half in Pakistan but left in a hurry after six months, because articles in government-controlled newspapers accused the "Harvard group" of being Zionist spies. The DAS closed its operations in Pakistan and sent Larry and me to Indonesia, where it had another group of advisers. Indonesia was like a breath of fresh air compared with Pakistan. While Indonesia is also an Islamic country, most Indonesians at that time seemed to be Muslim in name only and there was no purdah. Women worked, women owned businesses, women were seen on the streets and shopped in the bazaars – actually, they ran most of the bazaar stalls. Many of the wives of Indonesian civil servants I met worked or ran businesses (often beauty salons), because their husbands' government jobs were prestigious but poorly paid, and they needed to earn money to support their families. At the education planning project where I worked, many of the staff were women. The economy was less subject to government control than in Pakistan, where no investment project proceeded without government approval. Of course, not everything was rosy – a civil war and a period of hyperinflation had just ended and corruption was widespread. When I went to the port to pick up my shipment of household goods from Pakistan, I needed a dozen signatures and paid a dozen bribes.

While in Pakistan and Indonesia, I decided to apply to PhD programs in economics. (Amazingly, the GRE was offered in Islamabad.) Why did I decide to go to grad school in economics? One reason was that I realized I could collect facts and data but I had no idea how to analyze them. Another was that, unlike most men in the same situation, I didn't have a lot of good alternatives. I might have obtained that professionally rated job in the federal government, but in those days I wouldn't have been hired on Wall Street or even at a private firm. But the main reason is that I was inspired by the beginnings of the feminist movement to push the boundaries. I became aware of the women's liberation movement around that time, because someone gave me a copy of Betty Friedan's *The Feminist Mystique*. The book really resonated with me and made me rethink many aspects of my environment and my own behavior. Why were women in Pakistan kept in purdah? Why did women in Indonesia have better lives than those in Pakistan? Back in the United States, why did married women follow their husbands around? Why did universities like Harvard bar women students from its libraries and residence halls, while providing inferior substitutes? Why did law schools and medical schools admit so few women? Why shouldn't women get PhDs and take faculty positions on an equal basis with men?

Larry was offered an assistant professor position at Princeton, so I applied for admission to the PhD program in economics at Princeton. The department responded with a suggestion that I apply to Rutgers instead, where another faculty member's wife had recently received her PhD. The concern seemed to be that the roles of graduate student and faculty wife wouldn't mix very well and it would be awkward if I did badly. But I persisted and was admitted, although without the normal financial aid. Princeton at that time had been admitting women as graduate students for a few years, although it had just started admitting women at the undergraduate level. The Economics Department had just hired its first woman faculty member, but there weren't any other women in my PhD class after the first year. The facilities were also a reminder that women were rare. The economics building at Princeton in those days had two floors and a basement, and the classroom for the first-year PhD courses was on the top floor. Each floor had a men's room, but the only women's room was in the basement. So while my classmates strolled to the men's room between classes, I ran to the basement.

I enjoyed graduate school after the first couple of months of filling gaps in my mathematical background. Fortunately I did well and the department rewarded me by giving me an Earhart Foundation Fellowship for my second year. (No one told me about the Earhart Foundation's conservative bent.) But I was somewhat disappointed by the limitations of economic analysis – many of the issues that had interested me in Pakistan and Indonesia seemed to fall outside the boundaries of economics as they were then defined.

I had intended to specialize in development economics, but when I entered the PhD program, I agreed not to put myself in a position where Larry would evaluate my performance. Since he taught development economics, I needed to find a different area. So I gravitated toward the new field of urban economics. One of the founders of the field, Edwin Mills, had just moved to Princeton and he attracted a lively group of graduate students to work in the area. Several of us became interested in extending urban economics from central cities to the suburbs. My dissertation was a model of suburban local government behavior in which local officials made zoning and land use decisions. I assumed that local officials behaved like managers of profit-maximizing firms with market power and that they treated current residents/voters like shareholders. The model predicted that local officials would choose whatever land uses maximized additional property taxes paid minus the additional costs of providing local public services. Existing residents of the jurisdiction gained from this policy, since the surplus of revenues over expenditures generated by new development allowed local governments to lower property taxes or expand public services. But the model implied that apartments would be scarce in the suburbs, since they generate relatively little in property tax revenues and force local governments to build expensive new schools. Thus, while suburban local governments acted in the interest of their residents, their choices harmed nonresidents. The model's predictions seemed to work well, at least for suburban areas in the Northeast. The results suggested that inefficient behavior by local governments didn't just occur in countries like Pakistan.

When I went on the job market in 1972–1973, the research-oriented economics departments had very few women faculty members. The 1972 Committee on the Status of Women in the Economics Profession report claims that the departments in the "Chairman's Group" had an average of 1.2 woman faculty members per department, but I don't recall that there were any women in the departments where I interviewed.[1] I focused my job search on the Philadelphia–New York area and accepted an assistant professor offer from the Penn Economics Department, where I became the only woman in a fifty-person department. I liked the idea that I was an affirmative action hire, part of the effort to begin making up for past discrimination against women in academia. But my colleagues at Penn claim that there was no pressure on the department to hire women at that time.

I loved being at Penn. My first day in the department, one of the woman graduate students in economics, Elyce Rotella, knocked on my door and we became friends for life. Also the Regional Science Department, which was in the same building, had recently hired its first woman faculty member, Janice Madden, and we also became close friends. (As the only women faculty members in our respective departments, we were often mistaken for each other.) I got a lot of support from some of my senior colleagues, particularly Jere Behrman and Bob Pollak. I also interacted with faculty members in other departments at Penn, including the Public Policy Program, the Department of Urban Planning, the Department of Regional Science, and the Business and Law Schools. But I had difficulty breaking into (even finding out about) networks in my field. There was no senior faculty member in urban economics at Penn who might have given me advice. I wasn't invited to any small conferences and I didn't give more than a talk or two at other universities. None of this bothered me particularly, but I didn't realize at the time how important it was to get to know people in my field at other universities.

Tenure clocks ticked faster in those days, and I came up for tenure in the fall of my fifth year. I didn't get it. But I had published enough not to perish and, going on the market again, I received several offers. I moved the following year to NYU, where I became one of two women faculty members in the Economics Department of the Business School (now the Stern School). I think that the main negative effect of not getting tenure is that, afterward,

I never thought of any job as permanent even if it was tenured. That meant I tried to be a good citizen of my own department and a good citizen of the profession but tended to avoid getting involved in wider university activities or university governance.

I got divorced around that time, and later Roger Gordon and I got married. Also, I plunged into my own urban economics lesson by buying two lofts in an old factory building near NYU. They had most recently been used as a photographer's studio and a false teeth factory. The false teeth factory still contained the remains of a large kiln used for firing the teeth, complete with blackened walls and burned floors. I intended to renovate both, live in one, and rent the other. My first task after buying them was to set off half a dozen bug bombs to kill the large cockroach population. I came back a few days later to find the floors carpeted with dead roaches, but the walls still inhabited by live ones. So Roger and I enthusiastically proceeded to demolish everything. (Roger was surprisingly good wielding a crowbar.) This solved the roach problem but left us without a kitchen or bathroom. I converted the false teeth factory into a work-live space and found tenants who were starting a business selling music for advertisements, which they produced using a computerized piano instead of an orchestra. The building needed a new elevator, which meant a year of walking up many flights of stairs while construction proceeded. The lack of an elevator caused my tenants to go on a rent strike, which completely upset my financial plans. Eventually the elevator was finished, the tenants started paying rent again, and I was able to do the construction work on my own floor. But it took many years, much investment in construction and reconstruction, the hiring of "expeditors" to bribe the building inspectors, and lots of lawsuits before the lofts were legally converted from industrial to residential use. Inefficiency and corruption weren't features just of governments in developing countries.

Roger worked at Bell Laboratories in northern New Jersey while I was at NYU, but when AT&T lost its telephone monopoly, the Labs decided that it no longer needed economists. So in 1984 we moved together to the Economics Department at the University of Michigan, Ann Arbor. At Michigan, there was one other woman faculty member, Eva Mueller, who soon retired. The Michigan Economics Department remained almost entirely male for years, despite our best efforts to hire women. Being located in a small city made it easy for the department to hire men with trailing spouses but difficult to hire women because their spouses often had career demands that couldn't be satisfied. Eventually we succeeded, mainly by finding women economists with trailing spouses.

During the mid-1980s, I was on the board of the American Economic Association's Committee on the Status of Women in the Economics Profession. At that time, male students getting PhDs in economics tended to take academic jobs, while their female classmates more commonly took nonacademic jobs. Also, almost no economics journals had woman editors and very few had even a single woman on their editorial boards. The lack of women in these positions seemed both to discourage women economists from entering academia and to reduce their chances of success if they did. I persuaded Barbara Bergmann, who was then the chair of CSWEP, to pursue an initiative pressuring journals to appoint women to their editorial boards and organizations such as the National Bureau of Economic Research to appoint women as research affiliates. The initiative, however, was a complete failure.

My research in these years shifted gradually from mainly urban economics to mainly law and economics. The field of law and economics was just getting started at this time. Richard Posner's book, *Economic Analysis of Law*, had been published a few years earlier, and it raised new economic questions about the common law fields of torts, contracts, and property. The field attracted me because it took in the background behind the economy – the laws and customs that determine how efficiently individuals and firms behave and how well markets function. I liked the fact that the field was interdisciplinary and that almost no question was considered to be out-of-bounds. What I didn't like about the field was the commonly held view that the law encouraged parties to behave efficiently. My view was that law has mixed effects at best and often encourages inefficient behavior. I also didn't like the fact that – as usual – there were very few women in the field.

But working in an interdisciplinary field has its challenges. After writing my first paper on personal bankruptcy, I asked a bankruptcy law professor who was visiting Michigan to read the paper and give me comments. I got back a twenty-eight-page single-spaced set of comments criticizing the paper paragraph by paragraph – the comments ran longer than the paper! At the end of the comments, the law professor advised that I drop the topic completely and find a new area of research. Later, the same law professor prevented me from getting a research grant and tried to prevent an article of mine on bankruptcy from being published in a law review. The problem wasn't just the difficulty of communication across disciplines, but the fact that many law professors were extremely hostile to economics.

While being married to a colleague in the same department had drawbacks, one advantage was that Roger and I could take leaves together. In 1986 we went to Beijing to teach for a semester in a master's degree program sponsored by the Ford Foundation and the American Economic Association. I taught micro and Roger taught macro. I had to learn to *speak slowly and clearly*, since most of the students had never been taught in English before. The students were the best we ever had; they had been picked to attend the program from a dozen of the top Chinese universities. They worked very hard – most of them had learned all the material in the textbooks we ordered by the time we arrived. I enjoyed applying in my teaching what we learned about the Chinese economy just from being there. Many Chinese products were of low quality; for example, store clerks would individually test lightbulbs before selling them and often had to try several before finding one that worked. Bicycle tires leaked incessantly, so that we carried a large air pump whenever we rode our bikes. Lamps sometimes exploded when first turned on. So I discussed incentives in a market system for producers to improve quality and why these incentives didn't exist in the Chinese economic system. I also discussed the history of slavery in the United States and the similarities between it and the Chinese system of assigning workers to employers. Our Chinese students were assigned as employees to their universities and had no right to quit. As graduate students, they lived three to a dormitory room and, when they finished their PhDs, they would still have to live two to a dorm room.

We gradually learned that many of our students wanted to apply to PhD programs in the United States and Canada – not surprising given that their opportunities in China were so limited. So when Roger and I returned home, we contacted many PhD programs in economics to find out which ones would admit Chinese students with financial aid during the first year. We then advised students to apply to these programs, and we wrote many, many letters of recommendation. Eventually about half of our Chinese students enrolled in PhD programs abroad. The students have been extremely successful, some as professors in the United States and China, some in government in China, and many in business and finance. We have followed their careers with pride, staying in touch with many of them, giving advice where we could, and greatly enjoying getting together with them for reunions. Two of our students have become close friends and greatly enriched our lives, Wei Li and Xiaohong Chen.

My research in law and economics included topics in the core areas of torts and property law, but I also started working on bankruptcy, which became my special area of interest. This happened entirely by chance. John Shoven gave a seminar at NYU on his research on corporate bankruptcy. I found the subject of bankruptcy intriguing, because it seemed central to how economies operate. All introductory economics textbooks discuss how markets move from short-run to long-run equilibrium because more efficient firms drive less efficient firms out of business, leaving only those firms that produce at minimum average cost. Bankruptcy is the legal mechanism by which this transition occurs, but economists knew very little about it. My first papers concerned whether the bankruptcy process actually shuts down only firms that are inefficient. Because financial distress and bankruptcy can occur for a variety of reasons, firms in bankruptcy can be either efficient or inefficient, and it is often difficult to determine which firms fit which category. I found that bankruptcy law sometimes results in inefficient firms being saved and sometimes in efficient firms being shut down, with the specifics of the law affecting the importance of each type of error.

From corporate bankruptcy, I moved to thinking about personal bankruptcy. At the time, no household-level data sets included information on whether households had filed for bankruptcy. So I worked on a paper that examined whether households would gain financially from filing – which I could study without knowing whether they had actually filed. Because US bankruptcy law does not require borrowers to repay from future income and some states have generous exemptions for assets, I found that up to one-third of US households could gain financially from filing. I wrote up these results in an article called "Why Don't More Households File for Bankruptcy?"

I also looked for opportunities to create household-level data on bankruptcy filings and approached some of the household surveys about the possibility of adding questions on bankruptcy. The Survey of Consumer Finance turned me down, because they thought that asking questions about bankruptcy would embarrass respondents and reduce the quality of responses to other questions.[2] But the Panel Survey of Income Dynamics was interested, and it included questions about bankruptcy in the 1996 wave. I worked with the PSID staff to develop a module on financial distress that led gently from questions about difficulty in paying bills to questions about calls from credit collectors to a retrospective question on bankruptcy – an approach that we hoped would prevent embarrassment. These data were the basis for a paper explaining households' bankruptcy filing decisions. The results showed that households behaved rationally in making bankruptcy decisions – they were more likely to file if their financial gain was higher.

Lack of data on bankruptcy filings also led me to start thinking about other effects of bankruptcy law – particularly how bankruptcy law affects credit markets. Having the right to file for bankruptcy reduces the downside risk that debtors face when they borrow, because they can have their debts discharged in bankruptcy if their ability to repay turns out to be low. Risk-averse debtors therefore demand more credit when there is a bankruptcy procedure. But having a bankruptcy procedure also increases default, causing lenders to reduce credit supply. I thought these predictions could be tested. I searched for a coauthor in the usual economist's way, by talking about the project, and eventually I linked up with Karl Scholz and Reint Gropp. Our empirical work made use of the fact that states in the United States determine the maximum value of assets that debtors are allowed to keep in bankruptcy and these exemption limits vary widely across states. We found that in states with higher asset exemptions, lenders accommodate the increase in demand for credit by richer households but don't accommodate the increase in demand by poorer households, so that credit is redistributed from poor to rich. Thus, while policy makers adopt high bankruptcy exemptions in order to help poor borrowers, the actual effect of the policy is the opposite.

Exploring the effects of bankruptcy law has become a popular area of research, which I find very gratifying. My own recent papers explore the effect of bankruptcy law on whether individuals become self-employed and on whether financially distressed homeowners default on their mortgages. Other researchers have examined the effect of bankruptcy law on divorce rates (there are more divorces in high-exemption states), on whether people buy health insurance (more people go without health insurance in high-exemption states), on the variability of consumption (it's lower in states with higher bankruptcy exemptions), and on mortality (bankruptcy filers who partially repay their debts using a repayment plan live longer).

I also enjoy writing papers on policy issues in urban economics that seem important but neglected by economists. One study, with Richard Green, examined whether homeowning – which is highly subsidized by the federal government – generates any economic benefits. We did not expect to find anything when we started the project, but in fact found evidence that children of homeowners are more successful than children of renters – they are more likely to graduate from high school, less likely to have children of their own as teenagers, and less likely to be arrested. In another study, I examined the negative externalities imposed by large vehicles (pickup trucks and SUVs) on occupants of small vehicles, motorcyclists, bicyclists, and pedestrians. I found that while driving a large vehicle increases safety for the large vehicle's occupants, this safety gain comes at the cost of four lives lost outside the vehicle for each life saved inside.

The field of law and economics includes professors at law schools, economics departments, and business schools. A professional organization for the field – the American Law and Economics Association – was organized in 1990 and the first ALEA conference was held at the same time. I heard about the conference after the program was organized but sent in a paper anyway and it was accepted. At the business meeting, the members voted on a proposed charter for the organization and on a proposed slate of officers and directors. None of the proposed officers or directors was female. A woman law professor proposed an amendment that added three additional slots to the board of directors and nominated three women – including myself – for the additional slots. No one spoke up against the amendment, so it was adopted and, through this back door, I became one of the original directors of ALEA. I attended the ALEA conferences and presented a paper every year, which helped me get to know others in the field, become familiar with the range of topics that others were working on, and find an audience for my own research. Much later, I became the second woman to serve as president of ALEA, and I had the nerve-racking but fun experience of organizing the first and only ALEA conference to be held in San Diego.

As I indicated, the range of problems that economic theory could examine when I was in graduate school seemed quite limited. Empirical work was also limited in those days, since data sets were small and discrete choices couldn't be handled properly. Since then, the adoption of game theory has tremendously broadened the types of questions that economists can ask, economics has been applied to the behavior of governments as well as to that of firms and households, and behavioral economics has introduced the idea that people don't always behave rationally. Economists now study religion, culture, law, and most everything else. Empirical work has similarly advanced, since we now have a broad array of econometric tools and powerful computers that allow us to use huge data sets. All of these advances have posed something of a challenge for economists of my generation to keep up with (I sometimes wish I could start over). But the reward is being able to ask questions and use data that I could only dream of in the past. In my most recent work, with Wenli Li, we start with millions of mortgage and credit records at the individual household level.

It was only after Roger and I moved to the University of California, San Diego that I began to have more than a few female colleagues. The Economics Department at UCSD had two women faculty members when I moved there in 2001 but has since grown to nine women out of forty-two. I'm glad to have lasted long enough to progress from being a token to being a member of a minority. I've also really enjoyed seeing women economists finally become editors of prestigious journals and program directors at NBER, receive the Clark Medal and the Nobel Prize, and get superstar treatment. But I still wonder how long it will take for women economists to get to parity.

Notes

1 See www.aeaweb.org/committees/cswep/annual_reports/1972_CSWEP_Annual_Report.pdf.
2 A few years later, the Survey of Consumer Finance also introduced bankruptcy questions.

29

The Accidental Economist

Marina v. N. Whitman

I had a standard answer to the question with which adults love to torture adolescents: "What do you want to be/do when you grow up?" "I don't know," I would reply, "but I do know two things I won't do: marry an academic or become one myself." So what happened?

EARLY IMPRINTS

Like most accounts of "how I came to be what I am," mine begins with my parents and the environment, or environments – for they went their separate ways before I reached my third birthday – in which they immersed me. John von Neumann and his bride, Mariette, were both privileged, protected children of Budapest's Jewish but fully assimilated haute bourgeoisie, born at a time when that city was a flourishing second capital of the Austro-Hungarian Empire. This golden age came to an abrupt end with the shock of the First World War and its aftermath: the breakup of the Empire, the 133 days of "Red Terror" brought on by a Communist coup and the declaration of the Soviet Hungarian Republic, and the creeping anti-Semitism that characterized the regime of Admiral Horthy, who led a successful counter-coup and was installed as head of state. He held that position until 1944, by which time my parents had re-created their lives in the new world across the Atlantic.

My father, already a precocious star in the world of mathematics, accepted a Rockefeller Foundation teaching fellowship at Princeton in 1930, dividing his time between there and Berlin, for the most pragmatic of reasons. He had calculated that the likelihood of moving up the academic ladder was greater in the United States than in Germany, where he had begun his academic career and where full professorships were few and far between. My mother, spoiled, glamorous, and always ready for adventure, leapt at the opportunity to create a life with her handsome, brilliant new husband beyond the reach of her overprotective parents. By the time von Neumann became one of the founding members of the Institute for Advanced Study in 1933, though, Hitler was in power and the Nazis had passed laws mandating the firing of all civil servants, including university professors, of non-Aryan background.

Now there was no turning back. Throughout the 1930s, my father watched Europe "relapsing into the Dark Ages" and became convinced that only an Allied victory, led by the United States, could save civilization from destruction by the spread of totalitarianism from the right: Nazism and Fascism. Once that battle had been won, he became equally convinced that the threat now came from totalitarianism on the left, in the form of Soviet Communism. Haunted by memories of the "Red Terror" that had forced his family into brief exile during his adolescence, he became a super–Cold War hawk, even advocating preventive war against the Soviet Union before it, too, acquired the ultimate weapon.

My childhood played out against the background of my parents' all-out commitment to the Allied war effort – a commitment shared by the new partners each had acquired very quickly after their divorce. My father shuttled between Princeton and Los Alamos, where he played a major role in the Manhattan Project, in addition to working on the development of the stored-program electronic computer under the auspices of the army's Aberdeen Proving Ground in Maryland, with a secret side trip to England to apply the insights of the mini-max theorem to the problem of sweeping German mines in the English Channel. My mother, meanwhile, having accompanied her American husband to Cambridge, where he had been recruited to work at MIT's Radiation Laboratory, soon abandoned her life of leisure in favor of joining the army of Rosie the Riveters, assembling radar sets. She soon rose to foreman and, within the same year, joined her husband at Rad Lab, where she became the supervisor in charge of training women technicians.

My parents not only devoted their superhuman energies to the Allied war effort, they also tackled head-on some of the eruptions of man's inhumanity to man that characterized the times. My father pulled every string he could find, both in Princeton and in Washington, to help other Jewish intellectuals escape from Europe and to find them jobs here – the promise of a job being a prerequisite to acquiring the means of salvation, a US visa. My mother, told by her superiors to put to a vote of her supervisees the question of whether they would be willing to have "negroes" as co-workers, marshaled the force of her personality, combined with a judicious use of Hungarian profanity, to make sure that the winning vote was "yes."

After the war, cosmopolitanism suffused family life in the households of both my parents. Gathered around my father's dinner table were not only such eminent mathematicians and physicists as Edward Teller and Eugene Wigner, but also Europeans from the world of arts and letters like Arthur Koestler and Emery Reves, friend and publisher of Winston Churchill. Oskar Morgenstern, a non-Jewish refugee on principle from Hitler's Austria and my father's *Theory of Games*[1] coauthor, courted his bride in our living room. During those same early postwar years, when my mother had become the first employee of Brookhaven National Laboratory and its ambassador and hostess-in-chief, her Long Island home became the gathering place for visiting scientists from every corner of the earth.

CHOICES AND MORE CHOICES

So what has this background to do with the career path I ultimately took? At the most basic level, it enabled me to escape the "1950s trap" that ensnared so many of my female contemporaries, indoctrinating them from childhood in the belief that their only choice was that of full-time housewife or childless – and most likely unmarried – professional woman. On the contrary, my father impressed on me, virtually from my earliest conscious moment, the moral imperative of making full use of whatever intellectual capacities we were endowed with, whether man or woman, paid or unpaid. My mother, on the other hand, taught by example, combining brainpower and feminine charm to create a lifelong career that she made up as she went along.

My father's focus on intellectual achievement made him a strong opponent of my early marriage, fearing that it would condemn me to the housewife trap, an opposition that gained moral authority from the fact that he was dying at the time. Much of the competitive drive that has infused every stage of my career was born of the desire to prove him wrong, to show his reproachful ghost that I had managed to combine the marriage and family I craved with the professional achievements he had feared I was denying myself. At the same time, I was determined to escape from under the shadow of a world-famous genius parent, to establish an independent identity.

A year of working as a glorified clerk at the Educational Testing Service in Princeton persuaded me that my summa from Radcliffe in political theory was an inadequate base for a meaningful career and that further training in a more "practical" area was essential. But, given my determination to escape my father's shadow, what on earth made me choose economics, a field in which he had made more significant contributions than I could ever hope to? The answer is twofold. First, I didn't actually intend to become an academic economist. My initial goal was to get two master's degrees, one in economics and one in journalism, with a vision of writing articles for the business pages of the *New York Times*, the *Washington Post*, or the *Economist*. It was pretty much a toss-up that I chose to pursue the degree in economics first.

It wasn't until late in my first graduate year at Columbia that Gary Becker, in whose microeconomics course I had done surprisingly well, asked me if I had considered pursuing a PhD in economics. If so, he said, he was in a position to offer me an excellent award, the Earhart Fellowship. The only requirement imposed by its conservative donor was that I evince support for a free-market system. By that time, I had begun to rethink my dual-degree career plan, partly because it might be more interesting to participate in the shaping of economic ideas and policies than simply to write about them and also because the peripatetic life of a journalist didn't seem to combine well with family life. And a predilection for a nonstatist form of economic organization came naturally to me, grounded in my parents' conservative views and nurtured by my own study of political philosophy. So with no more reflection than a "Sure, why not?" the die was cast.

The other part of the answer lies in my incredible ignorance and naiveté at that stage of my life. Having somehow talked my way into Columbia's graduate program with nothing more than Harvard's Ec 1 under my belt, I had simply never heard of the turnpike theorem and knew nothing about the role of game theory in economics. I knew about my father's contributions to physics and to what has become computer science, but the fact that in choosing the economics route I was treading on dangerous ground never occurred to me.

Although my parents' impact on my career was primarily positive, it had its negative aspects. I hold the fact that I am von Neumann's daughter directly responsible for a degree of mathematical illiteracy that no first-year graduate student could get away with today. My experience in the first term of calculus (Calculus 1a) at Harvard was uneventful. But, just after the term ended, I had a hallway encounter with Garrett Birkhoff, chairman of the Harvard Math Department and a renowned mathematician who had coauthored articles with my father. Thinking that he was making small talk, he commented, "Well, Marina, I'm glad to see that you've upheld the family honor by getting an A in calculus." "Good God," I thought to myself, "what would happen to the family honor if I were ever to get an A minus?"

The result was that I never again took a math course for credit, though I did work my way through R. G. D. Allen's *Mathematical Analysis for Economists*[2] while giving my firstborn his midnight bottle and audited a course in matrix algebra at Carnegie Mellon when I was teaching at Pitt. To my delight, I discovered recently that Marty Feldstein's mathematics training at Harvard was identical to mine. Peter Kenen was way ahead of us; he actually finished Calculus 1b as well. So now the secret is out, and today's graduate students can roll their eyes in astonishment.

My training in the other major tool set economists are expected to have under their belts, statistics and econometrics, was every bit as inadequate. The single graduate course in statistics available in Columbia's Economics Department while I was there was taught by F. C. Mills, a great man in his day but then in his final year of teaching before heading into overdue retirement. The very next year, Jacob Mincer arrived and completely revamped the statistics course, bringing it up to the cutting edge, but by then I had passed my comprehensive exam and moved on. I eventually audited an econometrics course taught by one of my colleagues at Pitt, but the gap was never adequately filled.

My decision to concentrate in international economics, again, arose from considerations both intellectual and practical. As the child of émigré parents with cosmopolitan perspectives and networks, who spent my childhood years focusing their supercharged energies on ensuring victory for the forces of light in a global conflict, I had always been fascinated by relationships among nations and the factors that rendered them either peaceful or hostile. Although I had long since abandoned the naive vision of world government that had led me to join the World Federalists during my high school days, I had already developed an instinctive preference for open economies and freedom of transactions across international boundaries.

My choice of specialty was bolstered by the fact that all the teachers of international economics I encountered at Columbia – Ragnar Nurkse, my original dissertation supervisor; Albert Hirschman, who took over after Nurkse's sudden and untimely death; and the newly minted Peter Kenen, who became a valued informal adviser while I was in the writing stage – took me seriously as a potential teacher and scholar in the field. This was in contrast to several distinguished faculty members in other areas of economics, who made clear to me that they felt it was a waste of time to invest in a female student who would almost certainly abandon a serious career commitment in favor of husband and children. The dissertation Hirschman and Kenen mentored looked at the effectiveness of public funds – from both the United States and international institutions – in stimulating private investment in developing countries. In it, I combined my focus on international issues with my emerging interest in examining interactions between the public and private sectors. With Kenen's advice guiding my revisions, I turned this thesis into a book published by the Princeton University Press.[3]

TEACHING, RESEARCH, AND PRACTICE INSIDE THE BELTWAY

When my husband accepted an appointment in the English Department at the University of Pittsburgh, whose ambitious chancellor had gotten financial backing from the Mellon family to raise that streetcar college to the level of a nationally recognized research university, I went along as the trailing spouse. My dissertation completed, I was looking around for something to do when I was lucky enough to be taken on as a cleanup researcher by two leading regional economists, Ben Chinitz and Edgar Hoover, who were trying to complete a multivolume study of the Pittsburgh region. I assembled the final volume from the bits and pieces of research left behind by the study's participants when the money ran out and they returned to their home universities, prompting me to quip that I had written one more book in the field of regional economics than I had read. [4]

When Hoover and Chinitz returned full time to their positions in Pitt's Economics Department they took me along with them as an instructor, blithely ignoring the university's strict antinepotism rule; by the time the HR Department discovered this violation, I was too entrenched to be uprooted. The following year, when the senior professor in international economics dropped dead of a heart attack in the departmental office on the first day of the fall term, I found myself responsible for teaching the foundation courses in the field.

Having tested my own understanding of the basics by mentally correcting the proofing errors in the first edition of Charles Kindleberger's *International Economics* textbook during my first year as a graduate student, I turned to the next edition as the underpinning for my own undergraduate course.[5] This approach, standard at the time, focused primarily on the current account in the balance of payments, with various types of capital movements treated almost as an afterthought rather being integrated into a full equilibrium model. At the graduate level, I teamed up with my colleague Jerry Wells to teach a course on international trade and economic development. Jerry, a development economist who had written his dissertation at Michigan under Wolfgang Stolper, of Stolper-Samuelson fame, had done his field research studying agriculture in Nigeria. Our course stressed the positive contributions of trade to economic development and the resulting advantages of policies that increased a developing country's openness to such transactions. At a time when the *dependencia* theory of Raul Prebisch and others, urging developing countries to develop self-sufficiency in manufactured goods and reduce dependence on the outside world, held sway, this was a distinctly contrarian view for a development economist, but one that Jerry embraced courageously and enthusiastically.

Two things happened in the early 1970s to change my approach to understanding, teaching, and writing about international economics. Most crucially, I was plunged into the real world of economic policy making three times in quick succession: first as a senior staff economist at the Council of Economic Advisers, covering international economic issues; then as a member of the ill-fated Price Commission that grew out of President Nixon's New Economic Policy announced on August 15, 1971, a date best remembered for the closing of the "gold window" that marked the end of the Bretton Woods system; and finally as one of the three members of the CEA, where my remit included both the international economy and the wage-price controls program.

The most intellectually stimulating project I was involved in during this last assignment was the effort, led by Paul Volcker, to design an international monetary system to replace the now-defunct Bretton Woods arrangements. Our suggestions foundered on the clash of divergent national interests, and the world defaulted to a disorderly non-system of managed floats. But the problems our proposal was designed to relieve – by instituting symmetrical pressures for adjustment on surplus as well as deficit countries and reducing the instabilities inherent in the use of a national currency, the dollar, as the primary source of international reserves – continue to plague international currency relationships today.

These Washington assignments gave me a crash course in the intricate web of feedbacks between policies aimed at dealing with problems of the domestic economy and those directed at supporting our goals in the international trade and payments arena. I also learned more than I could have imagined about the political constraints on economic policy making, about the law of unintended consequences, and about the need to balance not only the interests of the United States against those of other nations but also those of the myriad departments and agencies of our own government, each fiercely defending its own turf and parochial interests.

How to organize this hard-won wisdom coherently enough to communicate at least some of its essence to students posed a real conundrum for me as I returned to academic life. By a stroke of luck, I found a useful organizing framework in Bob Stern's just-published (1973) book, *The Balance of Payments*.[6] To me, at least, his approach was revolutionary, and far more realistic than the one I had absorbed in graduate school and had incorporated into my own teaching ever since. Rather than analyzing international economic interactions using what was essentially a closed-economy model with the current account tacked on, adding the term $(X - M)$ to the definition of national income, Stern outlined a full-fledged model of an open economy, incorporating as endogenous shifts in both the current and capital accounts. Rather than defining balance-of-payments equilibrium in terms of a zero balance on current account, as I had absorbed from Kindleberger, he defined it as zero net flows of "accommodating transactions" or balancing items, that is, short-term flows of official capital and movements of international reserves. Finally, he incorporated into what was effectively a graduate-level textbook Mundell's two-instrument solution to achieving both internal and external balance under different exchange rate systems. Eureka!

My style of research was similarly formed by a combination of my natural way of thinking and the glaring gaps in my training in the standard tools of economic research. During my first few years of teaching, before my forays into government, I paid my dues to quantitative empirical analysis. But in the first such effort, an article in the *Journal of Money, Credit, and Banking* titled "Economic Openness and International Financial Flows,"[7] Peter Kenen kindly ran the rank correlations my analysis required because I was making such heavy weather of the task. In the early 1970s a junior colleague, Norman Miller, and I published a series of articles that attempted to separate outflows of portfolio capital from the United States into their stock and flow components. Again, it was someone else (in this case, Miller) who bore the brunt of the statistical work. The statistical techniques we used never went beyond simple OLS regressions; our work was innocent of any attention to issues of robustness, colinearity, endogeneity, or any of the other problems that empirical work today must wrestle with. Yet our articles were accepted by the *Quarterly Journal of Economics*[8] and the *Journal of Finance*[9] without even a requirement to "revise and resubmit." How times have changed!

I have, of course, used mathematical models to illustrate and develop ideas in many of my papers. But these were always simple systems of linear equations analyzing equilibrium states, and they did not require anything more than algebra and the techniques of simple differentiation I had learned in Calculus 1a. When dynamics were involved, I invariably reverted to verbal and/or graphical descriptions of the analysis. For me, mathematical modeling has always remained a "second language" into which I have had to painstakingly translate my economic insights.

I have made my primary contributions to the economic literature in the form of synthesis: absorbing bits and pieces from the theoretical and empirical work of others and pulling them together to discern and describe patterns that add up to a coherent whole. Sometimes the result has been to show how different models relate to one another; at others, it has been to develop an integrated explanation of apparently unrelated developments in the real world. One early synthesis was of various contributions to the targets-and-instruments literature on the assignment of macroeconomic policies in *Policies for Internal and External Balance* (1970).[10] In "Global Monetarism and the Monetary Approach to the Balance of Payments" (1975),[11] I provided a formal reconciliation of the then-conventional Keynesian approach to balance-of-payments analysis with the extreme assumptions of "global monetarism," laying bare their radically different implications for policy. Many years later, after I had circled back to the academic world at the University of Michigan, my book *New World, New Rules* (1999)[12] offered an underlying explanation for the transformation of the successful large American corporation from the secure, paternalistic, and globally dominant organization of the 1950s and 1960s into the lean, mean global competitor it had become by the century's end. If I deserve designation as an "eminent economist," it is works like these that provide the core of my intellectual contribution to the field.

LESSONS LEARNED

My reputation rests partly, of course, on the fact that I have plied the economist's trade in a variety of venues, government and business as well as academe. I have always regarded the discipline of economics as a sort of mental filing cabinet that enables its practitioners to break a complex question into its component parts, discard inessential details, and then reassemble the pieces in an orderly way to arrive at an answer or solution. I first tested the usefulness of this filing cabinet, as well as my own powers of communication and persuasion, when I ventured out of the classroom and the professional journals into the world of economic policy making inside the Beltway. This was a path that numerous economists had trod before me, with various degrees of success and satisfaction.

I took away from my own government experience a hard-won realism about real-world economic policies and those who formulate them, lessons that can be summarized in three observations. The first is that a technocrat can't expect to bring about dramatic changes in policy; if one moves the discussion a degree or two in one direction or another, that's a substantial accomplishment. Second, any success is bound to be covered with so many fingerprints as to make finding the partial derivative of one individual contribution impossible. Finally, I discovered that many of my achievements were negative; more than once I went home at night satisfied that I had prevented a move in the wrong direction. It was in this spirit of minimizing harm that I accepted membership on President Nixon's Price Commission, despite the fact that every economist's nerve in my body screamed that price controls were a terrible idea. Someone was going to fill the role, I told myself, and maybe I could help hold down the economic distortions such a program was bound to create.

Despite recognizing these inherent limitations on my effectiveness, I enjoyed every minute of my time as a member of the CEA, and it was with real regret that I resigned once the mounting evidence no longer allowed me to relegate to the back of my mind the growing evidence that the president himself was implicated in the Watergate scandal. But the satisfactions of the job did not come without costs. The contradiction inherent in the very existence of the CEA was spelled out by Carl Christ in his highly critical review of the 1973 Economic Report of the President: "[T]he report is inherently a somewhat schizoid document. It is intended to serve two purposes that are not entirely compatible – first to function as an apology for or celebration of the President's economic program, and second, to constitute a professional job of economic analysis and policy recommendation."[13] Every CEA, both before and since the one I served on, has been confronted by this dilemma, and none has fully resolved it.

The ambiguity of the CEA's role is but one example of a larger point. An economist, or any expert in a particular field, can be an adviser or shaper of policy inside an organization, be it an agency of government or a private company, or an outside critic, as academics generally are. Both are honorable roles, and I have played both at different times in my career. But one cannot fulfill both functions at the same time. You can argue as hard as you can for your position inside an organization. But once a decision has been taken, there is no alternative except either to support the organization's view on an issue or, if the disagreement is fundamental enough, to resign. Academic freedom exists only for academics; under any other circumstances, public criticism of or disagreement with the official position is bound to destroy one's credibility and effectiveness inside an organization. More than one distinguished economist has come a cropper by failing to recognize this home truth.

LIFE IN THE CORPORATE WORLD

I was enjoying a sabbatical blissfully free of responsibilities at the Center for Advanced Study in the Behavioral Sciences on the Stanford campus – the fellows seemed to devote a lot of energy to volleyball and spouse swapping, both of which activities Bob and I watched from the sidelines – when Paul McCracken, my old mentor from the CEA, called to say that a man named Roger Smith from General Motors wanted to talk to me. I couldn't imagine why Mr. Smith wanted this meeting, but I said fine; I'll invite him up for one of the Center's excellent lunches. After some small talk about his daughter's experience at the Stanford Business School, Smith – who, unbeknownst to me, had been anointed as GM's next CEO – suddenly asked if I would be interested in joining the company as a vice president and its chief economist. I really thought that this man with the fair hair and mottled complexion had been addled by too much California sunshine. But it turned out that he was serious.

When I recovered from my open-mouthed astonishment, I told Mr. Smith I'd think about it. For someone who had always regarded cars simply as a means of getting from here to there quickly and without getting wet, and who couldn't tell a Chevrolet from a Ford without a scorecard, his proposition looked outlandish. But to an international macroeconomist, the idea of working in the nation's biggest company – large enough to have a noticeable impact on our country's GDP – and with operations on several continents, was enticing. And finding out if my mental filing cabinet could be useful and persuasive in a world where no one shared the assumptions or the vocabulary of my profession seemed like an exciting new challenge. Finally, the offer would give me an opportunity to test in the private sector a conviction I had already carried into government, that the fundamental criterion for evaluating an economic theory should be the insights it yields regarding the economic environment in which people live and make decisions. After several months of sorting out the implications of such a move for our family life, I took a leap of faith and said yes.

Almost as soon as I had arrived at GM, I decided to focus on changing the role of the chief economist from serving as a personal assistant to the chairman and the financial staff to producing output that could be useful to the operating units, the profit-making side of the house. My focus and that of my staff would be, in broadest terms, to explain the economic and competitive realities of the world to GM, and those of GM to the outside world. This pithy mission statement turned out to be far easier said than done, stymied as it was by GM's deeply embedded and profoundly dysfunctional culture.

This culture, supported by the protective bubble in which the company's senior executives lived their daily lives, provided an effective bulwark against reality, enabling them to cling stubbornly to their belief in a stable, reasonably predictable world. The incursion of new Japanese competitors who happened to be in the right place with the right kind of cars when the oil shocks hit was seen as a temporary or at least reversible aberration. For most of them, furthermore, the only vehicle market that mattered was the one in the United States, which then accounted for some 70 percent of GM's production and sales. The idea that the markets and the competition relevant to the company's fortunes were rapidly becoming global was foreign to their thinking.

The picture of the world I tried to persuade GM's management and directors to accept was very different. Consistent with the change in my own views that had occurred as I read and absorbed Bob Stern's *Balance of Payments*, I shifted the forecasts and analyses of the economics staff from treating the United States as a closed economy to regarding it as an open one, that is, as interdependent with the rest of the world, rather than as an economically self-sufficient entity onto which international trade and investment were tacked almost as an afterthought.

This shift in perspective made an important difference in how we anticipated the impact of developments in the national economy on GM's business. When exchange rates were fixed, foreign competition nonexistent, and cross-border flows of capital relatively insignificant, as they were until the 1970s, an increase in interest rates caused by tightened monetary policy had affected GM mainly through a drop in total vehicle sales, brought about by a decline in economic activity and the reduced availability of financing to both dealers and customers. In the more financially integrated world of the 1980s, in contrast, and with exchange rates now flexible, the capital inflow created by Paul Volcker's drastic tightening of monetary policy forced a rise in the value of the dollar relative to other major currencies. The result was to make imports cheaper and exports more expensive, putting the company's products at a competitive disadvantage relative to imported vehicles and contributing to the ongoing decline in GM's market share. Both the business risks and the appropriate responses were different in an economy that was now far more open to the outside world.

This integrated worldview didn't directly challenge GM management's complacency until I spelled out its implications for the company in more detail in a couple of op-ed pieces in the *New York Times*. "The trend toward more fuel-efficient cars is worldwide," I wrote, and "This growing product overlap will create increased opportunities to achieve specialization and economies of scale wherever components are manufactured, and thus the development of 'world cars.' ... The bottom line ... will almost certainly be a stepped-up pace of innovation and competition in an increasingly global – rather than national – automobile industry." I stressed, too, some of the worldwide developments accelerated by the two oil shocks of the 1970s, including an uncomfortable transition from cheap to expensive energy and the diffusion of economic power toward the newly industrializing countries.[14]

With these forecasts as background, the economics staff I headed produced competitive analysis research demonstrating that the cost disadvantage suffered by American car companies vis-à-vis their Japanese competitors was not, as their top managements insisted, due primarily to factors outside their control, like an undervalued yen or differences in national systems of taxation, but due mainly to the more efficient and effective design and production processes developed by the Japanese manufacturers.

With these pronouncements, my staff and I were striking at the heart of GM management's deeply held beliefs. The result was that my entire career at GM was marked by growing frustration as my economist colleagues and I were unable to persuade our top decision makers that competition from foreign producers was here to stay, that it would only intensify, and that protection against imports offered no long-term solution. As we, along with a few other forward-looking managers, repeatedly tried to bring the fast-changing competitive dynamic to bear on senior management's thinking, I began to feel like the Trojan princess Cassandra, whose dire warnings about the true nature of the Trojan horse were fated to be ignored by her countrymen, with fatal results.

If describing the outside world and its potential impact on the company to GM's top management was frequently an exercise in frustration, explaining to the outside world GM's situation, its needs, and the difficulties it faced posed its own challenges. I gave these explanations in press interviews, in op-eds, and, above all, in testimony before various congressional committees and subcommittees. These encounters not only tried my patience and toughened my hide, but forced me to hone my skills as a communicator and persuader, unable to take refuge in my academic perspective and vocabulary when facing a row of politically motivated and often hostile interlocutors.

Sometimes, my two personas as a professional economist and a defender of GM's bottom line merged seamlessly. One didn't have to work for an automobile company to believe firmly, and insist unyieldingly, that corporate average fuel economy standards are among the most costly and least effective policies to curb fuel consumption and that increasing gasoline costs by raising the gas tax would be both more efficient, in terms of cost, and more effective in attaining the desired goal.

At other times, though, I had to make compromises. I was successful in persuading GM's chairman to avoid succumbing entirely to the protectionist stance adopted by the other two members of the "Big Three" and the United Auto Workers (although the company's president and the managers of the business units that reported to him never forgave me). But I did squirm a bit as I laid out a rationale for the so-called Voluntary Restraint Agreement that for several years restricted the number of automobiles that could be imported from Japan. This discomfort arose not only from my economist's conscience, but also from a conviction that the cartel-like conditions created by the restraints would ultimately redound to the benefit of the very competitors we were trying to neutralize – as they did.

I did a reasonably good job, I thought, of integrating my two personas in the Graham Memorial Lecture I gave at Princeton after I had been at GM for about a year.[15] But some qualms remained. As my father once put it, when one leaves the world of academic abstraction (mathematics in his case, economics in mine) to join the battles in the trenches of real-world policy making, one inevitably loses one's purity and falls into sin. So be it.

COMING FULL CIRCLE

Ultimately, it was not a desire to retrieve my virginity, but rather my frustration at the inability to make a perceptible dent in GM's culture, along with a growing conviction that my job as vice president and group executive was redundant in a company beset with too many layers of management, that led to my resignation/retirement. I returned to the academic world, this time at the University of Michigan as a pleasant way-station while I decided what I wanted to do with the rest of my working life. Some two decades later, I have to admit that the way-station has become a permanent home; I have completed the circle of (professional) life, ending up where I started half a century ago.

There are some significant differences, though. During the years I spent away from academe, teaching became an interactive sport, and students metamorphosed from a captive audience into customers to be satisfied. The lecture method has diversified into a variety of techniques for holding and capturing students' attention and even encouraging them to push back until the underpinnings of an assertion have been laid bare. My own choices have changed as well. During the years I spent working my way up the academic ladder at the University of Pittsburgh, I taught standard courses in a department of economics. Today, I have neither the competence – there is no way that I could pass PhD comprehensive exams in any first-rate graduate program, now that economics has become a field of applied mathematics or statistics – nor the interest in teaching those courses. Rather, I have appointments in two professional schools – the Business School and the School of Public Policy – where my teaching has an interdisciplinary flavor and where my experience in the worlds of government and business can be incorporated to good advantage.

My research interests have also evolved. I've always been attracted to studying the interactions between the public and the private sectors; today the questions I examine fall squarely into the realm of political economy. In my book *New World, New Rules*, I not only set forth an integrated explanation of the changing characteristics of American multinationals over the second half of the twentieth century, but also explored the implications of these changes for government policies. With the Cold War over and capitalism triumphant, I became interested in looking at different styles of capitalism, as practiced in the Anglo-Saxon countries, continental Europe, and Japan, respectively, and the extent to which they were or were not converging toward the American, or Anglo-Saxon, laissez-faire model. Most recently, I have been studying the emergence of the concept of global corporate social responsibility and how it has expanded, not only geographically, from a company's home community to all the countries in which it operates, but also to include issues of environmental sustainability and labor and human rights, as well as corporate governance. Furthermore, the definition of a company's responsibilities in these arenas has extended beyond the legal boundaries of the firm to encompass such "outside" actors as suppliers and host governments.

Finally, my political convictions have been refined by age and experience, although the beliefs underlying them remain the same. My politics may have moved a bit to the left as income inequality has sharpened, but mainly it's a case of "I didn't leave the Republican Party; it left me." The innovations in social policy introduced during the presidency of Richard Nixon, on whose Council of Economic Advisers I served, would never be countenanced by the Republican Party of today; quoting Bob Dole, "They were far too progressive." I continue to believe in the importance of the flow of goods, services, capital, and ideas across national boundaries – it was not for nothing that the president of the UAW once referred to me as "that free-trade bitch at GM" – but I have taken account, in both my teaching and my writing, of the darker aspects of globalization that accompany its many advantages.

Finally, I continue to believe firmly that, to paraphrase Winston Churchill's description of democracy, free-enterprise capitalism is the worst form of economic organization except all the others that have been tried and that market-based incentives generally offer a less costly and more effective means to achieve social goals than command-and-control directives. At the same time, such a system must be firmly embedded in a framework of laws and regulations that is widely perceived as both effective and equitable. Harry Truman will have to keep searching for his one-handed economist!

Notes

1 John von Neumann and Oskar Morgenstern, *The Theory of Games and Economic Behavior* (Princeton, NJ: Princeton University Press, 1944).
2 R. G. D. Allen, *Mathematical Analysis for Economists* (London: Macmillan, 1956).
3 Marina v. N. Whitman, *Government Risk-Sharing in Foreign Investment* (Princeton, NJ: Princeton University Press, 1965).
4 Pittsburgh Regional Planning Association, *Economic Study of the Pittsburgh Region: Region with a Future*, vol. 3 (Pittsburgh: University of Pittsburgh Press, 1963).
5 Charles P. Kindleberger, *International Economics* (Homewood, IL: Richard D. Irwin, 1953, 1963).
6 Robert M. Stern, *The Balance of Payments: Theory and Economic Policy* (Chicago: Aldine, 1973).
7 Marina v. N. Whitman, "Economic Openness and International Financial Flows," *Journal of Money, Credit, and Banking* 1, no.4 (1969): 727–749.
8 N. C. Miller and Marina v. N. Whitman, "A Mean-Variance Analysis of United States Long-Term Portfolio Foreign Investment," *Quarterly Journal of Economics* 84, 84–2 (May 1970): 175–196.

9   N. C. Miller and Marina v. N. Whitman, "Alternative Theories and Tests of U.S. Short-Term Foreign Investment," *Journal of Finance* 28-5 (December 1973): 1131–1150.

10 Marina v. N. Whitman, *Economic Goals and Policy Instruments: Policies for Internal and External Balance*, Special Papers in International Economics, no. 9 (Princeton University, 1970).

11 Marina v. N. Whitman, "Global Monetarism and the Monetary Approach to the Balance of Payments," Brookings Papers on Economic Activity 3 (Washington, DC: Brookings Institution, 1975).

12 Marina v. N. Whitman, *New World, New Rules: The Changing Role of the American Corporation* (Cambridge, MA: Harvard Business School Press, 1999).

13 Leonard Silk, "Peers Give Nixon's Advisers Bad Reviews," *New York Times*, October 17, 1973.

14 Marina Whitman, Op-eds, *New York Times*, September 3 and 5, 1980.

15 Marina v. N. Whitman, *International Trade and Investment: Two Perspectives*, Essays in International Finance, no. 143 (Princeton University, 1981).

Index